Christ, and His Sacraments

COLLEGE TEXTS IN THEOLOGY

General Editor
FRANCIS L. B. CUNNINGHAM, O.P.
S.T.Lr., S.T.D.

BASIC

GOD AND HIS CREATION

THE CHRISTIAN LIFE

CHRIST, AND HIS SACRAMENTS

SUBSIDIARY

TOWARD MARRIAGE IN CHRIST

THEOLOGY

A Basic Synthesis for the College

CHRIST,
AND HIS SACRAMENTS

by

Thomas C. Donlan, O.P.

Francis L. B. Cunningham, O.P.

Augustine Rock, O.P.

Lectors and Doctors in Sacred Theology

THE
PRIORY
PRESS

Dubuque—1960

Revisores Ordinis: Antonius A. Norton, O.P., S.T.P., Ph.D., Ricardus T. A. Murphy, O.P., S.T.D., S.S.D. Imprimi potest: Joannes E. Marr, O.P., S.T.M., Prior Provincialis. Nihil obstat: Ricardus T. A. Murphy, O.P., S.T.D., S.S.D., Censor. Imprimatur: ✠Leo Binz, Archiepiscopus Dubuquensis die 22a Augusti, 1958

Third Printing

Library of Congress Card No. 58-14187

© Copyright 1958 by THE PRIORY PRESS, Dubuque, Iowa

Printed in the United States of America

1146531

ACKNOWLEDGMENTS

Grateful acknowledgment is made to the Confraternity of Christian Doctrine for permission to cite their version of the Sacred Scriptures, and to Henry Regnery Company, Chicago, Ill., for copyrighted material quoted at the end of Chapter Seventeen. Unless otherwise noted, all translations from the Fathers, the documents of the Church and from St. Thomas are original.

Very heartfelt thanks are owed to many college teachers and administrators who, by their suggestions, corrections and recommendations, have made this volume so much better than it would have been without their invaluable assistance. In particular, I should like publicly to acknowledge my debt to Rev. David A. Dillon, S.T.D., professor of dogma at the St. Paul Seminary and lecturer at the College of St. Thomas and the College of St. Catherine, St. Paul, Minn., to Rev. William B. Murphy, O.P., S.T.Lr., professor of theology at Rosary College, River Forest, Ill., and to Bro. Frederick, F.S.C., of St. Mary's College, Winona, Minn., for their constructive and useful criticisms; to Rev. Bernard O'Riley, O.P., of St. Rose Priory, for his labors on the manuscript; and to Rev. Thomas A. Morrison, O.P., Ph.L., of De Paul University, Chicago, who worked out the scriptural harmony of the life of Christ contained in the Appendix.

THE EDITOR

TO THE STUDENT

Learn of me, he said. And centuries of loving labor, by saints and scholars, by the learned and the lowly, have heeded that command and recommendation under the direction of his Spouse, the Church. The fruits of this labor of love, of this learning of Christ, are incorporated in this volume.

Your business as a college student is to learn things; that is your special vocation. You have put behind the things of the child in order to obtain a man-sized grasp of reality. As in your other subjects, so also in your learning of Christ, the most vitally important of all your subjects (are not its rewards in the coin of the kingdom of heaven?), it is an adult's role you must assume. Here, too, here above all, yours must be a "higher" learning—a mature and scientific grasp of the truths about Christ, *theology,* cut and proportioned to your roles as college students and future leaders of the Christian community.

That is what this book attempts to do. Because it is about a big subject, it is a big book. Big, that is, in any way you look at it: over six hundred pages of material, a couple of pounds in weight, footnotes, definitions, divisions without number, seventeen full chapters in length. But its bigness is far more than a matter of statistics. It is a vastness of subject matter, who is Christ; and therefore it is about God, and about man, and about the relations between God and man, man and God, a summing up of all that you have previously learned in theology, as Christ recapitulates all things in himself.

Each page of this book has this one central figure of the ages as its theme: Christ in his incarnation, in his life, in his redemption, the historic Christ in his being and in his activity, and the mother of Christ who so perfectly resembles him; Christ as he walks among us today and all days until the end of time, in his sacrifice which is the Mass, in the sacraments which are his prolongation into the temporal and his extension unto the ends of the earth, and in that mystical realization of him which is his Body, the living and life-giving Church; Christ, finally, in the glorious triumph of his second coming on the great day of the Lord. Is it possible to conceive of a subject vaster in extent of time or space, bigger in implications for the present and the future?

This bigness directly concerns you. For this book is yours; and it is big, ultimately, in the demands it makes upon you—on your time, your interest, your ability. There is much in here which may never even be touched upon in class. The entire first chapter, for example, and in general many of the historical sections, cannot be covered in a class which necessarily concerns itself with essentials. Yet this is important background material, if you are to get the most, or even much, out of your study of Christ. There will be a great deal presupposed as already contained in your storehouse of wisdom from previous courses in theology; perhaps you will have to make up for lost time by review or supplementary reading. Your teacher will do all in his power to help you obtain that deeper, fuller knowledge of Christ which, at one and the same time, is your right, your need, your duty and your desire. Ultimately, however, this is your book: you get this wisdom yourself, or it is not gotten at all.

How about it? That is a silly question. We know the answer already, or we would not have gone to all the trouble to plan, write and publish this volume. You *are* aware of your responsibilities as leaders and of your commitments as Christians. You are not those who need to be milk-fed, who cannot stomach the solid food of sound doctrine.

Hence we can confidently say with St. Paul (Heb. 6:1), "Therefore, leaving the elementary teaching concerning Christ, let us pass on to things more perfect."

Here, then, is *your* book on Jesus Christ. In him "are hidden all the treasures of wisdom and knowledge" (Col. 2:3).

This is indeed a treasure, and it is yours—for the digging.

Francis L. B. Cunningham, o.p., s.t.lr., s.t.d.
General Editor, COLLEGE TEXTS IN THEOLOGY

CONTENTS

CHAPTER ONE

The Dogma of the Incarnation

CHAPTER TWO

The Fittingness of the Incarnation

CHAPTER THREE

The Nature of the Union of the Incarnate Word

CHAPTER FOUR

Perfections and Imperfections of Christ's Human Nature

CHAPTER FIVE

The Consequences of the Incarnation

CHAPTER SIX

Christ's Life and Ministry

CHAPTER SEVEN

The Passion, Death and Resurrection of Christ

CHAPTER EIGHT

Mary, the Mother of God

CHAPTER NINE

Sacred Signs

CHAPTER TEN

Baptism and Confirmation

CHAPTER ELEVEN

The Most Blessed Sacrament

CHAPTER TWELVE

The Holy Sacrifice of the Mass

CHAPTER THIRTEEN

The Sacrament of Penance

CHAPTER FOURTEEN

Extreme Unction and Holy Orders

CHAPTER FIFTEEN

Marriage in Christ

CHAPTER SIXTEEN

The Mystical Body of Christ

CHAPTER SEVENTEEN

The Consummation of the Work of the Incarnate Word:
The Glorification of the Just
and the Punishment of the Damned

GENERAL BIBLIOGRAPHY

The function of any bibliography is to help the student over the rough spots of the material at hand. Many times students find that they can conquer the summit of the subject matter more easily when it is approached from a different vantage point. Thus articles and books which may aid in the clarification of the doctrine proposed in this volume are included in this bibliography. When difficulties are seen in a different light they often lose their shadowy intimations and become clear to the observer. Again, some of the references pinpoint an important part of the doctrine, treating in more detail the splendor which is contained summarily in this book. However, caution should be used with regard to these fine points of doctrine, lest the student become too absorbed in a section of the picture and miss the extraordinary beauty of the whole.

The books embraced here in the General Bibliography have been selected because of their worth on two counts. First of all, some of them run parallel to this book in the treatment of the doctrine; in general they treat the same points contained herein. Secondly, some will be found useful to the student who, at the outset of his study, would like to get a more simplified conspectus of the matter to be treated. At the end of each chapter a Bibliographical Note will be found. These notes have been designed to aid the student in his desire for a richer understanding of Christ and his sacraments.

First and foremost among the items to be listed is the *Summa* of St. Thomas Aquinas. Latin editions of this great work of the Dominican saint may be found in most libraries. However, because of the linguistic barrier, editions of this kind are of little use to the student. Still, the *Summa* can be perused at length in the English edition brought out by Benziger Brothers, Inc. (New York: 1947) in three volumes. Volume II will be particularly valuable to the student. The numbers of the questions covered by each chapter will be found in the Bibliographical Note added to the individual chapters. Closely associated with the *Summa* and helpful because of its spirited examples is Volume IV of *A Companion to the Summa*, by Walter Farrell, O.P. (New York: Sheed and Ward, 1953). Volume III of the *Summa of the Christian Life* (St. Louis: B. Herder Book Co., 1958), a compilation of texts selected from the writings of the Venerable Louis of Granada, O.P., should also be an immense aid to the student. This book is one of a series brought out by *Cross and Crown,* a periodical which publishes articles designed to inform Catholics of the treasures which can be found in the spiritual life. Brief definitions of more difficult points can be found in the *Dictionary of Dogmatic Theology* (Milwaukee: The Bruce Publishing Co., 1951, by P. Parente, *et al.* or in the *Catechism of the "Summa Theologica"* by T. Pegues, O.P. (Westminster, Md.: The Newman Press, 1950.)

A particularly excellent book which treats of the matter under consideration is *The Mystery of Christ, Our Head, Priest, and King* (Westminster, Md.: The Newman Press, 1950), by Charles Héris, O.P. Along the same lines, but a more spiritual treatment of the mystery of Christ, is a work from the pen of the great Dom Columba Marmion, O.S.B., *Christ the Life of the Soul* (St. Louis: B. Herder Book Co., 1935). A technical work on the Incarnation and Redemption by the renowned Dominican theologian, Reginald Garrigou-Lagrange, O.P., entitled *Christ the Saviour* (St. Louis: B. Herder Book Co., 1950) offers a profound commentary on this third part of St. Thomas' *Summa*. Scheeben's magnificent work, *The Mysteries of Christianity* (St. Louis: B. Herder Book Co., 1946) contains many excellent chapters on the present material.

Two books can be recommended to the student who would like to augment his study by delving into the riches provided by the Christian liturgy. The first of these is *Christ in the Liturgy* (London: Sheed and Ward, 1952), by Illtyd Trethowan, a comparatively short book which treats in easy fashion the liturgical cycles. The second treatment, heartily recommended, is a five volume work entitled *The*

Church's Year of Grace (Collegeville, Minn.: The Liturgical Press, 1953), by Pius Parsch. It treats of the week-to-week liturgy of the Church in an admirable manner.

The final references which must be included in the General Bibliography are *The Teaching of the Catholic Church* in two volumes (New York: The Macmillan Co., 1949), edited by George D. Smith; and *The Collected Works of Abbot Vonier* in three volumes (Westminster, Md.: The Newman Press, 1952). Specific references to these will be listed in the Bibliographical Note of each chapter. Of course, the Bible should always be kept close at hand. One of the translations of the material available in Denzinger's *Enchiridion Symbolorum*—either *The Church Teaches* (St. Louis: B. Herder Book Co., 1955) or the revised work, *The Sources of Catholic Dogma*, put out by the same publisher—should be made readily accessible to the students.

Christ, and His Sacraments

Prologue

Our Savior, the Lord Jesus Christ, in order to save his people from their sins, as the angel testifies (Matt. 1:21), showed unto us in his very person the way of truth, whereby by rising again we may reach the beatitude of immortal life. Hence it is necessary for the completion of the work of theology that we should now consider, after our study of the ultimate end of human life and of the virtues and vices, the Savior of all men, and the benefits bestowed by him on the human race.

—Summa, III, Prologue

Thus does St. Thomas announce in unequivocal terms the "Christocentrism" of his theology. All of our previous studies in theology, of God and man in relation to God, have prepared us for the theological investigation of the God-man. All that has gone before enables us to grasp more deeply the great Economy of salvation, "the mystery which has been hidden for ages and generations, but now is clearly shown to his saints" (Col. 1:26). The work of Redemption, which we will now closely study, presupposes the creation of man, his first establishment in original justice, the fall of our first parents, the long sweep of the ages when man lived under the law of nature or under the Mosaic code. It presupposes also the faith with which men awaited the coming of the promised Redeemer, and the other virtues—necessary for any of the states of human life—which prepare mankind here on earth

1

for the eternal reward Christ wins for us. The study of Christ, then, who is the unique subject matter of this volume, is the culmination and the consummation of our previous theological investigations, as the following outline shows:

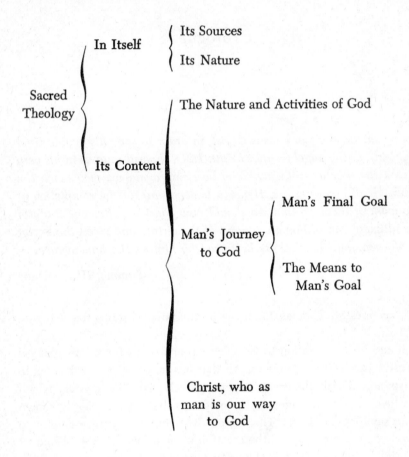

Sacred Theology

In Itself
- Its Sources
- Its Nature

Its Content
- The Nature and Activities of God
- Man's Journey to God
  - Man's Final Goal
  - The Means to Man's Goal
- Christ, who as man is our way to God

{ The Existence and Nature of God
The Blessed Trinity
The Creation and Governance of the Universe

{
In General { Human Acts
The Principles of Human Acts

In Particular {
Theological Virtues { Faith
Hope
Charity

Cardinal Virtues { Prudence
Justice
Fortitude
Temperance

The Word was made flesh and dwelt among us. St. John's simple statement enunciates one of the greatest mysteries of God's love. The Second Person of the Blessed Trinity—he who was in the beginning with God, without whom was made nothing that has been made—assumes, at a predetermined moment in the history of mankind, true human nature. Perfect God, he becomes perfect man—that he might save his people from their sins.

One person, the Son of God; and two complete natures, a divine and a human, each truly distinct from the other and yet most intimately united in, and according to, that divine person. This is the central fact of the universe, the fundamental fact of Christianity. It is an astonishing event, inexhaustibly rich in meaning and significance—too rich, too blinding, too divine for the poor weak reason of man. Today as in ages past, as in the beginning of Christianity, there are men who deny Christ's humanity, or his divinity, or the mysterious union of the two which we call "hypostatic."

Is it credible that God should take our flesh, become one of us, suffer and die for our sins? Not, certainly, to those who would perversely measure divine things by the finite capacities of their own mind. Yet theology can clearly show that it is most reasonable to believe the Incarnation and the Redemption—to *know*, that is to say, through the participated divine knowledge which is faith, founded on the infallible testimony of God himself. Christ fulfilled the prophecies revealed to God's chosen people. He himself claimed to be God, and this seemingly presumptuous declaration (which led to his death) was confirmed by the Father at his baptism and transfiguration. By his miracles (especially his own resurrection), by his prophecies, by his doctrine and his life, his love of God and of man, he established beyond reasonable doubt his right to divinity.

This is the fact, then, solemnly proclaimed by his Church—herself one of his miracles—time and again. In defense of his truth she rejects the attempts of misguided or malicious men to reduce this mystery to human dimensions, assimilable by human reason. The great Church councils of Ephesus (held in 431; cf. Denz. 111a-124) and of Chalcedon (held in 451; cf. Denz. 148) formally and solemnly declare what the Church has always held and still teaches today: the truth, toward, or from which all human history flows: the incarnational fact, the divine economy which opens heaven's gates. God became man, dwelt among us, suffered and died for our salvation. An ancient profession of Catholic belief insists on these fundamental points:

> The true Catholic faith is, that we believe and confess that our Lord Jesus Christ, Son of God, is God and man. He is God, begotten before the ages of the substance of the Father, and he is man, born in time of the substance of a mother. Perfect God, he is perfect man, with a rational soul and human flesh. Equal to the Father according to his divinity, he is inferior to the Father according to his humanity. Although he is God and man, there is but one Christ, not two—one, however, not by a change of divinity into flesh but by the assumption of humanity to God. He is one by unity of person, in no way by mingling of substance. For as a rational soul and flesh is one man, so God and man is one Christ.[1]

Following St. Thomas, we shall begin our investigation of Christ, of the Incarnation and the Redemption, by first studying the Savior himself (Chapters I-VII), concluding this phase of our study with a consideration of the Mother of the God-man, and our mother, Mary (Chapter VIII); then we will consider his sacraments, which are the prolongation in time of his Incarnation and the means by which we obtain salvation (Chapters IX-XV), realized in the mystery of his Mystical Body, the Church (Chapter XVI); finally we will consider the end Christ won for us: immortal life, which we reach through him by the resurrection (Chapter XVII).

The first point of this investigation embraces two considerations: the mystery of the Incarnation itself, whereby God was made man for our salvation; and the things done and suffered by our Savior, who is God Incarnate. Under the first of these headings three points must be studied: first, the fittingness of the Incarnation itself; second, the mode of union of the Incarnate Word; third, the consequences which flow from this union. These considerations will be prefaced by a pre-

---

[1] *The "Quicumque" Creed*, commonly called the Athanasian Creed; Denz. 40.

liminary chapter concerning the dogma of the Incarnation, its foundation in Sacred Scripture and its "development" by Christ's Church.

The order we will follow may be represented schematically as follows:

CHRIST
who as man
is our way to God

Christ himself, our Savior
(Chaps. I–VIII)

Christ's sacraments by which we obtain salvation
(Chaps. IX–XVI)

The end Christ won for us: immortal life, which we reach through him by the resurrection
(Chap. XVII)

The mystery of the Incarnation —God become man for our salvation
(Chaps. I—V)

The things which our Savior, God Incarnate, did and suffered
(Chaps. VI—VII)

Mary, God's mother and ours
(Chap. VIII)

The dogma of the Incarnation
(Chap. I)

The fittingness of the Incarnation
(Chap. II)

The mode of the union of the Incarnate Word
(Chap. III)

Perfections and imperfections assumed
(Chap. IV)

The consequences which flow from this union
(Chap. V)

CHAPTER ONE

The Dogma of the Incarnation

1. Introduction

Christ is God, and Christ is man, and there is but one Christ. These are the basic facts of the mystery of Christ, and our first theological task in investigating this mystery will be to search the sources of revelation—Scripture and/or Tradition—for God's own affirmation as to the existence of the Incarnation.[1] For here is another of those truths so intimately connected with the divine life that its very apprehension would escape man's powers of knowledge unless God himself chose to tell us about it. The gift of faith, of belief in God's

---

[1]The word *incarnation* literally means "enfleshment." Following the terminology of St. John (Jn. 1:14)—itself a reflection of the customary scriptural usage by which "flesh" through synecdoche stands for "body" and then for the whole man— the early Fathers adopt the word as the best expression of the revealed fact that God becomes man. Although abstractly not as clear a word as "inhumanation" which a few of them use, *incarnation* emphasizes against the Docetists (who declared Christ's body an illusion) the reality and integrity of Christ's human nature.

9

revealing himself, brings this divine truth to us, but even then the mystery so disclosed remains a mystery—incomprehensible, only its outlines perceptible behind the veil. Illumined, strengthened by this share in God's own knowledge which is faith, human reason can, to be sure, attain a deeper and more fruitful understanding of the mystery,[2] but never a complete and perfect comprehension of what is essentially infinite.

Object of a **revelation** from God, the Incarnation is also a **dogma** of Christ's Church, the infallible custodian and teacher of divine truth. In consequence, theology must also examine the Church's proposal of this mystery as a divinely revealed truth to be believed by all Catholics. Since these proposals have a history of increasingly more precise formulation of the terms of the mystery, this study of Catholic faith investigates "the development or evolution of dogma."

The primary purpose of this twofold investigation is that of **positive theology** (as explained in the first volume of this basic series), namely, "to *explain* and *defend* what is certainly revealed by God in the various sources of theology."[3] In accomplishing this end, however, the materials for another function of theology will be presented, although not developed. This is the work—here only secondary and subsidiary—of **apologetics**, which consists in defending divine revelation by showing that it is reasonable to believe the truths told us by God. By using our sources, not as witnesses of divine revelation, but simply as historical documents recounting historical facts and events, the theologian can show that the Incarnation is credible—that is, that it is reasonable to accept God's revelation and that objections against it can be solved.

The work of positive theology with respect to the Incarnation will be, then, the major concern of this initial chapter. Pursued under two headings, it will consider the following material:

---

[2]Cf. Vatican Council, Sess. III, *Dogmatic Constitution on the Catholic Faith*, Chap. 4, "On Faith and Reason"; Denz. 1796.
[3]Murphy, *et al.*, *God and His Creation* (Dubuque: The Priory Press, 1958), 57; cf. 53-57.

The Data
of Revelation
{
The Divinity of Christ
(Section 2)

The Humanity of Christ
(Section 3)

The Hypostatic Union
(Section 4)
}

The Development
of Dogma
{
First Period: Beginnings of Dogmatic Formulation
(Section 5)

Second Period: Theological Speculation
(Section 6)

Third Period: Crisis and Resolution
(Section 7)

Fourth Period: Christological Definitions
(Section 8)
}

THE DATA OF REVELATION

Sacred Scripture is the record of God's revelation to mankind. To determine the existence of a mystery such as the Incarnation, therefore, the natural first step is to examine that record for its evidence. This requires the determination of the literal sense[4] of any passage which may refer to the mystery in question, since this is the meaning principally intended by God himself.

Because the Incarnation involves three affirmations—the divinity of Christ, his humanity, and their union in the one individual—we shall successively consider the scriptural evidence with reference to each of these points.

---

[4]The "literal sense is that meaning immediately signified by the words" either in their usual meaning (the *proper* literal sense) or in figurative language (the *extended* literal sense). If definitely determined, it is an unanswerable argument in defense of Catholic dogmas for those who accept the Bible as inspired. Cf. Murphy, *et al., God and His Creation*, 10, 12-16.

2. The Divinity of Christ

A. Introduction

Accepting the existence of Jesus Christ as a historical fact beyond cavil,[5] the important question must still be answered: *who is he?* Search for that answer in the pages of the Bible will center on the basic dogma of Christianity, that Christ is the Son of God, true God of true God, the Second Person of the Blessed Trinity. We will conduct that search in three stages: the witness of the Old Testament; the revelation Christ makes of himself; and the testimony given by his disciples.

B. The Evidence of the Old Testament

Then the Lord God said to the serpent:
"Because you have done this,
      cursed are you among all animals,
      and among all beasts of the field;
On your belly shall you crawl,
      dust shall you eat,
      all the days of your life.
I will put enmity between you and the woman,
      between your seed and her seed;
He shall crush your head,
      and you shall lie in wait for his heel."[6]

Thus at the very dawn of history, following man's primal failure, does the Lord God bring the first good news to mankind. Eve and her descendants will withstand the serpent and his brood, and one of them in particular will crush the head of the Adversary in ultimate victory.[7] This is the initial announcement of the Deliverer, him

---

[5]In the past century, several writers, encouraged by their own prejudices and by evidence insufficient and ill-digested, attempted to show that Christ was only a fiction elaborated by Christians. Refutation of these critics by Christians of equal erudition and by incontestable evidence was so complete that today no serious historian, whatever his religious beliefs or non-beliefs, would call into doubt the existence of the central figure of the gospels.

[6]Gen. 3:14-15.

[7]This prophecy may be applied to Mary and her Son; common to many of the Fathers, such an interpretation is given by the dogmatic definitions of the Immaculate Conception and the Assumption.

who would bring salvation, the Anointed of God, the Messias (in Greek, *Christos*). Through long ages God will speak again and again through the mouth of his prophets to the descendants of the patriarchs, his chosen but often faithless people, revealing in ever greater detail the kingdom to come and the favored one who will inaugurate that reign.

That the inspired descriptions of the promised Messias are fulfilled in Jesus Christ there can be no doubt. Born in the little town of Bethlehem (Mich. 5:1), son of a virgin (Isa. 7:14), of Davidic ancestry (Isa. 9:6; Amos 9:11; Osee 3:5; Jer. 23:5, 30:9, 33:15; Ezech. 34:23-24, 37:24-25), truly a man (Isa. 7:14, 9:5; Ps. 21:10-11, 44:3), and a son of man (Dan. 7:13-14), the Messias fulfills his divinely appointed mission by ruling as a king,[8] by teaching as prophet,[9] and by satisfying for sin as priest.[10] Not only do the details mentioned above belong exclusively to Jesus Christ, but the Messias' mission is also his: he is king (Lk. 1:32; Matt. 2:2), although his kingdom is not of this world Jn. 18:36-37); he is prophet (Matt. 23:10; Lk. 4:16-21; Jn. 12:49; Lk. 24:19; Heb. 1:1-2), whose words are confirmed by the miracles he works; he is the great high priest (Heb. 4:14; cf. 7:27, 9:13-14, 28), and redeems his people from their sins by his sacrifical death (Matt. 1:21). He is the Servant of Yahweh (Isa. 42:1-7, 49:1-9, 50:4-9, 52:13– 53:12) whose suffering and death bring redemption, the terrible, sufferings already described in Psalm 21 of the "pierced one" of whom Zacharias speaks (12:10). But his also are the glory of the Servant of Yahweh (Isa. 52:13, 53:10-12), the subsequent exultation of the sufferer of Psalm 21 (23-32), the triumph over death and corruption (Ps. 15:9-11, applied to the resurrection; cf. Acts 2:25-32, 13:34-37). In very truth Christ is the Messias enthroned at the right hand of God who rules over the whole world (Ps. 2:8-9, 109:1-2). He is the son of man to whom "sovereignty and glory and kingship were given

---

[8]Gen. 49:10; Num. 24:17; Isa. 9:5-6; Ps. 2:6-9, 44:17, 71:8-11, 109:2; Zach. 9:9-10. These prophecies are no more to be understood of material kingship than the predicted kingdom of God is to be understood as an earthly reign; the prophets are quite clear on both points. Cf. P. Heinisch, *Theology of the Old Testament* (Collegeville, Minn.: The Liturgical Press, 1955), 324-335, 348-349.

[9]Deut. 18:15,18; Isa. 11:2, 49:1-6, 61:1.

[10]Ps. 109:4, Zach. 6:11-14 (the priest); Ps. 21:26-27, Isa. 53:5-12 (his sacrifice); Isa. 53:12 (his intercession).

so that all peoples, nations and tongues should serve him. And his kingship is an everlasting kingship" (Dan. 7:13-14).

If Christ is, then, the promised Messias,[11] does this prove that he was divine? Or, to rephrase the question: do the messianic prophecies ascribe divinity to the Deliverer who is to come? Although the matter is disputed, we unhesitatingly answer in the affirmative, on two scores:

1) The prophet Isaias declares that the Savior will not have a human father (Isa. 7:14) and that his name will be Emmanuel, "God with us" (Isa. 7:14 and 8:8). These hints as to the extraordinary nature of the Messias are amplified in a later passage (Isa. 9:6): "A child is born to us, a son is given to us, upon his shoulders rests the sovereignty, and his name shall be: Wonderful Counsellor, Strong God, Father Forever, Prince of Peace."

   All of these titles have the authentic ring of divinity about them, and the fact is quite starkly stated in the expression "Strong God," *'el gibbor*. This is a title exclusively reserved for Yahweh, the one true God,[12] and its deliberate use in this context can only mean that the Messias will himself be divine. Thus the *proper* **literal** sense of this prophecy proclaims the Messias as true God, possessing in truth the divine nature.[13]

2) The divinity of the Messias (and thus Christ's divinity) is clear from the text and the context of Isaias' prophecy. Two other prophetic passages—Ps. 2:7 and Ps. 109:1, 3—proclaim the superiority of the Messias in striking terms: he is begotten by Yahweh, a universal king and eternal priest who sits at his right hand. These expressions, however, may be understood in the *extended*, not in the *proper* literal sense, since neither the text nor the context assigns the reason for the superiority they prophesy.

---

[11]Only in Ps. 2:2 is this precise word used of the Deliverer in the Old Testament; Jesus seldom claimed the title (it occurs in Jn. 1:42 and 4:25), no doubt because the messianic hopes of the Jews were so exclusively concerned with an earthly kingdom.

[12]Deut. 10:17; Isa. 10:21; Jer. 32:18; Neh. 9:32.

[13]Cf. P. F. Ceuppens, O.P., *Theologia Biblica*, II (Romae: Marietti, 1949), 30-33, and III (Romae: Marietti, 1950), 27-28. Whether the Jews—or the prophet himself, for that matter—fully understood what is here predicted is another question which need not concern us at this juncture.

Hence they cannot be offered as Old Testament proofs of the divinity of Christ.

Nevertheless, their true meaning does become apparent when they are interpreted *in the light* of the New Testament. The author of the Epistle to the Hebrews teaches (1:5) that Ps. 2:7 speaks of a divine sonship by nature, and that in this is the superiority of the Messias found. Similarly, we know from the New Testament (Mk. 12:36; Matt. 22:44; Lk. 20:42-43) that the supereminent qualities ascribed to the Messias in Ps. 109:1,3 are his because he is God.

C. The Revelation of Jesus Christ

As already explained in connection with the dogma of the Trinity,[14] Christ as Messias-prophet slowly educates his listeners to receive the revelation he brings from the Father, and only after a considerable preparation does he proclaim himself true Son of God. Here, then, we can consider the evidence given by the Synoptics more summarily, without a detailed analysis of Christ's pedagogical method.

Objectively attested to by the Father on the momentous occasions of his baptism[15] and his transfiguration,[16] his divinity is proclaimed by Christ himself both by his manner of acting and by his express teaching.

(1) Christ's Manner of Acting

Christ claims for himself certain attributes which are proper to God alone, and clearly vindicates his right to them. In these actions he shows, then, that he is true God, not just a legate sent by God nor an inspired prophet.

[14]Cf. Murphy, *et al., God and His Creation,* 253-262.

[15]Matt. 3:16-17; Mk. 1:9,11; Lk. 9:35. In biblical as in classical Greek, the expression "beloved son" means "only begotten." The *proper literal* sense of the title, therefore, proclaims Christ's divinity, his consubstantiality with God the Father.

[16]Matt. 17:5; Mk. 9:7; Lk. 9:35. Christ is again called the "beloved son" of the Father.

1. **He claims for himself divine power.** By his own power he works miracles which demand his disciples' belief in him. Thus with respect to the blind men,[17] he asked: "'Do you believe that I can do this to you?' They answered him, 'Yes, Lord.' Then he touched their eyes, saying, 'Let it be done to you according to your faith.' And their eyes were opened."[18] "Power went forth from him and healed all" (Lk. 6:19), a fact Christ himself remarks on: "Someone touched me; for I perceived that power had gone forth from me" (Lk. 8:46). So properly is this divine power his, that miracles are worked in his name (Lk. 10:17; cf. Acts 3:6) and he bestows a share in it on his disciples (Lk. 10:9, 10:17; Mk. 16:17; Matt. 10:8).

2. **He arrogates to himself supreme moral authority.** As Jesus himself declares, his is a legal power equal to that of God.[19] He uses the divine power of forgiving sins (Mk. 2:5-12; Lk. 7:47-50); and the supreme power of judgment, likewise proper only to God, also belongs to him, for he declares that he has the power of judging all the actions of men, and the right of rewarding or punishing men for eternity.[20] All of these rights which he exercises and claims as his own are, according to the Old Testament and the doctrine of the Jews, the exclusive property of God alone.

3. **He claims absolute authority and demands that divine worship be paid to him.** For him, one should be willing to leave all things (Matt. 10:37-40; Mk. 10:29-30; Lk. 12:26), and those who wish to be saved should take up their cross and follow him (Matt. 19:29; Mk. 8:34-35; Lk. 22:29-30). Finally, "everyone who acknowledges me before men, I also will acknowledge him before my Father in heaven. But whoever disowns me before men, I in turn disown him before my Father in heaven."[21]

---

[17]Matt. 9:18.

[18]For similar incidents, cf. Matt. 8:5 ff. (servant of the centurion); Mk. 4:39 (quieting of the wind), 5:41 (girl "asleep"), 8:3 ff. (multiplication of the loaves), 9:24 (cure of possessed boy); Lk. 7:14 (son of the widow of Naim); etc. For examination of the miracles of Christ, see *infra*, Chapter Six, Sect. 8, and the appendix, "A Scriptural Harmony of the Life of Christ."

[19]In Matt. 5:21-48, he communicates his commands with the same authority as God did in giving the commandments to Moses; in Mk. 10:7-9, he restores matrimony to its pristine indissolubility; in Mk. 2:23-28, he proclaims himself Lord of the Sabbath.

[20]Matt. 24:30-31, cf. 25:34,41; Mk. 13:26; Lk. 21:27,36.

[21]Matt. 10:32-33; cf. Mk. 8:38.

(2) Christ's Explicit Teaching[22]

1. **His divine filiation.** Three times the Messias proclaims his filiation in words which cannot be otherwise interpreted: 1) before his disciples on the occasion of Peter's confession of faith;[23] 2) before the people, when he explains the allegory of the wicked vine-dressers, applying it to himself in so clear a manner that the chief priests and Pharisees perfectly understood him;[24] before the judges of the San-hedrin.[25] On this last occasion, Christ is asked a double question. First, is he the Christ, the Messias promised by the prophets? When he answers affirmatively, applying to himself the words of the messianic psalm (109:1), they put a second, even more solemn and vital question: is he, then, the Son of God? "Thou hast said it," Jesus replies. And the high priest rends his garments, shouts that he has blasphemed, and without further hearing condemns him to death—all certain signs of recognition of the fact that Jesus had solemnly affirmed his divine sonship.[26]

2. **His divine nature.** On two other occasions Christ taught explicitly that he possessed the divine nature. The first occurred in the presence of his disciples, just returned from their first mission. "All things have been delivered to me by my Father," he says to them. "And no one knows who the Son is except the Father, and who the Father is except the Son, and him to whom the Son chooses to reveal him."[27] *My* Father, Christ claims, stressing the entirely special relationship between himself and God, for he taught others to say *our* Father; hence his sonship is unique, not metaphorical or adoptive but proper and

[22]In this section we will consider only that teaching of our Lord recorded by the Synoptics, reserving to the final section his teaching as reported by St. John.
[23]Matt. 16:13-20; Mk. 8:27-50; Lk. 9:18-22. That this is beyond doubt a confession of Christ's divinity, and approved by him as such, is the common and solid conclusion of reputable modern exegetes. Cf. M.-J. Lagrange, O.P., *The Gospel of Jesus Christ*, I (Westminster, Md.: The Newman Bookshop, 1938), 257-263; F. Prat, S.J., *Jesus Christ*, I (Milwaukee: Bruce, 1950), 408-417; P. F. Ceuppens, O.P., *op. cit.*, III, 29.
[24]Matt. 21:33-44; Mk. 12:1-12; Lk. 20:9-19. Both Mark and Luke describe the son of the vineyard owner as his "beloved son"—the term, meaning "only begotten," as we have seen, is thus employed by Jesus to describe himself and his relations with the Father.
[25]Matt. 26:63-66; Mk. 14:61-64; Lk. 22:66-71.
[26]To declare oneself Messias or Son of God in a metaphorical sense would have been no blasphemy, nor would death have been the penalty for such a declaration.
[27]Lk. 10:22; cf. Matt. 11:25-27.

consubstantial. This is further brought out by the words which follow, for the peculiarly oriental formula, "no one knows who the Son is except the Father, and who the Father is except the Son," quite plainly teaches the perfect equality of nature of Father and Son and the equality and perfect reciprocity of the knowledge of Father and Son which is its consequence.[28]

The second occasion on which Christ affirms his divine nature takes place when he questions the Pharisees concerning the Messias and his origin. They answered, truthfully enough, that the Messias was the son of David.[29] Jesus then pursues the argument: "How then does David in the Spirit call him Lord, saying, 'The Lord said to my Lord: Sit thou at my right hand, till I make thy enemies my footstool'? If David, therefore, calls him 'Lord,' how is he his son?"[30]

None of the Pharisees, St. Matthew observes, could answer him a word. And no wonder. For our Lord is pointing out to them that David by divine inspiration ("in the Spirit") had called the Messias "Lord," a title reserved in the Septuagint (which is the text of Ps. 109:1, here cited by all three Synoptics) for God himself, Yahweh. Had the Messias been only the son of David, then regardless of the superiority of his kingship David would never have saluted him by the divine title of "Lord." Thus although the Messias is truly son of David according to the Old Testament prophets, he is also, as David recognizes, much more: son of David according to his human nature, he is Lord of David according to his divine nature. And the Messias, now proclaimed divine, is Christ—this he has several times declared before the Pharisees and the multitude.

D. The Testimony of the Disciples

For apologetic purposes—because some non-Catholics deny the authenticity or historicity of one or other group of writings attributed to Christ's disciples—we shall consider the witness which Christ's fol-

---

[28]So clear is this statement of Christ's divinity that non-Catholics who deny it on principle (Harnack, for example, and Loisy) are forced to impugn—quite fruitlessly—the authenticity of the text. Cf. P. F. Ceuppens, O.P., *op. cit.*, II, 105.
[29]Isa. 9:5, 11:1.
[30]Matt. 22:41-46. Cf. Mk. 12:35-37; Lk. 20:41-44.

lowers give to his claim of divinity under three headings: 1) the witness of the Catholic epistles; 2) the teaching of St. Paul; 3) the doctrine of St. John.[31]

(1) The Witness of the Catholic Epistles

"Let all the house of Israel know most assuredly that God has made both Lord and Christ, this Jesus whom you crucified."[32] Thus does the Prince of the apostles, he who first openly confessed belief in Christ's divinity, now after the powerful coming of the pentecostal Spirit proclaim boldly to the Jews that his Master was not only the promised Messias but also true God.[33] The good tidings here announced inaugurate the apostolic mission of Christ's disciples which will carry the Gospel to the ends of the earth. And in their extant letters these followers, in various ways and in differing circumstances, will all teach the central fact of the message of the Savior: he was God.

[31]It should be noted here, perhaps, that it is possible for the inspired writers of the canonical books of the New Testament to have added doctrinal complements to the personal teaching of Jesus—evangelic revelation does not come to a close until the death of the last apostle, St. John. Hence there is a dogmatic as well as an apologetic necessity to consider separately the teaching of the Master and of his disciples. Necessarily, of course, such teaching on the part of the disciples would be only complementary, i.e., it would presuppose our Lord's own doctrine as a first and indispensable basis and be perfectly harmonized with it. Thus theory confirms what the historical facts show us: that Christ himself affirms his unity of being and twofold nature, for this is the fundamental mystery of his coming and the cornerstone of his revelation and doctrine. But nothing will prevent his disciples from explaining and interpreting his teaching on so basic a mystery. On the contrary, everything will encourage them. To expose it in terms other than he used in attempting to reach other audiences, to fathom it more fully than the original recipients in order to elucidate more explicitly the simple terms of the original teaching—such "developments" are entirely in the nature of the case. When recorded under divine inspiration (as in the canonical books) their authority is of the same order as the teaching of Christ himself: it is the word of God.

[32]Acts 2:36.

[33]The term "lord" may be a purely human title, or it may be used as a synonym for "Messias" (cf. Lk. 1:43, 2:11); but most frequently in the Old Testament the word is used as a substitute for Yahweh (that name proper to God which the Jews were forbidden to pronounce) and it almost always has that meaning when applied to Jesus in the New Testament. Hence, although the immediate context of the sentence quoted does not necessarily demand that the title "Lord" used by St. Peter be interpreted as an affirmation of divinity, there is little doubt, from the customary New Testament usage of the word, that St. Peter here intends to give the ultimate reason for the exaltation of the Messias: the Messias is God.

"Lord of glory," St. James, "the servant of God and of our Lord Jesus Christ,"[34] calls him whom St. Peter declares to be Lord and Savior,[35] truly God,[36] of whom the Old Testament texts referring to Yahweh alone are affirmed.[37] "Of what was from the beginning I write," St. John states, "of the Word of Life,"[38] thus testifying to that divine pre-existence of Christ also preached by St. Peter[39] and St. Jude.[40] And the beloved disciple continues in a justly famous passage:

> Beloved, let us love one another, for love is from God. And everyone who loves is born of God, and knows God. He who does not love does not know God; for God is love. In this has the love of God been shown in our case, that God has sent his only begotten Son into the world that we may live through him. In this is the love, not that we have loved God, but that he has first loved us, and sent his Son a propitiation for our sins.[41]

The written witness of the apostles of Jesus Christ to his divinity is, then, unanimous and universal. The testimony of these so-called "Catholic" letters is all the more impressive because they do not directly set out to teach this doctrine but, on the contrary, obviously presuppose Christ's divinity as universally known and believed by the primitive Church. Moreover, these are circular or encyclical letters, sent by various apostles to different Christian communities scattered throughout the Near East; the unanimity of the writers, the universality of the churches to whom they are written—these are irrefutable proof of the belief of the primitive Church in the divinity of the Messias, Jesus Christ.

(2) The Teaching of St. Paul

To the zealous Jew converted on the Damascus highway was given this grace: "to announce among the Gentiles the good tidings of the unfathomable riches of Christ, and to enlighten all men as to what

[34] Jas. 1:1 and 2:1.
[35] II Pet. 1:11, 2:20, 3:2,18.
[36] I Pet. 1:1-2, 2:4-5.
[37] I Pet. 2:3, 3:15.
[38] I Jn. 1:1.
[39] I Pet. 1:11. Jesus had inspired the prophets, communicating his spirit to them, which is the spirit of Yahweh.
[40] Jude, v. 5: "Jesus, who saved the people from the land of Egypt, the next time destroyed those who did not believe."
[41] I Jn. 4:7-10; cf. 4:14-15.

is the dispensation of the mystery which has been hidden from eternity in God, who created all things."[42] Servant of Jesus Christ and his apostle by the will of God, he becomes the prisoner of Christ Jesus for the sake of the Gentiles,[43] to make known unto them the mystery of the redemption of all men by Christ and in Christ: this is the gospel of Paul.[44]

"Take heed to yourselves," he warns the presbyters of the church of Ephesus, one of his many foundations. "Take heed to yourselves and to the whole flock in which the Holy Spirit has placed you as bishops, to rule the Church of God, which he has purchased with his own blood."[45] So constant is this theme of redemption for all through the blood of the God-man that almost every page of his many letters bears witness to the divinity of Christ.[46] Christ is from the patriarchs "according to the flesh," he reminds the Romans (9:5), "who is, over all things, God blessed forever, amen." In Christ dwells "all the fulness of the Godhead bodily";[47] "image of the invisible God . . . in him were created all things in the heavens and on the earth. . . . All things have been created through and unto him, and he is before all creatures, and in him all things hold together."[48] To the Philippians he gives this magnificent example of humility:

[42]Eph. 3:8-9.
[43]Cf. Eph. 3:1; Philem. 1:1.
[44]Certain rationalistic schools of the recent past—Nietzsche, Loisy, Bötticher, Renan, and others less prominent—professed belief in a pretended antagonism between the teaching of Jesus and that of Paul, and this belief is still by no means purged from popular non-Catholic Christianity today, although it lacks any critical foundation and has been abandoned by competent Protestant students of the Bible. That there are differences between the two methods of teaching is obvious, but simple enough to explain in the light of different circumstances and different immediate aims. Cf. F. Prat, S.J., *The Theology of St. Paul*, I (Westminster, Md.: The Newman Bookshop, n.d), Chapter I, "The Definition of Paulinism" and Chapter II, "The Origins of Paulinism," 3-44. Besides this excellent work, the student may wish to consult *Paul of Tarsus* by J. Holzner (St. Louis: B. Herder Book Co., 1946) for a well written account of Paul's interesting life, or G. Ricciotti's *Paul the Apostle*, (Milwaukee: Bruce, 1953), a more recent work by a distinguished Catholic scholar.
[45]Acts 20:28.
[46]According to Prat (*op. cit.*, I, 13), the name "Lord" occurs about 280 times in his writings in its Old Testament use as a substitute for the sacred name of Yahweh; significantly, he considers the confession of the lordship of Christ a condensed profession of faith and a résumé of the Gospel (Rom. 10:9-10).
[47]Col. 2:9.
[48]*Ibid.* 1:15-17.

Have this mind in you which was also in Christ Jesus, who though he was by nature God, did not consider being equal to God a thing to be clung to, but emptied himself, taking the nature of a slave and being made like unto men. And appearing in the form of man, he humbled himself, becoming obedient to death, even to death on a cross.[49]

The faith of Paul, in short, preached in season and out, his hope and his love were in "our great God and Savior, Jesus Christ, who gave himself for us that he might redeem us from all iniquity and cleanse for himself an acceptable people, pursuing good works" (Tit. 2:14). In his name should every knee bend, and that name which is above every name all should confess: the Lord Jesus Christ, God and man.[50]

The author of the Epistle to the Hebrews professes in his own manner this gospel of Paul, particularly in the remarkable passage (1:1-14) which opens the letter. God has in these messianic times spoken to us "by his Son," "heir of all things, by whom also he made the world." "The brightness of his glory and the image of his substance, and upholding all things by the word of his power," it is he who has redeemed man. Infinitely superior to the angels, he sits at God's right hand, for he is the Son begotten from eternity, and the angels minister to him and adore him, the Lord who was in the beginning and whose years will never fail.

Here, then, as in St. Paul's own words, the divinity of Jesus Christ is explicitly professed. And in these letters, as in the Catholic epistles, that profession is made to diverse churches and different Christian communities and so testifies infallibly to the belief of the primitive Church in the divine nature of the Son of man.

(3) The Doctrine of St. John

"These are written that you may believe that Jesus is the Christ, the Son of God, and that believing you may have life in His name."[50a] Thus does St. John clearly state the purpose for which he composes his gospel, emphasizing in every possible way the transcendence and divinity of Jesus the Christ. From these sublime pages arises a Jesus more resplendent with divine light than the more human figure por-

[49]Phil. 2:5-8; cf. infra., 27-28.
[50]Cf. Phil. 2:9-11.
[50a]Jn. 20:31.

trayed by the Synoptics, but one no less historical for the careful selection of materials which underline this aspect of the Messias.[51]

Already in the Apocalypse the beloved disciple had asserted Christ's divinity—not in so many words, to be sure, but in naming him with divine names,[52] in ascribing divine offices to him,[53] and assigning him divine honors.[54] In the gospel the expressions are more direct and explicit. Christ is the Word who was in the beginning, who was with God, who was God (Jn. 1:1). He is life itself, and the fount and author of life.[55] He is light, the dispenser of truth,[56] and even truth itself,[57] that is to say, he is essential light and essential truth, insofar as he possesses the divine nature.

This testimony of St. John to the divinity of his Master is confirmed by what Christ has to say of himself. On three distinct occasions in this gospel he claims unity of nature with the Father:

1) *Before the Jews in the temple.*[58] In Jerusalem on the feast of the Dedication, Jesus replies to the insistence of the Jews that he state openly that he is the Christ. In his reply he declares that he and the Father are one. Astonished, the Jews would have stoned him for blasphemy. But he rejects their accusation and then calmly reaffirms his unity of nature with the Father: "If I do not perform the works of my Father, do not believe me. But if I do perform them, and if you are not willing to believe me, believe the works, that you may know and believe that the Father is in me and I in the Father." This was clear enough: again they sought to seize him, but his hour had not yet come.

---

[51]This purpose and character of the fourth gospel force those rationalist critics who reject the supernatural and dogmatic to deny the apostolic origin and historical validity of this narrative. The unprejudiced reader will recognize from internal evidence alone the authenticity and historicity of John's gospel. Cf. G. Ricciotti, *The Life of Christ* (Milwaukee: Bruce, 1947), 142-153.

[52]"The First and the Last": Apoc. 1:17, 2:8, 22:13; "he who lives": 1:18; "the holy one, the true one": 3:7; "the begining of the creation of God": 3:14; "Lord of lords and the King of kings": 17:14, 19:16.

[53]Lord of life and death: Apoc. 1:18; searcher of desires and hearts: 2:23; universal power: 1:4, 2:26,27, 12:5.

[54]Apoc. 1:6, 5:8-14.

[55]Jn. 3:16,17, 5:21,24-26,28-29, 11:25, 14:6,9, 17:2,24.

[56]Jn. 1:5,9-11, 3:17-21.

[57]Jn. 14:6. God is truth (I Jn. 1:5), the Holy Spirit is truth (I Jn. 5:6) and the Spirit of truth (Jn. 14:17, 15:26, 16:13; I Jn. 4:6).

[58]Jn. 10:22-39.

2) *Before the disciples at the Last Supper.*[59] To console his disciples on the eve of his departure from them, Jesus gently points out to them that they who have truly known him also know the Father to whom he is going. "I am the way, and the truth, and the life. No one comes to the Father but through me. If you had known me, you would also have known my Father. And henceforth you do know him, and you have seen him." When Philip then asked to be shown the Father, Jesus said to him: "Dost thou not believe that I am in the Father and the Father in me? The words that I speak to you I speak not on my own authority. But the Father dwelling in me, it is he who does the works. Do you believe that I am in the Father and the Father in me? Otherwise believe because of the works themselves."

3) *In his prayer to the Father.*[60] Having prayed to the Father for himself and for his disciples, Jesus now prays for all those who will believe in him. And what he beseeches is this, that they may be united one to another in a most perfect union, similar to the union of Father and Son, and that this intimate union be found also between these believers so united and themselves. Already he has begun this work of uniting men among themselves, to and in God: "And the glory that thou hast given me, I have given to them, that they may be one, even as we are one: I in them and thou in me; that they may be perfected in unity and that the world may know that thou hast sent me, and that thou hast loved them even as thou hast loved me."

3. The Humanity of Christ

Against the Docetists, those early heretics who denied the reality of the human nature of the Messias and claimed his body was only an illusion, St. John forthrightly asserts: "I write of what was from the beginning, what we have heard, what we have seen with our eyes, what we have looked upon and our hands have handled: of the

[59]Jn. 14:7-11.
[60]Jn. 17:20-23.

Word of Life" (I Jn. 1:1). Christ was truly divine, as the Docetists taught, the Son of God who was in the beginning with God; but, St. John insists, "the Word was made flesh" (Jn. 1:14).

The fact had been long foretold by the prophets. The "Son of man" (Dan. 7:13 ff.), the promised Deliverer, would be seed of Eve (Gen. 3:15), a descendant of Abraham of the tribe of Judah (Gen. 49:10), of the root of Jesse (Isa. 11:1). Born of a virgin (Isa. 7:14) in the Davidic town of Bethlehem (Mich. 5:1), he would sit on the throne of his illustrious ancestor (Isa. 9:7). "The most beautiful of the children of men" (Ps. 45:3) will suffer terribly (although patiently and willingly) (Isa. 53; Ps. 21) and die for our sins (Isa. 53:8-12; Zach. 12:10).

The true humanity of the Savior is superabundantly attested to by the gospels. Mary truly, albeit miraculously, conceives and bears a son, flesh of her flesh, fruit of her womb. The holy family returns to Nazareth from Bethlehem, and there, after the flight into Egypt, the "carpenter's son" (cf. Matt. 13:55; Mk. 6:3) "advanced in wisdom and age and grace before God and men" (Lk. 2:52). Simeon had held the child in his arms, the sinful woman dries the feet her tears had wetted and kisses them, John reclines on his breast. Wonderment is his, and anger, and pity, and sorrow—indeed, his soul is sorrowful unto death. He is wearied by his journeyings, he sleeps, he needs food and drink. And he suffers, in body and spirit, he gives up his spirit on an inhuman instrument of infamy, his pierced body is laid in the sepulchre.

After his predicted resurrection from the dead, solidly attested to by many witnesses, he says to the disciples who thought they saw a spirit: "Why are you disturbed, and why do doubts arise in your hearts? See my hands and feet, that it is I myself. Feel me and see; for a spirit does not have flesh and bones, as you see I have" (Lk. 24:38-39). As further proof of the reality of his risen body, he ate in their presence.

All this is very clear—so clear, that, as the Fathers did not hesitate to point out, a denial of Christ's humanity would make him who is God a liar, it would destroy his entire redemptive work, it would impugn the credibility of Sacred Scripture.

4. The Hypostatic Union

We do not find in the written word of God the technical terms which the Church will later use to define and specify, in precise and unambiguous language, the dogma of the Incarnation. But the doctrine thereby expressed is indubitably taught in the sacred pages, put forth in language proper and proportioned to the literary forms used and to the immediate recipients of these writings. The Hypostatic Union—i.e., the dogma of the Church that the Second Person of the Blessed Trinity subsists in two integral and unmingled natures, divine and human—has its solid foundation in Sacred Scripture. Proof of this fact will be found in the general teaching of the Bible and, more specifically, in the inspired teachings of St. Paul and St. John.[61]

A. General Teaching

The historical figure who dies for the sins of mankind is both God and man, both human and divine. He is a single concrete individual who possesses, in their fulness and integrity, the attributes both of divine nature and of human nature. Of one and the same identical physical subject, these qualities, seemingly contradictory, are predicated: the Messias, Christ, Jesus.

This is true from the first explicit announcement of the Deliverer's complex and paradoxical character by Isaias. Strong God, *'el gibbor*— this is the divine name given him (Isa. 9:6) who is yet a child to be born to us, a son to be given to us. A virgin shall conceive and bear him, and his name shall be called "God with us" (Isa. 7:14). The same basic unity of him who is both God and man is at least hinted at in the messianic psalms 2 and 109.

In the gospels the identical fact stands out so clearly as to obviate need for comment. No one could seriously maintain that the Synoptists ascribed divine qualities to one individual, and then predicated human qualities of another distinct physical subject, although heresies which amount to such a multiplication of individuals will later result. It is one and the same Christ who is born at Bethlehem and adored by

[61]Cf. footnote 31, p. 19.

the shepherds and Magi; one and the same who changes water into wine and shares in the wedding banquet; one and the same who claims oneness with the Father and is about to be stoned for blasphemy; one and the same who dies on the cross and arises from the dead.

"The author of life you killed," St. Peter remarks to the Jews in his first discourse (Acts 3:15). It is the Word of Life, declares St. John, whom we have looked upon and our hands have handled (I Jn. 1:1). Christ—yesterday, today and forever—is both God and man, the God-man.

B. The Teaching of St. Paul

Several passages of St. Paul's letters affirm at one and the same time both the divinity and the humanity of the one identical Christ. It is clear that Christ is from the patriarchs according to the flesh, he informs the Romans, but at the same time he is "over all things, God blessed forever" (Rom. 9:5). Writing to his disciple Titus, he speaks of "looking for the blessed hope and glorious coming of our great God and Savior Jesus Christ," and adds, in words unmistakably referring to Christ's humanity, "who gave himself for us that he might redeem us from all iniquity. . ." (Tit. 2:13-14).

Of equal clarity is the statement to the Galatians: "But when the fulness of time came, God sent his Son, born of a woman, born under the Law, that he might redeem those who were under the Law, that we might receive the adoption of sons" (Gal. 4:4-5). Thus of one and the same Christ he affirms an eternal pre-existence with God, as Son of God, and a temporal mission inaugurated by his birth of a woman, a man subject to the Law, in order to redeem the human nature: divine and human natures are united in the one person, in a hypostatic union.

Two passages are of particular interest and demand as well as merit a somewhat closer scrutiny.

1. Epistle to the Philippians, 2:5-11.

Have this mind in you which was also in Christ Jesus, who though he was by nature God, did not consider being equal to God a thing to be clung to, but emptied himself, taking the nature of a slave and being made like unto men. And appearing in the form of man, he humbled himself, becoming obedient to death, even to death on a cross. Therefore God also has exalted him and has bestowed upon him the name that is above every name, so that at the name of Jesus every knee should bend of those in heaven, on earth, and under the earth, and every tongue should confess that the Lord Jesus Christ is in the glory of God the Father.

Here, after declaring the pre-existence of Christ as God by nature (vv. 6-7), St. Paul points out that he renounced his divine honors and prerogatives to assume our nature, with its creaturely dependence, its mortality, its passibility. Developing this point as he next turns to consider the historical Christ (vv. 7-8), he gives a second example of his humility, his perfect obedience unto death. "Appearing in the form of man," i.e., exhibiting all the external appearances of a man— he eats, sleeps, walks, prays, etc.—in this way he manifests his humanity to those about him, a humanity that carries the humiliations of sufferings and death.

Thus St. Paul here teaches: 1) that Christ was God and equal to God, and therefore a person distinct from God although of the same nature; 2) that while retaining his divine nature he assumes a true human nature, both natures remaining complete even after their union; 3) that this union of two perfect natures is to be attributed to one and the same principle, to Christ.

In the last verses (vv. 9-11), it is the glorified Christ who is considered. Here again the perfect union of both human and divine natures in Christ is asserted, confirming the already stated doctrine of the Hypostatic Union in Christ. Because of the obedience of his death, Christ, whose divinity had been hidden in his assumption of human nature, now receives from his Father a singular reward. From this moment it will not only be his humanity which appears; now his divinity will be manifested in plain light before all, so that all, whether in heaven, or on earth, or under the earth, should confess the divinity of Christ and thus give glory to his Father.

2. The Epistle to the Colossians, 1:13-20.

He has rescued us from the power of darkness and transferred us into the kingdom of his beloved Son, in whom we have our redemption, the remission of our sins. He is the image of the invisible God, the first-born of every creature. For in him were created all things in the heavens and on the earth, things visible and things invisible, whether Thrones, or Dominations, or Principalities, or Powers. All things have been created through and unto him, and he is before all creatures, and in him all things hold together. Again, he is the head of his body, the Church; he, who is the beginning, the firstborn from the dead, that in all things he may have the first place. For it has pleased God the Father that in him all his fulness should dwell, and that through him he should reconcile to himself all things, whether on the earth or in the heavens, making peace through the blood of his cross.

In this passage St. Paul first teaches the divinity of Christ (v. 13). His is the kingdom described by the Synoptic gospels as the "kingdom of heaven" or "of God"; he is the "Son" of the Father, even more, the "beloved" Son (i.e., only begotten). Through him (the expression "in whom" is a Hebraism denoting a certain efficient causality), through this Christ who is true God, "redemption" comes to us—and here St. Paul uses a technical word which may be defined: "the liberation of the human race from sin and its effects and penalties, procured through Christ *by payment of the price of his own blood.*"[62] Thus (v. 14) Christ as man, by the shedding of his own blood, perfects the work of redemption.

In what follows Christ is described as "image of the invisible God" and "firstborn of every creature" (v. 15). The first expression denotes the equal perfection which Christ possesses with the Father, for he is not an imperfect likeness as are we who are made to God's image; he is the beloved Son of God, and in him the entire fulness of divinity dwells (Col. 1:19, 2:9), and therefore he is the most perfect possible image of the Father. By the second expression is designated Christ's eternal priority over every creature, because he is described (v. 16) as creator of every creature, "before all creatures"; it might be rendered, then, "begotten before any creature."

Hence the same Christ who is man, "the firstborn from the dead" (v. 18), and as man is the Redeemer (v. 14), "making peace through the blood of his cross" (v. 20); he is also the creator of all things, "in whom all things hold together" (v. 17), that is to say, true God of true

---

[62]F. Zorell, S.J., *Novi Testamenti Lexicon Graecum* (Paris: Lethielleux, 1911), 67. Thus the Vulgate text legitimately adds "through his blood" to the Greek text (no doubt under the influence of Eph. 1:7, "In him we have redemption through his blood, the remission of sins. . . .") to make explicit St. Paul's true doctrine.

God. This passage unequivocally teaches the Hypostatic Union of divine and human natures in Christ.

C. The Teaching of St. John

St. John's express purpose in writing his gospel was to proclaim the divinity of him whom he describes in that work as a fully and perfectly human being, the Savior and Messias who was Jesus Christ.[63] In the magnificent Prologue (1:1-18) which opens this sublime and profound work, he sets forth his essential doctrine of the Word of God[64] already briefly announced.[65]

[63]Jn. 20:31; cf. *supra*, 22-24.

[64]At one time the Johannine doctrine of the *Logos* or Word of God was considered by rationalist critics as a simple borrowing from the Platonic teaching of the Alexandrian Jew, Philo. Despite some similarities (both *words* play a role in creation, both are mediators between God and man), however—and these easily explainable on the basis of community of origin, found in the biblical sources both writers used—so great and essential are the differences in the two doctrines that even the most radical critics (Harnack and Loisy, for example) were forced to acknowledge that John owes nothing to Philo's ideas. A similar hasty reversal overtook other rationalists who held that the theological content of the fourth gospel derived from an obscure Oriental cult known as Mandeism; today it is commonly admitted that the case is exactly the opposite, that Mandeism was greatly influenced by Christianity.

What St. John did do was to deepen and transform the Old Testament personification of Wisdom. He used as his vehicle of expression the word "logos" which was known both to contemporary Jews and to the pagan Hellenic world, without being the exclusive property of any philosophical school or encumbered by false preconceptions. In this transformation the Logos is presented as a *person*, not a personification, who possesses the divine nature in the strict sense and is identical with the Messias of the Jews, him who is the Savior of all mankind, Jesus Christ.

Thus St. John translates and adapts and interprets the doctrinal data of the Synoptic gospels and the teaching of Jesus Christ for the Hellenistic Jews and the Greeks, for at his time the Church had spread far beyond the narrow Palestinian circle of her birth. To display the supereminent dignity of Jesus in full and plain light, he chooses the expression "Word of God." For "Son of God" (or any similar phrase) would have confused the pagans, to whom it would suggest one of the innumerable pantheon begotten of carnal relations between immortals and mortals; it would have alienated the Jews, for whom the title "Son of God" carried no messianic connotations. And not only does the phrase possess, in consequence, an admirable evangelical usefulness. More profoundly, it expresses the searching depth of St. John's own penetration of Christ's message and even suggests, beyond his unquestionably divine inspiration, a special revelation. For by this concept the infinite and unfathomable riches of the Blessed Trinity become more easily accessible to the searching mind of faith, "*quaerens intellectum.*"

All these points are more fully and authoritatively made in the works on Christ previously mentioned; for a more detailed study see J. Lebreton, *The Origins of the Doctrine of the Trinity*, I (London: Burnes, Oates and Washbourne, 1939), 420-433.

[65]Apoc. 19:13; I Jn. 1:1. Only in these three places does the word Logos occur in the whole New Testament; St. John in no way suggests that Christ himself or any one of his disciples used the expression or proposed the concept underlying it.

In the beginning was the Word,
  and the Word was with **God;**
  and the Word was God.
He was in the beginning with God.
All things were made through him,
  and without him was made
  nothing that has been made.
In him was life,
  and the life was the light of men.
And the light shines in the darkness;
  and the darkness grasped it not.
There was a man,
  one sent from God,
  whose name was John.
This man came as a witness,
  to bear witness concerning the light,
  that all might believe through him.
He was not himself the light,
  but was to bear witness to the light.
It was the true light
  that enlightens every man
  who comes into the world.
He was in the world,
  and the world was made through him,
  and the world knew him not.
He came unto his own,
  and his own received him not.
But to as many as received him
  he gave the power of becoming sons of God;
  to those who believe in his name:
Who were born not of blood,
  nor of the will of the flesh,
  nor of the will of man,
  but of God.
And the Word was made flesh,
  and dwelt among us.
And we saw his glory—
  glory as of the only begotten of the Father—
  full of grace and of truth.
John bore witness concerning him,
  and cried, "This was he of whom I said:
'He who is come after me
  has been set above me,
  because he was before me.'"
And of his fulness
  we have all received,
  grace for grace.

In the very first verse St. John asserts three singular facts about the Word: 1) his eternal pre-existence, for he already was, when as yet no creature was in existence; 2) his distinct personality, for the evangelist's use of the article to modify the word "God" indicates one divine person, while the phrase "the Word was with God" predicates a distinction between them; 3) his divine nature, for the Word is God, and here "God" appears without the article to denote the divine nature, the consubstantiality of the Word with the Father. Thus the Word is a distinct person truly divine. The same thought is repeated (v. 2), and then Christ's divinity is reaffirmed by a new argument (vv. 3-5): the Word is creator of all things, author both of the natural and of the supernatural orders—an irrefragable argument for the Jews.

It is this very Word, a divine person distinct from the Father, whom St. John declares to have been made flesh (v. 14). The word "flesh" in its primitive meaning denotes some organic material endowed with life and senses; but in common biblical usage it stands by synecdoche for the whole man, the composite of body and soul, connoting the mortality and passibility of human nature. The Word "becomes" flesh or "is made" flesh; that is, he is not changed into flesh or humanity (as heretics will later teach), but retaining all that he had, his divine personality, he assumes what before he did not have, a mortal and passible human nature. In this flesh "he dwelt among us" or—in the most literal sense of the Greek words—"he set up his tent among us," his humanity being, as it were, a tent hiding his divinity, and this tent established in our midst. Yet even so his glory was manifested through his human nature (by his miracles, for example, by his transfiguration, and most especially by his resurrection) to his earthly companions and particularly to his disciples, a glory such as belongs by proper right to one who is Son of God by nature (v. 15).

Thus throughout this Prologue St. John attributes to one and the same principle, the Word, who is a distinct divine person, qualities which are proper to both natures, human as well as divine. In the Word, human nature and divine nature are united in a personal, Hypostatic Union.

D. Conclusion

One and the same historical person, Jesus Christ, who is the Messias or Deliverer predicted by the Old Testament, is declared by the inspired word of God to be both divine and human. The essential facts of the Incarnation are stated only once, and somewhat obscurely, by the prophets of the Old Law. But the teacher whom God sends to mankind, "the only begotten Son, who is in the bosom of the Father, he has revealed him" (Jn. 1:21). Jesus Christ clearly and explicitly teaches that he is God and man, both human and divine; it is this revelation which ultimately leads to his redemptive death for mankind.

This teaching is a fundamental truth for the Church he founds in order to save men from their sins and bring them into the kingdom of heaven. His disciples refer to it briefly in the occasional letters they compose and send to various Christian communities, for it is a basic element of the oral catechesis which has led to the foundation of those churches. In different language and clearer light it is expounded at a deeper, more appreciated level by St. Paul and St. John in their writings.

But everywhere and always it is the identical truth which is preached: the union of divine and human natures in the one divine person, the Word of God, who is Christ Jesus, the Messias.

THE DEVELOPMENT OF THE DOGMA OF THE INCARNATION

Human understanding is not equal to the mysteries of faith it confesses; more is there than we can know; human words are even more unequal to expressing the objective reality which is the object of our faith, being barely adequate to communicate what our own mind conceives about them. Thus there is always (and infinitely) room for improvement of our knowledge of the divine and of our assertions about the divine, even though no new truth about the divine will ever be given to us or to the Church in this life.

With the death of St. John, the last apostle, God's revelation of himself to man comes to a close. It is the office of Christ's Church through the ages both to guard this deposit of faith and to expound it, that all men may hear the authentic voice of God and receive his call to salvation. *What* the Church has to say is always and necessarily the same: the divine truth given her by her founder. Thus the object of faith never varies, from the days of the primitive Church to our own times; nothing new is ever added, nothing is ever taken away, for the revealed truth exists in its fulness right from the beginning.

But the *expression* of that immutable truth can and does change. Without altering the essential meaning in the slightest, analysis of the terms of the mystery will lead to a deepening understanding, to a fuller appreciation of its wealth of meaning, to a more exact and precise determination of its significance, to a clearer insight into its perfection. In short, a firmer, more explicit, more profound grasp *on the part of the faithful* of the very same revealed truth will, in the course of time, result. The consequence of such an understanding is a restatement of the truth in an explanatory formula susceptible of one interpretation only, and that the orthodox interpretation. This the Church adopts as her own, to serve henceforth as the instrument of her positive teaching.

This continuous and progressive movement of Christian thought under the guidance of the Holy Spirit eventuates in a new dogmatic formulation of a revealed doctrine always professed by the Church. This process is known as the **evolution or development of dogma.** The inquiring mind of Christian thinkers is necessarily moved by their piety to probe the mysteries God has revealed, both to manifest their reasonableness to external critics, and even more to acquire a better understanding of them for themselves and for the Church. This is a delicate and even dangerous task, and it is no wonder that the Church carefully watches over such efforts, howsoever sincere. For as the thinking activity of Christians proceeds, there will be hesitations, uncertainties, inexactitudes, unfruitful adaptations; altercation and controversy will arise; some will go too far, slipping (perhaps unconsciously) into error or misrepresentation.

Nothing should surprise us in this. God did not promise infallibility and the unerring assistance of his Spirit to individual Christians, but to his Church and to her head. And the difficulty of choosing and formulating exact expressions, often in scientific and philosophic terms, of the revealed deposit of faith (which is itself completely new to the human mind) is obviously an enormous one, fraught with peril.

Thus the Church will carefully supervise these human efforts, conscious always of the essential truth to be safeguarded. At times she will reprimand these thinkers, if they prove themselves rash; or modify any expressions that distort or pervert the truth; or arrest, in definitive statements, any erroneous interpretations. The end result of this intellectual activity will be the precise definition of a revealed doctrine, authoritatively proposed by the Church of Christ.

Like the dogma of the Trinity, so also the dogma of the Incarnation exemplifies this advance in understanding of, and exposition of a revealed truth in itself unchangeable. Covering the earlier periods more rapidly (for much of this matter has already been treated at some length in studying the dogma of the Trinity),[66] we shall sketch this history in four stages: 1) beginnings of dogmatic formulation (**Section 5**); 2) theological speculation (**Section 6**); 3) crisis and resolution (**Section 7**); and 4) Christological definitions (**Section 8**).

5. The First Period, A.D. 100-200: Beginnings of Dogmatic Formulation

From the first moment of her inception, the Church of Christ insists on two indispensable elements of belief, the mysteries of the Incarnation and of the Trinity. These were revealed to us (as the Scriptures attest) by the Son of God made man, who came down from heaven "to declare" to us the intimate life of the Godhead in which he shares and which furnishes the basis for our redemption.[67]

---

[66]Cf. Murphy, et al., *God and His Creation*, 264-285.
[67]"No one at any time has seen God. The only begotten Son, who is in the bosom of the Father, he has revealed him" (Jn. 1:21).

A. "I Believe. . . ."

Modern historical research irrefutably confirms the fact of this witness of Tradition, expressed by the primitive Church, in the essential doctrines of Christianity. Baptismal formulas explicitly attest to the three (and among them Jesus Christ) who are one God.[68] The "rule of faith" is a creed, a summary of Christian doctrine. In its most primitive form, this creed is a Christological confession of faith (cf. Acts 8:37; I Pet. 3:18-22; I Cor. 15:3; Phil. 2:5-11; Rom. 1:3), although the trinitarian formula became dominant, doubtless because of its association with baptism.[69] Whatever be the exact origin of these creeds, whatever historical difficulties may attend the determination of their primitive form, the doctrines which they certify have a number of independent witnesses in this dawn of Christianity. St. Ignatius of Antioch (+107), whose "theology," founded on St. Paul and enriched by St. John, is centered on Christ incarnate, so puts these essentials:

> I give glory to Jesus Christ, the God who has imbued you with such wisdom. I am well aware that you have been made perfect in unwavering faith, like men nailed, in body and spirit, to the cross of our Lord, Jesus Christ, and confirmed in love by the blood of Christ. In regard to our Lord, you are thoroughly convinced that he was of the race of David according to the flesh, and the Son of God by his will and power; that he was truly born of the Virgin and baptized by John in order that all due observance might be fulfilled by him; that in his

[68]Cf. *Didache*, Chap. 7, n. 1. At a later date (c. 150), the same essential profession of faith is mentioned by St. Justin (*Apology*, I, n. 6), and thirty years after Justin by St. Irenaeus (*Proof of the Apostolic Preaching*, nn. 3 and 7). St. Hippolytus (c. 170-c. 235) indicates that a specific question was asked of the catechumen regarding each member of the Trinity (*The Apostolic Tradition*, XX, 12-17), and the Trinity in unity is expressed by the primitive ritual of triple immersion (or aspersion). Such continuity of profession and ceremony is inexplicable on any other ground than that of community of belief.

[69]The two most ancient of extant creeds—one contained in an obscure work dating from 150-180, the other that of an Egyptian ritual of the second century—clearly indicate the importance of the trinitarian profession: of five articles of faith, three relate to the Trinity (cf. Denz. 1). It thus appears likely that the Apostles' Creed in the form we now possess it (our text dates back no further than the early sixth century) was originally centered on trinitarian doctrine. The expanded teaching of the second article on Christ would then be a later explanatory addition to a simpler formula.

The history of the Apostles' Creed is uncertain, but it is probably of Roman origin, dating from the early part of the second century. It receives the name "Apostles'" both because it dates from this "Apostolic" age and because it is so closely linked in doctrine and language with the apostles.

body he was truly nailed to the cross for our sake under Pontius Pilate and Herod, the tetrarch—of whose fruit are we, of his most divinely blessed passion—so that, through his resurrection, he might raise for all ages, in the one body of his Church, a standard for the saints and the faithful, whether among Jews or Gentiles.[70]

But other of these earliest of Christian writers—whom we call "Apostolic Fathers" because they are linked so closely in time and teaching with the apostles—testify just as surely to the same fundamental facts of Christianity. Besides their trinitarian formulas, couched in scriptural terms,[71] they assert that Jesus is Son of God,[72] true God[73] and yet true man.[74] Thus they affirm—although they do not state it in these words—that Christ possessed both divine and human natures; and since these properties are predicated of one and the same historical individual, the Apostolic Fathers evidently suppose that there is unity of person. In brief, they teach, in all but the very words of the Scriptures, the basic facts about the God-man revealed in Sacred Scripture. They are important witnesses of Apostolic Tradition.

B. The First Denials

Despite this unanimity of teaching, heresies only too quickly appear on the scene. These arise from attempts, foredoomed from the beginning, to blend the unique message of Jesus Christ with pagan and/or Jewish preconceptions. Either denying his true humanity or rejecting his true divinity, in either form these errors have a con-

---

[70]*Epistle to the Smyrneans*, 1:1-2.
[71]St. Clement of Rome (+101), *Epistle to the Corinthians*, 42:3, 46:6, 58:2; St. Ignatius of Antioch, *Epistle to the Ephesians*, 9:1, *Epistle to the Magnesians*, 13:1, *Epistle to the Smyrneans*, title; the account of the martyrdom of St. Polycarp (disciple of St. John), *The Martyrdom of St. Polycarp* (156/7), 14:3.
[72]St. Clement, *op. cit.*, 36:2-5; Ps.-Clement, 1:1-2, 9:5; St. Polycarp (+156), *Epistle to the Philippians*, 2:1, 6:2, 12:2; *Martyrdom of St. Polycarp*, 17:3; *Didache*, 9:2-3, 10:2-3.
[73]St. Ignatius of Antioch, *Epistle to the Ephesians*, title, 15:3, 18:2, *Epistle to the Trallians*, 7:1, *Epistle to the Romans*, title, 3:3, *Epistle to Polycarp*, 8:3; *Martyrdom of St. Polycarp*, 14:1,3, 20:2; *Epistle of Barnabas*, 5:5, 6:12.
[74]Christ saves us by his blood (St. Clement, *op. cit.*, 49:6, 31:6; *Epistle of Barnabas*, 5:1, 7:3,5), which is the blood of God (St. Ignatius of Antioch, *Epistle to the Ephesians*, 1:11). He died for our sins (St. Polycarp, *Epistle to the Philippians*, 1:2, 8:1; *Martyrdom of St. Polycarp*, 17:2); he is truly man (St. Ignatius of Antioch, *Epistle to the Romans*, 7:3, *Epistle to the Ephesians*, 7:2 [*teaching on Mary, his mother*], 19:3, 20:2, *Epistle to the Smyrneans*, 1:1-2, 2, 3, *Epistle to Polycarp*, 3:2; St. Polycarp, *Epistle to the Philippians*, 7:1).

tinuous history during the first centuries of the Christian era. Two are of particular note in this first period.

1. **Docetism.** According to ancient oriental dualism, the cosmos was a vast arena wherein the struggle between two supreme principles, one of good and one of evil, was enacted. This philosophy supplies the theory for the first heresy, which held that Christ did not assume a real body but only an apparent or illusory body. Hence it received the name Docetism, from the Greek *dokein,* to appear. Since matter was evil, the very incorporation of the principle of evil, and God was absolutely transcendent, the very notion of a divine incarnation was unacceptable to them. Hence the necessity, on philosophical grounds, for their compromise with Christianity.

But so obviously destructive was this theory of the facts and the fundamental tenets of Christian belief that the Docetist error was quickly detected and refuted. St. Paul attacks it, insisting on the necessary mediatorship of the man Christ Jesus.[75] St. John declares bluntly: "Every spirit that confesses that Jesus Christ has come in the flesh, is of God."[76] Their disciples, the Apostolic Fathers, are quite as forthright, as the quotation from St. Ignatius given above indicates.[77] Somewhat later, St. Irenaeus, Tertullian (in a complete work on the subject, *On the Flesh of Christ*), and later still St. Augustine will vigorously refute contemporary versions of the Docetist heresy.

2. **Ebionites.** The Ebionites were a Jewish sect which taught that Jesus was only a man, the son of Joseph and Mary, upon whom the spirit of God descended at his baptism to raise him to the dignity of adopted son of God. No doubt it was such heretics that St. Paul had in mind in extolling Christ above all the angels in his letter to the Hebrews,[78] and St. John wrote his gospel precisely to prove the divinity so gratuitously denied by "deceivers . . . who do not confess Jesus as the Christ coming in the flesh" (II Jn. 7). Once again, the same

[75]II Tim. 6:20.
[76]I Jn. 4:3; cf. I Jn. 1:1, II Jn. 7, Jn. 1:14.
[77]Cf. *supra,* 36-37 and note 74.
[78]Heb. 1:1-14; cf. Col. 1:15-20, where he refutes those Jews who set the angels higher than Christ.

refutations will be made by the Apostolic Fathers.[79] But this is a heresy hard to kill, and it will reappear time and time again in the succeeding centuries under one guise or another.

3. **Gnosticism.** Of more imminent danger than either of the heresies just mentioned is a new movement, intellectual in character, seductive and persuasive for an age genuinely anxious for religious truth and absolute values. **Gnosticism,** it is called (from the Greek word *gnosis,* knowledge), for its claim to a superior, and secret, understanding of things. Pagan to the core, it synthesizes mythology, current philosophical systems and degenerate religious elements. But it promises to its initiates a knowledge of the sacred mysteries of Christianity higher than that offered by the common faith, and thus seduces many of the new converts and prospective converts of an expanding Christianity. The Gnosis constitutes a problem the Church has to face up to, if she is to win the age for Christ.

C. Apology and Controversy

(1) The Apologists

A group of learned and educated converts enter the lists in intellectual defense of Catholicism against paganism and Judaism, a feat which history honors by giving them the title of Apologists. Seeking to commend Christianity to a hostile world, they employ current philosophical notions and language to translate Christian truth into familiar terms. Their marshalling of evidence from the Scriptures, their attempts to explain the mysteries through philosophical concepts, their efforts to construct a more scientific vocabulary and formulate technical expressions—all this adds up to a genuine intellectual movement within the Church of prime importance for the development of dogma.

But since Christology does not enter explicitly into their discussions with pagan antagonists, and they strove in any case to underline points of contact, their consideration of the Incarnation is little developed beyond the traditional notions. They are a testimony to the faith,

[79]Cf. *supra,* 37 and notes 72 and 73.

nonetheless.[80] St. Justin (+ 165-166) in particular records all the essential elements of Christian belief in the Incarnation.[81]

Despite this adherence to dogmatic essentials, the attempts of the Apologists to explore and explain the origin of the Word and the relations between Father and Son are far from felicitous. Doctrinal inaccuracies, stemming from their philosophy, betray them into expressions which suggest a hierarchy in the Trinity, with the Son subordinate to the Father. This first sketch of a trinitarian doctrine, however orthodox for the Apologists themselves,[82] bears a warning of the difficulties and even dangers inherent in human explanations of revelation; certain of their formulas will develop at a later date into genuine heresies.

(2) St. Irenaeus

The work of the Apologists in justifying Christianity as a most lofty wisdom did much, at least indirectly, to counteract the influence of the Gnosis. But it is St. Irenaeus of Lyons (c. 140-c. 202), bishop and martyr, who refutes Gnosticism in so masterly a fashion as to drive it entirely outside the Christian pale. This he accomplishes, not by abstract and philosophical theorizing, but by appeal to the divine authority of Christ's Church. This alone is the "rule of faith," he in-

[80]Aristides sums up the scriptural history of Jesus Christ (*Apology*, n. 15 in the Greek text); Tatian, although he does not name Jesus, speaks much of the Word (*Discourse to the Greeks*, Chap. 5), and mentions the suffering God (*ibid.*, Chap. 13) and God in the form of man (*ibid.*, Chap. 21), both undoubtedly allusions to Jesus Christ of whom his special purposes preclude explicit mention; the *Epistle to Diognetus* acknowledges the Savior as God (Chap. 7:4, 8, 9), true and proper Son of God (Chap. 9:2, Chap. 10:2) who becomes man (Chap. 7:4) to save us (Chap. 9:5); Melito of Sardis in a remarkable passage affirms the two natures of him who is both God and man (Fragm. 7), identifies Christ with the Godhead itself (*Homily on the Passion*, 8-10), strikingly affirms his pre-existence (*ibid.*, 82), and is no less clear regarding his Incarnation (66, 70-71).

[81]Jesus Christ is the Word, the Son of God made flesh and become man (*First Apology*, nn. 5, 23, 32, 46, 63; *Second Apology*, n. 6; *Dialogue with Trypho*, nn. 45, 48, 63, 84) who is composed of body, Logos and soul (*Second Apology*, n. 10). His was a real body (*On the Resurrection*, nn. 1 and 2) in which he truly suffers (*First Apology*, nn. 31 and 32; *Dialogue with Trypho*, *passim*) in order to redeem us (*First Apology*, n. 63; *Dialogue with Trypho*, nn. 41, 134).

[82]Athenagoras no doubt speaks for their common belief when he clearly marks both the unity of nature and the distinction of Persons. The Christians profess, he declares, "a God and his Word, what is the union of the Son with the Father, what is the communication of the Father with the Son, what is the Spirit, what is the union and the distinction of those who are thus united, the Spirit, the Son, the Father" (*Supplication for the Christians*, n. 12; cf. n. 10).

sists, for the Church (and in particular the Church of Rome)[83] is the witness, the guardian, the organ of apostolic tradition and the genuine interpreter of the source of faith which is the Scriptures.

In the vast synthesis which he constructs of traditional truth taught by the Church, Christology is the heart and center of his theology. And the theory of "recapitulation" (unique with him, although an obvious development of Pauline theology) is the heart of his Christology:

> There is one God the Father, as we have shown, and one Christ Jesus our Lord, who comes by a universal dispensation and recapitulates all things in himself. But man also, a creature of God, is included in the "all things"; therefore he recapitulates man in himself. The invisible is become visible, the incomprehensible comprehensible, and the impassible passible, and the Logos becomes man, recapitulating all things in himself. Hence, just as he is the first among heavenly and spiritual and invisible things, so also is he the first among visible and corporeal things.[84]

Jesus Christ thus summed up in himself all mankind and became for it a new Adam, a new head in whom it recovered every blessing it had lost in the first Adam.[85] For Jesus is the Word,[86] identical with the Son of God,[87] begotten by the Father[88] by an eternal generation,[89] and thus truly God.[90] This Word, who is by his very essence immortality and incorruptibility,[91] becomes man,[92] takes our flesh and blood[93] and soul,[94] becomes as we are, of our race, our brother.[95] Born of a virgin, his was yet a totally human experience of temptation, passion, sorrow and suffering.[96] The work of our redemption and

[83]*Against Heresies*, Bk. III, Chap. 3, n. 2. Unless otherwise noted all future references to St. Irenaeus are to this work.
[84]Bk. III, Chap. 16, n. 6; cf. Chap. 18, nn. 1 and 7, Bk. IV, Preface, n. 2 and Chap. 20, n. 8.
[85]Bk. III, Chap. 18, n. 1, Chap. 21, n. 10, Bk. V, Chap. 23, n. 2.
[86]Bk. III, Chap. 16, n. 6, Chap. 9, n. 3, Chap. 16, nn. 7-9.
[87]Bk. II, Chap. 28, n. 6, Bk. III, Chap. 16, n. 6, Chap. 18, n. 2.
[88]Bk. II, Chap. 28, n. 6.
[89]Bk. II, Chap. 25, n. 3, Chap. 30, n. 9, Bk. III, Chap. 18, n. 1; this is a deliberate correction of the notions of some of the Apologists of a temporal generation of the Word.
[90]Bk. III, Chap. 6, nn. 1 and 2.
[91]Bk. III, Chap. 9, n. 1, Chap. 18, n. 7.
[92]Bk. III, Chap. 18, n. 1, Bk. V, Chap. 14, n. 2.
[93]Bk. III, Chap. 18, nn. 6 and 7, Chap. 22, nn. 1 and 2; etc.
[94]Bk. III, Chap. 21, nn. 1 and 2, Bk. V, Chap. 1, n. 1, Chap. 14, n. 3.
[95]Bk. III, Chap. 1, nn. 4-10.
[96]Bk. II, Chap. 22, n. 4, Bk. III, Chap. 17, n. 4, Chap. 18, nn. 1, 6, 7, Chap. 19, n. 2, Chap. 22, n. 2, Bk. V, Chap. 21, n. 2.

salvation, already begun with the Incarnation itself, is completed by his atonement for sin through his obedience unto death[97] and by the ransom of his blood.[98]

Thus the greatest of these early theologians explicitly affirms the union of divine and human natures in Jesus Christ, the duality of natures in the personal unity of the Word. "He has truly saved us," he declares. "He is the Word of God, he the only begotten of the Father, Christ Jesus our Lord."[99] And again, "The incarnate Word of God has been suspended on a tree."[100] But how this union (which he styles, quite inaccurately, a "commixtion" or "community" of God and man)[101] was accomplished, St. Irenaeus does not even attempt to explain, no more than he would dare to explain through philosophical speculation the generation of the Word.[102]

According to this exposition of the faith, Christ has a threefold mission: 1) to reveal the Father;[103] 2) to redeem mankind;[104] and 3) to sanctify, deify and so reconcile man with God.[105] So through Christ we are made once more in the image of God and his children, and immortality and everlasting life is conferred upon us.

From this résumé of St. Irenaeus' Christology it should be apparent that all the elements of future development are here present in germ, the fruit not of speculation but of the traditional faith. Thanks to his work, that unfolding of implicit and latent truths which is the development of the dogma of the Incarnation can take place in the West calmly and gradually, for it is based on the surest of foundations, the living teaching authority, the *magisterium* of the Church. His epochal work marks the highwater of these affirmations of faith which characterize the first period of dogmatic development.

---

[97]Bk. IV, Chap. 5, n. 4, Bk. V, Chap. 17, n. 1, Bk. III, Chap. 18, nn. 6 and 7.
[98]Bk. V, Chap. 1, n. 1, Chap. 2, n. 1, Chap. 16, n. 3.
[99]Bk. III, Chap. 16, n. 9; cf. Chap. 19, nn. 2 and 3; etc.
[100]Bk. III, Chap. 9, n. 3, Bk. V, Chap. 18, n. 1.
[101]Bk. IV, Chap. 20, n. 4.
[102]Bk. II, Chap. 13, n. 8, Chap. 28, n. 6.
[103]Bk. III, Chap. 11, n. 8, Bk. IV, Chap. 9, n. 3, Chap. 12, n. 2, Chap. 13, n. 2.
[104]Cf. *supra*, notes 97 and 98.
[105]Bk. III, Chap. 18, 19, 23, Bk. V, Chap. 1, n. 1, Chap. 12, n. 6, Chap. 14, nn. 1 and 3; etc.

6. The Second Period, A.D. 200-300:
Theological Speculation

The dogmatic reaffirmations of the early Christian writers, despite a lack of precision in their formulas and a fixed technical vocabulary, focus light on a fundamental question. How can one reconcile the divine unity with the divinity of the Son or Word and of the Holy Spirit? The third and much of the fourth centuries will be preoccupied with this basic problem; only after its resolution, first at the Council of Nicaea in 325 and definitively at the Council of Constantinople in 381, does the difficulty become a strictly Christological one.

The approach of the Christian thinkers and writers of this time will differ greatly from that of the Apostolic Fathers and the Apologists. No longer is there only defense and apology. Now the main concern is to explore the truths revealed by Christ, to seek answers and explanations, employing what human tools are available. This effort, to be sure, will constitute a defense of the mysteries—particularly of the Trinity and of the Incarnation—from critics without and heretics within; but it is primarily an attempt to obtain a fuller, richer understanding of God's revelation.

These Christian speculations are carried on both in the East and in the West. In examining these efforts for their teaching on Christ (necessarily entwined with their trinitarian theories), we shall first consider the Christological heresies which sprang up at Rome, then their refutation in the West, and finally the course of theological speculation in the East.

A. The Heresies at Rome

(1) Adoptionism

Toward the close of the second century, a new school of theology opened at Rome under the direction of a certain Theodotus. His teachings, based on a too literal and grammatical explanation of Scripture, were only a revival of the errors of Cerinthus and the Ebionites. Jesus was a mere man, born of a virgin, on whom the Christ descended at his baptism with special powers. Because of his merits, he was adopted by God as his son while still remaining only a man.

Immediately excommunicated by Pope Victor, Theodotus formed a schismatic community at Rome. As late as the middle of the third century the heresy was being defended by Artemon, but he is its last representative in the West. He seems, however, to have transmitted it to Paul of Samosata, friend of that Lucian who was the master of Arius, the heresiarch of the fourth century.

(2) Sabellianism

A more stubborn heresy, although obscure in origins, seeks to maintain the divine unity by denying any real distinction between the Father and the Son. The Word is only another name for the Father, who becomes Son by the Incarnation and suffers for mankind. First to have spread this heresy were Praxeas (against whom Tertullian wrote) and Noetus (refuted by St. Hippolytus). But it was a later heretic, Sabellius, who exercised the greatest influence and gave his name to the heresy.

In this later stage, moreover, the heretical doctrine took far more subtle forms. There is only one person in God, called Father, Son, or Holy Spirit according to the successive manifestations of his various attributes; thus the Persons are only *modes* of the one divinity. This theorizing gave the heresy its name of Modalism, as earlier versions had been called Monarchianism (because of the insistence on the "monarchy," the absolute divine unity) and Patripassianism (from the Latin *passio*, "suffering," and *patris*, "of the Father").

B. Refutations of Heresy

Serious as were the errors of Sabellianism (=Modalism=Monarchianism=Patripassianism), they were not at the time so clearly formulated as to demand a precise and specific condemnation by the *magisterium*. But the Church does authoritatively intervene: in an official papal pronouncement St. Callistus (+ 222) condemns Sabellius. He and his predecessor, St. Zephyrinus, had already proclaimed their faith and that of the Church in the unity of God and in the divinity of Jesus Christ, who (and not the Father) was born and suffered.[106]

While these papal formulas lack theological precision, they are official expressions of the Rule of Faith. Three western theologians, Hippolytus and Novatian at Rome and Tertullian in Africa, not only refute the new heresies by exposing their deviations from the same Rule of Faith, they also attempt explanations of the mysteries so grievously distorted by the heretics.

(1) St. Hippolytus (c. 170-c. 235)

A disciple of St. Irenaeus, the learned Hippolytus attempts to refute Modalism and Patripassianism by developing the trinitarian system of the Apologists. Desirous of emphasizing the distinction of the divine Persons against the Modalists, he adopts the theory of the temporal generation of the Word. He even goes so far as to add a third phase (the Incarnation) by which the Word, eternally present to the Father as immanent idea (*logos endiathetos*) and first begotten as spoken word of the Father (*logos prophorikos*) in the creation of the world, becomes perfect Son.

That such theories imperil the eternity of the Word, the immutability of God, the unity and equality of the Persons—these dangers St. Hippolytus does not seem to have recognized. In any case, they in no way detract from the orthodoxy of his Christological teachings. The Word becomes incarnate, becomes a true man, assumes not only our body but a rational soul and our infirmities and passions.[107] The eighteenth chapter of the *Against Noetus* emphatically affirms both the duality of the divine and human elements and their intimate union in the unity of the person of the Word.[108] Like St. Irenaeus, he sees in this Incarnation of the Word the "recapitulation" or summing up of mankind in the Word which is the beginning of man's salvation.[109]

---

[106]Cf. Denz. 42a.

[107]*Against Noetus*, Chap. 17; *Philosophumena* ("*Refutation of All Heresies*"), Bk. X, Chap. 33.

[108]Cf. *ibid.*, Chap. 6, 13, 14, 17.

[109]This work is completed by the death of the Savior: by dying, Christ has conquered death (*Treatise on Antichrist*, 26, 44; *Commentary on Daniel*, IV, 5, 11) and thus secured incorruptibility for us (*Treatise on Antichrist*, 26).

(2) Novatian (+c. 257)

A generation after Hippolytus, a Roman priest, Novatian, openly espoused his theology of the Word in a remarkable and influential treatise, *On the Trinity,* the first theological work composed in Latin at Rome. Dependent to a great extent on Tertullian, Novatian incorporates the subordinationist tendencies of his predecessors into his trinitarian doctrine. Hence despite the fact that he explicitly affirms not only the eternity of the Father (*On the Trinity,* Chap. 16 and 31), but also the "divine substance" of the distinct "second Person," the Son (*ibid.,* Chap. 31), and the "communion of substance" of Father and Son (*loc. cit.*), he subordinates the Son to the Father (*op. cit.,* Chap. 27) and makes him his subject (*ibid.,* Chap. 18) and servant (*ibid.,* Chap. 31).

But this defective trinitarian exposition does not impair his Christology. Chapters 9-28 of *On the Trinity* are a defense of the two distinct natures and their union in Christ. Against Docetists and Ebionites, against Adoptionism and Modalism, he reaffirms the Rule of Faith, the true humanity (*ibid.,* Chap. 10, 13, 21, 22, 23) and true divinity (*ibid.,* Chap. 11 and 17) of Jesus Christ, Son of God and son of man (*ibid.,* Chap. 11), promised in the Old Testament and revealed in the New. Undoubtedly this doctrine and its expression owe much to Tertullian, but Novatian himself formulated many phrases to express his full acknowledgment of the personal unity of Jesus Christ.[110]

(3) Tertullian (c. 150-c. 240)

A Roman advocate of repute, Quintus Septimius Florens Tertullianus, a native of Carthage, places his considerable talents and profound knowledge in the service of Christian truth after his conversion. A vigorous thinker, a master of rhetoric, he attacks and refutes the heretics: the Gnostics (*Against Marcion, Against Hermogenes, Against the Valentinians*); the Docetists (*On the Flesh of Christ, On the Resurrection*); Monarchianism (*Against Praxeas*). In these, and

---

[110]He describes the unity of the distinct two natures in Christ as a "harmony" (*concordia: ibid.,* Chap. 13, 16, 18, 19, 22), a "compacting" (*concretio: ibid.,* Chap. 11, 14, 19), a "conjunction" (*ibid.,* Chap. 14, 16), a "connection" (*ibid.,* Chap. 16, 19), a "confederation" (*ibid.,* Chap. 13, 16, 19), and even—although this must be understood in the context of the other descriptions—a "mixture" (*ibid.,* Chap. 11, 19).

in the numerous other works he composed, the great African creates a firm and precise theological language in Latin, which he was one of the first theologians to employ.

Thus in affirming the substantial divine unity of the three numerically distinct divine Persons, he composes, a hundred years before the Council of Nicaea, the definitive formula: *three Persons, one substance*. While Tertullian's trinitarian teaching is not entirely free from subordinating the Son to the Father, his insistence on the consubstantiality of the Trinity is a marked advance over his predecessors and a true corrective of the old confusions.

The defects of Tertullian's teaching on the Trinity find no place in his Christology, which has all of its merits. Against the Docetists he teaches the reality of Christ's humanity, against the Adoptionists the reality of his divinity. Without transformation of one into the other, without their fusion or combination into one substance, both natures are united in the single person of Christ while each retains its own distinct operations.

Here, too, the African strikes the exact word and creates the definitive formula. He states:

> We see plainly the twofold state, which is not confounded but conjoined in one person: Jesus Christ, God and man. . . . The property of each nature is so wholly preserved that the spirit [Christ's divine nature], on the one hand, did all things in Jesus suitable to itself, such as miracles and mighty deeds and wonders; and the flesh, on the other hand, exhibited the affections which belong to it. It was hungry under the devil's temptation, thirsty with the Samaritan woman, wept over Lazarus, was troubled even unto death, and at last actually died. If, however, it was only some third thing, some composite essence formed out of two substances . . . there would be no distinct proofs apparent of either nature. But by a transfer of functions, the spirit would have done things to be done by the flesh, and the flesh such as are produced by the spirit, or else such things as are fitting neither to the flesh nor to the spirit, but confusedly of some third character. Nay more, on this supposition—if the Word had been converted into flesh—either the Word underwent death or the flesh did not die, because either the flesh was immortal or the Word was mortal. Inasmuch, however, as the two substances acted distinctly, each in its own character, necessarily there accrued to each of them their own operations and their own issues.[111]

[111]*Against Praxeas*, Chap. 27: cf. *On the Flesh of Christ*, 5.

"The twofold state, not confounded but conjoined in one person, Jesus Christ, God and man"—this is already, two hundred years before the fact, the teaching of St. Leo and the formula of the Council of Chalcedon (451). Tertullian bequeaths to Latin theology forms of thought and of expression which will spare the West from the controversies and divisions which are to rend eastern Christendom.

C. Theological Speculation in the East

While the Latin Church was struggling with heresy, a Christian intellectual movement of prime moment was quietly developing in the East. At Alexandria in Egypt, cultural capital of the Roman world, a school of Christian learning was established about the middle of the second century. This resulted in the pioneering effort of one of its first masters, Clement (150-211/15), to employ philosophy systematically in producing a higher and more scientific knowledge of the faith, a Christian *gnosis* to offset the "pseudo-gnosis" of the pagans.

This highly original attempt had many faults. Orthodox affirmations of the doctrine of the Trinity do not prevent expressions which suggest subordination and modalism. Clement taught the incarnation of the Word, acknowledging that he is both God and man, but held that his body was free from the common necessities of eating and drinking and his soul free from the movements of the passions. But these flaws destroy neither his work nor his influence: he may well be regarded as the founder of speculative theology.

Origen (185-254), his pupil, was also his successor as master of the school of Alexandria. A genius of vast erudition, his prodigious and original efforts will influence other scholars for hundreds of years. While his speculations are not without error and some of his theories must be completely discarded, on the whole Origen's was an epoch-making contribution to theology.

His trinitarian doctrine, for example, not only affirms the unity of God but the three *hypostases* (persons?) of Father, Son and Holy Spirit. He explicitly teaches the eternal generation of the Son and his consubstantiality with the Father, thus refuting the heretic, Arius, a century before he appears. He identifies the Logos with the incarnate Jesus of the gospels, admitting the integrity of the two natures and the unity of the Person.

The orthodoxy of Origen's Christology can be gathered from the following passage concerning the interchange of divine and human attributes:

> The Son of God, through whom all things were created, is named Jesus Christ and the Son of man. For the Son of God is also said to have died—in reference, namely, to that nature which could admit of death; and he who is announced as about to come in the glory of God the Father with the holy angels is called the Son of man. It is for this reason that, throughout the whole of Scripture, not only is the divine nature spoken of in human words, but the human nature is adorned by names of divine dignity.[112]

These clear Christological notions, together with his emphatic assertion of the free soul of Jesus Christ,[113] make him a powerful ally of the cause of orthodoxy in the Christological controversies which are to come. For Origen, as for the Rule of Faith he so deeply respected, Christ is always *theanthropos,* the God-man.[114]

D. Conclusion

This second period in the development of the dogma of the Incarnation does not produce much theorizing or speculation concerning the Hypostatic Union itself. But in the rejection of persistent heresies— of Docetism which destroyed Christ's humanity, of Adoptionism which denied his true divinity—the fundamental characteristics of that revealed mystery are restated in ever clearer and more precise language. This will permit, in the following centuries, first of all a precise statement of the Christological problem, and ultimately a resolution of that problem that exposes the deeper significance of the Incarnation.

Nor are the theologians of the third century only continuing witnesses of Tradition. They have themselves made significant progress in the understanding of Christian faith. And in their exposition of the

---

[112]*On First Principles,* Bk. II, Chap. 6, n. 3.
[113]*Loc. cit.* and *ibid.,* n. 5.
[114]Clement had used the expression, man-God, *anthropos theos;* Origen himself invents the happier expression and is the first to use it, *Third Homily on Ezechiel,* 3.

gospel revelation they have assisted the Church in fixing the foundations of her belief so as to be ready, when occasion may demand it,
to define its great principles.

7. The Third Period, A.D. 300-400:
Crisis and Resolution

With the fourth century, stretching from St. Athanasius to St. Augustine, one enters into one of the greatest epochs of ecclesiastical history, the "golden age" of the Fathers of the Church. So rich a period
in doctrine and teaching and speculation, and one so agitated by controversy and politics, is little patient of the kind of summary sketch
that can be attempted here. But the highlights of that history and the
more outstanding contributions of its great theologians and doctors
must be touched upon, for they are of primary importance in the
development of the dogma of the Incarnation. Four main subjects
will occupy our attention: 1) the Arian crisis; 2) the Christology of the
Greek Fathers; 3) the heresy of Apollinarianism; and 4) Christological
doctrine in the West.

A. The Arian Crisis

From the first Christian century Adoptionism had been condemned
again and again—officially by the Church, and at length and in detail
by her theologians. Yet once more it appears, and now for the last time.
At Alexandria a popular and erudite preacher, Arius (256-336) by
name, formally proposes the doctrine that the Word was not God but
a created intermediary between God and the world, begotten of
God only by a sonship of adoption.

This trinitarian heresy with its obvious Christological implications
was by no means an original creation. It was the subordinationism
of the Apologists (of which even Origen was not free) carried to its
logical extreme. It was a direct inheritance from Arius' master, Lucian,
founder of the school of Antioch, an influential teacher who had defended the adoptionist teachings of his friend, Paul of Samosata, thrice

condemned (between 264-268) by synods of Antioch. But if Arius did not father the doctrine, he so furthered its dispersal after his condemnation at Alexandria as to plunge the East into violent theological controversy.

To remedy the intolerable situation the emperor, Constantine, took the unprecedented step of summoning the bishops of Christendom to sit in synodal judgment on the dispute between Arius and his powerful friends and Alexandria. The three hundred bishops and the papal legates who assembled at Nicaea in 325 condemned Arius and his doctrine and issued an official declaration of faith, a Creed, the first such since the baptismal formulas. In this postive statement of Catholic belief, Jesus Christ, "the Son of God," is declared "the only begotten of the Father: God of God, Light of Light, true God of true God: begotten, not made, consubstantial with the Father (*homoöusion to Patri*)." Negatively, the council anathematizes all those who profess Arian formulas of subordinationism or adoptionism.[115]

This definitive formulation of Christ's divinity should have ended the affair. But imperial sponsorship of the Arian cause, which hid under various guises and ambiguous professions of faith, not only maintained the heresy within the Church; what is more, the new Caesar by force and trickery imposed the court religion on the empire. Valiantly opposed by St. Athanasius (296?-373), patriarch of Alexandria, in the East, and by the popes and St. Hilary (c. 315-367) in the West, imperial policy by 359 apparently won complete victory over orthodoxy and Nicaea.

But the death of Constantius in 361 cleared the way for the ultimate triumph of Catholic truth. Although Valens supported Arianism much as his predecessors on the throne had done, the tide had turned. The great Cappadocian Fathers worked out precise theological formulae which avoid both extremes of Sabellianism and Arianism, and theoretically vindicate the faith of Nicaea and its expressions. Finally, in 381 the ecumenical Council of Constantinople sounded the death-knell of Arianism with the tocsin of Nicaea: the *homoöusios* or consubstantiality of Christ.

[115]Denz. 54.

The fathers of that Council declare their belief "in one Godhead
and power and *ousia* (nature) of the Father and of the Son and of
the Holy Spirit, of equal dignity and coeternal majesty, in three perfect *hypostases,* that is, three perfect persons. . . ."[116] With this
definition the victory of Nicaea over religious error is total and unconditional. Henceforth Arianism is a sect exterior to the Church, an
external enemy of Christianity taking refuge among the barbarians.
The *homoöusios* of Nicaea—the consubstantial divinity of the Son of
God—is accepted in the entire Christian world as a dogma of Christian faith.

B. The Christology of the Greek Fathers   •

In their vigorous opposition to Arianism, and in the struggle against
a later heresy, Apollinarianism (which we shall discuss in the following section), the Fathers in the East were brought to consider more
thoroughly and profoundly than heretofore the mystery of Christ.
Their theological speculations, while leaving much to be desired in
the way of accuracy of language and maturity of ideas, mark a
considerable step forward in Catholic understanding of the mystery.
We can but outline them here, reducing a complex body of doctrine
to a few simple and essential points.[117]

1) In their attacks on Arianism and defense of Nicene dogma, these
   great theologians unequivocally affirm their belief in the divinity of Christ, his consubstantiality with the Father and his
   eternity. Equally clear are their declarations of his true humanity. He possesses a true human body (against Docetism),[118] a

---

[116]This is taken from a letter of a local council held at Constantinople in 382
to Pope Damasus and the western bishops; the excerpt summarizes the lost doctrinal tome of the ecumenical Council of Constantinople of the previous year.
(Preserved in Theodoret, *Church History,* V, 9.)

[117]For the purposes of this survey we will limit ourselves to the teachings of
St. Athanasius (c. 295-373), St. Cyril of Jerusalem (c. 313-386), St. Epiphanius
(c. 315-403), Didymus the Blind (313-?), St. Basil (330-379), St. Gregory of
Nazianzus (330-c. 390), St. Gregory of Nyssa (335-c. 395), St. John Chrysostom
(344-407), St. Amphilochius of Iconium (340-c. 403).

[118]Athanasius, *Letter to Epictetus,* 5, 7; Cyril of Jerusalem, *Twelfth Catechesis,*
3, 13, 22, 24, 31, 33; John Chrysostom, *Homilies on St. John,* 11:2, 63:2; Amphilochius, Frag. X; Basil, *Epistle 261.*

created intelligent soul (against Apollinarianism),[119] and, except for sin, is subject to our infirmities, weaknesses and needs.[120]

2) Despite the union of divinity and humanity in Christ, there is no change of one nature into the other, nor any combination or fusion of them to constitute some third nature.[121] Hence even after their union the two "forms"[122] or natures remain distinct, each preserving its distinctive characteristics and properties.[123]

3) Distinct though Christ's divine and human nature are, their union in the Word constitutes a personal unity.[124] This important truth is most precisely stated in a definitive formula by St. Gregory of Nazianzus:

> If any introduce the notion of two sons, one of God the Father, the other of the mother, and discredits the unity and identity, may he lose his part in the adoption promised to those who believe aright. For God and man are two natures, as also soul and body are; but there are not two sons or two gods, as neither in this life are there two manhoods. . . . And (if I am to speak concisely) the Savior is made of [elements] which are distinct from one another (for the invisible is not the same with the visible, nor the timeless with that which is subject to time), yet he is not two— God forbid! For both [natures] are one by the combination, the deity being made man, and the man deified, or however one

[119]Didymus, *On the Trinity*, Bk. III, Chap. 4 and 21; Epiphanius, *Ancoratus*, 32-35, 76-80; ps.-Athanasius, *Against Apollinaris*, Bk. I, Chap. 15, 16, 17; Gregory of Nazianzus, *Epistle 101, First Theological Discourse*, 35, 42; Gregory of Nyssa, *Antirrhiticus adversus Apollinarem*, 32, 41.

[120]Athanasius, *Discourse on the Incarnation of the Word*, 8, *Second Discourse against the Arians*, n. 69, *Third Discourse against the Arians*, nn. 34 and 56; Basil, *Epistle 261*, 3; Gregory of Nazianzus, *Thirtieth Theological Discourse*; Epiphanius, *Ancoratus*, 33; John Chrysostom, *Homilies on St. John*, 11:2, 63:1, 67:1,2.

[121]Didymus, *On the Trinity*, Bk. II, Chap. 6, 13, 21; Epiphanius, *Ancoratus*, 75; John Chrysostom, *Homilies on St. John*, 11:2.

[122]Athanasius, Fragm. (P.G., 26:1256-1257).

[123]Gregory of Nazianzus, *Epistle 101, Second Theological Discourse*, 23; Epiphanius, *Ancoratus*, 75, 116, 117; Amphilochius, Fragm. II, VII, IX, XI, XII. Didymus explicitly affirms the existence of two wills in Christ, *On the Trinity*, Bk. III, Chap. 12.

[124]Athanasius (?), *Tome to the Antiochians*, 7, *On the Doctrine of Denis*, 9; Didymus, *On the Trinity*, Bk. III, Chap. 6, *On the Holy Spirit*, 52, *Commentary on the First Epistle of St. Peter*, II, 23, *Commentary on the First Epistle of St. John*, IV, 15; Cyril of Jerusalem, *Twelfth Catechesis*, 4; Epiphanius, *Ancoratus*, 120; Amphilochius, *First Sermon, On the Nativity*, 4, 6, *Fifth Sermon, On Holy Saturday*, 2, Fragm. III; Gregory of Nazianzus, *Second Theological Discourse*, 23, *Thirty-seventh Theological Discourse*, 2; Gregory of Nyssa, *Against Eunomius*, Bk. V.

should express it. And I say different [elements], because it is the reverse of what is the case in the Trinity; for there we acknowledge different [Persons] so as not to confound the Persons, but not different [elements], for the three are one and the same in Godhead.[125]

4) The first consequence of this personal union of divine and human natures in Jesus Christ, the Word, is the interchange of properties (*communicatio idiomatum*), i.e., the predication of what is human of him who is God, of what is divine of him who is man. Already outlined by Origen,[126] the theory is both stated and practiced by these fourth-century Fathers.[127] In the controversies of the following century it will be an important criterion to distinguish between orthodoxy and heresy.

5) A second consequence is the divine maternity of Mary. The designation, mother of God, *theotokos* (literally, "God bearer"), is not only an affirmation of Mary's dignity but a profession of faith in the divinity of the human son to whom she gave birth, Jesus Christ. As such it was a part of the traditional teaching of Alexandria.[128] Now reaffirmed in the same meaning by these theologians, it acquires an even more technical dogmatic significance.[129] It, too, will shortly serve as a test of Catholic Faith.

Thus the essential truths concerning the Hypostatic Union which are revealed by Sacred Scripture and the teaching of Tradition are more sharply and distinctly stated by the Greek Fathers of the fourth century. But even among the later Fathers the speculations on the nature of that union are incomplete, with a corresponding lack of precision in analyzing the doctrine. Add to this disadvantage a theological language as yet too immature for the truths it bears,

---

[125]*Epistle 101.*
[126]*On First Principles*, Bk. II, Chap. 6, n. 3, Bk. IV, Chap. 31.
[127]Athanasius, *Epistle to Adelphius*, 3; Gregory of Nazianzus, *Thirty-eighth Theological Discourse;* Gregory of Nyssa, *Against Eunomius*, Bk. V.
[128]Already known to Origen (cited by Socrates, *Church History*, VII, 32), it was used by St. Alexander of Alexandria, bishop from 312 to 328 (confession of faith in his letter to Alexander of Constantinople; Theodoret, *Church History*, I, 3) and St. Athanasius (*Third Discourse Against the Arians*, 14, 19, 33) in this very sense.
[129]Didymus, *On the Trinity*, Bk. I, Chap. 31, Bk. II, Chap. 4, Bk. III, Chap. 41; Epiphanius, *Ancoratus*, 75; Gregory of Nazianzus, *Epistle 101, Twenty-ninth Theological Discourse*, 4.

and a terminology not sufficiently accurate for incisive and necessary distinctions. The result is that the basic Christological problem, which these theologians have clearly exposed—in what manner divine and human are united in the Word without diminution or change—still lacks a definite and satisfactory solution.

Thus the earlier Fathers use expressions which suggest a merely moral union between the divine and human in Christ—the foundation of the future heresy of Nestorianism.[130] Even the Cappadocians fall into the same error; with them it is chiefly a matter of words, to be sure, but they furnish important ammunition for future deviations from the truth.[131] More seriously, their insistence on the absolute personal unity of Christ produces a disturbing tendency to unite the natures and eliminate the distinction between them.[132] The "one-nature" heresy of the next century (Monophysitism or Eutychianism) will employ the same phrases and push these tendencies to their logical limit of error.

Penetration of doctrine, clarification of terminology, precision of language—all must be achieved before the fundamental problem of Christology is definitely resolved. The time will come; it is not yet.

C. The Heresy of Apollinarism

One of the most redoutable opponents of Arianism, as courageous as he was profound and erudite, was Apollinaris, created bishop of Laodicea about 360. Zeal for the orthodox cause led him to suspect the views of Diodorus, head of the school of Antioch; the latter's emphasis on the human nature of the Savior seemed to Apollinaris to compromise the personal unity of Christ, and thus issue logically if indirectly in Arianism.

[130]Athanasius, *Third Discourse against the Arians*, 34, 52, *Epistle to Epictetus*, 2, 4, 10, *Epistle to Adelphius*, 3, 4. *Discourse on the Incarnation of the Word*, 42, 43, 44; Cyril of Jerusalem, *Twelfth Catechesis*, 1, 6.
[131]Gregory of Nazianzus, *Twenty-ninth Theological Discourse*, 18, 19, *Thirtieth Theological Discourse*, 1, 7, 8, 9, 10, 12, 13, 21; Gregory of Nyssa, *Against Eunomius*, Bk. V, *Antirrhiticus*, 54.
[132]Gregory of Nazianzus, *Second Theological Discourse*, 23, *Thirtieth Theological Discourse*, 3, *Thirty-seventh Theological Discourse*, 2, *Thirty-eighth Theological Discourse*, 13 (these tendencies can easily be detected in the quotation on pp. 53-54 from *Epistle 101*); St. Gregory of Nyssa, *Against Eunomius*, Bk. V, *Antirrhiticus*, 42.

Working independently on the problem, keenly aware of the dangers of exaggerated dualism and as keenly unconcerned about Tradition, the learned bishop came up with his own solution. Since two complete beings cannot be one, and Christ is unquestionably one, the humanity which he assumed was not a complete, a perfect and integral humanity. What element was lacking? Obviously the free and intelligent soul, which would have been a second principle of activity and in conflict with his divinity. A human body with an animal soul, plus the divinity—these were the "elements" of the one incarnate nature of the Word.

The consequences of this doctrine—and Apollinaris was bold enough, confident enough, even logical enough to draw them—are indeed appalling.

1) The Word did not become man; he was "enfleshed," in the most literal sense of the word. His humanity is only similar to ours (he has a human body), not consubstantial.

2) Our flesh is saved by Jesus' flesh, but without any merit on its part; our soul is saved, not by his death, but by moral union with Christ.

3) There is only one subject of our adoration, the one incarnate nature of the Word, and only one principle of operation and free activity—the future heresy of Monotheletism, now promulgated by Apollinaris two hundred years before its condemnation.

4) *The chief consequence:* there is but one nature in Jesus Christ, one single nature (*mia phusis*), one single substance (*mia ousia*). Without transformation or mixture, the divine nature now exists in another way, through the addition of a new, and incomplete, element.

Against these ideas, first propagated secretly through Apollinaris' numerous and dedicated disciples, the reaction was swift and total. St. Athanasius, pseudo-Athanasius, St. Epiphanius wrote tracts against the novel doctrine. When Apollinaris came out into the open, he was denounced by St. Epiphanius and St. Basil, and shortly after officially condemned by Pope Damasus in the Roman Synod of 377. This authoritative papal decision was received and promulgated by the councils of Alexandria in 378 and of Antioch in 379; in 381 it was ratified by the ecumenical Council of Constantinople and in 382 by another Roman council.[133]

Despite these measures (including imperial persecution), the sect continued for a time. In the fifth century, however, its adherents swell the ranks of the great Eutychian and Monophysite heresy. This is but the result of cause and effect: Apollinaris had taught the same doctrine decades before.

D. Christological Doctrine in the West

While these dogmatic developments were occurring in the eastern half of the Roman empire, Latin theology, firmly founded by St. Irenaeus on Tradition and the *magisterium,* and already possessing (thanks largely to Tertullian) the indispensable tools of language and terminology, was advancing less spectacularly and quarrelsomely in the understanding of the faith. Evidence of this progress is sufficiently attested by the fact that these theological efforts culminate in the greatest of the Fathers and one of the greatest minds of all times, St. Augustine.

A brief survey of this doctrinal development will be undertaken in two parts: first, the theological doctrine on Christ of the Latin writers in general; second, the Christology of St. Augustine.

(1) Latin Christology in the Fourth Century

Seven men comprise the subject of this study. St. Hilary (315-366), St. Ambrose (333-397) and St. Jerome (347-419) are the great figures of the period. St. Hilary is the ablest theologian of them all, victor over Arianism in France and Italy, a forceful writer and powerful thinker, for all his borrowings from Athanasius and Greek theology. Of lesser stature are Victorinus (born c. 300), Zeno (+ 380), Phebadius (+ c. 392) and Niceta (+ c. 402); but they too have an important word to say as witnesses of Catholic teaching in the Latin Church.

All were valiant fighters in the struggle against Arianism. In their defense of Nicene dogma all unhesitatingly affirm the consubstan-

[133]Cf. "Tomus Damasi," seventh anathema; Denz. 65.

tiality (*homoöusios*) of the Word, his equality with the Father, and his eternal generation.[134] "God the Father and God the Son are absolutely one, not by a union of person, but by a unity of substance," declares St. Hilary.[135] It is the accurate expression of Tertullian, endowed with a deeper significance and rinsed of all subordinationism.

Bringing this exact knowledge of the Word to their consideration of the mystery of Christ, these Latin theologians restate the traditional beliefs of the Church. St. Hilary presents the fullest and deepest exposition of Catholic doctrine, but they all teach the fundamental truths. The Word, fully divine, becomes incarnate.[136] He assumes a real humanity,[137] taken of the substance of Mary,[138] freely bearing our infirmities and capable of suffering.[139] St. Ambrose and St. Jerome, add to this the insistence, against their contemporary, Apollinaris, that Christ assumed a rational soul, using the now classical argument that the Word must have assumed all of man, "for what is not assumed is not healed."[140]

The fundamental question of the Hypostatic Union, the duality of natures and unity of person in Jesus, still remains to be treated. The fourth-century Latins teach the fundamental facts with perfect clarity and in precise formulas. "We preserve the distinction of divinity and flesh," declares St. Ambrose. "The one Son of God speaks in both, because both natures exist in the same [subject]; and if the same one speaks, he does not always speak in the one manner."[141] Without

---

[134]Zeno is an exception here, being betrayed by his master, Tertullian, into reviving the Apologists' theories of the temporal generation of the Son. Cf. Bk. II, Tract 3, Tract 4 and Tract 5, 1. Nevertheless, he teaches the unity of substance of Father and Son (Bk. I, Tract 1, Bk. II, Tract 2, Tract 3 and Tract 5, 1) and their equality (Bk. II, Tract 1, 1, Tract 3, Tract 5, 1, Tract 6, 3, 4).

[135]*On the Trinity*, Bk. IV, n. 42; cf. n. 40.

[136]*Ibid.*, Bk. II, n. 26, Bk. IX, n. 51.

[137]*Ibid.*, Bk. X, n. 25.

[138]*Ibid.*, Bk. II, n. 26, Bk. X, nn. 15-17, 22, 25.

[139]*Ibid.*, Bk. X, nn. 23, 55, 56.

[140]Ambrose, *On the Mystery of the Lord's Incarnation*, Chap. 7, 68, cf. 63-78; Jerome, *Apology against Rufinus*, Bk. II, n. 4, *Commentary on the Epistle to the Galatians*, Bk. I, Chap. 1, etc.

[141]*On the Faith*, Bk. II, Chap. 77; cf. Chap. 57, 58, 60, Bk. III, Chap. 10 and 65, *On the Mystery of the Lord's Incarnation*, nn. 23, 37-45.

transformation of nature,[142] or a mixture resulting in a third substance,[143] the Word has united a human nature to himself, in such a way that after the union there is only one person, the natural Son of God, and yet the divine and human natures remain distinct in their attributes and operations.[144]

But these theologians are little interested in the concepts of nature and person which so engrossed their eastern contemporaries. Stating the facts, they set down the problem in exact terms. But since they attempt no intellectual analysis of the mystery of Christ, they may hardly be said to have recognized that there was a problem in reconciling the two distinct natures with the personal unity of Christ. Certainly they attempt no solution, contenting themselves with a plain and forceful statement of what the Church believes and the Rule of Faith teaches.

(2) St. Augustine (354-430)

Of this great saint and scholar, pre-eminently Father and Doctor of the Church, little can here be said. With regard to the development of the dogma of the Incarnation he contributed little that was personal or original. Yet so accurately did he restate the essential facts, and upon them threw so clear a light, that neither of the future fifth-century heresies of Nestorianism and Monophysitism will obtain a hearing in the West.

Against the Arians he declares the oneness and identity of the three divine Persons,[145] each really distinct from the other by their distinct relations.[146] The Second Person of the Trinity, the eternal Word and

---

[142]Phebadius, *On the Divinity of the Son,* 8; Victorinus, *Against Arius,* Bk. I, Chap. 45.

[143]Phebadius, *Treatise against the Arians,* 5.

[144]Hilary, *On the Trinity,* Bk. IX, nn. 3 and 14, Bk. X, nn. 22, 34, 52, 62, 63; Phebadius, *Treatise against the Arians,* 4, 5, 18, 19, *On the Divinity of the Son,* 8; Victorinus, *Against Arius,* Bk. I, Chap. 14 and 45, *Commentary on the Epistle to the Philippians,* II:6-8; Zeno, Bk. II, Tract 8, 2, Tract 9, 2, Tract 7, 4; Niceta, *On the Notion of Faith,* 6, 7, *On the Creed,* 4; Jerome, *Epistle 120,* 9, *Commentary on the Epistle to the Galatians,* 1:1,11, *Commentary on Matthew,* 28:2.

[145]*On the Trinity,* Bk. V, Chap. 9, Bk. VII, Chap. 10, Bk. VIII, Chap. 11, *Epistle 120,* 13, 17.

[146]*On the Trinity,* Bk. V, Chap. 6, 16, 17, Bk. VII, Chap. 24.

Son of God, becomes man, assuming an earthly body of a virgin[147] and a rational soul,[148] which is the bond between the Word and the body.[149]

This human nature, complete and perfect in itself, is united to the Word, but not through a transformation of one nature into the other nor through their combination. The two natures, divine and human, remain distinct, but they are united in a personal and hypostatic union in the person of the Word:

> The plan by which Christ was born of the Holy Spirit, but not as son, and of the Virgin Mary, yet as son, manifests to us the grace of God. For it was by this grace that a man, without any antecedent merits, in the very inception of his existence, was so united in one person to God the Word that the very same person was Son of God who was Son of man, and the very same person was Son of man who was Son of God.[150]

St. Augustine draws three important conclusions from this hypostatic union of divine and human natures in the Word.

1) In Christ there is only one son, the natural Son of God: "One person, he is the Son of God and also the Son of man; one person, he is the Son of man and also the Son of God; not two sons of God, God and man, but one Son of God; God without beginning, man from a beginning, our Lord, Jesus Christ."[151]

2) The interchange or communication of divine and human properties of each other (*communicatio idiomatum*): God dies, man is God, etc.

3) The Word brings to the human nature he assumes his own divine personality.

Thus despite the fact that St. Augustine's Christology is not as profound or as original as his investigation of other theological subjects, his synthesis of the traditional data marks a notable step forward in the development of the dogma of the Incarnation. Far more

---

[147]*Concerning the Christian Combat*, 20, 24; *Against Faustus*, Bk. 26, Chap. 71; *Sermon 190*, 7.
[148]*Commentary on John*, Tract XXIII, 6, Tract XLVII, 9.
[149]*Epistle 137*, 8; *Epistle 140*, 12.
[150]*Enchiridion*, Chap. 12, n. 40. The same doctrine is affirmed in text after text.
[151]*Ibid.*, Chap. 10, n. 35.

perfectly than his Latin predecessors, in the clearest of lights he exposes the personal unity of Christ. His insistence on the single personality of the God-man will save the West from the deviations from truth that result in the Greek Church through the attempt to resolve the Christological problem of the two natures and one person.

St. Augustine does not attempt to solve that problem; the nature of the Hypostatic Union is never analyzed by him. But of all the theologians we have so far considered—even more perfectly than the great Greek Fathers of the fourth century, with less imprecision of language and ambiguity of thought—he has most lucidly set forth the revealed fact of its existence. Only after the controversies in the East which culminate in the Councils of Ephesus and Chalcedon will a truly theological explanation be possible. It is these we must now consider.

8. The Fourth Period: The Fifth Century: Christological Definitions

Once the trinitarian question had been definitively settled by the Council of Constantinople in 381, the attention of theologians was directed to another deep problem. Already touched upon in the Arian controversy, brought to the fore by the heresy of Apollinaris and the orthodox reaction against it, the problem was this: how was the Word, who was truly God, also a man? In what sense were divinity and humanity united in him? In other words, what was the nature of the union realized in the Word when he became incarnate, according to our way of conceiving things?

The examination of the attempts to answer these questions takes us into one of the most complicated periods of ecclesiastical history and one of utmost importance for the development of the dogma of the Incarnation. The study will center on three points: the heresy of Nestorius; the Council of Ephesus and its aftermath; the monophysite heresy of Eutyches and the Council of Chalcedon.

A. The Heresy of Nestorius

As so often happens, the heresiarch who gives his name to the heterodox theory is not its inventor but its popularizer. Nestorius depends on Theodore of Mopsuestia, and Theodore in turn on Diodore of Tarsus, who seems to have been, quite against his will and knowledge, the true father of the heresy known to history as Nestorianism.

(1) Diodore of Tarsus (c. 330-391/2)

Founder of the second great school of Antioch, Diodore was a faithful adherent of its scholastic methods, which favored Aristotelian realism over Platonic speculation and the literal exegesis of Scripture as opposed to the allegorical and mystical interpretations of Alexandria. In solving the Christological question, therefore, he began with the realistic and scriptural fact of the two natures of Christ. When Apollinaris attacked the integrity of Christ's humanity by denying it a rational soul, Diodore hastened to the defense.

Unfortunately, his reaction led him so to accentuate the distinction between Christ's divinity and his humanity as almost to make two persons of them. In explaining their union he used expressions like those of the Adoptionists, affirming only a moral union. These dangerous formulas, whatever his good intentions, contain implicitly the entire heresy of Nestorianism and play a large part in bringing that heresy to fruition.

(2) Theodore of Mopsuestia (350-428)

Theodore was a pupil of Diodore and became head of the school of Antioch, numbering John of Antioch, Theodoret of Cyr and Rufinus among his pupils. He was a staunch and able defender of orthodoxy against Arianism and Apollinarianism—but at the same time a true disciple of his master. "When we distinguish the natures we say that the nature of God the Word is complete, and that his Person is also complete, since it cannot be said that a hypostasis is impersonal; that the nature of the man is complete and his person complete also.

But when we consider the union we say that there is only one person."[152]

Thus does Theodore synthesize, develop and explicate the implicit declaration of Diodore. For the "one person" of which he speaks, the Christ, is the result of a purely moral union between two different personalities, the Word and the man. God was in Christ, but Christ was not God. In consequence of this theory, he denies the communication of properties and refuses to acknowledge that Mary is truly the mother of God (*theotokos*), although popular pressure forces him to modify this last position.

In the teaching of Theodore of Mopsuestia all of the errors of Nestorianism are contained. They constitute a denial of the reality of the Incarnation and a consequent destruction of Christianity. These things are not clear in his lifetime. They only become manifest when Nestorius and his teaching thrust the Church into yet another controversy.

(3) Nestorius

Nestorius was an Antiochian preacher who so favorably impressed the emperor as to be named patriarch of Constantinople in 427. Shortly after, he defended one of his priests, Anastasius, who had scandalized the faithful by denying the title of mother of God (*theotokos*) to Our Lady. This disclosure of the patriarch's views on the Person of Christ caused a great stir in Constantinople and precipitated a doctrinal crisis of first moment.

What did Nestorius teach? To an extent he tried to attenuate the divergences between Theodore's doctrine and that of tradition, but when the flurry of words was over the same basic errors were present. An Antiochian, he insists on the distinction of Christ's humanity and his divinity. Both God and man, Christ is one, *for from the union—* not in spite of it—*there results a unique person.* Thus this "person of union" who is Christ is not identical with the pre-existing person of the Word, there is no interchange or communication of properties,

---

[152]*On the Incarnation of the Son of God,* VIII.

Mary is not *theotokos*. In short, the man in Christ is not Son of God by nature; the union of the two natures is a superficial union, not one according to essence nor according to hypostasis, but a merely moral union of the physical persons (*prosopa*) of the humanity and the Word.

Fundamentally, then, Nestorius teaches a "hypostatic dualism," that is, the existence of two persons in Christ. The consequences of such a theory for the dogmas of the Incarnation and the Redemption are evident: God does not become man, is not born of a virgin, does not die for our sins.

B. The Council of Ephesus

(1) Cyril of Alexandria

Far across the blue Mediterranean from the upstart imperial city of Constantinople where Nestorius held sway, sat the ancient cultural capital of Alexandria of Egypt, together with Rome and Antioch the most venerable of the sees of Christendom. And on the patriarchal throne of that proud see sat the man providentially destined, like his predecessor Athanasius a hundred years before, to defend the traditional doctrine.

Cyril was named to succeed his nefarious uncle Theophilus (a bitter and unscrupulous enemy of St. John Chrysostom during the latter's term as patriarch of Constantinople) as bishop of Alexandria in 412. He was many things—national leader, ecclesiastical politician, organizing genius—but above all else he was, in the most formal sense of the word, a theologian. Not as erudite as his opponent Theodoret, and by no means his equal as an exegete, inferior to the Cappadocians in philosophy and to Latin theologians in precision, Cyril surpasses all the Fathers as a theologian, saving only Augustine in the West and perhaps Origen in the East. In particular, he penetrates more deeply than any of them into the mystery of Christ and achieves a solution of the Christological problem which will be incorporated in the Church's definition of the dogma.

Faith and tradition and the profound insight into supernatural reality which one calls "the Catholic sense" were rules of thought for Cyril's theological genius. He begins with the absolute unity of the Word, a *phusis* (in Cyril's terminology, the concrete, individual, autonomous, self-subsistent, incommunicable subject of a certain nature, the nature concretized at the peak of its perfection and dignity, so to say; what we would call a "person") of the divine *ousia* (essence, nature or substance). The Word becomes flesh, is born a man—but this is the incarnation and generation not of any new *phusis*, it is the Word himself, the divine *phusis*, who is born in uniting humanity so intimately to himself that nothing of his unity is lost.

Thus the personal unity of Christ in no wise suffers from this union with humanity, and the physical oneness of the humanity and divinity in Christ must be affirmed as the reality it is, not just as a matter of words. Precisely here, Cyril saw, lay the great error of the Nestorians. In distinguishing between God and man in Christ and admitting only a relative and moral union between them, in fact (whatever their verbal formulas and protestations) they divide Christ in twain. Since his humanity is attached to the Word in their theory only by a tenuous link, it acquires an autonomy which elevates it to the dignity of personality. God and man are two persons.

But in truth there is far more than a mere rapprochement or liason between Christ's humanity and his divinity, there is a true, real, physical union. Cyril describes this as a "union **according to hypostasis**," the humanity being drawn into (so to speak) the pre-existing hypostasis of the Word, the divine *phusis*. In a less felicitous phrase he calls it a union **according to "nature"** (*enosis kata phusin* or *enosis phusike*), not because a new "nature" (*phusis*=person) results, but because the humanity is so possessed by the Word incarnate that in spite of the plurality of elements only one *phusis* (concrete, autonomous "nature") results, that of God. Thus while the humanity of the Savior is integral and perfect (Cyril teaches this firmly against Apollinaris), it is not a *phusis* in the full sense of the word, since it lacks autonomy and self-existence, the characteristics of a person.

All of this is summed up in a famous phrase: *mia phusis tou Theou Logou sesarkomene,* **the single incarnate "nature" of God the Word.**[153]

The soundness of this doctrine is indicated by the fact that it leads surely and easily to the communication of properties and the divine maternity of Mary. But its orthodoxy and its profundity are unfortunately obscured and confused by the imperfections of his theological language. For all practical purposes, Cyril accepts as synonyms the words *hypostasis, prosopon* and *phusis;* all three signify something like what philosophers and theologians mean today when they use the word "person." But the Nestorians had abused the word *prosopon,* admitting one "person" in Christ, the *prosopon* of union by which God dwelt in Christ as in a temple; "person" signified only the outward appearance of unity. The word *phusis* (concretized nature) had the advantage of distinguishing orthodox doctrine from Nestorius' affirmation of a single moral person; it underlined the real (as opposed to verbal) and physical (as opposed to moral) nature of the union of divinity and humanity of Christ in the substantial order of personality.

But the disadvantages and dangers of the word *phusis* were many. It was customarily used in the sense of "nature," as a synonym for *ousia.* And despite all his explanations, Cyril never really convinced either many of his enemies or a considerable number of his friends that he was not affirming with Apollinaris the existence of only one nature in Christ. Hence the continuing opposition of Antioch even after the Council of Ephesus to his doctrine, and the claims of the

---

[153]Cyril takes this "slogan" from Athanasius, *On the Incarnation of the Word of God;* but, ironically, this is a spurious work, one of the numerous treatises of Apollinaris distributed under false auspices to gain their acceptance. The phrase will be interpreted in the heretical, Apollinarian sense by the Nestorians and later the Monophysites will similarly misinterpret Cyril's meaning. The true significance of the phrase is indicated in the eighth canon of the Second Council of Constantinople: "If anyone, confessing that the union was made from the two natures of the deity and the humanity, or saying 'there is one incarnate nature of God the Word,' does not take these expressions in the sense taught by the Fathers—that from the union of divine and human natures according to hypostasis one Christ results—but tries by such phrases to introduce one nature or substance of the Godhead and humanity of Christ, let him be anathema" (Denz. 220). In the fifth canon of the Lateran Council of 649 the same interpretation is given (Denz. 258).

Monophysites that they were professing his doctrine even after the correctives of the Council of Chalcedon.

(2) The Council of Ephesus

Cyril was almost immediately apprised of the heretical teachings of the patriarch of Constantinople. He sent Nestorius a strong letter of protest, denounced him to the emperor, and wrote to Pope Celestine to secure his assistance in suppressing the heresy. Finally a council at Ephesus was summoned by Theodosius II to settle the dispute. The pope approved, naming three legates and instructing Cyril to work to obtain Nestorius' retraction, meanwhile temporarily suspending his condemnation of the heretic. The main events of this complicated affair may be summarized as follows:

1. Despite protests, St. Cyril called the first session on June 22, 431, after a fortnight's delay to await the coming of the Antiochian delegation and the papal legates. Nestorius was summoned but refused to recognize the council. After examining his teaching in the light of approved orthodox expressions of the faith (including Cyril's second letter to Nestorius), the 159 bishops unanimously condemned it and, "urged thereto by the canons and the letter of our most holy Father and colleague, Celestine, bishop of Rome," deposed Nestorius.[154]

2. A few days later, John, patriarch of Antioch and friend of Nestorius, arrived in Ephesus with sixteen suffragan bishops. They held an independent synod of forty-three bishops, excommunicated the other council and St. Cyril, and condemned the twelve propositions of his third letter to Nestorius as heretical.

3. Shortly afterward the papal legates arrived from Rome and, under instructions from the pope, joined themselves to Cyril. In the second session of the legitimate council, held on July 10, the legates presented the pope's letter to the council demanding acceptance and execution of his decision against Nestorius. The council adjourned to permit the legates to examine the minutes of its proceedings.

---

[154]The letter of St. Cyril which the council adopts as an expression of orthodox faith will be found in Denz. 111a.

4. Reassembled on the next day for its third session, the council heard the Roman legates confirm all that had been done in the first session. Sentence was then declared against Nestorius.

(3) The Aftermath of Ephesus

After many complicated maneuvers the emperor finally accepted the decisions of the Council of Ephesus. He confirmed the deposition of Nestorius and selected a new patriarch of Constantinople. Not for two years more, however, were John, patriarch of Antioch, and his party brought to recognize the legitimacy of the council, its labors and definitions. Suspicion of the terminology of Cyril, which savored of Apollinarianism to the Antiochian school, was only removed when Cyril set forth his doctrine in language they could recognize as Catholic.

Finally a formula was found which expressed to both Cyril and John the faith they had always held in common. Once the formula was signed, John accepted the definition of Ephesus, the orthodoxy of the term *theotokos* and the deposition of Nestorius. The celebrated formulary, known as the "formula of union," was worked out only at the sacrifice of St. Cyril's favorite terminology—the phrases "one incarnate nature of God the Word" and "natural union." But the great Alexandrian willingly sacrificed his preferences for the good of the Church and for the sake of doctrinal peace.[155]

For the moment misunderstanding was at an end. After five stormy years calm settled upon the East, but it was a false calm, the unwitting presage of a coming tempest. Cyril died in 444, never even foreseeing the strange abuse the Monophysites would make of the formulas he had so triumphantly used to defend the true faith.

C. The Council of Chalcedon

(1) Eutyches

In 448 the superior of one of the numerous monasteries of Constantinople precipitated a new series of controversies. As zealous as he

---

[155]The formula of union and Cyril's letter to John accepting it can be found in *Christology of the Later Fathers* (Philadelphia: The Westminster Press, 1954), third volume of the Protestant-edited "The Library of Christian Classics," 355-358.

was ignorant, Eutyches wielded great influence at the court, where his godson was chief minister. His theories were a distorted version of Cyril's teaching: he refused to admit that Christ's body was consubstantial with ours or that after the union of human and divine natures they remained distinct. One nature only, the divine nature: monophysitism—that, the old monk proclaimed, was the teaching of Cyril, and it was heretical to depart from it.

Supported by Cyril's successor at Alexandria, Dioscoros, Eutyches launched a vicious attack against those he suspected of Nestorianism —chief among them the highly respected Theodoret, doctrinal leader of the Antiochian school—on the basis of his interpretation of St. Cyril. Denounced as a heretic to Flavian, the patriarch of Constantinople (and himself from Antioch), he was condemned. Once more Antioch and Alexandria were at doctrinal swords' points.

The pattern of 431 now reasserts itself. Events can be chronicled in the following succession:

1. Eutyches appealed to Alexandria and Rome. Dioscoros condemned the condemnation and demanded that the emperor call a general council. Pope St. Leo I agreed to the idea, selected his legates, and wrote his great dogmatic letter on the point at issue—the famous *Tome* of St. Leo. Not as profound a statement of the dogma as those of St. Cyril, this letter far surpasses any previous work in lucidity of thought and precision of language. Reproducing the doctrine of Tertullian and St. Augustine, the pope insists on the following points:

1) Jesus Christ is but one person. The Word and Christ are not two, but one individual.

2) Two natures, the divine and the human, exist in that single person without confusion or mixture.

3) Each of these distinct natures has its own faculties, its own operation, although these are not exercised independently of the other nature nor apart from the union.

4) In consequence of the unity of person, there is an interchange of properties (*communcatio idiomatum*).[156]

[156]The doctrinal essentials of the *Tome* of St. Leo can be found in Denz. 143-144.

2. The council met at Ephesus on August 8, 449, with Dioscoros of Alexandria as president. Excluded from the sessions were all who had condemned Eutyches or were suspected of hostility toward him. Ignoring the pope's directives, Dioscoros by threats of deposition and exile and physical violence enforced his will. Eutyches was restored; Flavian of Constantinople, Ibas of Edessa, Theodoret of Cyr, Domnus of Antioch, Eusebius of Dorylaeum—all of the Antiochian school and opposed to Eutyches—were deposed; Flavian, the patriarch of the imperial city, was so ill-treated that he died. "Not a council," cried the angered pope when he was informed of this assembly, "but a den of thieves (*latrocinium*)." And as the Robber Council this disgraceful synod has come down into history.

3. The Roman legates made their escape without signing and carried an appeal to the pope from Flavian and Eusebius. St. Leo held a council on September 29, 449, at Rome, and later sent unavailing protests to Theodosius II.

4. On July 28, 450, the emperor died; his successors were his sister Pulcheria and her husband Marcian, both of them Catholics. In a local synod at Constantinople in the fall of 499, the bishops (including Anatolius, the new patriarch) condemned Eutyches and subscribed to Leo's letter to Flavian.

5. A general council was convoked by Marcian on May 17, 451, and the pope was asked to preside.

(2) The Council of Chalcedon

In October of 451 five to six hundred bishops assembled at Chalcedon, together with three papal legates, one of whom presided. Dioscoros was condemned, deposed and sent into exile. Theodoret and Ibas were restored to their sees. In the second session, documents of unquestionable orthodoxy were publicly read and received with acclamation. These included the creed of Nicaea, that of Constantinople of 381, the second letter of Cyril to Nestorius and his letter of acceptance of the formula of union, and Leo's letter to Flavian ("Peter has spoken through Leo!").

Although the bishops protested that the *Tome* of St. Leo was a sufficient statement of the true doctrine, the emperor insisted on a new creed. The first draft was unacceptable to the Antiochian bishops and the papal legates. It omitted any reference to the *Tome*, and substituted for the precise Roman formula, "*in* two natures," the ambiguous expression favored by Dioscoros, "*of* two natures." A commission drew up another formulary, not as full or explicit as the pope's letter, but one which did away with all ambiguity. It was definitively received with acclamations by the assembly.

> Following, therefore, the holy Fathers, we all teach and with one accord confess one and the same Son, our Lord Jesus Christ, the same perfect in Godhead, the same perfect in manhood, truly God and truly man, the same of a rational soul and a body; consubstantial with the Father in Godhead, and the same consubstantial with us in manhood, like unto us in all things except sin. Begotten of the Father before all ages in his Godhead, and born in his manhood for us and our salvation in these last days of the Virgin Mary, mother of God. One and the same Christ, Son, Lord, only begotten, acknowledged in two natures without confusion, without change, without division, without separation—the distinction between the natures being by no means taken away because of the union, but rather the distinctive character of each nature being preserved, and uniting in one person and one hypostasis. Not divided or separated into two persons, but one and the same Son and only begotten God, Word, Lord Jesus Christ. This the prophets of old and the Lord Jesus Christ himself taught us about him; this the creed of the Fathers has handed down to us.[157]

(3) The Aftermath of Chalcedon

With the definition of the Council of Chalcedon the fundamental theology, the basic dogma of the revealed mystery of the Incarnation is brought to its perfection. Affirming in clear and definitive formulas the apparently opposing truths of Christian faith in Christ, and asserting their harmony without attempting to show the manner of that harmony, it marks the beginning of sound speculation on the mystery of Christ, and yet indicates the lines within which such speculation should proceed. The following chapters on the Incarnation will show how speculative theology gives us an ever deepening understanding of the dogma of faith with which it begins.

The controversy, unhappily, does not yet end. Anti-Chalcedonians or Monophysites remained strong in the Eastern Church for a century.

[157]Denz. 148.

The final result of the struggle is tragedy, a group of schisms which have endured to the present day. But the history of that tragedy adds nothing to our knowledge of the development of the dogma of the Incarnation. We need not consider it here.

9. Summary and Conclusion

From Sacred Scripture itself, the revealed word of God, comes our basic information concerning the mystery of Christ. An honest, critical and unbiased examination of the Bible discloses the central fact of the history of mankind: Christ, the promised Messias, is both God and man. "This the prophets of old and the Lord Jesus Christ taught us about him."

From the beginning of her life the Church has fought to preserve this precious heritage of her Master, condemning those who would pervert it, determining for the salvation of man an ever clearer and more accurate expression of his message. Her writers and theologians have assisted her in this labor of love, but always it is she who has the last and definitive word to say.

From this infallible presentation of doctrine, first undertaken against the Docetists and the Ebionites, the necessary and basic elements of the Incarnation emerge. Four things concur to make complete the whole state of our Lord Jesus Christ: his Godhead, his manhood, the conjunction of both in his Person, and the distinction of one from the other after the union. Four principal heresies withstood these truths of revelation: Arians by denying the Divinity of Christ; Apollinarians by disfiguring and misunderstanding that which belonged to his human nature; Nestorians by rending Christ asunder and dividing him into two persons; Eutyches and his ilk by confounding in his person the natures they should have distinguished. Against these heresies there have been four great general councils: against Arians the Council of Nicaea; against Apollinarians the Council of Constantinople; against Nestorians the Council of Ephesus; against Eutychians the Council of Chalcedon. In four words we may summarize the great definitions of faith which preserve and present the

truths of Jesus Christ: 1) *truly;* 2) *perfectly;* 3) *indivisibly;* 4) *distinctly*
—the first applied to his being God, the second to his being man, the
third to his being of both only one, and the fourth to his still continuing to be both in that one.

This study of the facts of revelation and of the development of the
dogma of the Incarnation leads to many interesting and important
conclusions, of which a representative few may be considered here.

1. History clearly shows the absolute necessity for a guardian and
infallible interpreter of the truths God has revealed to us. Men being
what they are, sons of the fallen Adam, heresy and schism always lie
just around the corner. To teach his truth, and preserve it free from
human disfigurement, is one of the chief purposes for which Christ
founded his Church.

2. Many subjects taken in college—languages, grammar, logic,
rhetoric, etc.—are considered lightly because they are only tools. But
the interpretation of Sacred Scripture and the history of the Christological controversies should show how important such tools are, and
how facility in using them to acquire and communicate truth is a
prime requisite for any advance in knowledge and wisdom.

3. The troubled waters of the first five Christian centuries indicate at what cost the truths about God he has given to man have
been preserved and handed down to us. We should be conscious
of our debt to past ages and the great Christian heroes of those days;
we should be personally conscious of the preciousness of the heritage
entrusted to our care; we should be aware of our duty to hand it on
unsullied to our children and our children's children.

4. Participation in the Church's liturgy brings home the essential
fact of the Incarnation: the sacraments and the Mass are, so to say,
the embodiment of Christ by which he as truly lives among us today
as he did in his own body two thousand years ago.

5. *From the homily of Bishop Paul of Emesa, given on the 29th
day of the month of Chaeac [December 25] in the great church of
Alexandria, in the presence of the blessed Cyril, on the Nativity of
our Lord Jesus Christ, and that the Blessed Virgin Mary is the mother
of God, and that we declare that there are not two sons but one Son,*

who is the Lord Christ, and in praise of the archbishop Cyril: "O most wondrous happening! A virgin brings forth, and remains a virgin; she becomes a mother, but suffers naught that all mothers must suffer. For the Virgin brings forth, as is the way of women; but she remains a virgin, contrary to what must happen to women who give birth. Isaias of old, foreseeing this wonder, exclaimed: 'Behold a Virgin shall conceive, and bear a son, and his name shall be called Emmanuel.' And making this known to us, the Evangelist interprets his name to mean *God with us.* Mary, therefore, the Mother of God, brought forth Emmanuel."

[The people here cried out: "This is our belief; this is the gift of God; O worthy teacher of the faith, Cyril. This we have waited to hear. Who denies this let him be anathema!" Bishop Paul continues.]

"Whosoever does not profess this, mean this, let him be shut out from the Church. Mary, therefore, the Mother of God, has borne unto us Emmanuel, who is God made man. For God the Word, who in a mysterious and ineffable manner was begotten by the Father before all ages, in these days was born of a woman. For having perfectly assumed our nature, and uniting mankind to himself from the moment of his conception, and making our body a temple for himself, he came forth from the Virgin fully God, and the same is fully man. For the meeting of two perfect natures, the divine, namely, and the human, has given to us one Son, one Christ, one Lord."

[The people cried out: "Welcome, right-teaching bishop! He is worthy of honor and praise." The Christians exclaim: "This is the gift of God, O true-teaching Cyril!"]

BIBLIOGRAPHICAL NOTE

There is no popular survey of the material of this chapter available in English, but the student may wish to consult some more or less specialized works for purposes of research or to clarify a particular point. Besides the studies mentioned in the footnotes—all highly recommended and a tribute to the growing consciousness of, and serious concern on the part of Catholics with high caliber scholarship —the following may be of special use.

On the analysis of the Old Testament, *Christ in Prophecy* by P. Heinisch (Collegeville, Minn.: The Liturgical Press, 1956). The doctrinal history is covered in considerable detail in the now classic *History of Dogmas* by J. Tixeront (St. Louis: B. Herder Book Co., 1930) and even more fully in J. Lebreton's *History of the Dogma of the Trinity*, of which unfortunately only the first volume is available in English (New York: 1939). Further information on the Fathers of the Church can be easily obtained from individual articles in The Catholic Encyclopedia; J. Quasten's *Patrology*, of which two volumes have so far appeared (Westminster, Md.: The Newman Press, 1950, 1953) and F. Cayré's *Manual of Patrology* (Paris: Desclée and Co., 1936) are more technical works. Philip Hughes surveys the history of these periods in *A History of the Church*, Volume I (New York: Sheed and Ward, 1952). The second two volumes of E. C. Messenger's translation of the famous Fliche-Martin *Histoire de l'Église* presents in even greater detail a study by contemporary scholars of the first rank of *The Church in the Christian Roman Empire* (London: Burnes, Oates and Washbourne, 1949-52).

Translations of many of the works of the Fathers of the Church are available in a new series by distinguished Catholic scholars entitled "The Fathers of the Church."

CHAPTER TWO

The Fittingness of the Incarnation

1. Introduction

Through the course of five centuries and at the cost of ceaseless vigilance and untold struggles, the Church has developed, under the guidance of the Holy Spirit, the definitive formulation of the mystery of the Incarnation. Revealed in Sacred Scripture itself, preserved and handed down by Apostolic Tradition, the complex fact of Christ is clearly determined, and now so expressed as to avoid all ambiguity. It is a dogma of Christ's Church.

In the main, the functions of that part of Sacred Doctrine which is called positive theology have been completed. But this, as we have said, is not an end, it is a beginning. Infallibly outlining the area within which speculation on the Incarnation should proceed, the Church's doctrine encourages the attempt to penetrate more deeply into the divine secrets God himself has invited us to ponder. The work of speculative theology here begins.

One of the most important of the theologian's tasks—important in terms of results, in the light it provides for grasping the mystery—is

76

to compare a mystery of faith with other truths, both those of the natural order garnered by reason itself and the revealed truths of the supernatural order. Our deeper inquiry into the mystery of Christ commences with just such an investigation. Believing through divine faith that the Incarnation is an existent fact (and explicitly contained in the sources of revelation; the previous chapter showed us this), we attempt to discover the relationships between this fact and other natural and supernatural facts.

Hence this second chapter is concerned with the "fittingness" of the Incarnation. The harmony of this mystery with others, its place in the divine scheme of things elaborated by the wisdom of God, the concordance obtaining among the facts as we know them—these are the things we seek to establish. Briefly, we shall try to see how the mystery of Christ "fits into" God's plan.

First, the appropriateness of the Incarnation in itself, abstracting from all circumstances and any hypothesis, will be considered; this will establish the true consonance of this mystery with God himself, its accord with his divine wisdom and goodness (**Section 2**). Next, the relation of the Incarnation to man will be taken up, its necessity relative to man's needs (**Section 3**) and its connection with the need of man for redemption (**Section 4**). Finally, the fittingness of the time God chose to become incarnate will be investigated (**Section 5**). Hence this order of inquiry:

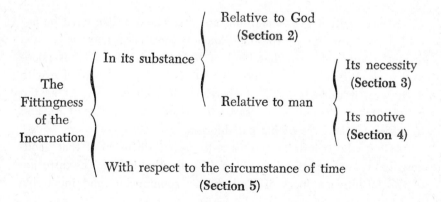

The Fittingness of the Incarnation

In its substance
- Relative to God (Section 2)
- Relative to man
  - Its necessity (Section 3)
  - Its motive (Section 4)

With respect to the circumstance of time (Section 5)

2. The Incarnation Considered in Relation to God

A. Introduction

We always expect a man to act rationally, that is, in accordance with his nature. Irrational behavior generally is considered improper in a man because it is unnatural and therefore unaccountable. A man acts like a man. To a man, too, certain actions come easily and naturally; man will think, laugh and love, because that is the kind of thing he is.

God, of course, is the cause of the Incarnation. It is he who becomes incarnate. In determining the harmony of the Incarnation, its place among other realities, the first point to be determined will be the relationship between this mystery and God himself. We are asking, in other words, *why* did God choose to become man? What is there in the very nature of God that makes this a fitting thing for him to do?

Obviously nothing external to him can motivate his choice or move him in any way. God is the freest of agents, and all of his acts are ruled by one sole object, his own infinite goodness. In consequence, the inquiry concerning the Incarnation's relation to him who wills it will be answered *in the most formal and proper sense* by determining the link between it and the infinite goodness of God.

B. The Fittingness of the Incarnation

God acts neither like a man, nor an angel; he acts like what he is— God. Was it appropriate that God become incarnate? The answer will depend completely on what kind of being God is—and he is goodness itself. When goodness acts characteristically, in accordance with its nature, it diffuses itself, it shares itself with others; just as the holiness, the spiritual goodness of the Curé of Ars, spread to, and transformed the lives of his parishioners.

In God, who is infinite goodness, there is a diffusion of that goodness that is necessary, and there is a diffusion that is free. The diffusion of the infinite goodness of God that is spontaneous and inevitable emerges within God himself in the relations of the three divine Persons; the divine love which God is, finds infinite satisfaction in the perfections of the Trinity, and has no need of extending itself further. However, divine goodness did not choose to rest there, but freely chose to communicate itself beyond divinity to God's creatures. And once God had so chosen, it was fitting that he, the supreme good, not only should communicate himself to others, but that it should be done in the most excellent manner possible. And the most excellent manner that divine wisdom could devise for God to communicate himself to his creature was for God to unite a creature to himself in a substantial union. The Incarnation is this kind of communication or diffusion of divine goodness. A greater way was not possible even to infinite power.

C. Theological Proof of the Fittingness of the Incarnation

The Incarnation, then, is perfectly in accord with God's nature, which is goodness itself, infinite goodness. We may reach this conclusion in a more scientific manner through the following argument:

Whatever pertains to the very nature of good is fitting for God.

And: it pertains to the very nature of good to communicate itself to others.

Therefore: it is fitting for the supreme good to communicate itself in a supreme manner.

But: the Incarnation is the supreme communication of God to others.

Therefore: the Incarnation is fitting for God.

(1) The Sharing of Goodness

The *first statement* of this argument (the "major") is clear from what we have already seen in theology of God's nature and attributes. As the perfectly subsisting being in whom all is actual, without a shadow of imperfection, he is goodness itself, infinitely desirable because infinitely perfect.

But that which is good, as the *second statement* points out, naturally draws others to share in its perfection, and in so doing gives of its goodness to them. The apple, for instance, attracts men and birds and insects, for it possesses a desirable perfection; its goodness, it is clear, consists in this *power* of attraction—whether it is actually eaten or

not does not lessen or increase its perfection, however much it may add
to the teacher's enjoyment. Thus *actual* communication of goodness—
i.e., actually causing goodness in others—is fully in harmony with the
nature of goodness, but the good is not driven to such a sharing and
without this actual participation retains its fundamental attractive-
ness, its nature. In a word, the good of its essence is **communicable;**
it is not necessarily **communicated.**

(2) The Sharing of Infinite Goodness

Since God is the supreme good, it follows (as our *third statement*
concludes) that his communicability must be supreme, and that if
he does communicate himself or his goodness in a supreme manner
it will be fully in accord with his nature. Does he do so? Here reason,
having taken us so far, must pause. But faith tells us, in fact, that
God's knowledge of himself and love of himself eventuate in a profound and equal possession of the divine goodness which is his very
nature. The Blessed Trinity—Father, Son and Holy Ghost—is comprised of .three divine Persons who are really distinct from each
other and yet each fully, equally God. Here is supreme and most
intimate communication of divine goodness within the Godhead,
pre-eminently the example of the diffusion of good. Is there any similar
communication of divine goodness *to others?*

It stands to reason that God has no need for such a giving of himself: it can add nothing to the perfection and goodness he already
possesses. If he does share his goodness—and all of creation witnesses
to the fact—he does so most freely, out of his infinite love and a
generosity without limits. On a higher plane, through sanctifying
grace, which is an accidental participation of God's own nature given
to his intellectual creatures, the partaking of divine goodness becomes
infinitely more perfect. Yet grace, tremendous reality that it is (for
it belongs essentially to the divine order of things, being a share in
God's own life), in no degree achieves the supreme communication
of divine goodness which is the Incarnation.

As the great commentator of St. Thomas, Cardinal Cajetan, points
out, the unique excellence of this singular sharing of divine goodness
is founded on three things:

1) The *infiniteness* of the goodness of God, to whose person (the Word) human nature is united.

2) The *supreme mode* of the communication itself. In the Incarnation God communicates himself to a creature not through some likeness or created gift, whether of the natural or of the supernatural order, but by elevating human nature to the divine personality, giving his own proper subsistence. This is a personal and substantial communication of his Godhead to others than which no greater would be intelligible.

3) The *creature* to whom this communication is made. Man, in the medieval phrase, is a microcosm of the macrocosm, i.e., since he is both of the material and of the spiritual orders, he sums up in himself corporeal nature and vegetative nature and sensitive nature, as well as the world of intellectual creatures. Thus the Incarnation is, in effect, the elevation of the entire created universe to personal and substantial union with the divine person. "The eager longing of creation," declares St. Paul, "awaits the revelation of the sons of God . . . because creation itself also will be delivered from its slavery to corruption into the freedom of the glory of the sons of God" (Rom. 8:19-21).

Two points revealed by this profound analysis of the meaning of the Incarnation should be emphasized:

1. The tremendous love God shows to man (and to the universe) by taking our flesh.

2. The eminent freedom God enjoys in choosing this way to man's salvation.

Is it any wonder that the Incarnation has been called "the gift of gifts" and "the mission of divine missions"?

D. Other Arguments of Fittingness

The vast range and variety of material things, from mighty oceans and mountains to microscopic insects, were made, so to speak, as a window through which men might look to the invisible things of God. St. Paul says: "For the invisible things of him, from the creation of the world, are clearly seen, being understood by the things that are made" (Rom. 1:20). As the Fathers never tire of pointing out, the Incarnation was a superlative device for the manifestation of the goodness, the wisdom, the justice and the power of God. The Incarnation, St. John Damascene declares, "makes known God's *goodness,* for he despised not the weakness of his own creation; his *justice,* for not by force did he snatch man from death, nor was the tyrant conquered save by a man; his *wisdom,* since for a most difficult matter he found a most fitting solution; his *power,* for there is nothing greater than for God to become man."[1]

3. The Incarnation and Man's Necessities

A. The Notion of Necessity

Anything is said to be **necessary** *when it cannot be other than it is.* There are various degrees of necessity, arising from various causes:

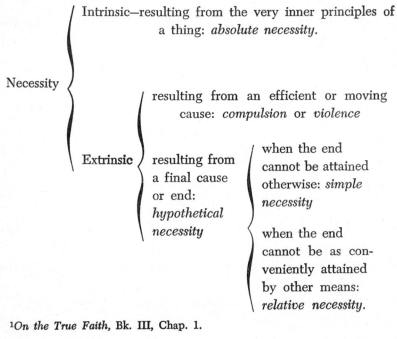

Necessity

Intrinsic—resulting from the very inner principles of a thing: *absolute necessity.*

Extrinsic

resulting from an efficient or moving cause: *compulsion* or *violence*

resulting from a final cause or end: *hypothetical necessity*

when the end cannot be attained otherwise: *simple necessity*

when the end cannot be as conveniently attained by other means: *relative necessity.*

[1]*On the True Faith,* Bk. III, Chap. 1.

B. The Necessity of the Incarnation

There is no question here of **absolute** necessity, of course; God remains sovereignly free with regard to all his works produced outside the divine essence. Nor can **violence** or **compulsion** enter the picture—the notion that a creature could coerce God in any manner, physically or morally, is patently absurd. The question of necessity arises only on the **hypothesis** that God chooses to redeem the human race, and thus that the Incarnation is somehow necessary in view of this end. But in no way was the Incarnation **simply** necessary. As a being of infinite power, God could have contrived numberless other ways in which man's redemption would have been accomplished. But the Incarnation is **relatively** necessary, in order to lead man to his destiny in the most effective way possible.

The effectiveness of the Incarnation in obtaining man's salvation is twofold: it prompts man to goodness, and it restrains him from evil.

1. **The Incarnation encourages us in good:**
    1) *Faith:* men could believe with greater ease and greater certitude, if God himself spoke to them. "In order that man might travel to the truth more confidently, the Son of God, who is truth itself, having assumed human nature, established the foundations of faith."[2]
    2) *Hope:* as St. Augustine says, "nothing was so necessary for raising our hope as to show how deeply God loved us. And what stronger proof of this love, than that the Son of God has deigned to share human nature with us?"[3]
    3) *Charity:* "God so loved the world as to give his only-begotten Son, that those who believe in him may not perish, but may have life everlasting" (Jn. 3:16). The most powerful persuasion for us to fulfill the supreme precept of the love of God is God's evident love for us, manifested in his Incarnation. "If once slow to love, at least let us hasten to return love."[4]

[2]St. Augustine, *The City of God*, Bk. XI, Chap. 2.
[3]*On the Trinity*, Bk. XIII, Chap. 10.
[4]St. Augustine, *Concerning the Instruction of the Unlettered*, Chap. 4, n. 7.

4) *Good actions:* Christ provided the perfect example of good deeds, showing us how God would live as a man in order that man could see clearly how to live so as to please God. "Man, who could be seen, was not to be imitated; God was to be imitated, but he could not be seen. In order, therefore, that one who could both be seen and be imitated might be shown to man, God was made man."[5]

5) *Full participation of the divinity:* the incredible gift of sharing in God's own life—that in which alone man's happiness and destiny lie—is given to man by reason of Christ's humanity. "God became man," declares St. Augustine, "so that man might be made God."[6]

2. **The Incarnation restrains us from evil:**

1) It makes man aware of his superiority to the devil, the author of sin, for God has deigned to honor human nature by uniting it to himself.

2) It makes man so conscious of his new dignity as to encourage him not to soil himself with the degradation of sin. "O Christian," cries St. Leo, "recognize thy dignity! And being made a partaker of the divine nature, refuse to return by evil deeds to your former worthlessness."[7]

3) It destroys man's presumption—without any merit on our part, any right, we are saved by the Incarnation.

4) It cures man's pride, for the profound humility and abasement of God's becoming man crushes this greatest obstacle to our union with God.

5) It frees man from the slavery of sin, and this in a way which satisfies fully and rigorously for man's offense.

C. The Need of Man for Christ

Could a man have accomplished the restoration of the human race by a heroic act or by a life of extraordinary sanctity? We may answer

---

[5]St. Augustine, *Sermon 371.*
[6]*Sermon 128.*
[7]*Sermon 21.*

this question by recalling just what it was that man had done and what effect Adam's rebellion had (and has) on his descendants.

First, all human nature had been corrupted by sin; no mere man could make adequate compensation for so vast an evil. Second, infinity was involved, and man could not encompass infinity. It was not a question of compensation for an injury to a man; the infinite majesty of God had been insulted. Sin acquires a gravity corresponding to the dignity of the person offended; a private soldier is not disciplined equally for punching a fellow private and for insubordination to the commanding general. Infinity was inseparable from the offense against God; it could no more be undone by a man than a child could, by donating his weekly allowance, undo the murder committed by his father. An infinite God had been affronted; there was just no proportion between the good that a man might then do, and the enormity of the evil that man had done.

Man needed reparation, but he could not manage it. God did not need reparation, but he alone could manage it. The Incarnation is God's answer to man in his desperate need. "Other ways were not wanting to God," St. Augustine observes. "All things are subject to his power. But a more fitting way of healing our misery did not exist."[8]

For by the Incarnation—and this could only happen in virtue of such a substantial unity with divinity—man was enabled to pay in the person of Christ *perfect satisfaction* for an offense which was universal in scope and infinite in injury.

4. The Motive of the Incarnation

Cur Deus homo? asks St. Anselm in his classic work on the Incarnation. The Creed of the Council of Nicaea answers: "**For our salvation** Jesus Christ descended from heaven."[9] Does this imply, then, that God would not have become incarnate if man had not sinned? The answer to this question is vigorously disputed by theologians,

---

[8] *On the Trinity*, Bk. XIII, Chap. 10.
[9] Denz. 54. Cf. also the First Council of Constantinople (Denz. 86); the Second Council of Constantinople, Canon 7 against Origen; the Council of Sens (Denz. 371); the Fourth Lateran Council (Denz. 429).

for it carries us into the mystery of the workings of God and of the divine economy. It is a difficult problem, one whose solution is of vital importance.

A. The Argument of St. Thomas

> Such things as spring from the will of God alone, over and above what is owed to any creature, can be known by us only insofar as they are revealed in Sacred Scripture, through which the divine will is made known. Hence, since everywhere in Sacred Scripture the reason given for the Incarnation is the sin of the first man, it is more fitting to say that the work of the Incarnation was ordained by God as a remedy for sin, in such a way that, there being no sin, the Incarnation would not have taken place. Yet the power of God is not limited to this—for God could have become incarnate even if sin did not exist.[10]

As we have seen, the Incarnation is a most free, a most generous outpouring of divine goodness, to which no creature has any right, of which no creature has any absolute need or reasonable hope. Not from creatures, consequently, can we find an answer to our question but from God alone. What does God tell us?

"The Son of Man came to seek and to save what was lost" (Lk. 19:10). "Jesus Christ came into the world to save sinners" (I Tim. 1:15). "God did not send his Son into the world in order to judge the world, but that the world might be saved through him" (Jn. 3:17).

These are typical passages from the Bible, God's own word. Beyond any doubt, of course, there are tremendous excellences connected with the Incarnation (God's glory and the glory of Christ, for example) which far exceed man's redemption, and to these intrinsic excellences Sacred Scripture frequently alludes. But St. Thomas is arguing formally: wherever a *reason* or a *motive* for the Incarnation is assigned it is always the same—the salvation of the human race. With this exegetical conclusion the best modern scripture scholars are in agreement,[11] just as the Fathers of the Church were in the past.[12] "Jesus" is the name which God himself bestows on the Word Incarnate, "for he shall save his people from their sins" (Matt. 1:21).

[10]*Summa*, III, q. 1, a. 3.
[11]Cf. P. F. Ceuppens, O.P., *Theologia Biblica* (Rome: Marietti, 1950), III, 7-24.
[12]Cf. *Dictionnaire de théologie catholique*, article *Incarnation*, cols. 1483 ff.

B. The Objection of Duns Scotus

Is not the Incarnation so great a work of divine love, so manifest a revelation of the wisdom and power of God that he *would*—not merely could—have become man in any event? Such is the feeling of theologians and pious authors who follow the great medieval thinker, Duns Scotus. And against St. Thomas and the Thomists they propose the following objection. *If man's redemption is the cause of God's Incarnation, then the entire order of things is perverted. Christ becomes a mere means for obtaining this end, his primacy above all creatures equivalently denied; the infinitely greater—God—is subordinated to that "abyss of nothingness," sinful man.* Hence it follows that, unless we are to deny the primacy of Christ, God would have become incarnate even if Adam had not sinned.

C. The Primacy of Christ

It is certain that God loves Christ, not only more than the whole human race, but even more than all creatures taken together. Proof of this is found in his decreeing for him a greater good, by assuming his human nature into union with the divinity and giving him "a name that is above every other name." This excellence is in no wise diminished by the fact that God delivered him over to death for the salvation of the human race; on the contrary, he has thereby become a glorious conqueror and, as Isaias says (9:6), "the government is upon his shoulder."[13]

St. Thomas, far from ignoring Christ's pre-eminence, insists that his glory (as subordinated, of course, to the glory of God) is the final cause of the Incarnation. In view of his principles how could he argue otherwise? Ultimately the only cause, the only motive for God's action, the only adequate object of his love and will-acts, is the divine goodness itself. Nothing outside himself can ever move him to will or to act; no creature is goodness itself.

But as far as God is concerned, nothing accrues to him, nothing can be added to his goodness; his remains a perfectly disinterested love, a liberality which is absolutely altruistic. Man on the other

[13]*Summa*, I, q. 20, a. 4, ad 1.

hand, fallen and sinful, is the infinitely indebted beneficiary of divine generosity. And man's sin is the occasion which leads God to such a supreme communication of his goodness; it is the matter, so to say, with which the work of the Incarnation is, in actual fact, engaged.

We may summarize these profound truths in technical theological terms in the following diagram:

The Incarnation

Its *end*
- that *on account of which* it takes place (finis cujus gratiae)
  - proximate: Christ's glory
  - ultimate: the glory of God
- that *for whom* it takes place—fallen man (finis cui)

The *matter with which* it deals—man's sin, original sin and personal sins (materia circa quam)

As the diagram indicates, the Word Incarnate is foremost and primary with respect to God's love and his action. Nonetheless, his primacy and pre-eminence are actually willed by God only in view of man's desperate need. The Incarnation is decreed by God as a "work," and the material with which it works *in actual fact* is the sin of man; the one whom it benefits is sinful man. If you had stolen Michelangelo's block of marble, no statue of David would now amaze the world. God freely chooses to become incarnate in view of man's sin. Subtract that "material" and no Incarnation would have taken place.

To appreciate this more fully, we must re-consider God's will-acts, especially as they concern things outside himself, his works *ad extra*.

D. The Divine Decree of the Incarnation

(1) Its Nature

It is important to insist at the outset that our investigation does not concern what God could have willed. We want to know what God *did* decree when he willed to become incarnate. Was that particular will-act so linked with man's fallen state as to exclude his Incarnation in other circumstances in virtue of the same act of the will? Our affirmative answer, founded on God's own testimony, takes into account the following truths about the divine decrees.

What God *effectively* wills—his **consequent will**, in scientific terms, as contrasted with his **antecedent will** (which views things in the abstract and in general and does not necessarily imply that the things so willed will take place)—embraces not only the end he desires and a choice of the best among possible means. This act also includes each and every circumstance in which the plan he decides upon will be executed. There are no unforeseen events to modify that plan, to change its direction, or to thwart it. To think otherwise is to interpret divine activity in terms of our human limitations; as if, like us, God chooses one thing and modifies the choice in view of later circumstances.

What God *efficaciously* decrees, then, is not the Incarnation **in the abstract**, apart from the means which will bring it to pass and the details in which it will be operative. On the contrary, his decree embraces from the beginning and at one and the same time the Incarnation of the Word, and the suffering and death his human body will undergo, and the fallen state of mankind which necessitates this sacrifice and satisfaction. **In the concrete**—that is to say, as actually willed and effectively realized—the Incarnation is directed toward the redemption and salvation of man. Man's sin is not an additional modifying circumstance, an unforeseen accident, an adventitious event which disturbs the divine economy and redirects it. From the beginning God foresees the fall, and he permits this evil as an occasion to manifest his tremendous love. "O happy fault," the Church sings on Holy Saturday, "which merited to have such a Redeemer!"

To think of the Incarnation as capable of realization under other conditions is possible, of course, but it means deviating from the plan God has designed, it means blinding ourselves to his actual decree. It reduces theology to idle speculation, for it deals only with a supposition, not with the facts determined by God.

(2) Its Significance

The Incarnation is indissolubly linked with the redemption of man. In the manner explained, man's salvation pertains to the very essence of the union of human and divine natures in the Second Person of the Trinity which is actually willed by God. By definition, this is a **redemptive Incarnation.**

Does this lessen the glory of Christ and minimize God's love for him? Quite the contrary, as St. Thomas points out in the passage cited above (p. 87). For to the double primacy of pre-eminence and finality which is his in virtue of the Hypostatic Union, the work of redemption adds yet further glory—the glory of being efficient cause of all the grace to be given man, and the glory of his merits and satisfaction. This resultant glory far surpasses that which would have been his in a sinless world. Without the redemption Christ would indeed have been King, but the grounds for that Kingship would have been less, its glory of an inferior order.[14]

The redemptive Incarnation brings greater glory and greater primacy to Christ, and through him it redounds to the greater glory of God. Such, St. Paul tells us, was God's eternal decree: "We see him who was made 'a little lower than the angels,' namely, Jesus, crowned with glory and honor because of his having suffered death. . . . For it became him for whom are all things and through whom are all things, who had brought many sons into glory, to perfect through suffering the author of their salvation" (Heb. 2:9-10).

E. Original Sin and Personal Sin

The Incarnation of the Word was to make men holy, and present them to God as a holy people. The initial step in that process was to blot out men's sins. St. John wrote: "Behold the Lamb of God, behold him who taketh away the sins of the world" (Jn. 1:29). Christ's work

---

[14]Cf. Pope Pius XI's Encyclical on Christ's Kingship, *Quas Primas;* Denz. 2194-2196.

was aimed at the destruction of all sins of all men, original and actual. The blotting out of original sin was the primary objective, because it was the greater fault, in that it was an infection that had spread to the entire human race.

As each grape on a vine is ripened by the sun exactly as if the sun were giving that grape its total, exclusive attention, so the infinite power of Christ's sacrifice works its effectiveness. The sin of all human nature is healed as perfectly as if the infinite power of the healing were applied exclusively to each man alone, and every man coming into this world is intended to share completely in what was won by Christ's victory. St. Paul says: "Christ . . . loved me and delivered himself for me" (Gal. 2:20).

Christ, the glorious conqueror, also destroys each man's personal sins. Since these are wholly the result of our own will they are *intensively* greater than original sin. This personal rebellion against God the God-man also crushes, in order to restore us to divine friendship.

Thus Christ's suffering and death are universally and infallibly effective in purifying a man of *all* his sins—except that God permits man to will it otherwise. Unfortunately, some men do so will, rejecting even Christ and his victory, wallowing, so to speak, in the slime of their own iniquity. "The light is come into the world, and men loved the darkness rather than the light" (Jn. 3:19). Yet even for these, and for their sins, he became incarnate, suffered and died. His is a universal medicine for the moral sickness, whatever it may be, of the human race; men have only to drink of this medicine, and they shall not taste death.

5. The Timing of the Incarnation

The exact moment at which the Incarnation took place in human history was selected with meticulous precision as the most opportune for the divine plan. We can more easily see this, perhaps, by considering the extreme alternatives God rejected.

A. The Incarnation at the Beginning of Mankind

In view of the actual divine decree on the Incarnation, it could not have taken place at the beginning of the human race before sin was commmitted. For at that time the situation was precisely that for which Christ himself says he did *not* come: "They that are in health need not a physician, but they that are ill. . . . For I am not come to call the just but sinners" (Matt. 9:12-13).

It would not have been advisable, either, for the Incarnation to have come quickly in the wake of sin—if a doctor somehow cured a lung cancer five minutes after diagnosis, the patient would be powerfully inclined to minimize his need of treatment. Originally, under the most favorable conditions, pride had proved man's undoing. Man must be taught humility. Left to his own devices, he would learn, with increasing clarity, the futility of his own efforts, as the evil in his history mounted. By bitter experience, man would be sharply reminded of the stupidity of his pride, and realize his desperate need to be delivered by God from the evil, the weakness, the helplessness that were his own doing. His lesson in humility must be long, if it was to be indelible.

Then, too, the infinite dignity of the Incarnate Word dictated that the preparation for his coming should be long and carefully arranged. God would send his prophets intermittently in the history of his chosen people; then, and only then, "when the fulness of time was come, God sent his Son, made óf woman, made under the law" (Gal. 4:4). Moreover, had the Incarnation occurred immediately after the sin, there would be danger, in the long later history of the human race, that it would become blurred and vague in men's memories, thereby jeopardizing the vividness of men's faith in the God-man.

B. The Incarnation at the End of the World

The appropriateness of the time actually chosen by God to inaugurate on earth the work of salvation is likewise underlined when we consider the possibility of his Incarnation at the end of time. Sin was the target that the Incarnation was designed to destroy. Man, enmeshed in his sin, was to be rescued by God-become-man, restored to the divine freindship, brought to perfection. So the timing of the Incarnation would take into account the sin at which it was aimed, and the means for the restoration of man.

The time must be exquisitely perfect. If it came too soon, man would be spoiled and complacent, as we have seen. If it came too late, however, he would be lost. It could not be withheld until the end of the world; there was a desperate urgency in man's need. Even the revelation of the Old Law had encountered scorn among the Gentiles and faithlessness among the Jews. Man's history provides only too abundant evidence that, when left to his own resources, his knowledge and reverence for God undergo a steady decline, and interest in morality deteriorates with the passage of time.

Had God's coming been postponed until the end of the world, man's interest in God and morality would have come close to the vanishing point. So at the moment exactly calculated to help man to the uttermost, at the fulness of time, God became man to save man from his sin.

In its details, as in its substance, the Incarnation, both from the divine and the human points of view, is most eminently fitting, truly a divine work.

6. Summary and Conclusion

At the beginning of human history, man was set upon a course which would lead him unerringly to the kingdom of God. This was God's plan, his means of showing divine friendship with man. But the perversity of man's free will, the desire of being autonomous in the moral order, caused man to veer from this true course, a deviation which resulted in the rejection of God's friendship. Man was cast into a nightmare of unrelieved desolation. Yet even in this darkest of hours God's love for man still shone like a beacon. He promised man a redeemer.

God is goodness itself and it pertains to the nature of goodness to communicate itself, to share itself with others. Since God is the supreme good, he shared his goodness with us in a supreme way. He became incarnate—that is, he united a creature to himself in a substantial union. A better way of sharing the divine goodness could not be devised. God freely elevated human nature to the divine personality, and, in effect (since man is the sum of corporeal, vegetable, sensitive and intellectual natures), in so doing elevated the entire universe to the divinity.

Certainly, then, the Incarnation was in accord with God's nature. However, it was not absolutely necessary that man be redeemed in this way; other courses could have been chosen. But God, by a kind of relative necessity, chose the way which would most surely direct man's eyes toward the heavenly horizon. The Incarnation encourages us in good through examples of faith, hope and charity, showing us the way to live as Christ lived and allowing us to participate in God's own life; it makes us humbly conscious of sin and the author of sin, restraining us from evil. It is the most effective way of redemption.

Man needed Christ in a profound way. God had been injured and man's corrupt nature had not the strength to shoulder the responsibility of setting things aright. No atonement that man might make could balance the scale which evil had set askew. The God-man alone could restore the inequality. This was the motive of the Incarnation: the salvation of the human race, the return of mankind to harmonious co-operation with God. Nevertheless, Christ is not merely the means for obtaining man's redemption. Rather, the Incarnation has for its end not only fallen man *for whom* it takes place, but also Christ's glory and ultimately the glory of God—the end *on account of which* the Incarnation takes place. The Incarnation is a "work" decreed by God, and the *material* upon which it works is the sin of man. If man had not sinned, there would have been no "material" for God to work upon.

The Incarnation is indissolubly joined with redemption: the union of human and divine natures is a **redemptive Incarnation.** Christ is glorified in it. Besides his primacy of pre-eminence, he obtains both the glory of being the efficient cause of all grace and the glory of his merits and satisfaction. Through Christ, original sin was obliterated, and, depending upon the acceptance of each individual man, personal sins are also destroyed by him.

Appropriately, the Incarnation came at a time neither too soon nor too late. The preparations were long and fastidious, and at the moment when man was seen to need the most help, God became man to save man from sin.

Flowing from this summary of the theological doctrine concerning the fittingness and necessity of the Incarnation are the following conclusions:

1. "What mind can comprehend this mystery? What tongue describe this wondrous grace? Iniquity returns to the ways of innocence, old age to newness of life. Strangers are received into adoption as sons, and they without claim enter upon an inheritance. Evil-doers begin to live as righteous, the parsimonious become bountiful, the incontinent chaste, and the earthly heavenly-minded. What is this transformation unless the witness of the hand of God? For the Son of man came that he might destroy the works of the devil, and has so joined himself to us and us to him that the descent of God to what was human has brought about the raising of man to what is divine."[15]

2. By taking unto himself human nature, God saved all men, sinners and saints alike, regardless of nationality or color. All men are ripened to perfection in the warmth of God's love, and no one is unwanted. The word "prejudice" is not in his vocabulary.

3. Speaking of personal sins, St. Thomas remarks: "Our Lord said, 'For if you will forgive men their offenses, your heavenly father will forgive you also your offenses' to those who ask that their debt be forgiven, but not to those who persist in sin."[16]

4. The words of St. John the Evangelist, "The light shines in the darkness" (Jn. 1:5), summarize the liturgy of the Christmas cycle. Advent is the dark night of the expectant waiting of the ages which is suddenly pierced by the light of Christ's birth, and a preparation for the glorious light of the Second Coming.

5. From a realistic point of view, the history of humanity has no meaning unless it is studied in relationship to God. The Incarnation

---

[15]St. Leo, *Sermon 27* (seventh on the Nativity), Chap. 2.
[16]*Summa, Supplement*, q. 99, a. 5, ad 3.

is a historical fact. It happened at the precise moment when mankind
had the greatest need. Redemption was for man, it is true, but on
account of Christ's glory and the glory of God. All major historical
events can, in this same way, be traced back to God.

BIBLIOGRAPHICAL NOTE

St. Thomas' treatment of the doctrine on the fittingness of the
Incarnation can be found in the first question of the Third Part of
the *Summa*, Volume II of the English edition. No one article or
book in the popular field treats the question without including other
aspects of the Incarnation. Thus the following two references can
also be used for the next several chapters. "Jesus Christ, God and
Man," an essay by the Rev. George D. Smith, can be found in *The
Teaching of the Catholic Church*. Although Fr. Smith's treatment is
more technical than popular, still, his succinctness will enable the
student to cover a lot of ground rapidly. A more popular analysis
of the same subject can be found in *The Collected Works of Abbot
Vonier*, Volume II, Book III, Chapter IV, "The Inner Meaning of
Christ's Victory." This chapter gives a very concise account of the
fittingness of the Incarnation.

The final work which deserves mention is *The Christ of Catholicism*
(New York: Longmans, Green and Co., 1947), by Dom Aelred Graham.
In this book, Dom Aelred gives the student ample material for contemplation. He himself calls it a "meditative study," not intending
that it be apologetical in character.

CHAPTER THREE

The Nature of the Union of the Incarnate Word

1. Introduction

We receive from divine faith the **fact** that the union of the Incarnation is a **hypostatic** one, that is, that one and the same divine Person (hypostasis) subsists in two distinct and complete natures, human and divine. This basic information, however, is neither analyzed nor explained by the sources of revelation or by ecclesiastical definitions. To give an explanation of this fact (which is far removed from attempting to prove it), to determine what sort of union this is and how it is realized—in a word, to render the mystery as understandable as possible, this is a possible, even a necessary task. It is the major *speculative* function of Sacred Theology.

So after having traced the revealed dogma of the Incarnation back to its sources (Chapter One), and seen its place in the divine plan and its harmonious relationship with other truths (Chapter Two), we begin with the present chapter to investigate the truth more deeply in order to obtain a deeper and better understanding of it. Here we shall attempt to determine the *nature* of the Hypostatic Union—just what kind of thing, according to our human way of grasping reality, it is.

We first know what a thing is *not* before we can determine what it is. So we commence our investigation with a brief summary of the principal errors concerning the Hypostatic Union (**Section 2**), recalling the matter treated more fully in Chapter One. Then we shall examine the Hypostatic Union from a positive aspect, both its essence (**Section 3**) and its characteristics or properties (**Section 4**).

Following this study of the Incarnation in its unity, the next point to be considered are the "parts" of which it is constructed. The person who assumes human nature is the subject of two sections, the first in which the analysis is an abstract consideration (**Section 5**) and then the concrete analysis of the actual person (the Word) who does assume (**Section 6**). The other extreme of the union, human nature, is studied under three aspects: in itself (**Section 7**); in its integrity (**Section 8**); and the order in which the constitutive parts of human nature were assumed (**Section 9**).

Hence the order of this chapter, indicated in outline on the opposite page.

2. What the Incarnation Is Not

Divine nature. Human nature. The union of these two distinct and unmixed natures in the person of the Word. These are the revealed facts of the Incarnation, solemnly defined by the Church; they are the object of belief of all Catholics. But historically, as we have seen, the Church's formal proposal of these truths follows upon the sometimes lamentable attempts of men (however well-intentioned) to explain this mystery in terms intelligible to other men.

The first centuries of Christianity are filled with such errors, which human obstinacy elevates to heresy. Considering the sublimity of the mystery revealed by Christ, and the fallen state of those destined to receive his revelation, it is not surprising, perhaps, that each of the constitutive elements of the revealed truth should have been denied,

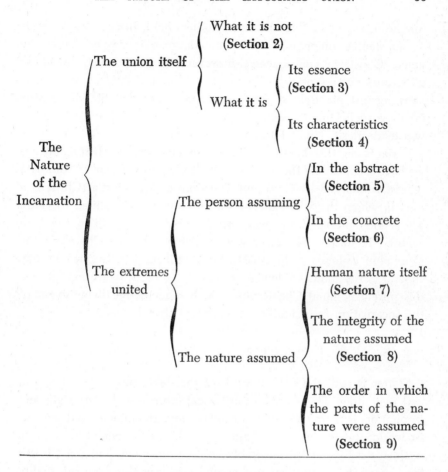

The Nature of the Incarnation
- The union itself
  - What it is not (Section 2)
  - What it is
    - Its essence (Section 3)
    - Its characteristics (Section 4)
- The extremes united
  - The person assuming
    - In the abstract (Section 5)
    - In the concrete (Section 6)
  - The nature assumed
    - Human nature itself (Section 7)
    - The integrity of the nature assumed (Section 8)
    - The order in which the parts of the nature were assumed (Section 9)

nor that even today many will deny them. An examination of the three classes of errors—concerning Christ's divinity; concerning his humanity; concerning the union of his divinity and his humanity—will help to indicate the lines within which lies the truth.

A. Errors concerning Christ's Divinity

In the earliest days of the Church a heretical sect, known as the Ebionites, taught that Christ was a mere man, lacking previous existence, who was adopted by God—at his baptism, say some; as a reward for the merits of his life and death, others hold. In any case there is no substantial union of God with man, man is simply deified by grace. Christ, in consequence, however highly endowed by God's gifts, does not essentially differ from any of the saints. It was, perhaps, against precisely so fundamental an error that St. John insists in his gospel: "In the beginning was the Word . . . and the Word was made flesh" (Jn. 1:1-14).

Variants on this heretical theme are numberless. Historically, as we have seen, among the most important are those of Paul of Samosata (Christ is adopted by God) and Theodore of Mopsuestia (Christ is a man in whom the Word dwells, and is thus morally united to God). These men prepared the way for the great heresiarch of the fifth century, Nestorius. The error was condemned by the Church in the Council of Ephesus (held in 431), but it still persists. In our own day "liberal" Protestants, following the dictates of Modernism,[1] profess this purely nominal Christianity, which reduces the divine event of the Incarnation to a significance no more than human.[2]

B. Errors concerning Christ's Humanity

Matter is evil, the flesh a work of the devil, physical reality foul and degrading. This extreme puritanical error, oriental in origin and inspiration, is hardly a danger for today's material-minded and secularist world. But in times past (and, no doubt, as the pendulum swings, in times yet to come) it inevitably led to a sweeping denial of Christ's true humanity. In the first and second centuries this false spirituality was embraced by Docetism. St. John in his writings and the Apostolic Fathers (especially St. Ignatius of Antioch and St. Clement of Rome) fought vigorously against this heresy which taught that Christ's body was a phantasm, his human life, suffering and death only illusory. St. Augustine in the fourth century, St. Dominic and St. Thomas in the

---

[1]Cf. the decree of the Holy Office, *Lamentabili* (Denz. 2027-2031), and the Encyclical *Pascendi* of Pius X (Denz. 2071 ff.).

[2]In a work devoted to a study of modern Protestant teachings, *The Protestant Churches of America* (Westminster, Md.: The Newman Press, 1956), John J. Hardon, S.J., shows that many sects today either deny Christ's divinity outright, or adopt ambiguous positions.

thirteenth, waged all-out war against the contemporary versions of so pernicious an error.

Christ, the Church declares firmly, is not only true God but also true and perfect man (Athanasian Creed, Councils of Ephesus, Chalcedon, Constantinople, Lateran, etc.). Otherwise God would have been deceiving man in evidencing human characteristics, and Christ would have lied in convincing his disciples after his resurrection that he was not a spirit (cf. Lk. 24:39, Matt. 14:27).

Errors equally destructive of Christ's humanity were those proposed by Apollinaris and Arius, who held that there was no human soul in Christ, the Word himself taking its place. To these men it mattered little that their teachings were by many and various councils condemned; but the justice of their condemnation is apparent: there can only be a true human being when the formal element of the human composite, the human soul, is present.

C. Errors concerning the Union Itself

In a small work entitled *On the Articles of Faith and on the Sacraments*, St. Thomas continues this unhappy catalogue of human frailty:

> The seventh error is that of Eutyches, who placed only one nature in Christ composed of the divinity and the humanity. This is contrary to what the Apostle affirms: "Though he was by nature God, he did not consider being equal to God a thing to be clung to, but emptied himself, taking the nature of a slave and being made like unto men" (Phil. 2:6-7). In this text the two natures of Christ, human and divine, are manifestly seen to be distinct.
>
> The eighth error is that of the Monothelites, who maintain that Christ had only one knowledge, one operation, one will. Against such as these our Lord himself says: "Not as I will, but as thou willest" (Matt. 26:39). Here it clearly appears that in Christ there is a human will, and a divine will which is common to the Father and to the Son.
>
> The ninth error is that of Nestorius. He admitted that Christ is perfect God and perfect man; but he stated that there were two persons, the person of God and the person of man. There would be a union of God and man in Christ only insofar as God dwelt in him by grace. Hence he denies that the Virgin can be called the Mother of God and says that she is the mother of the man, Christ. Against this error Scripture states: "the Holy One to be born shall be called the Son of God" (Lk. 1:35).

Considering the number of variations that have been played upon these major themes through the course of centuries, the providential role of Holy Mother Church as the custodian and guardian of truth is brought clearly into view. "In him was life, and the life was the light of men. And the light shines in the darkness; and the darkness grasped it not" (Jn. 1:4-5).

3. The Nature of the Hypostatic Union

Revelation teaches infallibly that the Second Person of the Blessed Trinity is God, because to him belongs the divine nature; in the Incarnation, the Second Person of the Trinity became man, that is, he assumed a human nature. It is readily evident, then, that an understanding of the Incarnation hinges on an understanding of the realities that underlie the terms: person and nature. Thus before we begin our inquiry concerning the Hypostatic Union a scientific knowledge of the realities signified by those terms is indispensable.

A. The Notions of Nature and Person

(1) The Notion of Nature

Three terms are customarily used by philosophers and theologians to designate one and the same reality: essence, nature and substance. **Essence** signifies the primitive reality, *that by which a thing is what it is,* that by which it is constituted and classified in the hierarchy of being. The identical reality, insofar as it is *the source and center of spontaneous activity,* is called **nature**. A third term, **substance**, designates the very same fundamental reality from another aspect: it is *that which exists in itself and serves as the basis for all else that belongs to it.*

It is this last aspect of essence or nature which concerns us here. But we should remember that the three words are basically synonyms and frequently used interchangeably, and that one and the same reality is determining and specifying principle (essence), source of activity (nature), and existential foundation (substance). As a nature or essence competent to exist in itself and not in another, substance is capable of supporting other realities in existence. A smile, for example, can exist only in another, never by itself; it is the face which supports a smile. The beautiful painting will cease to exist when the canvas disintegrates. But the reality of which we are speaking needs no such support, has no other foundation except itself, furnishes the ground for the **accidents** which modify it. Strength, agility, speed are in the dog, the dog is in itself; love, sorrow, delight are in my soul, my soul is in itself.

If such a reality, a substance, is so much *in itself*, so much *itself*, that it can be said of no other, it is known as *first* substance. It is so perfect in being that it does not exist in another, it cannot even be said of another. Socrates, for example, so exists in himself and is so much himself that he can be predicated of no other thing. On the other hand, a reality may in no sense exist in some subject but may be said of some other subject. Humanity is a substantial perfection and not an accident dependent for support on a more basic reality; yet it may be applied to others, to Socrates and to all those who are men: only Socrates is Socrates, but he is a man, and Plato is a man, and so is Aristotle. Humanity, the abstract, universal nature which exists only in our minds, is called *second* substance, for it has existence in reality only as concrete and individual, only when actualized as first substance. It is **first substance** which realizes in terms of actual existence the **essence** (that by which a thing is what it is) or **nature** (the principle and source of characteristic activity).

Obviously it is first substance we are concerned with here, when we affirm that Christ truly possessed human nature. We mean that his was an individual, concrete, existing nature, complete and perfect in all that pertains to human nature, existing so perfectly in itself that it needed no other support and could be predicated of no other thing. Yet it was not a person, it lacked the higher perfection of personality.

(2) The Notion of Person

What is it that distinguishes "person" from "nature"? What separates the first reality even from so complete and perfect a nature or essence as that expressed by the words "first substance"? That they are really distinct we know. The Church teaches that there are three persons in one divine nature, and yet only one person subsisting in two natures, the divine nature and the human nature of the Word. Right here lies the crux of the "Christological problem," to determine the distinction and relationship between person and natures of the Son of God.

What *is* a person? If we have that answer it should not be too difficult to settle our first difficulty. The great Christian philosopher of Rome, Boethius (470-525), summed up the insights of the Greek Fathers and of his Latin predecessors in the latter's precise and technical language to give a classical answer. A **person** is *an individual substance of a rational nature.*[3] For full understanding of what he means, we shall have to explore this lapidary definition.

1. First of all, a person is a *substance*. We have already seen what this means: a substance is a being of a certain nature, concrete, individualized and existent, which possesses the competence to exist in itself without the support of another and is so perfect that it can be predicated of no other. Socrates is such a being.

2. Second, this substance is *individual*. Here we are faced with an apparent difficulty. First substance is always individualized, concretized, realized in one single being; it is incapable even of verbal multiplication. What, then, does Boethius mean by an "individual" first substance? Evidently something more than is contained in the notion of first substance itself.

To resolve this difficulty, it is necessary to note that there are various degrees of individuality, graduated from the less to the more perfect:

1) Any real substance or substantial part (even so incomplete and imperfect a thing as the soul or vital principle of an animal) enjoys a true individuality. It is what it is and it is distinct from anything that is not it. But the brute soul is not such as to be able to exist and to act without being united to (although not supported in existence by) another substantial element. Separation from the animal body it informs ("death") means the fatal and irreparable ruin of the vital principle of dogs, cats, horses and (happily) mosquitoes.

[3] *Book on the Two Natures* [of Christ] *Against Eutyches and Nestorius,* Chap 3.

2) A real substance can be of such a kind as to be able to exist even when separated from a constitutive substantial element with which it forms a composite. Yet although it can live and act without being united to another, it does not form, by itself alone, a perfectly and completely constituted nature. The human soul possesses this kind of individuality; but a separated human soul (those in heaven, purgatory or hell) is not a human being nor a human person.

3) A real substance can be so much itself, and in and of itself, that it could form part of no other essence or nature, for in itself it constitutes a complete species. Angelic natures are this kind of first substance, and so is the human composite of body and soul; neither could form part of any other nature nor enter into union with any other nature. Despite this uniqueness, however, both angelic nature and human nature (we are still speaking of *first* substance) could be assumed by a divine person. The human nature of Jesus Christ, it is clear, although as fully perfect as possible in the order of nature and the order of grace, was assumed by the person of the Word. The summit of individuality, then, has not yet been reached, since such a nature is not so perfectly itself as to exclude all communications with another.

4) The highest perfection signified by individuality is achieved by a real substance which is so much itself, so exists in and of itself, that it is absolutely independent of any other; it belongs so exclusively to itself alone that no alien substance could appropriate it. Here, then, we have the full meaning of Boethius' definition of person: an individual so complete and perfect that it is entirely self-sufficient, of itself, *sui juris*, possessing its ultimate perfection and enjoying a finished individuality.

So perfected a substance or concrete nature is absolutely incommunicable to any other being. First of all, there is no possible communication of the general to the particular, such as that of the species (e.g., human nature as second substance) to the individual (Socrates). Nor is there communicability of part to the whole, as the hand or arm lives in the human composite, or the human soul lives in conjunction with the body; this kind of substance lives and exists by itself alone. Finally (and chiefly), there is no communicability of the person to another equally complete individual. Howsoever perfect a nature, essence or substance may be—even so perfect a nature as the humanity of Jesus Christ, recapitulating in itself, so to say, all the marvels of nature and of grace—it does not enjoy the crowning glory of personality. For it can become the property of another and subsist in that other.

This is what the Fathers meant by declaring the autonomy and self-sufficiency of a person: this is the being to which existence and action properly, fully and definitively belong. With reference to so independent a being, the nature no less than its accidents or qualities is only that *by which* the being itself exists and acts. Humanity is that by which Socrates is a man and by which he acts humanly; but that which is human, that which possesses existence, that which is beautiful—this is the hypostasis or person. Of themselves, neither subtantial parts nor faculties nor even the nature are or operate. The hand does not strike, but a man with his hand; the will does not love, but a man loves by his will; human nature does not act, but a man who has human nature. That which acts, which loves, which strikes is the perfectly achieved whole, the hypostasis or person.

3. A person is an individual substance *of a rational nature.* In this phrase Beothius indicates that the self-subsistent, autonomous being of which we speak is at the highest level of being, the level of intellectuality. Hence men are persons, and angels, and God. The word is used only in this restricted sense. If we wish to indicate the same autonomy and independence in lower creatures, the terms "supposit" or "hypostasis" may be used. Fido is a supposit, Felix is a hypostasis; so is Fred, but we usually give him the more honorable and meaningful title of "person."

(3) The Notion of Subsistence

From the foregoing analysis it should be clear that nature (even as first substance) and person are two really distinct realities, not mutually exclusive or repugnant, but the latter the crowning and perfection of the former which it presupposes. What is it, then, that constitutes such a perfection? What element is there in the constitutive make-up of things which brings nature to this crowning perfection? To this day philosophers and theologians argue the point. The following are the main theories which have been suggested.

1. **The theory of Scotus.** For Duns Scotus (1274-1308), the great Franciscan theologian, "personality" (that which constitutes a person in the metaphysical sense) is only a negative modality of the substance by which all communication to another hypostasis is excluded.[4] In other words, a human nature which is singular and complete becomes a person so long as it is not assumed by a more perfect hypostasis. Because it has been assumed by the Word, Christ's human nature is not a person, but it yet actually possesses all that would constitute a distinct person if there were no union.

Although this explanation has been accepted by some modern theologians, it enjoys little favor. The perfection which is implied by person is surely greater than that accounted for by a simple *de facto* negation. And if Christ's humanity does not lack anything positive, the theory does not really explain why it is not a person. And it is hard to see how the union could be a real and intrinsic one if there were no positive reality in which the two natures communicate.

2. **The explanation of Suarez.** Francis Suarez, S.J., (1548-1617) identified nature or essence with existence. An existing nature was rendered incommunicable (i.e., made a supposit or person) by the addition of a further modality which completes it and which is a substantial perfection.[5] But this solution is rife with difficulties. First of all, it denies the real distinction between essence and existence in created beings, a thesis which is a fundamental principle of the science of God as well as of any true philosophy. Moreover, existence is the *ultimate* actualization of substance; anything that comes after that can only be accidental. Furthermore, existence comes after the constitution of the person, not before; nature is not that which is but that by which the person or supposit is what it is. Finally, a union according to hypostasis implies a union according to existence

---

[4] *Commentary on Bk. III of the Sentences of Peter Lombard,* dist. 1, q. 1.

[5] *On the Incarnation,* disp. 11, sect. 3. The same opinion is followed by De Lugo (*On the Incarnation,* disp. 12, sect. 1, nn. 1-4) and Vasquez (*Commentary on the Summa Theologiae,* III, q. 4, a. 2, disp. 3, chap. 6).

(since existence properly belongs to the hypostasis); but such a union is impossible in Suarez' theory because he identifies nature and existence, and the union is not according to nature.

3. The theory of Billot. Many distinguished theologians hold a solution effectively proposed in our day by Cardinal Billot, S.J.,[6] although it may be traced back to Medina and perhaps even to an earlier renowed commentator on St. Thomas, Capreolus.[7] According to this explanation, it is the proper existence of a being which formally constitutes it a supposit or hypostasis. Thus only two realities suffice to explain this perfection: the essence or nature, and its own existence, which is separate and really distinct from the nature and renders it incommunicable. In the Incarnation the humanity is not a person because it lacks its proper existence, which is supplied by the personal being of the Word.

This theory is an attractive one. It maintains the fundamental truth of Christian philosophy; it explains with ease and naturalness the traditional expressions which affirm that the union was made according to subsistence, i.e., according to the subsistent being of the divine Person. Yet it poses another question: are the perfection which renders a nature incommunicable and the ultimate actuality which makes it exist one and the same? Are subsistence and existence truly identical? It does not seem so.

4. The theory of Cajetan. For the majority of those who follow St. Thomas, the previous solution seems insufficient. Following Cardinal Cajetan (1468-1534), greatest of the commentators on St. Thomas,[8] they hold that essence, subsistence and existence are three distinct perfections, not separated but superimposed one on the other and linked together in one perfected whole. The first perfection distinguishes the essence from accidents and constitutes it a substance; a second perfection renders this substance autonomous, self-subsistent, so independent and incommunicable as to prohibit its being assumed

---

[6]*On the Word Incarnate*, q. 2.
[7]*Defenses of the Theology of St. Thomas Aquinas*, III, dist. 5, q. 3.
[8]*Commentary on the Summa Theologiae*, III, q. 4, a. 2. Ferrariensis, John of St. Thomas, the Salmanticenses, Bannez, Gonet, Goudin, Billuart—all notable disciples of St. Thomas—adopt Cajetan's explanation, as do many modern theologians, like Garrigou-Lagrange and Héris.

by any other supposit; a final perfection gives the substantial whole so constituted its actuality, its existence. Nature is essentially perfected by subsistence, and subsistence is essentially perfected by existence, for which it supplies the preparation and by which it is crowned.

In this solution, then, subsistence is an intermediary between substance and existence. It may be defined: *a substantial modification of a particular and individual nature by which that nature is made (1) complete in itself; (2) incommunicable to others; and (3) capable in its own proper right of existing and acting.* It is a real, positive and intrinsic perfection which is the ultimate term of a singular substance. It is the necessary preamble and preparation which existence cannot supply; but it itself receives the completion and perfection proper to it from existence.

(4) Conclusion

The Church has never expressed, and probably never will express, a preference for one of these explanations over the others; one is free to hold any of them, or any other that does no violence to revealed truth. But the first two present insoluble philosophical difficulties which have their repercussions in the theology of the Incarnation. It seems wiser to abandon them.

The third and fourth solutions (those of Billot and Cajetan) labor under no such disadvantages. Both affirm and explain a fundamental truth: in Christ there is only one existence, one subsisting being, while the two essences or natures always remain distinct in the union. According to the third opinion, the Word supplies only one perfection to the human nature he assumes, his existence; the more common opinion holds that the Word supplies two distinct but subordinated perfections, subsistence as well as existence.

It is this last solution we shall follow in attempting to give a theological explanation of the nature of the Hypostatic Union, because it seems a better solution for analyzing the nature of reality and one more firmly rooted in the teaching of St. Thomas. But whatever solution is finally adopted, theologians are all at one in confessing that the union is real, substantial and immutable, and that Jesus Christ is truly the God-man, the divine Person of the Word subsisting in two distinct natures, divine and human.

B. The Union of Divine Nature and Human Nature
in the Person of the Word

(1) The Teaching of the Church

The third ecumenical council, held at Ephesus in the year 431, thus defines the teaching of the Church of Christ on the Incarnation:

> We do not say that the nature of the Word became man through a change in it, nor that it was transformed into a complete man constituted of body and soul. But we do assert that the Word, uniting to himself according to his hypostasis a body animated by a rational soul, became man in an inexpressible and incomprehensible way; that he existed as the Son of man, and not merely by a union of affection, nor merely by assuming a human person. Yet even though the natures are diverse, they are so brought together in a true union that they constitute one Christ and Son. Not that the difference of the natures was taken away by their union, but the divinity and the humanity, by their mysterious and ineffable conjunction in one person, produce one Jesus Christ, one Son.[9]
>
> Let him be anathema who does not confess that Emmanuel is truly God, and therefore that the holy Virgin is the Mother of God, for she bore according to the flesh the Word of God made flesh. And if anyone divides the natures in Christ after the union, joining them only by a simple connection of dignity or authority and power, instead of admitting a physical union between them, let him be anathema.[10]

And the fourth general council, the Council of Chalcedon, convoked in 451, declares:

> We confess one and the same Lord Jesus, only-begotten Son, whom we recognize to exist in two natures, without there being confusion or transformation or division or separation between them: for the difference of natures is in no way suppressed by their union; on the contrary, the attributes of each nature are safeguarded, and they subsist in one person alone and in one hypostasis alone.[11]

(2) The Significance of the Church's Teaching

From these divinely revealed facts defined by the Church we can see that, in the person-to-nature relationship, Christ presents a situa-

---

[9]From the second letter of St. Cyril of Alexandria to the heresiarch, Nestorius, read and approved at the first session of the council; Denz. 111a.

[10]These anathemas were written by St. Cyril a year previous to the council and were never officially approved by it, although of unquestionable orthodoxy; Denz. 113, 115.

[11]This official declaration of faith expresses in unambiguous language the traditional belief of the Church; Denz. 148.

tion that is clearly unique. In every other instance we know of, from the union of body and soul (a human nature), there always emerges a human person. Not so with Christ. His human nature does not give rise to a human person. The only person involved is the Word, the Second Person of the Trinity. To the person of the Word belongs the divine nature. The person of the Word assumed a human nature. In the Incarnation, the divine nature and a human nature are joined in the *person* of the Word. The Greek word for person is "hypostasis"; thus the term: **Hypostatic Union,** to designate the union of the two natures in Christ.

The two natures reside in the one person, the Son of God. I am a person, and I have a human nature. The Son of God is a divine person who, in the Incarnation, assumed a human nature. So, Jesus Christ is one person who, because of his divine nature, is God, and who, because of his human nature, is man. Jesus Christ is both God and man, or the God-man, or the man-God.

It is possible to conceive various ways in which God could have joined a human nature to himself; but, of them all, the most wonderful, the most intimate union possible, was the union that was actually established by God. We have some understanding of the intimacy that exists between our own person and nature; in Christ, the human person which is the normal complement of human nature is "supplanted" by the person of the Son of God. To imagine a closer union is not possible.

(3) A Theological Explanation of the Union of the Incarnate Word

The indispensable philosophical notions we saw in a previous section will throw some light on the mystery of the Hypostatic Union, without adequately expressing what is an essentially incomprehensible mystery. By the analogous application of these ideas taken from created things, however, we may reduce the teaching of theology on the Incarnation to a few statements of profound significance.

1. **The union of the Incarnate Word is not realized in the divine nature.** Christ's human nature is of its kind as perfect as his divine nature; Sacred Scripture and the Church both insist that the two na-

tures remain integral and perfect even after their conjunction. As a matter of fact, it is impossible, a contradiction, to hold that the incarnate union could be a union-in-nature, i.e., one from which a single nature results. We can see this if we examine the possibilities of such a union.

1) A unity formed out of two perfect and integral things which remain so after their union. This would only be an *accidental* union (like that of a rock pile or the union of the various substances that make up a building), and not a true single nature, except in the improper sense of the word. The union of the Incarnation, on the contrary, is (as we shall see) a *substantial* one.

2) The union of two perfect substances through the transformation of one into the other (a few drops of water added to a jug of wine) or of both into a third thing (hydrogen and oxygen uniting to form H_2O). But God cannot change, nor can human nature be converted into God (not only would human nature be changed but the Word also). Neither can the two natures form a third thing, for this new composite or mixture would differ from its component elements: Christ would be neither God nor man.

3) A union-in-nature may be formed—and this is the last possibility —by two imperfect things which remain themselves unchanged, as in the union of body and soul which forms a human being. In the Incarnation, however, both human nature and divine nature are perfect. Moreover, the result of this kind of union differs from the things united (man is neither body nor soul, but a composite); here too Christ would become neither God nor man.

Hence there can be no union-in-nature, for the three mentioned exhaust the possibilities. The heresy of Eutyches is self-contradictory, a denial of reason as well as of faith.

2. The union of the divine and human natures is *in* the divine person of the Word, the Son of God. Faith teaches us that human nature is intrinsic to the Word, not something exterior added on, so to say. But everything which is intrinsic to a person is united to it *in* the person: integral parts (arm, head); interior accidents (shape, color); the essence itself (humanity). If human nature is not united to the

Word in the supposit, it simply is not united to him at all—which denies the Incarnation completely. So the union is made in the person of the Word, but not in the nature.

3. Human nature is united in the person of the Word neither **essentially** nor **accidentally** but *according to* the hypostasis. This is the very center of the great mystery of the Incarnation. In Christ his divine nature and his human nature are united in the unity of one subsistent being, of one person—the Second Person of the Blessed Trinity. This union is not an *essential* one, according to the nature; nor is it an *accidental* one, according to some accidental connection. It is a *personal* union, in which the subsistence and the existence of the Word of God are given to a particular human nature, and this human nature thereby is drawn into his hypostatic oneness. It is a **Hypostatic Union.**

Let us try to explain.

1) *The human nature of Christ is complete in all that belongs to such a nature, wanting nothing for its integral perfection.* It is on the verge, so to say, of subsisting by itself, of being a human person; for subsistence is the usual, the ordinary sequel of so complete and perfect a thing. In this unique case, however, subsistence does not result, a human person does not eventuate: God steps in. Instead of human subsistence bringing this nature to its ultimate perfection in essence, an infinitely more perfect subsistence, that of the Word, completes and perfects this nature, closing it off, terminating it, making it incommunicable to all other things and divinely capable of existing and acting.

On the one hand, this human nature, its proper subsistence having been impeded by divine subsistence, forms with the divine nature, and in the person of the Word, a single being, a single supposit, a single hypostasis. On the other hand, Christ's divine nature, which is identical with the Word (the three divine Persons, really distinct as persons, are one in nature, which is identical with each), forms with him a single person. So, with no loss of his proper subsistence in the divine nature, the Word also subsists in his human nature, from the moment of his union with it.

2) *The perfection of this union should be evident.* This is not a mere accidental union, a superadded qualification or modification of the Second Person. Accidents, we have said, are "beings of being"—that is, they bring a subsidiary kind of existence to a subject already essentially constituted and pre-existing (at least in thought). They are outside determinations, so to say; they do not enter into the inner make-up of things, nor do they help to establish their subsistent unity.

Christ's human nature is not united to the Word and to his divine nature in this external fashion, like a suit of clothes God dons to masquerade in. Not even the marvelous union achieved through sanctifying grace can match this incarnate union, for the union through grace also is accidental, a supernatural but extrinsic determination of, and addition to human nature. In such accidental unions each of the things united retains its own unity of essence (and of supposit, if both subsist) and its own independent existence. The union of the Incarnate Word, on the contrary, is of a far higher order: it is a substantial union.

3) *In the Incarnation, the human nature, composed of body and soul, enters intrinsically, as an essential and substantial element, into the formation of the unique personal being who is the God-man.* The divine person of the Word, of course, eternally pre-exists his human nature; his person is in no wise the result of this union (as, for example, the human person is the result of the union of body and soul). But for the human nature he assumes, the Word fulfills the same functions of subsistence as he does for his divine nature. Human nature is united to the Word precisely from the point of view, and by the bond of subsistence: the hypostatic independence, incommunicability and unity of the Second Person of the Blessed Trinity. Human nature and divine nature are thus united by the very same divine subsistence, and they together form one same personal being.

Since the supposit is essentially specified by the nature in which it subsists and to which it brings subsistence (and its complement, existence); and since this supposit, the Son of God, subsists both in a divine and in a human nature; the consequence is that the Word is both God and man. As by his divine nature the Son of God is truly God, so on equal terms and with equal rights the Son of God is truly man—by his human nature. But the Word Incarnate is only one person, at once divine and human. Subsisting from all eternity in the divine nature alone, the Second Person in the fulness of time hypostatically unites a human nature to himself, and thus subsists in a human nature also. And this Son of man—this person subsisting in human nature— is thus *by nature* God. Jesus Christ: true God and true man, perfect man and perfect God.

(4) Differences between the Hypostatic Union and a Simply Personal Union

The union of divine and human natures in Christ has no counterpart in all of nature; it is unique, the only one of its kind. Our previous observations have enabled us to penetrate more deeply into this mystery of God's love for man, but like all divine things the Incarnation so exceeds the limited capacities of our minds that we can never fully understand it. A traditional comparison—necessarily defective, like all examples drawn from created things to illustrate the divine—may help to clarify what we have seen so far.

The Athanasian Creed points out: "As a rational soul and flesh are one man, so God and man are one Christ." In us body and soul are united to constitute a single person or hypostasis, a man: John Doe, Charlie Brown. So, similarly, in the Incarnation divine nature and human nature are united in a single unity, the unity of the one subsistent being, the person of the Word. As the immortal soul, the form of the body, communicates its own subsistence to the body at the moment of its creation by God and union with the body; so the Second Person, subsisting in divine nature, communicates to the human nature he assumes his own divine subsistence at a given moment of time, and so unites divine nature and human nature in his person.

Three similarities may be noted in this comparison. (1) Both unions are substantial ones, for in each there is a unity of subsistence which unites the two elements. (2) Each union has a decided and essential result: a new nature and person results from the union of body and soul; subsistence in a new nature results from the hypostatic union. (3) From neither union does a multiplication of persons result.

But the **differences** between the two unions are far greater than their similarities, and of special significance. They too may be reduced to three. (1) Body and soul are incomplete substances, related to each other as matter and form; divine nature and human nature are each integral and complete, and no relationship of matter and form is possible between them. (2) A person is newly constituted by the union of body and soul: John Doe; in the Incarnation, the person, the Word, is in no sense the result of the union, for he exists fully and perfectly from all eternity. (3) The union of body and soul is not only substantial, it is *essential:* a new nature or essence, human nature, is its formal result. On the contrary, the substantial union of divine and human natures preserves each in its proper perfection and integrity, and no new essence results.

4. Characteristics of the Hypostatic Union

Like all other realities, natural and supernatural, the union of the Incarnate Word manifests certain distinguishing notes which flow immediately from its nature as this particular kind of thing. Since these characteristics also help us more fully to appreciate God's gift of himself to us, we will consider them briefly in a series of statements and explanations.

1. **The incarnate union, as a real relation of Christ's human nature to his divine nature, is a created entity.**

The word "union" may be taken in three senses: (1) for the action which joins two or more things; (2) for the conjunction between them which results; (3) for the mutual relation of one to the other which follows upon their conjunction. Thus (1) by the uniting action produced by the exchange of marital vows, (2) a permanent bond arises between man and woman, in virtue of which (3) they are related as man and wife. By God's uniting action, human nature and divine nature are joined in the unity of the Second Person, and so related to each other.

Offhand it might appear that the doctrine of God's immutability is compromised by the Incarnation, because after the Incarnation God is man, which he was not before. The same difficulty arises in connection with every new relationship between a creature and God, beginning with the act of creation, which seems superficially to add considerably to God. But this change, we have previously noted,[12] was not in God but in the things created. Take the example of an artificial pond that is newly located at the foot of a tree: the tree's reflection in the pond is something new, but it adds nothing to the tree. Or, if someone in a room opens a shutter to let the sun shine into the room, the room is flooded with sunlight, but no one would suggest that the sun had undergone any change.

The human nature assumed by God was a creature made by God. As he assumed it, he did not become dependent upon it in any sense, but it was always totally dependent upon him. When he assumed it, he underwent not the slightest change, but it was transformed in a way that was incomparable. A new relation appears in the world, the real relation of Christ's human nature to God. But on God's part there is no change, and consequently no new real relation.

2. The incarnate union is the greatest of created unions.

Although the extremes which are united in the Incarnation—human nature and divine nature—are at infinite poles apart, they are united to each other in the very being of the Second Person. The oneness of the Word is the highest of all unities, for he is a divinely subsistent being, without any parts whatsoever, absolutely complete in himself and possessing all that properly makes a thing one. United in this supreme oneness, the unity of Christ's divine and human natures is surpassed only by the unity of the Trinity itself. As St. Bernard has pointed out: "Among all the things which can truly be called one, pre-eminence is held by that unity of the Trinity whereby three persons are one substance [the divine nature]; in the second place is that unity by which three substances [body, soul, divinity] are, in Christ, one person."[13]

---

[12]Cf. Murphy, et al., God and His Creation (Dubuque: The Priory Press, 1958), 157-158.
[13]Concerning Consideration, Bk. V, Chap. 8.

3. **The incarnate union is the greatest of God's gifts to his creatures, and hence is called "the grace of union."**

Grace, as you should remember, is a word with many meanings: it signifies God's free decision to bestow his gifts on creatures, his *effective* love for them; it signifies that habitual divine gift whereby the creature is made a partaker of God's own nature (sanctifying grace) and his transitory assistance of the moment (actual grace); it can mean also any gift of God, on which the creature has no claim whatsoever.

The elevation of human nature to substantial union with God as he is in himself is a manifest action of love on God's part, a pre-eminently "gracious" divine action. Its result is a gift beyond dreams and aspirations, even beyond man's conceiving: the greatest possible gift—a communication of the infinite Person of the Word and of the very existence of God, a communication which ennobles, elevates, enriches our nature in an ineffable manner. This is the **grace of union,** the exemplar and perfection of habitual grace and actual grace. As is obvious, no other divine gift—not even habitual grace—could be a bond or link in so direct and immediate a union with God as that given by the subsistence of human nature in, and by the subsisting divinity who is the Word. On the contrary, the greatest effusion of God's sanctifying grace and his actual supernatural assistance will be poured upon the nature he assumes, because of (and in some sense as a result of) this grace of union, the Hypostatic Union itself.

Two important corollaries derive from the above facts:

1) *The Incarnation was not merited or earned.* The Hypostatic Union is the source of all of the grace Christ is given, and of all those merits of his which earn grace for other men, including his own Mother. It is, in the theological phrase, *the* **principle of all supernatural merit.** Thus the Hypostatic Union cannot itself be merited, for the God-man (nor anyone dependent on him) cannot merit this gift until he exists, and he exists only at the moment of the Incarnation.

In a wider meaning of the word "merit"—as appropriate or suitable that one's desires and petitions should be heard and answered by one's friends—the saints of the Old Testament may be said to have "earned" this gift of God: "for it was fitting that God should hearken to those who obeyed him."[14] Similarly Our Blessed Lady, by the great grace given her in view of her Son's merits, won by herself, not to be the Mother of God (this too was a completely gratuitous gift, for to be God's mother is equivalent to God's becoming man), but "that degree of purity and sanctity which *fitted* her to be the Mother of God."[15] The prayers and works of the Virgin, her excelling co-operation with God's gifts, secure from him an outpouring of the gifts of divine love to adorn her in a fashion becoming his mother.

2) *The incarnate union is absolutely and singularly supernatural.* To be substantially united to God transcends in an inexpressible degree the entire natural order, and infinitely exceeds even the order of grace. The Incarnation is supernatural in its cause, who is God alone, the Blessed Trinity; and in itself, for it is the gift of the subsistence of the Son of God and of God's own existence: it is as far above nature and the whole of nature as God himself. Moreover, it transcends even the order of grace (and even the least grace, let us not forget, is of more value than the entire created universe). For grace, wonderful as it is, is but an accidental and analogous participation of God's nature and attributes. But the Incarnation is a substantial communion with divinity: this man, Christ our brother, is by substance, by nature God.

Thus is the divine economy revealed to us in the fulness of time. Three "orders" are established by divine wisdom and love:

(1) **The order of nature:** all the things, from the smallest particle of matter to the highest angel, created by God.

(2) **The order of grace:** the divine gifts (and those sanctified by them) by which God elevates his intellectual creatures to a participation in his divine life and ultimately in the beatitude proper to himself.

(3) **The hypostatic order:** Christ, only begotten Son of God, whose human nature is substantially divinized by its subsistence in the Word and its divine existence. All the things

[14]*Summa*, III, q. 2, a. 11.
[15]*Ibid.*, ad 3.

which are essentially linked with the Incarnation belong to this order also. Our Blessed Lady, in virtue of her divine maternity, intrinsically pertains to the hypostatic order; St. Joseph, as Christ's guardian, pertains to the same order extrinsically. The consequences of these facts concerning Mary and Joseph will be shown in a later chapter.

5. The Assumption of Christ's Human Nature

We have examined the union of the Incarnate Word in its essence, seen (as best we can in this world) what it is: two natures, human and divine, subsisting and existing in the singular unity of the Second Person of the Blessed Trinity. Now we will separately examine these elements of which this unique and single being, Jesus Christ, is "composed"—not as parts of a composite (as body and soul are substantial parts of the human composite) compose a single thing, but as your nature and your subsistence "compose" or constitute the metaphysically unique *you*. Thus we consider the person who assumes this human nature, and then study the nature so united to God.

A. The Notion of Assuming

We speak of the divine action by which the Incarnation took place in synonymous phrases: "God unites a human nature to himself"; "God assumes a human nature." Yet we find a modifying phrase in the first statement—"to himself"—which has no place in the second. *To assume* is a reflexive verb, i.e., one which refers the action back upon the subject rather than involving a second party: "I assume you are studying" means that I take it upon myself to reach a conclusion; you may find the conclusion ludicrous. Such is the etymological bearing of the word, *ad se sumere*, to take or draw to oneself. In the context of this mystery, it will mean to unite human nature to oneself in such a way as to form a personal and substantial union with it. By the very force of the word itself, both the *principle* responsible for the action is indicated and the object at which the action terminates, the *term* of the action; and principle and term are one and the same.

B. Who or What Assumes

With this strict meaning of the word before our eyes, we can reach some important conclusions with regard to the hypostatic union.

1. **In the most proper sense, only a person can assume.** To assume implies both principle and term, beginning and end of the action which eventuates in a subsistent union—and the identity of these two. But the supposit alone (called a "person" when we talk of intellectual beings) is *that which* acts, although the nature or essence determines and specifies the action—it is that *by which* a supposit acts. Moreover, this particular unifying action does not take place in the nature (for the natures united remain unmixed, each perfect and distinct) but in the person, the proper term of the action. To assume, in consequence, is an action proper to the person alone, for only the supposit can be both principle and term.

2. **Only a divine Person can assume another nature.** To give subsistence to a particular nature is the work of any supposit, but that nature specifies and determines the supposit to be this kind of thing and not something else—in a word, it limits, restrains, encloses the supposit. Created supposits, from angels to adzes, are necessarily finite, i.e., they subsist within the limits imposed on them by the nature they complete and terminate. But God knows no such limitations: a divine person is properly infinite, without any boundaries. And whereas the termination of a creature exhausts a created supposit, not one nor many natures can "use up" the completing, terminating potentialities of God.

3. **In a secondary sense, the divine nature may be said to assume.** The person that I am performs all my actions, from thinking to running. But, fundamentally, the thinking requires a mind, and the running requires feet; in other words, actions spring basically from the nature. Likewise for the assuming involved in the Incarnation: the person of the Word performs the action, but the divine nature is the source that makes it ultimately possible. The ultimate source of all divine acts—whether it be creation or the act of assuming— is the divine nature, which belongs to the Father no less than to the Son. But it is the Son who immediately assumes the human nature,

with the result that in him alone the human nature assumed "resides." **In the Incarnation, the three persons of the divine nature united a human nature to the Second Person of the divine nature.**

To put this conclusion in another way. Any nature exists only as subsisting in a supposit, for which it is the specifying source of activity —that by which and by reason of which the supposit acts, and acts in this way. The divine nature subsists in the three divine Persons, and is the principle or source of the unitive action by which human nature is terminated in and by the subsistence of the Word. Hence as principle the divine nature may be said to assume: to unite a human nature not to itself (the union is not made in the nature), but to one of its supposits, namely, the Word. It is in this restricted sense that the Fathers (St. Cyril of Alexandria, for example) speak of "one incarnated nature of the Word of God."[16]

The meaning of this phrase, badly distorted by the Monophysites (heretics like Eutyches who profess only one nature in Christ), is clearly indicated by the Church. In the words of the Second Council of Constantinopole:

> If anyone, confessing that the union was made from the two natures of the deity and the humanity, or saying that "there is one incarnate nature of the Word of God," does not take these expressions in the sense taught by the Fathers—that from the union of divine and human natures according to hypostasis one Christ results—but tries by such phrases to introduce one nature or substance of the Godhead and humanity of Christ, let him be anathema.[17]

A consideration of the facts mentioned above leads to a rather startling conclusion: that even abstracting from the Trinity of persons (as do those, pagans and Jews, unenlightened by revelation), God could still assume a human nature. For an impersonal God is a contradiction. Divinity must necessarily possess the ultimate perfection we call subsistence. God is subsisting divinity, a supposit or person who is identical with his nature—or else he is a mere non-existing abstraction, like any universal nature. As subsisting, he can assume human nature by giving it his own infinite subsistence and existence.

---

[16]*Against the Blasphemies of Nestorius*, Bk. II.
[17]Denz. 220; cf. Council of the Lateran, 649; Denz. 258.

C. Who Can Assume

It is proper to a divine Person to assume another nature, and to him alone. But there are three divine Persons, and human nature is in fact assumed only by the Word. This naturally raises questions concerning the possibility of such an action and termination on the part of the other Persons, and of restricting the action to one of them.

1. **One of the divine Persons can assume a created nature without the others.** Faith teaches this as a fact; we want to know, how come? "It must also be believed that the entire Trinity produced the Incarnation of the Son of God, because the works of the Trinity cannot be separated. Nevertheless, the Son alone 'took the nature of a slave'—in the singularity of his Person, not in the unity of divine nature; in that which is proper to the Son, not in that which is common to the whole Trinity."[18] This declaration points out that the uniting action is not exclusively the work of one Person, for it proceeds from the divine nature which is common to all and identical with each. But the term of the action is a Person; and since each divine Person is truly distinct from the others, and distinct precisely by reason of his subsistence, he could communicate his own proper subsistence to a created nature without involving the others or their subsistence.

2. **Any divine Person, not only the Son, could** assume a human nature. Each Person is omnipotent fully and perfectly; and Father and Holy Spirit are as fully and perfectly subsistent as the Son. As active principle, accordingly, the Father or Holy Spirit, together with the other Persons, could unite a human nature to himself by communicating his subsistence and his subsistence alone.

Actually it is a question of the capacity of divine power and where it resides, and of divine subsistence and where its resides. In a word, divine power is infinite, and it resides equally and totally in each of the divine Persons. The power of my free will is undetermined, and can be directed toward God or toward sin. The divine power is immeasurably less determined; by that divine power the assuming of a human nature could have been "channeled," so that it terminated in the person

---

[18]Eleventh Council of Toledo, 675 (Denz. 284); it is not clear that this provincial council was ever approved by the pope, but its creed (of which the quotation is an excerpt) undoubtedly is an expression of the ordinary *magisterium*.

of the Father or the Holy Ghost—each subsists with his own proper subsistence. No less than the Son, the Father or the Holy Ghost can become man.

3. **Two or three divine Persons could assume one and the same human nature.** As is evidenced by the Trinity itself, one divine Person does not exclude another from subsisting in the same divine nature. Each Person terminates one and the same divine nature by his own subsistence. In the same way, all three could subsist in one and the same human nature: each could terminate with his own proper subsistence one and the same human nature. In this event, because of the oneness of the nature assumed, the three divine Persons would be one man, not three; just as now they are one God, because there is only one divine nature. Each would still be distinct from the other, of course, except insofar as they subsist in this single human nature.

4. **One divine Person could assume several human natures.** The power of a divine Person is infinite: he is omnipotent; and the divine subsistence is infinite: no created nature can so encompass the subsistence of God as jealously to restrict its terminating and perfecting ability to itself alone. Neither from the point of view of principle nor of term, in effect, can a divine Person be so bound within created limits. The statement: God can only become incarnate once, is a patent absurdity.

In this case also, as in the preceding one, even though there are several human natures assumed, there would only be one man. For there is only one supposit subsisting in these several human natures. This man (who is God) would have several human natures, it is true; God could be said to have become incarnate several times. But there would only be a single God-man.

6. The Second Person Assumes

The possibilities just discussed show some of the ways which could realize God's substantial union with human nature for the purpose of saving mankind from his sins. In fact, however, the union is realized in the subsistence of the Second Person alone, whatever the possibilities. St. Thomas points out four reasons which show the special appropriateness of this union with the Word, and with him alone:[19]

1. On the part of the union itself.

1) *From the general similarity of the things united:* Even before the Incarnation, there was a deep "affinity" between the Son of God and creatures. The act whereby the Father generated the Son is the model of all later creative activity by God. And the Son is the Word, the mental word or eternal concept of the Father, according to which he fashioned all his creatures. St. John writes that without the Word "was made nothing that was made" (Jn. 1:3), and the idea of the Son's special connection with creation is enlarged upon by St. Paul in these words: "He is the image of the invisible God, the firstborn of every creature. For in him were created all things in the heavens and on the earth, things visible and things invisible. . . . All things have been created through and unto him, and he is before all creatures, and in him all things hold together" (Col. 1:15-17).

Since all things were made through him, it was singularly fitting that, when they proved wayward and wanton, they should be brought back, restored, redeemed through him. For so does any artist work to restore his damaged masterpiece: he recalls the artistic idea which inspired him and through it works to re-create the original.

2) *From the special affinity between the Son and human nature:* Man was made for wisdom, the knowledge of divine things. God, who is eternal wisdom, is the source of all man's wisdom, and the Word is the concept of that eternal wisdom. Men become more perfect, they acquire more wisdom, the more perfectly they share in the Word of God; just as students become more learned in a particular subject the more completely they assimilate the writings of an expert scholar. Students always consider it a priceless opportunity to be taught personally by the master; so, too, if the very Word of God united himself personally to human nature, men would have, to the perfect wisdom in which their perfection lies, an approach that could not be improved upon.

[19]*Summa,* III, q. 3, a. 8.

2. **On the part of the end of the union.** Further evidence that it was most appropriate for the Son to become man can be discerned in the precise purpose of the Incarnation, namely, to make men adoptive sons of God. It is unmistakably most suitable that the task of making men adoptive sons of God should be discharged by God's own natural Son. Who could better usher men into the dignity of divine adoption than their own divine brother? St. Paul wrote: "For those whom he has foreknown he has also predestined to become conformed to the image of his Son, that he should be the firstborn among many brethren" (Rom. 8:29).

3. **On the part of man's need.** And finally, the Incarnation was designed to undo the damage wrought by the sin of our first parent. That sin was the outgrowth of a disordered desire for knowledge expressly forbidden by God. So it was eminently fitting that man, who had abandoned God in a perverse seeking after forbidden knowledge, should be rescued and brought back to God by him who is the Word of the God of true wisdom.

7. The Human Nature of the Word

The Second Person of the Blessed Trinity is one element of this marvelous incarnate union. Human nature is the other. So we proceed from a consideration of the first element to a consideration of the second. This second study will be three-fold: the human nature itself (**Section 7**); its constitutive parts, body and soul (**Section 8**); and the order in which these parts are assumed (**Section 9**).

A. Human Nature Alone Can Be Assumed

Absolutely speaking, no creature possesses any innate quality which equips it to be hypostatically united to God. A stone, a bird, an angel— it does not matter, so long as the thing can be terminated by subsistence. Excepting a passive non-repugnance to being elevated to substantial union with God—common to all substances or substantial parts —no creature can contribute to such a union, none possesses any special powers or abilities which fits it better than another for the divine subsistence.

But *relatively* considered—in relation to man's redemption—the nature assumed must have special qualities: it must be endowed with intellect and will. For man's salvation is to be secured through the merit and satisfaction of the nature assumed; as free acts, both merit and satisfaction presuppose knowledge and choice. An angelic nature, or that of a separated soul, or human nature—all could be fittingly assumed by God, since each, hypostatically united to God, could merit and satisfy for man.

Yet only human nature perfectly fulfills all the requirements of appropriateness for the hypostatic union. As rational and intellectual (and this the angels possess in a far superior way), human nature already has a certain fitness: by its operations of knowing and loving it can approach the Word and be united to him. This is an advantage no lower creature can claim. At the very same time, human nature after Adam's fall stands in desperate need of redemption; and this no higher nature possesses, for the angels' sin is irremediable, as St. Thomas teaches.[20]

It remains, then, that *only human nature can be assumed with full appropriateness by God.* It alone has the double qualities of dignity and necessity.

B. A Human Person Cannot Be Assumed

Since the person is a complete and incommunicable substance, it cannot enter into substantial union with another supposit: either one person would be destroyed (and then how absurd to assume a person, when one is bound to be frustrated), or both persons would remain without substantially uniting (which is contrary to revelation and the Church's teaching). Properly speaking, it follows that the Word cannot be said to have assumed a man. This concrete term "man" means a supposit subsisting in human nature, a human person; there was none such, nor could there be, in the incarnate union.

[20]*Summa*, I, q. 64, a. 2; cf. Murphy, *et al.*, *God and His Creation*, 379.

C. A Particular Human Nature Is Assumed

Human nature as such exists only in particular human beings, for it is composed of body and soul, and what is material is necessarily singular, individual, particularized. Humanity itself is a pure abstraction, without existence in the world of reality; it is a universal idea which exists only in the mind. As a divine idea in the mind of God— the divine essence as imitable in this special way—human nature is identical with divinity itself: God is his knowledge. This "human nature" if assumed, would be the Son from all eternity, not something assumed in time. To assume human nature as it is an abstract, mental concept would be a mere fiction, a false assumption: Christ would not be a real man, he would only be thought of as a man. Such a deception by God is inconceivable.

To make the Incarnation a true incarnation, the Word assumes an individual human nature, concrete and particularized, and in this respect different from all other singular human natures, such as yours or mine. Although he could assume many or even all human natures, he does not do so. Respecting the nature he has made, which is born to exist in many supposits rather than in one alone, he takes to himself only one nature. This is befitting his dignity: of many brethren, he is, according to his human nature, the firstborn; just as according to his divine nature he is the firstborn of every creature. It is fitting, too, that his should be a maximum unity. As it was fitting that only one divine supposit should become incarnate, so is it that only one human nature should be assumed.

So the Word takes a particular human nature. And the one he chooses is, in fact, of the stock of Adam. It could have been otherwise, of course; God could have created a completely new human nature, descended from no human ancestors, or realized his plan in other ways. But there is a unique suitability in his actual choice of a nature derived from our first parents:

1) *Justice is served.* For justice demands that satisfaction should be paid by him who has sinned. Hence from the nature corrupted by sin should be taken that by which satisfaction for that whole nature would be fulfilled.

2) *The dignity of man is increased.* From the very race conquered by the devil is born the devil's conqueror.

3) *God's power is made more manifest.* God brings a nature deeply damaged and pitifully weak to undreamed of heights of power and dignity—the power and glory of God himself.

8. The Integrity of the Human Nature of the Word

Human nature is a composite, that is, a being composed of two elements, two substantial parts: body and soul, which are related to each other as material principle and formal principle. If one or other of these is missing, there is no human being. A cadaver is not a man, a separated soul is not a man. But Christ is true and perfect man—he said so himself many times, and the Church says so time and time again, and Holy Scripture witnesses on innumerable occasions to his human actions, both those proper to the body and those proper to the soul.

The Word assumes both parts of the human composite: a true human body and a true human soul.

A. The Human Body of the Word

There are probably few things in the New Testament for which there is such a great mass of evidence as the reality of Christ's body. Christ ate, drank, slept, prayed, got tired, walked, talked, suffered, died, etc. If the body was not real but only imaginary, the conclusion is inevitable: his human nature was unreal and God has misled men with the most monstrous hoax in all history. Further, his death was a fake and the salvation of the human race has never been won.

To suggest such fantastic behavior on the part of a person who is truth itself is absurd. Christ personally made a special point of dispelling any possible doubts on the matter, when he appeared to his apostles after his resurrection. "Jesus stood in their midst. . . . But they were startled and panic-stricken, and thought that they saw a spirit. And he said to them: 'Why are you disturbed, and why do doubts arise in your hearts? See my hands and feet, that it is I myself.

Feel me and see: for a spirit does not have flesh and bones, as you see I have' " (Lk. 24:36-39). Then he asked them for food and ate it in their presence.

Christ's body is a body like ours, flesh and blood like ours. It is not a special body, made of some "heavenly" material—those who have thought so, seeking to preserve God's dignity from the grossness of human earthiness, make God out to be a liar, destroy his humanity, deny the divine maternity of Our Lady.

B. The Human Soul of the Word

The reality of Christ's human soul is clear on three grounds: the authority of Sacred Scripture; the utility of the Incarnation; the truth of the Incarnation.

1) *The authority of Sacred Scripture.* The Evangelists have provided ample evidence for the genuineness of the other element of Christ's human nature—his soul. They report clearly that he experienced wonder, sadness, anger—all actions which conclusively show the reality of his human soul, as eating is proof of the genuineness of his body. St. Mark quotes Christ as saying of himself: "My soul is sorrowful even unto death" (Mk. 14:34). If his soul was not real, he was speaking nonsense or deliberately deceiving us.

2) *The utility of the Incarnation.* If the human soul of the Word was not real, the meaning of the Incarnation is seriously impaired. For its purpose was to free man from sin, and the liberation was aimed less at the body than at the soul which had spawned the sin and its attached miseries. But "what is not assumed is not cured"—this ancient patristic adage is apposite here. As an ancient writer says:

> If you look at its origin, the substance of the soul is more precious than the body; if at the sin of transgression, then because of its intelligence it is worse than the body. But I know, I do not doubt, that Christ is perfect wisdom and most loving. Because of the first, he did not despise that which was better and capable of prudence; because of the second, he assumed that which had been more deeply wounded.[21]

[21]Vigilius Tapsensis, *Against Felician,* Chap. 13 (a work at one time attributed to St. Augustine).

3) *The truth of the Incarnation.* If Christ's soul was not genuine, he was not a man at all; his body was not human, his mind was not human, his eyes were not the eyes of a man. Where these things are human, it is a human soul that makes them so. The soul is the determining form: without it, no man, no God-made-man.

C. The Human Mind of the Word

A man is a rational animal. This classic definition implies that this two-legged creature necessarily wears a thinking cap—the faculty or power of reasoning. Remove the thinking cap and you end up with a two-legged creature, and we are back swinging insouciantly from limb to jungle limb.

Yet, in effect, that is what some heretics have tried to do with Christ's human nature: strip it of its rationality, its own proper power of thinking. This blasphemy may have been unconscious or unthinking; it is a blasphemy nonetheless, a denial of God's own word and of the utility and truth of his Incarnation.

1) In the gospels, there are actions ascribed to Christ that are impossible of performance without a human mind. St. Luke records that, when Christ heard the centurion, he "marvelled" (Lk. 7:9). St. Matthew reports that Christ said of himself: "Learn of me, because I am meek, and humble of heart" (Matt. 11:29). Wonderment, meekness and humility are inconceivable in Christ, if he has no human intellect.

2) The Incarnation was designed to restore man from his sin; it is rationality that makes man capable of separation from God through sin and of union with God through grace. For Christ not to assume a human intellect would have been completely incongruous. *What was not assumed by him, was not redeemed by him.*[22]

---

[22]St. Gregory Nazianzen, *Letter 101, to Cledonius,* 7; St. Ambrose, *Letter 48 to Sabine.* St. Thomas states the same truth from a different angle: "Nothing that God planted in our nature was wanting to the human nature assumed by the Word of God" (*Summa,* III, q. 9, a. 4); this statement is derived from St. John Damascene, *On the True Faith,* Bk. III, Chap. 6, itself a re-wording of the identical truth expressed by earlier Greek Fathers and by St. Augustine, *Enchiridion,* Chap. 10.

3) Fundamentally a man's body is human because he has a rational soul; if Christ's soul was not rational, his body was less than human. The soul of a man differs from the soul of a beast precisely in this: that the human soul is rational. To deny rationality to the soul of Christ is an outrage to reason, and does violence thereby to faith.

D. The True and Integral Humanity of the Word

The most holy Roman Church anathematizes:

Manes and his followers, who take away the truth of Christ's humanity, dreaming that the Word of God did not assume a true body but an imaginary one.

And Valentine, asseverating that the Word of God received nothing from his Virgin Mother, but assumed a body of celestial material, and passed through the womb of the Virgin as water runs through an aqueduct.

Also Arius, who asserted that the body assumed of the Virgin lacked a soul and wished the "deity"[23] to take the place of the soul.

Also Apollinaris, who, understanding that the denial of a soul in Christ which informs the body would mean that he did not possess true humanity, yet held that the Godhead of the Word took the place of the rational soul.[24]

9. The Order of the Assumption

Whenever and wherever two or more things get together, the question of order spontaneously arises—ask any hostess. Order implies priority and posteriority, before and after. Did Jack get to the party before Jill? Is Jill before Jack in scholastic achievement? In athletic ability? Is Jack older than Jill?

As these questions indicate, we may speak of an *order of time,* in which one thing precedes another according to duration; or of an *order of nature,* where the question of time does not enter in but natural precedence is all important. Order of nature is subdivided into order of *dignity* (bishop precedes priest, soul precedes body: the more perfect the less) and order of *causality* (the cause is prior by nature to

[23]That is, the *Logos* who in Arius' sense is not cosubstantial or coeternal. Cf. Denz. 705.
[24]*Decree for the Jacobites,* Council of Florence, 1442; Denz. 710.

its effect, even though both may be simultaneous). When causal priority involves an intellectual agent, there is order of *intention* (the end is the first thing the agent has in mind) or of *execution* (to achieve the end certain means must first be taken). Hence this outline:

$$
\text{order}
\begin{cases}
\text{of time} \\
\text{of nature}
\begin{cases}
\text{of dignity} \\
\text{of causality}
\begin{cases}
\text{of intention} \\
\text{of execution}
\end{cases}
\end{cases}
\end{cases}
$$

These distinctions are most useful in considering the human nature of the Word. For this is composed of several things—the body and its parts, and the soul and its faculties. Since the Word unites all of these to himself, which does he assume first?

1. **In the very same instant of time, body and soul are assumed.** The body is not human unless it is informed by the soul; the human soul is created by God precisely as the form of the body, and thus at the very same instant is infused into the body. Since the Word becomes incarnate at the moment of the Annunciation, in that very instant, without the slightest time-gap, Christ's body is miraculously generated in the womb of the Virgin, his soul is created and infused in it, and both are assumed by the Word.

2. **In the order of nature, and of intention, human nature is assumed before its constitutive parts.** The Word intends to unite to himself a whole and perfect human nature, not just a body nor just a soul. On the contrary, it is by reason of this whole nature that the parts are assumed.

3. **In the order of execution, the parts are assumed prior to the whole.** By nature (not always in time by any means, as we have seen) the parts of a composite, the things out of which it is formed, precede its formation: they go into its make-up and hence come first. So body and soul, in the order of execution, are naturally prior to the whole, the complete human nature, which they constitute, even though it is this whole which the Word has first in mind.

4. In the order of dignity (*as the more perfect*) **and of causality (***as the specifying element***), the body is assumed by reason of the soul, and the soul itself by reason of its intellectual part.** Flesh is human only when, and because, it is informed by the determining and differentiating element of human nature, the soul. The human mind (intellect and will) gives the soul, in turn, its proper characteristics of rationality and spirituality, making it like to God and capable of knowing and loving God—for which reason the Word also assumes the other parts of human nature intrinsically and necessarily linked with the intellectual soul.

5. The Word does not assume human nature by means of grace. This merely repeats what we have seen earlier in this chapter.[25] "Grace" as indicating God's loving will freely to give himself to a creature is the effective cause of this union, but in no sense a connecting medium in which the union is realized. The *substantial* sanctification of human nature which is the **grace of union** is the term, not the medium, of the union: human nature is assumed in order that the personal being of the Word, terminating it, may be communicated to it. The *accidental* sanctification of human nature which is **habitual grace** is an effect consequent on the union: because this man is the Only-begotten of the Father, he is full of grace and truth.

10. Summary and Conclusion

Attempts to explain the words "God became man" have, throughout the ages, led philosophers and theologians alike into a bewildering labyrinth of errors. Some have proprounded the idea that Christ was merely man, albeit a man showered with extraordinary gifts; others that Christ was truly God but that his body was a phantasm, a make-believe body. On the one hand, fallacious ideas about Christ destroyed his divinity; on the other hand, ideas just as false concerning the humanity of Christ relegated him to the shadowy niche of illusion. Significantly, these same fruitless concepts can be found even today, devitalizing the real meaning of the Cross.

[25]Cf. *supra*, pp. 118-120.

The basis for an understanding of the meaning of the Incarnation is found in the use of the terms nature and person. A nature is that *by which* a thing is what it is. A person is *that which* subsists and exists. A human person who exists *has* humanity. The Church teaches that Christ existed as a person subsisting in two natures, human and divine. The person of Christ is the Second Person of the Trinity. This Person, the Word, assumed a human nature. Divine nature and human nature were welded together in the Person of the Word: thus they were united in a union called the **Hypostatic** (*personal*) **Union.** Jesus Christ is one Person who, identical with the divine nature, is God, and, possessing a human nature, is man. Christ is the God-man.

When we speak of the Hypostatic Union we are speaking of a mystery, and yet our concepts of nature and person throw a great deal of light upon how this union must have taken place in the Person. For everything which is intrinsic to a person is united to him. Nature is something intrinsic. Therefore, if human nature is not united to the Word in the supposit or person, it simply is not joined to him at all.

The unique union of the Incarnate Word is a substantial one. His human nature and divine nature have the same divine subsistence and together make up one same personal being. However, in this union, which as a relation is a created entity, no change takes place in God. Rather, God is always independent of human nature, because, after all, he created human nature and he created its union with divinity.

Without doubt the incarnate union is the most sublime of God's gifts. In what greater way could God show his love for mankind than by elevating human nature to the Godhead? This is the **grace of union,** the elevation of our nature to the heights of God. It is something which man could never merit by his own feeble efforts, but once the Hypostatic Union took place it became *the* principle of all **supernatural merit.**

God assumed human nature without destroying his further capacity for action. *In the Incarnation the three Persons of the Trinity united a human nature to the Second Person of the divine nature.* The Second Person of the Trinity assumed human nature because human nature alone had the requisite qualities of dignity and the need for redemption. Christ was God, but when he took human nature to himself, he gained both a true human body and a true human soul. Jesus Christ subsisted in the Word as true God and true man.

Adhering to the teaching of theology on the nature of the union of the Incarnate Word, certain practical conclusions can be drawn.

1. We would be astounded at the number of people who call themselves Christians but who, in reality, do not follow the God-man. To them Christ is merely a teacher of morality, a philosopher who led a good life and had a large following. They repeat his words and follow his example in the same way as the Chinese live according to the dictates of Confucius. Their self-complacency is bottled up in moral righteousness, a residue left over from the heretical ideas of early pseudo-Christian thinkers.

2. Modern educators should take a cue from the doctrine of the Hypostatic Union. No mind can assume knowledge unless it is intrinsic to the knower, united to the person, directing him to the heights of contemplation. Aristotle said that all men desire to know reasons for things. Today, teachers no longer try to give reasons for things but merely show the unwary pupil how to act in this or that situation. The solution lies in teaching pupils to be God-minded, not man-minded.

3. Within the last fifty years fiction writers, lost in the maze of a so-called realism, have forgotten the dignity of man, which follows from the doctrine of the Hypostatic Union. Today literature possesses no tragic heroes, no great kings or princes, no heroic leaders of state, no men who carry the fortunes of nations hinged to their fates. The modern hero is more like an animal, an amoral bumpkin who has no idea that God is the measure of all things. Shakespeare allowed his tragic heroes to be the masters of their own fates, but he never allowed them to think of themselves as the measure of universal action. Even Hamlet, the Prince of Denmark, could exclaim: "Angels and ministers of grace defend us!"

4. "As our word becomes in a way the voice of the body, assuming that by which it is made manifest to men's ears, so the Word of God becomes flesh, taking on that form in which it likewise is made visible to men's eyes. And as our word becomes a voice, yet it is not

changed into a voice, so the Word of God is indeed made flesh. But let no one say that it is changed into flesh: by assuming that form, not by being changed into it, does our word become a voice, and the Word of God become flesh."[26]

BIBLIOGRAPHICAL NOTE

The material covered in this chapter will be found in the second volume of the English *Summa,* Part III, Questions II-V inclusive. A highly technical study of the nature of the Hypostatic Union, and perhaps a little difficult for immediate consumption, is the essay "Created Personality: Unity of Thomistic Tradition," by T. U. Mullaney, O.P., in the *New Scholasticism,* XXIX (1955), 369-402.

Several chapters in Book II of *The Collected Works of Abbot Vonier,* Volume I, will be of use to the student. Particularly valuable are the chapters entitled: "The Metaphysics of the Incarnation"; "The Replacement of Human Personality by Divine Personality in Christ"; and "How Completely Our Lord's Human Nature Is Divine." No one of these chapters is more than three pages long and all three have the further advantage of being written in a less technical manner.

Although we have already mentioned the usefulness of *The Teaching of the Catholic Church,* Volume I, as a complement to the study of these chapters on the Incarnation, note here the special worth of Chapter II, entitled "An Outline of Catholic Teaching," again by the Rev. George D. Smith. Note also Section IV of Chapter XI, "Jesus Christ, God and Man," by the same author.

---

[26]St. Augustine, *On the Trinity,* Bk. 15, Chap. 11.

CHAPTER FOUR

Perfections and Imperfections of Christ's Human Nature

1. Introduction

In the two preceding chapters we have studied at some length and
in some depth the mystery of the Incarnation. But our investigation
is by no means complete. The essence or nature of this marvelous
union of divine and human natures in the person of the Word has
been considered; we have seen something of its divinely designed
appropriateness. But the Second Person does not assume an abstract
human nature. On the contrary, as we have seen, he takes to himself
a particular human nature, one so individualized that nothing like it
before or since has ever been seen. On the one hand, as befitting the
nature of the Son of God, it will possess a perfection conferred by
God's gifts which far exceeds that of any other man: the model, the
prototype, the apex of humanity supernaturally elevated by God's love.
On the other, this grace-filled nature will be perfectly adapted by
God to secure man's redemption through Christ's life and death: it
will possess certain defects (the ability to suffer, for example) incompatible with divinity, but only too natural for man—"one tried as
we are in all things except sin" (Heb. 4:15).

138

In substance, Christ's human nature is the same as any man's; by it he is a rational animal. But the work of this chapter is to study the special modifications this particular nature receives, the perfections and imperfections he co-assumes. Sacred Scripture and Tradition are the sources of this investigation. But our theological interpretation of the revealed facts will be guided by the all-important principles which are the fruit of our previous study. These are:

1. **The Incarnation is divinely designed to secure this end, man's redemption.** God has eternally decreed that this infinitely generous communication of himself, so befitting his own nature (Chapter Two, Section 2) and man's need (Chapter Two, Section 3), should take place precisely in order that fallen man might be restored to supernatural union with him and thus attain the happiness which is his own (Chapter Two, Section 4). This is the divine economy of salvation, and the perfections (as well as the imperfections) which the Word assumes together with his nature must be measured by this end.

2. **The union of divine and human nature in Christ is not an essential one—not in the nature.** Neither divine nor human nature undergoes the slightest change in essence in this union. Each retains its properties, its characteristics, its specific and determinate activity (Chapter Three, Section 3). No later modifying elements can be assumed by the Word which could essentially change either his human nature or his divine nature.

3. **The incarnate union is hypostatic: it is realized in, and according to, the subsistence of the Second Person of the Blessed Trinity.** This important conclusion (Chapter Three, Section 3) means that *this* human nature is, in the most intimate manner, the most personal possession of a divine person. It is God who is man, the Word of God who walks our earth and dwells among us, the Only-begotten who is lifted up on a cross between heaven and earth. His human nature will immeasurably "benefit" from this closest of all possible unions with God.

To elucidate the particular conclusions which flow from these principles as they are applied by theology to the facts of revelation, we shall follow the outline set down on the page which follows.

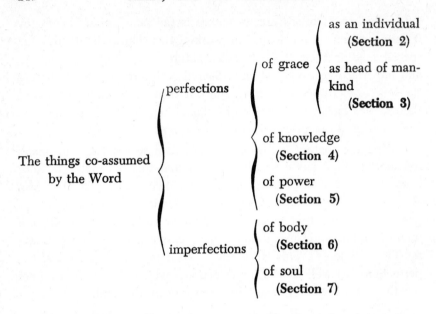

2. Christ's Grace as an Individual

By the omniscient providence of God, the whole universe, the world and all things in it, is divinely directed to the world of grace, and this in turn to the Hypostatic Union: "For all things are yours, and you are Christ's, and Christ is God's" (I Cor. 3:22-23). The Word as God is the firstborn before every creature; the Word as man is the first born among many brethren.

These are facts necessarily consequent on the Incarnation, resulting not only from God's will but from the very nature of things. The transcendent dignity and excellence of Christ as man, his singular role as link between God and man—these are effects of the gifts with which God endows his human nature, not of that nature itself. For Christ's humanity, perfect of its kind, is yet a little lower than the angels. Through grace, however, which the Word assumes together with his human nature, Christ is placed at the pinnacle of the created universe: he is the apex of the isosceles triangle of creation which through grace impinges on the Trinity:

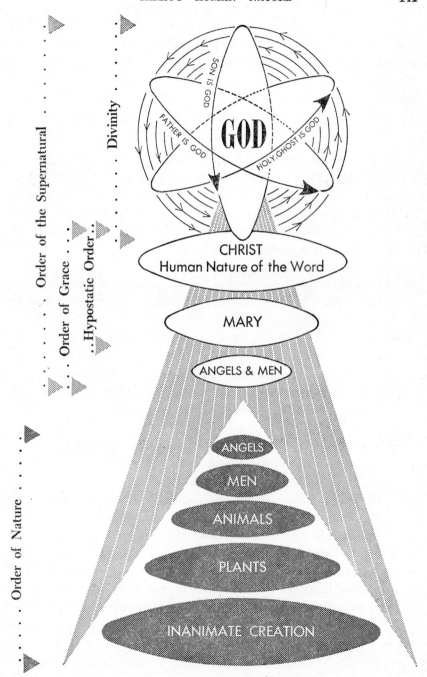

Christ's grace will be studied under two aspects: 1) as an *individual* perfection, insofar as it confers special dignity and excellence upon him; 2) as a *social* perfection, insofar as it constitutes him our head, through whom God's gifts come to us. It is the first aspect which interests us in this section.

A. The Work of Grace

All the various supernatural gifts which are denominated by the common term "grace," sanctify, elevate, divinize God's creatures, either in their essence, or in their faculties, or in their acts. In one way or another, in greater or lesser degree, these graces bring that which is finite and created to the perfection proper to God alone, to union with God as he is in himself.

This is **sanctity**: to be so united with God as to be separated from all that is not God or is opposed to him, and united firmly, stably, immutably.[1] Such holiness, which is essentially supernatural, may be realized in two ways:

1) **In the order of being.** God accepts a creature as his own, exclusively his. This act of divine benevolence is *effective* before it is *affective*. It first produces a definite reality in the creature which unites it to God and thereby sanctifies it, divinizes it. This in turn is the mark and the reason of God's affective love for it.

   This special singling out of divine predilection and wisdom is also known as *consecration*, for by the exclusive appropriation of this thing to God it becomes intrinsically ordained to his service and worship. Thus a chalice receives this special holiness in being—not from anything of its own, not alone from man's intention of reserving this thing to God's use, but precisely because God accepts this donation; and this acceptance makes the object his own by producing in it a new physical quality. Through certain religious ceremonies, man can concur in this act of consecration—but only as the instrument of God's love. True

---

[1] Cf. St. Thomas, *Summa*, II-II, q. 81, a. 8. Pseudo-Denis defines it: "A purity free from any fault, in every way perfect and entirely immaculate" (*On the Names of God*, Chap. 2).

holiness in being is always exclusively God's own work; it consists in an intrinsic, real, physical, supernatural quality in the creature so consecrated of which God alone can be the principal author.

2) **In the order of action.** Sanctity in operation is the privilege of God's intellectual creatures alone, for only men and angels can know and love God as their final end and direct their action to him. This dynamic holiness is a voluntary oblation of virtuous activity by which the creature becomes one with God and separate from all that is not God. Hence it is essentially supernatural. It likewise implies a certain firmness and stability and also involves a new, superadded, intrinsic and divine modification of the creature, of his powers and of his actions.

B. The Substantial Sanctification of Christ

By the **grace of union** the subsistence of the Word is given to his human nature, and in it human nature is united to divine nature. This fact leads to the following conclusions:

1. **By the grace of union Christ is** *substantially* **sanctified.** Christ is "the Holy One of God" *par excellence,* in a manner infinitely exceeding, not only in degree but also in kind, the sanctity of all other creatures. For in the measure that one is firmly and stably united to divinity, so to that degree is one sanctified. And Christ's humanity, by the grace of union, is perfectly and substantially united to his divinity. "In Christ," St. Thomas points out, "in whom humanity is joined to the divinity in the unity of subsistence, full and perfect union with God is found. For such was this union that all the actions both of his divine and of his human natures are acts of the divine person. He is full of grace, therefore, not in the sense that he received from God some special gratuitous gift, but in the sense that he is God himself."[2]

Here St. Thomas re-affirms the constant tradition which teaches that the grace of union brings a unique and pre-eminent holiness to Christ's humanity. Because of this substantial union with the Word and his Godhead, his human nature is anointed (i.e., sanctified) by the

[2]*Lectures on the Gospel according to St. John,* Chap. I, Lect. 8.

Godhead, not by an accidental consecration like other creatures, but by the substantial consecration of divinity itself. "He is called the Anointed (Christ)," says St. Gregory Nazianzus, "because of his divinity. For the divinity is the unction of his humanity, not by its action (as is true for other anointed persons) but by its sanctifying presence."[3] It is in this fuller sense of holiness that the Fathers commonly understand the scriptural texts which refer to Christ's sanctity.[4] And the Council of Frankfort, in 794, confirmed this traditional doctrine: "Christ is anointed by nature, we by grace; for in him in its fulness was the divinity."[5]

2. **The Hypostatic Union makes Christ absolutely incapable of sinning.** Christ's substantial sanctification is a consecration of his humanity—holiness in the order of being, not in the order of action. But the acts of this human nature belong to the Word. Hence perfect moral sanctity, complete immunity from sin, is a necessary consequence of the grace of union. The human actions of Christ proceed from his human faculties, and these powers are natural, totally lacking in the perfection conferred by supernatural grace; but they are nonetheless actions for which the Second Person is morally responsible, and moral imperfection is absolutely incompatible with divinity. God must, if he is God, ensure the absolute impeccability of his human nature.

This immunity from even the possibility of sin and from any tendency to sin in no way destroys or lessens Christ's freedom. Rather is it a *guarantee* that Christ will live his consecrated life in God's service in the most perfect manner possible, without defect or fall or possibility of failure. Through efficacious actual graces and divine enlightenment, he will infallibly perform acts of virtue. Thus even apart from the accidental sanctity conferred by habitual grace, Christ is, in

---

[3]*Fourth Theological Discourse*, n. 21.

[4]Ps. 45:8, Heb. 1:9, Isa. 61:1, Dan. 9:24. Cf. St. Irenaeus, *Against Heresies*, Bk. III, Chap. 18; St. Cyril of Alexandria, *Commentary on John*, Bk. XI, Chap. 10; St. John Damascene, *On the Orthodox Faith*, Bk. III, Chap. 3; St. Augustine, *Concerning the Trinity*, Bk. XV, Chap. 26; St. Gregory the Great, *Epistle* 67. For the examination of the texts of Sacred Scripture see P. F. Ceuppens, O.P., *op.cit.*, III, pp. 72-73.

[5]*Letter to the Bishops of Spain*; J. D. Mansi, *Sacrorum Conciliorum Nova et Amplissima Collectio* (Florence, Paris, Leipzig: 1759 ff.), XIII, 900.

virtue of the Hypostatic Union, holiness itself—in the order of operation as in the order of being. This is the inevitable corollary of our Third Principle concerning the Incarnation.

C. The Accidental Sanctification of Christ

(1) The Habitual Grace of Christ

1. **The necessity of habitual or sanctifying grace.** God's gift to Christ's human nature surpasses any other of the graces he bestows on those he loves, Yet, as the Second Principle concerning the Incarnation convinces us, this grace of union in no way intrinsically alters his human nature: inherently natural, even after its substantial union with the Godhead, his humanity had nothing by essence of the supernatural; whatever of the supernatural comes to it comes by way of gift, over and above the grace of union. The human nature of Christ, to be sure, depends on the subsistence and the existence of the Word. But subsistence is not the source of action; rather, it is the essence or nature which is the source. And the Word's subsistence does not mix the natures, but unites them in a unity of being, while preserving each intact in essence and in the properties which flow from it.

Hence the human powers of Christ—his intellect and will, the intrior and exterior senses, the sense appetites, etc.—remain human. They preserve their *natural* mode of action and remain ordained to their *natural* and proper objects. The acts produced in virtue of these powers will be essentially human acts; Christ's human activity will be restricted to the order of nature, intrinsically incapable of attaining the order proper to divinity.

2. **The presence of habitual grace in Christ.** If Christ's human nature is to be elevated in its essence and properties and actions to the supernatural order, sanctifying grace is necessary—as necessary for his humanity as for any of the creatures God's love chooses to sanctify and divinize by giving them a share in his own Godhead. Thus habitual and sanctifying grace is a necessary and immediate consequence of the grace of union, as the Church's theologians all but unanimously teach. St. Thomas assigns three reasons for this certain conclusion:

1. Because of the union of his soul with the word of God. For in the degree that a being, submissive to the action of a cause, is closer to that cause, the more does it partake of its influence. But the source of grace is God, according to the words of Psalm 83: "The Lord will give grace and glory." It is pre-eminently fitting, therefore, that his soul should receive the influx of divine grace.

2. Because of the dignity of Christ's soul. Its nobility demands that the soul should attain God as intimately as possible by acts of knowledge and love. This is only possible through the elevation of human nature by means of grace.

3. Because of the relation of Christ to the human race. For Christ, precisely as man, is the "mediator between God and man" (I Tim. 1:5). And consequently it was necessary that he should possess grace capable of overflowing upon others. As St. John states (Jn. 1:16): "Of his fulness we have all received, grace for grace."[6]

This is the classical interpretation of the testimony of Scripture and Tradition concerning Christ and his grace. He is "full of grace and of truth" (Jn. 1:14); on him rests the spirit of the Lord, communicating to him in fulness the gifts of the Holy Spirit which flow from grace (Isa. 11:1-3). He is "full of the Holy Spirit" (Lk. 4:1).[7] "The Lord Jesus has not only given the Holy Spirit as God," St. Augustine concludes, "as man he has received him. Therefore is he called full of grace. . . . For God has anointed him with the Holy Spirit—not, to be sure, by a visible unction but by the gift of grace, which is signified by the visible unction with which the Church anoints the baptized."[8]

3. **Christ's sanctifying grace and the Hypostatic Union.** It is clear from what has been said that the accidental sanctification of Christ's human nature which is brought about by habitual grace is an inevitable result of the grace of union. There is, however, no *physical* link between them: habitual grace does not emanate from the grace of union as, for example, the property of rationality flows physically from man's soul. Hence the reasons given by St. Thomas in the passage cited above do not conclude to any necessity for the presence of sanctifying grace in Christ's soul. It is within God's power (abstracting from

---

[6]*Summa*, III, q. 7, a, 1.

[7]For the exegesis of these texts, cf. P. F. Ceuppens, O.P., *op. cit.*, III, pp. 74-77.

[8]*On the Trinity*, Bk. XV, Chap. 26. Cf. also St. Athanasius, *First Sermon against the Arians*, n. 46; St. Ambrose, *On the Holy Spirit*, Bk. II, Chap. 6-8; St. Bernard, *Fourth Homily on Lk. 1:26*.

his wisdom and love) to unite a human nature to the Word which would not be elevated to the supernatural order by grace.

But if habitual grace is not a physical property of the Hypostatic Union, it is a *morally* necessary consequence. As Son of God, Christ has a strict right to the grace which will perfect, elevate, sanctify and supernaturalize his human nature. Otherwise God would love Christ much less than he does his other creatures; otherwise God would fail to give him the gifts necessary for the accomplishment of his predestined work as Savior. Habitual grace, in short, considering divine wisdom and love, is the natural and inevitable sequel of the grace of union.

4. **The infinity of Christ's habitual grace.** God gives to his beloved Son a fulness of created grace proportionate to the uncreated grace of union. As the first of all creatures, as the apex of the world of nature and supernature, Christ has an infinity of grace, which can never be surpassed nor equalled by anyone else. This is a relative infinity, of course, since it is that of a created thing, a circumscribed and limited being. But it is an infinity which attains, both in *intensive* perfection and in *extensive* perfection, the outermost limits of accidental sanctification.

1) *Intensive perfection.* Grace is possessed by Christ in the maximum perfection which, according to the wisdom of God, it can ever have. No greater union with God, no more excellent consecration by God, no higher knowledge and love of God than that which is Christ's in virtue of his sanctifying grace can be conceived. This created gift, it is evident, does not exhaust God's omnipotence, nor its participation his infinite perfection; a higher degree of grace than that given to Christ is, in the abstract, possible. Concretely, however, the intensity of his grace is of the degree proper to the Son of God, and to him alone. In consequence divine wisdom ordains that no more perfect or complete or excelling plentitude can or will be produced.

Thus while others of those God loves receive a fulness of grace commensurate with their roles and offices in the divine economy (so that Mary, from the moment of her conception, is given a greater grace than that of all other men and angels, because of her divine maternity), Christ's fulness, proper to him alone, is limited only by the relative perfection which grace itself can produce.

2) *Extensive perfection.* Infinite in intensity, Christ's habitual grace is also infinite in extent. This means that every form of divine activity of which grace can be the source is to be found in the God-man, and found most perfectly. The virtues and gifts and charismata which accompany grace supernaturally perfect his human nature to a degree that invites closer inspection.

(2) *The Virtues of Christ*

Habitual or sanctifying grace is frequently called by St. Thomas "the grace of the virtues and the gifts." For grace itself supernaturalizes the essence of the soul by making it share in God's own nature. And just as the natural properties which are our faculties and powers flow from the soul's essence, so from this second, divine nature which is grace flow supernatural properties, divine faculties and powers—the virtues and gifts. These permanent dispositions so elevate and divinize our human faculties as to enable us to act in a strictly supernatural way, in a manner similar to the inner vital activity of God. The degree of perfection of these virtues and gifts will be in direct proportion to the degree of excellence of their source, habitual grace.

Christ possessed a singular fulness of grace, the utmost perfection God in his wisdom can confer on a creature. Hence:

1. **From the instant of his conception Christ had in the highest degree all those supernatural virtues which imply no imperfection.** Charity, justice, prudence, meekness, humility, fortitude, religion, obedience—all these, and many more, are eloquently attested to by the pages of Sacred Scripture which recount the life history of the God-man. Nothing was or could be lacking in the supernatural perfection which is pre-eminently his, and which equips him so perfectly for his role as Savior of mankind.

2. **Christ did not possess the supernatural virtues of faith, hope or penance.** All of these virtues imply an imperfection which is incompatible with Christ's supernatural excellence. The proper object of *faith* is divine truth obscurely known, unseen; but Christ en-

joyed the vision of God from the first moment of his earthly existence. *Hope* is primarily concerned with God as not yet possessed, and Christ had the beatitude of full enjoyment of God. (He could, however, hope for the immortality and bodily glory not yet his; the source of this desire and expectation was, however, the virtue of charity, his love for God, whom he already perfectly possessed and fully enjoyed.)

Since the slightest shadow of sin could not touch him, *penance,* which is sorrow for one's own sin, could have no place in Christ, although his love made him mourn for others' faults and urged him to make satisfaction for them. Not even the tendency to evil existed in a nature so divinely perfected as that of the God-man, and consequently those virtues which work to correct the moral unbalance caused by original and personal sin could not be present.

(3) The Gifts of the Holy Ghost

"And there shall come forth a rod out of the root of Jesse, and a flower shall rise out of his root. And the spirit of the Lord shall rest upon him: the spirit of wisdom, and of understanding, the spirit of counsel, and of fortitude, the spirit of knowledge, and of godliness. And he shall be filled with the spirit of the fear of the Lord" (Isa. 11:1-3).

Thus does God himself testify through his prophet to the presence of the gifts of the Holy Spirit in the soul of his Son. These permanent dispositions, perfections of a higher and superior order even than that of the supernatural virtues, make the soul receptive of the impulses of the Holy Ghost which sweetly but strongly urge us to actions ever more Godlike. Through them man can act in a manner truly divine, above the earth-bound judgments of reason and the rules of human prudence.

This more truly divine life was present in its perfection in Christ. As a great commentator on St. Thomas explains:

> By the gift of *wisdom* he judged of eternal things through the highest causes and by divine reasons. *Understanding* read the inner meaning of things, penetrating all the truths God proposed to him. Of actions to be taken he judged securely and without doubt by *counsel,* having instantly that decisiveness which the counselings of prudence customarily produce. By *fortitude* he strengthened his body against all ad-

versity, and girded himself for the hard labor of our redemption.
Knowledge enabled him to judge of things through secondary causes,
so as to accommodate them to our grasp. His zealous worship of God
the Father was the result of *godliness,* as was his filial affection for
his Virgin Mother. Finally, by a *fear* not servile but chaste and filial,
he most deeply reverenced the immense eminence of the divine
majesty and its supreme power.[9]

(4) The Charismata of Christ

God gives to certain men very special divine gifts, transitory in nature, which are designed primarily to bring other men to salvation.
These charismata (called by theologians "gratuitous graces"—*gratiae
datae*—as opposed to sanctifying grace) are apostolic in character.
They do not necessarily flow from grace, for their first object is the
common or social good, and not the good of the individual. Ordinarily,
these extraordinary graces are given to the saints, since they are
God's special instruments for the salvation of the world and they
exercise a profound supernatural influence upon it.

These special gifts Christ must also have possessed in unique fulness. His singular role demanded that he have at his free disposal such
extraordinary supernatural powers as prophecy, cure of the sick, the gift
of tongues, etc., to use when occasion arises. As head of the Church he
possessed all the graces which are severally distributed to his members. And he was the first and principal preacher and teacher of the
truths of faith and of spiritual doctrine. Therefore these charismata
must have been his. It is their work to manifest the truths of God, to
propose them to others in a fitting manner, so that they may believe,
and to confirm the credibility of these truths in a supernatural fashion.
They are necessary equipment for him who is the Way, the Truth and
the Life.

(5) Actual Graces

To bring an inert, motionless object into activity some propulsion
is needed from outside. This is no less true in the supernatural order
than in the natural order; and so beyond sanctifying grace and its
properties the creature needs God's actual graces to produce super-

---

[9]Contenson, *Theologia Mentis et Cordis,* X, Diss. 5, Chap. 1.

natural acts, to pass from the state of being able to act supernaturally to actual performance. The same holds good for Christ. Despite his union with the Word, despite the supernatural fulness of grace and virtues and gifts which is his, he retains in his human nature the essential condition of the creature, its imperfection, its inability to actualize its potentialities without divine assisance.

To convert the potentiality of grace into actuality, actual grace is required. This is a transitory impulse from God which initiates supernatural action on the part of his creatures and guarantees its completion. No one can doubt that supernatural assistance of this kind was superabundantly Christ's. Not now and again, but always and efficaciously is his soul moved by God to supernatural operation, to human acts of their very nature good, perfect, meritorious, satisfying for sin, and divine in character. For by the Hypostatic Union his human nature is infallibly and indefectibly united with God, the First Cause of grace as well as of nature.

3. The Grace of Headship

Holiness begins from Christ; by Christ it is effected. For no act conducive to salvation can be performed unless it proceeds from him as its supernatural cause. "Without me," he says, "you can do nothing" (Jn. 15:5). If we grieve and do penance for our sins, if with filial fear and hope we turn again to God, it is because he is leading us. Grace and glory flow from his unfathomed fulness. Our Savior is continually pouring out his gifts of counsel, fortitude, fear and piety, especially on the leading members of his Body, so that the whole Body may grow daily more and more in spotless holiness. When the sacraments of the Church are administered by external rite, it is he who produces their effect in souls. He nourishes the redeemed with his own flesh and blood, and thus calms the soul's turbulent passions; he gives increase of grace and is preparing future glory for souls and bodies. All these treasures of his divine goodness he is said to disburse to the members of his Mystical Body, not merely because he, who is the eucharistic Victim on earth and the glorified Victim in heaven, lets his wounds and prayers plead our cause before the eternal Father, but because he selects, he determines, he distributes every single grace to every single person "according to the measure of the giving of Christ" (Eph. 4:7). Hence it follows that from our Lord as from a fountainhead "the whole body (being closely joined and knit together through every joint of the system according to the functioning in due measure of each single part) derives its increase to the building up of itself in love" (Eph. 4:16).[10]

In these words the late Holy Father delineates the workings of what is called Christ's capital grace (from the Latin *caput*, which means head) or *grace of headship*. This is a metaphorical term whose meaning we must explore to appreciate the significant reality it describes.

A. The Metaphor of Head and Body

In everyday conversation we use the word "head" in numerous contexts. There is a head in reference to a physical body; the head of a government; the boy who is at the head of his class; the head of a river; the head of a school; the colloquial expression: the head man. All of these are clues to the various reasons for identifying Christ as head of all men.

By divine inspiration, this familiar figure of speech, based fundamentally on the analogy of the human body, is used by St. Paul to describe the relations which obtain between Christ and the created universe. The major points of comparison are the following:

1) The Church is an organism in which dissimilar parts are united under one head. Rom. 12:4-5.

2) All the members of this organism are interconnected, and they grow, increase and act in virtue of their common union with the same head. Eph. 14:15-16; I Cor. 12:12-26.

3) Hence the Church is the body[11] of which Christ is the head. Eph. 1:22-23; Col. 1:18.

St. Thomas explains this divinely inspired analogy in this way:

> As the whole Church is called one mystical body from its likeness to the natural body of man, which has different acts according to its different members, as the Apostle teaches, so Christ is called the head of the Church from a likeness with the human head. In this head we may consider three things: order, perfection and power:

[10]Pius XII, Encyclical *Mystici Corporis* (N.C.W.C. translation).

[11]Later ages have added the word "mystical" to distinguish Christ's body which is the Church from his physical body and from his sacramental body, the Eucharist.

Order, because the head is the first part of man, beginning with the higher. And thus every principle is customarily called the head.

Perfection, because it is in the head that all the senses, interior and exterior, are found, whereas in the other members there is only the sense of touch.

Power, because it is the head which, by its sensitive and motive power, gives strength and movement to the members and governs them in their actions. It is in this sense that the ruler of the people is called their head.

These three functions of the head belong in a spiritual manner to Christ. *First,* by reason of his closeness to God, his grace is more exalted and prior to all other graces (even though not in time). For all have received grace on account of his grace, as St. Paul points out: "Those whom he has foreknown he has also predestined to become conformed to the image of his Son, that he should be the first born among many brethren" (Rom. 8:29). *Second,* he possesses the perfection of grace, the fulness of all graces, according to St. John (Jn. 1:14): "We saw his glory . . . full of grace and of truth." *Third,* he possessed the power of communicating grace to all the members of the Church, according to John 1:16: "Of his fulness we have all received, grace for grace."

So it is clear that Christ is fittingly called the "head" of the Church.[12]

B. The Qualities of Christ's Capital Grace

(1) Its Extension

The humanity of Christ is the organ of his divinity, i.e., the instrument by which God communicates grace to Christ's members. Not only his soul but his human body was used by him to satisfy for our sins and to merit our salvation by his passion and death. By his grace our souls live with divine life, and through the soul even man's body and its activity become supernaturalized, divinized. In this life, therefore, as St. Paul admonishes, you should "present . . . your members as weapons of justice to God" (Rom. 6:13); in the next life the soul's glory will overflow upon the body: "he who raised Jesus Christ from the dead will also bring to life your mortal bodies because of his Spirit who dwells in you" (Rom. 8:11).

By his whole humanity, then, body and soul, Christ is head of the whole man, body and soul. Moreover, his headship extends to each and every member of the human race—in varying degrees of perfection,

---

[12]*Summa,* III, q. 8, a. 1.

of course, since all men do not equally share in his grace, and hence
are not equally united to their head. Nonetheless he is the Savior
of all mankind, the propitiation for the sins of the entire world. Only
those in hell—the damned and the fallen angels—are completely
blocked off from the fire of his love, the light of his grace. From the
blackest sinner to the highest angel, all others share, at least potential-
ly, in the divine life of grace which comes through Christ.[13]

(2) Its Nature

What constitutes Christ the head of men and of angels? His grace
of headship is the very same grace by which his human nature is intrinsically modified, elevated and sanctified: his habitual grace. This
he possesses in fulness, in perfection, in the highest degree possible
to a creature. By it he merited our salvation; by it he satisfied for our
sins, winning for us a real and physical participation in the nature of
God, our divine sonship. His humanity, so sanctified, is the physical
instrument God uses to produce grace in the souls of men. Thus of
the fulness of grace which is proper to Christ we all receive, grace
for grace. Our justification and sanctification is by the grace of
Christ, which, in making us children of God, conforms us to the image
of God's only-begotten Son. Through him we become members of the
body of which he is the head; together with him, we become, body
and head, "the whole Christ."

Christ alone is our head in the full significance of the term, for only
he exercises an interior influence on his members, only his grace penetrates to the depth of our souls and so permeates the whole being of
man as to supernaturalize his essence, his powers and his acts. But
in the external governing of this body, which is a subsidiary function
of the head, he chooses to associate other members with himself and
through them rule his Mystical Body. Thus by divine authority the
ecclesiastical hierarchy governs the Church; through pope and bishops
passes Christ's own ruling of his members. In this secondary sense,
the bishop in his diocese, and the pope over the whole Church, may be
called "heads" of the Church. Yet their authority is limited to this life,

---

[13]For a fuller development of these points, cf. *infra*, Chapter Sixteen, "The
Mystical Body of Christ."

and even to certain places (like the bishops) or to certain times (like the pope during his lifetime). Moreover, they govern only *for* Christ, not in their own name nor by their own power: "On behalf of Christ, therefore, we are acting as ambassadors, God, as it were, appealing through us" (II Cor. 5:20).

4. The Knowledge of Christ

Christ is God; and his knowledge is the knowledge of God: infinite, omniscient, infallible. But Christ is also man. Is his knowledge the knowledge of man—limited, ignorant, capable of error? Of what use is any human knowledge to him at all, if he already knows all things? Does he have any human knowledge?

A. Christ's Knowledge as Man

Certain heretics assert that Christ was, as regards his human intellect, an ignoramus. The statement is absurd on three counts:

1) Christ assumes a genuine human nature, deficient in none of the perfections proper to such a nature. Thus he assumes a human soul which is perfect of its kind. But a human soul which owns none of the knowledge for which it was made is imperfect— the most stupid child possessing the use of reason is more perfectly human. Hence besides his divine knowledge Christ must also have a human knowledge proportioned to, and perfective of his human soul.

2) The human soul is made to know things: that is its proper work. Without created knowledge Christ's human soul would be frustrated in its most essential function. Why assume a human soul at all if it is only a useless appendage, so much excess baggage?

3) Knowledge of first principles pertains to the very nature of man's soul, it is as natural to man as breathing. But Christ receives human nature in its entirety, not just this or that selected element. So at least this much human knowledge must be his— and if this much, why deny him more?

B. The Kinds of Christ's Human Knowledge

The reason for the Church's continuing insistence,[14] against heretics of one type or another, that Christ possessed true human activity is simply this: otherwise he would be only imperfectly human, and, in fact, not really human at all. This is tantamount to a denial of the Incarnation, the fundamental and central fact of Christianity.

But just what were these human operations, so far as his knowing things is concerned? St. Thomas and the other Schoolmen, following the lead of St. Gregory and the holy Fathers, point out three general classifications of the human knowledge of Jesus: his beatific knowledge; his infused knowledge; and his acquired knowledge.

(1) Christ's Beatific Knowledge

1. **Christ possessed the beatific vision.** Christ's humanity is the cause of our beatitude, which consists in seeing God, through the light of glory, as he is. But the cause is always more excellent, more powerful than its effect. In short, the role of the God-man as our head, as king even of the angels, demands that he be given this ultimate perfecting gift, the light of glory, by which he possesses the beatifying vision of God. His is not only the uncreated happiness of being God, but the created beatitude of seeing God. Full of truth as well as of grace, he it is who tells us what he has seen in his vision of the Father.[15]

2. **The extent of Christ's beatific knowledge.** As man Christ sees the very essence of God, but this is not a "comprehensive" knowledge, i.e., he cannot know, or exhaust, all that can be known about God—this requires infinite intelligence. Neither, then, can he know all that God can do, for action follows upon being and he does not know all of God's being. Nevertheless, in seeing God's essence he knows all there is to be know about creatures, since he sees them in God who knows no limitations of time (past, present and future are all as one in the eternal *now* of God), or of place. As judge of heaven

[14]Cf. Lateran Council (649), Denz. 258, 262 ff.; Council of Rome (680), Denz. 288; Third Council of Constantinople (the sixth ecumenical Council), Denz. 290; Council of Florence (1442), Denz. 708.
[15]Cf. Jn. 1:14, 1:17-18, 3:31-32, 8:38.

and of earth, king and lord of all things, head of men and angels, his is a legitimate desire to know what concerns him, and all things do concern him; in the beatific vision this desire is fully satisfied.

By his beatific knowledge Christ not only knows many more things than anyone else; his is a deeper, more penetrating, and hence more perfect knowledge of God and of all things in God. For the beatific vision depends not on one's native intellectual power (any angel's is higher than that of any man's, including Christ's), but on the excellence of the supernatural gift of the light of glory. To his only-begotten Son the Father gives an immeasurably more perfect gift, one which is divinely proportioned to the fulness of grace which he enjoyed.

(2) Christ's Infused Knowledge

1. **The existence of infused knowledge in Christ.** To know as the angels know is far superior to the laborious acquisition of ideas characteristic of strictly human knowledge. In one glance they see all they will ever see about a certain subject. For at the moment of their creation they receive directly from God, together with their nature, all their ideas. In these infused ideas they perceive intuitively all the realities of the created world.[16]

As man Christ could not possibly possess such superior knowledge in virtue of his natural powers. But it could be given to him, directly infused into his soul by God. Did he receive such a gift? St. Thomas thought so, although there is no direct evidence from Sacred Scripture of this gift. But the opinion of the Angelic Doctor seems eminently reasonable. If Christ is above all creatures, the angels themselves being subject to him, should he be their inferior in so important an activity as that of knowing things? Should he not have immediate contact with the angelic intelligences, he who rules, governs and judges the whole universe? To deny him this perfection, and yet extoll his supereminent position and role over all creatures, seems theologically inconsistent.

2. **By his infused knowledge, Christ knows all things except the essence of God.** The extent of this angelic knowledge which God's

[16]Cf. *Summa*, I, qq. 54-58; Murphy, *et al.*, *God and His Creation*, 365-371.

free gift gives to Christ, his Son, is limited only by the horizons of creation. God himself he cannot directly know, of course; this is the ultimate gift, which not even the angels possess except through the light of glory. Yet Christ's "angelic" knowledge is likewise proportioned to the infinite excellence of his grace, of which it is the sequel, and to his position and role in the universe. All the wonders of grace and of nature, the secret desires and thoughts of men and angels, past events and things yet to come and present actualities (and thus his knowledge, being supernatural, exceeds the natural knowledge of the angels)—all these the son of man knows through this higher, angelic knowledge which is his in virtue of the ideas God infuses in his human intellect.

(3) Christ's Acquired Knowledge

1. **The God-man possesses acquired knowledge.** "And Jesus advanced in wisdom and age . . . before God and men" (Lk. 2:52). Man's natural mode of knowing is to acquire universal, abstract ideas from data supplied by the senses. By experience and by reasoning we advance, more or less slowly and laboriously, to an intellectual knowledge of all things. Did Christ so progress in the acquisition of ideas? Sacred Scripture certainly seems to say so, and the perfection of his human nature leads to the same conclusion. Otherwise the uniquely human power of abstracting such ideas (the agent intellect) would have been forever idle in him, frustrated in the very operation for which it was made. If Christ could not use his intelligence in this human manner, he could hardly be considered fully and perfectly man.

2. **The extent of Christ's acquired knowledge.** In a word, Christ, through the knowledge he humanly acquires, knows all that can naturally be known by man. This excludes a *direct* knowledge of the angels, and of concrete singular things (these he knew, however, through his infused knowledge), and of God (whom he knew directly through the beatific vision). Unlike his beatific and infused knowledge, however, which is perfect from the instant of his conception, Christ's acquired knowledge grows with the years; his intellectual capacity is such, nevertheless, that he acquires knowledge

quickly, easily, perfectly. Thus, for example, as St. Thomas points out, "by seeing the heavenly bodies he could understand their powers and the effects they exercise on lower bodies which cannot be apprehended by his senses."[17]

Yet if, in virtue of this knowledge, Christ was a student of the world his Father had created, he sat at the feet of no man nor angel. The whole point of his human acquisition of knowledge was to perfect his own intellect, not to acquire new truths (he could not learn anything he did not already know by his beatific or infused knowledge). By his own industry and acumen, with God through his effects as his only teacher, Christ acquires at each stage of his existence the perfection of knowledge proper to his human age, and thus at maturity has a universal knowledge.

C. The Qualities of Christ's Human Knowledge

(1) Its Infallibility

The Church has not explicitly and solemnly defined the fact that Christ was free from all possibility of error according to his human knowledge. But this is an obvious conclusion, and one affirmed by constant and universal tradition.[18] Ignorance is incompatible with God; but if Christ erred, even as man, the error would be imputable to God, since all his actions are those of a divine person. This is as unthinkable as to accuse him of moral error. To be sure, we have Christ's own word that no one, not even the Son, knows the day or hour of the Last Judgment except the Father.[19] But this can easily be understood as meaning that his knowledge of this event is not such as to permit him to reveal it to others (that is his Father's prerogative); or that his natural knowledge does not encompass a happening which only his supernatural knowledge makes known to him.[20] What-

---

[17]*Summa*, III, q. 12, a. 1, ad 2.

[18]St. Gregory the Great, *Epistle 39;* St. John Damascene, *Concerning Heresies,* Chap. 88; St. Bede, *Fourth Homily on Mark;* St. Anselm, *Cur Deus Homo?* Bk. II, Chap. 13; etc.

[19]Cf. Mk. 13:32.

[20]Cf. St. Augustine, *On the Trinity,* Bk. I, Chap. 12; St. Thomas, *Summa,* III, q. 10, a. 2, ad 1.; St. Gregory the Great, *loc. cit.*

ever the explanation, the Fathers of the Church, her theologians and her exegetes are in universal agreement. There is no ignorance, or error, or possibility of either in Christ, even as man.

(2) Its Suitability

He who is the term and end of creation synthesizes in the intellectual perfection of his humanity all the perfections of intelligence to be found in creatures. As he lived our intellectual life, so also did he live the intellectual life of the blessed in heaven and that of God, as well as that of the angels. Each of his ways of knowing is a stream of divine light illuminating his created intelligence; in harmony one with the other, they together enable him to participate, in the most perfect manner possible to a creature, in God's own knowledge of himself and of all things. In truth, Christ is the Master and Doctor of the universe. He is Truth incarnate.

5. The Power of the God-Man

Christ said: "All power in heaven and on earth has been given to me" (Matt. 28:18). And St. Luke observes that "all the crowd were trying to touch him, for power went forth from him and healed all" (Lk. 6:19). He walked on the waters, he stilled the storm, he gave sight to the blind, brought the dead back to life, raised himself after three days from the tomb. . . . Were these the actions of God or of man? Did they come from Christ's human nature, or were they the work of his divinity?

A. Christ's Power as Man

The Hypostatic Union is not a commingling of natures: divine nature and human nature remain distinct, each preserving in their union in the divine Person that which is proper to it, exclusively its own. But omnipotence is a property of the divine nature alone—an *incommunicable* property, for it is infinite power and thereby demands an infinite source of power, an infinite nature. Christ's humanity, on the contrary, is limited, circumscribed, finite. Perfect though his soul was by nature, perfected as it was by grace, he can, by his human power, do only those things (but all of those things, of course) which belong to the finite order, whether natural or supernatural.

Thus the soul of Christ informs and rules his body, and serves as the source of his human acts. His grace enables him to supernaturalize those acts, to merit grace and supernatural gifts for others, to satisfy for all the sins of all men. But there are definite limitations on his human power:

1. **There is no possibility of his creating or annihilating anything as man** (not even as God's instrument)—for to give being to a thing, or to reduce an existing thing to non-being, requires infinite power.

2. **He cannot as man be the principal cause of sanctifying grace.** Grace is a participation, real, physical and analogical, of the divine nature; only he who is by nature divine can communicate a share in that nature to others.

3. **He cannot by his own human power work miracles.** By definition a miracle is something produced beyond the entire order of nature, exceeding all created power either in itself or in its manner of production. God alone can work miracles.

B. Christ's Power as God's Instrument

(1) The Notion of Instrumental Causality

It is the very essence of an instrument to have an activity proper to its own nature and at the same time to participate in the power of a higher cause. Through this communicated higher activity the instrument produces results to which its own native effectiveness does not extend. A piece of chalk, for instance, being what it is, can make white marks on a colored surface if pushed into action: that is its proper power, its proper activity, its proper effect. In the hand of an intelligent agent, however, those marks become more than indiscriminate colored scratches, like hen tracks: they can be so formed as to compose words, intelligible signs. Subtract the principal cause, however, and the chalk, left to itself, ceases to be an instrument; it can only produce white marks, not words.

The essential characteristic of any instrument, then, is that it possesses two powers: 1) its own proper activity which belongs to its nature; 2) an elevated activity, of its nature transient, communicated by the principal cause.

(2) Christ's Humanity as Instrumental Cause

As St. John Damascene points out, Christ's humanity, indefectibly united to the Word, is "the organ of divinity"—somewhat as the members of our bodies are organs by which the soul carries out many of its functions.[21] It is, therefore, a most fitting instrument of divine omnipotence. For Christ's humanity is a living instrument, endowed with intelligence and will, filled up with grace; it is an instrument which can thus freely and fully put itself at God's service. By this living instrument, God's power of healing bodies and transforming souls is brought to the world. Christ's humanity is not an inert material instrument but a human instrument whose will is always that of his Father. Whatever he chooses to do, either by his own created power or as the organ of divinity, will always come to pass. Hence the following conclusions:

1. **As God's instrument, personally united to the Word, Christ as man worked innumerable wonderful miracles.** As we shall see in a later chapter, and as the gospels never tire of relating, Christ's human life is full of these happenings, events outside of the ordinary course of nature, which are clear and evident signs of divine power.

2. **As God's instrument, Christ's humanity is the physical cause of his grace in the souls of men.** Not only by his merits and satisfaction, but in the physical order as well, Christ produces in us here and now the physical reality of grace by which we are justified and sanctified. His sacred humanity, sanctified by grace, is the efficient and universal instrument in the hands of God of our salvation. "Of his fulness we have all received, grace for grace," for "grace and truth come through Jesus Christ" (Jn. 1:16-17).

3. **The soul of Christ as God's personal instrument had complete control over his body.** Had he so wished, Christ could have prevented any physical harm whatsoever from afflicting his body. His passion

---

[21]Cf. *On the Orthodox Faith*, Bk. III, Chap. 14.

and death, then, are most freely accepted, entirely voluntary: "No one takes my life from me, but I lay it down of myself. I have the power to lay it down, and I have the power to take it up again. Such is the command I have received from my Father" (Jn. 10:18). Such is the perfect harmony between the divine will and the human will in Christ, that he exercises his communicated divine power—his instrumental power as distinct from his properly human power—in fullest accord with the divine designs for our salvation, despite the fact that he is thus led to the terrible death of the cross.

6. The Imperfections of Christ's Human Nature

The gospels tell us of the weariness of the Son of God, of his thirst on the cross and his hunger after the desert-fasting, of the most cruel tortures he underwent which led to his death. We read of his mental agony in the garden, of his weeping, of his anger, his wonder, his fear. In a word, "we have not a high priest who cannot have compassion on our infirmities, but one tried as we are in all things except sin" (Heb. 4:15).

Marvelous as are the perfections of grace, of knowledge and of power which Christ assumed together with his human nature, it is at least as remarkable (and in many ways more difficult to understand) that the Son of God should also assume our imperfections, both of body and of soul. What is the reason for this divine abasement? for the awful humility which empties itself of Godhead to take the nature of a slave? which makes him to be sin who knew nothing of sin?[22]

A. The Fittingness of Assuming Human Defects

In the following words St. Thomas shows the appropriateness of Christ's assumption of our human imperfections:

> First, because it was in order to satisfy for the sin of mankind that the Son of God, having taken flesh, came into the world. But one satisfies for the sin of another by taking on himself the punishment

[22]Cf. Phil. 2:7; II Cor. 5:21.

due to that sin. Bodily defects of this kind—death, hunger, thirst and the like—are the punishment of sin, which was introduced into the world by Adam, as St. Paul points out: "Through one man sin entered into the world and through sin death" (Rom. 5:12). Hence, considering the end of the Incarnation, it was fitting that he who takes our place should receive these penalties in our flesh, according to the saying of Isaias (53:4): "Truly he has borne our infirmities."

Second, in order to engender belief in the Incarnation. Human nature, as we know it, is subject to these bodily defects. Hence if the Son of God had assumed a human nature free of such imperfections, it would have seemed that he was not a true man, and that he did not possess true flesh but, as the Manicheans claimed, imaginary flesh. Therefore, as the Apostle says, "he . . . emptied himself, taking the nature of a slave, and appearing in the form of man" (Phil. 2:7). Thus also was Thomas, by the sight of his wounds, called back to the faith, as St. John relates (Jn. 20:26).

Third, in order to give an example of patience, which he shows us by valiantly bearing up under human sufferings and infirmities. Therefore it is said in the Epistle to the Hebrews (12:3): "Consider him who endured such opposition from sinners against himself, so that you may not grow weary and lose heart."[23]

B. Bodily Defects Assumed by Christ

1. **Christ freely and voluntarily assumes these corporeal defects.** The Son of God takes a human body, and a human body by its nature is subject to certain imperfections. Yet such was his power as God and his participated divine power as man that he could have prevented these weaknesses—was not Adam, in fact, by the gift of integrity free of them? Because of his exceeding love for us, however, Christ does not remove the infirmities and imperfections of his human body.

Moreover, weaknesses of this kind are the effect and the penalties of man's sin. All men born into this world by human generation (Our Blessed Lady alone excepted) are under the debt of contracting these defects, for all are conceived in original sin. No such necessity may be placed upon Christ. On the contrary, he takes a human nature in the purity which it possessed in the state of innocence, without the shadow of any sin, for he is conceived of the Holy Ghost, not by human generation. He does not *contract* these bodily defects which result

[23]*Summa*, III, q. 14, a. 1.

from sin, in consequence, but for the reasons given freely *assumes* them.

2. **Christ takes all, and only, the defects which are commonly found in men as a consequence of Adam's sin.** Certain defects—ignorance, inclination to evil, difficulty in doing good—are incompatible with the perfection of Christ's grace and knowledge; these he cannot assume, for they would work against the very purposes for which he assumes our flesh. Others, however, such as disease, injury, inherited deficiencies, are not common to all men but result from particular causes—vicious living, or degenerated human powers, or the like. These causes, however, can have no place in Christ's human nature, and their resulting defects will not be found in him.

Death, suffering, fatigue, thirst—the common lot of fallen man—imperfections of this kind he does assume. And by taking up the corruptibility and passibility of our too mortal flesh, he has healed all the bodily defects of man, the particular as well as the common ones. In the glory of heaven after the Last Judgment, bodily perfection will be one of his gifts to us.

C. Defects of Soul

1. **The moral defect which is sin, whether original or actual, was never in Christ.** This obvious conclusion is the explicit statement of divine revelation. The "Holy One of God" (Lk. 1:35), God's own son, is our High Priest, "holy, innocent, undefiled, set apart from sinners" (Heb. 7:26), "who did no sin, nor was deceit found in his mouth" (I Pet. 2:22). Christ could himself declare, in all truth, that the prince of this world in him has nothing (Jn. 14:30), for he does always the things that are pleasing to his Father (Jn. 8:29). And with full right he can pose the unanswerable question: "Which of you can convict me of sin?" (Jn. 8:46).

Christ is not only free of all sin, original and actual, he has no possibility of sinning. This impeccability arises from three sources: 1) *in virtue of the Hypostatic Union,* for this human nature is God's, and God cannot sin; 2) *in virtue of his fulness of grace,* which so subjected all his powers to God as to render the deordination in which sin consists an impossibility; 3) *in virtue of the beatific vision,* for he who enjoys the intuitive vision of God can never turn away from him or against him. Moreover, Christ assumes our defects, as pointed out above, to satisfy for our sins, to demonstrate his true human nature, and to provide us with an example. But these ends would not have been furthered, they would have been impeded and frustrated, had he assumed the defect of sin.

2. **Concupiscence has absolutely no place in Christ.** Concupiscence in the moral sense (called also the fuel or source of sin—*fomes peccati*) is *the inordinate inclination to sensible good against the order of reason.* Not in itself sinful, it is yet a tendency to sin, and as such irreconcilable with Christ's humanity, which has no sinful potentialities. A sensuous inclination to what is contrary to reason implies a fundamental disorder; but all of Christ's human powers are so perfected and strengthened by his virtues, of which he possesses the absolute fulness, that not even the possibility of disorderly movement of the lower appetites can remain. By grace his is that perfect subjection of lower powers to reason, and of reason itself to God, which guarantees absolute sanctity.

3. **There was no ignorance in Christ.** His was a fulness of knowledge as well as of grace, so that this human imperfection is necessarily excluded from his soul.

4. **Christ possessed true human emotions and feelings.** It is natural to man to react, according to his human appetites, to the world around him and to its contacts with him. An unfeeling human being is an anomaly, something of a sideshow freak when not something of a monster. Yet with us the emotions all too easily get out of control, and they who should be servants of our reason frequently overpower their master, usurp his authority, and consequently misdirect our activities. In themselves these inevitable reactions, which are movements of the sense appetites, are neither morally good nor morally bad: they are simply part of our physical make-up, like hands or eyes. But they can and should come under the control of the will. In the measure that they do, they become reasonable and good. In the measure that they escape such direction, they become morally imperfect and even sinful.

Christ is truly and perfectly human, and thus necessarily subject to human passions. But, morally speaking, there is a vast difference between the movements of his sense appetites and those of other men:

1) They are never directed to what is morally evil or illicit.
2) They arise only at the behest of his will, never anticipating the judgment of reason.
3) They remain under perfect control, in no way disturbing his reason or impeding its proper function.

Hence theologians give a special name to Christ's passions, to underline the perfection they possess in him. They are called *propassions*, "beginning passions," since they never reach that wild, turbulent and unruly state, as often with us, where they overthrow reason.

7. Summary and Conclusion

One can only wonder at and admire the human nature of the God-man as it is endowed with these perfections which he assumes together with it. By its union with the Word of God, Christ's sacred humanity possesses an absolute holiness incomparably above that of any other creature. Beyond that, the fulness of grace is given to this nature—the highest degree of deification and sanctification possible to a finite being in the divine dispensation. All the theological and infused moral virtues, the gifts of the Holy Ghost, the charismata, and the plenitude of efficacious actual grace are his to a unique degree. His human intelligence is perfected by the beatific vision and by an infused knowledge comparable to that of the angels. And his power, as God's instrument, extends over the entire created universe, the worlds of grace and of nature, only creation being impossible for him.

Yet is he a man like us. His body bears our common weaknesses, for out of love he chooses to share the defects that result from man's sin. His soul suffers with our feelings and emotions, even though these are always under control. He walks our earth, one of us and yet infinitely above us, our brother but our example, son of man but God's Son also. And one sad day he will walk the way of torture to the Hill of the Skull, to the cross, to his death for our salvation.

From the first moment of his conception in Mary's virginal womb Christ, as man, enjoys the beatific vision: he is a *comprehensor*, one of the blessed, one of those who have the perfect happiness of seeing God face to face. But he is also a *viator*, a wayfarer, one who works toward the happiness of heaven in this vale of tears. For he miraculously impedes the overflowing of that heavenly blessedness on his body and the lower powers of his soul. Suffer he will, for us, that he might merit and satisfy, for us. Even on the cross, however, in the consummation of death, he will also rejoice. For his is the Kingdom of Heaven.

Apart from the scientific conclusions which have been drawn from the doctrine of this chapter, certain other conclusions can be cited as practical consequences, applicable to the Christian in his daily life.

1. Christ is the instrument of God. His humanity is the physical cause of his grace in the souls of men. When men reject this grace they are rejecting Christ, and they are rejecting even the meaning of redemption. Salvation came to man because the God-man assumed human nature and all of the common defects consequent on original sin. He alone could pay the price of redemption, and he alone, because of his remarkable degree of sensitivity, could experience the deepest agony of physical and mental torture. Christ suffered and died for all men. Those who realize it, but do nothing to accept his grace, are in reality scoffing at the misery of Calvary.

2. The ancient proverb, "God smiles on the rich man," is rooted in the Old Testament idea that God rewards the just in this life by riches, health and happiness. Christ and his saints are witnessess to the hollowness of this statement. He embraced poverty and suffering for our sakes, and his saints, following his example, welcomed the opportunities to show their love for him. Pope Pius XII underlines this fact: "The meaning of human destiny is not limited to the enjoyment or recovery of perishable health; it extends infinitely, even to the unspeakable realities of the other world."[24]

3. When Christ asked his apostles: "Whom do you say that I am?" Peter responded to the inquiry with the words, "Thou art Christ, the son of the living God."[25] By these words Peter publicly attested to

[24]Pope Pius XII, *On Radiology*, April 5, 1954.

the twofold nature of the God-man, and at the same time professed his belief in the oneness of the Person.

4. "Preserving, therefore, the substance of both natures, and uniting them in one person, lowliness is assumed by majesty; infirmity, by power; mortality, by immortality. And to pay the debt of our present state, an inviolable nature is united to our suffering one; and true God and true man are welded into the unity of one Lord, so that, as was needed for our healing, one and the same mediator of God and men, might, by the one, suffer death, and by the other, rise again from the dead."[26]

BIBLIOGRAPHICAL NOTE

Chapter IV should be of tremendous interest to all Christians because it shows how much Christ loved us when he took to himself the same clay out of which all men are made. For further study of this great mystery, Questions VII-XV, Part III of the *Summa* are suggested. Although St. Thomas presupposes a great deal of previous study before attempting these questions, still an adept student will be able to abstract much valuable information from them. Karl Adam gives a more popular presentation of the doctrine in his book *Christ Our Brother* (New York: The Macmillan Co., 1931).

The first volume of *The Collected Works of Abbot Vonier* yields many useful ideas on Christ as man. In particular, Book I, Chapter III, "The Rôle of Christ's Humanity," is recommended; as also Book II, Chapter VII, "The Permanence of Our Lord's Human Nature," and Chapter XV, "Christ's Knowledge." Specific references to the same subject can also be found in "Jesus Christ, the Model of Manhood," Chapter XII of Volume I of *The Teaching of the Catholic Church*.

[25]Matt. 16:16.
[26]St. Leo, *Sermon 21* (first on the Nativity), Chap. 2.

CHAPTER FIVE

The Consequences of the Incarnation

1. Introduction

In the preceding chapters of our study of Jesus Christ we looked at the Hypostatic Union as it is in itself. Our investigation embraced the following points:

I. The Fittingness of the Incarnation (Chapter Two).

II. The Nature of the Incarnate Union.
1. The union itself, its essence and characteristics (Chapter Three, Sections 2-4).
2. The extremes united:
   1) The Person assuming (Chapter Three, Sections 5 and 6).
   2) The nature assumed (Chapter Three, Sections 7-9).
   3) The perfections and imperfections co-assumed with human nature (Chapter Four).

It is obvious that so singular an event as this unique union of two natures in one person will have far-reaching repercussions. The task of the present chapter is to investigate the consequences which inevitably flow from the fact that God becomes man. These will first of all concern the unique being who subsists in these two natures, Jesus Christ; he, who was ever God, in becoming man acquires new properties and characteristics. New relations also spring up between the God-man and God himself, between the God-man and ourselves. These relative consequences are likewise of deepest import, and must be examined theologically.

The points to be considered in this chapter will be taken up according to this outline:

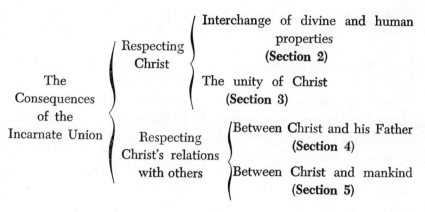

2. Mutual Predication of Divine and Human Properties

A. The Communication of Properties

Against Eutyches and the Monophysite ("one-nature") heretics, the Church has defined that the human nature and the divine nature of Jesus Christ remain, even after their hypostatic union in the person of the Word, without any "confusion or transformation or division or separation between them: for the difference of natures is in no way suppressed by their union; on the contrary, the attributes of each nature are safeguarded, and they subsist in one person alone and in one hypostasis alone."[1] Hence it would be heretical to maintain that the attributes of divinity are physically communicated to Christ's humanity, or the properties of his human nature to his divine nature

[1]Council of Chalcedon, 451; Denz. 148.

But it remains equally true that only one person is both God and man, subsisting both in divine nature and in human nature. And thus what can be said of Christ's human nature—that he suffers, that he sleeps, that he prays—may in fullest truth be said of him who subsists in divine nature. Similarly, what can be said of Christ's divine nature—that he creates, that he is omnipotent, that he is incorporeal—may with equal right and equal truthfulness be said of him who subsists in a created, a human nature. This is the foundation for what Chesterton has called "the paradox of Christianity."

Theologically speaking, this consequence of the Incarnation is known as the **communication of idioms or properties:** *the mutual predication of Christ's divine and human natures, and their respective properties, of each other.* For since there is only one supposit in Christ, subsisting in two natures, the attributes of God can be attributed to this man, and the attributes of man to God. The son of man is in heaven; the Son of God is born of a woman.[2] "The Lord of glory is said to be crucified," remarks John Damascene, "although his divine nature has in no way suffered; and again, before his passion the son of man was said to be in heaven, as our Lord himself stated. For the Lord of glory is one and the same as he who by nature was truly the son of man. We acknowledge that both miracles and prayers are his, even though he worked miracles by reason of one nature and offered prayers in virtue of the other."[3]

B. Rules for This Mutual Predication

Precision of language when speaking of so divine a reality as the mystery of the Incarnation is an absolute necessity. For human words are but inadequate expressions of human concepts and ideas, and human concepts can at best but inadequately represent the divine. Inaccuracy of expression will inevitably produce a result at variance with reality, with the divine facts God has revealed to us. The following rules are the bare essentials for accurate predication in regard to the Hypostatic Union.

---

[2]Cf. Jn. 3:13; Gal. 4:4. This manner of speaking of Christ is found everywhere in the New Testament; hence the necessity for carefully determining whether the statement applies to Christ precisely as God, or precisely as man.
[3]*On the Orthodox Faith,* Bk. III, Chap. 3.

1. *In order to predicate the divine nature and its properties of Christ's human nature and its properties (and vice versa), concrete terms must be used, and abstract terms excluded.* Concrete words designate the person or supposit, who is essentially one in the Hypostatic Union, the divine person of the Word. Abstract words, on the contrary, designate the nature; since there is no identity of natures in Christ, an abstract term signifying one nature ("humanity") cannot be said of the other nature. Hence one may say: God is man (or suffering, or mortal); but not: God is humanity, or divinity is humanity.

2. *But in negative statements, abstract terms should be used, to exclude any identity of natures; concrete terms should not be used, lest the unity of the person be denied.* "God is not man" is untrue; "God (or divinity) is not humanity" is an accurate statement of fact.

With these rules in mind, the meaning of certain paradoxical statements can be easily ascertained: "The eternal is born in time, the omnipotent made weak, the immortal dies, the immutable is changed." These are equivalent to less startling statements expressing the same truth: one and the same person who (according to his divine nature) is eternal, omnipotent, immortal, immutable; this same person becomes (according to the human nature he assumes) temporal, weak, mortal, changeable. In short, God becomes man.

Stated according to the rules which are laid down above, the communication of properties becomes an effective expression of revealed truth concerning the Hypostatic Union and an equally effective denial of error. The first rule affirms the unity of the Person against Nestorius, who held that Christ was both a divine person and a human person. The second affirms the duality of natures in Christ, to the confusion of the Monophysites who mixed and fused Christ's divine and human natures and their properties.

C. Applications

The following statements, therefore, are **true and accurate** expressions of the revealed facts about the Incarnation:

1. God is man.

2. Man is God.

3. God becomes, or is made, man.

4. Humanity is deified.

The following are as **false** as the above are true:

1. Man is made God.

2. Humanity becomes divinity.

3. Christ is the Lord's man.

4. Christ as man is God.

3. The Unity of Christ

Two natures, one person. Should Christ be considered two things, God and man, because of the duality of natures? Or is he only one, because of his personal unity? Does a unity of person mean a unity of operations, and of the source of operations, the will? Just what were the results of the Hypostatic Union with respect to multiplying or unifying things in Christ?

A. Christ's Unity of Being

(1) Christ Is One

"If anyone does not confess that Christ is one, one being possessing his own flesh, i.e, one person who is both God and man, *let him be anathema*."[4] Thus St. Cyril of Alexandria anathematized the Nestorian error which taught that Christ was two things, two beings. Since there is only one supposit (the Word), and only the supposit truly subsists in completeness of essence, his duality of natures does not make Christ two beings, but one being subsisting in two natures. It would be otherwise, of course, if each nature was self-subsistent. But it is the very nature of this hypostatic union of natures that it is a unity according to subsistence. No more than you are two things because you have both a body and a soul is Christ two.

[4]*Second Anathema against Nestorius;* Denz. 114.

(2) Christ Has Only One Existence, Divine Existence

On the basis of St. Thomas' principles respecting subsistence and existence,[5] it follows immediately from the conclusion above that there is only one existence, the divine existence, in Christ. Existence is the ultimate perfection or actuality of a thing which already possesses, in the line of essence, its full complement of being: a subsisting supposit or person. Christ is substantially one, not accidentally so, because he is but one person, one divine supposit. Hence he exists by one personal existence alone, his divine existence; he does not acquire a new personal existence when he becomes incarnate, simply because he does not become a new person. Rather is the contrary true: *from the moment of its assumption, his human nature begins to exist in virtue of his pre-existing (from all eternity), divine, personal existence.*

B. Christ's Unity of Will

After seeing that Christ is one in being, we must determine whether he is one in his activity. Here certain philosophical axioms would seem to be of assistance: "Action follows being"; "as a thing is, so does it act." With these friends at hand, it follows that Christ's action, its unity or multiplicity, will logically concern us after our consideration of the unity of being in him. But since the will is the principle or proximate source of action in intelligent beings, our first question will be a more basic one: Did Christ have one will (his divine will) or two wills (divine and human)?

(1) The Church's Decision

There are apparently good reasons for insisting on the singleness of Christ's will:

1) The will is the motivating and commanding faculty, and in all that is human, Christ is clearly not in command but subject to the divine will—so much so that we have described his humanity as the instrument or organ of his divinity.
2) He is one in being; therefore, one in activity.
3) Holy Scripture insinuates the same fact.

[5] Cf. *supra*, Chapter Three, 108-109.

On such specious grounds as these, certain Greek churchmen, ambitious for political unity in the Byzantine empire between Catholics and the heretical Monophysites (even at the expense of orthodoxy), denied the duality of wills in Christ. Opposition to this new heresy—which was only a thinly disguised form of Monophysitism—was prompt, wholehearted and effective. The sixth ecumenical council, the Third Council of Constantinople (680-81), presided over by Pope St. Agatho through his legates and its acts confirmed by his successor, Pope Leo II, declares:

> Acording to the teaching of the holy Fathers, we proclaim that there are two wills in Christ, and two natural operations, neither divided nor changed, neither separated nor intermingled. The wills of the two natures are not opposed, as godless heretics assert; far from it. But Christ's human will follows his divine and omnipotent will, not reluctantly and with resistance, but rather in subjection to it.[6]

(2) Christ's Human Will

The theological soundness of the Church's definition is easy to defend. Christ himself testified to the existence of his human will: "Father, if thou art willing, remove this cup from me; yet not my will but thine be done" (Lk. 22:42). "His will," comments St. Ambrose on this passage, "he refers to the man; the Father's, to the Godhead. For the will of man is temporal, but the will of the Godhead is eternal."[7] Christ's prayer, his supplications, his obedience, his merits—these are all human actions which can only proceed from a human source of action.

It stands to reason that if, while conserving his perfect divine nature, the Second Person assumes a perfect human nature, he must have both a perfect human will and a perfect divine will. Like the intellect, the will is a characteristic power of human nature, an essential property without which that nature would not be human. That Christ's human will is fully subject to his divine will does not prevent its own proper motion and activity; its very value consists in this, that having its own activity it exercises it at God's behest, under (and in accord with) divine influence. And this much is true

---

[6]Denz. 291; cf. the Council of the Lateran, 649, Canons 10-18 (Denz. 263-272); *Dogmatic Epistle of Pope St. Agatho*, Roman Council, 680 (Denz. 288).
[7]*Exposition of the Gospel according to St. Luke*, Bk. X, n. 60.

of all human voluntary activity when it is morally good. It is in this precise manner that Christ's humanity becomes a *living* instrument in God's hands, autonomous and self-determining, moved by its own will to serve God as his minister.

(3) Christ's Sense Appetite

Man is an animal, albeit a rational one. He has powers which are properly of the sense order, for his life must be lived, in part at least, on the sense level. These capacities for sense activity come under the sway of his higher powers, so that his animal life can be lived in full accord with the dictates of right reason. One of man's sense powers is his **sense appetite**—the faculty of reacting to sense stimuli and sensuous goods and evils. Subject to his will as it should be, directed by it, subservient to it, the sense appetite participates in the higher activity of the will and becomes not merely an animal, but a truly human power.

Christ possesses such a power: he is a man; it is part of the natural equipment of man, without which he would not be human. In him, however, (as pointed out when we discussed his human passions) the subjection of this lower appetite to his higher, rational appetite—the will—is perfect. There is no movement of this power which escapes or anticipates his deliberate will, none which contradicts reason.

(4) The Human Liberty of Christ

1. **Christ has free will.** The will is an intelligent drive or tendency toward the good as apprehended by the intellect. By its nature it will always move with necessity to absolute goodness, for this is its fulfillment; the honey-bee will be drawn irresistibly to honey. But there are many things which are less than absolutely perfect and good, their goodness being participative, particularized and limited. With respect to these created goods, the will remains free: it can choose or reject them, move toward or away from them. Free will is the necessary companion of an appetite which is satisfied only with the infinitely perfect. On this solid ground one must affirm human freedom of Christ as well as the freedom of his divine will.

2. **Christ's impeccability perfects his human liberty.** It is a typically modern error to equate freedom with the ability to sin. Nothing could be more absurd. The will is oriented only to that which is good according to reason; to choose evil, to sin, is to elect that which at least appears as good. Basically, then, sin involves a wrong choice, and it is a sign of deficiency rather than of perfection: the sinner does not use his liberty as he should, he abuses it, because his free will is too imperfect to select what is truly good from what is only apparently so. This being clear, it is obvious that Christ's impeccability in no way impairs his sovereign human freedom. Like the saints in heaven, who are confirmed in good but remain at liberty to talk now with St. John, now with their next-door neighbor, Christ has unqualified freedom of choice among the host of goods which confront him. Perfect freedom demands that he not fail in tending and moving to good; his impeccability guarantees this freedom.

(5) The Harmony of Wills in Christ

"My food is to do the will of him who sent me" (Jn. 4:34). So does Christ express the fact of the absolute accord between his human will and his divine will. Endowed with all the supernatural moral virtues in an ineffable degree, he could will only what God wishes and as God wills it. His human will, fixed irrevocably in God, is nevertheless sovereignly independent with regard to created objects; it makes its own decisions. But these choices are always exclusively for God, in perfect conformity with the divine wishes made known to him from on high, without the slightest deviation from the straight way plotted by God's eternal decrees. His is the perfect obedience of which St. Paul speaks, obedience unto death, and yet the obedience of a man.

In the garden, for example, his will and his sense appetite naturally recoiled from the prospect before him, the agony of his passion and death. But this shrinking of his sensibility, and the horror spontaneously arising in his will, occasion no conflict within him. For love of his Father and for us, he freely wills, with no compulsion whatever, to drink of this dreadful cup to its last dregs. His natural reaction of fear, of horror, of sorrow is not suppressed; "but Christ's human will follows his divine and omnipotent will, not reluctantly and with resistance, but in full compliance with it."[8]

C. Christ's Unity of Action

Did Christ as man possess autonomy of action? Or was his dependence on God so complete as to rob him of all initiative in his strictly human activity? His perfect obedience so wholehearted as to make him an automaton for the execution of God's predestined plan? So it seemed to those heretics who denied any duality of active principles in Christ, declaring he possessed but one will, and that divine. But the Church on innumerable occasions has severely censured this lessening of Christ's human dignity, this equivalent denial of his true, integral and perfect humanity.[9]

(1) Christ's Divine Activity and His Human Activity

The existence of two activities in Christ may be proved by the following argument:

Whenever a mover and a thing moved have proper and distinct forms, there are necessarily proper and distinct activities. For the form is the principle *by which* a thing acts, and its power of acting; thus as many forms as there are, so many will there be types of activity.

But: in Christ there are two distinct forms—his human nature which remains integral and perfect after its union with divinity; and his divine nature itself.

Therefore: there is a proper and distinct *divine* activity in Christ, and a proper and distinct activity which is *human*.

The Godhead, it is true, uses Christ's human activity as its instrument; and his humanity participates in his divine activity as an in-

[8]Third Council of Constantinople; Denz. 291.
[9]Cf. *Letter of Pope St. Leo to Flavian*, 449 (Denz. 148); *Letter of Pope Honorius to Sergius*, 634 (Denz. 251 ff.); Lateran Council, 649 (Denz. 264 ff); *Dogmatic Letter of Pope St. Leo and the Roman Synod to the Emperors*, 680 (Denz. 288); Third Council of Constantinople, 680-681 (Denz. 291 ff.); *Creed of St. Leo IX*, 1053 (Denz. 344); Council of Florence, *Decree for the Jacobites*, 1442 (Denz. 710); *Profession of Faith for the Orientals*, 1743 (Denz. 1465).

strument participates in the higher action of the principal cause. But this proves the point rather than denies it. For every instrument has two activities: its own proper operation which flows from its nature; and a sharing of the activity of the higher, principal cause using it, a sharing which elevates and perfects its own activity. Unless we are to hold that Christ's human nature lacks its proper form and its principle of action (which is heretical: for his human nature would then be neither perfect nor integral), or that his power is only one, composed of divine and human powers (which would be heretical: for then there would be a mixture of natures), we must hold on divine faith that Christ had both divine operations and human operations.

(2) The Kinds of Christ's Activity

1. Some of Christ's actions were **strictly divine:** the creation and conservation of the universe, for example; his divine governance of all things.

2. Some proceed from his human nature alone, and were thus **strictly human:** his suffering, his prayer, his eating, drinking, sleeping and walking.

3. Other actions of Christ were both **divine and human,** his divinity being the principal cause and his humanity the instrument used by the Godhead to produce the effect. The miracles he worked are an example of this class of activity: his divine nature communicates to his human powers the transient power of restoring to health; his human nature by words or touch applies this communicated power to the one to be cured. These actions are called *theandric,* from the Greek for "divine-human," because both his divine power and his human power are engaged in producing the effect. In a wider and less accurate use of the word, even his strictly human actions are sometimes called theandric, since they are those of a divine person, even though in this case divine power does not come into play.

(3) The Merit of Christ's Human Activity

1. **Christ by his human action can merit.** The conditions for meriting a supernatural reward are the following: 1) free action; 2) pro-

ceeding from grace and charity; 3) by a man living in this life; 4) offered to, and accepted by God. But Christ's human actions are most perfectly free (every single one springs from his will, for even the lower powers of action are under the perfect dominion of his will); his grace and charity have the fulness of perfection; he is a wayfarer, living our human life on this earth; his actions are performed only for the Father, and are most pleasing to him.

2. **Christ merits for himself.** Whatever is of greater perfection should be attributed to Christ, unless it would derogate from the perfection he possesses from the beginning. But to merit something for oneself (if this is possible) is obviously more perfect than to receive it as a gift. Christ cannot merit grace—(as the source of merit, grace itself cannot be merited, but only an increase of grace; and Christ's grace is perfect from the moment of his conception and thus admits of no increase). Nor can he merit the essential glory of his soul, for the lack of glory would seriously detract from his perfection as man. But he does merit superabundantly the accidental glory of his body, his resurrection and ascension, the exaltation of his name, his position at the right hand of God, etc. Made obedient unto death, it is precisely on account of this meritorious action that God exalts him.[10]

3. **Christ merits for us.** Christ's human actions are of superabundant supernatural value, not only for himself, but for all of mankind. For he is the head of the body of which we are members; of his moving force, his life, his interior influence all have received. Grace is given to him in absolute fulness and perfection, both intensive and extensive —not for himself alone, but for all his members, for all mankind. Such is this capital grace that by his human actions (which culminate in, and are specified by his passion and death) he *earns* from God this supernatural reward: a superabundance of sanctifying grace, more than sufficient for the salvation of each and every human being, for the remission of all the sins of all men, for the sanctification and deification of all, and for their eternal glory in the happiness of the beatific vision.

[10]Cf. Phil 2:8-9; Lk. 24:26.

4. The Relations between Christ and His Father

If the consequences of the personal union of divine nature and human nature in Christ are of considerable moment respecting Christ himself, they will be equally momentous with regard to his relations with others. The Second Person is the Only-begotten of the Father, identical with him in nature, in power, in all things except his distinguishing personal property of sonship. But now the situation radically changes, for he is not only God but also man; the relations between him and his Father will be radically different. Similarly, Christ's relations with us undergo a fundamental revision: he who is our creator, our first cause and last end, becomes one of us, flesh of our flesh, our brother; and the implications of this fact are tremendous indeed.

When a man marries, a host of new elements enter his life, affecting him deeply, and changing also his relationships with his own family and with his newly acquired in-laws. We have already considered the consequences of the marriage between God and man which is the Incarnation, so far as these affect Christ himself. Now we shall see in this section how this intimate union affects Christ's relations with his own family, with God. What may be determined by our study will necessarily depend on the principles already enunciated concerning the Incarnation (cf. Chapter Four, Introduction), and these indicate that the following points need special investigation:

$$
\text{Relations between Christ and his Father}
\begin{cases}
\text{Of Christ to his Father}
\begin{cases}
\text{His subjection} \\
\text{His prayer} \\
\text{His priesthood}
\end{cases} \\
\\
\text{Of the Father to Christ}
\begin{cases}
\text{Christ's sonship} \\
\text{Christ's predestination}
\end{cases}
\end{cases}
$$

A. Christ's Subjection to His Father

As God, Christ is in every way equal with the Father: "identical is their divinity, equal their glory, coeternal their majesty. Such as is the Father, such also is the Son, such also the Holy Spirit."[11] But according to his human nature Christ is subject to God. Since his is a created nature, and a created intelligent nature, this will be a three-fold subjection: he will, as man, be subject to the divine goodness and perfection; subject to God's power; and subject, in a manner characteristically human, to God's commands by his own will.

1) God is the very essence of goodness, of perfection; Christ's human nature is but a participation of the divine goodness, in no way attaining the infinite degree of perfection which is God's. Christ himself gives testimony to this subjection of inferiority on the part of his human nature: "The Father is greater than I" (Jn. 14:28).

2) All that happens to Christ in virtue of his humanity takes place by divine appointment. For every creature, being subject to the divine ordination, is God's servant. In taking a human nature, the Son of God assumes "the nature of a slave" (Phil. 2:7), abandoning himself utterly to the divine good pleasure.

3) "I do always the things that are pleasing to him" (Jn. 8:29). Christ's ultimate subjection as man—and the subjection most typically human, in which true human perfection is to be found, and man's destiny—is that of his human will, his perfect and pre-eminent obedience to the will of God. He is made obedient to his Father unto death, even to the death of the cross (cf. Phil. 2:8).

Thus is Christ, in St. Augustine's phrase, "less than himself," just as he is less than the Father; and as he is subject to God the Father, so also he is subject to himself as God. For according to his human nature he is man; but he who is man is, in actual fact, also God, the Second Person of the Blessed Trinity.

B. The Prayer of Christ to His Father

That Christ prays is the clear testimony of Sacred Scripture. "He went out to the mountain to pray, and continued all night in prayer to God" (Lk. 6:12). "I pray for them; not for the world do I pray, but for those whom thou hast given me" (Jn. 17:9). "He lives always to make intercession" (Heb. 7:25). The facts are evident enough: Christ

[11]The "Quicunque" Creed, commonly called the Athanasian Creed; Denz. 39.

prays, for himself and for us. We must see what these facts mean and what they imply.

1. **It is fitting for Christ to pray.** Prayer (of petition) is nothing else than the expression of one's legitimate desires to God, in order that he may fulfill them. Since Christ's human will is created and finite, it cannot, except through divine power, accomplish that which it desires; accordingly, it is entirely right that he, a human being with a human will, should beseech God's assistance. His prayer—which is an act of his reason and his will—embraces even those things which his sense appetite desires, for these also are human desires. In praying in this manner he accomplishes many things: 1) he manifests his true human nature, complete with human needs and feelings; 2) he indicates that it is permissible to desire even what God does not want (when such desires are legitimate in themselves, and God's will is not known to us); and 3) he teaches us that the desires of our lower appetites must always be subjected by our will to the will of God.

2. **Christ prays both for himself and for us.** In recognition of his Father's power and authority, Christ in his prayer explicitly acknowledges God as the author of his human nature and thanks him for the gifts he has received (cf. Matt. 26:27; Jn. 11:41). So also does he beg his Father in prayer for those gifts still lacking to him in his human nature: the glorification of his body, the exaltation of his name, and so forth (cf. Jn. 17:1). Here, as in all his actions on this earth, he himself gives the example, in order that we should imitate him in prayer—by thanking God for the benefits we have received, by asking God for the gifts we do not yet have. In still another way his prayer is beneficial for us. "The very glory which Christ by praying sought for himself pertained to the salvation of others: 'He rose again for our justification' (Rom. 4:25). And therefore that prayer which he offered for himself was also in a certain way for others. Just as anyone who asks a boon of God that he may use it for the good of others prays, not for himself alone, but also for them."[12]

3. **Christ's prayer is always heard.** No sane man asks for things that cannot possibly be his, much as he might wish such things. No good man asks God for what he knows God will not grant; this would

[12]St. Thomas, *Summa*, III, q. 21, a. 3, ad 4.

be to oppose his will to God's, a procedure as futile as it is sinful.
Christ knows all of God's wishes, and his will is in perfect harmony
with the divine will. So he beseeches God by prayer only for the things
God has chosen to give him, and consequently his requests are always
heard and answered by God. At times, of course, (as in the garden)
he expresses the desires of the sensitive part of his human nature,
even though these may not be according to God's will; but then his
prayer is always conditional—*if* it be possible, *if* it pleases God—that is,
he would have it so (and hence prays God for its fulfillment) if nothing
stood opposed to it in God's designs.

C. The Priesthood of Christ

(1) The Notion of the Priesthood

A priest, in the true sense of the word, is one who is basically *an
official mediator between God and man, chosen by God to link
heaven and earth.* The Latin word for priest, *sacerdos,* means one
who gives sacred, divine things (*sacra dans*). That which is essentially
sacred is the Godhead itself; all other things are denominated sacred
because of their reference to God: either because they are God's gifts
to man or because they are man's "gifts" to God. The priest is said to
give sacred things inasmuch as he brings to man the sacred things of
God which descend from above—his truth and his grace—and presents
to God the sacred things of man which ascend from this earth and
are directed to God—man's prayer and, above all, man's sacrifice.
"For every high priest taken from among men is appointed for men
in the things pertaining to God, that he may offer gifts and sacrifices
for sins" (Heb. 5:1).

As minister of this mutual exchange of sacred things, the priest joins
God and man, unites heaven and earth, mediates between the infinite and uncreated and the finite and created. Two essential notes
of this holy and sacred office must be clearly understood.

1. **The priest is an** *official* **mediator.** The priest does not act in
his own name but in that of human society: he is a public personage,
not a private individual. Not by himself or any other private person,
then, can he be deputed to this divine service, but only by legitimate

authority. And since his service consists precisely in dealing with supernatural things, he can be called to his eminent role only by the author of the supernatural order: "No one takes the honor to himself; he takes it who was called by God, as Aaron was" (Heb. 5:4). But God's love, which prompts his selection of this man as his priest, is effective, as we have repeatedly said. This vocation produces a new physical supernatural reality in the individual chosen; by it he is appropriated exclusively by God, intrinsically ordained to God's service and worship, and accepted by God as his own, and his only. Man's priesthood, in short, is the result of divine *consecration*.

2. **The principal duty of the priest is to offer** *sacrifice.* "Every high priest is appointed to offer gifts and sacrifices" (Heb. 8:3). **Sacrifice,** as previously defined,[13] is *an offering which a priest makes to God by changing or destroying some object in order to manifest God's dominion and our subjection.* Special emphasis must be given to the various elements of this definition to grasp this unique religious reality.

1) Since man is a dependent being, naturally subject to a higher power, he must give explicit recognition of his inferiority and God's supremacy.

2) But he must pay homage to God *in his own human way.* Now it is natural to man to convey his sentiments by perceptible signs. So to express the submission of his being to God (and this is the spirit and heart of true sacrifice), he will externalize his homage through signs.

3) Basically, then, sacrifice is an *offering,* a giving up or surrender of self. This interior sacrifice is symbolized when man offers God one of the inferior creatures placed at his disposal. For man is God's steward, and hence given dominion over the things of this world; to give up such a sensible object to God appropriately represents his self-giving.

4) But as his spiritual sacrifice is entire and complete, the symbolic action must express this perfect submission. Hence the sensible object which is offered must be so removed from ordinary human

---

[13] F. L. B. Cunningham, ed., *The Christian Life,* 579; and, St. Thomas, *Summa,* II-II, q. 85.

use by his action as to be placed entirely at God's disposal. The external sacrifice thus always involves a kind of destruction of the thing offered, and in this way it truly signifies the interior, total surrender of self to God in recognition of his dominion over all things, especially over man himself.

5) The primary purpose of sacrifice is to give this visible sign of our recognition of God's superiority and our submission to him. But it is also an act of thanksgiving, out of gratitude for the gifts God has given us, and of impetration, powerfully beseeching the gifts we have not yet received. Most important of all, in many ways, is the fact that it is an act which reconciles sinful man to God—an act of expiation for past sins which is pleasing to God because of the totality of man's surrender to him.

6) Sacrifice is, then, natural and necessary for man, an act of religious worship clamored for by his nature. But the private individual cannot satisfy this need, since it is basically a social need: man must protest before others his recognition of the relations between God and himself, and must act as a member of the human race and of human society. It is for this reason that the rite expressive of sacrifice must be external, signifying publicly his interior sentiments. In consequence, sacrifice is properly the work of the religious head of the community, the priest; he will, as the official mediator between themselves and God, make a sacrificial offering for all. **Sacrifice is the principal duty of the priest.**

(2) Christ, Our High Priest

Under the former covenant, as the apostle Paul attests, there was no perfection, because of the powerlessness of the Levitical priesthood. Hence it was necessary—God the Father of mercies so ordaining—that another priest "according to the order of Melchisedech" (Gen. 14:18; Ps. 109:4; Heb. 1:11) should arise. This was our Lord Jesus Christ, who could perfect all who would be sanctified and lead them to perfection. He, therefore, our Lord and our God, was to offer himself to God the Father once and for all by his death on the altar of the cross, there to accomplish an everlasting redemption.[14]

[14]Council of Trent, Sess. XXII, 1562, *Doctrine . . . concerning the Most Holy Sacrifice of the Mass*, Chap. 1; Denz. 938.

This important conciliar definition enunciates these truths about Christ's priesthood:

1. **Christ is a true priest.** The prophecy of the Psalmist is a messianic one, as Christ himself declares (Matt. 22:42-45; cf. Heb. 5:10): "The Lord hath sworn and he will not repent: 'Thou art a priest forever according to the order of Melchisedech'" (Ps. 109:4). The Epistle to the Hebrews examines profoundly and at length this special priesthood of Jesus Christ, the "great high priest" (Heb. 4:14), "a high priest over the house of God" (Heb. 10:21). Divine revelation thus fully confirms the fact that Christ as man fulfills in the most perfect manner the qualities of a priest.

1) He is a *mediator* between God and man. In the Second Person divine and human natures are conjoined. Through him the gifts of God, divine teaching and divine grace, come to man; his fulness of grace enables him to offer God man's gift, man's prayer and his acceptable sacrifice (cf. Col. 1:20).

2) He is *called* by God to this official role: "So also Christ did not glorify himself with the high priesthood but he who spoke to him, 'Thou art my son, I this day have begotten thee'" (Heb. 5:5).

3) He is *consecrated* by God. By nature the son of man is the Son of God, in virtue of the grace of union; so he is substantially sanctified, and becomes in the most exclusive manner possible God's own, and his alone. Through the fulness of sanctifying grace, he actively mediates between God and men: he is the efficient, meritorious and satisfactory cause of grace in men; he is the man who offers man's perfect prayer and sacrifice to God.

2. **Christ is not only perfect priest but perfect victim.** Through Christ's humanity, by the visible sacrifice of the cross which is the sign of his invisible offering of himself through perfect love and perfect obedience, our sins are completely wiped out, we receive the grace of salvation, and the perfection of glory becomes man's possession. He who could have prevented his death in innumerable ways allows his persecutors to have their way with him, that he might voluntarily offer himself for our sake as a most pleasing victim to God. In his offering

was thus accomplished all that had been shadowed forth in the imperfect sacrifices of the Old Law. He who offers, offers himself: as a victim for sin, as a victim for peace-offering, and as a holocaust.

3. **Christ offers a perfect sacrifice, of which all other sacrifices are but figures.** This is clear on all counts: 1) on the part of him who offers; 2) on the part of the victim offered; 3) on the part of the mode of the offering; 4) on the part of the effects secured and the purposes served by this sacrifice.

4. **Christ's priesthood is the perfection of the priestly office.** This conclusion, implicit in the declaration of the Council of Trent, is an obvious sequel of what we have said of his role and of his accomplishment of that role.

(3) The Qualities of Christ's Priesthood

1. **Christ's priesthood is one of adoration of God, thanksgiving and impetration; but above all it produces a perfect expiation of sin.** His grace, infused in the souls of men, abolishes all stain of sin. His sacrifice is a superabundant satisfaction for the sins of the entire world, taking away the entire debt of punishment under which man was burdened. Since he himself is entirely sinless, he does not receive this expiatory effect of his priesthood himself; rather does he communicate it to all other men.

2. **Christ's priesthood is eternal.** Although Christ's sacrificial offering takes place once and for all on Calvary, its power and effect endure forever. For through his priesthood the eternal goods of heaven are won for mankind.

3. **Christ's priesthood is according to the order of Melchisedech.** This prophetic expression indicates the perfection of Christ's office as compared with that of the Old Law. As Abraham paid homage to his superior, the priest Melchisedech, so the Levitical priesthood (whose ministers were descendants of Abraham according to the flesh), which never cleansed from sin and was far from eternal, must acknowledge the superiority of Christ's priesthood, of which it was but a faint image.

D. The Sonship of Christ

"Behold what manner of love the Father has bestowed upon us, that we should be called children of God; and such we are" (I Jn. 3:1). But Christ also is God's son, his only-begotten Son. Since we are sons by adoption, is not he who by nature is God's Son now become, according to his human nature, God's adopted son?

(1) Divine Adoption

God adopts us as his sons, as is revealed in many places in Sacred Scripture (e.g., Eph. 1:5; Jn. 1:12; Rom. 8:15; Gal. 4:5; I Jn. 3). But what is the meaning of divine adoption? By considering the nature of human adoption, and removing from it all that is imperfect, we may form some notion of this act of God's love for us.

1. **The nature of adoption.** Adoption is *the gratuitous and free assumption of a stranger as a son with the right of inheritance.* Out of his goodness and with the utmost freedom, God assumes as his sons, with full rights to his inheritance (eternal beatitude), those who are strangers to him so far as the supernatural order of grace and glory is concerned. In giving us his sanctifying grace, he makes us participate in his very nature; and by reason of that likeness we acquire a true right to his riches, that inexhaustible spiritual wealth of knowing and loving him as he knows and loves himself in which perfect eternal happiness consists.

Thus there are significant differences between divine adoption and its human counterpart.

1) Human adoption is a legal fiction, effecting no physical change in the one adopted; it supposes, too, that the "stranger" is in some measure worthy of being adopted. God, on the contrary, gives a physical share in his own nature to his adopted son (sanctifying grace), and thus his love makes this "stranger" worthy of adoption, which he was not before.

2) Human adoption is, in most cases, a substitute: an attempt to supply the lack of natural children. But God's only motive in

adopting is his superabundant goodness; nothing accrues to him at all from his action.

3) Man adopts a child so that an heir may succeed him; God adopts us so that we may share his infinite spiritual riches, which he himself enjoys for all eternity and which is the proper inheritance of his natural Son.

2. The act of adopting sons is common to all three divine Persons. Divine adoption is accomplished by the production of a divine effect in the souls of men: the real, physical and analogical participation of the very nature of God which is habitual grace. Because of their unity of nature, which is the source of all divine activity outside of the divinity itself, any effect worked on a creature is common to all three Persons, and cannot be the exclusive prerogative of any one of them.

3. Only those possessing divine charity are adopted sons of God. Adopted divine sonship implies a certain likeness to the natural sonship of the Word. All creatures bear some resemblance to the Word, for as perfect image of the Father he reproduces the divine ideas according to which all creatures are formed. In this respect, intellectual creatures more perfectly correspond to the Son. But the likeness requisite for sonship is of a far higher order: it must reflect that unity of nature which exists between Father and Son and which is essential to such a relationship. Only grace and charity can produce this higher conformity and more perfect resemblance.

(2) Christ's Sonship

Since Christ in virtue of his divine nature is the natural Son of God, he cannot also be an adopted son, even though grace, the principle of divine adoption, is given to his human nature in fulness. The reason for this is simple. Christ is only one person, a person divine by nature and not by some lesser title. Just as we never call the natural son of a certain man his "adopted" son, even though he is willed a share of his father's property, so we should not call Christ an adopted son, when he is, in fact, God's natural son. Otherwise we imply that there are two persons involved in the Incarnation. This would be heresy.[15]

E. The Predestination of Christ

1. **Christ is truly predestined.** Predestination is *the eternal pre-ordination of God concerning those things which will take place in time through his grace.* This divine action implies two things: 1) priority of time with respect to the thing to take place; 2) a gratuitous divine gift given in time to a creature. But in the fulness of time the person of Christ, *precisely as subsisting in human nature* (not, of course, as subsisting in divine nature: thus he is eternally Son, by nature and not by gift), becomes the Son of God through the grace of union. That is to say, that God eternally preordains this Hypostatic Union of divine and human natures in the Second Person. But human nature was not eternally united to the Word, and its personal union to the Second Person takes place only by divine gift, by the grace of union. By reason of his human nature, then, Christ is predestined to be the Son of God.

2. **Christ's predestination is the cause of our predestination.**

1) As man Christ is predestined to natural divine sonship; we too through grace are destined to be God's sons, his sons by adoption. Christ's more perfect sonship is thus the *exemplar* and model of ours. This is true, not only with respect to the reality given, but also with respect to the way it is received. For Christ as for us, divine sonship is, with respect to his humanity, an absolutely gratuitous gift, in no manner or degree earned or merited. In the words of St. Augustine, "The Savior himself, the very mediator of God and man, the man Jesus Christ, is the most brilliant light of predestination and of grace."[16]

2) Christ's predestination, moreover, is the *efficient cause* of ours. By divine ordination the merits and satisfaction and instrumental

---

[15]Cf. *Letter of Pope Hadrian I to the Bishops of Spain*, 785 (Denz. 299); Council of Frankfort, 794 (Denz. 311-314).
[16]*Concerning the Predestination of the Saints*, Chap. 15.

efficiency of his humanity obtain our salvation. "He predestined us to be adopted through Jesus Christ as his sons" (Eph. 1:5).

3) Finally, Christ's predestination is the *final cause* of our predestination. Our salvation is ultimately ordained by God to manifest his own glory and the glory of Christ, his predestined Son, King of heaven and of earth.[17]

5. The Relations between Christ and Us

A. The Adoration of Christ

In testimony of another's excellence and superiority, man is accustomed to manifest his submission to such superiority by certain signs. Thus a baseball crowd will rise to its feet when the President enters the ball park; the enthusiastic crowd in St. Peter's will fill the basilica with applause as the Pope is carried down the middle aisle. Obviously it is the internal act of reverence which is important here—standing on one's feet during the seventh inning stretch does not count as an act of reverence of the President; but, as with sacrifice, such is man's composite nature that he seeks to express this interior sentiment by perceptible signs.

If reverence is due to men, it is obvious that adoration pre-eminently is owed to God, for his excellence and superiority are uncreated and supreme. But since there are varying degrees of excellence and superiority we may distinguish different grades of adoration:

Civil—based on natural, created excellence[18]

Religious
(based on supernatural excellence)

latria: adoration given to God alone

dulia: veneration given to saints and angels

hyperdulia: veneration given because of some unique supernatural but created excellence, as, e.g., to Our Blessed Lady

---

[17]Cf. the Encyclical of Pope Pius XI on the Kingship of Christ, *Quas Primas*.
[18]The honor and reverence paid to one's superiors in any field of human life is governed by the virtue of *observance;* cf. St. Thomas, *Summa*, II-II, q. 102.

Insofar as Christ is God, unquestionably he should be honored with the adoration of *latria*. But what kind of reverence should be paid to his humanity?

(1) The Worship of Christ's Humanity

Christ is a divine Person, subsisting both in divine and in human nature. This is the necessary fact underlying the conclusions which concern the worship which his intellectual creatures owe to him.

1. **Christ's humanity precisely as united hypostatically to the Word of God must be worshipped by the same adoration as his divinity, not for itself but as subsisting in the divine Person.** We have only to take the human attitude toward burial to appreciate the basis of this conclusion. Even though a dead human body is not even human any longer (for the soul has departed), we still pay the cadaver human honor and reverence (this is why cremation arouses such horror in right-thinking men), for once this disintegrating material thing was united to someone we knew and respected, and his possession. But Christ's humanity is the humanity of God, personally united to him in the closest of unions. Would any other reverence except that of *latria* be worthy?

2. **Considered only in itself (abstracting from its hypostatic union with God), Christ's humanity does not merit the adoration of latria.** The corpse has nothing of itself to warrant our respect: it is a piece of putrefying matter. Christ's humanity, howsoever perfect it is, whatever its endowments of grace, of wisdom, of power, remains human: created and finite, it is not divine. Adoration of this humanity for itself alone would properly be that of *hyperdulia*, not of *latria*.

(2) The Sacred Heart of Jesus

The heart of man has always been considered as the symbol of human love. "Love the Lord thy God with thy whole heart" is a meaningless phrase when understood literally; in figurative language, however, it well expresses the divine command to offer all our love to God. When we honor the Sacred Heart of Jesus, then, it is not the physical organ only which receives our adoration, but rather that heart precisely as it is the heart of Jesus: 1) a part of his humanity hypostatically united to the Word, and thus worthy by its union of *latria;* 2) the emblem and symbol of the love which the Word Incarnate showed for man. In adoring the Sacred Heart we worship the humanity of Christ, the human love of this divine Person for us, and his divine love as well. Thus in this way our reverence is ultimately the adoration of the Second Person of the Blessed Trinity. Necessarily, then, this adoration is the worship of *latria.*

(3) Images, the Crucifix, Relics

The veneration which Catholics offer to sacred pictures, medals, statues, etc., is a favorite point of attack for non-Catholics, from the iconoclasts of the seventh century, through the Protestant innovators of the sixteenth, to the Nazi and Communist image-breakers of our own day. Yet these same people, so vociferous against Catholic religious practices, will inconsistently deny their theological position in their everyday lives. What man does not treasure a picture of his loved ones? What state does not honor its famous dead with statues and memorials? These are images and relics, revered by men, not for what they are, but for the sake of those they represent. Basically, the Church's devotion is based on the same sound human recognition of man's dependence on these sensible mementos. Hence we may legitimately conclude:

1. **The use of sacred images by the Church is both legitimate and useful.** Such reverence is *legitimate,* because these images are not worshipped for themselves (this would be pagan idolatry), but for the person (God, Christ, Mary, the saints) they represent, who is worthy of honor.[19] This is a *useful* practice, because by means of such representations the faithful are instructed, we are moved to devotion and meditation, and by them we may be inspired to imitate the example of those represented.

2. **Images are worshipped with the same veneration as that given to their prototypes.** Since the person represented is the reason for giving honor to these images, and not their physical natures (whatever be their material value or artistic merit), the adoration awarded them will be of the same kind as that given to the person they image.

[19]Cf. Second Council of Nicaea (Denz. 302); Council of Trent (Denz. 986).

This will be a *relative* adoration, i.e., given to the image because of its relation to the person represented; *absolute* adoration, on the contrary, is given to the person himself, on account of his superiority and excellence. A picture of Christ, for example, will be worshipped with relative *latria* because it **represents** one whose excellence is such as to be worthy of *latria;* Christ himself will be worshipped with absolute *latria* because **he** is worthy of such worship.

3. **The Cross of Christ should be reverenced by the relative adoration of latria.**

1) The True Cross by a double title (as an image and because of its uniquely special contact with Christ) is owed the relative worship of *latria,* because of Christ.

2) Crucifixes and images of the cross are true representations of the Crucified. So they are honored because of him, and not for their own excellence; the relative cult of *latria* is the proper worship with which to honor them.

B. The Mediation of Christ

The essential role which Christ holds with respect to mankind is that of mediator. It is for this that he came into the world: to join God and man, separated by man's sin. Once friends in divine fellowship, God and man now stand apart in enmity. To mediate between these enemies is Christ's chief work, and one uniquely his. "There is one God," declares St. Paul, "and one Mediator between God and man, himself man, Christ Jesus" (I Tim. 2:5). This is the ultimate consequence of that gift which conjoined human nature to divine nature in the person of the Word—that one of us, flesh of our flesh, should bridge the infinite chasm which yawns between him who is and us who are not.

(1) The Office of Mediator

Modern disputes between industry and labor make the role of mediator familiar to us. A consideration of the nature and workings of this office reveals the following characteristics:

1) The mediator should belong to neither of the separated (and disputing) factions.

2) The mediator should be accepted by both of the parties to the dispute.

3) The mediator by his action unites or reconciles the disputants, bringing what is proper to one party to the other faction, and vice versa. (If only one party gives something—if management yields to all of labor's demands—then no *mediation* is necessary; the person who nominally holds the office in this instance has failed in his job, for a complete concession could be made by one of the parties without him.)

(2) Christ, Our Mediator

As man, Christ perfectly fulfills the conditions laid down above for a true mediator:

1) Insofar as the Second Person subsists in human nature, he is distant both from God (by nature) and from man (for this nature is hypostatically united to the Word, and thus infinitely above other men in the dignity of grace and of glory).

2) In the eternal decree by which God ordains his Son to be the Savior of mankind, he accepts him as mediator; in our name, Our Blessed Lady at the moment of the Annunciation consents to his fulfilling this office for us.[20]

3) Through the humanity of Christ, God's gifts and instruction come to man; through Christ's humanity, and especially through his saving death, man's satisfaction and prayer are brought to God. By the actions of his life, his passion, his death and his exaltation, Christ unites those who were separated and at enmity. God and man once more are joined in eternal fellowship.

In the truest and fullest sense of the word, then, Christ as man is alone Mediator between God and man. In a secondary sense, other men—the prophets and priests of the Old Law, and especially Christ's priests of the new covenant—may be designated as mediators, since

[20]Cf. St. Thomas, *Summa*, III, q. 30, a. 1 and ad 1.

they co-operate with him in uniting men to God. In a very special way, as we shall see in a later chapter, this title belongs to Our Blessed Lady: Mediatrix of all graces and Co-redemptrix.

6. Summary and Conclusion

As the preceding analysis has indicated, the consequences which flow from this singular union we call the Incarnation are many and of vast importance—to Christ himself, to God, to man. We may summarize these consequences in a few statements, but their implications will never be fully explored or exhausted.

1. *Consequences with reference to Christ himself*:

1) Because of the indissoluble, substantial and personal union of divine and human natures in the person of the Word, the properties of one nature may be predicated of the person subsisting in the other nature.

2) Although Christ is necessarily one, despite the duality of natures, and exists with the single existence of a divine Person, he nonetheless possesses two distinct powers of action, his divine will and his human will, and two distinct activities, divine and human. His humanity, however, may be used as the instrument of his divinity to produce divine-human actions which surpass his human powers alone.

2. *Consequences with reference to others*:

1) As man Christ is subject to his Father, prays to him, and acts in his service as his priest. Although even as man he is not God's adopted son (for his sonship is by nature), he is, nevertheless, predestined as man by God to be the natural Son of God.

2) We owe to Christ's humanity the divine worship of *latria*, since his is the human nature of God. By this selfsame humanity he, on his part, is constituted mediator between God and ourselves; through his humanity he reconciles us with God.

These considerations thus lead us naturally to the material to be studied in the next two chapters: Christ's life on earth (Chapter Six), and his passion, death and exaltation (Chapter Seven). For it is by these human actions which culminate in his death and resurrection that the God-man actively fulfills—most perfectly and most completely —the office his Father entrusted to him: his role as Mediator. For this he came into the world; this is his meat and his drink; this is the model, the efficient and meritorious and satisfactory cause of the salvation of the human race. This accomplished, he returns to his Father's house, there to await our coming, that we may share with him forever the blessed happiness of the sight of God.

A marvelous array of practical conclusions can be taken from the doctrine displayed in this chapter. Among them are the following.

1. Due to the nationwide circulation of newspaper comics and humor magazines, plus the inanities of T-V "comedies," the social prestige of the American father has taken a sudden plunge. Formerly fatherhood was looked upon as a position which required strength, integrity and intelligence. Today the father-image pictures a weak and ludicrous personality who cannot outwit his own four-year-old. If a child were taught to look upon his father as the representative of God the Father, much disrespect and delinquency would be avoided. Christ was God, and yet as man he was subject to his Father in all things.

2. "Today after so many centuries which were centuries of civilization because they were centuries of religion, the need is not so much to reveal God for the first time as it is rather to recognize him as Father, reverence him as a Lawgiver, and fear him as a Judge. If they would be saved, the nations must adore the Son, the loving redeemer of mankind, and bow to the loving inspirations of the Spirit, the frutiful Sanctifier of souls."[21]

3. True Christian prayer is an act of worship. Worship should never be reduced to a catalogue of idle reflections, nor become a practice that is donned and doffed at the door of the church. Christ was not too good to be in constant communion with his Father. Rather, he prayed to his Father at all times in all places and even taught us how to pray.

[21]Pope Pius XII, *Modern Science and Existence of God*, Nov. 22, 1951.

4. Respect for priests is one of the greatest ways to show faith in the Incarnation. Christ is the High Priest, to be sure, but every priest has the power to offer sacrifice. The enormity of this power is seen at the altar, when, at the command of the priest, Jesus Christ, true God and true man, becomes present on the altar.

5. The dignity of the professor is a reflection of the dignity of Christ. Christ was the teacher of mankind, the mediator between earth and heaven. The professor is also a servant of God, mediator between ignorance and wisdom.

6. Too often, our mind's eye portrays Christ as the "Man of Sorrows," to the exclusion of Christ, "Man of Joy." He came, of course, to atone for sin, but it is important to keep in mind that he had something else to give mankind. He also lived his life as a means of teaching all men how to find happiness on this earth. For Christ, although he worked diligently, toiling with his hands for the major portion of his earthly existence, lived a happy life. He carried through each day in a perfectly natural way, living as God wishes each man to live. By being completely subject to the will of his Father, he fulfilled the purpose of man's existence. This was the guiding principle of Christ's labors and no sorrow could diminish the happiness he found therein.

BIBLIOGRAPHICAL NOTE

In the second volume of the English *Summa*, Part III, Questions XVI-XXVI, St. Thomas considers the material taken up in this chapter. A book which might be easier to manage in the beginning of this study is *Christ, Priest and Redeemer* (New York: The Macmillan Co., 1928), by Martin C. D'Arcy, S.J. Fr. D'Arcy's book is valuable on two counts: first, it was written for laymen; and secondly, it exhibits clarity of exposition and theme. Another book which expresses at least part of the doctrine in a very understandable fashion is *The Sacred Heart and Modern Life* (New York: P. J. Kenedy and Sons, 1952), by Francis Charmot, S.J.

"Christ Our Mediator," a short article by D. Schlegel in the *Clergy Review*, XLI (1956), 409-412, proposes yet another consequence of our Savior's Incarnation. The student might also check Volume I, Book II, "The Personality of Christ," in *The Collected Works of Abbot Vonier*. Several chapters of Book II deal directly with the subject at hand.

CHAPTER SIX

Christ's Life and Ministry

1. Introduction

Many people are quite willing to acknowledge that God is present in the world in some vague manner. At the same time they are opposed to the whole idea of the Incarnation. A God whose presence in the world is vague and indefinite can be easily shunted out of the way whenever his influence threatens the pursuit of what men fancy to be their happiness. But when God acquires a face, a family, a birthday, a recognized voice and a familiar step, he is not so easily ignored. He becomes "real" in a new sense, he becomes relevant to everything human in a more perceptible manner, he is no longer so easily dismissed.

St. Thomas does not attempt to write a life of Christ. It is his purpose rather to offer explanations of the principal points of the gospel narrative from a theological viewpoint. He draws many of these explanations from the works of the various Fathers of the Church and from the official teachings of the Church Councils. Throughout he adheres to the principles already set forth regarding the mystery of the Incarnation. A grasp of this treatment requires careful collateral reading of the gospels and of certain parts of the Old Testament and the epistles, to which reference is frequently made.[1]

The principal details of Christ's earthly life and ministry will be treated according to the outline on the following page.

2. The Birth of Christ

That Jesus Christ is absolutely unique becomes apparent from the instant of his birth. The ordinary mortal is born once; he simply becomes a man. But before his birth at Bethlehem, Christ is the eternal Son of God, he is constantly the subject of an eternal generation. At Bethlehem the same Person of Christ becomes the subject of another generation, he becomes the child of Mary. It is this second birth which makes him truly a man without prejudice to his eternal Godhead.[2]

A. Christ's Virgin Mother

The birth of Christ made him a man; it also made Mary his mother in the true and proper sense of that term. Now since there is but one Person in Christ, and precisely because that Person is divine, we say that Mary is truly the Mother of God, for she conceived him and gave him birth.[3] Thus Christ is the Son of God because of the real relation existing between himself and his Father; he is the Son of the Virgin Mother because of the real relation of her motherhood to Christ.

It is the constant teaching of the Church, based upon the Scriptures, that Mary remained a virgin before, during and after the birth of Christ.[4] St. Thomas teaches as a consequence of this that Mary endured no labor when she brought her son into the world. For Christ came forth miraculously without destroying the seal of her virginity and without causing her the pain which is part of the heritage of sin.

---

[1]For a summary of the various scriptural passages with reference to the points considered in the following two chapters, see the Appendix, "A Scriptural Harmony of the Life of Christ."
[2]Cf. Second Council of Constantinople, 553; Denz. 214.
[3]Cf. *ibid.*; Denz. **218.**
[4]Cf. Lateran Council, 649; Denz. 256.

The Things Christ Did and Suffered for Us

His entrance into the world
- His birth (Section 2)
- The attendant legalities (Section 3)
- His baptism (Section 4)

His earthly life
- His manner of living (Section 5)
- His temptation (Section 6)
- His preaching (Section 7)
- His miracles (Section 8)

His departure from the world (CHAPTER SEVEN)
- His passion
- His death
- His burial
- His descent into hell

His exaltation (CHAPTER SEVEN)
- His resurrection
- His ascension
- His place at the right hand of the Father
- His power of judgment

Thus we perceive the significance of the words of St. Luke that she ". . . brought forth her firstborn son, and wrapped him in swaddling clothes, and laid him in a manger . . ." (2:7).

B. The Circumstances of Christ's Birth

Of all cities, Bethlehem enjoyed a special suitability as the birthplace of the Savior. Bethlehem was the birthplace of King David, from whose lineage Christ came and to whom a special promise of the Messias was made (II Kings 23:1). His birth in the city of David indicated that the promise was fulfilled. Then, as St. Gregory points out, "Bethlehem means 'The House of Bread.' It is Christ himself who said, 'I am the living bread which came down from heaven.' "[5]

The simple fact that Christ chose the time of his own birth is sufficient proof that it occurred at the moment best suited to the divine plan. St. Thomas offers some reasons which point up the suitability of the time of the Nativity. Christ became man to lead us from bondage to spiritual liberty, and by being born at the time when he would be enrolled in Caesar's census, he thus submits himself to bondage for the sake of our freedom. He was born at a time when the world was at peace, a fitting time for the birth of him who ". . . himself is our peace . . ." (Eph. 2:14). Again, at the time of Christ's birth Augustus was the sole ruler of the civilized world, and this was a suitable time for him who came ". . . that he might gather into one the children of God who were scattered abroad . . ." (Jn. 11:52), that there might be ". . . one fold and one shepherd . . ." (Jn. 10:16). Finally, tradition tells us he chose to be born in winter to begin at once his sufferings for us.

C. The Manifestation of Christ's Birth

The gospel account of Christ's birth indicates that this most important event was made known to few people. It seems strange that the Savior of mankind should enter upon his work so quietly. Yet the fact

[5]*Eighth Homily on the Gospels.*

that his coming was not heralded immediately to all men fits in well with the plan of Redemption. Universal knowledge of Christ would have interfered with the crucifixion, ". . . for if they had known it, they would never have crucified the Lord of glory" (I Cor. 2:8). Secondly, widespread manifestation of Christ's birth would have deprived mankind of the merit of divine faith, which is ". . . the evidence of things that are not seen . . ." (Heb. 11:1).

Christ's birth was manifested to a few, and through these to many, for ". . . faith depends on hearing . . ." (Rom. 10:17). The universality of the salvation which Christ brought was reflected in those to whom his birth was first made known. The shepherds were Israelites; the Magi were Gentiles. The shepherds were simple and humble; the Magi wise and powerful. Simeon and Anna were saintly; the Magi were sinners. Thus the first messengers of the Incarnation represented all classes and conditions of men. It would not have been suitable for Christ himself to manifest his birth, for that would have shaken confidence in the reality of his human nature, because no human infant manifests his own birth.

The very means used to signalize the birth of the Savior were carefully chosen. To Simeon and Anna, who were leading an interior life, his coming was made known by the inspiration of the Holy Spirit. To the shepherds who, as Jews, were accustomed to divine signs in religious matters, he was made known by the message of angels. To the Magi, who were astrologers, he was manifested by a star. The order in which the Incarnation was revealed is most suitable. The shepherds represent the apostles and the first Jewish converts, among whom ". . . there were not many wise according to the flesh, not many mighty, not many noble" (I Cor. 1:26). The faith of Christ came next to the fulness of the Gentiles, represented by the Magi. Finally, faith came to the fulness of the Jews, represented by the righteous Simeon and Anna, who learned of Christ in the temple at Jerusalem.

It is the opinion of St. Thomas that the star which led the Magi to adore Christ, as a presage of the faith and devotion of the nations who were to come to Christ from afar, was a heavenly body created specially for this purpose.

3. Christ's Birth and the Law

The Old Law prescribed certain observances and ceremonies at the time of the birth of children (cf. Lev. 12). All of the prescriptions of the Law were fulfilled in the case of Christ. Eight days after his birth, the infant was circumcised. Thus the reality of his humanity was demonstrated; his approval of the ancient Jewish rite was given; his membership among the children of Abraham was indicated; his rejection by the Jews was forestalled; his teaching on obedience was exemplified; his acceptance of the divine remedies for human weakness was shown; and his willingness to accept the burdens of the Law to secure our freedom was proclaimed. At the same time he was named Jesus. And this name signifies the special prerogative of grace by which he is the Savior of all men, for the name Jesus means Savior.

The Old Law contained two precepts regarding newborn children. The first of these commanded that the mother should offer a sacrifice for every child when the time of her purification was over (Lev. 12:6). The second prescribed that the firstborn male should be consecrated to God (Exod. 13:12). Both of these precepts were fulfilled regarding Christ (Lk. 2:22-24). Although these observances among the Jews contained an acknowledgement of their sinfulness, they were fulfilled by Jesus and Mary rather as an example of humility and obedience, and to show the divine approval of the Law, and to forestall his rejection by the Jews on grounds that he rejected the Law. For he was sent to bring salvation ". . . to the Jew first, then to the Greek" (Rom. 1:16).

4. The Baptism of Christ

Besides the legal rites of the Jews, Christ submitted to the baptism of St. John as a prelude to his public ministry. This was not a true sacrament, but rather a kind of sacramental. In receiving this rite, Christ sanctified baptism and gave St. John the opportunity to fulfill his role as Precursor by announcing the coming of Christ to the multitudes. St. John also accustomed men to the rite of baptism in preparation for the institution of the sacrament, and he encouraged men to do penance in preparation for receiving the baptism of Christ.

The rite of the baptism of St. John was the result of a divine inspiration (cf. Jn. 1:33), but its efficacy came entirely from the dispositions of those who received it, and thus it differed essentially from the sacrament instituted by Christ which produces its effects by virtue of the rite itself, *ex opere operato*. The baptism of St. John did not cause grace in those who received it; his whole mission was to prepare men to receive the grace of Christ. This he did by his preaching, by getting them used to the rite of baptism, and by calling them to repent so that they could receive Christ's grace worthily. It is clear that those who had been baptized by St. John would have to be rebaptized sacramentally in order to share in the saving grace of Christ (cf. Acts 19:1-6).

5. Christ's Manner of Living

The suitability of any course of action must be judged in terms of the end in view. Now Christ came to ". . . save his people from their sins" (Matt. 1:21). It is in the light of this principle that St. Thomas inquires into the way in which he chose to live on this earth.

Christ's role as Savior demanded that he live among men, rather than as a solitary apart from the ordinary ways of life. He came to enlighten men with divine truth. "This is why I was born, and why I have come into the world, to bear witness to the truth" (Jn. 18:37). He came to save sinners, and that implies that he must go about and find them. "For the Son of Man came to seek and to save what was lost" (Lk. 19:10). He came to give us confidence in being able to approach God through him. "Let us have peace with God through our Lord Jesus Christ, through whom we also have access by faith unto that grace in which we stand, and exult in the hope of the glory of the sons of God" (Rom. 5:2). To accomplish these ends, it was most suitable that Christ should dwell among men as one of them.

The life of Christ was not one of unremitting activity. Rather did he live a life of action which flowed from the abundance of his contemplation. In view of the principle that Christ's action is our instruction, the way Christ lived teaches all those who engage in apostolic activity that there is a great need to retire periodically for rest and prayer and to avoid the pitfall of courting the favor of men.

In his association with others, Christ conformed to the common social customs. "The Son of Man came eating and drinking . . ." (Matt. 11:19). His example was later to be expressed by St. Paul, "I became all things to all men, that I might save all" (I Cor. 9:22). He gave a perfect example regarding all things that relate to salvation. "For the kingdom of God does not consist in food and drink, but in justice and peace and joy in the Holy Spirit" (Rom. 14:16). It is not the use, but the abuse of such things that makes them sinful. When Christ was with men, he used food and drink in the manner that would best serve his purpose of salvation. When he withdrew into the desert, he fasted and abstained to teach us the lesson that fasting is a powerful means of resisting evil.

By his own testimony, Christ was poor. "The Son of Man has nowhere to lay his head" (Matt. 8:21). This poverty was in keeping with his role as preacher of divine truth. Those who preach God's word should give themselves up entirely to this work; they cannot afford the care of wealth. His poverty was part of the price he paid for our redemption. "For you know the graciousness of our Lord Jesus Christ— how, being rich, he became poor for your sakes, that by his poverty you might become rich" (II Cor. 8:9). His poverty precluded the charge that he worked for earthly gain. Finally, the lowliness evidenced by his lack of worldly possessions manifested his divine power more effectively.

Throughout his life, Jesus Christ remained a devout Jew, faithful to all the precepts of the Old Law. Thus he showed approval of the Law. "Do not think that I have come to destroy the Law or the Prophets" (Matt. 5:17). By his obedience, Christ was able to show that the Law was ordained to himself and his mission.

"I have not come to destroy, but to fulfill" (Matt. 5:18). He also prevented the Jews from rejecting him on grounds that he rejected the Law. He delivered his followers from the bondage of the Law by his own obedience to it. "God sent his son . . . born under the Law, that he might redeem those who were under the Law . . ." (Gal. 4:4-5).

6. The Temptation

The temptation of Christ by Satan is one of the events in the gospel history that is full of meaning for every Christian. The temptation took place in the desert after Christ had fasted for forty days. He was alone. There were no witnesses. Whatever we know of this event must have been disclosed by Christ himself. In view of the principle that Christ's action is our instruction, the temptation deserves careful study.

Under the inspiration of the Holy Spirit, Christ went into the desert as to a battle-field to be tempted by the devil. Four reasons can be assigned for this:

1) He wished to strengthen us against our temptations. By his temptations he wished to overcome our temptations, just as by his death he conquered our death.

2) He wished to warn us that no degree of holiness insures anyone against temptation. "Son, when thou comest to the service of God, stand in justice and in fear, and prepare thy soul for temptation" (Sirach 2:1). The devil desires to overcome the virtuous above all.

3) He wished to give us a practical example of the means to be used in overcoming temptation.

4) He wished to strengthen our confidence in his mercy. "For we have not a high priest who cannot have compassion on our infirmities, but one tried as we are in all things except sin. Let us therefore draw near with confidence to the throne of grace, that we may obtain mercy and find grace to help in time of need" (Heb. 4:15-16).

The devil was unaware of the reality of Christ's divinity because he lacked the faith necessary to perceive this mystery. He was impelled by hatred and by envy to destroy the sanctity of this man whose works gave evidence of his holiness. The devil showed his ingenuity in choosing the lonely desert as the place for the temptation, for men are weakest when they are alone. "And if a man prevail against one, two shall withstand him" (Eccles. 4:12).

It was the devil's perception of Christ's hunger, the sign of his human frailty, that led him to begin the temptation. The fast which was the prelude to, and the occasion of the temptation also has an instructive value. It teaches the value of fasting as a source of strength against temptation. The fact that the temptation followed the fast indicates that all works of mortification are means of avoiding falls, not ways of escaping trials. Finally, Christ's temptation shows that the suggestion of the enemy is specially contrived to suit the individual's inclination. The devil does not begin to tempt spiritual men to great sins, but he begins with lesser ones so as to lead them almost imperceptibly to destruction.

St. Thomas finds an interesting parallel between the temptation of our first parents and the temptation of Christ:

Temptation of Adam and Eve (Gen. 3)	Temptation of Christ (Matt. 4:1-11; Lk. 4:1-13)
"Why has God commanded you, that you should not eat of every tree of paradise?" He appeals to common human curiosity, and suggests unreasonable means to satisfy it.	*"If thou art the Son of God, command that these stones become loaves of bread."* He appeals to hunger, and suggests unreasonabe use of power to satisfy it; Christ could have found bread in a nearby village.
"Your eyes shall be opened." He appeals to vainglory by promising them something new that is beyond the divine restrictions.	*"If thou art the Son of God, throw thyself down."* He suggests a vain display involving a presumptuous dependence upon God's protection.
"You shall be as gods, knowing good and evil." He appeals to their unbridled love of their own excellence and promises that they can become independent of God.	*"All these things will I give thee, if thou wilt fall down and worship me."* He appeals to pride that would lead to contempt for God by offering unjust dominion to be obtained by rejecting God.

The temptations are progressive. From the desire for food the devil sought to lead him to the vanity of the needless working of a miracle; and from this desire of vainglory, he tried to lead him to tempt God through pride by casting himself headlong from the mountain-top.

Christ emerged as victor after a remarkable struggle. Satan had seen Christ preparing to establish the kingdom of God, and he perceived that this might mean the end of his own reign. He hoped to deter Jesus from his purpose of becoming a spiritual savior. Satan can coexist with a military dictator or with a political ruler, but he has no part with a spiritual savior. With the man who is rash, ambitious or proud, he can come to terms. He was willing, in the last temptation, to forego part of his own kingdom to have such a man. But the offer was rejected and a battle was joined of which the ultimate outcome is as certain as was the decisive victory with which it began.

7. The Teaching of the Master

Christ came to save men from their sins. One of the principal means to accomplish this mission was to preach his divine message of truth. Yet the very methods of Christ's teaching seem rather to defeat his purpose. He spoke almost exclusively to the Jews. Much of what he said was offensive to the most powerful leaders of the people. Most of his teaching was couched in parables and figures that were not easy to grasp in their fulness. He left no written record of anything he said. Yet withal he was the greatest and most influential teacher in the history of the race. How can these apparent contradictions be reconciled?

St. Thomas invokes the principle that it is a sign of greater, and not lesser power to accomplish something through others rather than to do it by oneself. This principle can be applied to solve the questions about Christ's manner of teaching.

A. The Subjects of Christ's Teaching

It is true that Christ's teaching, although intended for the salvation of all, was directed first to the Jews. "I was not sent except to the lost sheep of the house of Israel" (Matt. 15:24). The Messias was promised first to the Jews, and divine providence directs everything in order. The divine message came first to those who believed in and worshipped the one true God, and through them to the Gentiles, just as the lower angels are enlightened by the higher. "I will send of them that shall be saved, to the Gentiles . . . to them that have not heard of me, and have not seen my glory. And they shall declare my glory to the Gentiles" (Isa. 66:19). If Christ and the apostles had gone first to the Gentiles, the chosen people would have had grounds for rejecting their teaching. Finally, it was by the Cross that Christ merited power over the Gentiles, and his Gospel was not preached to them until after the Passion, when he sent his disciples to men of all nations.

Christ came as the universal savior, first to the Jews and through them to the Gentiles. The salvation of all was preferable to the peace of any individuals whomsoever. Now the Scribes, Pharisees and leaders of the Jews were generally a hindrance to the preaching of the Gospel, and by their evil example they corrupted the morals of the people. Christ was undeterred by their taking offense, and he preached the truth which they hated and condemned the vices which they loved. Thus did he set the common good above the preference of even the leaders of the people.

B. The Manner of Christ's Teaching

Christ did not set out to conceal his teachings, nor did he propose different doctrines to different groups. But he did propose much of his doctrine in parables which the people were either unable or unworthy to grasp. Yet it was better for them to have his spiritual doctrine in parables rather than be deprived of it altogether. Then he instructed his disciples in the meaning of the parables so that they might hand it down to those who proved themselves worthy. "The things that thou hast heard from me through many witnesses, commend to trustworthy men who shall be competent in turn to teach others" (II Tim. 2:2).

In omitting to write down his teachings, St. Thomas says that Christ showed himself the most excellent of teachers, for he impressed his doctrines on the hearts of men. Then, too, his doctrine was so sublime that it cannot be captured fully by the written word. Had Christ written his message, men would have no deeper thought of it than what appears on the written page. Finally, he strove to spread his teaching in a most orderly manner, instructing his own disciples personally so that they could teach others by their words and writings.

The deeds of God are stamped with the impress of divine order, and that order is reflected in the method by which Christ taught. At first glance, it may strike us as less wise and less effective than the modern methods of publicity and propaganda. But how many men can remember last week's newspaper or last semester's texts? And how many have been instructed unto salvation by the methods employed by the greatest teacher the world has ever known?

8. The Purpose of Christ's Miracles

Miracles are here viewed by St. Thomas as among the instruments Christ used to fulfill his mission. The reality and possibility of miracles is assumed. The consideration follows a threefold division.

Miracles
  - In general
  - Specifically, the different kinds
  - Particularly, the Transfiguration.

A. Miracles in General

There are two reasons why God allows anyone to work miracles: first, to confirm what the man teaches; secondly, to indicate the presence of grace in an individual.

The teachings of faith are above and beyond reason; consequently, they must be confirmed by arguments that are divine rather than human. Now when a man performs works proper to God, we may safely believe that his message is divine. By a similar process of reasoning, we may safely conclude that God dwells by grace in him who does the works of God. Christ drew these two conclusions from his own miracles. (Cf. Jn. 10:34-38).

A **miracle** is defined as *an event perceivable by the senses and caused by God alone outside the ordinary course of created nature.* Many of the saints have performed miracles in the name and by the power of God. But Christ performed them in his own name and by his own divine power. And although the miracles were wrought both to confirm his teaching and to manifest his divine power, these purposes were subordinated to the needs of the salvation of mankind, which was the whole purpose of his having become man. Thus his first miracle, the changing of water into wine at Cana, was performed before he began to teach publicly, but it was a manifestation of his divine power that led his disciples to believe in him. (Cf. Jn. 2:1-11).

St. Thomas assigns three reasons to explain why the miracles of Christ gave sufficient grounds to believe in his divinity:

1) Because of the very nature of the things he did. Among the miracles of Christ were some which surpassed the entire power of nature and, consequently, could not be done except by divine power. (Cf. Jn. 9:32-33).

2) Because of the way in which he worked miracles on his own authority and by his own power, without dependence on prayer. (Cf. Jn. 5:19-21).

3) Because he clearly taught that he was God. This would never have been confirmed by miracles if it were false. (Cf. Mk. 1:27).

St. Thomas concludes this general consideration by saying: "When a particular work is proper to some agent, then that particular work is sufficient proof of the entire power of that agent. Thus, because the act of reasoning is proper to man, the mere fact that someone reasons about any particular proposition proves him to be a man. Similarly, since it is proper to God to work miracles by his own power, any single miracle worked by Christ through his own power is a sufficient proof that he is God."[6]

[6]*Summa*, III, q. 43, a. 4, ad 3.

Christ's miracles are not, however, a strict proof of his divinity, i.e., an argumentative proof based on principles known by natural reason. His divinity is of the supernatural order, which cannot be attained by reason but is known only on authority through faith. Nonetheless, these miracles are so clearly a sensible manifestation of his divine power that it becomes most reasonable to believe (i.e., to know through supernatural faith) his divinity and most rash to deny it.

B. The Kinds of Miracles Christ Performed

St. Thomas considers the miracles of Christ according to the four-fold division of subjects upon which they were worked:

1) He worked miracles by casting out *demons* to rescue by his divine power those who would believe in him.

2) He worked miracles on *heavenly bodies* which are subject to no earthly control and thus manifested his divine power.

3) Christ's miracles performed on *men* were a suitable demonstration that he was the savior of all men.

4) Christ's miracles worked on *irrational creatures* showed the universality of his power over all creation.

All of the miracles recorded in the gospels fall into one or another of the above categories. Taken together, they show the universality of Christ's divine power; singly, any one manifests by a sensible sign the truth of his teaching and the reality of his divinity.

C. The Transfiguration

St. Thomas singles out the Transfiguration as the most exceptional miracle of Christ and worthy of special attention. (Cf. Matt. 17:1-8; Mk. 9:2-8; Lk. 9:28-36). Our Lord had foretold his passion and had exhorted the disciples to follow the path of his sufferings (Matt. 16:21-24). Now when anyone is urged to undertake a hard and painful task, he must know something of the end that gives purpose to his suffering. Christ's passion is the road to the manifestation of his physical glory.

Thus he gave Peter, James and John a glimpse of his glory to strengthen them for the persecution they would endure in sharing in his passion.

For a moment he allowed the glory of his Godhead and of his beatified soul to shine forth in his body and to become visible to his disciples. This was a miraculous occurrence, because this quality of clarity was not natural to Christ's body before his resurrection. He appeared in the presence of Moses and Elias as the representatives of the witnesses who preceded him, and to Peter, James and John as witnesses who would come after him. In the midst of the vision they heard the voice of the heavenly Father, "This is my beloved Son, in whom I am well pleased; hear him" (Matt. 17:6). Thus did the Father give personal testimony to the natural sonship of Christ.

9. Summary and Conclusion

The reality of a theocentric universe becomes terribly important when God is given a face and a name. For God became man. The Second Person of the Blessed Trinity, generated before all ages in the womb of eternity, became the Son of a virgin, and lived out his life as true Son of God and true son of Mary. The living God who said, "I am the living bread," was born in Bethlehem, the "House of Bread," at a time appointed in the divine plan of redemption.

By a curious paradox, the Savior who came to lead all men to the vineyards of heaven manifested his coming to a mere handful of the race of man: the shepherds, the Magi, Simeon and Anna. Those who were given this singular privilege, however, were a carefully chosen cross-section of the totality of humanity. The shepherds represented the simple men who became the wise apostles of Christ; the Magi, the Gentiles who would be given the light of faith; and Simeon and Anna, the Jews whose faith in a redeemer had been fulfilled.

One important consideration crowds in upon the narrow room of our knowledge concerning the life of the child Jesus. From the moment of his birth he subjected himself to the maze of religious legalities which were the code of life for all Jews. He was circumcised, his mother offered sacrifice for him when the time of her purification was completed, and he, as the first-born male child, was consecrated to God. Even though he was above and beyond the bonds of any law, Christ had good reason for fulfilling the Jewish code. He wanted to show humility and obedience as an example to all men; he wanted to give his approval of the Law; and he wanted to give evidence that he did not reject the Law, a denial which in later years might have been used against him.

At the time of his baptism in the Jordan by John, Christ began to manifest his divine mission. He sanctified the rite of baptism by submitting to it at the hand of John. He took a sacramental, a rite whose efficacy depended upon the dispositions of the receiver, and made of it a sacrament, a rite whose efficacy is produced by virtue of the rite itself.

In order to teach men, Christ had to live among them and talk with them. He ate and drank and slept, and carried on all of the physical functions necessary to life. He was an active man, seeking out sinners and preaching the truth. And yet his activities flowed from a life of intense contemplation, for his was at all times the vision of God. Christ was also a poor man in order that he could spend all of his time in the pursuit of his Father's business without the burden of wealth to distract him.

Like our first parents, Christ underwent a series of temptations. He allowed himself to be tempted by the devil to show us that it is the lot of man to be tempted and that resistance depends upon the strength which comes to us through confidence in the mercy of God.

Christ, in his role as redeemer, both taught men his claim to divinity and proved his teachings by working miracles on his own authority. He showed that his power was universal, and in the miracle of the Transfiguration gave an irrefutable sign that God was his Father.

The following conclusions are derived from our discussion of Christ's life and ministry.

1. The first of Christ's numerous miracles was, in a sense, the prototype of those which followed. For Christ commanded the servant

to fill the jars with water, and having done this, to draw a sample from one of the jars and give it to the chief steward of the feast. The reaction of the steward was immediate: "Every man at first sets forth the good wine, and when they have drunk freely, then that which is poorer. But thou hast kept the good wine until now."[7] These words of the servant, when applied to Christ's other miracles, signify that the end product of Christ's power is greater than what nature can produce herself. Thus when Christ raised men to life, he also raised them to the life of the spirit, and when Christ healed the sick, he healed the soul along with the body.

2. The social workers who devote their lives to bettering the living conditions of the poor and sick of every race cannot perform efficacious works without contemplating the life and ministry of Christ. Christ is *the* exemplar for those who would learn compassion for the sufferings of others.

3. "Oftentimes God threatens us, not that he may inflict evils upon us, but to draw us to himself. And when we return to him, immediately he banishes our fear; for were we to feel the same security in temptations as when at peace, then there would be no need for us to be tempted. But why do I speak of *us*? For even holy men for this purpose were grievously tried: 'It is good for me that thou hast humbled me' (Ps. 118:71). And he himself has said to the apostles: 'In the world you shall have distress' (Jn. 16:33). And Paul implies the same thing when he says: 'There was given me a sting of my flesh, an angel of Satan to buffet me' (II Cor. 12:7). Even though he had prayed to be delivered from temptation, yet his prayer was not answered, because from his very temptation he drew great profit."[8]

4. Christ's life and ministry is reported to us in the liturgy of the Church through the Sunday epistles and gospels. These are designed to teach the faithful of today in the same manner that Christ taught the Jews of old.

5. "It is in the days of trial, rather than in untroubled hours, that men of all nations should realize that they are brothers. The real

[7]Jn. 2:10.
[8]St. John Chrysostom, *Tenth Homily on the Gospel according to St. Matthew.*

meaning, the lofty mission and the power to reconcile of this brotherhood has never been, nor shall ever be, extolled with such force as it
was by 'the firstborn among many brethren' (Romans 8:29), who from
Bethlehem to Golgotha preached by his example more than by his
words that great and universal brotherhood of man."[9]

BIBLIOGRAPHICAL NOTE

An overall picture of the life of Christ can be found in the second
volume of the English *Summa,* Part III, Questions XXXI-XLV. Many
technical reviews of his life have been written throughout the ages.
However, mention will be made here of those whose origin is more
recent. *The Life of Christ* (Milwaukee: The Bruce Publishing Co.,
1952), by Guiseppe Riciotti is an example of scholarly research; a
book which is exclusively historical and documentary. Père M.-J.
Lagrange, O.P., has written a highly recommended book entitled
The Gospel of Jesus Christ (London: Burns, Oates and Washbourne,
Ltd., 1950). In this work, Père Lagrange attempts to solve the
difficulties presented by the gospel narratives of Christ's life, work
and ministry.

Perhaps more popular in style is the two volume work *Jesus Christ*
(Milwaukee: The Bruce Publishing Co., 1950), by Ferdinand Prat,
S.J. In this book Father Prat combines scholarly research and intelligible phraseology. *The Son of God* (London: Sheed and Ward,
1934), by Karl Adam, is an example of a life of Christ written from an
apologist's point of view.

The Bible, of course, is the greatest source for meditation on the
story of Christ. Among commentators who approach Christ's life as
a subject of meditation is Romano Guardini. His work, *The Lord*
(Chicago: Regnery, 1954), selects this or that event or teaching, plucks
it out of chronological order, and proceeds to show points for meditation without referring to scientific documentation.

[9]Pope Pius XII, *Christmas Message,* Dec. 24, 1947.

CHAPTER SEVEN

The Passion, Death and Resurrection of Christ

1. Introduction

St. Thomas treats of the sufferings and death of Christ immediately after his consideration of Christ's miracles. We are thus confronted successively with an insight into Christ's divine power and a consideration of his most profound abasement. Christ's death was decreed by the heavenly Father, and yet he laid down his life freely. In this lies the mystery of our redemption.

But the death of Christ is only an apparent defeat; in reality it is the greatest of triumphs, a victory over death, over the devil, over the bondage of sin and sin itself. It is followed in quick succession by Christ's resurrection and ascension, and by his exaltation in heaven at the right hand of his Father.

Reserving this exaltation of Christ for later theological consideration, we will now examine the mystery of his passion and death—the reception of our redemption—and the problems connected with these mysteries. They will be considered according to the outline which follows on the next page.

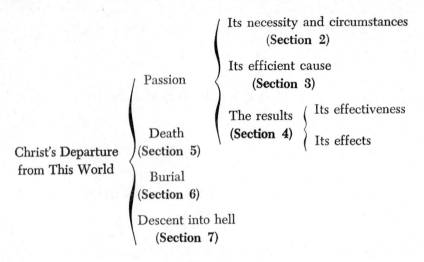

Christ's Departure from This World
- Passion
  - Its necessity and circumstances (**Section 2**)
  - Its efficient cause (**Section 3**)
  - The results (**Section 4**)
    - Its effectiveness
    - Its effects
- Death (**Section 5**)
- Burial (**Section 6**)
- Descent into hell (**Section 7**)

2. The Necessity of Christ's Passion

Was the Passion truly necessary for our salvation? To answer, it is essential to grasp the various meanings of the term *necessity*.

Anything is said to be necessary when it cannot be other than it is. There are various degrees of necessity:

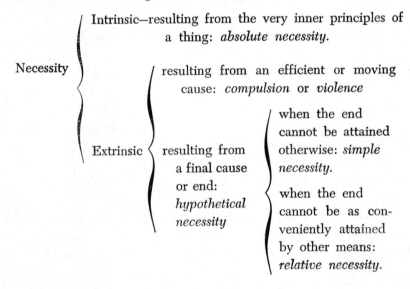

Necessity
- Intrinsic—resulting from the very inner principles of a thing: *absolute necessity*.
- Extrinsic
  - resulting from an efficient or moving cause: *compulsion* or *violence*
  - resulting from a final cause or end: *hypothetical necessity*
    - when the end cannot be attained otherwise: *simple necessity*.
    - when the end cannot be as conveniently attained by other means: *relative necessity*.

A. The Passion Itself

(1) Its Relative Necessity

With this understanding of the kinds and degrees of necessity, we may reach the following conclusions with respect to the necessity of Christ's sufferings:

1) It is clear that there was no **absolute** necessity for Christ's passion, either on God's part or on man's.

2) There was neither **compulsion** nor **violence**, because the Father was not compelled to decree the passion, and Christ undertook his sufferings willingly.

3) Granted God's will to free mankind from sin, there was still no **absolute** necessity for the passion, because the divine omnipotence was not limited to this one means.

4) There was, however a **relative** necessity for the passion—i.e., from the point of view of the end proposed by Almighty God—for three reasons:

   a) because we were delivered by the passion (Jn. 3:14);

   b) because Christ merited the glory of his exaltation through the humiliation of his passion (Lk. 24:26);

   c) because the Father's decree of Christ's passion, as foretold by the Scriptures, had to be fulfilled (Isa. 53:4, 5; cf. Lk. 22:22, 24:44, 46).

The passion was uniquely suited to manifest both Christ's mercy and his justice. His sufferings and death were a true payment for the offenses of mankind, and thus men are made free by the justice of Christ. The passion discharged a debt which man unaided could never pay, and thus men are redeemed by his mercy. Indeed, Christ's payment for sin by his passion was more merciful than a simple dismissal of the debt, for greater mercy is shown in assuming an obligation than in remitting it.

Absolutely speaking, then, it was possible for mankind to be delivered from sin by some means other than Christ's passion. But on the supposition that God foreknew and decreed the passion as the means of salvation, then it was not possible at the same time for man to be saved in some other way and for Christ not to suffer. To maintain the contrary, one must assume that God's foreknowledge can be deceived and that his decrees can be frustrated.

If God had decreed to dismiss the debt of sin without any satisfaction, he would have acted mercifully, but not unjustly. The reason is that God is absolutely supreme and above every right. Thus if he forgave a sin committed against himself he would injure no one. Similarly, anyone can forgive a personal affront without injuring the rights of anyone.

(2) The Eminent Fittingness of the Passion

The passion emerges as the most suitable means of redemption, for not only does it obtain our deliverance from sin (this was possible in other ways, as we have seen) but it produces many concurring means which are helpful to man's salvation:

1) It was a compelling demonstration of God's love which calls for a return of love, and love is the perfection of human salvation. (Cf. Rom. 5:8.)

2) It exemplified obedience, humility, constancy, justice and the other virtues necessary for salvation (I Pet. 2:21).

3) It not only delivered man from sin but merited justifying grace and glory for mankind.

4) It provided a stronger reason for avoiding sin (I Cor. 4:20).

5) It enhanced human dignity by showing that the devil, who had overcome men, would in turn be overcome by a man; and that as men had deserved death, a man would conquer death by dying (I Cor. 15:57).

B. The Circumstances of the Passion

The purpose of St. Thomas' inquiry into the circumstances of the passion is to show how every last detail conspired to further the Redemption and to bring about the greatest good for mankind. The circumstances to be considered are these: the crucifixion; the extent and intensity of his sufferings; the time and place of his death; his association with thieves on Calvary.

(1) The Crucifixion

The purpose of the Redemption was to save mankind from sin. Death by crucifixion was especially suitable for this purpose because of these reasons:

1) Crucifixion, which is the most fearsome of deaths, gave an example of virtue that strengthens upright men against fear of death by any means whatsoever.

2) Adam's sin consisted in taking fruit of the forbidden tree against the divine command. It was fitting that Christ should be fastened to the tree of the cross in atonement, as if to restore what Adam had taken.

3) By being raised on a cross, Christ symbolized his sanctification of the elements and his preparation of an ascent into heaven for us.

4) His position on the cross, with outstretched arms, indicated the universality of the salvation he brought for all men.

5) As St. Augustine indicates, he turned the tree of the cross into the chair from which the Master gave his final teaching.

The cross, then, is a symbol and an expression of the immeasurable love which is the source of the redemption. "For God so loved the world that he gave his only-begotten Son, that those who believe in him may not perish, but may have life everlasting" (Jn. 4:16).

(2) The Extent of Christ's Sufferings

Did Christ endure all human suffering? Certainly he was not afflicted by the evils which directly affect the welfare of the soul—sin, loss of grace, ignorance. Nor did he endure the suffering caused by internal disorders, like tuberculosis, leprosy, cancer, etc. St. Athanasius remarks that it was not befitting him who healed the infirmities of others to have his own body afflicted with the same.[1]

Of the sufferings of Christ inflicted by external forces, he could not have endured every specific suffering, because some of them, like burning and drowning, are mutually exclusive. But he did endure each *kind* of suffering, and this in three ways:

[1] *Discourse on the Incarnation of the Word*, nn. 22, 23.

1) On the part of men who tormented him, he suffered from Jews and Gentiles; men and women; rulers, servants and the mob; friends and acquaintances.

2) On the part of the ways man can suffer, he suffered from his friends who abandoned him; in his reputation, from the blasphemies hurled at him; in his honor and glory, from the mockeries and insults heaped upon him; in his possessions, when he was stripped of his garments; in his soul, from sadness, weariness and fear; in his body, from wounds and scourging.

3) On the part of the members of his body, he suffered in his head, from the crown of thorns; in his hands and feet, from the nails; on his face, from blows and spittle; and throughout his body, from lashes. Every one of his senses was afflicted: touch, by the nails and scourges; taste, by vinegar and gall; smell, by being crucified in a malodorous place of execution; hearing, by the shouts of blasphemers; sight, by the tears of his mother and the disciple whom he loved.

There was, then, a kind of universal extent to the sufferings of Christ in a generic, rather than a specific sense. Any one of his actions, even a wave of his hand, would have sufficed to redeem us. But Christ's action is our instruction, and he underwent the entire weight of his passion to teach us the horror of sin from which he saved us because of his love.

(3) The Intensity of Christ's Sufferings

Did Christ suffer more than any other man? St. Thomas replies that both the sensible pain and the interior pain of the Passion were the greatest in this life. He offers four reasons:

1) Because of the sources of his pain: the frightful pain of crucifixion; the sadness arising from the weight of the sins of the world, from the rejection of his own people, and from the cowardice of his disciples.

2) Because of his special susceptibility to suffering, both in soul and body: Christ's human nature was the miraculous result of the power of the Holy Spirit; it was more perfect than that of ordinary mortals. His sense of touch, which experienced pain,

and his interior faculties, which apprehended the causes of sadness, were more acute than ordinary.

3) Because he abandoned himself wholly to his passion, without
any effort to mitigate his sufferings or to distract himself from
his pain.

4) Because he embraced an amount of pain proportionate to the
fruit of the Redemption, and that was universal.

Christ's sufferings, great as they were, did not interfere with his
free will. Indeed, throughout the passion the higher faculties of his
soul continually enjoyed the beatific vision. But this supernatural
peace and joy did not mitigate his sufferings, for it was not allowed
to overflow either into the lower faculties of his soul or into his senses.

(4) The Other Circumstances of the Crucifixion

In speaking of himself under the figure of the Good Shepherd, Christ
said, ". . . I lay down my life that I may take it up again. No one
takes it from me, but I lay it down of myself" (Jn. 10:18). Every detail
of Christ's death was subject to his will, and his will was ruled by the
divine wisdom which ". . . orders all things sweetly" (Wis. 8:1).
It follows that the Passion occurred at the most suitable time and
place for the purposes of the Redemption.

By crucifying him between two thieves, the Jews hoped to associate
him in their guilt. But this failed, because the thieves are forgotten
while Christ's cross is honored. There is also a symbol of the Last
Judgment here. The converted thief on Christ's right symbolizes the
elect who will stand in the same place at the Judgment, while the im-
penitent thief on the left represents the reprobate who will stand
there on the Last Day.

C. The Passion of God

In considering the principal details of the passion, we may well
inquire if all this suffering may be attributed to Christ's divinity. To
answer this question some basic notions of the Incarnation must be
recalled. The union of divine and human nature was effected in the
person of Christ in such a way that the distinction between the natures
was preserved. The passion must be attributed to the person of

Christ, because actions are proper to a person, not to a nature. Yet nature is a principle in virtue of which the person acts. Now Christ's divine nature could not become capable of suffering. Consequently, we must say that the sufferings and death of Christ are to be attributed to his person because of the human nature he had assumed. This doctrine is summarized in one of St. Cyril's anathemas against Nestorius: "If anyone does not confess that the Word of God suffered in the flesh, and was crucified in the flesh, and experienced death in the flesh, . . . let him be anathema."[2]

3. The Cause of Christ's Passion

Because of the admixture of human and divine elements in the passion, it is necessary to make several inquiries into its causes in order better to understand the plan of Redemption.

A. The Role of Christ and of His Father

The first and most obvious problem is to determine Christ's own role as a cause of his passion. It is evident from the gospels that Christ could have prevented his enemies from putting him to death (cf. Lk. 4:30; Jn. 10:18, 18:8). Christ, then, is the *indirect* cause of his passion, because he did not prevent it when he could have done so. But it was his persecutors who were the *direct* cause of the Passion—they inflicted mortal wounds, and thereby deliberately brought about his death.

Christ endured his passion in a spirit of obedience, he died voluntarily of his own free will, ". . . becoming obedient to death, even to death on a cross" (Phil. 2:8). This voluntary obedience was perfectly suited to the end of the Redemption:

1) "For just as by the disobedience of the one man the many were constituted sinners, so also by the obedience of the one the many will be constituted just" (Rom. 5:19).

2) It reconciled man to God by a sacrifice, for obedience is the most acceptable of sacrifices. (Cf. I Kings 15:22.)

[2]Cf. Denz. 124.

3) Thus Christ became victorious over death and over the devil who is its author, for "an obedient man shall speak of victory" (Prov. 21:28).

The heavenly Father, who ". . . has not spared even his own Son but has delivered him for us all" (Rom. 8:32), was also a cause of the passion. This is evident in three ways:

1) The Father preordained the passion as the means of redeeming mankind. (Cf. Isa. 53:6, 10.)

2) The Father inspired Christ by charity with the will to suffer for us. (*Ibid.*, 7.)

3) The Father did not protect him, but abandoned him to the fury of his persecutors. (Cf. Matt. 27:46.)

It would be a grave mistake to conclude that the Father decreed the passion to satisfy his severity, after the manner of Shylock. The divine purpose in the passion was to impress mankind with a proper horror of sin and to offer a compelling example of love to reclaim men from sin. The motive of the Father in decreeing the passion, and of Christ in accepting it, was a motive of love.

The motives of some of the others who were intimately concerned were wicked and blameworthy. Judas betrayed him because of greed; the Jews because of envy; Pilate because of worldly fear. But even some of this evil was turned to good, because the effects of the passion were foreshadowed in the way it was accomplished. The passion wrought its first effects among the Jews (Acts 2:41; 4:4), and it was at the hands of the Jews that Christ first began his sufferings. Later, the effects of the passion were spread abroad among the Gentiles who completed the work of crucifixion after the Jews delivered him up.

B. The Responsibility of His Persecutors

Did Christ's persecutors recognize him? Various texts of the Scriptures seem to give contradictory answers to this question. "But now they have seen, and have hated both me and my Father" (Jn. 15:24; cf. Matt. 22:38, 45). On the other hand, Christ prayed, "Father, forgive them, for they do not know what they are doing" (Lk. 23:34; cf. I Cor. 2:8; Acts 3:17).

To solve this difficulty, St. Thomas distinguishes first between the rulers and the common people, and, secondly, between knowledge of Christ as Messias and Christ as God.

Now the Jewish leaders, who were well versed in the prophecies which foretold the coming of the Savior, knew that he was the promised Messias because they saw all the signs fulfilled in him. But they did not recognize the mystery of his divinity. In this sense St. Paul says that, if they had known it, they would not have crucified the Lord of glory. Their ignorance, however, did not excuse them from crime, because it was *affected* ignorance. This rather increases guilt, for it manifests a will to sin so strong that it pretends ignorance to facilitate sinning.

The common people, who had not grasped the meaning of the scriptural prophecies, did not understand either that he was the Messias or that he was the Son of God. Only a minority believed in him, and when others were impressed by his miracles or by the force of his teaching, they were promptly deceived or threatened by their rulers. (Cf. Jn. 9:1-41.)

This perceptive analysis reconciles the various passages of the Scriptures and demonstrates the falsity of those teachings which would conclude that the gospels give a wholesale condemnation of the Jews.

We may now make an assessment of the objective gravity of the sins of those who were implicated in the crucifixion:

1) The most grievous crime was that of Judas. He shared the basic malice of the rulers, and even surpassed it. He was an apostle, a witness of Christ's miracles, and himself a worker of miracles in Christ's name. By approving of St. Peter's words, "Thou art Christ" (Matt. 16:16), he professed his faith. Thus to greed and envy, he added the malice of ingratitude and betrayal. The gravity of his sin was compounded into the most grievous crime of all Christ's persecutors.

2) The rulers and chief priests delivered him up out of envy and hatred, to which was added the malice of affected ignorance.

3) The common people sinned also, but their guilt was mitigated by their real ignorance.

4) Pontius Pilate condemned Christ, but he was not only ignorant but also afraid of Caesar.

5) The crime of the Gentile executioners was least of all, for they carried out the orders of their leaders and had no knowledge of the Law.

4. The Effects of Christ's Passion

A. The Manner in Which It Procures Our Salvation

Sacred Scripture speaks of mankind's salvation in different ways, as a sacrifice, a redemption, a payment, etc. Thus there are various ways in which our salvation was procured by Christ, even though the entire work of salvation is basically a work of love, and all other modes derive their efficacy from the charity of Christ.

St. Thomas examines in detail the several ways that Christ's passion brought about our salvation, proceeding carefully from the more to the less universal.

1) By his passion Christ **merited** salvation for all his members. Christ received grace as an individual and also as head of the Church; thus Christ's works redound both to himself and to his members. Now whoever suffers for justice's sake while he is in the state of grace merits his salvation. Consequently, by his passion Christ merited salvation for himself and for all his members. This teaching has been defined by the Council of Trent.[3]

2) By his passion Christ made **atonement**, i.e., **satisfaction**, for all sins. Atonement is made whenever someone offers as recompense something the offended party loves as much or more than he detested the offense. But by suffering through love and obedience, Christ offered God more than was required to compensate for the offenses of all mankind:

    a) because of the intense love with which he suffered;

    b) because the life he laid down was both human and divine;

    c) because of the magnitude of his sufferings.

---

[3]Sess. VI, 1547, *Decree on Justification*, Chap. 7 (Denz. 799); cf. Can. 10 (Denz. 820).

Consequently, the Passion was a superabundant atonement for all sin. (Cf. I Jn. 2:2.)

3) In his passion, Christ procured our salvation by **sacrifice.** Properly speaking, a sacrifice is something done for the honor of God alone, in order to appease him. Now Christ's free submission to his passion was most acceptable to God because it resulted from his great love. It is manifest, then, that Christ's passion is a true sacrifice. It is a matter of faith that Christ is a priest and that he offered himself as a true sacrifice. (See Chapter Five, Section 4.)

4) By his passion, Christ paid our **redemption.** In this context "redemption" is restricted to mean "liberation from the bondage of sin, from the debt of punishment and the slavery of the devil." Sin creates a double servitude: the bondage of sin (Jn. 8:34), and the obligation to undergo punishment. Now Christ's passion was a satisfaction for both of these. Therefore it redeemed us from both bondages, because in the Passion, Christ paid the price of himself to redeem us.

5) Since Christ's humanity is the instrument of his divinity (cf. Chapter Four, Section 5), his passion accomplishes man's salvation as **efficient cause,** operating instrumentally in virtue of his Godhead for the salvation of mankind.

In summary, Christ's passion caused our salvation by way of merit, satisfaction, sacrifice, redemption and efficiency. It was Christ's life which was the price of redemption, and it was Christ himself who paid it, under the inspiration he received as man from the Blessed Trinity.

B. The Benefits Acquired by Christ's Passion

After considering precisely *how* the Passion secured our deliverance from sin, St. Thomas seeks to determine exactly *what* particular benefits we received in the redemption.

(1) Its Effects

The Church teaches that Christ redeemed us in such a way that he repaired the nature which Adam had lost.[4] Further, it teaches that

---

[4]Cf. Second Council of Orange, 529 (Denz. 194); Council of Trent, *ibid.* (Denz. 800).

Christ, by his crucifixion, redeemed mankind from sin and reconciled him with the Father.[5] The passion satisfied for the sins of the whole world, even for the sins of the damned.[6]

The following are the effects of Christ's passion:

1) The passion **delivered us from sin.** Christ is the Head, we are the members of his Mystical Body. By laying down his life through love and obedience, he paid the price of our sins. Similarly, a man may repair by the work of his hands the damage he has caused by his feet.

2) The passion **freed us from the devil's domination.** Man became a slave of the devil through sin (Jn. 8:34; II Pet. 2:19). The Passion paid the price of our sins, and hence freed us from the dominion of Satan. Although, God so permitting, the devil can still tempt men's souls and harass their bodies, a remedy is found in Christ's passion for men to defend themselves against the devil's snares so as to avoid eternal destruction.

3) The passion **freed us from the debt of punishment.** Christ's passion made superabundant satisfaction for all sin, and thus discharged the debt of punishment. Even should one fall into sin after baptism, by the co-operation of Christ's passion a much lighter penalty (e.g., sacramental penance) suffices than one proportionate to the sin.

4) The passion **reconciled us to God.** Sin made us enemies of God. But the passion destroyed sin and thus restored us to the divine friendship. This was not done by working a change in God, but by taking away the source of the divine hatred, and by making compensation through a more pleasing offering.

5) The passion **opened the gates of heaven.** Christ satisfied both for original and actual sin, which had kept the gates of heaven locked to mankind (Heb. 9:11-12). Although the saints of the Old Testament had merited, by faith and works, the kingdom of heaven, enjoyment of the beatific vision was denied them until the barrier had been removed at the cost of Christ's blood.

[5]Cf. the constitution of Pope Paul IV, *Cum quorundam;* Denz. 993.
[6]Cf. Second Council of Valence, 855 (Denz. 323); Council of Trent, *ibid.,* Chap. 2 (Denz. 794).

6) The passion merited **Christ's exaltation.** "He humbled himself, becoming obedient to death, even to death on a cross. Therefore God also has exalted him . . ." (Phil. 2:8-9). This exaltation was fourfold: the humility of his passion and death was rewarded by his resurrection; the humility of his burial and descent into hell, by his ascension; the shame and mockery he endured, by his place at the right hand of the Father; his subjection to man's power, by the power of judgment given him over all men.

(2) Its Universality

It is clear that Christ's redemption is universal. That means that the passion was sufficient to redeem all men, from all sins, and to restore all good things that were lost by sin.

The Church teaches that Christ died for all men. "But, although he died for all, yet all do not receive the benefit of his death, but those only to whom the merit of his passion is communicated."[7] Theologians generally maintain that Christ died even for unbaptized infants, because he merited the grace of baptism for them, even if its reception was prevented by some failure permitted by God in secondary causes. The Scriptures simply maintain in a general way that Christ died for all (Rom. 5:18; I Jn. 2:2).

Although Christ satisfied sufficiently for all sins, this satisfaction must be effected in each individual by having the merits of Christ applied through faith, charity, the sacraments and good works. No adult is ever saved without his co-operation. The means which Christ established must be used by each one.

Christ's passion restores to mankind all the goods lost through sin. This is a work begun in this life and completed in the next. Christ sufficiently merited for all not only habitual grace but also the actual graces that precede and follow justification, and eternal life itself. Likewise he merited whatever natural goods are conducive to salvation. The reason he did not merit the restoration in this life of the preternatural gifts of freedom from death, sickness, error and concupiscence is to leave us with the opportunity to be united to his own suffer-

---

[7]Council of Trent, *ibid.*, Chap. 3; Denz. 795.

ings. He did merit that these defects should not conquer us, and that they shall be completely eliminated in heaven.

5. The Effects of Christ's Death

The reality of Christ's death is clearly taught in the Scriptures; it is incorporated into the teaching of the Church.[8] His death was prophesied by Caiphas: "It is expedient for us that one man die for the people, instead of the whole nation perishing" (Jn. 11:50).

It was fitting for Christ to die for the redemption of mankind for several reasons:

1) By dying, Christ satisfied for the entire human race, which was sentenced to die for its sins. To undergo the penalty deserved by another is a suitable way of making satisfaction for him.

2) Christ's death manifested the reality of his human nature.

3) By dying, Christ delivered men ". . . who, throughout their life, were kept in servitude by the fear of death" (Heb. 2:15).

4) By dying because of the penalty of sin, Christ teaches us to die spiritually to sin. (Cf. Rom. 6:11.)

5) The reality of his death, which was overcome in the resurrection, gave us a real hope of arising from the dead.

Christ's death was real, and his body and soul truly separated. Was his divine nature also separated from his body at the time of his death? The union of the divine nature to human nature in the person of Christ was the result of the special grace of the Hypostatic Union. This grace was the greatest gift ever bestowed; it made Jesus Christ the natural Son of God. It was immeasurably greater than the grace by which men are sanctified and become the adopted sons of God. Now sanctifying grace is never lost except through sin; much less would the greater gift of union be lost without fault. Christ, however, was without sin. Therefore, the union of the divine nature with the body of Christ, a substantial constituent of his human na-

[8]Cf. the anathemas of St. Cyril of Jerusalem against Nestorius, Can. 12 (Denz. 124); not a statement of the solemn magisterium, these anathemas yet enjoy, properly interpreted, the authority of the Church's ordinary teaching office.

ture, was not dissolved by his death. The body of Christ remained personally and hypostatically united to the divine nature in the Word of God even after his death.

By the same token, the soul of Christ, although separated from his body by death, remained personally and hypostatically united to the divine nature in the Word of God. The union of his soul to the Word is more immediate and primary than that of his body. Thus we say in the Creed: "He descended into hell." Now this refers to his soul, for the body remained in the tomb. Yet we say "*he* descended," denoting the person who remained united to his soul.

The person of Christ is eternal. He did not result from the union of the human and divine natures; he did not result from the union of his body and soul. When the union of body and soul was dissolved by death, each separately remained united to his Godhead in, and according to his divine personality.

Christ's body, dead in the tomb, still remained an instrument of his divine nature; it still remained a cause of our redemption. The dead Christ could not merit for us, it is true. But because his body remained the instrument of his divinity, it continued to remove the obstacles to our salvation which are the death of the soul and the death of the body. Christ's death destroyed sin, which is the death of our souls, because he ". . . was delivered up for our sins" (Rom. 4:25). And our bodily death, which is the result of sin, was conquered by his death, for "death is swallowed up in victory" (I Cor. 15:54).

6. The Lessons of Christ's Burial

As St. Thomas points out, there is much for Christ's followers to learn from the burial of their Master. He says:

> It was fitting for Christ to be buried. First of all, to establish the truth of his death; for no one is laid in the grave until the certainty of death has been established. Thus we read (Mk. 15:44-45) that Pilate, before he would grant leave for Christ to be buried, determined by diligent inquiry that he was dead.
>
> Secondly, to give hope to those in the grave, by his arising from the tomb, that they would rise again through him. This he himself prophesied: "Amen, amen, I say to you, the hour is coming, and now is here, when the dead shall hear the voice of the Son of God, and those who hear shall live" (Jn. 5:25; cf. 28-29).

Thirdly, to give an example to those who, through his death, die spiritually to their sins—those, that is, who are hidden "from the disturbance of men" (Ps. 30:21). Hence it is said, "You have died and your life is hidden with Christ in God" (Col. 3:3). For this same reason, the baptized, who are dead to sin through Christ's death, are as if buried together with Christ by immersion. This is what St. Paul points out: "Do you not know that all we who have been baptized into Christ Jesus have been baptized into his death? For we were buried with him by means of baptism into death, in order that, just as Christ has arisen from the dead through the glory of the Father, so we also may walk in newness of life" (Rom. 6:3-4).[9]

Even in the tomb, however, the body of Christ remained incorrupt, in order to manifest his divine power and show that he died, not from weakness, but through the voluntary acceptance of the sufferings inflicted on him. For two nights and a day his body remained in the tomb, clearly showing the reality of his death.

7. The Descent into Hell

"Neither was he abandoned to hell, nor did his flesh undergo decay" (Acts 2:31). These words of St. Peter's first sermon (cf. Acts 2:14-36; especially v. 24 and v. 27) state the defined truth: while his body remained in the tomb, Christ's soul "descended into hell."[10]

This fact may seem puzzling to us unless we realize two things:

1) The word "hell" is not restricted to the place of the damned but may signify any of the "lower regions"—purgatory, limbo, or the temporary abode of the saints of the Old Law.

2) A thing is said to be present somewhere either *by its essence* (**substantially**) or *by its effect* (**in virtue of its power** to produce an effect somewhere).

[9]*Summa*, III, q. 51, a. 1.

[10]The Fourth Lateran Council, Chap. 1, 1215 (Denz. 429), explicitly states: "he descended into hell, arose from the dead, and ascended into heaven; but he descended in his soul, arose in his body, and ascended equally in both." The essential truth had already by the fifth century been incorporated in the Apostles' Creed (Denz. 6) and in the "Athanasian" Creed (Denz. 40) and was an explicit belief of the primitive Church (cf. St. Ignatius, *Letter to the Magnesians*, 9:2; St. Justin Martyr, *Dialogue with Trypho*, 72 and 99; St. Irenaeus, *Against Heresies*, Bk. III, Chap. 20, n. 4 and Bk. IV, Chap. 22, n. 1; Tertullian, Clement of Alexandria, Hippolytus; etc.). St. Peter's clear testimony, and the witness of St. Paul (Rom. 10:6, f.), as well as more dubious texts (Eph. 4:9 f.; I Pet. 3:19 f.; the interpretation of the "sign of Jonah," Matt. 12:40), are the revealed basis for this belief.

With these distinctions in mind, we may reach the following conclusions:

1) Christ's soul was **substantially** present (and hence Christ himself, for his person is hypostatically united with his soul as with his body) only in the "hell" of the just, and this throughout the time his body remained in the tomb. By this "descent"—to be understood metaphorically, for the spiritual soul does not move as bodies do—he delivered the saints of the Old Law from the penalty of original sin which excluded them from the life of glory, applying to them the fruits of his passion.

2) Since Christ's descent into hell produces deliverance through the power of his passion, those only are delivered who were united to his passion through faith quickened by charity. Hence neither the damned, nor children who died in original sin shared in the deliverance from hell, but those in purgatory who were cleansed sufficiently were delivered. Nonetheless, he was present to them **by his effect**, the damned feeling shame and confusion, those in purgatory and not yet cleansed receiving renewed hope and consolation.

8. The Resurrection of Christ

Having considered the events which comprise Christ's departure from this world, our next point of theological inquiry concerns his exaltation. As we have seen,[11] the humility of his departure brings him by way of merit and reward a fourfold exaltation:

His resurrection
(Section 8)

His ascension
(Section 9)

His place at the Father's right hand
(Section 10)

His power of judgment
(Section 11)

[11] Cf. *supra*, p. 234.

St. Thomas considers the first of these exaltations, the resurrection of his body which is the reward for the humility of his passion and death, from four aspects: the resurrection itself; the quality of Christ's risen body; the manner in which the resurrection was made known; and the causality the resurrection exercises upon us.

A. The Resurrection Itself

It is a matter of faith that Christ arose from the dead on the third day. This teaching is contained in the gospels,[12] in the open teaching of his disciples,[13] and in all the official Creeds. The Church has also defined certain particulars about the resurrection: that Christ arose by his own power; that his was a true resurrection of the body; that his soul and body were reunited; and that he ate after the resurrection, although he had no need to do so.[14] St. Thomas offers a theological background for these and other facts connected with the resurrection.

(1) Its Necessity

Absolutely speaking, the resurrection was not necessary. But in view of the divine plan, the prophecies, Christ's merits and our needs, it is necessary relative to the attainment of these ends.

There are five reasons to explain the suitability of the resurrection:

1) It is becoming to divine justice to exalt the humble. Now Christ humbled himself on the cross. It was fitting that God should exalt him to a glorious resurrection.

2) The resurrection strengthens our faith in his divinity (I Cor. 15:12).

---

[12]Christ's prophecies of his own resurrection on the third day (Matt. 12:40, 20:19, 27:63, etc.) are borne out by the testimony of the angel (Matt. 28:6), the evidence of the empty tomb and his frequent apparitions after the event (cf. Matt. 28:5 ff.; Mk. 16:1 ff.; Lk. 24:1 ff.; Jn. 20:1 ff.; etc.).

[13]Cf. Acts 2:22 ff., 3:15, 4:33, 13:30 ff., 17:3; I Cor. 15:4; etc.

[14]Cf. Eleventh Council of Toledo, 675 (Denz. 286); Creed of Pope St. Leo IX, 1053 (Denz. 344).

3) It confirms our hope in our own resurrection (*ibid.*).

4) The resurrection directs the faithful away from the death of sin to a new life in God (Rom. 6:4).

5) By the resurrection the work of salvation was completed, for afterwards the Holy Spirit was given and the Gospel preached (Rom. 4:25; Lk. 24:47; Jn. 7:39).

(2) Its Circumstances

Christ arose on the third day after his death. Had his resurrection been delayed until the end of the world, men would have doubted his divinity. If he had arisen immediately, they would have doubted the reality of his humanity and death. The three days precluded all these doubts.

While it is true that others, like Lazarus, arose from the dead before Christ, nonetheless Christ's was the first perfect resurrection. These others were rescued from actual death by an imperfect resurrection, for they had to die once again. Both the necessity and possibility of dying again were removed in the perfect resurrection of Christ.

St. Matthew records that many of the saints arose from the dead at the time of Christ's death. This is a very mysterious matter. St. Thomas observes that there are two opinions regarding this resurrection. Some hold they arose to die no more. On the contrary, St. Augustine holds that they arose to die again. The view of St. Augustine is favored by St. Thomas. It is a commonly held view among the faithful that Christ and his Mother were the first to ascend bodily into heaven.

(3) Its Cause

When it is said that Christ arose by his own power, this does not refer to the power of his human nature. As true man, his separated soul and body had no power of reuniting. The reference is to the divine power of Christ. Both soul and body remained united to his divine nature even in death, and in virtue of his divinity the body took back the soul and the soul took back the body. Christ's divinity was the principal efficient cause of his resurrection; his body and soul were instrumental causes; his passion was the meritorious cause.

B. Christ's Risen Body

Regarding the quality of Christ's risen body, there are four conclusions:

1) He arose with a *true* body which was of the same nature as it was before, differing only in glory. If his risen body had been imaginary, it would not have been a true resurrection. (Cf. Lk. 24:39.)

2) He arose with a *glorified* body, because his soul communicated its glory to his body once the mystery of the redemption was completed by his passion and death; moreover, Christ's resurrection is the examplar of our own, and ours will be a glorious resurrection (I Cor. 15:43). As glorified, his body possesses the qualities of **impassibility** (security from all injury and corruption), **subtlety** (complete domination of the body by the soul, making it independent of all things material), **agility** (unresisting obedience to the soul's commands, with a speed of movement comparable to thought), and **clarity** (a splendor and translucency of the body originating in the soul; this may be hidden at the will of the soul).[15]

3) He arose with a *complete* body. Christ's body was of the same nature after the resurrection as before, but it differed in glory. Whatever pertains to the nature of a human body was restored in the resurrection.

4) He arose with a *scarred* body as a permanent trophy of his victory, as a confirmation of his disciples' faith that the same body arose, as a manifestation of what he endured when he prays to the Father for us, and as an instrument on the Day of Judgment to evoke the love and gratitude of the just and to rebuke the reprobated.

C. The Manifestation of the Resurrection

We learn from the Acts of the Apostles (10:40) that "God raised him on the third day and caused him to be plainly seen, not by all the

[15]Cf. St. Thomas, *Summa*, III, q. 54, a. 2, and *infra*, Chapter Seventeen.

people, but by witnesses designated beforehand by God." Great supernatural events like the Nativity and the Transfiguration, which pertain
to future glory and exceed the common knowledge of men, are revealed to the few and then preached to all. This law of divine revelation is found throughout the Scriptures and is verified in the manifestation of the resurrection.

(1) Christ's Appearance

Christ's great affection for his mother is the solid foundation for
the ancient pious belief that he first appeared to her after the resurrection. But his first recorded appearance was to Mary Magdalen
(Mk. 16:9-11; Jn. 20:11-18). A woman had been the first to bring the
source of death to man; now a woman becomes the first to announce
the glorious life of the resurrection. Thus the more persistent love
of women, who did not desert Christ even when the disciples fled, is
rewarded by the first glimpse of his glory.

No human being witnessed the resurrection, and this is in keeping
with the procedure of providence, which reveals supernatural reality
through the ministry of angels.

While the risen Christ appeared several times to his disciples to
assure them of the truth of his resurrection, yet he did not live with
them continually as before, lest they might think he had returned to
an identical way of life as before. St. Thomas points out that there
were appearances not recorded in the gospels, two of which St. Paul
mentions in his First Epistle to the Corinthians (15:6-7). The Scriptures
do not tell us where Christ lived when he was not with his followers.
There is a probable opinion that he spent some of this time with his
mother.

(2) Proof of the Resurrection

In view of the unique importance of the resurrection as the foundation of faith in the divinity of Christ, it may well be asked if the
truth of this great mystery was sufficiently demonstrated. Now proofs
are of two kinds: proof strictly so called employs reason to confirm
some matter of doubt; less strictly, a proof is a sensible sign used to
manifest the truth.

No strict argumentative proof of the resurrection was given to the disciples, for no such proof is communicable to humans in supernatural matters. Argumentative proofs must be based upon known principles. But the principles of the supernatural order cannot be comprehended by reason; they must be accepted on authority by faith.

But sensible signs of the resurrection were supplied sufficiently to manifest the fact of the resurrection. First, to move their reluctant hearts to accept the faith (Lk. 24:25; Mk. 16:14), and secondly, to strengthen the testimony that the disciples would give to others (I Jn. 1:1-3).

The resurrection was manifested in the first place by the irrefutable testimony of the angels at the tomb and of the Scriptures (Lk. 24).

In the second place, many signs were given to show the truth of this mystery, as indicated in the diagram on the following page.

D. Christ's Resurrection Causes Our Resurrection

St. Paul clearly teaches that Christ's resurrection is the cause of ours (I Cor. 15:21). And this is reasonable, for Christ's was the first perfect resurrection, and whatever is first in any order is the cause of all that comes after it. In the natural order established by God, every cause operates first upon what is closest to it, and through that, upon things more remote. Thus the Word of God first bestowed immortality upon the body united to himself, and through his own body as an instrument, he bestows immortality upon others. The efficacy of Christ's resurrection does not extend to others by some physical power of his body, but rather through the power of the divinity to which it is personally united.

Christ's resurrection is the *exemplar* of our own. It is also the *efficient instrumental cause* of our resurrection, because Christ's body is the instrument of his divinity. And his divine power is in virtual and dynamic contact with all places and times. Why, then, do not the dead arise at once? Because the Word of God disposes that we must first be conformed to the sufferings and death of Christ in this mortal life so that afterwards we may share in the likeness of his resurrection.

PROOF OF CHRIST'S RESURRECTION

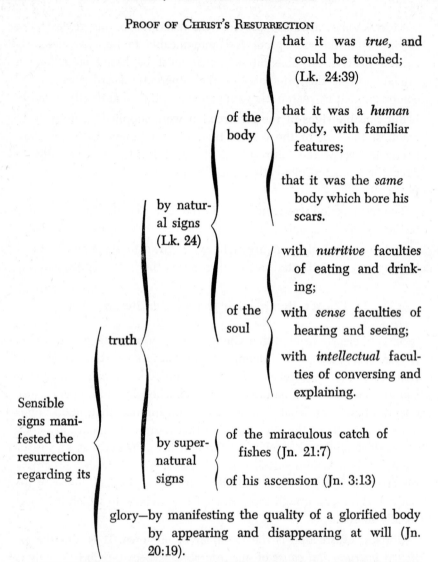

Sensible signs manifested the resurrection regarding its

truth

by natural signs (Lk. 24)

of the body
- that it was *true*, and could be touched; (Lk. 24:39)
- that it was a *human* body, with familiar features;
- that it was the *same* body which bore his scars.

of the soul
- with *nutritive* faculties of eating and drinking;
- with *sense* faculties of hearing and seeing;
- with *intellectual* faculties of conversing and explaining.

by supernatural signs
- of the miraculous catch of fishes (Jn. 21:7)
- of his ascension (Jn. 3:13)

glory—by manifesting the quality of a glorified body by appearing and disappearing at will (Jn. 20:19).

The efficiency of Christ's resurrection extends to the good and wicked alike, for no one arises except through the power of Christ. But the exemplarity of Christ's resurrection is reserved for those who will arise unto glory; those who will arise unto condemnation do not arise after the likeness of Christ whom they have rejected.

9. The Significance of the Ascension

The Scriptures clearly teach the fact of Christ's bodily ascent into heaven (cf. Mk. 16:19; Lk. 24:51; Acts 1:9; Eph. 4:8; Col. 3:1). The teaching of the Church, particularly in the Apostles' and the Nicene Creeds, declares that Christ ascended body and soul to sit at the right hand of the Father in his natural manner of existing, that his kingdom is without end, and that he will come physically to judge the living and the dead.

On the basis of faith in Christ's ascension, St. Thomas inquires into the suitability, manner of occurrence and effects of this mystery.

When Christ arose with a glorified body, it was fitting that he should ascend into heaven, which is the normal abode of incorruptible beings.

Moreover, Christ was able to bestow greater blessings by withdrawing his bodily presence through the ascension than would have been possible by his remaining upon earth:

1) He *increased our faith,* which is of things unseen. "Blessed are they who have not seen, and yet have believed" (Jn. 20:29).

2) He *raised our hope* of reaching heaven by dwelling there in his human nature (Jn. 14:3).

3) He *directed the fervor of our love* to heavenly things. "Seek the things that are above, where Christ is seated at the right hand of God. Mind the things that are above, not the things that are on earth" (Col. 3:2).

Christ ascended as man by his own power; first by the power of his divine nature, and secondly by the power of his glorified soul which moved his body at will, because his body was enhanced by the gift of agility.

Christ ascended above all the heavens, and this was befitting his supreme dignity (Eph. 4:10). Now the divinity is said to be in heaven, not as if heaven contained God, but rather that it is contained by him. Christ the man was exalted ". . . above every Principality and Power and Virtue and Domination—in short, above every name that is named, not only in this world, but also in that which is to come" (Eph. 1:21).

Christ's ascension, like his resurrection, is the cause of our salvation, not by way of merit—for this was the work of the Passion—but by way of efficiency.

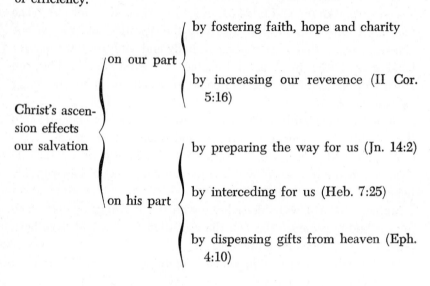

Christ's ascension effects our salvation

on our part
- by fostering faith, hope and charity
- by increasing our reverence (II Cor. 5:16)

on his part
- by preparing the way for us (Jn. 14:2)
- by interceding for us (Heb. 7:25)
- by dispensing gifts from heaven (Eph. 4:10)

10. The Kingship of Christ

A. The Fact

Several of the messianic prophecies of the Old Testament indicate that Christ is to be a king (cf. Ps. 2:2, 71:7; Isa. 9:6; Dan. 2:34 f.; Zach. 9:9). At the moment of the annunciation, the angel declared: "The Lord God will give him the throne of David his father, and he shall be king over the house of Jacob forever; and of his kingdom there shall be no end" (Lk. 1:32 f.). Christ himself declared that he was a king (Jn. 18:33 f.). The title affixed to his cross proclaimed him "King of the Jews" in three languages.

Faith teaches that after his ascension Christ sits at the right hand of the Father and reigns forever.[16] The liturgy salutes Christ as king.

[16]Council of Trent, Session XIII, 1551, *Decree on the Holy Eucharist*, Chap. I, "Concerning the Real Presence of Our Lord Jesus Christ in the Sacrament of the Holy Eucharist"; Denz. 874.

In the hymn *Te Deum:* "Thou, O Christ, art the king of glory"; in the Invitatory of the Office of Corpus Christi, which St. Thomas composed: "Let us adore Christ the King, Ruler of Nations." The various litanies hail Christ as king of angels, apostles, martyrs, etc. In the Nicene Creed we chant of Christ "whose reign will never end."

Modern times have witnessed the publication of the encyclical of Pope Pius XI on Christ the King (*Quas Primas,* Dec. 11, 1925), which established the feast of Christ the King for the universal Church. The theological background for this teaching of the faith is explained in St. Thomas' inquiry into Christ's position at the right hand of the heavenly Father.

B. The Meaning of Christ's Kingship

A king is one who rules and governs. Universal government belongs to the king, whose duty it is to order all things to a good end. The king is in his kingdom as God is in the world and as the soul is in the body.

Christ's claim to kingship rests upon three titles: 1) the Hypostatic Union; 2) the fulness of created grace; 3) his redemption of mankind. Of these titles, the first two are natural rights, and the third is a right acquired by his sacrifice on the cross.

1) By virtue of the Hypostatic Union, Christ as man transcends every creature, even the highest angels who must adore and serve him.
2) By virtue of his fulness of grace, Christ excels all creatures and is the head of the Church. He enjoys the highest degree of glory and of charity.
3) By virtue of the redemption, he acquired the right of kingship. The angels are the ministers of his kingdom and they assist the redeemed in attaining their final goal.

Christ sits at the right hand of God. That means that he shares the glory of divinity with his Father, and that he possesses perfect happiness and judiciary power unchangeably and royally. This prerogative belongs to him first as the Son of God who has the same divine nature; secondly, it belongs to him as man because of the Hypostatic Union; thirdly, it is his because of the fulness of grace which is uniquely his.

Thus no one else, angel or man, can rightly be said to sit at the right hand of the Father, or to be king over all creatures.

C. Its Implications

The following conclusions, commonly taught in the light of the foregoing principles, are confirmed by the encyclical on Christ the King:

1) Christ as God rules as Lord and King of all, both spiritually and temporally (Col. 1:6).
2) Christ as man is spiritual king of all men, all societies and of all angels (Apoc. 17:14). It follows, then, that there is an obligation upon civil governments to recognize this kingship, and to reflect its rights in their legislation.
3) Christ never exercised his temporal power as king of the entire world (Jn. 6:15, 18:34; cf. Denz. 2195 f.).
4) Pius XI teaches that Christ as man is king by legislative jurisdiction, coercion and administration. He enjoys this right over the members of his spiritual kingdom, over all men and all civil affairs. For this reason, secularism must be condemned.
5) Christ's kingdom is especially spiritual, and concerns spiritual things. At the same time, Christ enjoys absolute empire over all creatures committed to him by the Father, and all things are in his power. It would be a grave error to assert that Christ has no authority whatever in civil affairs, even though he never exercised such authority during his earthly life.

11. Christ as the Universal Judge

The Scriptures teach that Christ ". . . has been appointed by God to be judge of the living and the dead" (Acts 10:42 f.). This same truth is taught officially by the Church in the Apostles' and the Nicene Creeds.

There are three things required for passing judgment: 1) the power of coercing subjects (Sirach 7:6); 2) an upright zeal to administer justice (Prov. 3:12); 3) wisdom, which is the standard of just judgment (Sirach 10:1). Now all of these requisites are found in Christ, for he has complete power and jurisdiction, his zeal is manifest in that he died for love of justice, and he is wisdom incarnate. Consequently, the judiciary power which is common to the Blessed Trinity is attributed to the Son by special appropriation.

There are three reasons why judiciary power also fits Christ as man:

1) by reason of the Hypostatic Union;
2) because of his fulness of grace and his dignity as head of the Church;
3) because of his infinite merits.

While it is true that the primary authority of judging rests with God, the power to judge is shared with men in regard to those who are subject to their jurisdiction. Now Christ as man is head of the Church, and God has subjected all things to his jurisdiction. It is clear, then, that Christ as man is the universal judge. This power he merited by fighting and conquering for divine justice, for the sake of which he endured an unjust condemnation.

Christ's judiciary power extends to all human affairs. Christ will judge all men in relation to eternal salvation (Matt. 25:31, 40), and all human affairs are as means in relation to eternal salvation, to which men are admitted or from which they are excluded by Christ's judgment. Thus he judges the means as well as the end.

The judgment of Christ is twofold: one for each particular individual at the moment of death; another for all in general on the Day of Judgment. The judgment of each individual falls upon the soul and is unchangeable. Over and above this, there is required a general judgment, because the effects of an individual's life do not terminate with his death. A man's life continues:

1) in the memories of others, in which good or evil reputations linger, sometimes contrary to the truth;
2) in a man's descendants, whose lives are affected by their forebears;
3) in the results of their actions, both good and evil;
4) in their bodies, which are sometimes buried with honor and sometimes abandoned;

5) in the things on which they set their hearts during this life; some endure and others perish.

While a man neither merits nor loses merit after his death, these things which remain affect his reward or punishment in some measure. Since these effects are subject to change until the end of time, their judgment is reserved until then. On Judgment Day everything concerning every man in every respect will be judged perfectly and publicly.

Even the angels are subject to Christ's judgment. From the beginning of the world, the eternal Son of God in his divine nature meted out everlasting happiness to the good angels and eternal damnation to the wicked. But even in his human nature, Christ judges the angels. By the Hypostatic Union, Christ's soul is more filled with the truth of God's word than any angel. By the humility of his passion he merited to be exalted above them all. Because Christ is the head of mankind, he exercises power over the angels who minister to men. To the good angels, he dispenses the special joy which comes from co-operating in the salvation of the just. To the wicked, he administers the galling defeats which they suffer in his name, and the imprisonment in hell which removes them from the world of men. These joys and sorrows are accidental to the essential bliss or condemnation which the angels have already received from the Word of God.

12. Summary and Conclusion

The real challenge offered by the mystery of the Redemption cannot be discovered in the simple narration of facts. Rather it is found in this profound truth: Christ died by divine decree, while at the same time he gave up his life freely. Chapter Seven considers the difficulties arising from this mystery. First, we must say that Christ's passion was necessary in a relative way. That is, it was the most convenient way for the attainment of our redemption. The passion of Christ paid a debt which man, unaided, could never have paid. Moreover, it demonstrated God's love for us and showed us the virtues necessary for salvation; justifying graces were merited and the dignity of man was made clear.

It is a gross understatement to say that Christ underwent terrible punishments. The extension and intensity of his sufferings cannot be imagined by the modern mind. He suffered the most fearsome death the ancient world could offer, death on the cross. He was pitifully tortured by an aggregation of external forces. Men and women from every walk of life prodded him to Calvary and hung him there, displaying his torn body to a voracious world. He underwent it all— the crown of thorns, the nails, the jeers of the mob—to teach us two things: the love of God and aversion for sin. And yet, during the horror of his passion, Christ still possessed the beatific vision. At the height of his sufferings, while his senses and the lower faculties of his soul bore the brunt of unmitigated agony, his higher faculties saw God. For the sufferings of Christ, although they are to be attributed to his Person, are attributed to it because of the human nature he assumed.

As the day drew to a close and the earth groaned in travail at the death of Christ, our redemption was bought. Christ's work of love had produced salvation. He sacrificed himself and in doing so atoned for the totality of sin and merited the grace of salvation for all and each of us. Thus Christ's humanity was God's instrument and the efficient cause of our redemption. Man became God's friend once more.

In the tomb, Christ's incorrupt body was disjoined from his soul, and yet both body and soul were still hypostatically united to the Word of God. His soul descended into purgatory and limbo and he delivered the righteous to glory. And then on the third day Christ arose from the dead by his own power, his glorified soul and body reuniting at that instant. He appeared to a chosen few to manifest once and for all the reality of his resurrection, and because of these appearances strengthened our faith in the promise of our own resurrection: his immortal body will be the instrument of our own immortality.

His ascension continued the work of salvation. By it, Christ showed us that heaven is attained through faith, hope and charity. He reigns there now as King and Judge, preparing the mansions of the elect, interceding to the Father for us, and showering gifts upon us from the abundance of his treasury.

The following thoughts are rooted in the doctrine of this chapter.

1. Christ in no way compromised the horror of his passion. He bowed under the fury of the lash; he remained silent during the derision of the Roman soldiers; he accepted the mock royal cloak and crown of thorns; and he stood calmly when faced with the hatred of the Jews. He suffered all of these outrages silently that we might have an example of steadfastness under torture. Christ persevered to the end for the entire human race. Now it is our duty to follow his lead by persevering through the dozen daily hardships of human existence, offering each tiny cross in expiation for the hundreds of faults we commit.

2. Even during his death agony Christ still remained the Good Shepherd, seeking out his lost sheep. Moreover, he did not merely hold the shepherd's staff in his hands, he was nailed to it; a sign that his sovereignty over every flock is eternal.

3. The phoenix is the most common symbol of Christ used during the Lenten and Easter seasons. According to legend, the phoenix is consumed in flames and dies, only to rise again from the cold ashes. During Lent Christians are reminded that through fasting they may put an end to their old sinful existence and rise to new life with Christ on Easter morning.

4. "Since the disciples supremely desired that he might live, they could not listen to anything concerning his death; since they knew he was not alone an innocent man, but truly God, they could not conceive that he would die. And as they were accustomed to hear him speak in parables, they believed that as often as he said anything concerning his passion, this must be applied allegorically to something else. And so there follows: 'And this word was hid from them, and they understood not the things that were said.' But the Jews, who were plotting against his life, knew that he was speaking of his passion when he said: 'The Son of man must be lifted up' (Jn. 3:14). Because of which they said: 'We have heard out of the Law, that

Christ abideth forever; and how sayest thou: the Son of man must be lifted up' (Jn. 12:34)?"[17]

5. ". . . salvation will not come for the world until mankind, deriving its inspiration from the teachings and example of Christ, comes to recognize that all men are children of the one Father who is in heaven, destined to be truly brothers through union with his divine Son whom he sent to be redeemer of us all. Only this brotherhood gives to man, with the highest sense of personal dignity, assurance of true equality, the necessary basis of justice."[18]

BIBLIOGRAPHICAL NOTE

The doctrine contained in Chapter VII is expressed by St. Thomas in the *Summa*, Part III, Questions XLVI-LIX inclusive. For a more popular account, read *The Passion and Death of Our Lord Jesus Christ* (New York: P. J. Kenedy and Sons), by Archbishop Alban Goodier, S.J.

"The Passion, Death and Resurrection of Christ," by J. S. Considine, O.P., an article in Volume III of the English *Summa*, complements St. Thomas' treatment of the subject and will certainly be an aid to the interested student. Several articles from a variety of periodicals can also be recommended as helpful reading for this chapter. E. Graef has written a concise piece called "Christ's Passion: Sacrament, Sacrifice, Satisfaction," in *Homiletic and Pastoral Review*, LVII (1957), 539-540. "Meaning or Motive of the Resurrection," by Vincent McNabb, O.P., in *Blackfriars*, XXIV (1943), 132-139, is another short article, restricting itself to the resurrection of our Lord. Also recommended as an interesting account of the resurrection is "Resurrection of Our Savior," by P. J. Hamell in the *Irish Ecclesiastical Review*, LXXXVII, 276-284.

An article expressive of the liturgical value of the Passion is "Liturgical Aspects of the Passion," by J. Kreuter in *Orate Fratres*, VI (1932), 193-201. And, from a different point of view, the student is urged to read "Faith, Sacraments, and Calvary," by Christopher Kiesling, O.P., in *Cross and Crown*, VIII (1956), 430-441. This article can also be of use when studying the ninth chapter.

[17]St. Bede, *Exposition of the Gospel of Luke*, Bk. V, Chap. 18.
[18]Pope Pius XII, *Answer to President Truman's Letter of Dec. 17, 1949.*

CHAPTER EIGHT

Mary, the Mother of God

1. Introduction

Devotion to Mary, the Mother of God and our blessed mother, has existed in the Church since the earliest times and is based on a solid theological foundation. A study of Mary's position in the divine plan is of tremendous importance if we are to get a clear notion of her role in our redemption and her place in our salvation.

Stimulated by the definition of the Assumption, which was proclaimed by Pope Pius XII on November 1, 1950, much theological thought and writing have been devoted to the study of what has come to be called "Mariology." The best of what modern theologians have written about Mary is securely based upon the principles clearly enunciated by St. Thomas, and will be presented in summary form in this chapter. What is known of St. Joseph, the husband of Mary, will complete this study. Our plan, therefore, will follow this outline:

The divine maternity
(Section 2)
- Physical and metaphysical aspects
- Moral and spiritual aspects
- Divine maternity and the hypostatic order

Mary's fulness of grace
(Section 3)
- Divine maternity and fulness of grace
- The fulness of grace in Mary
- The purity of Mary
- Mary's perfection

Mary, our mediatrix
(Section 4)
- Divine maternity and doctrine of the New Eve
- Mary's co-redemption
- The role of Mary in the distribution of grace
- The exercise of Mary's mediation

Cult to the Mother of God
(Section 5)

The role of St. Joseph
(Section 6)

The logic and reasons for this division of the matter of the chapter and the order which is followed will become apparent as we pursue our investigation of the mystery of Mary, God's Mother and ours.

2. The Divine Maternity:
Fundamental Principle of Mariology

Perhaps no theological tract has given rise to so much fruitful investigation in recent years as that concerning Mary. Indeed, the very basis upon which the theology of Mary rests has been a matter of lively controversy. However, thorough discussions have made clear to the vast majority of the foremost theologians that Mary's divine motherhood is the source from which all of her other prerogatives flow.[1]

Some theologians claim that Mary's fulness of grace is greater and more fundamental than her divine motherhood. To the woman who cried out to Jesus that the mother who bore him was indeed blessed, Jesus replied, "Rather, blessed are they who hear the word of God and keep it" (Lk., 11:28). Using these words, they argue that Mary's true worth is to be found in the fact that she is full of grace and holiness, rather than in the fact that she is the Mother of God.

However, this opinion does not take into account the circumstances of the conversation. The very expression used by the unknown woman is evidence that she was referring only to a natural motherhood. She refers to the "womb that bore thee, and the breasts that nursed thee." She is not thinking of the divine maternity, of the supernatural consent to the Incarnation. Christ was, however. His answer implicitly refers to the humble consent of his Mother to what she heard and believed. His general terms suit the occasion, since they serve the further purpose of calling to our attention the wisdom of imitating Mary by humble consent to God's plan.

A. Physical and Metaphysical Aspects

(1) What Is Maternity?

Maternity or motherhood refers to the activity of the female principle in bi-sexual animal generation. The female animal produces an egg, a living organism, which begins to develop into a living being of the same species as the mother when stimulated by an adequate external force. The force involved is generally provided by a male of the same species, but it could, of course, be provided by God. He is

---

[1]Cf. the excellent article, "The Unitive Principle of Marian Theology," by Paul Mahoney, O.P., in *The Thomist*, XVIII (1955), 443-479; see also, "The Fundamental Principle of Mariology," by C. Vollert, S.J., and "Mary's Divine Motherhood," by G. Van Ackeren, S.J., in *Mariology*, ed. by J. Carol, O.F.M., II, (Milwaukee: The Bruce Publishing Co., 1957), 30-87 and 177-227.

not restricted in the production of effects in creation to the ordinary, secondary causes he established to achieve them.

In the various forms of animal life, the total life cycle of the female is ordained to, and therefore governed by the bearing of offspring. This is so completely the case that in those species in which the care of the mother is unnecessary after the young have been hatched, the mother often bears her young and then simply goes off to die. The point to be noted is that the whole potentiality of the species is involved in motherhood.

Because the potentiality of a human being extends far beyond purely animal functions, it can easily be understood that a purely physical maternity in a human being is incomplete, imperfect. That it achieve the nobility that belongs to it, maternity in a human mother must involve reason and will, the highest human faculties, as well as the reproductive organs. The intellect must know what is being accomplished and the will must consent to its accomplishment.

(2) What Is the Divine Maternity?

When we speak of the divine maternity of Mary, we speak of a dignity that belongs only to the noblest human maternity. Mary, knowingly and willingly, conceives and bears a son—and he is God. Through the faith and charity which well from her fulness of grace, she consents to receive this unmerited gift of God—to be his mother. Hence, her maternity is not only *physical* (as would be the case if God had been conceived in her without her knowledge); nor is it only *human* (as would be the case if she had not been elevated by grace and yet gave human consent to be God's mother). The motherhood of Mary is also a *supernatural* maternity, because she conceives her son, the Son of God, not only physically and humanly, but through supernatural acts of faith and love. Not only does she fulfill completely the physical role of woman in human generation, acting in a manner fully and perfectly human; she is God's mother in the most perfect sense of the word by reason of her supernatural maternity.

Moreover, her consent, which merits bounteous graces for herself, is of primary importance for us all. Had she withheld her consent, there would have been no Incarnation. Mary's consent to become a mother was accepted by God as the consent of mankind to the Incarnation.[2] It was for this purpose—that she might be worthy to be asked, and capable of accepting—that Mary was prepared by the fulness of grace.

This is the reason that Mary's divine motherhood is looked upon as the source of all the glories that belong to Mary, of all that Mary is.

B. Moral and Spiritual Aspects

It is inconceivable that the Mother of God would have borne the infant Jesus without love and without consciousness. Deep spiritual sentiments must have accompanied the reality accomplished in her body. By willing to ennoble one woman, God ennobled all women. God chose one for this dignity from among those creatures who resemble him. This is the sole reason why secondary causes exist in general, and mothers in particular. Neither the grandeur nor the beauty of the Incarnation would have been achieved if God had entered into this mystery by means of a woman who would give her consent but not her love. Indeed, her intimate physical union with Christ fulfilled her union of love with him.

To conceive the Word of God in the soul is certainly of greater spiritual value than to conceive him physically. The divine maternity implies much more than the physical conception of the Son of God. A worthy mother devotes all of her powers to motherhood. Thus, although Mary's motherhood includes physical conception, it encompasses also the complete devotion of her spiritual powers. For this reason it is fitting that she should have been asked for her consent, so that by her deliberate conformity to the divine will she might conceive spiritually in conceiving physically.

C. Divine Maternity and the Hypostatic Order

Further proof for the view that Mary's divine maternity is the basis of Mariology can be found by relating her maternity to the hypostatic order. Many strong arguments support the view most theologians hold that her motherhood is the source and principle from which her

[2]Cf. *Summa*, III, q. 30, a. 1 and ad 1.

graces, her privileges and her role in the redemption all arise. We will give only two of the strongest.

1. **The relation between the divine decree of the Incarnation and Mary's motherhood.** All grace depends upon the divine decree by which the Son of God became man. Included in that decree, as an integral part, is Mary's divine motherhood.[3] Therefore, since Mary's grace, like all other grace, depends upon the Incarnation, and since her divine motherhood is part of the Incarnation, it follows that her fulness of grace depends upon the divine maternity.

2. **The relation between the Hypostatic Union and the divine maternity.** A second reason for giving pre-eminence to the divine maternity is that it is ordained to the Hypostatic Union—the substantial union of her son's humanity with divinity—which is far superior to the term to which grace is ordained, the accidental union of eternal glory. This second reason seems conclusive.

3. Mary's Fulness of Grace

A. Divine Maternity and Fulness of Grace

Grace is an entirely free gift of God upon which no created nature has any claim. By it we are born again into a new life, a share in the very life of God. Grace is rooted in the essence of the soul, and from it the infused virtues and the gifts of the Holy Spirit flow into the various faculties. This second nature, this supernature, makes our acts significant in the supernatural order and is the beginning of eternal life in us. Grace is so completely superior to created nature that the whole of created nature, including the angels, does not approach the value of the slightest degree of sanctifying grace.

Because Mary was chosen to be the Mother of God, she was filled with grace beyond all other creatures. This is the order of the divine plan: God, having willed to manifest his goodness, willed Christ and his glory. This was an act of divine love, a love which permits original sin for the greater good to follow upon it. When he willed that his

[3]As Pope Pius IX pointed out in his definition of the Immaculate Conception (*Ineffabilis Deus*, 1854).

Son become man, God also willed that it happen through Mary's motherhood. Thus, he willed her glory, along with the grace and merits by which she would attain that glory.

The divine maternity itself did not sanctify Mary.[4] However, it would have been incredible if God had been born of a mother who was not holy. Thus, the divine maternity demanded fulness of grace in the mother for the following reasons:

1) in order that despite the sufferings foretold in the Scriptures, she might accept the motherhood of the Messias with the greatest generosity;

2) in order that she might remain virginal while becoming a mother;

3) in order that she might give him the most holy motherly devotion;

4) in order that she might blend her will most perfectly with his; and,

5) in order that she might complete her acceptance of motherhood most perfectly on Calvary.

B. The Fulness of Grace in Mary

When the angel appeared to Mary, he addressed her as if her very name were *Full of Grace*. Yet certainly Mary was holier when she came to the end of her life on this earth than she was when she was first conceived; indeed, at the end of her life, she must have been far holier than when the angel came to her.

Mary's fulness of grace does not compare to the fulness of grace which is ascribed to Christ, for every grace finds its origin in the grace of Christ. Yet Mary's grace is something far greater than the fulness of grace that belongs to other saintly human beings, for through her grace all the graces which come to us from Christ must pass. Christ is full of grace *absolutely*, in such a way that no increase is possible. Mary is full of grace *relatively*, in the sense that her grace

---

[4]Christ's humanity is sanctified by its substantial union with his divinity (cf. *supra*, 143-145). Mary, however, is not directly united to the divinity by her motherhood but to the humanity of her son, and through it to the Godhead. Hence, her divine motherhood itself does not intrinsically make her holy, although this special relationship to God clearly demands her sanctification as its fitting complement.

is superabundant, but it was capable of increase until the end of her life.

We can reconcile these facts with the scriptural attestation to Mary's fulness of grace by recalling a simple distinction. Fulness can be understood in two senses: either one has all there is of something (**absolute fulness**), or one has all he can hold at the moment (**relative fulness**). Only Christ possesses an absolute plenitude of grace, perfect both intensively and extensively. Mary's fulness of grace is relative to her subordinate role (but because of her primacy of office, it is greater than that of all men and angels); it admits of increase as she more perfectly fulfills in her life the function God has given her in the divine economy. At each moment she possesses the fulness of grace commensurate with her status at that time.

By considering both the negative and the postive aspects of the grace given to Mary and its consequences, we shall better appreciate the supernatural adornment with which God has graced his Mother.

C. Purity of Mary

The purity of Mary is a negative aspect of her holiness. One becomes holy in the degree that one has control over the free and spontaneous movements of the soul in its flight to God. The perfect and universal purity of Mary is founded upon her fulness of grace, and is found in her perpetual virginity, her sinlessness, and in her Immaculate Conception.

(1) Mary's Perpetual Virginity

The Church teaches that Mary was a virgin when she conceived her Son, a virgin when she gave him birth, and a virgin throughout the rest of her life.[5] Virginity refers to a constant disposition of the soul never to consent to venereal pleasure of body or mind. It can also mean a perfect ordering of the sense appetites, which frees them from any movement of sexual desire. Lastly, virginity means a state of bodily integrity. While the doctrine of the Church refers

[5]Council of Lateran, 649 (Denz. 256); Paul IV, *Cum quorundam*, 1555 (Denz. 993).

primarily to bodily integrity, we know from Mary's own answer to the angel, from her preservation from original sin and its effects, and from her plenitude of grace that she was virginal in the first two ways as well. Mary's virginity remained perfect:

1. **In conceiving Christ.** All the ancient Creeds say that she conceived of the Holy Spirit. Luke tells us that she was a virgin when the angel appeared to her. In the "Emmanuel prophecy" it is foretold: "Therefore the Lord himself shall give you a sign. Behold the virgin shall conceive and bear a son, and his name shall be called Emmanuel" (Isa. 7:15). Scripture scholars have shown that the Hebrew word translated "virgin" means a maiden, nubile but virginal. The obvious meaning of this prophecy is that a virgin, while remaining a virgin, shall bring a son into the world. Otherwise, what would be the sign? The Fathers of the Church are completely unanimous in defending the virginal conception of Jesus.

2. **In giving birth to Christ.** This has always been taught by the Church. The Fathers, both Greek and Latin, and most theologians, together with St. Thomas, teach that Christ's birth did not violate the seal of her virginity and hence was miraculous.[6]

3. **For the remainder of her life.** This is denied by most Protestants. Why do they deny it in the face of widespread patristic teaching in its favor? Where were Mary's supposed other children when the dying Christ committed her to the care of John? What they achieve by this gratuitous denial of a teaching so traditional to Christianity is the lessening of Mary's dignity. In some mysterious way, Mary seems to be the "Scepter of Orthodoxy."[7] Claiming to find

[6]Some modern theologians have claimed that this conclusion is based upon a physiological error concerning what is necessary to preserve bodily virginity. They assert that, according to modern scientific knowledge, physical virginity is preserved as long as the marriage act remains unfulfilled and the ovum uncontacted by the sperm. They hold that the words of the gospel, "she brought forth" (Matt. 1:25; Lk. 2:7), indicate the true activity involved in giving birth. Since the pain of childbirth is a punishment for sin, Mary must have given birth without pain, but this does not make it necessary to posit a miraculous birth. This theory ascribing a normal but painless parturition to Mary can be held, since it does not accuse the Fathers of a doctrinal error, but of a scientific one, and it seems to preserve the doctrine of the Church. The more common opinion, however, is that of the Church Fathers.

[7]Cf. *Mary in Protestant Theology and Worship*, by P. F. Palmer, S.J., reprinted by "The Marian Library," Dayton, Ohio, from *Theological Studies* (December, 1954).

scriptural justification for their error, Protestants refer to such expressions as "the brethren of Jesus" and "her firstborn son." But their interpretation is based on unscientific exegesis. It is well known now that the term "brethren" is used to designate relatives and brothers. Furthermore, an only child was referred to by the Jews as the firstborn son because of the special dignities and obligations attached to the firstborn.

Mary would not have protested her virginity to the angel if she had not intended to preserve it. It has always been Christian teaching that virginity is the holier way.[8] Since Mary was "full of grace" when she conceived Christ, she would not have chosen a lesser way later.

(2) Mary's Sinlessness

Such was the purity brought Mary by her fulness of grace, so virginal in soul as in body, that hers was a holiness fully befitting the Mother of God. It is the teaching of the Church that she was granted the special privilege of complete sinlessness, or confirmation in grace. The Council of Trent says: "If anyone says . . . that he can during his whole life avoid all sins, even those that are venial, except by a special privilege from God, as the Church holds in regard to the Blessed Virgin, let him be anathema."[9] Mary's confirmation in grace means that she could not sin, but it does not mean that she was not free to sin. The reconciliation of her freedom and her confirmation in grace is a problem analogous to that which arises in the consideration of Christ, and has been equivalently discussed in that connection already.

(3) Immaculate Conception

Mary possesses the highest purity, an absolute innocence, a created holiness absolutely perfect: these are the gifts God gives his Mother in the fulness of grace. Just what they imply is made clearer in the light of her Immaculate Conception: not for an instant did sin ever stain her soul; every moment of her life, from the second she was

[8] Cf. I Cor.: 7.
[9] Session VI, Can. 23 (Denz. 833); cf. J. J. Schroeder, O.P., *Canons and Decrees of the Council of Trent* (St. Louis: B. Herder Book Co., 1950), 45.

conceived in the womb of St. Ann, was spent in most intimate union with God.

In the Bull *Ineffabilis Deus* of Pope Pius IX, issued on December 8, 1854, Mary's Immaculate Conception is defined in these words:

> We declare, announce and define that the doctrine which states that the Blessed Virgin Mary, by a singular grace and privilege of God omnipotent and because of the merits of Jesus Christ the Savior of the human race was, in the first instant of her conception, preserved free from all stain of original sin, is revealed by God and must therefore be believed firmly and with constancy by all the faithful.[10]

Three important points are to be noted in this definition:

1. Mary was not *cleansed* **from original sin, she never** *contracted* **it.** When her soul was created and joined to her body, it was entirely without sin. Original sin, man's heritage from Adam, ordinarily is contracted at the moment of conception (we are children of wrath), but by a great and unique privilege Mary was preserved from this moral infection of the human race.[11] For grace and the divine friendship belonged to her from the beginning, and where grace is there can be no sin.

We do not know exactly what original sin is, but we do know what it does. It stains the soul and makes us worthy of being rejected by God. Spiritually the soul is dead (this is why an unbaptized person is incapable of receiving any sacrament other than baptism). Enslaved to Satan, the soul is subject to the law of concupiscence, suffering and death. Since she was free from sin, Mary was completely free from these effects insofar as they were *punishments* for sin, even though she endured suffering and perhaps death as a consequence of nature, for our salvation.

2. Mary was *redeemed* **by Christ.** Since Mary was a human being, born by human generation, and a child of Adam in every natural way, she was *in need of* redemption from sin. Only Christ, who was conceived by the Holy Spirit and not by carnal generation, is excepted from this law of the human race. Mary, too, was redeemed by the

---

[10]Denz. 1641.

[11]Protestants frequently confuse the two privileges of the Virgin Birth (Mary remains a virgin even while truly bearing her Son) and the Immaculate Conception (Mary at her conception preserved from sin, through her fulness of grace). It is an error no Catholic should be guilty of.

merits of Jesus Christ, yet by being *preserved* from sin rather than by being *cleansed* from sin. God would not permit sin to mar the soul of his most pure Mother for the slightest instant.

3. This dogma of faith is revealed by God. The Church proposes Mary's Immaculate Conception as a revealed truth. It is at least implicit in Scripture and explicit in tradition. Two scriptural texts imply the Immaculate Conception. The first of these texts reads: "I will put enmity between you [the serpent] and the woman, between your seed and her seed; he shall crush your head and you shall lie in wait for his heel" (Gen. 3:15). Since the earliest days, the Church has applied this text to Mary. Such an application would not have been made if the faithful had not believed that Mary's victory was complete, that she was never subject, even for an instant, to Satan.

The second text is: "Hail, full of grace . . . blessed art thou among women" (Lk. 1:28). This is the angel's greeting to the future Mother of God. If Mary had not been immaculately conceived, this salutation would be meaningless. Furthermore, the Fathers of the Church as well as the universal agreement of the hierarchy testify to the fact that the belief of the Church has always been in accord with this implication.

Theologically speaking, it was most fitting that this honor be conferred upon Mary. For the Immaculate Conception increased her glory over the glory of those, like St. John the Baptist, who were sanctified while still in the womb. A singular privilege of this kind is a most becoming spiritual adornment for God's Mother.[12]

We can list two main consequences of the Immaculate Conception:

1) *Freedom from the consequences of original sin.* Since Mary was never subject to sin, she was never subject to the consequences of sin. She was free of concupiscence and of the errors and il-

---

[12]It is often said that St. Thomas taught that Mary was not immaculately conceived. As a young man he seems to have taught that she was (I *Sent.*, d. 44, q. 1, a. 3, ad 3); as a mature scholar, concentrating on her need of redemption, he appears to deny that she was (*Summa*, III, q. 27, a. 2 and ad 2); but just before his death he again seems to affirm it (*On the Angelic Salutation*). Considering the notion of *preservative* redemption, the principles of St. Thomas actually lead to the conclusion that Mary was immaculately conceived. But it was the glory of the Franciscan, Duns Scotus, who was born the year St. Thomas died, to have made the notion of preservative redemption explicit. Cf. Thomas U. Mullaney, O.P., "Mary Immaculate in the Writings of St. Thomas," *The Thomist*, XVII (1954), 433-468.

lusions which result from darkness of the intellect. Preserved
from original sin, she never committed an actual sin, nor even
had an inclination to sin. She did suffer pain, and perhaps she
died. However, these sufferings were not punishments for sin
but arose from perfect conformity to her Son, who suffered
these things freely for our redemption. Mary not only never com-
mited a sin, but she was also privileged never to choose a
lesser good. She always made the best possible choice on every
occasion.

2) *Fulness of grace.* "Grace and truth came by Jesus Christ," says
St. John (1:17). Since no one was closer to Christ than Mary,
she must have received more grace and known more truth than
any other creature. By her fulness of grace: (1) she was able to
avoid every sin and practice every virtue most perfectly; (2)
her body was prepared for the Incarnate Word, since the effects
of grace overflowed from her soul into her body; and (3) grace
was able to flow through her to all men.

D. Mary's Perfection

(1) Growth and Degree of Grace

The perfection to which the Mother of God attained is the positive
aspect of her holiness. Both Jesus and Mary possessed the fulness of
grace. However, the grace of the Son was acquired in an instant,
while the grace of the Mother was acquired progressively.

Mary did not possess the beatific vision on this earth. Nevertheless,
she began her life with a more perfect charity than the greatest
saints attain at the end of theirs. Her growth in charity was very
rapid because she lacked even the slightest attachment to, or desire
for anything not perfectly ordained to divine union. Her rapid growth
was not impeded by the slightest obstacle. She grew in charity by
means of:

1) Meritorious acts. Whenever we act under the influence of charity
we gain title to an increase of grace. When the act of charity
is sufficiently intense to dispose us for such an increase, it is

given immediately by God. Every act of charity performed by Mary (and her every human act flowed from charity) was more intense than her previous act of charity. Therefore, with her every act Mary merited an increase of charity.

2) Prayer. Prayer asks more of God than what is deserved or merited. Oftentimes, charity and growth in grace are increased more by prayer than by meritorious acts. Prayer is always answered if it is humble and persevering, and if it asks those things which are necessary for our spiritual development. Mary's prayer fulfilled these conditions and contributed powerfully to her growth in grace.

3) Mary's communion with God. Mary's union with God was more perfect and more constant than that of any of the saints. Her union of knowledge and love led her onward to more fervent acts of love and a more heroic practice of the virtues, and thus to an ever-increasing perfection in grace.

4) Reception of the sacraments. The sacraments are divine channels of grace. They are fountains of divine life for those who are properly disposed to receive God's gifts. We may be certain that Our Lady used these efficacious means of growing in grace, and that they wrought wonders of grace in her perfectly disposed soul. Theologians generally hold that she received baptism and partook devoutly of the sacred banquet of the Eucharist.[13]

As a result of her constant growth in grace, Mary attained the degree of charity necessary for her role as Mother of the Son of God. However, she did not merit the divine maternity, for that would be equivalent to meriting the Incarnation. Since the Incarnation is the principle of merit, it would violate the principle of contradiction to merit the Incarnation.

At the instant of the Incarnation, Mary's grace vastly increased. Three points clarify and substantiate this statement:

[13]She would receive these sacraments of the New Law only, of course, after their institution by her Son.

1) Her grace was to prepare her for the divine motherhood. Since Mary grew in grace, it is reasonable to conclude that the perfection of grace necessary for her preparation would be finally achieved at the instant it became necesasry.

2) When Christ comes in the Eucharist, he grants as much grace as the recipient is disposed to receive. Since Mary was perfectly disposed for the divine motherhood, his coming to her must have resulted in a vast increase in grace.

3) The love of a mother for her child blossoms during pregnancy and unfolds beautifully at the birth of the child. Mary's motherhood, however, was in full bloom at the instant of conception, because, at that moment, the divine infant was fully possessed of his faculties. (This does not, of course, preclude an increase of love at the time of the Nativity.) When we consider the love a mother has for her child, and then consider Mary's capacity for love and the fact that she loved her God in her child; and when we think of how supernaturalized her every human act was, then we can gain some insight into the vast extent of the grace which perfected the nature of the Mother of God.

At the Visitation, Elizabeth was given the knowledge that Christ, through his mother, was already beginning the work of sanctification in the world. "The babe in my womb leapt for joy. And blessed is she who has believed, because the things promised her by the Lord shall be accomplished" (Lk. 1:45). In her reply, the *Magnificat*, Mary shows how well she understood her place in God's plan, and how complete was her submission to his will. She is filled with gratitude to God in whom alone she finds her joy. Having come to set right the wrongs of the world, he chose to come through her. As a result he has raised her to so great a dignity that men will sing her praises until the end of time. But in praising her, mankind will be praising God, because all that she is she owes to him.

Two other events of Mary's life mark an especially significant increase of divine life in her soul. On Calvary she shared her son's suffering and death, offering him to God for our salvation. She did this with the same sentiments which inspired his sacrifice. God will not be outdone in generosity, and showers his Mother with gifts in a measure beyond our comprehension. Again, the mystery of Pentecost notably increases the sublime perfection of the grace she already possesses. Yet she does not cease to grow in grace until her assumption into heaven.

(2) Mary's Principal Virtues of Mind and Soul

Since the virtues are properties of grace, we can expect to find a wonderful array of virtues in Mary. Furthermore, her exemption from original sin and its effects left her intellect clear and bright, and her will strong. All the virtues were hers in a more perfect manner than they are to be found in any of the saints, but in what is revealed to us of her life certain virtues are especially evident.

Read the account of the Annunciation and of the Visitation in the first chapter of the gospel according to St. Luke. Note the wonderful virtues manifested by Mary in her consent to the divine will. Several are particularly evident. There is no doubt of the marvelous virginity of her soul. She had a perfect desire to forego the pleasures which normally belong to marriage. Her humility also shines forth in her perfect willingness to accept the place alloted to her in the divine plan. This is beautifully enunciated in the *Magnificat*. Her wonderfully simple faith is so evident that Elizabeth comments upon it, saying: "Blessed is she who has believed." Her courage and her confidence in God are clearly manifested in her *Fiat*, because she well knew the prophecies concerning the suffering of the Messias, which would be hers too. We must not forget that she was well aware of the punishment reserved in Jewish law for women who conceived outside of marriage. Her self-forgetfulness was complete. Gifted beyond all other human beings both in nature and in grace, Mary did not look to herself for her greatness, but only to God.

1. The theological virtues. Mary manifested the divine virtues of faith, hope and charity most clearly in her life. She was in a special

way a woman of faith. We have already seen that the demonstration
of her faith at the Annunciation was so marked as to merit comment
from Elizabeth. During the hidden life and the trials of the public
life of our Lord, her faith must have been sorely tried. Yet we see
it operating again at the marriage feast of Cana and especially at the
foot of the cross. Without a word she accepted what could only have
seemed a dismal failure, for hers was the confidence born of faith
that the world's greatest victory was being won.

Twice in the second chapter of the gospel according to St. Luke
we are told that Mary kept the memory of the mysterious things that
were said and done carefully in her heart. She pondered them under
the influence of the gifts of understanding and knowledge. Her hope,
too, perfected by the gift of piety, sustained her during these days.
Finally, we find in Mary the perfection of charity and the gift of wisdom. Her perfect charity will become clearer when we consider her
assumption. The wisdom of the ages has named her "Seat of Wisdom."

2. The moral virtues. Mary's humility has already been mentioned. Her courage was evident at the Annunciation and again at
the foot of the cross. Supernatural prudence and justice shine throughout what we know of her life. But these are only the most outstanding of a collection of precious gems whose beauty is surpassed only
by that of her Son's.

(3) Mary's Charismatic Graces

The charismatic graces are not given for the sanctification of the
individual. Therefore, they were granted to Mary only insofar as they
were needed for the accomplishment of her mission. Certainly she
possessed a special gift for the understanding of the Scriptures. Christian tradition shows her humbly and sweetly encouraging and ad-
vising the apostles and first disciples of our Lord. Despite their fear,
which normally gives rise to flight, they remained gathered together
with her until the coming of the Holy Spirit. Whether (as some have
suggested) she was given the gift of tongues on the flight into Egypt
and when she went with John to Ephesus is not known. It seems more
likely that this gift would have been given to Joseph and to John.

However, we do know that she possesses this gift now, since in recent years she has spoken in Portuguese and in at least two French dialects.

4. Mary, Our Mediatrix

We have considered Mary's relationship to God by her divine maternity and by her plentitude of grace. Now we begin our consideration of Mary's role as mediatrix between God and man.

A. Divine Maternity and Doctrine of the New Eve

(1) Mary's Maternal Mediation

Since God became man for the sake of men, everything about Christ has some significant effect on men. Mary's whole glory is found in her association with Christ. Thus we can expect to find in this union of Mary with Christ some understanding of the role she plays in our affairs.

Mary is intimately involved in the work of redemption. She freely and deliberately consented to be the Mother of the Savior. With knowledge of the complete self-sacrifice that this would exact from her, she accepted the role that God had prepared for her.

Thus Mary is in a spiritual sense the mother of all men by an adoptive motherhood. Since grace comes to us through her, she is more than merely our sister in grace. Since divine adoption (unlike legal adoption) causes an intrinsic change in the adopted, namely, the new life of grace, Mary (as we shall see later) causes grace in us.

When Mary gave her consent at the Annunciation she became the mother of our spiritual regeneration, but by her perfect union with the redemptive act on Calvary she became our mother in a more perfect way. It was here that Christ proclaimed Mary's universal motherhood by sacramental words which effected what they signified. Together with the universal motherhood she received the grace and maternal love necessary to achieve it. It was also here that the devotion of the Church to Mary was born in the heart of the beloved disciple.

(2) Mary as the New Eve

Christ is the new head of the human race, the new Adam. Thus, in some sense, Mary can be called the new Eve. Her part in the Redemption can be compared to Eve's part in the fall. Eve was a secondary and subordinate cause of the fall of man. Had she alone fallen, original sin would not have been passed down to her children, for she was not the head of the human race. Mary, too, is a secondary and dispositive cause of our redemption. Not merely because of her physical motherhood is she the new Eve, but by a moral association with the Redeemer through her free and meritorious acts. She disposes us for the action of her Son, who effectively causes our salvation.

Traditionally, the Fathers of the Church speak of Mary as the new Eve. As early as the middle of the second century we find this beautiful passage in St. Justin's *Dialogue with Trypho the Jew* (Chapter 100):

> We understand that he [Christ] became man by means of the Virgin, so that the disobedience caused by the serpent might be destroyed just as it began. Eve, a virgin, having conceived the word of the serpent, gave birth to disobedience and death. Mary, on the other hand, conceiving faith and joy, when the Angel Gabriel announced to her that the Spirit of the Lord would come upon her and the power of the Most High would overshadow her so that the Holy One born of her would be called the Son of God, answered: "Be it done unto me according to thy word." He is then born of her, he of whom the Scriptures so often speak. By her, God destroyed the empire of the serpent and of all the angels and men who became like to the serpent, and frees from death those who repent of their faults and believe in him.

Other Fathers wrote in a similar manner, pointing out various ways in which the antithetical comparison between Mary and Eve can be made.

(3) Consequences of This Doctrine

Mary is our mother, as well as God's; she is not only Mother of the Word, she is her Son's associate in the work of redemption. From this fact, which a deeper understanding of the divine maternity has given us, flow consequences of the highest importance. Three of these are the key doctrines containing the implications which fully reveal Mary's mediation: 1) her *acquisition* of grace, frequently called by theologians her "co-redemption"; 2) her role in *dispensing* grace to us; and 3) the actual *exercise* of her role of distributing grace to mankind.

Each of these points will be separately examined in successive subsections.

B. Mary's Co-redemption

Whereas God seeks the co-operation of other men in *applying* the grace acquired by his Son to mankind, Our Lady has the special privilege of co-operating (although in total dependence on Christ) in the very *acquiring* of grace. This co-operation is the proximate basis for her universal participation in the distribution of the graces so acquired to mankind. Mary's fruitful association with Christ in the work of redemption begins with the Incarnation and is exercised throughout her life with him. But it reaches its climax in her co-operation with the very work for which he became incarnate, his bloody sacrifice on the cross for us. In her consent to his redeeming death which is the prolongation of her *Fiat*, she acquires rights, over and above those belonging to her as God's Mother, to the distribution of the fruits of the Redemption.

We will examine Mary's acquisition of grace under two aspects, her merit and her satisfaction.

(1) The Merits of Mary

Merit is *a right to compensation,* the payment of a price for a work accomplished. In the supernatural order, the right of man for compensation from God is founded about the gift of grace, by reason of which man's free acts are pleasing and acceptable to God and merit an appropriate reward. There is only an approximate equality here, of course (except for the acts of Christ), for perfect equality exists only between equals; hence there is only *relative* justice, insofar as God rewards man for doing what he is able to do with the gifts God bestows on him. Further, since it is fitting that God should reward those who act freely and generously, there is a "merit of suitability" by which we can gain grace and even salvation for others.

These considerations lead to the division of merit:

Merit
{
  Strictly deserving (worthy in justice)
  {
    Perfectly deserving (**de condigno perfecte**)—belongs only to the acts of Christ. Since he is God his acts are at least as valuable as the reward given for them.

    Deserving (**de condigno**)—the good acts of a man in the state of grace deserve a reward, not because they are as valuable as the reward, but because they are proportionate to it.
  }

  Properly fitting (**de congruo**)—by which one earns title to reward for another. This title is based on friendship rather than strict justice.
}

Mary merits for us at least *de congruo.*[14] This is theologically certain. Probably it is revealed and can be defined; St. Pius X in his encyclical, *Ad Diem Illum,* says:

> Mary, since she surpassed all in sanctity and union with Christ, and since she was joined to Christ in the work of human salvation, merited for us *de congruo,* as it is called, what Christ merited *de condigno,* and she is the chief minister in dispensing graces.

All the graces which Christ merited for us—justification, final perseverance, eternal glory, as well as all others—Mary merited for us **de congruo**.

(2) Mary's Satisfaction

The purpose of satisfaction is to repair offence against God and to restore the sinner to his favor. Because God is infinite, offence against him requires infinite satisfaction, and this can come per-

---

[14]Some modern theologians even hold that Mary merits graces for us and our salvation in relative justice (*de condigno*). But the basis for such merit seems difficult to establish, and the more common opinion is that Mary's merit is *de congruo*.

fectly from God alone. Man offended, it was for man to repair. Yet God alone could repair. This is the dilemma perfectly solved by the Incarnation: God became man so that his acts would be the acts of a man and still have the value of divine acts. Since meritorious acts are satisfactory when they are physically or morally painful, the sufferings of Jesus were infinitely satisfactory. Jesus associated with his perfect satisfaction the fitting satisfaction of his Mother.

Since Mary is a human being, the satisfaction she offered was finite. Justice did not require that God accept it, and yet it was fitting that he should. The satisfaction Mary offered is greater than that of all the saints together. Since satisfaction carries with it the notion of pain, we can gather from the extent of the satisfaction she offered some idea of the suffering she endured. Her pains were accepted as satisfaction for the offences of mankind because of the immensity of her love, the intensity of her pain, her maternal dignity, and because no fault of her own had to be expiated. Like the satisfaction paid by her Son, Mary's proceeds from the deepest obedience to God's decrees, and yet is perfectly free and voluntary.

Mary's sufferings were the direct effect of man's sin. Precisely in this is found their quality of satisfaction. Mary understood sin as only the holy can. She knew that the scourge and thorns and nails which tormented her Son were as nothing in comparison to the effects of sin in a sinner's soul. She suffered in proportion to her love for God and for souls.

Pain alone does not make an act satisfactory. The spirit with which pain is accepted must also be taken into account. On Calvary we see in Mary a peerless example of faith, hope and charity. To human eyes all that her Son stood for was being destroyed. Yet by faith she knew that the words "It is consummated" were a cry of victory; she saw the hand of God where others saw only darkness and desolation. Mary was also filled with hope on Calvary, because she saw the opening of the gates of heaven, attested to by the words of Jesus to the good thief. Her act of charity on Calvary was surpassed only by that of Christ himself. Giving all that she had, she retained nothing for herself. There was no sorrow like her sorrow because there was no love like her love. Through her affliction on Calvary she became the "Comforter of the Afflicted."

Despite her offering her own Son on Calvary, Mary was not a priest. The priesthood is not conferred precisely for the salvation and glory of the priest, but to fulfill the mission of the Church. But her dignity is greater than that of any priest, for it is greater to give the Son of God human nature than to make him present in the Eucharist. And it is theologically certain that her consent to the sacrifice of the cross was in some way a co-operation in the principal act of the priesthood of Christ. Though she was not a priest, the fulness of the *spirit* of the high priesthood of Jesus Christ was hers. That is why she is rightly called the Co-redemptrix of the human race.

C. The Role of Mary in the Distribution of Grace

(1) Mary's Mediation

Tradition sees in Mary a universal and perpetual subordinate mediatorship, which extends to all men and to all graces. St. Pius X in his encyclical, *Ad Deum Illum,* affirms that Mary is the mediatrix between her divine Son and the whole world. Her mediation is founded entirely on Christ's. This does not mean that our redemption is partly the work of Christ and partly the work of Mary. Our redemption is entirely from God, the first cause of grace; it is entirely from Jesus, the principal and perfect mediator; and it is entirely from Mary, a mediator fully subordinated to Christ. The position given to Mary is both an honor conferred upon her, which gives her a share in the divine causality, and a concession to our weakness. Her mediation is higher than that of the saints, both because it is universal and because Mary alone gave us a Savior. She merited for us and she made satisfaction for us.

Mary's mediation adds nothing necessary to the universal, infinite mediation of Christ. It is, however, of great help to us.

In the first place it serves to accent the great glory of Mary. It is a great honor to be taken into partnership by God in the production of offspring. It is an even greater honor to share in the production of spiritual offspring. The priest does this, and so we call him "Father." Mary, however, has a far more universal share in God's causality than any priest, and this by reason of her own merit.

We should know Mary's glory so that we can pay her the reverence due to her. Many Protestants know that she is the Mother of God; the Scriptures are clear on this point. Yet they seldom honor her as she should be honored, because they do not realize (not having the teaching Church to instruct them) the significance and the consequences of her divine maternity. Mary is a perfect example of how God favors those who are faithful to him.

Mary's mediation is also very useful to us because of our weakness. Despite all that Christ did to become one of us and to show his love for us, he is still God. Thus, he can strike such fear and terror into the heart of a sinner that the sinner will be driven to despair. No sinner who turns to Mary can be terrified of her. Through her, the sinner is led to understand Christ's love for him. As the Jesuit poet, Hopkins, says: "Through her we may see him / Made sweeter, not made dim."

(2) Mary, Dispenser of Grace

A rich man's mother does not necessarily have the right to dispense his riches. But if he desires his riches to be dispensed, and if his mother is a good and wise woman who stood by him and assisted him during all the perils, sufferings and anguish by which his riches were amassed, it would not be unreasonable for him to give her a share in dispensing what she had a share in acquiring. We have already seen that Mary, by a certin fittingness, merited all that her son merited in strict justice. Tradition further teaches us—in a manner so certain that this doctrine has been widely suggested as definable—that every grace granted in this world is granted through Mary.[15]

(3) Mary, Help of Christians

Eve was given to Adam to be his helpmate. Therefore, she was made to love him, for there is no better helper than a lover. But she re-

---

[15]The question may arise concerning sacramental graces. These, too, come through Mary, at least to the extent that she provides the necessary conditions of fruitful reception and perhaps the necessary circumstances (e.g., the presence of a priest, etc.).

jected her vocation. Because she did not love Adam sufficiently, she led him into sin. Mary's love for men is without defect. That is why she well deserves the title, "Help of Christians." The whole history of Christianity shows the increase of this helpfulness and the growing appreciation of it by the Church and by individual Christians.

In order to appreciate more fully the actual and universal role of the Mother of God in the exercise of mediation, it would be well to consider how she accomplishes, here and now, this mediation.

D. The Exercise of Mary's Mediation

That Mary possesses an actual and universal role in the distribution of grace seems now established beyond reasonable doubt. But precisely in what manner is this special office put into practice by Our Lady? To answer this important question we must first consider her present, actual state in heaven. Then we may more clearly see how she intercedes for us, how she actively intervenes in our behalf, how in very truth she is Queen.

(1) The Assumption of the Blessed Virgin

Mary's final plentitude of grace, her beatitude, since it is proportioned to her grace on earth, is greater than that of all the angels and saints combined. Although the angels have far greater natural powers of knowledge than any human being, even Mary, the vision of God is not proportioned to native capacities; it is essentially supernatural. The beatific vision depends upon the light of glory, which is proportioned to grace rather than to nature. Not only is Mary's vision of God greatest in intensity, it is also greatest in extent, for her mission is a universal one.

Mary's happiness in heaven is such as befits the Mother of God and the Co-redeemer of man. Essentially this consists in the full realization of her divine maternity, union with her Son in his divinity. But the Church teaches that she is present in heaven in both body and soul. We must examine this mystery of Mary's assumption more in detail.

1. The dogma of the Assumption. On the feast of All Saints, 1950, His Holiness Pope Pius XII solemnly announced to the world: "We pronounce, declare and define it to be a divinely revealed dogma: that the Immaculate Mother of God, the ever Virgin Mary, having completed the course of her earthly life, was assumed body and soul into heavenly glory."[16]

Because of her Immaculate Conception, Mary was not condemned to the corruption of the tomb. The perfect victory won by Christ over sin and death makes it unfitting that death should have won a victory over her. Death should not have crushed her but should have merely transformed her pure body to the lightness of glorification so that it would no longer weigh her soul down to earth. Love seeks union. The most perfect union with God in the beatific vision drew Mary's grace-filled soul heavenward. Only the grossness of the unglorified human body could restrain Mary's soul from being perfectly united with her Son. Once the impediment was removed she was in heaven, body and soul. At that instant she achieved her final fulness of grace.

2. The death of Mary. The Church has not defined the fact of Mary's death, although the more common opinion holds that she died. This opinion seems more in accord with the general tenor of the Apostolic Constitution by which her assumption was defined. The following are to be noted if we accept this opinion:

1) Since she was preserved from original sin, Mary was not subject to death as a penalty for sin.

2) Her death would be fitting, since it was in accord with her nature and with the death of her Son.

3) Neither of these points concludes to the *necessity* of her death.

The effects of original sin did not fall upon Mary. She was not subject to bodily corruption. Immortality, which in the state of innocence was a preternatural gift, was withdrawn after Adam's sin. It was not an endowment of man's nature. Death, therefore, is not

[16]From the translation of the Apostolic Constitution, *Munificentissimus Deus,* by Msgr. Joseph C. Fenton, S.T.D., in *The Thomist,* XIV (1951), 21.

necessarily a punishment for sin. If Mary did die, it was certainly not as a punishment for sin.

Because he has a body, a man shares animal nature. Death normally concludes an animal's life. Therefore, the death of a human being is quite normal. Thus in view of the fact that her Son chose to die, there would be nothing incongruous about the death of Mary. Mary had already suffered the terror of death on Calvary. There was no need for her to suffer again. Yet because of her perfect conformity to her Son she may have wished to die before her glorification. If she did die, it was the most peaceful death of love. If Paul could speak of himself as "desiring to depart and to be with Christ" (Phil., 1:23), how much more must Mary have longed for the beatific vision!

Although these considerations may lead us to think that Mary died and was raised again to be assumed into heaven, the evidence is not conclusive. She shares in the work of our redemption by her living spiritual death on Calvary, not by her physical death. Nothing essential is added to her work by her death.

(2) Mary's Intercession in Heaven

Mary is the mother of us all. Her mediation, as we have seen, is universal. It extends to all men and to all the favors God grants to men. It follows from this that everything we obtain from God, whether we ask it of Mary or not (even those things we did not think to ask for at all), we obtain through Mary. When we ask anything of the saints they seek it for us through Mary. This does not mean that we have to ask explicitly for everything through Mary. It does mean that when we ask anything of God, we desire that it be granted according to God's plan. And God's plan is to grant it through his Mother.

Even during her life on earth, Mary was powerful with God. Indeed, God seems to have deliberately provided that her power should be called to our attention. The sound of her greeting caused Christ in her womb to sanctify John in the womb of Elizabeth. His first miracle performed at Cana was at her behest. She is explicitly mentioned as having prayed in the midst of the disciples for the coming of the Holy Spirit. Her power of intercession since her assumption into heaven is unquestionably greater than that which she enjoyed upon earth.

Every spiritual and temporal need that we have is known to our spiritual mother. We have the assurance of the Council of Trent that the saints are able to help those who call upon them, and this implies confirmation of the traditional teaching that the blessed in heaven know those things which concern them on earth. Since Mary's concern is universal, she has knowledge of all needs, even the most immediate and personal. This is why we ask her to "pray for us sinners *now* and at the hour of our death."

(3) Mary's Direct Action

"For there is one God and one mediator of God and men, the man Jesus Christ" (I Tim., 2:5). The purpose of mediation is to unite two extremes, not to separate them. The mediator between God and men raises man's offerings to God, and distributes God's gifts to men. In the proper sense only Christ does this, but that does not prohibit Christ from generously associating others with himself in his work of mediation. The close union of Mary to Christ, which is the consequence of her divine motherhood, results in her perfect share in his universal mediation. This has long been taught by the Church's ordinary *magisterium*, and in 1921 the feast of the Mediatrix of All Graces was approved for the Universal Church.

(4) The Queenship of Mary

In the Litany of Loretto, the Church addresses Mary as a Queen. Indeed, the Church has always considered Mary to be, in the strict sense, a queen. Certainly she is a queen in the wide sense of the word, since she is the Mother of Christ the King. Also the title can be given to her by reason of the exalted qualities of her soul. But more than this. She has both a *primacy of honor* over angels and men, and a real *power* to command them. Thus she is a queen in the strict sense of the term.

Several reasons can be given for this statement:

1) As Mother of God, she belongs to the hypostatic order and so truly shares the universal kingship of Christ.

2) Christ won his kingship by his victory over Satan, a victory in which Mary intimately shared. Thus she has a true right to queenship.

3) She is the first adopted child of the eternal Father and conceived her Son by the overshadowing of the Holy Spirit.

Her physical motherhood alone does not give Mary her royal title. Her title belongs to her by reason of her intimate association with his mission, an association which brought her motherhood to complete fulfillment. The radical right to queenship belongs to her by reason of her divine motherhood. However, she was to merit its perfection by suffering in union with her Son. Her full exercise of this power was to await her assumption.

Mary exercises her queenship in heaven by contributing to the accidental glory of the angels and saints. In purgatory her power results in lessening the sufferings of the faithful departed by prompting the faithful on earth to pray and have Masses offered for them and by offering them herself to God, thus increasing their value. In hell, she limits the powers of the devils to tempt. Although she seems to have been given no share in inflicting punishment for sin, she does so accidentally, since the devils suffer more from being conquered by her humility than by the omnipotence of God.

5. Devotion to the Mother of God

The Church and the faithful have always called upon Mary to intercede with God and dispense his graces on earth. After having studied her divine motherhood, her plenitude of grace, her function as principal subordinate mediator, and her spiritual motherhood of all men, the necessity of devotion to Mary is obvious. But it remains for us to study the nature of the devotion that is owed to Mary.

1. The devotion we owe to Mary. The usefulness of invoking the saints is a doctrine of the Church. The saints are able to obtain from God, through Christ, the answer to our prayers. It is, therefore, fitting that they should be worshipped with a form of worship known as **dulia.** This form of worship is owed to those whose great supernatural excellence derives from the fact that they are glorified with Christ.

If this is true of the saints, it is even more true of Mary. She is the spiritual mother of us all, and knows all of our needs. It was fitting that she merit everything that Christ merited, even though he merited by strict right. In a special way she shared his task of making satisfaction for us. Through her intercession, all the means of salvation come to us. For these reasons it is not difficult to see that we owe special devotion to her, because her supernatural dignity as the Mother of God is unequalled by all the angels and saints.

The worship which we owe to God is called **latria**. We pay reverence to those things which pertain to God by *relative* latria. For example, we adore the crucifix on Good Friday, knowing perfectly well that we are not adoring a piece of wood and metal. Adoration of any sort pertains essentially to a person. The adoration given to the crucifix is obviously given essentially to God. Persons closely joined to God are, as we have seen, adored because of this proximity. Yet because they are themselves persons, and as such deserve reverence in themselves, they cannot be given that reverence which is applicable to God alone. They cannot, then, be given relative latria. They are given a reverence essentially less than that given to God, but it is an *absolute* reverence, truly given to them, not to someone they represent.

The reverence owed to Mary is of this kind. Yet since it is greater than the reverence owed to the other saints, and since her glory exceeds that of all the angels and saints combined, the reverence owed to Mary is given a special name, **hyperdulia**.

2. **Means of giving devotion to Mary.** The devotion of hyperdulia is given to Mary in the following ways:

1) by honor and veneration proportionate to her excellence in grace and glory;

2) by invoking her in prayer, since she is the universal, though secondary, mediator through whom all graces come to us;

3) by love and filial devotion, since she is our mother;

4) by gratitude for the benefits we have received from God through her;

5) by imitation of her virtues and conforming ourselves to her by
our intellects and wills; and

6) by consecration and reparation.

Mary is the exemplar of our predestination and is charged with the
distribution of all graces. Therefore, to be devoted to Mary and to
strive to imitate her is to adhere to the certain source of salvation.
For this reason it has been said that devotion to Mary is a sign of
predestination.

There is no better way to grow in devotion to Mary than by the
frequent recitation of the Rosary. The constant testimony of the popes
joins with her own witness in proclaiming the efficacy of this, the
greatest of Marian prayers. The Rosary has transformed countless
souls and, in the minds of the faithful, is intimately associated with
her name. She will surely be the Mother of those who carry her
Rosary and recite it frequently.

The Church especially commends devotion to Our Lady's Immaculate Heart.[17]

6. The Role of St. Joseph

Many theologians have devoted their efforts in recent years to the
study of the place of St. Joseph in the theology of our redemption.
Only a brief summary of St. Joseph's role can be presented here.

We have seen that Mary's place in our redemption is unique. Although Joseph's part cannot begin to compare with Mary's in importance, nevertheless, his is a very special role. We saw that the
foundation upon which the whole theology of Mary rests is her
divine motherhood. The whole theology of Joseph rests on the fact
that he was the husband of Mary.

We intend to speak here of the three immediate consequences of
his marriage to the Mother of God.[17a] As a result of this marriage,
Joseph

1) was in a sense the father of Jesus;

[17]Cf. AAS, XXXVII, 1945, 44 ff.
[17a]It is the teaching of tradition and the common teaching of theologians that
this marriage, even though not consummated, was real and true. In short, the
exercise of the rights conferred by the matrimonial contract does not pertain to
the essence of marriage. Cf. *infra*, p. 507.

2) shares in the order established by the Hypostatic Union; and,

3) has a special place in the work of the redemption.

1. Joseph is, in a sense, the father of Jesus. It is perfectly apparent from the Bible that the conception of Jesus was effected by the power of the Holy Spirit in the womb of a virgin. Joseph, therefore, has nothing directly and immediately to do with the generation of Christ. Yet human fatherhood does not consist in generation alone. The office of fatherhood consists also in accepting the child as one's own and educating him to take his place in the adult world. With regard to these functions, Joseph was truly the father of Jesus.

But he was not entirely eliminated even with regard to generation. Mary was his wife. No man can consent to the violation of his wife by another man. However, a man can certainly consent to the Supreme Lord of creation miraculously effecting conception in his wife. There-fore, what she conceives is truly his because she is his. Joseph certain-ly consented to the conception of Christ. He had agreed to Mary's perpetual virginity and he accepted her before the world and before God.

Thus it is somewhat misleading to call Joseph the "foster father" of Jesus. He is much more than that. Mary herself calls him the "father" of Jesus: "Thy father and I have been seeking thee sor-rowing" (Lk. 2:48). He is called the father of Jesus on other occasions too, and he exercises the dominion of a father over Christ. It was Joseph who, at the direction of God, gave Jesus his name.[18] Joseph, therefore, since he was the husband of Mary, was, in a very real, though restricted sense, the father of Jesus.

2. Joseph shares in the order established by the Hypostatic Union. Joseph's real share in the hypostatic order is a consequence of his real and natural marriage to the Blessed Virgin. Union can be estab-lished at three levels. At the *metaphysical* level the Word of God established the hypostatic order in himself. Since the Incarnate Word was formed in the womb of the Virgin Mary, her union with the hypostatic order is *physical*. Joseph, because of the moral bond of

[18]Cf. Matt. 1:25.

matrimony which united him to Mary, shares in the hypostatic order at the level of *moral* union.

His marriage, therefore, joins him to the mystery of the Incarnation, since it is part of the eternal decree that Joseph's matrimonial consent should be the protection of Mary's motherhood. Moreover, by his consent, Joseph's matrimonial union designated him as the direct and immediate agent for the fulfillment of the office of fatherhood in rearing the child Jesus. Thus since he was married to Mary, Joseph had a real moral share in the order established by the Hypostatic Union.

3. Joseph has a special place in the work of redemption. The redemption of mankind was the reason for the Incarnation. Thus anyone involved in the Incarnation is involved in the Redemption as well. We have already seen that Mary is the physical cause of Christ, who is the first cause of our redemption. The root of her spiritual maternity relative to all human beings is to be found in her "Fiat" at the Annunciation. Her part in our redemption is rooted in being the Mother of our Redeemer.

There is an analogy between Mary's part in our redemption and the part played by Joseph. Just as her part is founded upon her divine motherhood, his part is founded upon his marriage to Mary. By this marriage, the life of St. Joseph was intimately bound up with the life of Jesus. Since the whole life of Jesus is ordained to our redemption, we can see that the singular association of Joseph with Jesus and Mary gives him a special place in the work of the Redemption. Although his part in the mystery of the Incarnation and in the work of the Redemption is inferior to hers, still it is much superior to that of all the other saints. He had a special role to play in the Incarnation, a role ordained by God in his very act of decreeing the Incarnation of the Word. Since Joseph's place depends on his marriage to Mary, his special union with Christ is through Mary.

It is the growing consciousness on the part of the Church, both laity and hierarchy, of the implications of these theological considerations that has led to an ever-increasing devotion to St. Joseph in modern times. Truly, he is the patron of the Universal Church.

7. Summary and Conclusion

To summarize this chapter on the Mother of God, little more need be said than that **she is the Mother of God.** Because she is, by her free consent, the Mother of God, she is full of grace. This means that, from the time of her Immaculate Conception, she continually grew in her capacity for grace, and her capacity was constantly filled, until she was worthy to be assumed into heaven and crowned as its Queen. Because she is the Mother of God, she shared in our redemption, and is the spiritual mother of us all, charged with dispensing all the graces which God showers upon the earth. Because she is the Mother of God, she deserves special honor from men—the devotion of hyperdulia—and this devotion is a sign of predestination in those who possess it. Because she is the Mother of God, her husband, too, has a unique role to play in our redemption.

> Parce que vous êtes là pour toujours, simplement parce que
>   vous êtes Marie, simplement parce que vous existez,
> Mère de Jésus-Christ, soyez remerciée![19]

Consequent on the teaching of the Church concerning the Mother of God, are these conclusions:

1. The greatest single attraction that Mary should have for us is her normality. There is no record of her having performed extraordinary penances or noteworthy austerities. She was a human mother who washed and cooked and cleaned for her husband and son. And yet, she is above all of the angels in holiness; for whatever task was given to her as Mother of God, she accepted wholeheartedly as the will of God. It does not take much common sense to realize that our own lives could reach the heights of heroic sanctity if only we would give ourselves completely, body and soul, to the workings of grace, as she did.

2. "It is indeed the way of nature that a woman in wedlock brings forth; when an unwed virgin, after she has born a child, is still a virgin, then nature is here surpassed. Of that which happens in accord with nature we may inquire; what passes above it we honor in silence;

---

[19]The last lines of Paul Claudel's poem, *La Vierge à Midi.* They might be translated: "Because you are always there, simply because you are Mary, simply because you exist, O Mother of Jesus Christ, thank you!"

not as something to be avoided, passed over, but as that which we venerate in silence, as something sublime, beyond all telling."[20]

3. The words of Gerard Manley Hopkins, "The world is charged with the grandeur of God," apply in a very significant way to Mary. For, next to her divine Son, she approaches a perfection unequaled in creation. She flows with the grandeur of God as no other creature can. Heaven and earth are her playthings and mankind is her slave.

4. The anguish that St. Joseph felt when he first learned that his wife, a virgin, was to become a mother, must have been acutely painful. But because he was a just man, he decided to put her away privately so that the sword of scandal would not wound the public conscience. His course of action should be a pattern for us. When we discover the faults and idiosyncrasies of others, we should not be quick to judge and condemn, but rather keep our knowledge secret. After all, facts which seem true on the surface may be only part of the reflection of character. Silence concerning matters we cannot explain or understand does not cost us anything.

5. The liturgy connected with the feast of the Annunciation centers wholly around the Mother of God. This feast is the first reminder of the approach of Advent and Christmas. It gives us a chance to focus our meditation on the part Mary played in the Incarnation and consequently in the work of redemption. The liturgy seems to say: several months hence we shall again stand before the newborn King of Peace.

6. Just as we salute God with the title of "Father," we have the privilege of greeting Mary under the title of "Mother." For by adoption we are sons of God and brothers to Christ.

[20]St. John Chrysostom (?), *Second Homily on the Birthday of Our Lord Jesus Christ.*

BIBLIOGRAPHICAL NOTE

St. Thomas' analysis of Mary's role as virgin Mother of God is put forth in the *Summa*, Part III, Questions XXVII-XXX. For a more popular account, consult *The Mother of God* (Westminster, Md.: The Newman Press, 1953), by M. M. Philipon, O.P. In his book, Fr. Philipon gives a happy combination of solid content and appealing devotion. *Mary in Our Life* (New York: P. J. Kenedy and Sons, 1954), by William G. Most, is a study of the dogmas which show Mary's exalted position in the plans of God. Fr. Most's work also points out the means whereby sincere Catholics can make their own lives harmonize with God's plans.

The fullest work available in English on Our Lady is a collection of distinguished essays by competent scholars on all aspects of Marian study. Entitled *Mariology*, it is edited by J. Carol, O.F.M.; two volumes have already been published (Milwaukee: Bruce, 1955-57). A book of the same nature by the great Dutch theolgian, C. X. V. M. Freithoff, O.P., has been recently translated into English as *A Complete Mariology* (London: Blackfriars, 1958).

An account of the divine and human maternity of Mary, and the meaning of this maternity, is expressed in "Mother of the Mystical Body," by G. Geenen, O.P., in *Cross and Crown*, II (1950), 385-402. "Mary's Assumption: History, Theology, Dogma," by L. Russell in *Homiletic and Pastoral Review*, LVII (1956), 31-37, is apologetical in character. It answers the charge that, in defining the dogma of the Assumption, the normal means of appeal having failed, the Catholic Church attempted to prove a historical fact by theological speculations.

A highly technical but very valuable article on the theology of Mary is "Unitive Principle of Marian Theology," by P. Mahoney, O.P., in *The Thomist*, XVIII (1955), 443-479. Chapter XV of *The Teaching of the Catholic Church*, Volume I, yields an article entitled, "Mary, Mother of God," by O. R. Vassall-Phillips, C.SS.R. Abbot Vonier gives his reflections on Mary in Volume I, Book IV of *The Collected Works of Abbot Vonier*. From the abundance of his personal devotion to Mary and his intellectual grasp of the doctrines concerning her, he has produced a fitting tribute to Our Lady.

CHAPTER NINE

Sacred Signs

1. Introduction

It is consummated. Outside of the walls of the Holy City a condemned criminal, suspended on a gibbet between earth and sky, gives up the ghost. But the criminal is Christ, God and man; and the gibbet is the Cross, the altar of salvation; and the death is the Sacrifice which our High Priest offers of himself as most perfect Victim, the culminating, synthesizing, specifying, consummating action of his predestined mediation between the foresworn enemies, God and man. "Christ, our passover, has been sacrificed. Therefore let us keep festival, not with the old leaven or with the leaven of malice and wickedness, but with the unleavened bread of sincerity and truth" (I Cor. 5:7-8).

We should rejoice. And why? "Since, brethren, we are free to enter the Holies in virtue of the blood of Christ, a new and living way which he inaugurated for us through the veil (that is his flesh) . . ." (Heb. 10:19). "The passion of Christ," St. Thomas concludes, "works our salvation: insofar as it is compared to his divinity, it acts as *efficient cause;* insofar as it is compared to the will of his soul it acts as *meritorious cause.* Considered with respect to his flesh, it *satisfies* for us, freeing us from our debt of punishment, and *redeems* us, liberating us from the servitude of sin. It is, finally, a *sacrifice* by which we are reunited with God."[1]

Why should we not keep festival? Christ, to be sure, has ascended above the highest heavens, to sit at the right hand of the throne of majesty, to judge the quick and the dead. But he enters "into heaven itself, to appear now before God on our behalf" (Heb. 9:24), as the glorified Victim of divine love, most pleasing and most acceptable to God.

From our study of Christ's life and death, then, (which presupposes the theological investigation of the God-man conducted in the first five chapters of this volume) we can draw the following momentous conclusions:

1. By his passion Christ *causally* delivered us from sin. "This is to say that Christ, by his passion, has set up the cause of our liberation in virtue of which any sins, whenever committed—in the past, the present, or the future—can be remitted, just as if a doctor should concoct a medicine by which any sick person, even at a future time, could be cured."[2]

2. Christ in heaven is the cause of our salvation. The sacred humanity of the Word is exalted above every creature and bears now the marks of his suffering as glorious signs of his victory. But he remains the victim immolated for our salvation, and his humanity remains the instrument of God and the organ of divinity. Here and now he is our salvation, not only through his moral intercession (cf. Heb. 7:24-25), but through his physical action. The power of our High Priest, the divine energy and causality of his passion and death, remains forever, to exercise its salutary influence on every man who comes into the world. Everything Christ did and suffered for us in his humanity contributes to our salvation by the power of his divinity, as St. Thomas points out,[3] regardless of the passage of time or the distance of space; divine power transcends the restrictions of time and space. So the glorious Christ, the God-man, is, even in heaven, the cause of our

---

[1]*Summa*, III, q. 48, a. 6, ad 3.
[2]*Ibid.*, q. 49, a. 1, ad 3.
[3]*Ibid.*, q. 56, a. 1, ad 3.

salvation—the meritorious and satisfactory cause, the redeeming, reconciling and impetrative cause, and the instrumental efficient cause. In the fullest possible sense, *Christ is our Savior.*

3. Man must unite himself with Christ. God, who created man without his co-operation, will not re-create him by grace without his co-operation. As beings dignified by the power of free will, we who are by nature children of wrath can only become brothers of Christ and God's sons by freely uniting ourselves with our Savior. God takes the initiative in our salvation, calling us to divine fellowship through the grace which is the fruit of his sacrifice; but we must respond, at least to the extent of placing no obstacle to this pouring forth of the infinite riches won by Christ's blood. We must become one with our High Priest to share the fruits of his redemption.

4. Man unites himself with Christ through faith and the sacraments of faith. "Although Christ's passion is corporeal, from its union with divinity it possesses a spiritual power. And therefore it obtains its efficacy through spiritual contact—i.e., through faith and the sacraments of faith."[4]

1) *Faith.* To know our Savior, the God-man, through the supernatural light of faith (not with the eyes of our body or of our reason) is to establish vital contact with him, our first response to God's invitation to unite ourselves with his Son. But knowledge alone is not sufficient to bring two persons together; the psychiatrist, fortunately for him, does not become one with all the characters who pour out their sad stories on his couch. When the supernatural knowledge of faith is vivified by divine love— God's outpouring of charity in our hearts to which we must also give our free acceptance—then truly does the union of God and man achieve consummation. For then and then only is the whole man, precisely according to the powers most characteristically his, his intellect and his will, in vital, fruitful contact with Christ. Participating in his divine life of light and of

---

[4] *Ibid.,* q. 48, a. 6, ad 2; cf. q. 49, a. 1, ad 4 and 5, a. 3, ad 1, etc.

love, we become members of his Mystical Body, his brothers and his Father's sons and heirs. Since his divine life already circulates in our souls, every good act, every good work performed or accepted out of love for him, unites us ever more intimately with him and intensifies this life within us and our love for God. Then is realized Paul's fervent prayer (Eph. 3:14-19):

> For this reason I bend my knees to the Father of our Lord Jesus Christ, from whom all fatherhood in heaven and on earth receives its name, that he may grant you from his glorious riches to be strengthened with power through his spirit unto the progress of the inner man; and to have Christ dwelling through faith in your hearts: so that, being rooted and grounded in love, you may be able to comprehend with all the saints what is the breadth and length and height and depth, and to know Christ's love which surpasses knowledge, in order that you may be filled unto all the fulness of God.

For Catholics, then, faith is a far more sublime, more embracing, more meaningful thing than the emotional response in which Protestants seek to find union with Christ. Faith is not a simple blind trust in our justification, a confidence we *feel* that we have contacted Christ. It is a truly vital and vitalizing union of intellect and will (elevated and supernaturalized by God's real physical gifts) with our Savior in true knowledge and true love. Faith is an ontological modification of our power of knowing which issues through the virtue of charity in supernatural love. Our good human acts, which proceed under the directive force of these supernatural principles, are thus themselves interiorly suffused and vivified supernaturally. This is Christian action, man's living the life of Christ which is in him, truly one with Christ and perceptibly participating in the fruits of his passion.

2) *The sacraments of faith.* But if the living faith of the Christian is his fundamental contact with Christ and the root of his union with his Savior's redemptive work, it is by no means his only contact. God in his wisdom made man a composite of spirit and matter; in his wisdom he draws man to himself through the

visible world in which he places him. To redeem fallen man he sends his Son in our visible flesh. And he provides for our participation in Christ's redemption not only through the invisible contact of faith but through the visible contact of the sacraments.

So true is this that we must not think of these two channels of Christian grace as diverse and isolated avenues of approach to God. On the contrary, although different streams of divine life which flow from the foot of the Cross, they so intermingle and interpenetrate that there is no redemption by faith alone or by the sacraments without faith. Man's loving belief in God includes as a necessary minimum for salvation at least an implicit desire to receive the sacraments. And the sacraments are **sacraments of faith:** they are not magical rites which produce their effects regardless of man's attitude toward them and toward God. The adult who receives them must be properly disposed, i.e., he must believe in Christ, for they are external protestations of that faith, meaningless and empty if it be wanting. This necessary minimal faith is demanded even of infants receiving baptism, but here faith is not the result of their proper activity but of the Church, of whose fruitful womb they are reborn.

The remainder of this book (with the exception of the last two chapters) will treat of these divine channels of grace called the sacraments. We shall first consider the sacraments in general and then each of the seven sacraments of the New Law—baptism, confirmation, Holy Eucharist, penance, extreme unction, holy orders and matrimony.[5]

With respect to the general treatment of the sacraments we shall follow the scientific order of St. Thomas in his *Summa* (III, qq. 60-65) which examines these supernatural realities through an investigation of their intrinsic and extrinsic causes:

---

[5]Cf. the *Decree for the Armenians* of the Council of Florence (Denz. 695), Council of Trent, Sess. VII, Can. 1 (Denz. 844).

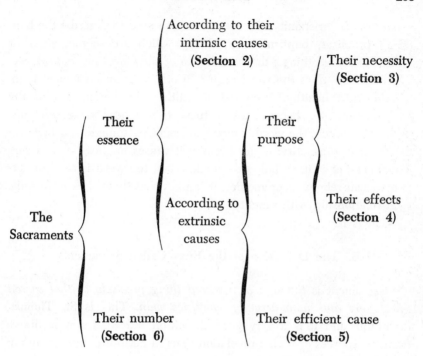

The Sacraments
- Their essence
  - According to their intrinsic causes (Section 2)
  - According to extrinsic causes
    - Their purpose
      - Their necessity (Section 3)
      - Their effects (Section 4)
    - Their efficient cause (Section 5)
- Their number (Section 6)

2. The Nature of the Sacraments

A. The Meaning of the Word

Although for us the word "sacrament" signifies the special, sanctifying rites bequeathed us by Christ with which we are familiar from our youth—baptism, confirmation, etc.—it was centuries before this word acquired so exclusive and restricted a meaning. The Church's lexicographer, St. Isidore, believed it meant something hidden or secret; others trace its etymology to the Latin word meaning "to make sacred or holy"; while still others maintain it has its origin in the word designating something in itself sacred.

The Romans called the oath taken by their soldiers a "sacrament," and they used the same word to describe the money which parties to a litigation left on deposit in the temple treasury. With early ecclesiastical writers the word was adopted to mean something mysterious (the mysteries of Christianity). Hence it was also used to describe the baptismal promises, baptism itself, things which are sacred, signs or figures of sacred things, the sacred rites of the Christian religion, etc.

What, then, *does* the word mean? Briefly, it is an analogical term, like the word "healthy." We speak of healthy color, healthy air, healthy environment, etc., because all of these things bear some reference to health. So, too, the word "sacrament" signifies something which has a reference to sanctity: either because it causes holiness, or is a sign of holiness, or is itself holy or sacred. When the word is used of certain special religious ceremonies, it implies that these rites have some such relationship with sanctity.

What is it?

B. The Definition of the Rites Called Sacraments

A sacrament is *the sign of a sacred thing precisely as that sacred thing here and now actually sanctifies man.* This is St. Thomas' definition, and it is a very good definition indeed, for it is drawn from the sources of divine revelation (Sacred Scripture and Tradition) and only God can tell us what these supernatural realities truly are. The better to understand these great Christian mysteries, we must examine this definition in detail.

(1) The Sacraments as Signs

A sacrament is a sign. Following St. Augustine,[6] theologians call "signs" all those realities whose whole point in existing is to inform us of some reality besides themselves, over and beyond whatever impression they make on our sense faculties of knowing. Signs are essentially intermediaries between ourselves as knowing beings and an object to be known; self-effacing and modest by nature, they are of value only to the degree they notify and instruct us about this other reality they make present to us. The black figures left by the printing-press on these pages, for example, are of little worth in themselves; their whole importance is to convey an idea, the mental expression of some other reality, to your minds. Similarly, the yellow

[6]*On Christian Doctrine*, Bk. II, Chap. 1.

octagonal piece of metal on the street corner, with the black letters S T O P on it, is of little importance in itself; its business, its nature, is to let people know they should halt their cars at this intersection.

To this general class of things the sacraments belong. They are signs —that is, realities which, in forcing their attention on our faculties of sense knowledge, tell us about other things than themselves. In the Old Law circumcision was such a reality—the sign of the pact between God and man.[7] Christ himself describes the Eucharist as a commemorative sign of his passion and death,[8] while St. Paul speaks of baptism as the sign of our spiritual rebirth and of matrimony as a sign of Christ's union with the Church.[9] This is a vital point, for it indicates that the importance of these divine realities is determined not by what they are in themselves but—as is the case with all signs— by what they signify.

All the sacraments will manifest the following notes, which are characteristic of all signs, or at least of certain types. They will be:

1) *Sensible* signs, i.e., material realities which can be seen or heard, smelled or touched or tasted—or any combination of these. For only man obtains knowledge through the use of signs, and man's knowledge begins with his senses.

2) *Conventional signs.* Some things are by their own nature signs of something else—weeping of sorrow, smoke of fire, etc. The sacraments are not such **natural** signs, for the material elements of which they are composed cannot of their nature express the spiritual and supernatural. On the contrary, they become signs of sanctity only by a convention, because they are instituted as such either mediately or immediately by God. Since God chooses as his sacramental signs certain sensible realities which have a certain aptness to signify this or that (thus the washing with water in baptism suggests the spiritual cleansing of the soul), the sacraments are not simply arbitrary signs but rather *symbolical* signs.

[7] Cf. Gen. 17:11; Rom. 4:11.
[8] I Cor. 11:24.
[9] Rom. 6:3, Tit. 3:5, Eph. 5:32.

(2) *What the Sacraments Signify*

A sacrament is a sign **of a sacred thing.** All signs have in common the fact that they represent something other than themselves. *What* they signify, then—the object represented—will distinguish one sign from another. The sacraments signify something sacred or holy—this is why they have the name they bear. But there are many other things which are sacred signs too: crucifixes, statues, certain ceremonies, etc. So we must find a more determining signification than this if we are to define the sacraments as the unique divine realities they are.

A sacrament is distinct from other signs of a sacred thing precisely because it signifies that **that sacred thing here and now sanctifies man.** Here truly is the distinctive and distinguishing note of these special supernatural signs. They signify holiness—not the sanctity of God or his saints, but the holiness of this man receiving the sacrament. From this fact flow two important consequences:

1) At one and the same time a sacrament signifies 1) the *cause* of man's holiness, the passion of Christ; 2) the *form* or intrinsic principle of man's holiness, sanctifying grace; and 3) the *goal* of man's holiness, his future glory. Since man here and now is sanctified by grace, this is the thing principally signified by these signs. But sacramental signification means even more yet than this; it means that man's holiness is **produced at the very moment the sacramental sign is present**—in the presence of this sacred sign God causes sanctifying grace in the soul of the one using this sign, the recipient. Hence:

2) The sacraments are **practical** signs, ordained not only to instructing man about holiness but to obtaining man's holiness. Just as a stop-and-go light is intended to halt vehicles or permit them to proceed, and not only to inform us of these facts, so the purpose of the sacraments is to secure this end, man's sanctification, not just to give us information. Whether the sacraments effect this result of themselves does not matter (the stop-and-go light does not stop the cars, the drivers do). The point is that they

Mystery of Christ
Do research + Expand Hogan
thesis

Schillebech

signify that the effect is actually produced here and now in their presence; man is sanctified. And this is the great, the overwhelming difference, which distinguishes these sacred signs from all other signs of sacred things—the sacramentals, statues, stained glass images, etc.

C. The Physical Nature of the Sacraments

The sacraments are signs. But signs are realities useful only for human beings, and human knowledge proceeds from sense objects to intellectual comprehension. Hence, God in his wisdom gives man material, sensible realities as signs of the spiritual and supernatural, for these are accommodated to man's nature. We will analyze this fact more in detail.

(1) The Material Element of the Sacraments

The sacraments are constituted by certain sense-perceptible realities which are the subject of sacramental signification. The pouring of water in baptism, for example, signifies (together with the accompanying words) the spiritual cleansing of the soul by grace. Man can see and hear, and even feel this action; it affects his senses. By it he knows that holiness is being effected in him, grace is given him. So, too, with all the sacraments, even those (like circumcision and the sacrifice of the paschal lamb) of the Old Law. Some sense-perceptible religious ceremony, which is symbolic of his interior sanctification by grace, takes place, and the proper use of this sacred symbol guarantees that the sanctifying work which is signified will itself take place within him. It should be noted that the ritual **use** of a certain thing (water, oil), the ceremonial or liturgical action, is the true sign; the material thing itself only *remotely* suggests the intended meaning, but the use made of it by man's action makes it *proximately* meaningful.

Every sacrament, then, is a composite of two things: the sensible element, and the special meaning which this sense-perceptible action conveys. This sacramental signification does not belong by nature to these sensible actions (the sacraments are **conventional** signs, not natural signs), even though they possess a certain aptness or congruity to express what they do (the sacraments are **symbolical** signs).

This means that some intelligent being must determine what sensible things and actions will be used, and what they will mean in spiritual, supernatural terms. And since man's sanctification is not of himself and his power, but from God, then it follows that the sense-perceptible realities which are the subject of sacramental signification will all be determined by God. In the ages which preceded God's revelation to Moses, God inspired man to select some particular ritual which would be expressive of belief in him and signify man's redemption from original and personal sin through the foreseen merits of Christ. With the revelation of the Law came also the revelation of God's selection of certain sensible ceremonies as sacramental signs, and these were promulgated by Moses. The New Law, the perfection and consummation of the Old Law, witnesses to the institution of more perfect sacraments by Jesus Christ.[10] It is the common teaching of theologians (and hence theologically certain) that all the seven sacraments of the New Law were instituted immediately by Christ, without the mediation of the apostles or of the Church.[11]

(2) The Words of the Sacraments

The greater perfection of the sacred signs instituted by Christ himself demands that that their subject be more expressive and manifestive of the sacred reality they are chosen to signify. Because of this, the subjects of the sacramental signification of the New Testament are composed not only of sense-perceptible actions but also of *words*.

For us human beings words are the chief and most powerful of all signs, i.e., the most meaningful. In the Old Law the "weak and needy elements" which were sacraments consisted in certain ceremonies alone, like eating the paschal lamb. But Christ designates words for his sacraments, so that, together with the ceremonial action, the full significance of what is taking place may be clearly realized. In confirmation, for instance, the anointing with chrism only vaguely con-

[10]Council of Trent, Sess. VII, Can. 1; Denz. 844.
[11]Cf. Emmanuel Doranzo, O.M.I., *De Sacramentis in Genere*, pp. 397-404.

veys the supernatural strengthening which is conferred; this is made explicit by the words of the Bishop, "I confirm (strengthen) you with the chrism of salvation." The words thus perfect the meaning of the action.

The sacraments of the New Law, in consequence, are far more perfect signs; but this perfection depends on a more elaborate and complex composition:

Sacramental Sign
- Sensible sign
  - Material element (sacramental action)
    - Thing
    - Use of thing
  - Words
- Signification or meaning

(3) The Matter and Form of the Sacraments

All of the sacramental signs of the New Law are composed of a double element, both of sense-perceptible actions and of words. Since the words clearly state what the liturgical action means, they may be said to perfect or determine the action in the line of signification. Water may be used, for example, to refresh, or to nourish, or to cleanse, etc.; the baptismal words tell us just what meaning is intended by the use of water in that sacrament. By comparison with the hylomorphic composition of material objects, in which form specifies and determines matter, the sacramental *words* are known as the **form** of the sacrament and the sacramental *action* as its **matter**. The matter itself is composed of the things used (called the *remote* matter, because less determined and significative) and the actual use of these things (known as the *proximate* matter).

This analogy of the sacraments with the hylomorphic composition of material objects enunciates the following truths:

1) Actions and words are essential and intrinsic parts of the composite subject of all New Testament sacraments.
2) Together they constitute one essence; if one is missing there is no sacrament. Hence there must be a *moral* unity of words and

actions, i.e., they must be so closely united in time and space that it is clear that the words apply to the action and that the action is specified by the words.

3) The words, being more expressive, perfect and specify the meaning of the less determinate element in the signification, the ceremonial action. So they are called the "form" of the sacraments, and the actions their "matter."

From this analysis of the physical nature of the sacraments an important fact emerges.

Since the sacraments are instituted by God, no one, not even the Church, can *substantially* change a sacrament. It should be clearly understood that a slight change in the form—a mispronunciation, addition, omission, etc.—which does not change the sense of the words does not alter the essence of the sacrament. Similarly, a merely accidental change of the matter—water from a faucet rather than from the baptismal font, for example—does not change the essence of the sacrament.

3. The Necessity of the Sacraments

Something of the tremendous importance of these sacred signs to our journey to God should now be clear. The omnipotent God could, of course, redeem and save us without making us dependent on these sensible signs, just as he could have redeemed us without becoming incarnate.[12] That he does not do so—that, on the contrary, he carefully institutes the sacraments—reveals both his infinite wisdom and his tremendous love for man. As St. Thomas points out, there are three reasons which manifest the necessity (in the sense of a most fitting means for securing the end, our salvation) of these symbols of sanctification:

> *The first reason: from the condition of human nature.* It is characteristic of human nature to be led to spiritual and intellectual things by means of corporeal and sensible things. Now it belongs to divine providence to provide for each thing according to its characteristic nature. Therefore divine wisdom fittingly gives man the aids for salvation under certain corporeal and sensible signs which are called sacraments.

[12]Cf. *supra*, Chap. Two, Sect. 3, 82-85.

The second reason: from man's state. By sinning man subjected himself to corporeal things through his affection. But there where he suffered disease ought a medicinal remedy be applied to him. Hence it was fitting that God should apply spiritual medicine to men through certain corporeal signs. For if spiritual things had been nakedly proposed to him, his soul, being given over to bodily things, could not have been applied to them.

The third reason: from the inclination of human action, which concerns itself chiefly with material things. Lest it should be hard for man to be withdrawn entirely from bodily actions, bodily exercises were offered to him in the sacraments. By these he could be so healthfully exercised as to avoid superstitious practices (which make up the worship of devils) and all manner of harmful activity (which consists in sinful deeds).[13]

These reasons underlie a rather startling conclusion of St. Thomas— that there would have been no sacraments in the state of innocence. For Adam was so perfected by God's supernatural and preternatural gifts that he was completely independent of material, corporeal things. To be subject to them in the most important matter of all, his spiritual and supernatural welfare, would have contradicted the special perfection of this state.

After man's fall through Adam's sin from his high estate, however, sacraments were necessary for his salvation. Since that salvation comes only through Christ, these visible signs would be protestations of belief in the Redeemer. Before Christ's coming these sacraments would be visible protestations of man's belief in the future Redeemer. After his mission was accomplished, other sacraments would be necessary to signify man's belief in the work of salvation the Redeemer had already accomplished.

4. The Efficacy and Effects of the Sacraments

There are seven sacraments of the New Law: Baptism, confirmation, the Eucharist, penance, extreme unction, holy orders and matrimony which greatly differ from the sacraments of the Old Law. For they did not cause grace but were only figures of the grace to be given by Christ's passion; but our sacraments both contain grace and bestow it on those who receive the sacraments worthily. . . . Among these

[13]*Summa,* III, q. 61, a. 1.

sacraments there are three—baptism, confirmation and holy orders—
which imprint an indelible character on the soul, i.e., a certain spiritual
and distinguishing sign.[13a]

Sacramental grace, sacramental character—these are the effects of
the sacraments of the New Law, the first their principal effect, the
second a secondary one. But before we examine these effects, it is
first necessary to consider the manner in which the sacraments produce them in our souls.

A. The Efficacy of the Sacraments

The gift of God which sanctifies us, which makes us holy and pleasing to God, is the divine life of our soul; the *form* or formal principle
of our supernatural life as the human soul is the form of our natural
life. This is grace—*a habit which modifies the very essence of the
soul, giving us a real, physical (although analogical) participation of
God's own nature.* By it we truly become divine, brothers of Christ
and sons of God; from it supernatural virtues and gifts which are the
proximate sources of our divine life flow into our human powers.

All sacraments of the Old Law, as well as of the Christian dispensation, signify the presence of this grace within the souls of those using
them. Our sacraments—the sacraments of Christ and the Church—
further signify *that they themselves effect this marvelous change in
the souls of men.* **The sacraments of the New Law cause the grace
which they signify.**

(1) The Fact

This astonishing notion, that the sacraments *contain* and *cause*
grace is a fact. It is a revealed dogma based on no less authority than
the word of God himself.

1) The efficacy of baptism is clearly taught by St. Paul (Rom. 6:3-
   11), and is the basis for Christ's insistence, in his conversation
   with Nicodemus, on its necessity (cf. Jn. 3:1-7). Christ himself
   promises, in a saying too hard for those of little faith, that they
   who eat his flesh and drink his blood, and they alone, shall

[13a]Council of Florence, *Decree for the Armenians;* Denz. 695.

possess eternal life (Jn. 6:32-59). The Sacred Scriptures explicitly affirm the efficacy of confirmation (cf. Acts 8:17) and penance (Jn. 20:23).

2) The Tradition of the Church universally and unanimously declares the same truth. To cite only one of a thousand examples: Tertullian states unequivocally: "The body is washed, that the soul may be cleansed; the body is anointed, that the soul may be consecrated; the body is signed, that the soul may be strengthened; the body is overshadowed, that the soul may be illuminated by the Spirit; the body is fed with the body and blood of Christ, so that the soul may be nourished even with God."[14]

3) Against the doctrinal innovations of the so-called reformers, the Church solemnly proclaims the truth: "If anyone says that the sacraments of the New Law do not contain the grace which they signify or that they do not confer that grace on those who place no obstacle (as if they were only external signs of the grace or justification received through faith and a sort of mark of Christion profession by which the faithful are distinguished by men from infidels), *let him be anathema*."[15]

(2) The Statement of the Fact

The causality and efficacy of the sacred signs instituted by Christ is succinctly expressed in a classical formula: **The sacraments of the New Law confer grace** *ex opere operato* **on those who place no obstacle to its reception.** Two phrases of this statement demand further explanation.

1. **Ex opere operato.** Literally translated this means "from the work worked," i.e., from the sacramental sign itself, the ceremony or sacred rite composed of actions and words. The objective, impersonal accomplishment of the sacramental sign effectively causes grace of itself alone. It is not the labors of man (**ex opere operantis**, "from the work of the worker") that produce the effects of the sacraments; no matter how good and holy a man is, or how meritorious his action,

---

[14]*Concerning the Resurrection of the Body*, Chap. 8.
[15]Council of Trent, Sess. VII, Can. 6 (Denz. 849); cf. Council of Florence, *Decree for the Armenians* (Denz. 695).

he does not of himself cause the sacramental effects, although he can impede them. When water is poured on the head of a child in the name of the persons of the Trinity, the child by the very performance of that act ceases to be "a child of wrath" and becomes a son of God.

In this manner Christ himself acts through the signs he has instituted. The grace which he won by his passion and death is transmitted through these objective realities and applied to the individual Christian. It is not the human element in the Church which sanctifies mankind, but the power of Christ alone. Man does not baptize, man does not absolve, but Christ alone, through the sacraments themselves.

2. On those who place no obstacle. These Christian symbols are signs of faith, and by their use the Christian protests, publicly and perceptibly, his living faith in Christ, in his passion and in his Church. The recipient who has attained religious and moral consciousness, however, must prepare himself subjectively for the grace objectively implanted by the sacraments. Else he places an impenetrable obstacle to the flood of divine life Christ would pour on his soul; his protestation of faith is a mockery, and he himself a hypocrite who sacrilegiously abuses sacred things.

Briefly, man must open his soul to the grace offered by the sacraments through his own acts (which presuppose the divine movement and assistance of actual grace) of faith, hope and love; if he be in the state of mortal sin, he must also produce acts of contrition (at least imperfect contrition or attrition) and repentance. *Impenitence* would effectively bar the grace conferred by the "sacraments of the dead" (baptism and penance). Similarly, the *consciousness of mortal sin* impedes the fruitful reception of the "sacraments of the living."

The sacraments, then, are not magical rites which confer grace automatically, regardless of man's attitude toward them and toward their source, Jesus Christ. They are God's instruments, and God does not sanctify us without our co-operation. On the other hand, man's preparation (*opus operantis*, "the work of the worker") is not the *effective* cause of the grace of the sacraments and his sanctification, it only removes the obstacles to its reception. Opening a window lets the freshening breath of spring into the room, but does not produce the freshness; by his preparatory, dispositive acts man opens his soul to the quickening breath of the Spirit, but he does not cause his sanctification.

It is the *work worked*, the sacramental rite, that effects this participation of divine life which is his sanctification.

(3) Explanation of the Fact

The sacraments, not the man, truly cause grace. To account for this singular fact, divinely revealed to us, various theological theories have been proposed. These, naturally enough, are of very unequal merit in explaining the causality of the sacraments, and the only theory which seems fully satisfactory is that of St. Thomas and his disciples: *the sacraments are physical instrumental causes of man's sanctification by grace.*

1. **The sacraments of Christ are instrumental causes.** As we have seen in our discussion of the efficient causality of Christ's humanity,[16] an instrument has two powers: one which is proper to its nature as a physical reality (the power of a pencil to make dark marks, for example); and a higher power which is proper to the principal agent and only transiently communicated to it (the power of a clarinet to make music when played by a musician). The sacraments of the New Law have their own proper power and activity: they *signify,* i.e., they notify and instruct us of our supernatural sanctification through Christ's passion which will lead to our eternal glory. More than this, they *cause:* God, the principal author of grace, through Christ uses their power of signification to produce what they make known to us. This he does by elevating their natural activity, giving these sacred signs a participation in his own infinite activity and power. Just as the piano is the true cause of the music you hear (although not its principal cause), so the sacraments of Christ are true causes of his grace in us.

2. **The sacraments of Christ are physical causes.** Unlike other practical signs, these symbols of the Christian religion themselves work (as instruments) the effect which they represent as being accomplished here and now. *They are direct and immediate (physical) causes of*

[16]Cf. *supra*, Chap. Four, Section 5, 160-163.

man's sanctification; that is, they have a true share with God in the physical production of the physical being of the effects of the sacraments. This conclusion is based on several facts:

1) The strong words of Sacred Scripture, which attribute to the baptismal "bath" itself, for example, the spiritual regeneration of man.[17]

2) The statements and examples of the Fathers, who ascribe an intrinsic power to the sacraments, "The sanctified waters," declares Tertullian, "absorb the power of sanctifying."[18] "Whence such a power in water," asks St. Augustine, "that it touches the body and washes the heart?"[19] And St. Ambrose answers that question by stating that divinity itself is present in the baptismal waters.[20]

3) The definitive expressions of the Councils of Florence and Trent. While these do not directly affirm the physical causality of Christ's sacraments (nor were they meant to), they not only permit but almost demand such an interpretation. These sacramental rites themselves "contain and confer grace";[21] they themselves possess a sanctifying *vigor*,[22] a spiritual *power*,[23] so that by the **power of the words themselves** bread and wine are changed into the body and blood of Christ.[24]

In view of these descriptions of the efficacy of the sacraments of the New Law, any other explanation than that of true physical efficient causality seems insufficient. Certain medieval theologians thought that they were **occasional causes**, i.e., the use of the sacraments would present occasions for God's causing grace in us, or a necessary condition for obtaining such graces.[25] Obviously, however, an occasion or condition is not a true cause, but rather an opportunity.

---

[17]Cf. Jn. 3:5; Ephes. 5:26; Tit. 3:5; II Tim. 1:6; Jn. **6:56.**
[18]*On Baptism,* Chap. 4.
[19]*Tract LXXX on the Gospel according to St. John,* n. 3.
[20]*On the Christian Mysteries,* Chap. III, n. 8.
[21]Council of Florence, *Decree for the Armenians* (Denz. 695); Council of Trent, Sess. VII, Can. 6 (Denz. 849).
[22]Council of Trent, Sess. VII, *On Baptism,* Can. 1; Denz. 857.
[23]*Ibid., On Confirmation,* Can. 2; Denz. 872.
[24]*Ibid.,* Sess. XIII, Chap. 3; Denz. 876.
[25]Such was the opinion, in substance, of William of Auvergne, St. Bonaventure and Scotus, among others.

Hence others propose the sacraments as **moral causes**, which move God to confer grace on the one using them.[26] Yet in this case the sacraments themselves, whatever their intrinsic worth or dignity, do not cause grace (God produces grace directly, not *through* or *by* the sacraments), and it is difficult to see how they could be called intrinsically efficacious.

A more modern theory (that of Cardinal Billot, S.J.), known as **intentional causality,** seems even more deficient. In this explanation, the sacraments, as purveyors of Christ's intentions, produce a disposition in their recipients which demands as its complement the grace God himself will cause. Here, again, the explanation seems to attenuate the true dignity and efficacy of the sacraments which is attested to by Scripture and Tradition. All of these "systems," in short, seem to reduce the sacraments of the New Law to mere signs, like the sacraments of the old dispensation.

St. Thomas' theory, on the contrary, admirably accounts for the revealed facts. The sacraments of Christ are real physical causes—*direct and immediate causes*—of the supernatural effects of justification, of the grace which sanctifies. In the other theories God alone produces and causes these physical effects, while the sacraments, in one way or another, move or induce him to do so; for St. Thomas, both God and the sacraments are true causes of sacramental grace and sacramental character in their physical existence, both produce and attain the physical being of these effects. The sacraments, however, produce their effects not in virtue of any native power but as Christ's instruments, applying the fruits of his passion here and now to the individual Christian. They are, so to say, the prolongation of the Incarnation among us; they extend to this time and this place the salvific mission wrought by the God-man through the instrumentality of his humanity.

B. The Grace of the Sacraments

Grace, considered in itself, perfects the essence of the soul, since it is a participation of a certain likeness of the divine essence. And as the powers of the soul flow from its essence, so certain perfections

[26]This theory, first proposed by the Dominican, Melchior Cano, is still held by many today.

(called the virtues and gifts) flow from grace into the soul's powers, and by these the powers are perfected with respect to their actions. Now the sacraments are orderd to certain special effects in the Christian life. Thus baptism is ordered to a kind of spiritual regeneration, by which a man dies to vice and becomes a member of Christ—a special effect over and above the acts of the powers of the soul. And the same ordination to these special effects is found in the other sacraments.

Consequently, just as the virtues and gifts add to grace commonly so called a certain perfection specifically ordained to the acts proper to the various powers of the soul, so sacramental grace adds, both to grace commonly so called and to the virtues and gifts, a certain divine assistance in obtaining the special end of each sacrament.[26a]

An analysis of this doctrine, commonly held by the Church's theologians brings out several points worth considering more in detail.

(1) Sanctifying Grace

All the sacraments confer sanctifying grace, a participation of the divinity of God. Baptism and penance produce divine life in the soul which is supernaturally dead by reason of serious sin, either original sin or actual mortal sin. Hence they are called *sacraments of the dead.* The other sacraments increase and intensify the life of grace in those already supernaturally alive through sanctifying grace. Hence they are called *sacraments of the living,* and may be fruitfully received only by those in the state of grace.

Sometimes, however, the "sacraments of the dead" will cause an increase of divine life, namely, when they are received by those already in the state of grace. Conversely, the "sacraments of the living" will occasionally cause grace to exist in the soul spiritually dead. This would happen only if a man, truly not conscious of a mortal sin he was guilty of, would in good faith receive one of the sacraments of the living, with sorrow for sin and other necessary dispositions of soul, but without perfect contrition.[27]

(2) Sacramental Graces

As St. Thomas teaches, each sacrament confers a grace proper to itself alone. This is not, however, a new supernatural *habit.* Rather,

[26a]St. Thomas, *Summa,* III, q. 62, a. 2.
[27]Cf. *Summa,* III, q. 72, a. 7, ad 2; q. 79, a. 3.

the special grace conferred by each sacrament, known as **sacramental grace,** may be defined: *an intrinsic perfection so modifying sanctifying grace as to add a special vigor, as well as the right to actual graces when occasion demands, in order to obtain its special end relative to the Christian life.*

To understand what this means we will treat each point individually.

1) Each sacrament of Christ confers *a special grace.* This follows from the very fact that there are several sacraments which differ in their signification and hence also in their causality. Otherwise one sacrament would suffice.

2) This sacramental grace *is not a new habit.* Sanctifying grace and the virtues and gifts which emanate from it are fully sufficient for the divinization of the soul and its faculties; any further habit would be superfluous. There is no act of the Christian which cannot be accounted for by his state of grace and the supernatural virtues and gifts of grace.

3) This grace *intrinsically modifies sanctifying grace, giving it a special force or vigor to obtain the end of each sacrament.* St. Thomas describes these sacramental graces as "different medicines for the defects of sin."[28] His great follower, Cardinal Cajetan, explains: "The proper effect of baptism is not sanctifying grace absolutely considered, but so to be re-born by grace as a member of Christ as if one had suffered together with the suffering Christ. And this means the remission of every sin and of every penalty for sin."[29] Thus baptismal grace brings together whatever in sanctifying grace, in the virtues, and in the gifts has reference to spiritual regeneration, and it orders these supernatural habits under its force to procure Christian regeneration. And the same is analogously true of every other sacrament.

4) This grace also confers *a special title to God's actual graces to enable the recipients, when need arises, to achieve the end of each sacrament.* For all their life together, the sacramentally married couple, for example, have a true right to God's special

[28]*De Veritate,* q. 27, a. 5, ad 12.
[29]*Commentary on the Summa,* III, q. 62, a. 2, n. 3.

help to fulfill their matrimonial obligations: to deal charitably with each other, to raise their children prudently, etc., etc.

(3) The Causing of Sacramental Grace

Not by "the work of the worker" (*ex opere operantis*), the actions of the subject receiving the sacrament, is grace produced in his soul; on the contrary, the sacrament itself causes grace. But the dispositions of the subject are of great importance, his faith, hope and charity or contrition. For sacramental grace is received in the measure of the disposition of the recipients. Just as the same amount of heat will cause a greater fire if the wood is drier, so the fire of divine love which is caused by the sacraments will be greater in the souls of those whose more perfect spiritual preparation removes obstacles to God's grace and prepares them better for its reception.

There is, of course, a cause of this effect other than the sacraments: every sacramental grace is derived from Christ's passion. As we have seen, [30] Christ's passion, as the culminating action of his divine-human life, is the universal cause of man's salvation. His sacred humanity is the organ of his divinity in producing grace in us, but it is an instrument hypostatically united to the Godhead. As a great artist communicates his artistic power to the piano (separated instrument) by means of his fingers, hands and arms (conjoined instruments); so God communicates his power to the sacraments (separated instruments) through the sacred humanity of Christ (conjoined instrument), which procured our redemption on the cross. In very truth, Jesus Christ acts through our sacraments: they are the separated instruments of his humanity which is the conjoined instrument of his divinity.

C. Sacramental Character

The Schoolmen insist that the sacraments of faith produce another effect besides grace, a secondary effect which is yet as real as grace and prior to it by nature. Thus there are three elements in every sacrament: the exterior rite which signifies, this intermediate effect

[30]Cf. *supra*, Chap. Seven, Sect. 4, 231-234.

caused by the sensible sign and itself signifying the further effect which is caused, and the final reality (sacramental grace) produced and signified by the exterior rite and the intermediate sign-effect. In the language of the Schools, now adopted (as is this doctrine) by all theologians, we may represent these various elements in this way:

1) **Sacramentum tantum**—the sensible sign (*sacramentum*) or exterior rite which directly both signifies and causes two effects, and is not itself signified in any way. The rite of baptism or confirmation is such a *sacramentum*.

2) **Res et sacramentum**—the first effect (*res*) signified and caused by the sensible sign. It is not only a physical, spiritual reality, however; together with the *sacramentum tantum* and dependent upon it, it is both a sign and a cause (*sacramentum*) of the sacrament's further effect. Thus it is both signified and signifying, caused and causing. The sacramental characters of baptism, confirmation and holy orders; the body and blood of Christ in the Eucharist; the interior penitence of sacramental penance— these are both *res* and *sacramentum*, effect and sign.

3) **Res tantum**—the ultimate and principal effect, sacramental grace. It is signified and caused by both the *sacramentum tantum* and the *res et sacramentum*, but is itself neither a sign nor a cause of any further sacramental effect.

A closer, more penetrating, and more scientific study of the sacraments, and of the revealed data concerning them, convinced the medieval thinkers that all our sacraments produce this intermediate reality-sign (*res et sacramentum*), as well as the effect it signifies, sacramental grace. Although it is a spiritual thing, a physical but supernatural ornamentation of the soul, it can be a sign because of its infallible link with the exterior sensible reality; it is also a preparatory cause which disposes for the grace which the *sacramentum tantum* effectively produces.

Every sacrament of the Christian faith produces this secondary effect, as we shall see when we consider the individual sacraments. But for some sacraments the *res et sacramentum* is of such a special

nature that it is given the special name of **sacramental character.**
These will be the subject of our present investigation.

(1) The Existence of Sacramental Characters

The word "character" is of Greek origin, and originally described
the mark or brand physically impressed on animals and later also on
soldiers. Through usage it came to mean any distinguishing note,
sign or image, particularly those which set off things or persons
deputed to public use or functions. Legal documents and money bore
official seals called "characters"; the insignia of public office were
known by the same word.

St. Augustine adopted the word as an apt description of the
effects worked by some of the sacraments which distinguished Christians from non-Christians, and even one Christian from another. The
reality so described was, of course, known to others before him, as
the practice of the Church in refusing to baptize again clearly shows.
Unlike sacramental grace which can be lost (and hence its sacramental cause can be repeated), this distinguishing mark can never be
effaced; so there can be no reiteration of the baptismal rite.

This traditional doctrine, insinuated by Sacred Scripture,[31] dates
from apostolic times. Errors and heresies forced the Church to proclaim the existence of this sacramental reality in various solemn
declarations, chief of which is that of the Council of Trent: "If anyone says that in these sacraments (baptism, confirmation and holy
orders) a character is not imprinted on the soul—i.e., a certain indelible spiritual sign, that makes them incapable of being repeated—
let him be anathema."[32]

(2) The Nature of the Sacramental Character

In the Church's statement quoted above, the sacramental character
is equivalently declared to be something real (it is impressed on the

---

[31]Cf. II Cor. 1:21-22, Ephes. 1:13-14.

[32]Sess. VII, Can. 9 (Denz. 852); cf. the letter of Pope Innocent III to Humbert,
Archbishop of Arles, 1202 (Denz. 411), Council of Florence, *Decree for the
Armenians* (Denz. 695).

soul), spiritual, ineradicable. What sort of thing is it then? St. Thomas
makes the following points:

1) The sacraments of the New Law imprint a character on the soul
   insofar as they establish the true worshippers of God, i.e., those
   men who participate in the divine worship inaugurated on the
   cross by Christ's sacrifice, of which all the sacraments are commemorative signs. Not by their natural powers can men share in
   this supernatural religion; the pagan in the jungles cannot worship God in the manner determined by Christ. Christian worship,
   in fact, consists either in receiving divine things procured by
   Christ or in giving divine things offered through Christ, and for
   both some special spiritual power is necessary, passive in the first
   case, active in the second.

   The Christian worships God according to the acceptable rite
   established by Christ. The non-Christian does not. Hence some
   superadded quality must be given the Christian, an ability he
   does not possess by nature. This is not a habit (for the Christian
   can abuse this divinely bestowed gift by sacrilegious reception
   or administration of the sacraments, while a good habit guarantees morally good acts); it must be something like the faculties
   of our soul, the will or intellect, which can be badly used but
   yet continue to give a capacity for a particular type of action.
   Character, then, is a certain *spiritual faculty or power* ordained
   to the things which pertain to divine worship.

2) In virtue of this spiritual power, the Christian participates in
   Christ's worship of God: in perpetuating, actively or passively,
   Christ's sacrifice, in communicating by his reception or administration of the sacraments in Christ's activity of praise and
   propitiation, of thanksgiving and petition. He does not act in
   his own name but in the name of Christ; he does not worship
   as a private individual but as a member of Christ. His ability so
   to act cannot be the principal cause of Christian worship; rather
   does he act as Christ's minister. His power is an *instrumental* one.

Sacramental character, then, is *a physical, spiritual, instrumental
power for performing acts of Christian worship.*

(3) *The Properties of Sacramental Character*

1. This physical, spiritual, instrumental power is **a distinctive sign.**
The character is infallibly connected with the exterior sacramental
rite. Unlike grace, which presupposes the proper dispositions of its
recipients, sacramental character is infallibly conferred by a valid
sacrament. Hence it is not only a reality effected by the sacrament
but also a sign: whoever validly receives baptism by that very deed
gives sensible evidence of the fact that he possesses the power of
receiving the things belonging to Christian worship.

1) It is a sign *configuring man to Christ,* the High Priest of the
   Christian religion. The power of receiving or giving sacred
   things is derived from, and a participation of the priesthood
   of Christ, who alone offers a worship acceptable to God. So by
   this character men bear on their souls the likeness of Christ,
   the priest.

2) It is a *distinguishing* sign. The citizens, soldiers and priests of
   the Church of Christ are marked by his mark. This forever sets
   them off from the angels and devils, and from all other men.
   By these signs the faithful are also distinguished from one another, as confessors of the faith of Christ (baptism), as its de-
   fenders (confirmation), and its leaders (holy orders).

3) It is a sign *disposing for grace.* Together with the sacred ceremony, the character is both a sign and a cause of sacramental
   grace. Of its nature this power demands from God the grace
   which will make the religious acts of Christian worship supernaturally good and morally fruitful. The objective ability to
   perform these acts of worship requires the perfection of the
   subject which only grace can give.

2. The character is **a perfection of the practical intellect.** This
power is ordained to the protestation of faith which is accomplished
by the ceremonies of the Christian religion. Faith is an intellectual
virtue, i.e., a supernatural, habitual modification by which man's
cognoscitive power is perfected and elevated to know divine things
revealed by God. But the work to be accomplished by the sacra-

mental character is not primarily that of knowing things alone; rather is it the effective direction and ordering of man's other powers, including his external faculties, for the correct performance of the exterior acts in which divine worship consists. Properly speaking, this type of work is the job of the practical intellect, of the intellect under the moving force of the will. Thus the practical intellect is the subject of this supernatural instrumental power.

3. The character is **indelible.** This spiritual power is a *participation* of Christ's eternal priesthood; it is a *consecration* of man's eternal and immortal soul. It is incorruptible both *per se* (as a spiritual power it has no contrary which could destroy it: neither sin nor apostasy nor any other cause can change it) and *per accidens* (its subject, the intellect, is incorruptible). "And therefore after this life the character remains both in the good, to their glory, and in the wicked, to their shame."[33]

The eternal indelibility of sacramental character is a certain theological conclusion; that it is ineradicable in this life is a fact revealed by God and proclaimed by the Church.[34] It is the basis for the practice of never repeating those sacraments which imprint such a sacred power on the soul.

(4) The Number of Sacramental Characters

The ecclesiastical practice mentioned above was, from the beginnings of the Church, restricted to the sacraments of baptism, confirmation and holy orders; repetition of the other sacraments, on the contrary, is not merely permitted but even (in due circumstances) encouraged. This clearly attests to the fact enunciated by the Council of Florence: "There are three among these sacraments—baptism, confirmation and holy orders—which imprint an indelible character on the soul, that is, a certain spiritual and distinguishing sign. Hence these are not given more than once to the same person. But the other four do not imprint a character and admit of repetition."[35]

---

[33]*Summa*, III, q. 63, a. 5, ad 2.
[34]Cf. the Council of Trent, Sess. VII, Can. 9; Denz. 852.
[35]*Decree for the Armenians*, Denz. 695.

As St. Thomas points out, only these three sacraments are directly concerned with, and ordained to divine worship through the further reception or administration of the sacred ceremonies of Christ. Baptism confers the spiritual ability to receive the other sacraments, a truly new power not previously part of man's equipment, but a passive power. By confirmation a passive-active principle of Christian worship is given to the baptized: the capacity to receive special divine aids for the active and official confession of the faith of Christ; by this power the child becomes an adult, the citizen a soldier. Holy orders constitutes the leaders and religious heads of Christ's Church, by indelibly imprinting the active power of administering the sacred things which belong to Christ's worship of God.

5. The Cause of the Sacraments

Who can bring a sacrament into existence? Could the Church invent a new sacrament, one especially adapted to the pressing spiritual needs of the day? In case of emergency could a layman administer extreme unction? Can a Hindu nurse validly baptize? Are Protestant sacraments true sacraments?

Detailed answers to these questions (and the thousand like them) will not be attempted here. We will establish, however, the necessary general principles from which the properly conclusive answers to them can be drawn. This means the determination of certain fundamental distinctions.

In the first place, when we speak of *causing* a sacrament, we have reference either to its **institution** or its **administration.** To **institute** something is to bring it into existence for the first time; with respect to the sacraments, it would mean the determination of their essence as causative signs and the consequent conferring of power on them. The **administration** of the sacraments, on the other hand, means the effective production of the sacramental, causative sign already instituted.

Secondly, we must recall the distinction between a *principal* cause (one which has an inherent native ability to produce a certain effect) and an *instrumental* cause (one which produces an effect, not in virtue of its native power, but by sharing in the power of the principal cause). Our ambassadors, for example, act for our country in virtue of the power given to them by the government: they are *ministers* (a name of honor given to free and intelligent instruments), acting as instruments of the United States, not as private citizens.

With these distinctions in mind, the questions concerning the efficient causes of the sacraments can be answered in general by considering both the institution and the administration of the sacraments.

A. The Institution of the Sacraments

(1) The Authority of God

It is obvious to any theologian that God alone possesses authoritative power with respect to the sacraments; he alone can be their principal cause, whether we speak of their administration or of their institution. This is evident both from the kind of thing God is, and from the kind of thing the sacraments are. From the first point of view, it is clear that only God can give and preserve the being of all things. It immediately follows, therefore, that he alone is immediately and intrinsically present to the soul, for no created substance can infringe upon a spiritual substance like the soul. Therefore he alone can affect the spiritual soul of man in any direct manner. Since the sacraments do affect man's spiritual soul directly, in causing their effects within it, they must possess a power derived from God alone as the principal cause or author.

From the point of view of the sacraments, the same conclusion follows. According to the teaching of the Church, they both contain and cause grace. But grace is a participation or sharing of the divine nature precisely as it is in itself. And the sacramental character of which they are also causes is a real participation of Christ's priesthood, which is founded on the Hypostatic Union of his humanity with the Godhead. Thus from the point of view of the effects produced, it is equally clear that only God could be their principal cause. They can be authoritatively produced by him alone from whom they derive.

(2) *The Power of Christ*

Since Christ is God, he is the author of the sacraments or their principal cause both as to their institution and as to their administration. But precisely as man, precisely in virtue of the fact that his sacred humanity is hypostatically united to his Godhead and used as its instrument, he enjoys a special and unique dominion with respect to the signs which convey his grace to mankind.

To designate the special excellence Christ as man possesses with respect to the sacraments, theologians attribute to him the *power of excellence*. This power is founded on the fact that Christ is constituted our mediator, and the Head of his Mystical Body of which we are members, according to his human nature. He merits and satisfies for all men, and thereby becomes the principal moral cause of our salvation and of the sacramental effects which are the means of our salvation. Furthermore, as man he is the physical, instrumental, efficient cause of grace and sacramental power. As once he used his humanity to work miracles in the bodies and souls of men, so now the Word uses his humanity as his instrument to produce these supernatural effects in our soul.

In what does this "power of excellence" of Christ consist? St. Thomas points out that it comprises four elements: 1) the merit and power of his passion to work in the sacraments in producing their effects; 2) the sanctification of all the sacraments through his name, since they are protestations of faith in his passion made evident by our calling on his name; 3) the right and ability to institute the sacraments (subordinated, of course, to God as principal cause); 4) the power to confer the effects of the sacrament without using the exterior rites by which these effects are now bestowed on men.

These elements forcefully underline the ministerial or instrumental power which Christ possesses with respect to the sacraments, both as regards their institution and as regards their use. This excellence is further underlined by St. Thomas' teaching that Christ could communicate this power to other ministers. Endowed with such power himself, he could give to some man such a fulness of grace as to constitute that man the spiritual head of the human race. In virtue of such a fulness of grace, this man would be capable of meriting in justice (*de condigno*) the salvation of mankind. Such a man would, then, truly be our savior, and salvation would come to us through effects conferred by sacraments this individual would have a participated right to institute. In him, therefore, the four prerogatives of Christ's power of excellence would be realized, in virtue of Christ's communication.

Such a minister of Christ, to be sure, would possess the power of excellence in a far less perfect manner than Christ himself. Christ's power and his merit are those of a divine person; his instrumentality is that of an instrument conjoined to his divinity. On all counts, then, the minister of Christ would be inferior to the master: his fulness of grace relative, and not absolute; his merit not one of strict justice: his instrumentality that of a separate, rather than of a conjoined cause.

Nevertheless, this minister could do what Christ could do: he could, for example, as Christ's minister, institute the sacraments. This brings up the question: has any individual (the apostles, for example) or the Church herself acted in Christ's behalf to establish our sacraments?

(3) The Institution of the Sacraments

It is the universal opinion of theologians since the time of the Council of Trent that Christ, in fact, *immediately* instituted all of the sacraments of the New Law. Only such an interpretation realizes the full signification and implications of the Tridentine declaration that all the sacraments of the New Law were instituted by Christ.[36] But one may legitimately inquire: what is meant by immediate institution?

Immediate institution means the personal determination by Christ himself of the essence of a sacrament of the New Law and the bestowal on the sacred sign which he has selected of the power to effect what it signifies. No intermediary intervenes here, in contrast to the possible situation where Christ would appoint one of his disciples or inspire the Church to create a new sacrament. The institutor performs the institution himself.

[36]Sess. VII, Can. 1; Denz. 844.

This does not mean, however, that the determination of the sacred sanctifying rite need be complete down to the last physical detail. But it does mean that the meaning to be conveyed by the sacred sign must be specified, and that the elements suggesting this signification (matter and form) must be determined in at least a general way. Otherwise the institution would not be immediate but mediate. Thus, for example, Christ could have instituted the sacrament of holy orders by determining that some sensible rite, comprised of ceremonial action and signifying words, would convey the idea of a transference of sacerdotal power. This might be expressed by the imposition of hands or by a handing over of the instruments proper to the office of priest. Christ leaves it to the Church to select the specific ceremony, but he himself has instituted the sacrament immediately.[37]

Is Christ "jealous" of his power of excellence, so to reserve the institution of the sacraments to himself? In a sense, yes; and rightly so. As the author of the new Economy of salvation, the right of establishing the intrinsic constitution of that Economy properly belongs to him alone; and the sacraments are the very columns of the spiritual edifice which is the Church. Moreover, his dignity as conjoined instrument of the Word practically demands that he retain this power for himself. Then, too, there would be real danger in entrusting it to another man: danger of man's placing his trust in the creature who possessed such power, rather than in the Creator who gave it to him; danger of factions and schisms arising, as men adhered to this or that minister of Christ.[38]

B. The Administration of the Sacraments

As God is the principal cause and author of the institution of the sacraments, so also is he the chief and principal cause of their ad-

[37]This distinction and its application is taught by many theologians: Soto, Gonet, Billuart, Billot, Hugon, Galtier, etc. Although it is denied by other theologians, it seems fully in accord with the nature of the sacraments (to determine the reality to be signified and, in a general way, the things which will signify this reality is to determine the essence of the sacrament); moreover, it sufficiently accounts for the historical facts which seem to indicate that the Church has changed the matter or form of one or another sacrament.

[38]Compare the unhappy experience of St. Paul with the factious Church of Corinth, I Cor. 1:10 ff.

ministration. As Christ according to his human nature is the principal
minister of God in instituting the sacraments, so also is he principal
minister in administering them. But God customarily works through
secondary causes to achieve his effects, and Christ established his
Church to perpetuate his work among men and communicate the
fruits of his passion. Thus it is entirely in accord with the divine
scheme of things, and with the divine economy planned by God and
executed by the God-man, that secondary ministers should be employed in bringing the gifts of God which were won by Christ to
mankind. The chief channels of these graces are the sacraments of
Christ.

But what is necessary for one to be a minister of Christ, to distribute his gifts through the sacraments? We will answer this question
in discussing the physical qualities and the intention of a true minister
of the sacraments, and the role played by moral qualities.

(1) Physical Qualities

God could, if he chose, administer the sacraments by means of
angels or of departed souls, just as he can confer the effects of the
sacraments directly and without their mediation. But in fact, in the
present providence of God he associates men in this work of salvation.
Since the power of the sacraments is derived from Christ's passion,
and his passion was accomplished through his humanity, it is most
fitting that the application of the fruits of that passion through the
sacraments should be carried out through the agency of human beings.

Except for the sacraments of baptism and of matrimony, however,
not any man or all men can be true ministers. For the other sacraments, only he who has been officially deputed to the office by
the Church of Christ through sacred orders is a true minister.

(2) The Intention of the Minister

A "minister" is an instrument whose own proper power is that of
an intelligent being, namely, acts of intellect and will. Since the
principal cause uses the native power of the instrument, and the
instrument participates in the higher power of the principal cause
only as used by it, it follows that this instrument, the human being

who is the minister, must subject himself freely (and thus knowingly) to Christ.

How is this accomplished? By the formulation of an **intention**, i.e., a free act of the will by which one determines to do something. The "something to be done" in this case is to make a sensible sign representative of, and efficacious of man's sanctification, after the manner determined by Christ's institution and transmitted by him to his Church. To confer a Christian sacrament, it is therefore sufficient if the man, using the proper matter and form, **has the intention of doing what the Church does** by this sacred ceremony. For then a man submits himself freely and knowingly to Christ, thereby giving these sensible realities their true (i.e., sacramental) signification; by his action he can be used by Christ as his instrument. The limited intention of merely performing certain ritual actions and saying certain prescribed words, deliberately excludes, in fact, the intention of doing what the Church does. The Church does infinitely more: she makes a *sacramental sign*. On the other hand, one does not have to intend what the Church *intends*, for that implies the conferring of grace, which lies beyond the native power of the instrument to be used.

The minister must have at least a **virtual** intention. The will-act of doing something, formulated here and now and immediately effective of this action, is called an **actual** intention. If this intention were made some time in the past and never retracted, but is not productive of this action which takes place here and now, it is known as a **habitual** intention (the habit of justice may remain in a sleeping man; it does not account for his snoring). If the power (*virtus*) of a previous intention, however, does cause the present action, the will-act is said to be virtual—this action is performed *in virtue of* the previous will-act, even though the will is not brought explicitly to bear at this moment on the action performed.

For the valid administration of the sacraments a habitual intention does not suffice (the action would take place not because of, but in spite of a habitual intention). An actual intention is not required, for all that is necessary is that the minister produce this action (the application of a sacrament) as Christ's instrument. For this a previous intention of doing what the Church does which truly motivates his present action—*a virtual intention*—suffices.

(3) *The Moral Qualities of the Minister*

Neither faith nor sanctity is required in the minister for the valid administration of a sacrament. For writing, a golden pencil is of no more value than one made of plastic. So also, the spiritual worth of the minister, the human element, neither adds to nor subtracts from the objective value or power of the sacramental sign, which works *ex opere operato*. All that is required is that one be a minister, an instrument humanly subjected to the principal cause in virtue of intending to do what the Church does. Personal belief need not enter in; the most benighted pagan could intend (at least implicitly) to do what the Church does as effectively as the most enlightened Catholic. A case-hardened sinner can administer a sacrament as validly as the purest of saints. For many of the sacraments, of course, the sacramental character as well as the intention is required. But given these, it matters not, so far as the valid "making" of a sacrament is concerned, how badly or well the minister lives his life. Regardless of his state of soul, he can always validly confer a sacrament.

But since the minister acts in the name of Christ and of the Church, and the sacraments are themselves sacred things, the mortal sinner commits grave sacrilege in administering the sacraments. In virtue of their special consecration, priests are given the power to pass these divine things on to others. It is only fitting that those to whom such sacred and holy things are entrusted by Christ should manifest themselves spiritually worthy of these gifts, their lives and actions conformed to their holy office and sacred trust. The official and solemn minister of the sacraments acts in the person of Christ and of the Church; their holiness should be his.

An exception to this rule, generally admitted by theologians, is that of administering baptism in the case of necessity. In this instance the minister does not act as an official, consecrated person, but only comes to the assistance of one in dire spiritual need. His sinful state of soul, consequently, offers no injury to Christ or to his Church; his action is not itself gravely sinful or sacrilegious.

6. The Number of the Sacraments

There are seven sacraments of the New Law, and only seven, all of them instituted by our Savior: baptism, confirmation, Holy Eucharist, penance, extreme unction, holy orders and matrimony. This is a dogma revealed by Almighty God and infallibly taught by the Church of God.[39]

But since in the economy of salvation divine wisdom always works by disposing all things sweetly and powerfully, we may legitimately seek to determine (so far as it is permitted to the participated divine wisdom which is theology) the reasons which illustrate the suitability of the institution of these seven sacraments, no more, no less. And a better explanation cannot be found than that given by St. Thomas in a classical passage of theology:

> The sacraments of the Church are ordered to a twofold end: to perfecting man in the things which belong to the worship of God according to the religion of the Christian life; and also as remedies for the defect caused by sin. In both ways it is fitting that there be seven sacraments.
>
> I: The life of the spirit has a certain similarity to the life of the body, just as other corporeal things have a certain likeness to spiritual things. Now a man is perfected in his bodily life in two ways: first, with respect to his own person; secondly, with respect to the whole social community in which he lives. With regard to his private self, man is perfected both *per se*, by acquiring some vital perfection, and accidentally, by removing sickness and the like which are hindrances to his bodily life.
>
> There are three ways by which the life of the body is directly (*per se*) perfected:
>
> > First, by generation, by which a man begins to exist and to live. Corresponding to this in the life of the spirit is *baptism*, which, according to the Epistle to Titus (3:5), is a spiritual regeneration.
> >
> > Secondly, by growth, by which one is brought to full size and strength. Corresponding to this in the life of the spirit is *confirmation*, the sacrament in which the Holy Spirit is given to strengthen men. Because of this the disciples already baptized were told (Lk. 24:49): "Wait here in the city, until you are clothed with power from on high."

[39]Cf. the Council of Trent, Sess. VII, Can. 1; Denz. 844.

Thirdly, by nourishment, which conserves a man's life and his strength. The *Eucharist* corresponds to this in the life of the spirit. Thus Christ said (Jn. 6:54): "Unless you eat the flesh of the Son of man and drink his blood, you shall not have life in you."

If man's life, both bodily and spiritual, were inaccessible to harm, this would suffice. But since man at times suffers infirmity, both bodily infirmity and the spiritual infirmity which is sin, he needs a cure for his malady, and this is a double one:

One is the healing which restores health. And corresponding to this in the life of the spirit is *penance,* as the psalm (40:5) points out: "Heal my soul, for I have sinned against thee."

The other cure is the restoration of former vigor by suitable exercise and diet. In the spiritual life *extreme unction* corresponds to this, for it removes the remains of sin and prepares a man for his final glory. Hence in the Epistle of St. James (5:15) it is said: "If he be in sins, they shall be forgiven him."

With respect to the whole community, man is perfected in two ways.

First, by receiving the power to govern the community and to exercise public office. In the life of the spirit the sacrament of *holy orders* corresponds to this. As the Epistle to the Hebrews points out (7:27), priests offer sacrifice not for themselves alone but for the people.

Secondly, by natural propagation. Both in the corporeal and in the spiritual order this is accomplished by *matrimony,* which is not only a sacrament but also a function of nature.

II: From these considerations we can likewise see why the sacraments insofar as they are remedies for the defects caused by sin, are seven in number. For baptism is intended as a remedy for the absence of spiritual life; confirmation is ordained against the weakness of soul found in the newly born; the Eucharist, against the soul's proneness to sin; penance, against actual sin committed after baptism; extreme unction, against the remains of sin, which are not sufficiently removed by penance, due to ignorance or negligence; holy orders, against divisions in the community. And matrimony is intended as a remedy against concupiscence in the individual and against the decrease of the community through death.[40]

Although the traditional enumeration of the sacraments is that given by the Council of Trent, being based on the natural order in which they are usually received, from other points of view it would be necessary to list these seven sacraments in a different order. Thus

---

[40]*Summa,* III, q. 65, a. 1.

the Eucharist is the chief of all the sacraments, the most powerful of them all, their end and consummation. For it contains Christ himself, substantially present under the sacramental species, whereas the other sacraments contain rather a participated power of Christ; all the others, in one way or another, in greater or lesser degree, are ordained to the Eucharist, preparing man for its administration or its reception, or (in the case of matrimony) signifying this greatest of all sacraments. From the point of view of the necessity of reception (a point we shall consider more in detail with respect to the individual sacraments), baptism is absolutely necessary for all, and penance for those who have fallen into serious sin committed after baptism. Holy orders is necessary for the Church as a whole, since by it the religious leaders of Christ's Mystical Body are constituted.

7. Summary and Conclusion

St. Thomas has given us a justly famous definition of the divine realities which bear the name "sacrament": *the sign of a sacred thing precisely insofar as it here and now sanctifies man.* The pouring of natural water, the anointing with chrism through the imposition of hands—these rites are signs, not natural signs but symbolic signs, of the effect transpiring in the soul of the recipient, and their meaning is made clear and unmistakable through the sacred formulas which interpret them. In this way, through these instruments, does man come into physical contact with Christ himself, with his saving passion and, by anticipation, with the glory Christ won for us on his cross. Grace is poured out upon the soul, configuring the sacramentalized human being to the God-man; and power is given him so to unite himself with Christ's liturgy as to offer through his sacramental actions true and acceptable worship to God.

Thus in truth it is Christ who acts through these sacraments he alone has instituted. For they are his sanctifying tools; material and sensible realities elevated by his participated power to work, in the souls of those who use them, the essential transformation on account of which God became man: that man might become Godlike. This salvific process is begun in the regenerating waters of baptism and carried to spiritual maturity in the confirming fulness of the Spirit. But all through his life the Christian will maintain his contact with Christ, not through faith alone, but also through the sacraments of faith. For our Savior has provided numerous sacred symbols by which man's sanctification can be daily deepened and intensified, and his special circumstances provided for in a Christian manner. These sacraments will occupy our attention for the next several chapters.

Hence the following conclusions:

1. The sacraments confer grace not only to make us holy and bolster up our confidence in doing great things in life for Christ, but also to render us humble. Christ had to distill the supernatural strength of the sacraments into the tiny cup of our human understanding. We are like children who cannot believe the cake to be real until they have tasted the frosting. Thus Christ gave signs—water, bread, oil— as proof to the senses that what he has done for us is not just an illusion.

2. There would be no supernatural life and no sacraments as we have them if it were not for the sacred humanity of Christ. Supernatural life flows from God through the God-man as a channel, and branches off from him into sacramental springs which irrigate the parched earth of our souls.

3. The sacraments are not only channels of grace and remedies for sin. They are essentially *signs,* and they are protestations of our faith in Christ. Hence the Church surrounds their administration with the beauties of the liturgy to express the sacramental meaning as fittingly as possible. The Catholic conscious of these things will not sit dumbly by while the sacred rites are being celebrated, but will participate in them as actively as possible: reading up on the ceremonies beforehand, following the sacred actions closely, taking part in the communal singing or reciting, etc.

4. The center of all Catholic devotion is the Mass and the sacraments. These are the Christian "exercises" by which the life of the spirit grows daily unto the fulness of the manhood of Jesus Christ. All our other devotional practices—the Rosary, stations of the cross,

novenas, private prayers, etc.—should be connected with, prepare for or flow from, these pivotal practices of our religion.

5. For the Catholic, all of nature is, in a sense, sacramentalized, i.e., charged with a divine meaning and significance. Contrariwise, he will be aware of, and critical of the sham and the artificial, and deeply concerned about the materialism and secularism of our day and our country. He has but to reflect on the sacraments to realize the true and good use which can be made of material things, and how far we have strayed from Christ's view and use of the things of this world.

BIBLIOGRAPHICAL NOTE

Part III, Questions LX-LXV, of the *Summa* contain St. Thomas' teaching on the sacraments in general. For a more popular account of this doctrine, an exceptionally fine work of A. M. Roguet, O.P., called *Christ Acts through the Sacraments* (Collegeville, Minn.: The Liturgical Press, 1953), is highly recommended. Students who are interested in the spiritual and practical applications of the doctrine would do well to consult *The Sacraments in the Christian Life* (Westminster, Md.: The Newman Press, 1954), by M. M. Philipon, O.P. Another book brimming with practical insights applicable to the day to day life of the apostolic Catholic is *The Sacraments of Daily Life* (New York: Sheed and Ward, 1943), by Bernard J. Kelly, C.S.SP. The student who has a deep interest in the historical background of the sacraments can spend many hours of enjoyable study by taking in hand *Sacraments and Worship* (Westminster, Md.: The Newman Press, 1955), by Paul F. Palmer.

An article in Volume III of the English *Summa*, entitled "The Sacraments in General," by Urban Nagle, O.P., can be used for quick reference. Two other technical discourses on the subject are, "Spirituality for All: Channels of Grace," by Christopher Kiesling, O.P., in *Cross and Crown*, X (1958), 87-107, and "Two Approaches to Understanding the Sacraments: Sign and Cause," by G. Diekmann in *Worship*, XXXI (1957), 504-520. Writing from a different viewpoint, John Feoron, O.P., has produced *Graceful Living* (Westminster, Md.: The Newman Press, 1955), a course in the appreciation of the sacraments.

CHAPTER TEN

Baptism and Confirmation

1. Introduction

We have already discussed the nature of the sacraments in general. A sacrament is a sign of a sacred thing precisely as that sacred thing here and now sanctifies man. Now we shall begin to use our knowledge by applying this doctrine to the sacraments of baptism and confirmation. These are particular sacraments which in particular ways signify the cause of sanctifying grace, Christ's passion; signify the intrinsic principle of man's holiness, sanctifying grace; and signify the purpose of man's holiness, eternal glory. We shall see that their effect, man's sanctification, is produced here and now when they actually signify that effect. We shall also examine the sensible realities which God has chosen to bear the sacramental signification expressive of baptism and confirmation.

Baptism and confirmation are prime examples of this doctrine on sacred signs. But, and foremost, they are tremendously important in themselves. Through baptism man is reborn spiritually: he begins to live in union with Christ. Through confirmation he is brought to his spiritual maturity and given a spiritual strength to confirm him in that maturity.

Our method of proceeding will be the same as that used for the sacraments in general. An outline has been placed in the introduction to each of the two sacraments.

THE SACRAMENT OF CHRISTIAN INITIATION

> Do you not know that all we who have been baptized into Christ Jesus have been baptized into his death? For we were baptized with him by means of baptism into death, in order that, just as Christ has arisen from the dead through the glory of the Father, so we also may walk in newness of life. For if we have been united with him in the likeness of his death, we shall be so in the likeness of his resurrection also. For we know that our old self has been crucified with him, in order that the body of sin may be destroyed, that we may no longer be slaves to sin; for he who is dead is acquitted of sin. But if we have died with Christ, we believe that we shall also live together with Christ; for we know that Christ, having risen from the dead, dies now no more, death shall no longer have any dominion over him. For the death that he died, he died to sin once for all, but the life that he lives, he lives unto God. Thus do you consider yourselves also as dead to sin, but alive to God in Christ Jesus.[1]

"Dead to sin, but alive to God in Christ Jesus"—thus does St. Paul describe the wonders wrought in the Christian by the first and most necessary of the sacraments of faith instituted by the Savior of mankind. Baptism is the sacrament of Christian initiation, of the illumination of the Spirit, of the foundation of the Church of Jesus Christ. It is the indispensable contact with Christ's passion of which we spoke in the beginning of the preceding chapter, the sacred symbol which in sense-perceptible terms expresses all that we have previously seen regarding the wondrous signs God's love and wisdom establish, to bring to each man, throughout his life, the fruits of Christ's redemption. Baptism reveals all the characteristics of a sacrament of the New Law, and a theological consideration of it will deepen, in a practical manner, our previous investigation of the sacraments in general.

A thorough study of this vital and fundamental reality of Christian life is, of course, impossible here; but the essentials of the sacrament

[1]Rom. 6:3-11

can be disclosed in this investigation. Our study of baptism will follow this plan:

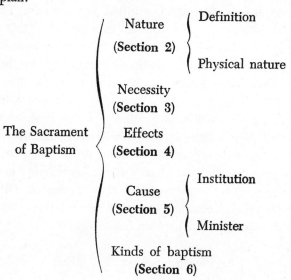

The Sacrament of Baptism
- Nature (Section 2)
  - Definition
  - Physical nature
- Necessity (Section 3)
- Effects (Section 4)
- Cause (Section 5)
  - Institution
  - Minister
- Kinds of baptism (Section 6)

2. The Nature of Baptism

Just what kind of reality this thing is can be a very important question. The answer will disclose the nature of the thing investigated, what makes it up, what distinguishes it from all other realities. We know already that all the sacraments are sacred signs of man's sanctification. We know that the sacraments instituted by Christ are composed of certain formulas (the *form* of the sacrament) together with certain sense-perceptible actions (analogously called the *matter* of the sacrament). The union of these two elements constitutes the sacred symbol, and this symbol efficaciously produces what it signifies. In the case of baptism, then, we must determine just what constitutes the matter and form of this sacred sign, if we wish to know what this particular sacrament is and how it differs from the other sacraments. Our investigation of the essence of baptism will necessarily center on the determination of its matter and form, but we shall first make an inquiry as to its metaphysical definition.

A. The Metaphysical Definition

Baptism is *the sacrament of spiritual regeneration.* This is the metaphysical definition of baptism. An explanation of this definition follows easily on what we have learned about sacraments in general. Baptism is a sacrament, and sacraments belong to that broad class of things which we call signs. It is a reality which tells us about another reality. Thus the external washing with water in baptism tells us that the sins which have soiled the soul have been washed away. Baptism is the sign of our spiritual regeneration. In this, we find baptism's special way of here and now sanctifying man. Through spiritual regeneration, man is given a special sanctifying grace, effective at the moment the sacramental sign is present. Other sacraments signify other means of sanctification and thus differ specifically from the sacrament of baptism.

B. Physical Nature of Baptism

All of the sacraments of the New Law are composed of **matter** and **form** (cf. Chapter Nine, Section 3, The Physical Nature of the Sacraments). For the greater number of the sacraments, the matter is itself composed of a twofold element: the sensible thing with which the sacrament deals (the *remote* **matter**), and the actual use which is made of this remote matter (the *proximate* **matter**). So also with baptism.

(1) The Remote Matter

The remote matter of baptism is all natural water, and it alone. This is clear from Christ's own words ("Unless a man be born again of water and the Holy Spirit. . . ."), from the practice of the apostles (cf. Acts 8:27-39, 10:44-48) and their teaching (cf. Eph. 5:26; I Pet. 3:20), and from the constant practice of the Church. Natural water is the sensible material instituted by Christ himself as one of the constituent elements of this particular sensible sign. It is a material whose natural qualities well fit it for its signifying role: as a cleansing agent it can symbolize the spiritual washing from sin; as a cooling substance it indicates the tempering of the fires of concupiscence; as a translucent, reflecting material it is well suited to represent the illumination it confers. Moreover, it is a most common and easily obtainable material, and so admirably chosen for a sacrament of such vital necessity as baptism.

Two further principles specify in a more determined manner the remote matter of this sacrament:

1) *For validity natural water in a liquid state is required.* "Natural water" means such as is usually judged to be water by men in general and so given that name. Regardless of taste, color, smell or previous state, if this substance is commonly considered to be water it is valid matter for the sacrament. Other liquid substances, however, not commonly recognized as water (fruit juices, distilled liquors of herbs, flowers, etc., urine, saliva, etc., etc.) would be invalid as matter, or at best of doubtful validity. Water in other than a liquid state—ice, hail, snow—would also be invalid, since then it would be unfitted for its baptismal use.

2) *For the lawful administration of baptism, clean and pure water is required, and for solemn baptism water especially consecrated for this purpose.* The dignity of the sacrament demands that only fitting materials be used, and one would sin gravely through a lack of reverence to ignore this fact by using unsuitable matter without necessity.

(2) The Proximate Matter

The proximate matter of baptism is the exterior washing of the body with water. As the very name of this sacrament indicates; as the effects it is supposed to symbolize declare; as the constant liturgical practice of the Church attests—the ceremonial action which constitutes this sacrament is one of washing, symbolic of the interior cleansing of the soul. This may be accomplished in three ways: 1) by *immersion* (common in the early Church and still practiced today by some sects and in the Eastern rites, in which the catechumen's whole body is moved through a pool or body of water; 2) by *sprinkling* with a sufficient quantity of water so that it flows on the person; 3) by *pouring* water on the one to be baptized. All of these are valid methods of using the remote matter, but the following conditions must be observed:

1) *The action should truly be one of washing.* The water must physically and directly touch the body, flowing over some part of it. A very small quantity of water will suffice for this—there is no necessity that an actual physical cleansing be accomplished.

2) *It must be performed by the one baptizing.* The words of the form clearly indicate this.

3) *It must be a washing of the one to be baptized,* i.e., of his body, either the entire body or its principal part, the head. The baptism of any other part would be of doubtful validity (cf. Can. 746, §§ 2 and 3). The water must touch the body itself, not merely the hair or the garments.

Although a triple washing (in honor of the Trinity) is prescribed by the Church (and for the Latin Church this should be done by pouring the water in the form of a cross, not by immersion or sprinkling, for the ceremony to be lawful), one such ceremonial washing suffices for validity and in case of necessity even for liceity.

(3) The Form of Baptism

I baptize you in the name of the Father and of the Son and of the Holy Ghost. These are the words which constitute the sacred formula of this sacrament of Christian initiation, expressing as they do the causes which make *this* human being, through *this* sacred action, a member of Christ and of his Church. No substantial change of the form can take place, and for the sacrament to be valid these five elements must be at least equivalently expressed:

1) *The person baptizing*—"I." This must be at least implicit in the formula. (The Greek Church uses the words, "The servant of God is baptized . . . ", and from the attendant circumstances it is clear that the words "by me" are equivalently expressed.) For greater certainty the one baptizing should always be explicitly indicated by the words.

2) *The action of baptizing—*"**baptize.**" Since water can be poured for various purposes, the use made of it in this ceremony should be specified. A synonym (wash, bathe) would express the same fact, and the baptism would be valid.

3) *The person baptized—*"**you.**" Here again any word indicating the precise one being baptized—the child's name, for example —would suffice for validity.

4) *The unity of the divine nature—*"**in the name.**" The central mystery of Christianity is that of the Trinity. Thus the sacrament which initiates a human being into the mysteries of Christianity fittingly professes the belief of the one being baptized in this chief and fundamental dogma of Christian faith. The use of the singular word, "name," states the essential unity of the three divine persons; any deviation from the phrase, "in the name," runs the grave risk of making the formula invalid.

5) *The trinity of Persons—*"**of the Father and of the Son and of the Holy Ghost (Spirit).**" Each person of the Trinity should be distinctly mentioned, with a clear indication that one is speaking of three distinct persons (hence the repetition of the "and"). The proper names of the divine Persons should be used, for in this case synonyms would lead to doubt as to the precise meaning intended, and hence make the sacrament of doubtful validity.

This formula, so full of meaning and of such vital importance for the effects it causes, should be pronounced as the water is being poured on the head of the one to be baptized. It is not necessary that water be poured all the time during the saying of the words, but at least while some of the words are being said the sacred action of washing should take place.

C. The Ceremonies of Baptism

The sacrament of baptism comprises three essential elements: the **form**, which designates the principal cause of the sacrament, the Blessed Trinity; the **minister**, who is Christ's instrument in conferring the sacrament; and the **use** or application of the matter, the washing with water, which symbolizes the principal effect of the sacrament. In case of necessity, only these three elements are required for the conferring of a true sacrament, but all of them are necessary.

The Church of Christ, however, surrounds these essential elements with some of her most beautiful prayers and ceremonies, and solemn baptism, in which her full ritual is observed, is one of the most impressive and significant of the Church's liturgical actions. In this way she inspires her children with devotion and reverence for the sacred ceremony of Christian initiation, and instructs them concerning its profound symbolism and the tremendous effects it works in the soul of the one baptized.

It would well repay parents and sponsors, and all those in attendance at baptism, to read these ceremonies before the actual baptism takes place, and to attend closely to the ritual while it is performed (much of it now is given in the vernacular). In fact, it is a revealing experience for *all* who have been baptized to read over the ceremonies which made Christians of them, perhaps many years ago. A realization of the true meaning of Christian baptism at long last, disclosed by the rites themselves, cannot but make better Christians of them now.

3. The Necessity of Baptism

Baptism is so necessary a sacrament that, after the promulgation of the New Law, no man can be saved without it. No adult can be saved without the actual reception of its saving waters or at least an implicit desire to receive the sacrament; saving only the case of martyrdom, no one without the use of reason can be saved, except by actually receiving baptism. Baptism is the necessary means for salvation, and both the natural law and divine positive law make its reception a matter of precept as well. As Christ himself told Nicodemus, "Unless a man be born again of water and the Spirit, he cannot enter the kingdom of God" (Jn. 3:5). "He who believes and is baptized shall be saved, but he who does not believe shall be condemned" (Mk. 16:16). It is for this reason that Christ commanded his apostles and disciples to go, not to the Jews alone, but to all nations, "baptizing them in the name of the Father, and of the Son, and of the Holy Spirit" (Matt. 28:19).

Several conclusions may be immediately drawn from this universal necessity of baptism:

1) There is a grave obligation not to delay the baptism of infants longer than necessary, lest they should die without the sacrament. To postpone the ceremony beyond a week or two after birth without good reason would probably be gravely sinful. Although the same urgency is not present in the case of adults, neither should their baptism be deferred unreasonably.

2) Every unbaptized human being, infant or adult, is capable of receiving this sacrament. For infants, and those perpetually without the use of reason, no disposition of soul is necessary for the valid and fruitful reception of the sacrament—as is obvious, they place no obstacle to its reception, and the faith and intention of Christ's Mystical Body brings them to the sacred font which is the womb of the Church. Adults, on the other hand, must be spiritually disposed: they must have the intention of receiving the sacrament (at least habitual and implicit); they must have faith, i.e., supernatural assent to the chief mysteries of Christianity, and they must have supernatural sorrow (at least attrition or imperfect contrition) for their past sins.[1a]

3) If an infant's parents are non-Catholics, the child should not, as a general rule, be baptized by a Catholic, except when there is proximate danger of the child's death. This general norm (which admits of several exceptions) is based on the following points: 1) the children of infidels remain in the care of their parents until they attain the use of reason; 2) there should be a solid hope that the baptized children would be raised as Catho-

[1a]Adults who are in danger of death, and cannot be more carefully instructed in the principal Christian mysteries, may nevertheless be baptized if in some way they show their assent to these mysteries and make a serious promise to observe the precepts of Christianity. Moreover, if they cannot ask for baptism (e.g., if they are unconscious), they may be baptized conditionally, if they had in the past indicated an intention of receiving the sacrament. However, if they should recover and a doubt of the validity of the previous baptism should persist, they should be re-baptized conditionally. Cf. Can. 752.

lics (hence although the Church possesses rights over the children of heretics, schismatics and apostates, she ordinarily does not exercise them, because of the grave danger of defection on the part of the baptized children who will be raised in a non-Catholic atmosphere). It should be noted, however, that the baptism of all these children would be valid if conferred; and that this general rule does not apply to the children of indifferent Catholics, nor where one of the parents is a Catholic.

4) The necessity of receiving baptism makes it clear that unborn children in danger of death, aborted foetuses and the like should be baptized insofar as possible. This is a matter of particular importance for Catholic doctors and nurses, who should receive special instruction on the subject; it is of too technical a nature to be discussed here.

4. The Effects of Baptism

By baptism man is born again to that life of the spirit which is had through the faith of Christ, as the Apostle says (Gal. 2:20), "The life that I now live in the flesh, I live in the faith of the Son of God." But life exists only in those members which are united to the head, from which they derive sensation and movement. And thus it necessarily follows that by baptism man is incorporated in Christ, as if one of his members.

Moreover, just as the members derive sensation and movement from the head of the natural body, so from their spiritual head (who is Christ) his members derive spiritual sensation—the knowledge of truth —and spiritual movement, under the inspiration of grace. Hence it is said: "We saw him full of grace and of truth; and of his fulness we have all received" (Jn. 1:14,16). And thus it follows that the baptized are illumined by Christ as to the knowledge of truth, and made fruitful by him with the fruitfulness of good works through the infusion of grace.[2]

"Dead to sin, but alive to God in Christ Jesus." This great sacred sign produces these three major effects of incomparable value: 1) the remission of all sin; 2) the conferring of divine life through grace; and 3) incorporation in Christ. Each of these effects merits a few words of explanation.

[2]St. Thomas, *Summa,* III, q. 69, a. 5.

A. Remission of All Sin

In all those who place no obstacle to the fruitful reception of this sacrament, sin is entirely removed by the power of the sanctifying waters. This means:

1) The remission of original sin.

2) The remission of any actual sins that have been committed, whether mortal or venial.

3) The remission of every penalty due to sin, not only eternal punishment but all temporal punishment as well, so that the person who dies immediately after baptism will enter heaven directly.

4) Consequently, the opening of the gates of the kingdom of heaven, closed to us by sin and the punishment due to sin.

5) The removal of concupiscence and all the penalties which flow from original sin. This will be perfectly accomplished only in heaven; they are permitted to remain in this life, not as punishments, but as opportunities for the practice of virtue by which we become more like to our Savior.

B. Conferring of Divine Life in Christ Jesus

All the sacraments of faith signify and thus effect man's sanctification, which is accomplished by the grace Christ won for us on his cross. Baptism initiates this life in us. Hence in those who place no obstacle to its fruitful reception this sacrament causes:

1) Sanctifying grace, which makes the soul holy and pleasing to God by conferring a physical but analogous participation of God's own nature. In those already in the state of grace, this means an increase of grace; for those not yet justified, it produces this first and fundamental participation of divine life.

2) All the infused moral and theological virtues and all the gifts of the Holy Spirit, for these are properties of habitual grace and the proximate principles of supernatural action for the Christian.

3) A special sacramental grace corresponding to the special end of this sacrament, namely, man's death to sin and rebirth in Christ Jesus.

C. Incorporation in Christ and in Christ's Church

This is accomplished through the consecration of baptismal character (which is caused by the sacrament even in those who do not receive it fruitfully because of some obstacle). Through this spiritual and indelible power man receives a participation of Christ's priesthood which enables him to join in the official worship of God, which derives from Christ's passion and is perpetuated by his Mystical Body. Only those who possess this mark of a Christian may receive the other sacraments validly, for only they can share in the divine liturgy which is constituted by the sacraments.

Two important corollaries flow from this doctrine concerning the effects of baptism:

1) *Baptism cannot be repeated.* It is a spiritual rebirth, and man is born but once; it is a death to sin through a washing in Christ's death, and Christ dies but once; it is chiefly a remedy for original sin, which is not committed again; and finally, it imprints an indelible character. This last reason, as the Church declares, is definitive; it makes one incapable of receiving the sacrament again.[3]

2) *When the obstacle to fruitful reception of baptism is removed (as, e.g., by penance), the sacrament "revives,"* i.e., it then and there causes man's sanctification through the remission of sin and the infusion of grace, or produces one of the secondary effects of grace previously impeded by the lack of disposition on the part of the subject.

5. The Cause of Baptism

A. Its Institution

The word *baptism* is derived from the Greek word meaning "to immerse," and by human usage came to acquire the more general signification of "to bathe" or "to wash." St. Paul describes Christian baptism as a "bath of water" (Eph. 5:26), a "bath of regeneration and re-

[3]Cf. the Council of Trent, Sess. VII, Can. 9; Denz. 852.

newal of the Holy Spirit" (Tit. 3:5)—a meaningful phrase which indicates the vast difference between this Christian washing and all other ceremonial washings, those of pagan religions, or of the Old Law, or even the penitential baptism of John.

The question before us, then, is this: did Jesus Christ himself institute such a ritual of washing with water as a true sacrament, as a sacred sign of man's sanctification efficacious of the effect it signifies? With the entire Christian tradition, with all the Fathers and all theologians, we unhesitatingly answer "yes." Baptism is one of the seven sacraments of the New Law instituted by our Savior—this is a dogma of faith.[4]

Sacred Scripture clearly attests to the fact of the institution of baptism by Christ, but the exact moment of its institution is not so clear. Four have been suggested by various theologians:

1) Christ's baptism in the Jordan (Lk. 3:21 ff.; Matt. 3:16 ff.; Mk. 1:10 ff.).

2) At the time of the conversation with Nicodemus (Jn. 3:5 ff.).

3) When the first disciples were sent to baptize (Jn. 3:22-26, 5:1 ff.).

4) At the time the apostles received the solemn command to baptize all nations (Matt. 28:19).

With most of the Fathers and with most theologians, both old and new, St. Thomas maintains that the occasion of his baptism likewise was the occasion of Christ's institution of this sacrament.[5] For "by Christ's infinite power, the contact of his body gave a regenerative force not only to those waters which touched him but to all waters everywhere on earth and through all ages."[5a] Whatever be the case, the essential fact remains that Christ is the true author of this sacred efficacious sign, as the gospels themselves point out.

B. The Administration of Baptism

(1) The Minister of Baptism

Man becomes God's agent in the distribution of the graces of his love, Christ's instrument in applying the fruits of his passion to in-

---

[4]Cf. Council of Trent, Sess. VII, Can. 1; Denz. 844.
[5]Summa, III, q. 66, a. 2.
[5a]Ibid., q. 78, a. 2.

dividual men. This fact, which is verified in a most special manner in the administration of the sacraments, is perhaps most evident with respect to baptism, the most necessary of all the sacraments. No one can administer baptism to himself, all men are dependent on the agency of some other man, but in case of necessity any man will suffice. For solemn baptism, however, the Church designates special ministers.

The minister of the sacrament of baptism may be indicated by means of the following outline:

Valid—any human being whosoever with the use of reason having the intention of doing what the Church does

Lawful
    Solemn baptism
        Ordinary—a priest
        Extraordinary—a deacon
    Private baptism (in case of necessity)—any human being (as for valid administration)

By the law of the Church, the Local Ordinary or the local pastor alone have the right to baptize (they are officially entrusted by the Church with the care of souls in their territories). But with the permission of one or the other any priest may legitimately baptize (his sacerdotal power over Christ's eucharistic body is the source of this power over Christ's Mystical Body). For a just reason, this permission may even be granted to one who is ordained a deacon. In either case the permission may be lawfully presumed if it is a case of necessity.[6]

Although anyone may baptize privately when there is danger of death (provided only that he uses the correct matter and form and has the proper intention), "if a priest is present he is preferred to a deacon, a deacon to a subdeacon, a cleric to a layman, a man to a woman (unless for the sake of modesty it would be more fitting for a woman

[6]Cf. Can. 738, § 1; 741.

than for a man to baptize, or unless the woman knows the form and manner of baptizing better)."[7] The baptism of adults should be referred to the Local Ordinary, in order that, if he wishes, baptism may be more solemnly conferred by him or by his delegate.[8]

(2) The Baptismal Sponsors

St. Thomas considers the **baptismal sponsors** as a kind of minister of the sacrament, for by their sponsorship they assume the grave responsibility of nursing and instructing the newly born Christian in the faith and in Christian practices; they become, as it were, spiritual parents. For solemn baptism at least one sponsor is required (unless this is impossible); two may be furnished, one of either sex, but no more than two. If a sponsor can be supplied for private baptism, this should be done.

Since the role of the sponsor is an important one and may, due to the death or neglect of the parents, in the future become one which is vital for the spiritual welfare of the baptized, the Church legislates carefully in order to provide worthy sponsors:

1) For *validity* a sponsor must: a) be baptized, have the use of reason, and possess the intention of fulfilling this office; b) be a practicing Catholic; c) be one who is not the father, nor the mother, nor the spouse of the one being baptized; d) be designated as sponsor by the one baptized or by his parents or guardians or, if they should be lacking, by the minister; e) hold or touch the one being baptized (by himself or by proxy) during the action of baptizing, or immediately take up the one baptized from the sacred font or from the hands of the minister. (Cf. Can. 765.)

2) For *liceity* the sponsor must possess these further qualities: a) be at least 14 years old; b) be free of ecclesiastical penalties; c) know the basic principles of Catholicism; d) not be a novice or a professed religious (unless it is necessary, and the express

[7]Can. 742, §§ 1 and 2.
[8]Can. 744.

permission of the superior, at least the local superior, is obtained); e) not be in holy orders, unless his Ordinary gives express permission. (Cf. Can. 766.)

The baptismal sponsors contract a true obligation of caring for the spiritual welfare of their charge, although only in case of necessity where their care and instruction would be needed does the obligation arise. Moreover, they contract a spiritual relationship with the one baptized, which between sponsor and baptized of opposite sexes results in an impediment to their valid marriage (cf. Can. 1079).

6. The Kinds of Baptism

From what we have seen of the essence of the sacrament of baptism, we may formulate the following definition: **baptism** is *a sacrament of the New Law instituted by Jesus Christ, by which a man, through the washing with water under the invocation of the most holy Trinity performed by the minister, is reborn to divine and supernatural life and made a member of the Church.*

This is sacramental baptism, called *baptism of water.* By analogy with the sacrament, two other kinds of "baptism" are recognized by the Church—*baptism of blood* (martyrdom undergone for Christ, for the faith, or for some Christian virtue) and *baptism of the spirit or desire* (an act of divine charity or of contrition perfected by charity, which includes at least implicitly the desire of receiving sacramental baptism). Baptism of blood takes the place of sacramental baptism, even for children (see our Lord's explicit teaching on this, Matt. 10:32,39; Lk. 9:24; it is for this reason that the Church recognizes the Holy Innocents as saints); it is a true imitation of Christ's passion, configuring the martyr to him in a most real fashion and thus obtaining for him the application of the merits of Christ's passion and the supernatural sanctification produced in others by the sacrament. Similarly, baptism of desire unites one to Christ through the love inspired by the Holy Spirit, and thus also procures man's salvation; it is, however, necessarily limited to adults.

It should be noted that neither baptism of blood nor baptism of fire is a sacrament, nor does either confer all the effects of the sacrament—sacramental grace is not given by them and the sacramental character is not imprinted on their souls. Thus the man already justified by baptism of desire still remains under serious obligation to receive the sacrament.

THE ANOINTING OF THE LAITY

It must have been a trying moment for St. Paul when he inquired of some of his hearers at Ephesus, "Did you receive the Holy Spirit when you became believers?", only to be told, "We have not even heard that there is a Holy Spirit" (cf. Acts 19:1-3). A complete lack of understanding of the role of the Holy Spirit in Christian life exists today. It is particularly noticeable in the widespread failure to understand the meaning and purpose of the sacrament of confirmation. This ignorance is no less trying to the Church now than it was in the time of St. Paul.

The widespread ignorance of, and indifference to the sacrament of confirmation is itself an indictment of the vitality of Catholicism in our day. Confirmation is the soldier's sacrament; it is tailored to produce apostolic fighters against the spirit of worldliness which Christ condemned so severely. Perhaps the fact that Catholics have come to terms with worldliness, that they have forgotten Christ's promise of enmity with the world, that they have ceased to fight; perhaps this explains their apathy toward confirmation and the relatively few apostolic souls in our day. The last thing a complacent man or a slacker wants is a uniform. The last thing some Catholics seem to want is a summons to battle.

Yet that is precisely what confirmation is, and it is exactly what our age needs. These matters become clear in this treatment, which will be developed according to the following outline:

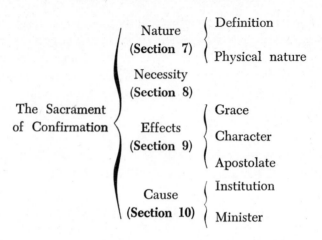

7. The Nature of Confirmation

The investigation of the nature of confirmation follows the same pattern as that for baptism. The object of our inquiry will be to discover what kind of reality the sacrament of confirmation is. In accomplishing this, we shall be able to know what this particular sacrament is, and the way in which it differs from baptism and the other sacraments.

Thus, since the sacrament of confirmation is a symbol which effects what it signifies, we must determine its matter and form. But first we shall give a metaphysical definition of confirmation.

A. The Metaphysical Definition

Confirmation is *the sacrament of spiritual strength.* This is its metaphysical definition. Like baptism, confirmation belongs to the general class of things we know as signs. It is a symbol of our reception of spiritual strength, actually accomplished at the moment when the symbol is present. Thus, confirmation sanctifies man in a special way by giving man spiritual strength and produces a special mode of sanctifying grace. In this, confirmation is a sacrament which is specifically different from the other sacraments.

B. Physical Nature of Confirmation

We must deal with the matter and form of the sacrament of confirmation, because these are the elements which make up the physical nature of any sacrament. Remember that sacraments are signs, and signs are of value to human beings alone. That is, only human knowledge proceeds *from* sense objects *to* intellectual comprehension. In confirmation, the sense objects which we must consider are the **matter** (both the sensible thing itself, the *remote* **matter**, and the use of the remote matter, the *proximate* **matter**), and the **form**, the words spoken at the moment of confirmation.

(1) The Remote Matter

The *remote* matter of this sacrament is sacred chrism. Chrism is an admixture of olive oil and balsam, and each of its elements has special significance. The lustre of the olive oil signifies the brightness of the Christian's conscience; its strength-giving qualities indicate the spiritual strength of the fulness of the Holy Spirit which is conferred by the sacrament. The fragrance of the balsam, which permeates to the far corners of the church, is a sign of the fulness of the spiritual life given to the Christian, in virtue of which he passes beyond the individual life of spiritual infancy into adult, social Christian life, wherein he communicates his spiritual riches to others.

The chrism must be consecrated, not simply blessed. The reason for this consecration lies in the fact that Christ himself probably did not use chrism, and hence a special consecration is needed to adapt it to become the instrument of grace. The special blessing prescribed for the consecration of sacred chrism on Holy Thursday is administered only by a bishop, who most fully represents Christ and takes his place.

(2) The Proximate Matter

The *proximate* matter of confirmation is the anointing with chrism on the forehead in the form of a cross through the imposition of hands. By this ceremony, the one confirmed is signed like a soldier with the mark of his Chief. He bears proudly the stamp of his Christianity upon his brow, which is the most prominent and obvious part of his body. It is on the forehead that one first notices the blush of shame or the paleness of fear, which might prevent the public protestation of faith. It is thus fitting that the forehead should bear the chrism, the sign of the Christian adult and soldier of Christ, rather than the signs of human fear and shame.

(3) The Form of Confirmation

The *form* of this sacrament is found in the words: "I sign you with the sign of the cross and I confirm you with the chrism of salvation, in the name of the Father, and of the Son, and of the Holy Spirit." St. Thomas points out that this simple but solemn formula expresses the three necessary elements of this sacred symbol, clearly determining the material sign.[9] It expresses the principal cause of the fulness of spiritual strength, the Trinity, and the instrumental cause, the minister, as well. The formula delineates the effect conferred by the visible sacrament, the spiritual strengthening unto salvation, "I confirm (i.e., strengthen) you with the chrism of salvation." It also makes clear that the Christian fighter is given the sign of his Chief, the cross on which the King won his victory, just as in worldly combat soldiers are given the insignia of their leaders.

8. The Necessity of Confirmation

As the fact that there is a special matter and a special minister of this sacrament suggests, confirmation is not of such absolute and universal necessity as baptism. The Christian may attain salvation without it. Such is the tremendous grace it confers, however, and such its power, that the Christian who deliberately neglected so important a channel of Christ's perfection could hardly be excused from fault. The man who remains physically or mentally a child in the natural order is to be pitied; the child of Christ who fails to reach his destined maturity through neglect of confirmation is in a comparable condition.

All of the baptized—and only the baptized—who are not yet confirmed are capable of receiving the sacrament validly. In the present

[9]*Summa*, III, q. 72, a. 4.

discipline of the Church, it is usually given, apart from danger of death, only to those who have reached the age of reason. It is clear, however, that confirmation could be given at any chronological age. For the fruitful reception of confirmation, the subject should be in the state of grace, and, if he has attained the use of reason, be instructed in the Christian religion and in the matters which pertain to this sacrament. Only then can he be properly disposed to receive the great graces of this outpouring of the Holy Spirit.

9. The Effects of Confirmation

The existence of a special sacrament implies a special effect of grace. Confirmation, then, will produce distinctive effects, and these we will consider according to this division:

The Effects of Confirmation
$\begin{cases} \text{Grace} \\ \text{Sacramental character} \\ \text{Preparation for the apostolate} \end{cases}$

A. Grace

Confirmation, like all the sacraments of the living, confers an increase of sanctifying grace upon those who receive it worthily. In addition, confirmation brings special sacramental graces which are designed to enable the recipient to attain the end for which the sacrament was instituted. By this sacrament, spiritual infants become spiritually mature, and the simple citizens of Christ's kingdom become his soldiers and athletes. These things are clearly indicated by the symbolism of this sacred rite, which implies the following effects:

1) A substantial and notable increase of sanctifying grace, of the infused moral and theological virtues, and of the gifts of the Holy Spirit—in recipients who place no obstacle to the reception of grace.

2) A special sacramental grace so strengthening the Christian that he will firmly and bravely live his faith in public before all men, defending it and fighting for it when circumstances demand.

3) The right throughout his life to the actual graces necessary for this conflict, whenever occasion arises.

B. Sacramental Character

A sacramental character, as explained above, is a special power whereby men are made able to participate in the divine worship inaugurated by Christ on the cross. Confirmation imprints an indelible character of this kind on the souls of all who receive the sacrament validly. We will consider in detail its characteristics.

(1) Its Indelibility

The sacramental character is indelible; nothing can efface it from the soul. Because of this, confirmation can be received only once. The character is impressed even upon those who receive the sacrament unworthily, in the state of serious sin. But in these cases, the permanent character remains as a pledge of the sacramental graces which will flow into the soul once the obstacle of sin is removed. Like baptism, confirmation "revives," i.e., comes back to spiritual life by producing its effects of grace at the time the soul becomes properly disposed to receive them.

Because the character is a permanent quality which effects a real change in the soul, we may rightly say that the confirmed Christian is a different *kind* of person than one who has not received the sacrament. This difference in being will normally be manifested by a difference in action.

(2) Its Activity

The character of baptism is a passive power to partake in the worship of Christ through the reception of the other sacraments. The character of holy orders is an active power to administer those sacred things which belong to Christ's worship of God. The character of confirmation holds a kind of middle-ground between these two. It is a kind of passive-active power, first, to receive special divine aids for the active and official profession of the Christian faith, and secondly, to bear witness by the public profession of faith, in words and deeds suited to edify the faithful.

In this sacrament of the fulness of grace, there is a special conformity to Christ, who from the first instant of his conception was ". . . full of grace and truth" (Jn. 1:14). The role of the confirmed in Christ's worship is quite different from that of those who are only baptized or those who are ordained. The ordained have a spiritual dominion over others; they are the official teachers of faith. Confirmation grants no authority over others. Yet its effects are social, insofar as a witness borne to Christ must necessarily affect others: it is related to building up the faith of Christ's Mystical Body. The baptized profess the faith, but as a personal thing, as an exercise of self-survival in the spiritual life to which they are regenerated by baptism. The confirmed professes the faith *ex officio,* he is like a soldier who defends the republic as one officially charged to do so. The character of confirmation does not bring any dominion to the recipient, but it does bring a special excellence, just as maturity brings to a man an excellence he did not possess as a boy.

It is upon the confirmed that Christ's Mystical Body must rely ". . . to do those things which pertain to the spiritual combat with the enemies of the faith."[10] Thus, although the salvation of the individual may be obtained without confirmation, it is clear that the sacrament is necessary for the Church. The workings of the character of confirmation are strikingly evident in the apostles, who were changed from cowards into fearless confessors of the faith at Pentecost, but they are no less real in the multitudes who bear witness for the faith today. This includes not only the countless victims of persecution throughout the Communist world, but also the Christian parents who sacrifice for their families, the Christian workers who strive for justice, the Christian officials who labor for good government, the Christian students who defend the truth, and countless others who bear witness to Christ.

(3) Its Divine Effects

The confirmed compose the normal majority of the faithful. It must be the divine intention to perfect the body of the Church by bringing its members to the perfect spiritual age, just as nature intends a race

[10]*Summa,* III, q. 72, a. 5.

of men, not dwarfs.[11] Even if all the members of the Mystical Body
were spiritually mature through confirmation, there would still be a diversity of works and duties among them, as St. Paul clearly teaches.[12]
The confirmed will be distinguished by differences in outlook, responsibility and action, corresponding to the maturity which the
sacrament causes.

In outlook, those confirmed should have an awareness of the corporate good of the Mystical Body; they should not be spiritually
self-centered like children. The confirmed should be characterized
by a willingness to accept responsibility for others, a great sign of
maturity in the supernatural family of Christ's Mystical Body, whose
whole character is militant and social. And, finally, confirmed Christians should be characterized by apostolic action proportioned to
their mature outlook and sense of responsibility. Such apostolic action will be the subject of the following section.

C. Preparation for the Apostolate

Pope Pius XII has stated: "Today more than ever and as in the
first days of its existence, the Church's need is above all for witnesses,
even more than apologists; witnesses who, by the whole of their
life, will make the true face of Christ and of the Church shine out
in splendor in the eyes of a paganized world." The perennial need
for apostolic action is here expressed in terms of its contemporary urgency. Any realistic hope for the fulfillment of this call must be
rooted in a knowledge of the power of the character and of the
graces of the sacrament of confirmation.

(1) The Meaning of the Apostolate

The term "apostolate" must be understood clearly for a proper
appreciation of the meaning of the apostolic activity which should
characterize the confirmed Catholic. Etymologically, "apostolate"
refers to the work of Christ's apostles, which was carried out in virtue of special powers he bestowed upon them. Some of these divinely

---

[11]*Summa*, III, q. 72, a. 8.
[12]Rom. 12:4,5. cf. *Summa*, II-II, q. 183, a. 2.

granted powers were *extraordinary,* and in virtue of these special powers the apostles become the founders of Christ's Church. Among these are the charisms—the special graces enjoyed by the apostles, not for their personal sanctification, but rather for the good of the Church as a whole. For example, the apostles had the gifts of tongues and prophecy, the power to work miracles, and the privilege of infallibility in matters of faith and morals. These gifts were necessary for the preservation and growth of the infant Church. The apostles also enjoyed wider jurisdiction than their successors, the bishops, whose jurisdiction is limited to their own dioceses. None of these extraordinary powers were transmitted by the apostles to their successors.

Besides these special powers, the apostles received *ordinary* powers which made them pastors of the faithful. By these they were enabled to teach, govern and sanctify their flocks. These ordinary powers attached to their office as bishops, and not to their persons. Hence, these ordinary powers received from Christ are transmitted to the bishops who suceed them in office.

The bishops, then, continue the work of the apostles. They have the fulness of priestly power by which they can ordain other priests. They enjoy supreme jurisdiction in their own dioceses, subject, of course, to the Holy Father.

Not only do the bishops continue the work of the apostles, but they also carry out the apostolic mission. That mission is to devote themselves to the salvation of souls because of their love for Christ. The bishop, like his Master, must be willing to lay down his life for his flock. The apostolic mission, then, is supernatural and spiritual in its essence and purpose. Whatever else it may embrace must be pursued for the purpose of the salvation of souls. It is the same purpose for which Christ came into the world.

All apostolic action is in some degree a sharing in the mission of the hierarchy, and the mission of the hierarchy is to accomplish the salvation of souls. Consequently, apostolic action, howsoever diversified it may become, will find its unity in the apostolic mission, which is to continue the work of Christ in the world for the salvation of souls.

(2) *The Foundation of the Apostolate among the Laity*

The work of Christ demands workers who are like Christ. That likeness is provided among the laity by the sacramental characters received in baptism and confirmation. By these characters, the soul is configured to Christ, especially as he is the great High Priest offering perfect worship to his Father. Apostolic action, then, is simply the flowering, the vital and active expression of this special oneness with Christ which results from the bond of unity founded upon these sacramental characters. Because of this union with Christ, the apostolic activity of Christians enjoys a certain sacredness, for it is a real contribution to the work of Christ in which the laity share the apostolic mission of the hierarchy.

The apostolate is the Christian warfare, the struggle and sacrifice to extend the work of redemption into the world. It is for this warfare that Christians become "soldiers of Christ" at confirmation. By this sacrament they become available for, and capable of Christ's work in the world; they co-operate in bringing the world to the worship of God through the priesthood of Christ by sharing in the mission of the hierarchy.

This teaching is summarized in these words of Pope Pius XI:

> In reality it is the sacraments of baptism and confirmation themselves which impose, among other obligations, that of the apostolate, that is to say, the obligation of giving spiritual help to one's neighbor. It is true that by confirmation one becomes a soldier of Christ, and everybody recognizes that a soldier must bear fatigue and battles for others rather than for himself. But, in a way that is much more hidden from the eyes of the uninstructed, baptism too imposes the duty of the apostolate, since by it we become members of the Church, that is to say, of the Mystical Body. Among the members of the Body—and this is true of every organism—there must be a solidarity of interests and mutual communication of life. "We, the many, are one body in Christ, but severally members one of another" (Rom. 12:5). One member should aid the other; none can remain inactive, each should contribute in his own turn.
>
> Every Christian has received the supernatural life which flows in the veins of the Mystical Body of Christ—that abundant life which Christ, as he himself says, came to bring on earth: "I came that they may have life, and have it more abundantly" (Jn. 10:15). And con-

sequently, every Christian must pass on that life to others who do not possess it, or who possess it only in small measure and only in appearance.[13]

(3) Different Kinds of Apostolate

There is a universal summons to the apostolate and it is binding upon all. As Pope Pius XII pointed out, "All have the obligation of collaborating in the restoration of the kingdom of Jesus Christ, because all are the joyful subjects of that merciful King. . . ." To dispense oneself from doing at least something is a sin of omission which, in certain circumstances, could become grave. In Lacordaire's phrase, everyone is called upon to become, by all his being, an apparition of Jesus Christ.

This general kind of apostolate is as old as the Church. The apostles had their faithful collaborators among the laity; this is clear from the many laymen mentioned in the epistles of St. Paul and in the Acts. The same co-operation has been true in every age down to the present day.

The exercise of this general apostolate by the faithful is the private fulfillment of a social obligation. Over and above this ordinary apostolate, laymen may be officially summoned or deputed to collaborate actively in the apostolate of the hierarchy. This is a special apostolate; this is Catholic Action in capital letters, Catholic Action properly so called.

Pope Pius XI ". . . after due thought, deliberately, indeed, one may say not without divine inspiration . . ." defined Catholic Action as ". . . the participation of the laity in the apostolate of the Church's hierarchy."[14] In this strict and proper sense, Catholic Action is an official institution of the Church by which and in which the ordinary apostolate of the faithful is organized and directed by the hierarchy. Thus the apostolate of the laity, founded upon sacramental charac-

[13]Letter to the Cardinal Patriarch of Lisbon, Oct. 11, 1933; cf. E. Guerry, L'Action Catholique (Paris: Desclée, 1936), 58 f.

[14]Discourse to the Young Women's Section of the Catholic Action of Italy, March 19, 1927. Cf. Civardi, A Manual of Catholic Action (New York: Sheed & Ward, 1936), 4 ff.

ters and grace, is elevated and assimiliated into the divine work
of the hierarchy.

Catholic Action becomes a special apostolate in virtue of the man-
date of the bishop, who is himself a successor of the apostles. By
this hierarchical summons, laymen are officially commissioned to
work for the glory of God and the salvation of souls. This is essentially a work of the laity in which the faithful act in an organized
fashion under the direction of the hierarchy as auxiliaries to further
the reign of Christ in individuals, in families and in society.

(4) Apostolic Works

If it be asked: What are the works of the apostolate?, many answers
may be given. Any good works which tend to further the kingdom
of Christ on earth are within the scope of the ordinary apostolate
of the laity. The spiritual and corporal works of mercy, for example,
could all be apostolic works for anyone.

For official Catholic Action, the works will be determined by the
needs of the Church as interpreted by the hierarchy. The organized
groups will fit themselves to the surroundings in which they work.
There are no ready-made forms. As a living organism, Catholic Action
will adapt itself to the situations in which it operates to establish
the human race under the rule of our Lord Jesus Christ.

Catholic Action is essentially missionary action, designed to bring
Christ to others. This demands that its participants shall themselves
lead an intensely Christian life. The call to Catholic Action is a
summons to a more perfect spiritual life, for no one can impart what
he does not possess. It is perhaps because of the personal demands
that a more perfect Christian life must make that the numbers engaged in Catholic Action are relatively few. But this apostolate is
not for the sake of personal salvation; it is missionary and concerned
with others. Hence, there must follow from a more abundant spiritual
life an effective Christian action upon others to draw them to Christ.

The works engaged in by Catholic Action are practically innumerable. There are the multiple works of the family apostolate: conduct-
ing conferences to prepare the young for marriage; preparing meet-
ings to improve schools; looking after neglected children; providing

opportunities for family recreation. There are many social works: laboring for good working conditions; striving for the passage of just laws; providing adequate family housing; promoting good literature and wholesome recreation; assisting in the works of the parish apostolate; encouraging vocations; promoting Catholic education; and similar works. There are specialized groups working among students, in the various unions, among members of the professions and occupational groups. But throughout this great array of diverse undertakings there is a great unity derived from the common goal of restoring all things in Christ.

10. The Cause of Confirmation

A. Its Institution

The Church has repeatedly defined that confirmation is a sacrament of the New Law instituted by Christ.[15] It is clear from the Scriptures that the apostles employed a sacred rite of anointing: they imposed their hands on the baptized faithful in order that they might receive the Holy Spirit (cf. Acts 8:12-18, 19:1-6), and it is hardly conceivable that they would have dared to introduce such a ceremony on their own authority.

Neither Sacred Scripture nor Tradition assign a determined time for the institution of this sacrament, but theologians generally hold that this occurred in the period between the resurrection and the ascension. It was during this time that Christ spoke to his followers of the kingdom of God (cf. Acts 1:3), and made a solemn promise of the coming of the Holy Spirit (cf. Acts 1:4; Lk. 24:49).

St. Thomas expresses this theological consensus regarding the institution of confirmation:

> It must be said that Christ instituted this sacrament, not by producing, but by promising it, according to John 16:7: "For if I do not go, the Advocate will not come to you; but if I go, I will send him

---

[15]Cf. the Second Council of Lyons, *Profession of Faith of Michael Paleologus,* 1274 (Denz. 465); the Council of Florence, *Decree for the Armenians,* 1429 (Denz. 695); the Council of Trent, Sess. VII, 1547, *On the Sacraments in General,* Can. I (Denz. 844), "On Confirmation," Can. 1 (Denz. 871).

to you." And this is so because in this sacrament the fulness of the
Holy Spirit is given, which was not to be bestowed before the resurrection and ascension of Christ, according to John 7:39: "For the
Spirit had not yet been given, seeing that Jesus had not yet been
glorified."[16]

Keeping in mind the parallel between growth in the natural and
supernatural orders, the suitability of confirmation becomes evident.
The infant grows gradually and matures until he reaches the state
of manhood; he becomes fully and perfectly human, capable of adult
responsibilities. Similarly, the spiritual infant arising from the baptismal waters must grow into the state of the mature Christian. This
comparison is beautifully expressed in the words attributed to Pope
Melchiades:

> The Holy Spirit came upon the waters of baptism, bringing salva-
> tion in his downward flight. In the font, he gave beauty to innocence;
> in confirmation, he brings an addition to grace. Because in this world
> at every age those who are to live on must walk amid invisible enemies
> and perils, we are reborn to life in baptism, and, after baptism, we
> are confirmed for the fray. We are washed in baptism; after baptism
> we are strengthened. But if the benefits of rebirth suffice for those
> who are immediately to pass on, the helps of confirmation are neces-
> sary for those who continue to live. Rebirth of itself saves those who
> are soon to be received into the peace of the blessed world, but con-
> firmation arms and instructs those reserved for the struggles and battles
> of this world.[17]

B. The Minister of Confirmation

Only a bishop, who alone possesses in virtue of his sacred office
the fulness of Christ's power, is the **ordinary minister** of this sacrament. This befits its nature as the spiritual consummation of baptism:
the work of perfecting anything belongs properly to a supreme
power, although preparations and beginnings may be initiated by
those of lesser ability or capacity.

By delegation from the Holy See, given by special indult or by
the law of the Church, a priest may be constituted the **extraordinary
minister** of confirmation. So anxious is the Church that the faithful

---

[16]*Summa*, III, q. 72, a. 1, ad 1.
[17]*Letter to the Bishops of Spain;* cf. *Catechism of the Council of Trent*, Part II,
Chap. 3, q. 5.

should receive this sacred sign of spiritual fulness and strength, that she delegates the power of confirming to pastors (when the bishop cannot perform the ceremony) for those Catholics in their parish who, because of serious illness, are in danger of death and have not yet been confirmed.

A **patron** or **sponsor** of the same sex as the one receiving the sacrament should be provided, although the bishop for sufficient reason may permit one to stand for all the men and one for all the women. The conditions required for valid sponsorship and those for lawful sponsorship are comparable to those required for baptism (cf. *supra*, pp. 345-346). The sponsors are *responsible* for bringing the confirmed to spiritual maturity through instruction, advice and example. This is a grave obligation, and they must fulfill it themselves if the one confirmed needs such training and it is otherwise unavailable. It must be noted that the spiritual relationship engendered by sponsorship at confirmation is *not* an impediment to matrimony as is the relationship of baptismal sponsors.

11. Summary and Conclusion

The focal point around which any of the sacraments revolves is the fact that sacraments are symbols of something holy and that they sanctify man at the instant they are used. Baptism symbolizes the rebirth of the Christian. Born to sin, he is reborn to the life of grace. He is initiated into the divine life of Christ himself. The character of baptism leaves an indelible mark on the soul of the baptized, a mark which is at the same time a tremendous power, enabling the baptized to take his first gigantic step into sacramental life.

Without baptism man is spiritually stillborn. He cannot even begin to grow and wax strong, "full of wisdom and the grace of God" (Luke 2:40). He cannot be incorporated into the Mystical Body, but must live a spiritual outcast, and an alien to the kingdom of God.

Whether or not there are still many who "have not even heard that there is a Holy Spirit," Christ has, in fact, sent the Paraclete. While his channels into souls are many, and while he has not disclosed them all to us, we do know by faith that the sacrament of confirmation is the ordinary means for the Christian to become spiritually mature.

This maturity is a reality; it is a growth in grace and a change in life. The soul of the confirmed Christian is sealed with God's mark; he is set apart, he is different. And just as he is different in what he *is*, so also should he be different in what he *does*, for the actions of a being manifest its nature. "By their fruits you will know them" (Matt. 7:16).

If the theology of confirmation is accurate, why is there so little evidence of the effects of these marvellous graces and of this character that makes men more like to Christ? Perhaps there is more than one would think. A great deal of what one sees depends on where one looks and what one seeks. Surely, however, the accomplishments fall short of the opportunities. Men can always resist grace, and that is a terrible thing. But there are many who do not realize the treasures they possess. And how can they begin to understand the power of confirmation and the need for the apostolate unless some man show them? What a tragedy to miss the privilege of a full life in Christ just because no one bothered to explain its meaning. There is an apostolate of the well-educated Catholic layman on behalf of those who are not so favored.

The following conclusions follow directly from our study of the doctrine concerning baptism and confirmation.

1. The permanence of the sacrament of baptism is something which colors the entire life of the Christian. No diversion can fill up the hollow left in his soul by the loss of grace through sin. Although a man may be the most hardened sinner, he can never completely shake off his Catholic common sense. Baptism incorporates man into the Mystical Body of Christ, and he who tries to forget this, falling back on his puny natural strength, is fighting a losing battle with the omnipotent power of God.

2. "This is what happens with us, whose model the Lord made himself. When we are baptized, we are enlightened; being enlightened, we become adopted sons; becoming adopted sons, we are made per-

fect; and becoming perfect, we are made divine. 'I have said,' it is written, 'you are gods and all of you the sons of the most High' (Ps. 81:6).

"The ceremony is often called 'free gift,' 'enlightenment,' 'perfection' and 'cleasing'—'cleansing,' because through it we are completely purified of our sins; 'free gift,' because by it the punishments due to our sins are remitted; 'enlightenment,' since by it we behold the wonderful holy light of salvation, that is, it enables us to see God clearly; finally, we call it 'perfection' as needing nothing further, for what more does he need who possesses the knowledge of God?"[18]

3. The liturgy of the paschal vigil contains a ceremony of profound significance. After the baptismal water has been blessed, the faithful renew their baptismal vows. Lighted candles in hand, they rededicate themselves to Christ by renouncing once again Satan, his works and his pomp. Just as the darkness of Christ's death is pierced by the light of his resurrection, so also the darkness of sin is pierced by the brilliance of baptism.

4. The Catholic adult living in the world needs to bring to perfection the graces given him in confirmation. Too often the sacrament of confirmation is looked upon as a child's toy; a present to be played with during childhood and then pushed aside and forgotten at the approach of maturity. We must understand that confirmation makes us apostles of Jesus Christ, in order that we might profess our baptismal faith to the world. This does not mean that the lay apostle must go about the world preaching and working miracles: rather, he must make use of the intellectual gifts of the Holy Spirit—wisdom and understanding, counsel and knowledge. Without perfecting these gifts through a continual growth in grace, he cannot be a healthy organ of the Mystical Body.

5. "The knowledge of our holy religion will enkindle in you a love of the Church. . . . It is the Church, not of one race or of one nation, but of all those who truly believe in his name. The more you dwell upon its teachings, its practice and its history, the stronger will be

[18]Clement of Alexandria, *Christ the Educator.*

your unity with the multitude of believers throughout the world. You will clearly understand that the true interests of each part, of each diocese and parish, are the interests of the Church Universal."[19]

6. ". . . Whoever lives by the spirit of Christ refuses to let himself be beaten down by the difficulties which oppose him, but on the contrary feels himself impelled to work with all his strength and with the fullest confidence in God. He does not draw back before the straits and the necessities of the moment, but faces their severity, ready to give aid with that love which flees no sacrifice, is stronger than death, and will not be quenched by the rushing waters of tribulation."[20]

7. "For a Christian who is conscious of his responsibilities even toward the least of his brethren, there is no such thing as slothful tranquillity; nor is there question of flight, but of struggle, of action against every inaction and desertion in the great spiritual combat where the stakes are the construction, nay the very soul, of the society of tomorrow."[21]

BIBLIOGRAPHICAL NOTE

The sacrament of baptism is treated in Part III of the *Summa*, Questions LXVI-LXXI. A technical review of the first two sacraments can be found in an apologetical work called *Baptism and Confirmation* (St. Louis: B. Herder Book Co., 1929), by Adhémar d'Alés. A simple, clear, yet adequate and comprehensive account of baptism, called *The Sacrament of Baptism* (New York: The Macmillan Co., 1929), has been written by John P. Murphy.

L. Bright, writing for the periodical *Life of the Spirit*, XI (1956), 158-163, gives a particularly fine view of Christian baptism in his article "Sacraments: I—Baptism." Consult also in the same issue the same sacrament looked at from a different angle in an article called "Sacrament of Faith," by Conrad Pepler. "Baptism, Confirmation and the Holy Eucharist," by Charles Keenan, S.J., in Volume III

---

[19]American Bishops, *Joint Pastoral*, 1919.
[20]Pope Pius XII, Encyclical *Summi Pontificatus*.
[21]Pope Pius XII, *Christmas Message*, 1942.

of the English *Summa,* can be used to great advantage, both for the material in this chapter and that of the next. A perceptive and illuminating pamphlet by A. M. Carré, O.P., *Baptized in Christ,* is published by The Liturgical Press, Collegeville, Minn.

For confirmation, plus the books in the General Bibliography, the student may consult the *Summa,* III, q. 72. There are two particularly valuable articles by James R. Gillis, O.P., "The Case for Confirmation" in *The Thomist* (April, 1947, 159-184), and "Unless They Be Sent" in *From an Abundant Spring* (New York: Kenedy, 1952), 110-136.

The following articles, all taken from *Theology Digest,* will be found helpful in developing the ideas of this chapter: Yves Congar, O.P., "What Is a Layman?" (I [1953], 8-12); A. A. Lobo, O.P., "The Social Character of the Church," (II [1954], 39-42); Emilio Sauras, O.P., "Is There a Priesthood of the Laity?" (IV [1956], 110-114).

A great deal has been written on the subject of Catholic Action. L. Civardi, *A Manual of Catholic Action* (New York: Sheed and Ward, 1936), is an excellent basic statement; much of its contents, however, have been amplified by the pronouncements of Pius XII. John Fitzsimons' *The Christian in a Changing World* (Chicago: Fides, 1950) is a very clear and brief statement on the apostolate in booklet form. One of the simplest ways to obtain an up-to-date bibliography on the apostolate is to write to Fides Publishers, Chicago 10, Ill. From its inception, that firm has been distinguished by its excellent list of books directed to the apostolate.

Several anthologies of papal documents are readily available in any good library. Particularly noteworthy among these because of the variety of topics covered through well selected excerpts are: R. C. Pollock, ed., *The Mind of Pius XII* (New York: Crown Publishers, 1955), and F. J. Powers, ed., *Papal Pronouncements on the Political Order* (Maryland: Newman Press, 1952).

Chapter XIII, "The Sacramental System," by C. C. Martindale, S.J., in the second volume of *The Teaching of the Catholic Church,* will also be most helpful to the student.

CHAPTER ELEVEN

The Most Blessed Sacrament

1. Introduction

This is the *Mystery of Faith*—the most august sacrament of the altar, the sacred sign of Christ which contains not his power only but Christ himself, his body and blood truly and substantially present under the veil of the outward appearances of bread and wine. It is a wonder of divine wisdom and divine love, the heart and center of the worship of Christ, the perpetuation of his sacrifice and the preeminent source of the graces of his sanctification. God, having given us all good things, gave us, his enemies, yet more than all else. His Son became man to save us from our sins by the sacrificial gift of himself to God, and by his sacrifice won God's gift of himself to us through grace; and his Son, the God-man, daily gives himself to us, his flesh and his blood, our daily and supersubstantial bread for the constant nourishment of our souls in grace, our daily and superabundant sacrifice of praise and propitiation and petition, of thanks.

This is *The Thanksgiving*, the Eucharist:

> When he who presides has celebrated the Eucharist . . . the deacons permit those present to partake of the eucharistic bread and wine and water; and they carry it also to those absent. We call this food the

366

Eucharist, of which he alone can partake who has received the truth of our teachings, who has been cleansed by baptism for the remission of his sins and for his regeneration, and whose life is lived according to the principles laid down by Christ. Not as ordinary bread nor as ordinary drink do we partake of them; but just as Jesus Christ our Savior became incarnate through the word of God and took flesh and blood for our salvation, so (as we have been taught) this food, become our thanksgiving by the prayer of his word and by assimilation the nourishment of our flesh and blood, is both the flesh and the blood of that Jesus who was made flesh. For the apostles in their memoirs (called gospels) have handed down what Jesus commanded them to do: he took bread and, after giving thanks, said, "Do this in commemoration of me; this is my body"; in like manner he took the chalice, and, having given thanks, he said, "This is my blood."[1]

Of the many descriptive names by which men have sought to express the tremendous reality of this sacrament of Christ's body and blood, the term "Eucharist," first used so long ago, remains still, perhaps, the best. Yet so various are the aspects under which it may be considered, so full of divine mystery is the reality itself, that no name can be regarded as exclusively proper; in the pages which follow these synonyms will be multiplied, as one or another facet is explored. But always it should be remembered that it is one and the same reality which is described, the sacred symbol which is the sacrament of sacraments.

For similar reasons it is hardly surprising that the Old Testament should foreshadow this promised sign of sanctification under various figures. Melchisedech's sacrifice of bread and wine[2] foretells the matter to be used in the sacramental rite, as do the twelve loaves of fine flour (Lev. 24:5). All of the sacrifices of the Old Law—particularly the sacrifice of expiation (Lev. 23:27)—are figures of the *res et sacramentum* of the Eucharist, Christ himself as sacrificed. And the *res tantum* or effect of this sacrament is clearly foreshadowed by the manna showered upon the Israelites in the wilderness (Ex. 16:13), for, like the sacramental grace which refreshes the soul in all things, it possessed "all that is delicious and the sweetness of every taste."[3]

---

[1]St. Justin Martyr, *The First Apology*, n. 66; see also *The Doctrine of the Twelve Apostles*, Chap. 9, n. 1, Chap. 10, n. 1; etc.

[2]Cf. Gen. 14:18.

[3]Wis. 16:20.

But the paschal lamb prefigures the great, sanctifying sign of the future best of all. It represents the *sacramentum tantum* of the Eucharist, the external rite, for it was eaten with unleavened bread; it represents the *res et sacramentum,* Christ crucified, for it was immolated by the entire Jewish people at the time of the Passover; it represents the *res,* the ultimate effect of the Eucharist, for by the blood of the paschal lamb the children of Irael were preserved from the destroying angel, and delivered from slavery.

Its names, its figures suggest the supernatural reality we shall now consider, and its inexhaustible spiritual richness of meaning. Theology —"faith seeking understanding"—shall lead us to a fuller appreciation of this mystery of faith, and we shall have St. Thomas, the poet of the Eucharist and its greatest theologian, as our teacher and guide. We shall consider the Eucharist under these headings:

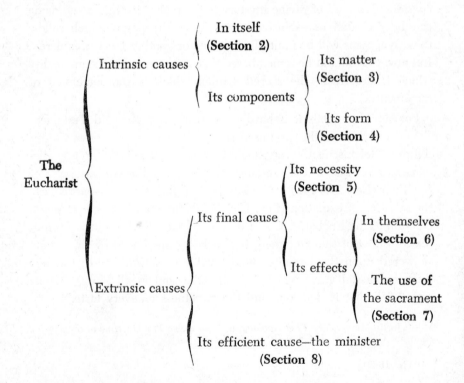

The Eucharist

Intrinsic causes

In itself (Section 2)

Its components

Its matter (Section 3)

Its form (Section 4)

Extrinsic causes

Its final cause

Its necessity (Section 5)

Its effects

In themselves (Section 6)

The use of the sacrament (Section 7)

Its efficient cause—the minister (Section 8)

The Eucharist is a sensible sign which sanctifies man, and thus a sacrament; but at the same time it is pre-eminently a liturgical action (as are all the sacraments), an act of worship of God, *the* act of worshipping God, the Mass: a re-presentation of Christ's sacrifice on Calvary. The sacrament of the Eucharist as sacrifice—as *the* sacrifice, the sacrifice of Calvary—will be studied in the following chapter.

2. The Essence of the Eucharist

The several aspects of the Eucharist which may be considered can be expressed in the following definition: the Eucharist is *a sacrament of the New Law instituted by Jesus Christ which, under the consecrated species of bread and wine, contains the body and blood of Christ for the spiritual nourishment of man.* The rest of this chapter will be devoted to a detailed consideration of the elements of this definition. For the present, however, the points which follow will suffice to emphasize the uniqueness and sublimity of this sacrament.

1. The Eucharist is a *sacrament* of the New Law. This dogma of faith is so clearly taught by Sacred Scripture, so constantly held sacred by the Church, both in the East and in the West, that not for centuries was it necessary to make a solemn and definitive pronouncement of this revealed truth.[4] It is a **sense-perceptible sign** (the physical appearances of bread and wine and the words of consecration) **of a sacred thing** (the accidents of bread and wine do not signify the substance of bread and wine but the body and blood of the crucified Christ and the sanctification and ultimate glory thus brought to man) **precisely as that sacred thing here and now sanctifies man** ("If anyone eat of this bread he shall live forever"—Jn. 6:52), **instituted by Christ as a permanent thing** ("Do this in remembrance of me"— Lk. 22:19).

2. The Eucharist is *one* sacrament, not several. Although there is a double matter and form of the sacrament, they ultimately signify only

---

[4]Cf. the Fourth Lateran Council, 1215 (Denz. 430); the Council of Florence, *Decree for the Armenians,* 1439 (Denz. 698); the Council of Trent, Sess. VII, Can. 1, 1547 (Denz. 844), Sess. XIII (the whole of which is concerned with the *sacrament* of the Eucharist), 1551 (Denz. 873a-893).

one thing, the end to which the sacrament is ordained, namely, the spiritual nourishment of man. *Formally,* therefore, (precisely as a sign) there is only one sensible sign (man's physical nourishment through food and drink, indicated by the outward appearance of bread and wine, precisely as specified by the words of the consecration), and hence one sacrament.[5]

3. The Eucharist is a *permanent* sacrament. That is, unlike the other sacraments which do not have the power of sanctifying until someone makes use of them, the Eucharist is constituted by the very consecration of the matter, for at that moment Christ's body is present under the appearances of bread and his blood under the appearances of wine. So long as these species remain the sacrament continues in existence, since the form—the words of consecration—perdures as determining and specifying the matter.

4. The Eucharist is *necessary* for salvation. Union with Christ and his Mystical Body through sanctifying grace is of absolute necessity for one to be saved. But this union is exactly that which is signifed and effected by this sacrament, the end to which all the sacraments are ordained as their consummation and perfection. Hence at least an implicit desire of receiving the Eucharist is necessary for salvation, although its actual reception is not. Baptized children have this desire, not of themselves, but through the intention of the Church; for by their very baptism they are ordered to its actual reception in due course.

5. The Eucharist was *instituted by Christ* at the Last Supper. This fact is explicitly taught by the Scriptures[6] and by the Church.[7] It is singularly appropriate that Christ should institute this commemorative banquet of love, the Eucharist, as he takes his last meal with his disciples.[8]

---

[5]The Eucharist is one *kind* of sacrament, but there will be as many *numerically* different sacraments of the Eucharist as there are spiritual nourishments signified and caused: two Masses, two sacraments; five persons receiving Communion, five sacraments.

[6]Cf. Matt. 26:20-26; Mk. 14:17-22; Lk. 22:14; I Cor. 11:23.

[7]It is proclaimed in the Canon of the Mass and defined by the Council of Trent, Sess. XIII, Chap. 1 (Denz. 874).

[8]Cf. St. Thomas' beautiful commentary on this fact, *Summa,* III, q. 73, a. 5.

3. The Matter of This Sacrament

Under this heading we must study some of the most profound doctrinal truths which concern the Eucharist—some of the deepest truths and mysteries of Christianity, in fact. Our inquiry will be undertaken according to four main subjects: 1) the materials used; 2) the change of the bread and wine into the body and blood of Christ; 3) the manner in which Christ's body and blood exist in this sacrament; and 4) the accidents of bread and wine which remain after the change.

A. The Material Elements of the Sacrament

Anyone familiar with Christ's institution of the Eucharist at the Last Supper knows that he took common bread and wine, separately consecrated them after offering thanks to God, and commanded his disciples to perpetuate this religious ceremony in his memory. In consequence of Christ's determination, therefore, bread and wine are the proper matter of this sacrament. That they are eminently suited to be the outward sign of the Eucharist is clear on three counts:

1) *So far as the use of the sacrament (which consists in eating) is concerned.* As water is used in baptism for the purpose of spiritual cleansing (since the cleansing of the body is usually done with water), so bread and wine—the common fare of the generality of men—are employed for the use of spiritual eating.

2) *In relation to Christ's passion,* wherein the blood was separated from the body. In this memorial of the Passion, the bread is received apart as the sacrament of the body and the wine as the sacrament of the blood.

3) *Considering the sacrament's effect,* the union of the faithful with Christ and with one another in the unity of the Mystical Body. As the bread is composed of many grains and the wine flows from many grapes, so the whole Church is constituted by many members.

From the fact that common bread and wine are to be used it follows that:

1. The bread should be made from wheaten flour, mixed with water, and baked, and not substantially corrupted. Bread from any other grain or fruit is not common bread, nor is that mixed with any other fluid except water, nor is an uncooked mixture; none of these would be valid matter. It is customary in the Latin rite to use unleavened bread; the Church also prescribes that the host be clean, whole, recently made and round in shape.

2. The wine must be true wine made from grapes. Liquors from any other grain or fruit are invalid; liquids made from grapes but not true wine are invalid. The Church prescribes that a small amount of water be added to the wine. This mixture 1) symbolizes the union of the faithful with Christ; 2) represents his passion, for water flowed with the blood from his side; and 3) imitates Christ's institution, for in keeping with Jewish custom he probably mixed a little water with the wine he used. But this addition of water to the wine is not essential to the sacrament.

3. The matter to be consecrated should be physically present to the priest and determined as the matter to be consecrated by his intention. Since he will use the demonstrative pronoun "this" to designate the matter, it must be clear by the physical presence of the matter that it is this bread and wine he is talking about. Moreover, "this" refers to some specific thing, and hence he must intend to consecrate some specific matter.

B. The Change of Bread and Wine into the Body and Blood of Christ

In this mystery of faith which is the Eucharist, the material elements of bread and wine are, through the consecratory power of the sacramental formulas, so changed in their very substance that, although their accidental qualities persist, the bread becomes the body of Christ and the wine becomes his blood. In this defined doctrine of the Church of Christ,[9] three marvels of divine power and wisdom and love need to be further explained: 1) the real presence of Christ in the Eucharist; 2) the mystery of transubstantiation; 3) the accidents of bread and wine which remain even after the change of substance.

(1) The Real Presence of Christ under the Species

Not until the eleventh century did any Christian cast the slightest doubt on the revealed truth the Church had always taught and which Christ himself had made so plain: that his true physical body was contained in this sacrament under the outward appearances of bread and his true physical blood under the outward appearances of wine. But from the time of Berengarius there have been men calling themselves Christians who, paying little heed to Christ's words or to his Church, contend that Christ's body and blood are not in this sacrament except as in a sign. This heresy was most vigorously proposed by Luther's successors and followers, and is found today among many Protestant sects. Against such as these the Church solemnly proclaimed, in the Council of Trent, the true faith: **in the sacrament of the Eucharist Christ is present truly** (not only as represented in sign), **really** (not only figuratively or symbolically or as the object apprehended by faith), **and substantially** (not only through his effects or by his action or power.)[10] His presence under the sacred species is as true, as real, as substantial as your presence in this room while you read these words.

The truth of this tremendous fact is manifest both from Sacred Scripture and from Tradition. A brief examination of each of these sources of God's revelation to man will suffice to indicate the solidity of the Catholic position.

1. Sacred Scripture. The revealed written word of God expressly teaches that Christ is truly, really and substantially present in the

[9]Cf. the Sixth Council of Rome, the profession of faith prescribed for the heretic, Berengarius, 1079 (Denz. 355); the Fourth Lateran Council, Chap. 1, 1215 (Denz. 430); the Second Council of Lyons, the profession of faith prescribed for the Greek schismatic, Michael Palaeologus, 1274 (Denz. 465); the Council of Florence, *Decree for the Armenians*, 1439 (Denz. 698); the Council of Trent, Sess. XIII, Chap. 4, 1551 (Denz. 877).
[10]Sess. XIII, Chap. 1; Denz. 874.

Eucharist, contained under the perceptible appearances of bread and wine.

1) *From Christ's words promising this sacrament to men:* In the sixth chapter of the Gospel of Jesus Christ according to St. John, the promise of this sensible sign composed of bread and wine containing his true body and his true blood is given by our Savior. After the multiplication of the loaves, evidence of his divine power and a figure of the future sacrament (vv. 1-15), he performs a miracle for his disciples by walking on the waters (vv. 16-21). On the following day, Christ discloses to the multitude the true spiritual nature of his messiahship. In this instructive discourse (vv. 27-51) he uses the symbol of bread to explain the sublime and lofty doctrine he has come to reveal to mankind: he is the spiritual bread come down from heaven, and whosoever eats of this bread through the impulse and light of faith which the Father gives, he shall never die. And then Christ states, not in figurative language but in literal truth (vv. 52-59):

> I am the living bread that has come down from heaven. If anyone eat of this bread he shall live forever; and the bread that I will give is my flesh for the life of the world. . . . Amen, amen, I say to you, unless you eat the flesh of the Son of man and drink his blood, you shall not have life in you. He who eats my flesh and drinks my blood has life everlasting and I will raise him up on the last day. For my flesh is food indeed, and my blood is drink indeed. He who eats my flesh, and drinks my blood, abides in me and I in him. As the living Father has sent me, and as I live because of the Father, so he who eats me, he also shall live because of me. This is the bread that has come down from heaven; not as your fathers ate the manna, and died. He who eats this bread shall live forever.

This is no allegory, no parable, no extended figure of speech; the stylistic difference between this passage and the figurative discourse which precedes it is as evident to any unbiased critic as it was to the startled Jews who heard it. It announces a mystery, to be sure, beyond human understanding, an impossibility and a scandal for all who measure things in human terms. Many in his audience doubted, his disciples murmured, but Christ let them go: they had heard aright, they had taken his words literally, they were under no false impression. And Christ in no way softens this hard saying by explaining it away as a symbolic manner of speaking. His body will be man's food, his blood man's drink for the spiritual nourishment of those who believe his words of everlasting life.

2) *From Christ's words instituting the Eucharist:* The Synoptics and St. Paul are in complete agreement in reporting Christ's institution of the sacrament of his body and blood: he takes bread and declares, "This is my body"; he takes the cup of wine and declares, "This is my blood." And he commands his followers to eat and to drink, and to perpetuate as the memorial of his coming passion the sacred ceremony he has thus instituted.[11]

To attribute a metaphorical meaning to these straightforward statements does violence to the words themselves and to the context in which they were uttered; it is a simple subterfuge for those whose faith is so weak that they cannot accept anything exceeding their human grasp. Either Christ spoke the literal truth, or he was deceiving his apostles.

2. Apostolic Tradition. The constant faith of Christ's Church attests to the fact of Christ's real presence in the Eucharist. St. Ignatius of Antioch (+ 107) reprimands the Docetist heretics because they do not believe that the Eucharist is "the flesh of the Savior which suffered for us."[12] The most ancient liturgies—of St. Hippolytus, of Egypt, of St. Cyril of Jerusalem, of the Apostolic Constitutions—are in universal agreement with the perpetual testimony of the Fathers to the fact of Christ's true presence under the sacramental species. Not until eleven hundred years after the fact was revealed did anyone directly call it into question; until the time of Berengarius the universal Church possessed this fundamental Christian truth in immemorial and tranquil belief, assured and unchallenged.

[11]Cf. Matt. 26:26-29; Mk. 14:22-25; Lk. 22:15-20; I Cor. 10:16-21, 11:23-29,
[12]*Epistle to the Smyrnaeans*, VII, 1.

(2) *The Mystery of Transubstantiation*

Because Christ our Redeemer declared that what he offered under the species of bread was truly his body, it has always been the faith of the Church of God (and this holy Synod now again states it) that by the consecration of the bread and wine a change takes place in which the entire substance of bread is changed into the substance of the body of Christ our Lord and the entire substance of wine into the substance of his blood. This change the Holy Catholic Church fittingly and properly entitles "transubstantiation."

If anyone says that the substance of bread and wine remains in the holy sacrament of the Eucharist together with the body and blood of our Lord Jesus Christ, and denies the wonderful and unique change of the entire substance of the bread into Christ's body and the entire substance of the wine into his blood—only the appearances of bread and wine remaining—a change which the Catholic Church most appropriately calls "transubstantiation": *let him be anathema.*[12a]

The marvel which is the eucharistic conversion can never be grasped by the human intellect; we can only assent to it through the supernatural light of faith. But we may make more explicit this mystery of love revealed to us by God and definitively proposed by the Church by considering the elements of which it is composed, and by separately restating and examining them.

1. In the Eucharist nothing remains of the *substance* of the bread and wine. It is a matter of common-sense experience that the appearance of things changes while the thing itself remains substantially the same. The fertilized ovum in the womb of the mother will one day be president of the United States; but regardless of the vast difference between the embryo and the future president, he is one and the same human being. You yourself are conscious of the fact, if you reflect on it, that it is the same fundamental you which underlies and unifies all the various changes, physical, moral, spiritual, which you have experienced. The leopard may change his spots; he is a leopard still. Appearances may come and go, but there is a substratum of things which is so basic that it survives all these changes.

In scholastic terminology, the word **substance** describes the reality underlying all the surface qualities of a being, the basic foundation

---

[12a]Council of Trent, Sess. XII, Chap. 4 and Can. 2; Denz. 877 and 884.

which preserves the thing's identity through any number of transitory changes. Substance requires no extrinsic substratum to sustain its existence, it sustains itself (more accurately, it is sustained in being in itself); it is a reality which of its nature possesses independence in being, requiring no subject in which it inheres in order to exist. A man is a substance, so is a tree, a stone: each has independent existence, no other subject sustains its being.

Accidents, on the other hand, are realities of a much different stamp—of their nature they call for a support, for a subject in which to inhere, for a foundation to sustain their being. Colors, for example, do not go around existing by themselves; they find their being by modifying some subject, some substance. A white horse is a substance (horse) supporting an accidental modification of color (white). The case is similar with a wise man, a tall tree, running water, leaping frogs, studious students: a substance plus an accident, a being competent of independent existence plus a being to which *per se* existing does not belong, but existence in something else as its subject of inherence. And the accident may change—the white horse become black by dirt or dye or physical alteration—while the substance remains the same. You yourself suffer innumerable such changes throughout your life; the fundamental you remains the same.

Material substances (stone, stick, man) are, unlike purely spiritual substances (the human soul, the angels), *composed* realities: matter enters essentially into their make-up, but so does form (spiritual substances are pure forms, without any matter). Thus man is composed of body and soul; take one or the other away, and you do away with man—without the soul this body ceases to be human, it is a cadaver; without the body, man's spiritual form, the soul, continues to exist, but not as a human being. All other material things—bread and wine, e.g.—also are composed of matter and of form as their intrinsic principles; if you change one of these elements, even while retaining the other, the transformation will be a substantial one, not merely an accidental modification. These ashes may once have been a fine piece of brocade; fire has so changed the cloth that it becomes a new substance, the matter remaining but the form of ashes succeeding the form of cloth.

With these preliminary notions in mind, we may restate our defined truth thus:

1) The change is not an accidental one but a *substantial* one. The accidents of bread and wine are not transmutated, but their very substances, the underlying realities which supported those accidents in being.

2) The change is a *total* one. It involves the whole substance, the entire substance, not just a part of the substance; since bread and wine are material substances, composed of both matter and form, this means that both the matter and the form of the original substance is changed. There is no parallel to such a wholehearted transformation in all of nature, for in all the substantial changes with which we are familiar at least the matter of the original substance persists through the transforming activity to receive the new form which makes it a new thing. This points up the uniqueness of the eucharistic conversion; it cannot, however, alter the fact.

The truths so far enunciated (as well as those soon to be considered) are implicit in the words of Christ's institution of the Eucharist which constitute the formula of consecration: "This is my body, this is my blood." "*This*," Christ equivalently declares (and the priest acting for him), "this substance which I hold in my hand and is directly contained under these sensible appearances of bread, this is substantially identical with my true physical body." To affirm such a substantial identity between bread and his body would be patently false—substantial identity means one substance, not two. If there is any truth to God's words, therefore, the entire substance of the bread and the wine must have ceased to exist under their outward appearances.

In what manner is this accomplished?

2. The entire substance of bread is converted into Christ's body and the entire substance of wine into Christ's blood. Bread becomes the body of Christ, wine is made his blood—this, as the consecratory words imply, is a true change, not annihilation (where nothing remains of the previous substances), nor creation (where no previous substance existed at all), but a mutation of the total substance of bread and wine, a *transubstantiation,* of which Christ's body and blood is the term. Hence:

1) Transubstantiation is a **converting action** by which God, the infinitely powerful cause of all being, changes whatever there is of being in the substance of bread into whatever there is of being in the substance of Christ's body, form into form and matter into matter; the same is analogously true of the conversion of wine into Christ's blood. So total a change is impossible for finite, created agents; limited, determined, specified by their forms, their activity cannot extend to the entire being of a thing. Hence every substantial change effected by a natural agent is a partial one: requiring a subject on which to work the change, a creature effects only a change of form, but the matter of the substance changed remains to receive the form of the new substance. But God who is infinite being and infinite act possesses unlimited power, infinite activity. He is the source of all being and his action extends and penetrates to the whole nature of being and to all its elements. His ability to effect this change, *transubstantiation,* is unquestionable.

2) The substance of bread and wine is **totally changed** into Christ's body and blood, without the latter undergoing any intrinsic change. Through the power of the words of consecration, the substance of bread and wine ceases to be *in order that* it may become the substance of Christ's body and blood which is pre-existent to the change: Christ becomes present under the species of bread and wine not through a change of his body and blood but through the change of the bread and wine. This implies:

   a) Transubstantiation is not an action which *produces* (nor even, properly speaking, which *reproduces*) the body and blood of Christ.

   b) It does not merely *substitute* Christ's substance for the substance of the bread and wine which has ceased to be. Nor can it be a simple *change of place* on the part of Christ's body and blood through local movement. On the contrary, by one and the same action of God's omnipotence Christ's substance becomes present and the substance of bread and wine ceases to be.

c) As a result of this divine action, Christ's body and blood acquire a new *manner of being:* they are truly present now under the sacramental species, where before they did not so exist.

d) This change is necessarily *instantaneous,* no single instant intervening between the cessation of the substance of bread and wine and the real presence of the body and blood; in one and the same instant both things happen.

(3) *The Accidents of the Eucharist*

Despite the total change of substance, the accidents of bread and wine continue to exist in objective reality. Although this truth is not directly defined by the Church, it is nonetheless presupposed by the conciliar definitions concerning the nature of the eucharistic change, which become unintelligible without it; it is at least theologically certain, it would be rash to question, doubt or deny it.

In other words, what we see with our eyes, touch with our hands, taste and smell—these are truly present in the Eucharist. The outward appearances (species or sense-perceptible accidents) of bread and wine continue to exist, they are real, they are bread-accidents and wine-accidents even though bread and wine have ceased to exist. They are not mere subjective impressions conjured up by our senses which fool us into thinking that there is whiteness and shape and taste and the rest. Our senses do not deceive us: their object is not the inner reality, the substance of things, but rather the extrinsic qualities. In the Eucharist the extrinsic qualities of bread and wine manifest themselves to the sense faculties and hence constitute the external sense-perceptible sign which is the sacrament.

To be sure, only God's miraculous intervention could sustain these accidents without their proper substratum or subject. But, as St. Thomas points out, it is entirely fitting that he should so intervene:

1) Because it is not customary but horrible for men to eat human flesh and drink human blood; hence Christ's flesh and blood are

given to us under the species of those things more commonly consumed by men, bread and wine.

2) Lest this sacrament might be derided by unbelievers, were we to eat our Lord under his own proper species.

3) That while we receive our Lord's body and blood invisibly, this may redound to the merit of faith.

C. The Way in Which Christ Is Present

Faith teaches us that the entire substance of bread and wine is changed into the body and blood of Christ. But the body and blood are not the entire Christ. Are the other integral parts of his body contained in this sacrament? Is the whole Christ contained therein, soul as well as body, divinity as well as humanity? Is the whole Christ under the species of bread or only his body? Is only his blood under the species of wine, or is his body there likewise, and his soul, and his divinity? And if the whole and integral Christ is present under each species, how is this so?

In the Council of Trent the Church answers these and similar questions in an illuminating summary of Catholic faith:

> This has always been the faith of the Church of God: that immediately after the consecration the true body and the true blood of our Lord, together with his soul and divinity, exist under the species of bread and wine. But by the power of the words the body exists under the species of bread, the blood under the species of wine. However, by the power of their natural connection and concomitance (by which the parts of Christ the Lord, who has already risen from the dead to die no more, are joined together), his body exists under the species of wine, his blood under the species of bread, and his soul under both species. Moreover, because of that admirable hypostatic union with body and soul, his divinity is present. It is therefore perfectly true that just as much is contained under either species as is contained under both. For Christ, whole and entire, exists under the species of bread and under any part of that species, and the whole Christ likewise exists under the species of wine and under its parts.[13]

A distinct statement of the several truths here proposed by the Church will make them easier to understand, although we should remember that no full human grasp of this mystery of faith can be expected; God asks only for our assent to what he has revealed.

[13]Sess. XIII, Chap. 3; Denz. 876

1. In the Eucharist the whole Christ is present under each species.
Christ himself declared: "He who eats me, he also shall live because
of me" (Jn. 6:58). It is not only his body we eat or his blood we drink,
but Christ himself. For Christ is not divided: body and blood, soul
and divinity are intimately linked together; in the state of glory they
are united in natural indissolubility.

2. *By the power of the sacrament* **(by the power of the words of
consecration) Christ's body alone is present under the species of
bread and his blood alone under the species of wine;** *by concomitance,* **however, the rest are contained.** The words of the sacrament
effect what they signify; by their power, therefore, there is contained
only that at which the conversion effected by them is terminated. That
which is signified as being contained under the species of bread by
the words, "This is my body," is the substance of Christ's body, and
it alone—not its accidents, nor his blood, soul or divinity. And the
same is analogously true for the species of wine.

On the other hand, whatever is naturally or supernaturally united
with Christ's body or blood will be concomitantly present (not by the
power of the words) wherever the body or blood are present (by the
power of the words). The body is naturally united with the blood, the
blood with the body, and both are united with the soul and the accidents proper to them; Christ's divinity is hypostatically united with
his body, blood and soul.[13a]

**3. The whole Christ is present under each and every part of
the sacred species, whether they are divided or not.** Just as before
the consecration, bread was truly present in every part of the piece
of bread and wine in every drop of the cup of wine, so after the
conversion into Christ's body and blood, each and every part of the
bread contains Christ's whole body, each and every drop of wine
Christ's entire blood. Thus a priest may break a large host into pieces
and distribute the pieces to several communicants; each would receive
Christ's whole body (and by concomitance its accidents, his blood,

[13a]So true is this principle, that if Mass had been celebrated while Christ was
in the tomb, only his body would have been present under the species of bread,
only his blood under the species of wine; his soul would not have been present
at all, but his divinity would have been present under both species, since it remained hypostatically united to both the body and the blood.

soul and divinity). So, too, Christ distributed the consecrated chalice to his apostles, which clearly shows that under each part of the species of wine the entire Christ was consumed.

The reason for this is that Christ's body and blood are present (by the power of the words) *as substances,* not by reason of quantitative dimensions. This is a point to be separately developed.

4. In the Eucharist, Christ is not present in a quantitative manner under the species but after the manner of a substance. Every corporeal substance possesses dimensions (length, depth, width) and distinct parts, one of which is not the other and is beyond or apart from the other; dimensions, parts, extension belong to corporeal substances *in virtue of their quantity.* The entire substance is present in the whole, and in every one of its parts: the entire glass of water is water, and ever drop of liquid in the glass is water. Because of its quantitative dimensions, however, one part of the water will be on top, another on the bottom; one will touch the side of the glass, another will be in the middle; its quantity, morever, contacting the glass's resistance, will make the water assume the shape and position determined by its container.

Only the substance of Christ's body is present through the power of the words. By reason of its natural connection with the body, however, the entire quantitative dimensions of his body will be present; but since quantity is there not properly, but by concomitance, it will exist there not according to its proper manner (part corresponding to some part of space, part to another) but *in the way in which the substance is present,* i.e., the whole present in every part, and in the whole as well.

Several important corollaries flow from this theological conclusion:

1) Christ is **sacramentally** present in the Eucharist. He is not present as in a place (by the extension of his parts to the various parts of space); nor is he circumscribed and measured by the limits of the species containing his body and blood (as if he were somehow squeezed into the confines of a small host); nor is his presence limited to the one place; nor is he present after the manner of spirits, by operating on bodies. Because he is contained under the species (being present there after the man-

ner of a substance), and these species are themselves quantified, and thus located in a certain place by reason of their dimensions, he may be said to be in a certain place *by reason of the species:* where the accidents of bread or wine are present, there also is Christ (without ceasing to be elsewhere).

2) Since extension in space through dimensive quantity is a necessary condition for all bodily changes, Christ in the Eucharist neither undergoes any such intrinsic changes himself nor produces any in other things.

3) Christ's body cannot directly undergo local movement in the sacrament, but only by reason of the species. When the sacramental species are moved, then he ceases to be where they were and begins to be where they now exist; his body does not itself undergo any movement.

4) Because he is not present in the Eucharist according to bodily extension, Christ cannot be seen by the eyes, nor can he see or hear (although through the beatific vision and his infused knowledge he knows all that occurs with respect to his sacrament and his sacramental presence). Nor can any created intellect by its natural power know of his presence: it is a supernatural reality, knowable only by faith or by the beatific vision.

D. The Accidents Which Remain in This Sacrament

Our senses attest to the fact enunciated by the Council of Trent: that the accidents (species or outward appearances—size, shape, color, taste, odor, etc.—which affect the senses) of the bread and wine remain after the consecration of the Eucharist. Since the substance of bread and wine which was their natural subject and necessary support has been totally converted (so we are taught by faith), we are faced with some apparent problems which, as theologians, we must consider.

1. By divine power the eucharistic species remain without any subject in which they inhere. Two truths are contained in this statement which demand explanation:

1) There is no subject of inherence of the accidents of bread and wine which remain after the consecration.

Their proper subject, the substance of bread and wine, has ceased to be, being converted into Christ's body and blood. Christ himself cannot be the subject of these accidents, for his glorious state prohibits any change or alteration of his body and blood, and these accidents do not belong to a man in any case. Nor can the surrounding air or any other thing be assigned as a subject: accidents do not pass from one subject to another, and much less can accidents of one kind of being become those of an entirely other class of being.

2) The permanence of the eucharistic accidents is accomplished by God.

Of their nature accidents cannot exist of themselves; it belongs to them to exist in another as in a subject. If, however, some superior cause could supply the power of sustaining them which their nature demands, then they could actually exist without inhering in their natural subject (a substance); this would happen, not in virtue of their own power to exist by themselves, but in virtue of this superior power which sustains them. But God, who gives to substances the power of sustaining and supporting accidents, can certainly supply that power without the intermediary of a substance. Such is the case here: God by his own omnipotence produces this effect, that accidents exist without any subject to support them. This is entirely beyond the ordinary laws of nature, of course; it is a result of God's miraculous intervention.

2. In consequence of their miraculous conservation, the accidents of bread and wine can produce any action or undergo any change possible to them while their substance remained. Since activity flows from a thing's nature and existence, and the sacramental species are divinely preserved in their (accidental) nature and existence, they can, in virtue of this miracle, likewise act on other things (e.g., truly nourish those who eat or drink) and be acted on by them (they can change shape or color, etc., even be totally corrupted by the power of natural agents). This fact, testified to by experience, implies that anything which could normally happen to accidents of bread and wine may likewise happen to the eucharistic species.

4. The Form of the Eucharist

The form of a sacrament of the New Law is the determining and specifying element of the sacred sign, that which makes most explicit the meaning the symbol is to convey. For human words (or the signs which are their equivalent) most perfectly express for us the ideas that can only be communicated to one another through the use of sense-perceptible realities. Consequently we must now ask: what are the words which constitute the form, or sacred formula, of the Eucharist?

To answer this question—which is obviously a vital one if we are to gain a theological appreciation of this sacrament of sacraments—two important facts about the Eucharist must be recalled and insisted upon:

1) Unlike all the other sacraments, the Eucharist is not perfected or accomplished in its actual use or application, but in the very consecration of the material elements. This consecration is not a blessing of the material but the transubstantiation of bread and wine, the miraculous conversion of their substance into Christ's body and blood.

2) Unlike the forms of all the other sacraments, the eucharistic form is not expressed in the person of the minister (whether by way of command: "I baptize . . ." or by way of prayer: "May this holy anointing . . .") but in the person of Christ himself speaking the words.

From these facts we may reach these important conclusions:

1. The form of the Eucharist is the words of Christ which first perfected the sacrament. Hence the words: *hoc est corpus meum, hic est calix sanguinis mei* ("This is my body, this is the chalice of my blood")[14] are absolutely essential to the form of the Eucharist; no

[14]By a common and familiar figure of speech (technically known as metonymy), Christ uses the containing thing (chalice) to signify the thing contained (his blood). The expression is the precise equivalent of: "This is my blood."

one of them may be omitted. It is probable, however, that the words which follow in the consecration of the chalice ("of the new and eternal covenant, the mystery of faith: which shall be shed for you and for many unto the remission of sins") are not essential. Since the words effect what they signify, the consecratory conversion would take place as soon as the word "blood" has been pronounced. These last words certainly pertain to the full meaning of the consecration, nonetheless, bringing the sacramental signification to its perfection.

2. The words of the consecration are eminently suitable, for they express precisely what they accomplish. Transubstantiation implies three things: 1) the substantial change; 2) the cessation of the substances of bread and wine; 3) the resulting presence of the substance of Christ's body and blood. These essential elements are clearly indicated by the formulas, "This is my body, this is the chalice of my blood."

1) The substantial conversion. Since this change is instantaneous, it must be expressed not as happening, but as having taken place. It would not be right to say "This is *becoming* my body"; the correct expression is "This *is* my body."

2) Since the substances of bread and wine cease to exist, only their accidents remaining, it is false to say "This bread is my body." The use of the pronoun, however, without any reference to the substance of bread and wine, preserves the miraculous truth of the sacrament: "This—i.e., what is before me, that which is contained under these accidents—is my blood."

3) The last words of the form also convey the truth: that it is Christ's whole body and entire blood into which the bread and wine are converted by the efficacious power of these words, the substance of his body and of his blood.

4) The additional words in the consecration of the chalice are also most appropriate. For they express the three-fold purpose of the shedding of Christ's blood: that ours may be the reward of his promises and contract with man; that faith may be ours, and the reward of faith; that our sins may be forgiven us.

3. These words are not only significative but causative. In this respect the sacramental formula of the Eucharist is like that of all the other sacraments: it is an instrument, a tool which Christ, the God-man, uses through his minister to accomplish the effect which it signifies. While being pronounced by the minister, these sacred words possess a true created power, physical and ontologically real, participated and transient, which enables them to accomplish this miraculous effect, entirely beyond the natural power of words. This is true, not of the individual words, of course, but rather of the whole statement; like any grammatical sentence, the formula has meaning only when the essential parts of the statement have all been uttered. Hence if the words of the consecration of the bread alone were said, Christ would be truly present under the appearances of bread, even though the wine were never consecrated.

5. The Necessity of Receiving the Eucharist

Since the Eucharist is the fountainhead and the end of all the other sacraments, all Christians are led by their baptism to the consummation and perfection of their union with Christ through grace (begun in the sacrament of initiation) which is obtained through this sacramen. For adults, this necessity is supplied by the desire, at least implicit, of receiving the Eucharist; for children it is fulfilled in virtue of the intention supplied by the Church. All men are bound *spiritually* to eat the Eucharist, i.e., to be united with Christ, for without such union there is no salvation; and this includes the desire, at least implicit, of receiving the Eucharist sacramentally. **Hence by divine precept adults are obliged, given the opportunity, to receive this sacrament:** "Amen, amen, I say to you, unless you eat the flesh of the Son of man and drink his blood, you shall not have life in you" (Jn. 6:54).

Three points should be noted:
1) This divine precept is binding on all adults, the faithful and infidels as well (in virtue of baptism, which they are obliged to receive); it is *of grave obligation,* because the Eucharist is necessary to persevere as a Christian.
2) It obliges one to receive *several* times during his life. As spiritual food, it should be received whenever the powers of the spirit

need refreshment and nourishment. Christ, however, lets his Church determine how often and when the Eucharist should be received.

3) It obliges *especially* when there is proximate danger of death. At no other time is the conservation of one's spiritual life so necessary as when approaching death.

The Church has prescribed that Holy Communion should be received at least once a year by all the faithful without exception who have reached the use of reason, during the Paschal season.[15] This ecclesiastical precept (Can. 859) is likewise of grave obligation.

6. The Effects of the Eucharist

First of all and principally, the effect of this sacrament should be considered from what is contained in this sacrament, which is Christ. Just as when he came visibly into the world he bestowed upon the world the life of grace (according to Jn. 1:17: "Grace and truth came through Jesus Christ"), so also, coming sacramentally into man, he produces the life of grace in man ("He who eats me, he also shall live because of me"—Jn. 6:58). Hence Cyril says: "God's life-giving Word by uniting himself with his own flesh made it life-giving also. For it was becoming that in some way he be united with our bodies through his sacred flesh and his precious blood, which we receive in vivifying blessing in the bread and the wine."[16]

Secondly, the effect of this sacrament is to be considered from what it represents, the passion of Christ. And therefore the effect which Christ's passion wrought in the world is produced in man by this sacrament. Therefore Chrysostom comments on the words, "Immediately there came out blood and water" (Jn. 19:34): "Since the sacred mysteries derive their origin from this, when you draw near to the awe-inspiring chalice, so approach as if you were going to drink from the side of Christ."[17] For this reason also our Lord himself said (Matt. 28:28): "This is my blood, which shall be shed for you unto the remission of sins."

Thirdly, the effect of this sacrament is to be considered from the way in which the sacrament is given, for it is given by way of food and drink. And therefore every effect which material food and drink produce with respect to the life of the body—sustaining life, giving increase, renewing, giving delight—all of these this sacrament produces

[15]Usually Palm Sunday to Whitsunday, but the Local Ordinary may extend the period for a just cause.
[16]*Commentary on the Gospel according to St. Luke,* Chap. 22:19-20.
[17]*Eighty-fifth Homily on the Gospel according to St. John.*

with respect to the life of the spirit. Accordingly, Ambrose says: "This is the bread of eternal life, which supports the substance of our soul."[18] And Chrysostom remarks: "To us who long for him does he give himself, to be touched, to be eaten, to be embraced." And thus our Lord himself also states (Jn. 6:56): "My flesh is food indeed, and my blood is drink indeed."

Fourthly, the effect of this sacrament is to be considered from the species under which it is given. Hence Augustine says: "Our Lord committed his body and blood to those things which are a certain unity of many parts: for one thing (bread) is made out of many grains, and the other (wine) flows from many grapes."[19] And for this reason he elsewhere observes:[20] "O sacrament of piety, O sign of unity, O bond of charity!"[20a]

Unquestionably the sacrament which contains our Lord Jesus Christ himself, which is the renewal and re-presentation of that fountainhead of all grace, his passion, will work marvelous spiritual effects in the souls of those who receive it. The saints and doctors of the Church have vied with one another in extolling the wonders of grace which this sacred symbol effects in those who are properly disposed. To set them down, as we must, in the dry language of principles and conclusions is not enough; they must be pondered, meditated upon, brought constantly back to mind if we are truly to attain any understanding of this divine reality and its importance for our lives as Christians. Consider these things:

1. The Eucharist **immediately effects** man's **union with Christ,** through charity transforming him into Christ.

While all the sacraments give or increase the divine life of our souls, the Eucharist directly nourishes our divine friendship with God, the supernatural love by which God and we become as one. The fervor of love—love springing into action and activity—is aroused by this bread of angels, and egoism, the inordinate love of self, is thereby diminished, suppressed, expelled. The soul is refreshed spiritually by this union through charity with Christ. For whereas natural food is changed into our own substance, this supersubstantial food so transforms us that we may say: "It is no longer I that live, but Christ lives

---

[18]*Concerning the Sacraments,* Bk. V, Chap. 4.
[19]*Tract XXVI on the Gospel according to St. John,* n. 17.
[20]*Ibid.,* n. 13.
[20a]St. Thomas, *Summa,* III, q. 79, a. 1.

in me" (Gal. 2:20). Thus the life of God is made fuller and fuller within us, not only at the moment when we receive Christ's body as food but for the future as well. For the sacrament entitles us to receive constantly the graces which will intensify and increase God's friendship by acts of love.

2. Since the Eucharist transforms us into Christ, assimilating us to him through the union of charity, it:

1) Sustains the divine life within us. Sanctifying grace is given to preserve the supernatural life of our spirit from future sins. This it accomplishes by arousing the fervor of love to the performance of acts of charity toward God and toward our neighbor (are we not made one with him in Christ Jesus?), by diminishing our self-love, and by bestowing the actual graces necessary for our perseverance;

2) Increases our sharing of God's own life through its supernatural nourishment;

3) Restores the spiritual vigor weakened by passion and wasted by daily carelessness, and repairs the damage done by venial sin;

4) Fills the soul with supernatural delight. This spiritual rejoicing, which is an effect of love, may not be sensibly felt by the recipient; but the soul is filled with Christ, nonetheless, and he is the soul's delight.

3. The Eucharist in a special way causes us to attain heavenly glory: it is the earnest of our celestial heritage and of our glorious resurrection.

Through Christ, whom this sacrament contains, and his passion, of which it is the memorial, this sacrament bestows on us the power of coming to our eternal happiness. The refreshment of this spiritual food unites us to Christ in a union which is the necessary prelude to the perfect and consummate union with God in heaven. The Eucharist is already the beginning of that happiness which is eternal life both for soul and for body.

4. The Eucharist remits venial sin directly, preserves us from mortal sin, and lessens the drive of our flesh to evil.

The flood of divine love poured out on the Christian by this sacrament moves him to charity so fervent and active that he despises (at least implicitly and virtually) all that offends the one he loves, including his own past defections, the affection for which is destroyed. This eucharistic fervor strengthens the spirit, for by notably increasing one's appetite for the things of God, it correspondingly decreases the desire and affection (rooted in concupiscence) for the things contrary and offensive to God. Furthermore, the sacrament is the sign of Christ's passion, his victory over Satan: thus it wards off all the attacks of the devil.

But the Eucharist is spiritual food (and hence also medicine), and food is of use only for the living. By Christ's own determination, no one spiritually dead by reason of mortal sin may be nourished by this angelic banquet; on the contrary, to receive the Eucharist in this state would be a desecration of sacred food, a sacrilegious mockery of the sacred sign which proclaims one's intimate union with Christ. Since, however, the sacrament contains Christ himself, the source of the remission of all sin, it will restore to divine life the mortal sinner who is not conscious of his sin and retains no affection for it. Infallibly the sacrament of Christ's body and blood produces grace in the souls of those who place no obstacle to its reception; grace perfects his contrition and causes the remission of his sin.

5. The Eucharist as sacrament **does not directly remit** the temporal punishment due to sin.

This sacrament was not divinely instituted to satisfy for sin, but to nourish the soul spiritually through union with Christ and with his members. This union is realized in charity, however, and the fervent acts of love to which it inspires the Christian may by their very fervor satisfy for the penalties due to past offenses. According to the measure of one's devotion and fervor, then, satisfaction may be paid and temporal punishment remitted. *As sacrifice* (insofar as the sacrament is offered to God as the memorial of Christ's passion), the Eucharist of itself satisfies for all sins; but it becomes of satisfactory value for those who offer it or for whom it is offered according to their devotion.

6. The Eucharist as sacrament **confers grace only** on those who partake of it.

Holy Communion is food, which can only nourish those who receive it: it is to be enjoyed, and cannot be offered to others. Yet this nourishment so increases our union with God that we may more properly and successfully beseech our divine friend for our other friends; and since receiving Communion is an act of divine worship, and thus of satisfactory value before God (*ex opere operantis*), the act itself may be offered for others.[21]

7. The Use of the Sacrament

As the Council of Trent, following St. Thomas, points out,[22] one may participate in this sacred banquet in three ways:

1) Only *sacramentally*—when one truly and validly receives the sacred species (i.e., truly performs the natural functions of eating or drinking) but, because of some obstacle, does not receive the fruit of the sacrament, sanctifying and sacramental grace.

2) Only *spiritually*—when one in the state of grace partakes of the sacrament through desire and affection, and thus in virtue of his own acts is united with Christ through faith and charity ("spiritual communion").

3) Both *sacramentally and spiritually*—when the sacramental species are truly consumed and fruitfully received, so that the sacrament produces its effect *ex opere operato*.

The use of the Eucharist is most perfectly realized in this last reception of the sacrament. We shall consider under four headings the matters which pertain to its use: the requisite dispositions, both of soul, and of body; frequent Communion; the necessity of receiving Holy Communion.

A. Dispositions of Soul

As we have seen (Chapter Nine, Section 4), for the fruitful reception of the sacraments, the recipient "must open his soul to the grace offered by the sacraments." Any baptized man living in the world is *capable* of receiving Christ under the sacramental species (but only men in this life: angels do not have bodies; the blessed are already

---

[21] It is in this sense, and only in this sense, that "offering up a Communion" (e.g., in "spiritual bouquets") is to be understood: it is a promise to plead for others during the sacred moments of our sacramental union with Christ.

[22] Sess. XIII, Chap. 8 (Denz. 881); cf. *Summa*, III, q. 80, a. 1.

most perfectly united with Christ through the beatific vision and perfect charity). For adults, the intention of receiving the sacrament is required for its *valid* use.[23] But for *fruitful* reception further conditions must be fulfilled, and in the measure of their fulfillment will the sacrament work its wonders of grace in the recipient.

1. **One must be in the state of grace.** The Eucharist is a "sacrament of the living": food is not given to those who have died, and sanctifying grace is the supernatural life of the soul while mortal sin is the death of divine life in man. Moreover, he who receives the Eucharist thereby professes his union with Christ and his members; if he does not have charity, the principle of this union, he falsifies the sacred sign and thus commits a grave sacrilege, a serious abuse of a sacred thing. "Whoever eats this bread or drinks the cup of the Lord unworthily, will be guilty of the body and the blood of the Lord. But let a man prove himself, and so let him eat of that bread and drink of that cup; for he who eats and drinks unworthily, without distinguishing the body, eats and drinks judgment to himself" (I Cor. 11:27-29).

Anyone conscious of serious sin must, therefore, receive the sacrament of penance before he receives Holy Communion. No matter how contrite he judge himself, or what sorrow he have for his mortal sins, confession before Communion is prescribed, a matter of grave precept (cf. Can. 856). In the extraordinary case where, at the same time, one was obliged to receive (e.g., in danger of death, profanation of the sacrament, serious scandal, fulfillment of a public office) and also confessors were unavailable (either physically unavailable or morally so, insofar as confession would be gravely disadvantageous to another party), the precept would no longer bind; one would be obliged, however, to make an act of contrition as perfect as possible.

2. **One must be sufficiently instructed as to the nature of this sacrament in particular, and of the truths of faith and the duties of Christians, and possess the use of reason.** Although anyone who is baptized, whatever his age or mental condition, may be nourished by

---

[23]To receive Viaticum—Holy Communion when one is in danger of death—an habitual and implicit intention suffices; he who wishes to live as a Christian certainly wishes implicitly not to die without the sacraments.

the Eucharist, the Church out of reverence for the sacrament insists that one be able to distinguish the Eucharist from common and material bread and approach the sacred table with becoming devotion.[24] Thus it is necessary that even children should, according to their capacity, understand those mysteries of faith which are necessary for salvation (cf. Can. 854). A perfect knowledge of the articles of faith is not, of course, necessary, although the fervent Christian will see in this fuller knowledge a more perfect preparation for receiving the sacrament more fruitfully.

3. One should have great reverence and actual devotion. Fully to open one's soul to God's gift of himself under the appearances of bread and wine, so as more perfectly to obtain the graces of this banquet, one should dispose himself to receive the Eucharist. This implies:

1) Serious preparation by acts of faith, of hope, of desire, of divine worship, proceeding so far as possible from intense love for God and accompanied by humility and true sorrow for sins.

2) Suitable thanksgiving according to each one's strength, circumstances and duties. Christ remains physically present in the soul until the sacred species are digested, a process ordinarily taking about fifteen minutes. For all that period our God is in a most special manner our guest.

3) Freedom, so far as possible, from venial sins (especially from such as are fully deliberate) and from any affection to them. (It is sufficient, of course, if one is free of mortal sin and has the intention of never sinning mortally again; Holy Communion may then help those who communicate frequently to emancipate themselves from venial sins and from affection for them.)

4) The right intention. He who approaches this holy table should do so, not out of routine, or vainglory, or human respect; his motive should be one of pleasing God, or of being more closely united with him by charity, of seeking this strengthening food for his weaknesses and defects.

---

[24]These dispositions are not required to receive Viaticum, although the sacrament may never be given to those who have never attained the use of reason.

B. Dispositions of Body

So sacred is the banquet to which the Christian is called, that his whole being should be fittingly prepared to receive his Savior. No more than a king's guest would dishonor his host by his disgraceful vesture or physical appearance should the Christian, by his manner of dress or of bodily cleanliness, evidence irreverence for Christ. Certain garments may not be out of place on the dance floor or the bathing beach, or for hauling rubbish; excessive make-up may accentuate the effect a circus clown or stage actress may wish to obtain—are they signs of one's attitude toward the Most Blessed Sacrament? Surely the King deserves above all others the small respect that can be given by men by proper dress and appearance; surely his love merits a little effort on our part to prepare ourselves for the banquet to which we are invited.

Similar reasons are at the basis of the Church's legislation for the eucharistic fast. This small mortification—to fast entirely from solid food and alcoholic beverages for at least three hours, and from all other liquids (except water) at least one hour before receiving Communion—not only safeguards us from dishonoring the sacrament through excess in food and drink, it also manifests our reverence for the bread of angels: it signifies that our food is Christ, the bread of life who is eternal life, and that our hunger is for him.

This law of fasting is, however, only a prohibition that the Church enforces to encourage proper preparation for the sacrament. Wise with two thousand years of experience, she may change her legislation to fit the special needs of particular times, and her modern regulations take full cognizance of the circumstances of our times, while they seek to promote the more frequent reception of Christ's body and blood by the faithful through less stringent prohibitions. Today, in virtue of the ruling of the Holy Father, water does not break the fast, and it is *sufficient* to abstain from solid foods and from alcoholic beverages for three hours, and for one hour from non-alcoholic beverages. But one is *exhorted* to observe the complete fast, through devotion or a spirit of mortification, as it formerly prevailed.[25] Moreover, the law ceases to oblige when there is probable danger of death (one need not be fasting to receive Viaticum), or reverence for the sacrament demands its consumption, or there is danger of grave scandal or infamy.

C. Frequent Communion

The sacred Council of Trent, having in view the ineffable treasures of grace which are offered to the faithful who receive the Most Holy Eucharist, makes the following declaration: "The holy Synod would desire that at every Mass the faithful who are present should communicate not only spiritually, by way of interior affection, but sacramentally, by the actual reception of the Eucharist."[26] These words with sufficient clarity state the wish of the Church that all Christians should be daily nourished by this heavenly banquet, and should derive therefrom abundant fruit for their sanctification. . . .

The desire of Jesus Christ and of the Church that all the faithful should daily approach the sacred banquet is directed chiefly to this end, that the faithful, being united to God by means of the sacrament, may thence derive strength to resist their sensual passions, to cleanse themselves from the stains of daily faults, and to avoid those graver sins to which human frailty is liable. . . .[27]

Daily to increase in God's love of friendship, daily to intensify the divine life of our souls, daily to become more closely, intimately united with Christ and his members—this must be the burning desire of every Christian worthy of the name he bears. He has but to have a right and devout intention and to be in the state of grace, and then his may be that daily bread for which we beseech the Father, that supersubstantial food, come down from heaven, "having in it all that is delicious, and the sweetness of every taste" (Wis. 16:20): Christ Jesus our Lord.

8. The Minister of the Sacrament

Such is the dignity of this sacrament that it is performed only as in the person of Christ. Now whoever performs any act in another's stead must do so in virtue of the power given him by that person.

[25]Cf. the Motu Proprio *Sacram Communionem*, Jan. 19, 1957.
[26]Sess. XXII, Chap. 6; Denz. 944.
[27]Decree of the Sacred Congregation of the Council, *Sacra Tridentina Synodus*, Dec. 20, 1905.

> But just as the power of receiving this sacrament is conceded by Christ
> to the baptized person, so likewise the power of consecrating this sacra-
> ment on Christ's behalf is bestowed upon the priest at his ordination.
> Through ordination the priest is placed in the rank of those to whom
> Christ said (Lk. 22:19): "Do this in remembrance of me." And there-
> fore it must be said that it is the prerogative of priests to perfect this
> sacrament.[27a]

While in certain circumstances a deacon may distribute Holy Communion (in case of necessity even a layman may administer Viaticum),
consecration of the sacred species—the liturgical action which is at
once both sacrifice and the perfecting of the sacrament—requires a
special instrumental power. Without that power, which is the indelible character conferred by ordination to the priesthood, no consecration can take place, no sacrifice can be performed, no sacrament can be perfected. Given that power, a man, no matter how unworthy he might be of his lofty office, can always validly consecrate;
in spite of the spiritual damage the unworthy priest might do himself through his illegitimate use of this power, the sacrament-sacrifice
is as objectively valid and intrinsically as priceless as the Mass of a
St. Thomas Aquinas.

This is the great office of the priest, and the source of his transcendent dignity: through his Mass he offers God the acceptable
sacrifice of Christ and his members and brings to men the gift of
God, Christ himself under the sacramental species, his grace and his
love. This is a privilege of which the priest will avail himself as often
as he can, but (except in certain circumstances) it is not a matter of
obligation—there is no need for him to be forced to share in that
great action of Christ which is the world's salvation.

9. Summary and Conclusion

The most colossal stumbling block which has confounded millions
of non-Catholics throughout the centuries is the same block upon
which the Catholic Church is built—the sacrament of the Eucharist.
Christ really present upon the altar, called down by the words of
consecration, is the sacrament *par excellence* of the Christian faith.

[27a]St. Thomas, *Summa*, III, q. 82, a. 1.

For Christ instituted this sign of his own sacred body and blood so that man, here and now, might be made holy by being united to him.

The truth of Christ's real presence in the Eucharist is attested to both by his own words as found in Sacred Scripture, and the firm and constant tradition of faith. In this tremendous mystery the bread and wine are placed upon the altar, offered to God, and then consecrated by the words of a priest. At the instant of consecration, the bread is no longer bread and the wine no longer wine, but the substance of bread becomes the substance of the body of Christ and the substance of wine becomes the substance of the blood of Christ. That which was bread is now the body of Christ, and that which was wine is now the blood of Christ, with only the accidental qualities of bread and wine remaining. The converting action by which this change takes place is called *transubstantiation,* an action which brings forth the whole Christ to man; body, blood and, concomitantly, soul and divinity.

The eating of the body and blood of Christ is not only a foreshadowing of the joys of eternal life, rather it is the real beginning of eternal life. For the power of being united to Christ is bestowed upon us in this sacrament as the prelude to perfect union with God in heaven.

Our share in the fruits of Calvary, however, depends upon our fitness to receive them. It depends upon the fulness of our participation in this sacred banquet. When we eat worthily, our status as children of God makes us also brothers of Christ and the true heirs of heaven.

The following conclusions have been derived from the doctrinal summary just presented.

1. " 'The Lord is with you, breathren! Brethren are you with me?
   'It is not only the paten, not only the chalice and the wine,
   'It is you, my little flock, I want to hold up in my hands.' "[28]

2. Sometimes Catholics deplore their lack of spiritual fervor, which they feel should be the consequence of their reception of the Eucharist. Although it is true that God at time does give us the sense of inner

---

[28]From a poem entitled "The Offertory," by Paul Claudel.

happiness when we receive him, spiritual joy should not be the thermometer by which we measure our progress in the spiritual life. The real gauge of the benefits of Communion is holiness of life itself. Do we fall into sin less frequently? Are we more charitable to our neighbor? Is God's will supreme in our lives?

3. Nations of the world will never live at peace until they sit side by side at the banquet table of Christ, the Prince of Peace.

4.　　　*O sacred banquet in which Christ is received!*
In which the memory of his passion is recalled,
the soul is filled with grace, and a pledge
of future glory is given to us.

℣. *Thou has furnished us bread from heaven*
℞. *Possessing in itself every delight.*

Let us pray

O God who didst bequeath us in this marvelous sacrament a memory of thy passion, grant, we beseech thee, so to venerate the sacred mysteries of thy body and blood that we may continually experience in us the fruit of thy redemption: who liveth and reigneth forever and ever.

Amen.

BIBLIOGRAPHICAL NOTE

Questions LXXIII-LXXXIII of Part III of the *Summa* were followed when this chapter and the next were composed. Also of interest as an aid to the study of these two chapters is Book III of the second volume of *The Collected Works of Abbot Vonier*. The title of this selection is "A Key to the Doctrine of the Eucharist." And, again, we must refer to *The Teaching of the Catholic Church*, wherein George D. Smith has written a chapter called, "The Sacrament of the Eucharist." In this short chapter Fr. Smith treats in a marvelous way the doctrine and history of the Blessed Sacrament, the meaning of transubstantiation, the manner of the real presence, and the moral and spiritual implications of Holy Communion.

The Blessed Sacrament or *The Works and Ways of God* (London: Burns), by F. W. Faber, is noteworthy for its admirable attempt to popularize the theology of the Eucharist. College students should find *The Kingdom Is Yours* (Chicago: Fides Publishers, 1954), by P. Forestier, especially appealing. The book was written for the youth of today, and in the section entitled, "Gospel of the Holy Eucharist," you will discover Christ's personal love for you in the wonderful sacrament by which he makes himself your Bread of Life, and the source of all the graces you need. Another book from the popular field is *God's Good Cheer* (London: Burns, Oates and Washbourne, Ltd., 1936), by Vincent McNabb, O.P., a collection of short paragraphs on the Eucharist.

"Blood of the Covenant," an essay by E. F. Siegman in the *American Ecclesiastical Review*, CXXXVI (1957), 167-174, is also recommended as auxiliary reading.

CHAPTER TWELVE

The Holy Sacrifice of the Mass

1. Introduction

We have seen that the Eucharist is perfected as a sacrament not, as is the case with all the other sacraments, through its use by men or in its application to men, but in the very consecration of the sacramental species: by the divine power of the sacred formulas, the substance of bread is totally changed into the substance of Christ's body and the substance of wine into the substance of his blood. In this manner the celebration of the Eucharist is an image representing Christ's sacrifice on the cross, which was accomplished in a bloody manner by the physical separation of his sacred body and blood. Thus also this ceremony (together with the preparatory and accompanying rites traditionally called the Mass) is itself a sacrifice: "By the consecration of this sacrament sacrifice is offered to God."[1]

Sacrifice, as we have seen, is the principal external act of the virtue of religion, that special virtue whereby man gives to God, insofar as in him lies, the honor owed to his singular excellence. In recognition

[1]St. Thomas, III, *Summa*, q. 82, a. 10.

of God's supreme authority and dominion and man's dependence, a gift is offered which represents ourselves, and the victim so offered is changed or destroyed in some manner to express the totality of the giving of ourselves and of the reparation man desires to make for his sin. Thus sacrifice, the external and sensible representation of man's interior immolation to his God, springs from the very nature of things, from the necessary and essential relationship existing between the Creator and his free and intelligent creature. Even had there been no revelation from God, man would have been impelled to make sacrifice, as we read of Cain and Abel doing in the Old Testament, as the anthropologist discovers in the history of religions.

Yet it is a fact—and a most powerful apologetic argument for the existence of the one true Church—that today true sacrifice is offered only in the Church of Christ. Jewry, Islam, the various Protestant sects have no sacrifice at all, nor is it offered by the great oriental religions. Degraded forms of sacrifice may be found in certain primitive pagan religions, but these rites are offered to strange gods, not to the one true God. Only in the Church of Christ whose earthly head is the Pope does there exist a realization of man's need, rooted in his very nature, to acknowledge God's sovereignty and expiate man's offenses against him. The Mass, the sacrifice of Christ, is the sacrifice of Christ's Church, the sacrifice of us Christians.

To obtain a clearer understanding of this sacrificial aspect of the sacrament of the Eucharist we shall concentrate on four points: its existence (**Section 2**); its essence (**Section 3**); its minister (**Section 4**); its fruits or effects (**Section 5**). So much could be said about this tremendous mystery of God's love which is the Mass that we can obviously but touch the surface of the matter, speaking only of the most essential points; but it is hoped that, through the liberal use of the Church's official teaching, the main features can be sufficiently outlined and the student thereby inspired to search for himself these deep things of God, a study whose fruits of grace will merit his attention throughout his life.

But besides these essential elements there are other things to consider. Christ himself gave the Church this precious jewel, his living memorial, which makes present in our midst his sacrifice on the cross and provides a sacred banquet imparting eternal life. But while the essential elements of the Mass are contained in the Last Supper and bequeathed to the Church, the Church herself has seen fit to provide, over the course of the centuries, a setting for them worthy of so priceless a heritage. The prayers and ceremonies of the Mass which constitute this setting are not, however, precisely the same at all times and in all places.

Better to understand the Mass, therefore, we shall briefly see something of its historical development (**Section 6**) and examine the theological aspects of the liturgy with which the Church surrounds Christ's sacrifice and ours (**Section 7**).

2. The Existence of the Sacrifice of the Mass

A. The Statement of the Church

The earliest ecclesiastical documents we can discover, the writings of the earliest Church Fathers, bear unfailing witness to the constant and perpetual tradition of the Church: **the Mass is a true sacrifice, the sacrifice of Calvary re-presented on the altar of this place,** at this moment of time. With the doctrinal innovations of the Protestants, a definitive statement of this dogma of Christ became necessary, and the Council of Trent restates the faith of Christ in these memorable words:

> As the apostle Paul testifies, there was no perfection under the former testament because of the insufficiency of the Levitical priesthood. It was, therefore, necessary (according to the merciful ordination of God the Father) for another priest to arise according to the order of Melchisedech (cf. Gen. 14:18; Ps. 109:4; Heb. 7:11), our Lord Jesus Christ, who could perfect all who were to be sanctified (cf. Heb. 10:14) and bring them to fulfillment. He, then, our Lord and our God, was once and for all to offer himself by his death on the altar of the cross to God the Father, to accomplish for them an everlasting redemption.
>
> But death was not to end his priesthood (cf. Heb. 7:24,27). And so at the Last Supper on the night on which he was betrayed, in order to leave for his beloved spouse, the Church, a sacrifice that was visible

(as the nature of man demands), declaring himself constituted a priest forever according to the order of Melchisedech, he offered his body and blood under the species of bread and wine to God the Father and he gave his body and blood under the same species to the apostles to receive, making them priests of the New Testament at that time.

This sacrifice was to re-present the bloody sacrifice which he accomplished on the cross once and for all. It was to perpetuate his memory until the end of the world (cf. Cor. 11:23 ff.). Its salutary strength was to be applied for the remission of the sins that we daily commit. He ordered the apostles and their successors in the priesthood to offer this sacrifice when he said, "Do this in remembrance of me" (Lk. 22:19; I Cor. 11:24), as the Catholic Church has always understood and taught. For after he celebrated the old Pasch, which the assembly of the children of Israel offered in memory of the passage from Egypt (cf. Exod. 12:1 ff.), Christ instituted a new Pasch. He himself was this new Pasch, to be offered by the Church through her priests under visible signs, in memory of his departure from this world to the Father when by the shedding of his blood he redeemed us from the power of darkness and transferred us into his kingdom (cf. Col. 1:13).

This is that clean oblation which cannot be defiled by any unworthiness or evil on the part of those who offer it, and which the Lord foretold through Malachy would be offered in all places as a clean oblation to his name, for his name would be great among the Gentiles (cf. Mal. 1:11). It is evident that the apostle Paul also refers to this oblation in writing to the Corinthians when he says that those who have been defiled by partaking of the table of devils cannot be partakers of the table of the Lord. By table he understands altar in both cases (cf. I Cor. 10:21). Finally, this is the oblation which was represented by various figures in sacrifices during the time of nature and of the Law (cf. Gen. 4:4, 8:20, 12:8; 22; Exod., *passim*). For it includes all the good that was signified by those former sacrifices; it is their fulfillment and perfection.[2]

B. The Teaching of the Church

The Church, the infallible custodian and teacher of God's truth, thus declares three truths about the Mass: 1) it is a true sacrifice; 2) it is identical with the sacrifice of Calvary; and 3) these truths have been revealed by God himself. These important facts will be considered in greater detail.

[2]Sess. XXII, Chap. 1 (Denz. 938); cf. Can. 1, 2, 3 (Denz. 948, 949, 950) and the Tridentine Profession of Faith (Denz. 997).

(1) The Mass as Sacrifice

Since sacrifice is the essential rite of any religion (cf. *supra,* pp. 186 ff.), the true religion instituted by Jesus Christ must possess just such a liturgical homage as its basic act of religion—and there is none such in God's Church, nor ever has been, except the Mass. For the sacrifice of the Cross, permanent as to its effects, was nevertheless accomplished at a particular moment of time, and Christ dies no more. To the eyes of faith, moreover, it is evident that the Mass fulfills all of the qualities of a true sacrifice:

1) *It is the offering of a sense-perceptible thing:* under the sensible appearance of bread and wine Christ's true body and true blood are offered to God the Father.

2) *It was legitimately instituted and is effected by a legitimate minister.* Christ himself instituted this sacrifice at the Last Supper and founded a new priesthood whose essence would be found precisely in its relationship to the Eucharist. The successors of the apostles by valid ordination receive a participation of Christ's own priestly power in virtue of which they act for him in offering this sacrifice to God.

3) *It is accomplished by the immolation of the victim:* through the power of the words of consecration, Christ is made present on the altar in the state of sacrificial victim, the words themselves effecting the separate presence of his body under the species of bread, his blood under the species of wine.

(2) The Mass and Calvary

The Mass is essentially the same sacrifice as the sacrifice of Calvary. It is a memorial of Christ's passion, its commemoration and re-presentation, not an innovation. "In the divine sacrifice that is offered in the Mass, the same Christ who offered himself once in a bloody manner on the altar of the cross is present and is offered in an unbloody manner. . . . For it is one and the same victim: he who now makes the offering through the ministry of priests and he who then offered himself on the cross; the only difference is in the manner of offering. The benfits of this oblation (i.e., the bloody one) are received in abundance through this unbloody oblation. By no means, then, does the sacrifice of the Mass detract from the sacrifice of the cross."[3]

(3) The Revelation of Almighty God

The Mass was prefigured by the sacrifices of the Old Law and prophesied by the psalmist (109:4) and by Malachy (1:10-11). Figure became reality, prophecy became fact when the Son of God became man. At the Last Supper Christ instituted a true sacrifice in the proper sense of the word. And he commanded his apostles and their successors to perpetuate this memorial of his passion through the celebration of the Eucharist. These things are evident from the very words of institution of this sacrament (cf. Matt. 26:26-28; Mk. 14:22-24; Lk. 22:19-20).

St. Paul shows that all the elements of the true sacrifice are to be found in the Eucharist: the altar (I Cor. 10:21), the immolation of the victim and its memorial (I Cor. 10:26), the pact between God and man which is the end of sacrifice (ibid., 25), and the union of those offering sacrifice with the victim (ibid., 10:18-21). Thus he bears witness to the perpetuation of Christ's sacrifice in the early Church through the celebration of the Eucharist.

From the time of the apostles through all the intervening centuries the Tradition of the Church has constantly, perpetually and universally taught these truths.

3. The Essence of the Mass

On the cross [Christ] completely offered himself and all his sufferings to God, and the immolation of the victim was brought about by the bloody death which he underwent of his free will. But on the altar, by reason of the glorified state of his human nature, "death shall have no more dominion over him" (Rom. 6:9), and so the shedding of his blood is impossible. Still, according to the plan of divine wisdom, the sacrifice of our Redeemer is shown forth in an admirable manner by external signs which are symbols of his death. For by the "transubstantiation" of bread into the body of Christ and of wine into his blood, his body and blood are both really present: now the eucharistic species under which he is present symbolize the actual

[3]Council of Trent, Sess. XXII, Chap. 2; Denz. 940.

separation of his body and blood. Thus the commemorative representation of his death, which actually took place on Calvary, is repeated in every sacrifice of the altar, seeing that Jesus Christ is symbolically shown by separate symbols to be in a state of victimhood.[3a]

In harmony with this teaching of the Church and with the doctrine of St. Thomas, we may offer this explanation of what the Mass is, of the essential elements which constitute it both a true sacrifice and the same sacrifice as that of the Cross:

1. **In the sacrifice of the New Law which is the Mass, Christ is made present formally as victim, together with the eternal power of his passion.** By the power of the words of consecration, Christ is not made present according to his glorified state (although he is so present in virtue of real concomitance), but precisely *as having suffered*. He is immolated sacramentally inasmuch as under the species of bread and under the species of wine there are separately placed the body and the blood of the perpetual victim immolated in a bloody manner on the cross.[4] Moreover, Christ as victim is present together with his passion: by reason of his sacramental presence, his divine power and the power of his passion, through the communication of its fruits, here and now work man's redemption.

2. **In the sacrifice of the Mass Christ is made present as the perpetual victim of the one oblation of the eternal High Priest sacramentally perpetuated by the ministry of his priests.** The very same act of offering by which the High Priest offered himself on the cross in a bloody immolation is perpetuated sacramentally. Through the ministry of his priests who offer in his name and by his power, the offering made at the altar is the very same (except for the unbloody manner of this offering) as that made once for all on Calvary. "As Ambrose says, 'There is but one victim'—namely, that which Christ offered and that which we offer—'and not many victims, because Christ was offered but once: and this latter sacrifice is the pattern of the former. For just as what is offered everywhere is one body, and not many bodies, so also is it but one sacrifice.' "[5]

[3a]Pope Pius XII, *Mediator Dei.*
[4]Cf. St. Thomas, *Summa,* III, q. 73, a. 3, ad 3; a. 5, ad 2; a. 6; q. 75, a. 1; q. 79, a. 7.
[5]St. Thomas, *Summa,* III, q. 83, a. 1, ad 1.

There is one oblation and one immolation of Christ, that which he completed once for all on the cross. But by the will of the Incarnate Word expressed in instituting this sacrament, this sacrifice is sacramentally perpetuated in his Church. It is not a new sacrifice—there is no new priest, no new victim, nor are the oblation and immolation essentially and substantially new; rather it is Christ's very sacrifice as communicated to the Church, as participated in by the Church in a sacramental manner. The principal one who offers is the same: the eternal High Priest who perpetually offers sacrifice as head of the Church through the Church's ministers, who are his instruments acting in his power. The victim is always the same: the body and blood of Christ which, through the power of the sacrament, are sacramentally placed apart and separated under the species of bread and wine.

By the fact that Christ's oblation now takes place through the ministry of his priests, it becomes likewise the oblation of the Church; otherwise it is the same offering.

4. The Minister of the Sacrifice of the Mass

The unbloody immolation at the words of consecration, when Christ is made present upon the altar in the state of a victim, is performed by the priest and by him alone, as the representative of Christ and not as the representative of the faithful. But it is because the priest places the divine victim upon the altar that he offers it to God the Father as an oblation for the glory of the Blessed Trinity and for the good of the whole Church. Now the faithful participate in the oblation, understood in this limited sense, after their own fashion and in a twofold manner, namely, because they not only offer the sacrifice by the hands of the priest, but also, to a certain extent, in union with him. It is by reason of this participation, that the offering made by the people is also included in liturgical worship.

Now it is clear that the faithful offer the sacrifice by the hands of the priest from the fact that the minister at the altar in offering a sacrifice in the name of all his members represents Christ, the Head of the Mystical Body. Hence the whole Church can rightly be said to offer up the victim through Christ. But the conclusion that the people offer the sacrifice with the priest himself is not based on the fact that, being members of the Church no less than the priest himself, they perform a visible liturgical rite; for this is the privilege only of the minister who has been divinely appointed to this office. Rather, it is based on the fact that the people unite their hearts in praise, impetration, expiation and thanksgiving with the prayers or intention of the priest, even of the High Priest himself, so that in the one and same offering of the victim and according to a visible sacerdotal rite, they may be presented to God the Father. It is obviously necessary that the external sacrificial rite should, of its very nature, signify the internal worship of the heart. Now the sacrifice of the New Law signifies that supreme worship by which the principal offerer himself, who is Christ, and in union with him and through him all the members of the Mystical Body, pay God the honor and reverence that are due to him.[5a]

5. The Fruits of the Mass

By his sacrifice on Calvary, Christ "by one offering has perfected forever those who are sanctified" (Heb. 10:14). The perfect immolation of the God-man, both priest and victim, head of the human race, was accomplished in perfect obedience and love, and thus earns in measureless profusion the graces that are meant for all men of every time and place. But men must individually come into vital contact with the sacrifice of the Cross, in order that the merits which flow from it may be communicated to them. Hence the tremendous importance of the Mass in the life of the Church and of each individual Christian. It is, as Pope Pius pointed out, "the supreme instrument whereby the merits won by the divine Redeemer upon the cross are distributed to the faithful."[6]

For the ends of the sacrifice of Calvary and the sacrifice of the Mass are the same. Both give glory to Almighty God, in recognition of his universal dominion and our subjection as creatures; both render thanks to God for the great goods he has bestowed upon us, most perfectly fulfilling the debt of gratitude we owe to so bountiful a Father; both expiate for our sins, propitiating him whom we have so grievously offended and reconciling us again with God; and both

---

[5a]Pope Pius XII, *Mediator Dei.*
[6]*Ibid.*

the sacrifice of the altar and that of the Cross effectively beseech God in our behalf for the blessings and graces we need each day of our lives.

By the Mass, then, honor and thanksgiving are properly given to God, and this directly and infallibly, for it is Christ's own worship of his heavenly Father, the perfect immolation of Calvary. But its other effects are not infallibly produced, for they are secured for men, and man has the ability to make himself unfit to receive them. Hence the Christian must participate as fully as he can in this august sacrifice, if he is to receive from this font of graces an ever increasing share of the fruits won by Christ on his cross.

> Nothing can be conceived more just or fitting than that all of us, in union with our Head who suffered for our sake, should also sacrifice ourselves to the eternal Father. For in the sacrament of the altar . . . the Church is made to see that in what she offers she herself is offered.[7]

> Let the faithful, therefore, consider to what a high dignity they are raised by the sacrament of baptism. They should not think it enough to participate in the eucharistic sacrifice with that general intention which is fitting for members of Christ and children of the Church. But let them further, in keeping with the spirit of the sacred liturgy, be most closely united with the High Priest and his earthly minister at the time the consecration of the divine victim is effected, and especially at that time when those solemn words are pronounced: "By him and with him and in him is to thee, God the Father Almighty, in the unity of the Holy Spirit, all honor and glory for ever and ever"; to these words, in fact, the people answer "Amen." Nor should Christians forget to offer themselves, their cares, their sorrows, their distress and their necessities in union with their divine Savior on the cross.[7a]

6. The History of the Mass

Only in the most cursory and superficial manner can we here discuss the complicated but highly interesting and significant story of the Church's solicitude through the centuries for the treasure which

[7] St. Augustine, *The City of God*, Bk. X, Chap. 6.
[7a] Pope Pius XII, *op. cit.*

is the Mass.[8] Attempting only to highlight the main developments in the liturgy of the Mass as an aid in grasping its theological significance, we shall break up our study into six periods. This division is necessarily arbitrary, shallow and non-exclusive. But only in ignoring the nuances and complications of history can a simplified presentation achieve its chief purpose of stressing the major changes which have occurred, in order to indicate clearly the bearing of history upon our understanding of the sacramental sacrifice of Christ.

With this end in mind, the following periods will be considered successively: the primitive ritual of the Mass (first century); the period of transition (second and third centuries); the classical formulation of the Roman Mass (fourth century to the pontificate of St. Gregory the Great, c. 600); Carolingian changes (seventh to eleventh centuries); developments in the Middle Ages (twelfth century to the reform of St. Pius V, 1570); the Mass in modern times (1570 to the present day).

A. The Primitive Ritual of the Mass

(1) The Last Supper

The history of the Mass begins in the Cenacle, when our Lord instituted the Eucharist in the course of the ritual paschal meal. Both this solemn ritual and the simpler Sabbath service had important features in common. The head of the household took bread, spoke a blessing over it, and broke it into pieces to distribute among the participants; in this way those who were present were symbolically embodied in one company. After the banquet, the head of the household took a cup (known as the "cup of blessing"), elevated it slightly above the table, and pronounced another prayer of blessing, in the

---

[8]The classical work on this difficult subject is *The Mass of the Roman Rite*, by J. A. Jungmann, S.J., (New York: Benziger, 1951); he summarizes his highly scholarly findings in a popular work, *Public Worship: A Survey* (Collegeville. Minn.: The Liturgical Press, 1957), which includes a good deal of additional information on the liturgy. The third edition of *The Liturgy of the Mass* by one of the liturgical movement's foremost representatives, Pius Parsch, (St. Louis: B. Herder, 1957) incorporates Jungmann's erudition into a less technical approach to the history and meaning of the Mass; this, too, is readily available in summary form in a long pamphlet, *Study the Mass* (Collegeville, Minn.: The Liturgical Press, 1953), which is unreservedly recommended to the student for its presentation of a difficult subject and its insights into the deeper significance of the Mass.

course of which thanks were given to God for all that he had done for his people. So closely linked are Christ's actions and words in instituting the Eucharist with these rituals that it seems likely that he deliberately connected the new Pasch with the ancient rites. He took bread, broke it, pronounced the words of consecration over it, and gave it to his apostles; then, "after supper was over" (Lk. 22:20; I Cor. 9:25) he took the (third) cup, said the words of consecration over it, and handed it to his disciples.

Externally, therefore, the primitive Mass ritual was that of a banquet or meal. The essential elements of the celebration were the Consecration and the Communion, and the fixed framework for the sacred action was the prayer of thanksgiving with which our Lord himself had united the words of consecration,[9] accompanied by the breaking of bread and the distribution of the bread and cup.[10] Other less essential features of the first celebration will also be preserved in variant liturgical ceremonies: purification (the washing of the feet—Jn. 13:1-5); sermon (the great sacerdotal prayer of Christ—Jn. 14—17); the hymn of praise sung after the Last Supper (recorded by Matt. 26:30 and Mk. 14:26; this consisted of the so-called Hallel psalms (112-117) and Psalm 135, which formed part of the paschal rite).

(2) The Mass of the Apostles

Undoubtedly the first Christians celebrated Mass after the example set them by our Lord. It was a simple ceremony, consisting of a love-banquet or charity-repast (agape), where the whole community gathered together to feast in unison, during the course of which the "breaking of bread" would be repeated in commemoration of him who died on the cross. But it was not a simple memorial: the agape was a sacred meal in common, whose whole significance was derived from the fact of the unity of the sacrifice of the assembly (ecclesia) and the unity of their communion in that sacrifice "Whoever eats this

---

[9]The very name of this sacrament-sacrifice, the Eucharist, derives from the "blessing" and "giving thanks" of Christ in instituting it; this custom is the origin of our "Eucharistic Prayer," the Preface and Canon of the Mass.

[10]The "breaking of bread" still survives in present liturgical practice; so significant a feature was it of the eucharistic rite that the celebration of the Eucharist was called by this name. Cf. Acts 2:42, 2:46, 20:6-21; Didache, Chap. 14, n. 1.

bread," says St. Paul, "or drinks *the* cup of the Lord unworthily, will be guilty of the body and the blood of the Lord" (I Cor. 10:27).

Yet the natural difficulties such a ceremony might give rise to only too quickly eventuated. Abuses inevitably crept in (cf. I Cor. 11:17-24), and with the rapid spread of Christ's worship led to an impracticable situation. Sts. Matthew and Mark, for example, make no mention in their accounts of the institution that the chalice was taken *after* the meal. And the Didache (A.D. 80-100) clearly distinguishes between the *agape* and the Eucharist. Within the first century, the festival meal as an essential component of the divine service of the Christian community had completely disappeared.

B. Period of Transition: Second and Third Centuries

If the external celebration of the Eucharist quickly and fundamentally changed from the form observed in the upper room, not so the essential elements it was expressive of. The prayer of thanksgiving remained and it was the necessary ceremonial skeleton of the development which continues through the ages down to our own day. Practical considerations had eliminated the banquet as an appropriate setting for the sacred action; practical considerations also suggested the considerable external evolution which followed in quick succession this early exclusion of an impracticable and non-essential ceremony. We may regret that we no longer have the simplicity and fervor of those early converts whose charity was never better expressed than in their mutual feasting and drinking together; the facts of original sin and its consequences, of a charity grown cold, are already manifest in the first century, and few of us would care in this day to deny them.

What new external form would the Eucharist take? First of all, it would necessarily continue to be a thanksgiving, an *action* of gratitude (the sacrifice, the gifts given in thanks) expressed by *words* of gratitude. This, as Christ himself suggested, is the proper setting for his offering in which man shares. St. Ignatius of Antioch (+ 110) implies just such a ritual action.[11] Herein is found the primary

[11]*Epistle to the Smyrnaeans*, VII, 1.

source of Christian unity, the center of that isolated and reviled community which is the early Church among the hostile Jews and pagans.

But St. Justin (+ c. 165) more clearly indicates the development which had ensued. Separated from the *agape*, the Eucharist was preceded by a series of readings. The service proper consisted of the kiss of peace, followed by the offering of gifts to the bishop; then followed the great eucharistic prayer, improvised by the celebrant, during which came the consecration through the words of institution; it was concluded with the great "Amen" of the people. This action was followed by the distribution of the consecrated bread and wine, provision for communion in the sacrifice (i.e., reception of the sacred species) being made for those who were absent.[12]

Recorded here is the union of the Jewish tradition respecting the worship of God with the specifically Christian service. The Synogague had always had a "service of the word," readings from the sacred books (cf. Lk. 4:16-21; Acts 13:14-16), followed by a communal prayer of petition; preserved by the Christians, this sacred observance is now (the dangers of the Judaisers being past) incorporated in Christian worship. At this early time, however, the instruction service was not a necessary prelude to the Mass proper. It substituted for other liturgical observances which would, on special occasions (solemn baptism, confirmation, ordinations, etc.), precede the usual celebration of the Eucharist.[13]

Two features of the ceremonies described by St. Justin and St. Hippolytus are to be noted. The first is the bringing forth of the offerings of the people, although as yet there is no offertory procession. The second is the distribution of the consecrated elements to the people; this is an office executed in St. Justin's time by the deacons, but only a half century later, St. Hippolytus describes a procession in which the faithful approach the sacrificial table themselves to receive Holy Communion, singing meanwhile a hymn of praise. After the Communion there was a prayer of thanks, a blessing through the imposition of hands, and the dismissal: "Go in peace."

[12]*First Apology*, 65, 1-5.
[13]Cf. Hippolytus, *The Apostolic Tradition*, Chap. 4, 7 and 22; the description of St. Justin already referred to is of the Roman rite of Mass for Easter Sunday, when baptism was solemnly conferred.

Thus in these very early centuries was already established the basic structure of our Mass today, what we may call, with Doctor Parsch, the "groundplan" of the eucharistic sacrifice, the basis of all the liturgies:

I: The Foremass: service of the word of God
  1. Readings from the Old and New Testament.
  2. Sermon by the bishop.
  3. Communal prayer (petitions) and kiss of peace.
II. Sacrifice—Mass
  1. Offertory (procession).
  2. Eucharistic prayer with the people's Amen.
  3. Reception of Holy Communion (procession).

This was a universal pattern, acceptable not only in Rome but equally in the East. But these liturgical essentials having been so determined during this period of transition, we now enter on a third stage of the celebration of the Eucharist. In this later period East and West will part company, for the Roman Church will adopt Latin as the language of her liturgy, while the Greek and Eastern Churches will retain their own liturgical traditions, including the use of language. Thus from a common starting point East and West will develop through the centuries many accidental modifications of the essential celebration. We shall ignore the former (although they are of great importance), in order to concentrate on the latter, for these are of greatest moment to our present liturgy.

C. The Classical Period of Roman Formulation

From the end of the third century until the end of the pontificate of St. Gregory the Great (+ 604), the accidental modifications of the essential Mass structure already established are of great import. Not only is Latin a substitute; the special Roman genius pervades all the prayers and ceremonies of the liturgy from now on, pervasive in its conciseness, incision, concentration, precision, its sober and honest approach even to supernatural reality, its minimal and dogmatic use of all—gesture, vesture and ceremonial—that involves emotionalism and sentimentality.

The important contribution of this period in the development of the Roman liturgy is to determine fixed forms for the celebration of the Mass; this is accomplished, not by arbitrary choice, but through a perceptive artistic genius, as appreciative of the doctrinal significance of what it was doing as of the proper use of the artistic means it selected. Thus the great Eucharistic Prayer was no longer left to the discretion of the celebrant; the Canon of the Mass, including the Preface and Sanctus, was composed in its essential outlines (the petitions for the living and dead and the lists of saints were a later insertion of this same period into the course of the older prayer of thanksgiving and of offering). Both Preface and Canon were the special prerogative of the celebrant, the former being sung solemnly, the later at first chanted and then recited aloud; the great doxology at the end of the Eucharistic Prayer was climaxed by the "Amen" of the people.

There were changes in the liturgical structure, too, although not such as to affect the essential outline. The solemn entry of the clergy was accompanied by the singing of a psalm by the choir, which continued until the action taking place was ended. In the early Mass the reading of the Word of God had preceded the great common prayer of petition; in the Roman liturgy these prayers disappear from this spot, and a number of other prayers (*Kyrie, Gloria,* Collect) are inserted before the readings. Psalms were also sung when the faithful brought up their bread and wine after the readings (after receiving these gifts, the priest washed his soiled hands) and during the Communion of the faithful; in both instances (as after the entry chant) there was a concluding prayer by the priest—the prayers we today call the Collect, the Secret and the Postcommunion.

Even in the early Mass there had been sung interludes after the Epistle, usually entire psalms appropriate to the feast being celebrated. During this period, with the singing of special chants taken over by the choir, these interludes (Gradual and Alleluia or Tract) were considerably shortened but musically elaborated, and frequently sung as solos for the meditation of the people, who joined in only in the responses.

For all its solemnity, the Roman Mass of this golden era of the liturgy was marked by simplicity, sobriety and harmony. It was a meaningful ceremony for both priests and people.

D. Carolingian Developments, Seventh to Twelfth Centuries

With the barbarian invasions came the Dark Ages and the decline of Rome as the cultural center of Europe. In the lands to the north, however, which would be the possession of the great Charles, the Roman Mass reached a further step in its development. It was transplanted into the kingdom of the Franks in preference to the local rituals, which varied considerably from place to place but were all influenced by the eastern liturgies. Although the Roman rite prevailed, it was inevitably modified by these Gallican customs, so much so that our Mass today may be more properly styled Roman-Frankish than purely Roman.

Chief among the obvious changes was the practice of reciting certain prayers silently. Up to this time all the prayers, including the Canon, had been declaimed in a loud voice so that they could be understood by the people. Now new silent prayers, to be said by the priest alone or quietly with his ministers, were inserted at the beginning at the foot of the altar; when the gifts were received from the faithful and placed on the altar; and at the Communion. Even the Canon was recited inaudibly. Moreover, a tendency grew up to emphasize each ritual gesture with explanatory words; kissing the altar, washing the hands, the breaking of bread, all previously carried out in silence, came to be accompanied by (inaudible) prayers which emphasized their significance. The practice of saying the Creed on great feasts was also introduced.

This important development (and a more subtle change in style and tone) had a most important effect: the separation, if not exclusion, of the people from the altar. They were now an audience, a group of spectators, and no longer participants in the sacred action and its witnesses.

E. The Middle Ages: 1200-1600

The contribution of the Ages of Faith to the liturgy of the Mass was not an entirely happy one. The changes, however, were in the main minor. Since the people no longer brought bread and wine (unleavened bread was used from the ninth century, which had to be supplied by the clergy) but now made their offering by way of a collection, the procession was suppressed and the psalm reduced to a short antiphon. The entry psalm (Introit) and Communion psalm were also curtailed to our present antiphons. The wording of the Canon was not changed, but the rite of the elevation of the host began at the end of the twelfth century, the elevation of the chalice in the fifteenth, and genuflections were made by the priest every time he touched the Blessed Sacrament.

There were several additions made during this time. Chief among these were the Sequences, extensive and sometimes very beautiful commentaries on the themes of the feast sung to simple melodies by the people after the Alleluia. The composition of "tropes," amplifications of the original text by insertions, was also much practiced in the late Middle Ages. All of this was but an intensification of the earlier tendency to relegate the celebration of the Mass proper to the priest as his work and supply private devotional practices for the people.

F. Modern Times: 1570-

The multiplicity of local variants and customs, the abuses and exaggerations which had crept into the Mass liturgy in the late Middle Ages, led the great Council of Trent to take action to purge the liturgy of questionable accretions. In 1570 St. Pius V imposed the text of the Missal of the Roman Curia everywhere.[14] Subsequent changes in the celebration of the Mass have been concerned with the way in which Mass is celebrated rather than with the fixed rite

[14]Those liturgies which could show a full two hundred years of existence were permitted to continue; thus the liturgies of the Dominicans, calced Carmelites, Carthusians, and of several dioceses still remain.

itself. Thus High Masses have become more prevalent, and the celebration of Low Mass has become a universal custom. The revival of interest in the liturgy, one of the spiritual phenomena of our day, has witnessed many attempts to secure the participation of the faithful and to render that participation more active and vital.

7. The Liturgy of the Mass

> Wherefore, O Lord, we thy servants, as also thy holy people, calling to mind the blessed passion of the same Christ thy Son, our Lord, and also his resurrection from hell and glorious ascension into heaven, offer unto thy most excellent majesty, of thy presents and gifts, a pure ✠ host, a holy ✠ host, a spotless ✠ host, the holy bread ✠ of eternal life, and the chalice ✠ of everlasting salvation.

This prayer, which immediately follows the Consecration, is our answer to Christ's request: "Do this in memory of me." It expresses the very essence of the Mass, which is a memorial ("calling to mind"), a sacrifice ("we . . . offer a host") and a sacrificial and eucharistic banquet ("bread of eternal life"), of priests ("we thy servants") and of people ("thy holy people"). These are the elements we must keep in mind in briefly setting forth in general lines the theological aspects of the liturgy of the Mass.[15] Before we do so, however, it would be well to outline the general plan of the Mass.

A. An Outline of the Mass

As has been noted, the Mass is composed of two principal parts, the Foremass ("service of prayer and instruction") and the Sacrifice-Mass ("the sacrificial action"). The main parts are subdivided as follows:

THE FOREMASS
(also known as the "Mass of the Catechumens," because in olden times the catechumens were dismissed at its close, since they could not take place in the offering)

[15]No detailed analysis will be attempted. There are several fine works available in English, especially those mentioned in footnote 8, to which may be added a valuable pamphlet, *What Is the Mass?* by H. Chéry, O.P. (Westminster, Md.: The Newman Press, 1952).

I. The Prayer Service:

1. THE PRAYERS AT THE FOOT OF THE ALTAR—*repentance*.
2. INTROIT—entry chant, formerly an entire psalm.
3. KYRIE—a shortened litany, expressive of *desire*.
4. GLORIA—the people's hymn of acclamation to the Blessed Trinity, an exultant expression of *praise*.
5. COLLECT—the climax and term of the prayer service, a solemn summing up by the priest of the prayer of the people, presented by him before the throne of God: *petition*.

II. The Scripture Service:

1. EPISTLE: God speaks to us through his prophets and apostles.
2. GRADUAL: a sung interlude providing meditation material for the people.
3. ALLELUIA: a sung interlude which serves as an invitation to the Gospel and a preparation for it.
4. GOSPEL: God speaks to us through his Son made man.
5. SERMON: God speaks to us through his Church.
6. CREED: a renewal of faith by the people, a witness to Christ and confession of his faith.

THE SACRIFICE-MASS
(also known as the "Mass of the Faithful")

I. The Offertory (originally constituted by the bringing of gifts of bread and wine and other stuffs—symbolic not only of material creation but of man's work and of his life—and their hallowing on the altar; thus it was the people's act of surrender of self, expressive of their sharing in the sacrifice).

1. OFFERTORY—the antiphon which is the curtailed processional chant.
2. OFFERING BY THE PRIEST OF THE SACRIFICE-GIFTS:
   1) Of the bread: *Suscipe sancte Pater*.
   2) Of the wine: *Offerimus*.[16]
   3) Of ministers and people: *In spiritu humilitatis*.

---

[16]Here occurs the ancient ceremony of the mixing of a little water with the wine (in imitation of Christ, for this was a Jewish custom). Symbolically, as the prayer *Deus qui humanae substantiae* expresses, the wine is Christ, and we are the water (which is therefore blessed by the priest); the mingling recalls the Incarnation and Redemption (Christ took our nature that we might be made partakers of his divinity) and signifies what this sacrifice and the whole work of Redemption accomplish: our divine adoption, and the transfiguration of our human nature through the Eucharist.

3. INVOCATION TO THE HOLY SPIRIT to sanctify these offerings ("epiclesis"): *Veni Sanctificator.*[17]
4. WASHING OF HANDS—now symbolic of the necessary purification of the heart for a worthy offering of the sacrifice: *Lavabo.*
5. OFFERING TO THE TRINITY, associating the saints with our gifts: *Suscipe sancta Trinitas.*
6. INVITATION TO GREATER DEVOTION AND RECOLLECTION: *Orate fratres.*
7. PRAYER OF DEDICATION OVER THE SACRIFICIAL GIFTS: Secret (like the Collect and Postcommunion, this is proper to each Mass).

(The redirection of this preparatory service, the Offertory, should be evident from this analysis; it is now an offering to God of the gifts to be consecrated which looks eagerly forward to the coming consummation of the sacrifice, rather than an expression of the people's sharing in the sacrifice. But its beautiful prayers, and the repeated acts of oblation, are still a most excellent preparation for offering the sacrifice well, and through them the faithful can approach the altar at least in spirit and make the necessary offering of themselves.)

II. The Great Eucharistic Prayer: the prayer of thanksgiving which is the right and proper setting for the sacrifice and from which it springs.

1. INTRODUCTION: it should be emphasized that the Preface and the Canon are *one* prayer, constitutive elements of a single prayer of praise and thanks which ends with the great "Amen" of the people.
   1) Acclamations: a preliminary dialogue ("Lift up your hearts," etc.) of priest and people.
   2) Preface: a majestic chant of praise to the Father through Christ for the works of our salvation; a solemn prologue to the Canon, this crescendo of thanks climaxes and reverberates in the
   3) *Sanctus*: a hymn of angelic praise (Isa. 6:2), in which we join the choirs of angels, continuing our praise in the

---

[17]At High Mass, the incensation occurs at this point (there had been a previous incensing of the altar after the prayers at the foot of the altar). The offerings, the altar, the celebrant, the ministers and the people are all incensed in turn, solemnized and purified and enveloped in the aromatic smoke as in an atmosphere of holiness; the rising cloud of incense is also symbolic of our prayers and expressive of our dispositions during the sacrifice.

4) *Benedictus*: an acclamation of the faithful to Christ on his coming to us, as once he entered Jerusalem on Palm Sunday.

2. PRAYERS BEFORE THE CONSECRATION (at this point the Canon begins, the "Rule" of eucharistic prayer and sacrifice first composed in the fourth century and unchanged since the time of St. Gregory).

1) Prayer of petition: a request that God will accept "these gifts" as an expression of our thanks and transform them by his heavenly blessing into what they are to become, and a petition:

a) For the Church as a whole, and especially for those who have charge of it: the pope, our bishop, and all the bishops of the world: *Te igitur.*

b) For the Church militant, in particular those who are near and dear to us, and all who are present at Mass, our co-offerers of the sacrifice: *Memento Domine.*

c) For our communion with the saints, a memento of the Church triumphant: *Communicantes.*

2) Prayers of sacrifice:

a) A plea for the gracious acceptance of our oblations; renewing the initial idea of the *Te igitur*: *Hanc igitur.*

b) A prayer for consecration, that the offerings may become *for us* the body and blood of our Lord Jesus Christ: *Quam oblationem.*

3. THE CONSECRATION: the sacred narrative of the institution of the sacrament-sacrifice, in which the very words of our Lord are used to effect the change of bread and wine into his body and blood, thereby accomplishing the sacrificial action which is the offering of the Son of God which we present to the Father together with Christ.

4. PRAYERS AFTER THE CONSECRATION.

1) Prayer of remembrance ("anamnesis"): while celebrating the redemptive work sacramentally, we must also call to mind its decisive steps: *Unde et memores.*

2) Prayers of sacrifice:

a) A plea that God will accept Christ's sacrifice precisely as offered with him by the Church, as it is *our* sacrifice in token of our gratitude and homage: *Supra quae propitio.*

b) An expression of our desire for the carrying up of our offerings in Christ and a preliminary petition for a fruitful share in the sacrificial banquet: *Supplices te rogamus.*

3) Prayer of petition:

a) Intercession for the dead, those near and dear to us but also the entire Church suffering: *Memento etiam.*

b) Intercession for "us sinners," beseeching fellowship with the saints: *Nobis quoque peccatoribus.*

c) Intercession for inanimate nature, represented by bread and wine: *Per quem haec omnia.*

4) The final elevation: taking the sacred host, the priest describes three crosses over the chalice, from lip to lip, followed by two crosses in front of the chalice, and then raises host and chalice slightly. He accompanies these gestures with a solemn doxology to the Holy Trinity: *per ipsum.* This is the solemn conclusion of the Canon, and the elevation of the sacred elements an invitation to the people to share in the sacred banquet. The concluding words of the prayer are chanted or recited aloud by the priest.

5) **Amen:** the people express their identity with what has been accomplished through the priest. The prayer of **thanks**giving and the liturgical action of sacrifice have always been the sole prerogative of the celebrant. But this "Amen" shows that it is the people's sacrifice as well, offered by them through the hands of their priest.

III. The Sacred Banquet (this is the *communion,* the fellowship or union of the members of Christ's Mystical Body with their Head, and with one another, sealed and cemented and manifested through the eucharistic body of Christ in this sacrificial meal).

1. PREPARATION:

1) The *Pater Noster,* the most sublime and precious of prayers, taught us by our Lord himself, links the Canon and Communion together. The first three petitions summarize the preceding action, the acceptance of the divine will which is the heart of all sacrifice; the other petitions beseech not only the "bread of eternal life," but all the

fruits of the Mass—it is a synthesis of all our desires and all our needs.[18]

2) Prayer for deliverance: a development of the final thought of the *Pater Noster*: freedom from the evils, especially from every moral evil, of past, of present and of future: *Libera nos.*

3) The breaking of bread: the ancient ceremony symbolic of Christian unity (I Cor. 10:17), also expressed by the subsequent commixture of the elements as the priest announces the kiss of peace: *Pax Domini.* People and clergy chant a litany-like greeting to the Lord, concealed under the species as the sacrificial Lamb, a salutation of the Blessed Sacrament: *Agnus Dei.*

4) The kiss of peace: expression of the fraternal charity which is a necessary prerequisite for the reception of the divine mystery of love, prefaced by a prayer amplifying the theme of peace: *Domine Jesu Christe.*

5) Preparation prayers before Communion:

   a) Confession of faith: *Domine Jesu Christe Fili Dei vivi.*

   b) Profession of humility: *Perceptio Corporis tui.* Both prayers ask for a worthy and fruitful reception of the sacrament.

   c) Exclamation of joy (Ps. 115): *Panem coelestem.*

   d) Humility and confidence (Matt. 8:8): *Domine, non sum dignus.*

2. THE SHARING OF THE BANQUET:

1) The Communion of the priest: the celebrant receives the sacred host, "May the body of our Lord Jesus Christ preserve my soul to life everlasting. Amen." After a short meditation he expresses his thanks and gratitude (Ps. 115): *Quid retribuam,* and receives the precious blood, for only with the Lord's own gifts can adequate thanks be rendered to him.

2) The Communion of the faithful: after the *Confiteor* in the name of all the faithful, and the priest's *Misereatur* and absolution, he shows the host to them, saying, *Ecce*

---

[18]Traditionally the *Pater* has always been the prayer of preparation for Communion—the only prayer in ancient times; it is the table prayer recited by the children of God before the sacred meal. Hence the new rubrics for Good Friday prescribe that this prayer should be recited by all the faithful.

Agnus Dei and then repeats for the faithful the *Domine non sum dignus.* Finally he distributes the Eucharist, using the same prayer with which he communicated, *Corpus Domini Jesu Christi.*

3. THE THANKSGIVING.
   1) The ablutions: purification of the sacred vessels and of his anointed fingers by the priest, together with prayers:
      a) *Quod ore sumpsimus.*
      b) *Corpus tuum.* Both prayers ask that the effects of this sacrificial banquet may be accomplished in the souls of the communicants: purification of all sin and eternal possession of spiritual consolation.
   2) The Communion: the antiphon which is a relic of the processional chant sung by the faithful as they approached the sacred table.
   3) Postcommunion: a final prayer (variable, like the Collect and Secret), petitioning that the graces of the sacrament may be experienced and shown forth in our daily life.

IV. The Conclusion.
1. THE DISMISSAL: *Ite, missa est.*
2. CONCLUDING PRAYER FOR ACCEPTANCE OF THE SACRIFICE: *Placeat.*
3. FINAL BLESSING IN THE NAME OF THE TRIUNE GOD.
4. LAST GOSPEL (St. John's prologue).

B. Theological Aspects of the Liturgy

(1) The Drama of the Mass

From the summary of the Mass liturgy just completed, and in the light of the theology of the Mass, certain general features stand out. The Mass is, as it were, a great five-act drama which celebrates and memorializes and re-creates the "admirable exchange" between God and man accomplished by the Incarnation and Redemption of the God-man. In THE FIRST ACT we go to God through prayer, expressing our sorrow for our sin (prayers at the foot of the altar), our deep desires (*Kyrie*), the joyous praise of Christ and the Trinity (*Gloria*), and our petition for our material and spiritual needs (*Collect*). God stoops to us, so to say, in THE SECOND ACT, exchanging for the word of man the word of God, through his prophets and apostles (*Epistle*), through his only-begotten Son (*Gospel*), through his Church (sermon); this divine instruction is the best possible preparation for the sacred mysteries themselves, into which we are introduced by our public confession of the divine truths God has revealed (*Creed*).

THE THIRD ACT is the offering (*Offertory*) or self-giving and self-surrender of ourselves, symbolized by our gifts which are to be the matter of the sacrifice. In the great Eucharistic Prayer which comprises THE FOURTH ACT, we (the Church through the ministry of the priest) offer in sacrifice the immaculate Victim whose immolation is made present by the Consecration. In this tremendous mystery the bread of man has become the Lamb of God and the Bread of God; in THE FIFTH ACT we receive the sacrificial victim as members of one another united in our Head, the supersubstantial Bread God gives to us in a sacrificial banquet.

It should be well understood, however, that we are not the principal actors in this sacred drama, although the sacramental characters of baptism and confirmation enable us to have a true share in it. But it is Christ himself who effects all these actions here on earth: it is his Spirit who prays in us, his Word that instructs and vivifies us; the gifts we offer (ourselves) we have first received from him, and it is Christ who presents his pleasing and acceptable sacrifice to the Father, incorporating our self-surrender in his. Finally, it is Christ himself who gives himself, that we may all be one Body deeply one with one another and our one Head.

(2) The Significance of the Mass

Several important considerations arise from this reflection on the theological significance of the Mass. It will be worthwhile to analyze them in greater detail.

1. The Mass is an **action**. For all of its wealth of symbolism and the splendor of the magnificent prayers which surround it, the Mass is essentially an act of *giving*, a sacrifice. Who does the giving? It is we, together with Christ, i.e., the Church, who offer to God through the hands of the priest of the assembly. What do we give? We offer

God the *whole Christ,* Christ principally, but ourselves in him, united with him as consecrated victims (by sacramental character). Hence of its nature the Mass demands our active participation, as active a sharing through word and gesture, eyes and lips and limbs as permitted to us. Only the priest can accomplish the sacramental sacrifice (the Eucharistic Prayer and action are his special divine privilege), but our external activities should express the interior sentiments which unite us with the offering, so that we can truly give voice to our identity with the sacrifice and our agreement with the priest's action in the great "Amen" at the end of the Canon. But, most importantly of all, we will share by participating in the sacrificial meal. For Communion, by which we partake of the Victim that is offered, is the normal, the natural, even (in some sense) the necessary completion of our share in the Mass. Christ sacrificed should become Christ our food, for only then are we completely united to the sacrifice.

2. **The Mass is a thanksgiving.** About the tremendous central act of sacrifice the liturgy brings together a number of petitions, in order that our needs and desires may be inserted more deeply into the sacredness of the celebration, and thus acquire a greater urgency and even a greater efficacy. But this should not obscure the fact that Christ's sacrifice and ours, like all sacrifice, is an expression of man's recognition of his relations to God: of his dependence and God's eminence, of his nothingness and God's excellence; primarily and above all, sacrifice is an offering of thanks in the form of a gift. And thus the Mass is accomplished from the very beginning in the midst of a verbal offering of thanksgiving, and its chief prayer is concerned in the first place with the thanks which we offer to God for his great mercies; only then do our verbal thanks resolve into adoration and sacrifice. This by no means excludes the fact that the Mass is also a sacrifice of impetration, and above all of expiation and propitiation; but it is a corrective for the forgetfulness and egocentrism of modern man. Our duty toward God is first absolved by our participation in Christ's sacrifice, before we think of the benefits that can accrue to us from so perfect an offering.

3. **The Mass is the concern of the whole Church.** To insist on the active participation of the individual Catholic in the Mass emphasizes

the truth that it is not the act of the priest alone. But it is *my* Mass precisely because I am a member of the Mystical Body of Christ, marked with the very likeness of Christ through the baptismal character (and more perfectly through the seal of confirmation) which is common to all the members. Thus the prayers in the Mass (except for the private prayers introduced later) are all in the plural: it is the Church who prays, who offers, who receives. At the sacred moment of Consecration she gathers about the altar the entire Mystical Body— the hierarchy and the faithful of the Church militant, but also the Church suffering and the Church triumphant, the angels even, and all of material creation. And in the Mass we pray not for ourselves only, and for those close to us, living and dead, but for the entire holy Catholic Church in the first place, and for all Christians, and especially "for all here present." Communion, too, is not an accidental gathering of individuals each busy with his personal piety, but above all the communal sharing of the assembly in a common sacrificial banquet, wherein our separatedness and divisions are destroyed by our assumption into the unity of Christ. In the Mass is fully realized, in a manner prognostic of eternal glory, that oneness for which Christ so fervently prayed (Jn. 17:11,20-23), for which he became man, for which he hung between heaven and earth, that he might draw all things to himself.

8. Summary and Conclusion

Sacrifice is the keynote of the Eucharist. The changing of bread and wine into the body and blood of Christ is celebrated in an unbloody manner as a re-presentation of Christ's bloody sacrifice on the cross. Thus the rite used, the ceremonies of the Mass, is truly a real sacrifice; that is, Christ's true body and true blood are offered to God. He is made a sacrificial victim through the power of the words of consecration which bring about the separate presence of his body and blood upon the altar. Both the sacrifice of Calvary and the sacrifice of the Mass are attuned to the one purpose of giving glory to God. Through sacrifice we pay to God the honor due to him as our Creator and Master. This is an infallible effect of the Mass, produced infallibly because of the fact that the Mass is the way in which Christ himself adored his heavenly Father. We sacrifice as Christ sacrificed, and thus obtain the fruits that he so perfectly picked for us from the tree of Calvary.

Unde et memores—memorial, sacrifice, banquet, the Mass is the solution of divine wisdom for the problem of bringing man deep into the heart of the redemption won for him by Christ, Son of God and of man. It is our opportunity to share fully in the sacrifice of Christ and obtain the fruits of redemption—and share we shall, in the measure of our giving, in the surrender of self to God through Christ Jesus our Lord. And through our participation in the Mass, climaxed in our union with the sacrificial victim at his sacred banquet, we can truly wax strong in the grace and wisdom of God, filled unto all the fulness of God, to the mature measure of the fulness of Christ.

From this analysis of the *Mystery of Faith* innumerable practical conclusions can be derived. Only a few are offered here, as suggestions for further meditation and reflection and as examples for your own thinking.

1. The modern world has discovered "togetherness" as a necessary complement of man's life: no man is an island. But compared with the profound unity established through, with and in Christ, this worldly union and community is shallow and evanescent. St. Cyril of Alexandria points out: "To merge us in unity with God and among ourselves, even though we each have a distinct personality, the only-begotten Son devised a wonderful means: through one only body, his own, he sanctified his faithful in mystical communion, making them one Body with him and among themselves. Within Christ no division can arise. All united to the single Christ through his own body, all receiving him, the one and indivisible into our own bodies, we are the members of this one Body. And thus he is for us the bond of unity."[19]

2. To the celebration of Christ's sacrifice the Church brings all that human resources can offer. Here are unified all the finest contributions of the arts, of man's mastery of the material and sensible as signs and ministers of the spiritual and supernatural. Once again in our day, as

[19]*Commentary on John,* Bk. II, Chap. 2.

in the glorious past, the artistic homage of man should surround our central act of worship, not with ersatz, sham and plaster, but with the finest products of mind and imagination.

3. As the grains of wheat must be crushed in the mill to provide the bread and the grapes crushed in the wine-press to yield the wine, so in each of us there is much to be pressed and crushed that we may be one with Christ and his members.

4. The more active our share in the communal sacrifice, the more fully we may realize its significance and effects in our daily lives. The formation of parish groups to learn the Mass chants, the dialogue, the reverential movements which express the congregation's attitude—this will be of great assistance to enable the parish to live more fully the liturgical life planned for it by Christ and his Church. Such a project could well be undertaken as an apostolic work by existing parish societies, as is already done in many places. But at least each individual can assist at Mass in a more active way by using a Missal, and synchronizing his prayers, in time and meaning, with those of the Church.

5. If we cannot assist daily at Mass, it is highly recommended that we unite our intentions with those of Christ and his Church at the very time when Mass is being celebrated in the parish. It is a growing and commendable custom for at least one member of each family to attend daily Mass, that the family itself may be represented: "Be mindful of all here present," says the priest at the *Memento*. "For them we offer up to thee this sacrifice of praise, as they too for themselves, *their households* and all dear to them. . . ."

BIBLIOGRAPHICAL NOTE

There have been innumerable books published on the Mass, both from the dogmatic and the liturgical point of view. Of these we select only a few which seem most useful for the college student. Besides the works by Jungmann and Parsch already mentioned in a footnote, the following are of note.

An excellent booklet, a brief introduction to the study of the Mass, has been written by H. Chéry, O.P., and is entitled, *What is the Mass?* (Westminster, Md.: The Newman Press, 1952). Fr. Chéry does not claim to treat the subject exhaustively in his book, but students will find it suitable for their present needs. *Holy Mass, Approaches to the Mystery* (Collegeville, Minn.: The Liturgical Press, 1953), by A. M. Roguet, O.P., appeals to a large audience of readers because of its popular mode of expression. This work is a study of the Mass, not from its origins and theories, but from its ritual acts. Another book written in the popular vein and a great source for meditation on the Mass is *The Spirituality of the Mass* (St. Louis: B. Herder Book Co., 1952), by Adolph D. Frenay, O.P. Its fifty chapters take their inspiration from the approximately fifty prayers which make up the Ordinary and the Canon of the Mass. A further advantage to this book is its use of St. Thomas' tract on the Eucharist.

The Teaching of the Catholic Church contains a fine essay entitled, "The Eucharistic Sacrifice," by B. V. Miller. Other sources for study are the article on the Mass in The Catholic Encyclopaedia and the encyclical *Mediator Dei* by Pius XII.

CHAPTER THIRTEEN

The Sacrament of Penance

1. Introduction

The history and the literature of the human race are witnesses to the universality of man's concern with sin and guilt. The concomitant idea of penance under some form or other is as ancient as the race itself. By various kinds of penance men have striven to undo their evil deeds and to set right their wrongs. Penance answers the deep human desire to be rid of personal evil, to be cleansed of sin.

The Old Testament is filled with references to penance, and the idea of atonement and satisfaction was deeply rooted among the Jews. Many of their religious practices were designed to bring about freedom from guilt, and the practice of penance was highly cultivated among them.

433

Yet withal, there is no such universal record of *security* in forgiveness. There is no sign of real assurance that the penance was fruitful and that the sins were truly forgiven. For ultimately sin is an offense against God, and satisfaction must be made to him. Only a divine assurance of the acceptability of penance can bring security of forgiveness.

It was Christ who first spoke with authority to say: "Your sins are forgiven." And it was precisely for this reason that he came into the world. The forgiveness that he directly dispensed was limited by the span of his life, by the extent of his journeys, by the number of people he directly contacted on this earth. The entire number of those he forgave is infinitesimal when compared to all who exist now or who have existed since his death. Yet he promised never to leave us orphans, and he fulfilled that pledge in part by making his divine forgiveness available to all who wish to have it. He instituted the sacrament of penance, and thus extended the hand of his healing forgiveness beyond the boundaries of time and space. He made the divine assurance of forgiveness available to all.

St. Thomas began a profound analysis of this sacrament of mercy in the *Summa Theologiae,* but he made only a beginning. He set up the order of his treatise (which differs somewhat from the customary order we have followed previously) and had finished seven questions of the tract when he experienced some kind of vision or revelation which caused him to regard all his writing as hopelessly inadequate. Three months later he died.

The unfinished *Summa* was completed from portions of his earlier work. Most probably the compiler was Brother Reginald, a Dominican who had been his disciple, secretary and companion for many years. The order of the completed tract, which we shall follow, is contained in the outline on the opposite page.

This theological investigation of the sacrament of forgiveness will be concluded by a historical survey of penitential discipline in the Church (**Section 8**).

Penance
- In itself
  - As a sacrament (Section 2)
  - As a virtue (Section 3)
- Its effects (Section 4)
  - Remission of mortal sins
  - Remission of venial sins
  - Return of sins forgiven
  - Revival of virtues
- Its parts (Section 5)
  - Contrition
  - Confession
  - Satisfaction
- Its recipients (Section 6)
- Its minister (Section 7)
  - Power of the keys
  - Excommunication
  - Indulgences

2. The Essence of the Sacrament of Penance

A. Its Nature

A sacrament of the New Law is an external sign instituted by Christ to give grace. It is evident that penance as practiced in the Church is such a sign, because something sacred is signified both by the acts of the repentant sinner who shows that his heart has renounced sin, and by the act of the priest whose absolution signifies God's forgiveness of sin.

The Council of Trent teaches that "our Lord instituted the sacrament of penance particularly at the time when, after rising from the dead, he breathed upon his disciples and said, 'Receive the Holy Spirit; whose sins you shall forgive, they are forgiven them; and whose sins you shall retain, they are retained' (Jn. 20:30). The consent of all the Fathers has always understood that by this striking act and by these unequivocal words there was communicated to the apostles and to their successors the power of remitting and of retaining sins for reconciling the faithful who have fallen after baptism. . . ."[1]

In penance, as in every sacrament, it is possible to disinguish the sacred sign from the interior spiritual reality which it signifies and effects.

Penance
- The sign or sacred rite itself—the external acts of penitent and priest (*sacramentum tantum*).
- The sign and the reality signified—the sinner's repentance (*res et sacramentum*).
- The reality itself—the forgiveness of sin (*res tantum*).

Of these elements, the first causes the second, and the first and second taken together cause the third.

In some sacraments the sacred, signifying action involves a material element, a physical object to which the form is applied by an authorized minister. For instance, in baptism the priest applies the form, "I baptize you, etc.," to the water which is the material element of the sacrament. In penance, there is no such physical object as water. Human actions take the place of matter in penance, and these actions proceed from the internal inspiration of grace. Hence God applies the matter by interior inspiration, and the minister supplies the completion of the sacrament when he applies the form of absolution, "I absolve you, etc." The elements of the sacrament of penance may be seen in this outline:

[1]Session XIV, Chap. 1; Denz. 894.

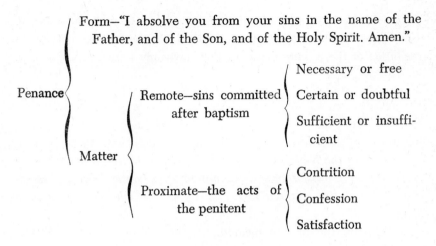

Form—"I absolve you from your sins in the name of the Father, and of the Son, and of the Holy Spirit. Amen."

Penance

Matter

Remote—sins committed after baptism
- Necessary or free
- Certain or doubtful
- Sufficient or insufficient

Proximate—the acts of the penitent
- Contrition
- Confession
- Satisfaction

B. Its Necessity

Absolutely speaking, a man can be saved without receiving the sacrament of penance. The reason is that penance is designed as a remedy for sins committed after baptism, and no one is compelled to commit sin. But on the assumption that some of the baptized will commit mortal sins, then penance becomes necessary for their salvation. (Cf. Denz. 894.)

As we have seen, baptism and the Eucharist are, in different ways, indispensable to salvation for all; penance is indispensable for all who have mortally sinned after baptism. Thus penance becomes a "second plank after shipwreck." It is absolutely necessary, when one has heedlessly tossed aside the "first plank of baptism" and the Eucharist which rescued him from sin, lest he should perish in the moral shipwreck of personal sin.[2]

Whereas baptism is a spiritual birth, and thus can occur only once, penance is a spiritual medicine, and thus can be repeated. This is clearly the teaching of Christ, for when Peter inquired how often he should forgive those who offended him, our Lord answered, "I do not say to thee seven times, but seven times seventy" (Matt. 19:22).

[2]This metaphor, first used by Tertullian (*On Penance*), and repeated by St. Jerome (*Letter 130 to Demetrias*), was approved and used by the Council of Trent, Sess. VI, Chap. 14 (Denz. 807) and Sess. XIV, Can. 2 (Denz. 912).

When Christ instructed his disciples in prayer he told them to ask daily for forgiveness (Matt. 6:12), and he told them to be merciful in imitation of the infinite mercy of their heavenly Father (Lk. 6:36).

C. Its Definition

From what has been said in the preceding sections, we can formulate a definition of this important sacrament. **Penance is *a sacrament of the New Law instituted by Christ in the form of a judgment for the remission of sins committed after baptism through sacramental absolution granted to a contrite person who confesses those sins.***

To explain the precise meaning of the various elements of this definition will be a major work of this chapter.

3. The Virtue of Penance

When a man repents, he deplores something he has done. This may be nothing more than an emotional reaction to evil, or it may be a deliberate act of the will based upon free choice. Now it is reasonable for men to grieve over evil with due moderation and for a good purpose. The man who sorrows in this way over his past offenses, with the intention of removing them, performs a good action. Thus penance is a good act and may be the act of a virtue.

Penance is a distinct virtue because it aims at a special object—the destruction of past sins. Penance is a kind of sorrow for having offended God, and it includes the intention of making amendment. Now to make amendment is to offer some kind of repayment; it includes the notion of debt and hence pertains to the virtue of justice.

While the virtue of penance is properly a species of justice, it is closely related to many other virtues, as St. Thomas shows:

> Although penance is directly a part of justice, it includes whatever pertains to all the virtues. Inasmuch as there is a kind of justice between man and God, it is fittingly a part of the matter pertaining to the theological virtues which have God for their object. Consequently, penance is exercised with *faith* in the passion of Christ by which we

are freed from our sins, with *hope* of pardon, and with hatred of vice which is an effect of *charity*. As a moral virtue, it partakes of the nature of *prudence* which directs all moral virtue. And from the very nature of justice, penance embraces not only the matter of *justice*, but extends to both *temperance* and *fortitude*, because whatever causes pleasure (which pertains to temperance) and whatever causes fear (which fortitude regulates) have something in common with justice. Accordingly, it belongs to justice both to abstain from pleasure, which pertains to temperance, and to sustain hardship, which pertains to fortitude.[3]

The exercise of the virtue of penance is dependent upon many other virtues. It is not a matter of experiencing some emotion of sorrow, or of being moved to tears. These things may be present as signs of the intensity of penance, but essentially penance is an act of the deliberate will proposing to amend an offence against God.

For Christians, penance is a supernatural, infused moral virtue whose object is the destruction of past sins precisely as they are offences against God. It is a part of relative commutative justice. It pertains to commutative justice because it involves reparation to another, to God; it is a part of relative justice because it is not between equals, but between Creator and creature. Accordingly, penance cannot attain the perfect compensation that absolute justice requires, but it represents the habitual will to do whatever can be done to make amends for past sins. As a part of justice, penance is in the will, but the exercise of this virtue may be accompanied by feelings of sorrow in the lower appetite.

In keeping with his general doctrine on God as the First Cause of all reality, St. Thomas teaches that God infuses the virtue of penance as the principal cause, but not without man co-operating dispositively by certain acts. The exercise of a particular act of the virtue of penance originates in this order:

1. God turns the heart of the sinner by grace. "Convert us, O Lord, to thee, and we shall be converted" (Lam. 5:21).
2. The sinner makes an act of faith.
3. The sinner makes an act of servile fear by which he dreads just punishment.

[3]*Summa*, III, q. 85, a. 3, ad 4.

4. The sinner makes an act of hope and proposes amendment in
   hope of obtaining pardon.
5. The sinner makes an act of charity by which sin becomes de-
   testable in itself, and not only because of the punishment.
6. The sinner makes an act of reverential fear and offers to make
   amends to the God who has loved him so much.

In concrete cases, most of these acts are implicit and not easily
distinguished, but all are necessary, and they furnish a practical guide
for increasingly fruitful exercise of the virtue and reception of the
sacrament of penance.

4. The Effects of Penance

In general, it may be said that the effect of penance is the destruction or forgiveness of past sins. But this is not sufficiently detailed
to answer many questions. Does penance affect the different kinds
of sins in the same way? In other words, are the effects of penance
the same on venial sins as on mortal sins? If sins are once forgiven
do they ever revive and plague the repentant sinner with new guilt?
Can penance remove all the effects of sin? Will penance restore to
the repentant the virtues they lost through sin? Can one merit by
penance?

A. Penance and Mortal Sin

Mortal sin is the "perfect" type of sin. It consists in deliberately turning away from God to seek happiness in some thing or in some way
that is opposed to the divine will. It results in the supernatural death
of the soul. No man can repair the disorder of mortal sin by himself,
any more than he could bring his dead body back to life. The restoration of man to divine friendship must be a divine work.

By the virtue of penance, man performs certain acts to obtain
God's pardon for his sins. These acts, taken together, are the **matter**
of the sacrament of penance. To these acts of the penitent the priest
applies the form, "I absolve you, etc," From the union of the matter

and form the *sacrament* is perfected, and it is the effect of this sacrament to restore the sinner to God's friendship by forgiving his mortal sins. The acts of the *virtue of penance* are subordinate to the form of the sacrament, and have their efficacy in blotting out sin precisely because of their relation to the sacrament. Consequently, for the forgiveness of mortal sin, both the acts of the virtue of penance and the sacrament itself are necessary, but in different ways.

(1) The Virtue and the Sacrament

A man may forgive his enemy without thereby making him his friend, but God's forgiveness acts differently. It brings about a change in the sinner who receives it, causing him to desire God's friendship, to seek divine pardon. Thus there is never forgiveness without the acts of penance, because the divine grace of pardon is the principal cause of forgiveness, and it moves the sinner to repent freely.

The necessity of the virtue of penance is expressed by the Council of Trent: "Penance has been necessary at all times to obtain grace and justification for all men who have stained themselves with mortal sin."[4] In other words, the exercise of the virtue of penance is absolutely necessary for forgiveness, and this applies to everyone who commits mortal sin, whether he be pagan, Jew or Christian. Without the will to repent, there can be no divine pardon. Forgiveness may be granted; it is never imposed. This bears out the remark of St. Augustine that God made us without ourselves, but he will not save us without our co-operation.

Now for the baptized, God provides the sacrament of penance, and for them, this is also necessary for the forgiveness of mortal sin. It may sometimes happen that the baptized cannot approach the sacrament, as, for example, when no priest is available. In such cases, their repentance must include the desire to receive the sacrament; otherwise their sins are not forgiven. For the exercise of penance by the baptized, there must be an actual reception of the sacrament, or, if this is not possible, there must be a sincere desire and intention of receiving it.

For the faithful, then, penance includes the exercise of the virtue *in union with* **the sacrament.** Hereafter the word is used in this sense.

[4]Sess. XIV, Chap. 1; Denz. 894.

(2) *The Sins Forgiven by Penance*

There is no sin which cannot be pardoned by penance in this life. While the wills of the damned remain fixed in the evil they have freely embraced, the wills of the living remain flexible to good and evil. In this regard it is true that where there is life there is hope, both because the will remains free to repent and because God's grace can move it freely to repent. "The heart of the king is in the hand of the Lord; whithersoever he will he shall turn it" (Prov. 21:1). Moreover, if there were some "unforgiveable sin," its existence would frustrate the power of Christ's passion through which penance has its effect, for "he is a propitiation for our sins, not for ours only but also for those of the whole world" (I Jn. 2:2).

Penance cannot remove one mortal sin while another remains. No sin can be forgiven without divine grace, and every mortal sin excludes grace. Neither could a man renounce one sin and not another, because all mortal sins are opposed to God. A penitent must reject sin because it is contrary to his loving God above all else, and no one can both reject and embrace at the same time what is contrary to God's love. Finally, it is contrary to God's perfection that he should pardon one sin and not another, for thus his forgiveness would be imperfect.

(3) *The Extent of Forgiveness*

How complete is the forgiveness obtained through penance? To answer that question, the doctrine on the nature of mortal sin must be recalled. There are two elements in every mortal sin: there is a turning away from God and an inordinate turning to some creature. Now whoever turns away from God turns away from eternal goodness, and he justly contracts a debt of eternal punishment for this. By turning his heart inordinately to some creature, man incurs a debt of temporal punishment, for self-indulgence is undone only by some measure of self-denial. "As much as she glorified herself and gave herself to wantonness, so much torment and mourning give to her" (Apoc. 18:7).

Penance remits the debt of eternal punishment, but the debt of temporal punishment remains in varying degrees, depending upon the circumstances. Adam and Eve were afflicted with sorrow and labor; Moses was denied entrance to the promised land; the innocent son of David's iniquity perished for his father's sin; and all these penalties befell after the guilty had repented and had been delivered from the debt of eternal punishment.[5]

Every act tends to be repeated. This principle holds true of mortal sins, and is verified particularly in habitual sins. The repentant drunkard is absolved of guilt, but he is not freed of his inclination to drink. Penance involves a turning of the will from evil, and this conversion of the will destroys the *essence* of the bad habit which is in the will. But the *tendency* to the habit remains. Clearly, renewed repentance will diminish the strength of evil inclinations, but the healing of the wounds of sin must be completed by many acts of self-denial. One who writes with his right hand could learn to write with his left, and the beginning can be traced to an act of his will. But how long will it take him, and how much effort will he expend, before he is freed of the inclination to reach for a pen with his right hand? Old dispositions must be broken down and a contrary habit must be built up. That is generally a long and painful process.

B. Penance and Venial Sin

A woman's beauty may be impaired in either of two ways: she may be permanently disfigured, for example, by being scalded; or she may suffer some temporary setback in her appearance, for example, by being drenched with rain. Similarly, the soul may lose the beauty of grace altogether by the disfigurement of mortal sin; or the radiance of its grace may be obscured by the disordered affections that are manifest in venial sin.

All sin separates man from God in some degree. Mortal sin effects a total separation from God, because by it the will acts against the love of God and turns away from him completely. Venial sin, on the other hand, causes an incomplete separation, because by it the will

[5]Cf. Gen. 3:16 ff.; Num. 20:11 f.; II Kings 12:13.

does not turn completely from God but rather becomes sluggish in seeking God through dawdling with disordered affections for some creature or pleasure.

(1) The Need for Penance

Neither mortal nor venial sin can be forgiven as long as the will remains attached to the sin, because sin separates man from God, and as long as the cause remains, the effect remains. But it is the effect of penance to reunite man to God after sin. Consequently, penance is required for the forgiveness of venial sin.

It is important to note, however, that the penance required for the forgiveness of mortal sin must be more perfect because the separation is greater. There can be no forgiveness of mortal sins without actually detesting each one of them as far as possible. This detestation must always be united to the sacrament of penance, either by actual reception, or, if this is impossible, by the intention to receive it.

Venial sin can be forgiven without receiving the *sacrament* of penance. An exercise of the *virtue* of penance suffices to forgive venial sin. It is not necessary for this that the sinner recall and detest each venial sin actually. It is enough if he should arouse a desire to seek God and divine things that is strong enough to make him detest whatever may hinder him from reaching God, even if he does not recall each specific venial sin. To this desire there should be joined the intention of taking practical steps to commit fewer venial sins, because if a man does not make progress in the spiritual life, he necessarily falls back. Among those who live habitually in the state of grace, the lack of a strong will to remove the obstacles to spiritual progress which arise from venial sins is the greatest cause of mediocrity.

(2) Grace and Sin

All forgiveness of sin is traceable to divine grace. A man in the state of venial sin remains supernaturally alive, he remains in the state of grace. Consequently, the forgiveness of venial sin in such a man does not require a new infusion of sanctifying grace, because that principle of divine life is not nullified by venial sin. With the aid of a movement of actual grace, the venial sinner is able to perform an act of supernatural sorrow, and thus the venial sins can be forgiven. The movement of actual grace impels the sinner to turn away from the obstacle of venial sin which slows his progress to God.

What of the man who is guilty of both mortal and venial sin? Can venial sin be forgiven while mortal sin remains? In view of the fact that sanctifying or habitual grace is the principle of forgiveness, and because the mortal sinner is not supernaturally alive with such grace, there cannot be any forgiveness of venial sin while mortal sin remains. Such a one would have to receive the sacrament of penance in order to regain the state of grace; only then could his venial sins be forgiven.

On the other hand, mortal sin could be forgiven while venial sin remained, in someone who would cling to the attachment for venial sin. For instance, a man can repent of having deliberately missed Mass without being sorry for a habit of lying by exaggeration. In this case, the mortal sin would be forgiven, but not the venial sin, because his will remained attached to it.

(3) Extra-sacramental Forgiveness

Practically speaking, there are many ways to insure the forgiveness of venial sins apart from confession. The principal requisite is to make some act which proceeds from grace and which involves a turning away from the sin. Consequently, the following acts will forgive those venial sins for which one is truly sorry:

1) The fruitful reception of any of the sacraments. Every reception of a sacrament implies an infusion of sanctifying grace, and this will remit the venial sins for which there is sorrow.

2) The devout recitation of the Our Father, the Confiteor, the Act of Contrition, and similar prayers can occasion the forgiveness of venial sin because they express a detestation of sin.

3) Any action that implies an impulse of reverence towards God can occasion the forgiveness of venial sin. Thus the use of sacramentals like holy water, or receiving a priest's blessing, can evoke a movement of grace in the soul which draws it to God and away from venial sin.

C. The Return of Sins Already Forgiven

Is it possible for past sins to revive when new sins are committed? Do man's present sins renew the guilt and the debt of punishment once due to past sins which have been forgiven? These are simply inquiries into the extent and the perfection of the divine forgiveness. It is common for men to treat offenders in the light of their former crimes, even in cases where the past and the present are separated by sincere repentance and satisfaction. But is the same true of God? This is surely a matter of great importance for every sinner who ever lived.

(1) The Perfection of God's Forgiveness

Each sin, like every human act, is distinct from all others by reason of some circumstance or other. Each is marked with its own malice or ignorance or weakness; each seeks its own goal. Considered in terms of their distinctive qualities, no sin ever returns once it is forgiven, "for the gifts and the call of God are without repentance" (Rom. 11:29). Indeed, God forgives the repentant sinner more perfectly than the sinner can forgive himself. "I will forgive their iniquity, and I will remember their sin no more" (Jer. 31:34).

For God's forgiveness is complete and perfect, penetrating deeply into the soul of the sinner to work a radical change in him. This is not just an attitude or pose on God's part, nor for man is it only a superficial change in appearances. Rather is it a change in the very being of a man, because God's friend is a different kind of person than God's enemy. "If your sins be as scarlet, they shall be made as white as snow; and if they be red as crimson, they shall be white as wool" (Isa. 1:18).

(2) The Danger of Sinning Again

Yet the man who sins seriously after repeated forgiveness surely adds the gravity of ingratitude to his recent sins. All mortal sins turn man away from God. Sins that follow forgiveness are worse than former sins, and are more deserving of punishment, because they imply a contempt for the divine mercy. The more numerous or the greater the sins previously pardoned, the greater must be the debt of punishment incurred by all subsequent mortal sins.

St. Thomas points out that there are four sins which connote contempt for past pardon and which are specially deserving of punishment because of their ingratitude:

1) Persisting hatred, which refuses to others a share in the forgiveness which the sinner has received from God.

2) Apostasizing from faith in the God whom the sinner formerly approached for forgiveness.

3) Regret for having repented of past sins.

4) Rejecting a previous intention of confessing one's sins.

D. The Revival of Virtues through Penance

We have seen that mortal sin destroys charity and sanctifying grace in the soul. It renders the soul spiritually dead, so that a mortal sinner can no more perform meritorious works in the sight of God than a corpse can speak. As long as one remains in the state of mortal sin, he can do nothing that merits salvation.

Moreover, mortal sin is a kind of spiritual bankruptcy that wipes out all previous assets. By mortal sin man rejects God and embraces something other than God as the goal of his life. In so doing, he destroys the principle of his union with God; he passes, so to speak, out of the light of divine love into the darkness of some kind of disordered self-love. In this state, all of his past acts by which he merited the divine favor lose their value. There is nothing left upon which he may fall back. He is a spiritual suicide.

(1) Grace and the Virtues

While the sinner is unable to restore himself to divine friendship, Almighty God can impel him to repent freely by divine grace. When the sinner repents and is restored to divine favor through the sacrament, do any of his past deeds revive so that they become once again his title to a divine reward?

To answer this problem, we must first recall that mortal sin is forgiven only by an infusion of divine grace. Grace is to the soul what the soul is to the body. Just as the soul is equipped with certain faculties, like the intellect and will, through which it operates, so does sanctifying grace bring with it an array of virtues and gifts through which man is enabled to lead a supernatural life. Through penance, then, the repentant sinner recovers all of the infused virtues and gifts, he is restored fully to spiritual life.

Grace, however, is recovered in proportion to the devotion of the penitent. Those who repent with greater fervor, whose wills move toward God and away from sin with greater devotion, will receive a greater measure of grace. Thus the repentant sinner may arise to a degree of grace equal to, less than, or greater than what he possessed before. The same is true of the perfection of the infused virtues which are regained together with grace.

(2) The Penalties of Sin

Like the returned prodigal son, the repentant sinner regains his dignity as a child of the heavenly Father. But no penance can remove the experience of sin, nor destroy its memory. It is incompatible with divine wisdom that what has been done should be undone. Innocence lost is not regained in the order of experience, but sometimes something greater can be recovered, as St. Gregory explains. "Those who admit they have strayed from God may recover their previous losses by subsequent gains. Therefore, there is more joy in heaven over such as these, just as a general in battle regards more highly that soldier who, after deserting, returns to attack the enemy more bravely, than some other who never turned his back but who never did anything courageously."[6]

Certain public and scandalous sins bring special penalties provided by canon law. For example, the commission of certain crimes will bar a man from holy orders. These penalties are not removed by simply repenting. They are provided to deter sinners and also to safeguard the holiness of certain offices. They pertain more to the province of law than to the domain of grace.

[6]*Homily 34 on the Gospels.*

(3) The Revival of Merit

Every good deed done by one in the state of grace establishes a claim to the eternal reward of heaven; all such deeds are *meritorious.* But when man commits a mortal sin, he prevents his past meritorious acts from actually earning heaven for him. The works remain worthy of eternal life, but the worker has made himself unworthy of that reward by his sin. He is like a criminal whose assets are impounded by the government which will not restore them until he has paid the penalty for his crimes. When the impediment of sin is removed by penance, these meritorious works revive, they come back to life, so to speak. Now that they exist once again in a worthy man, they again establish his title to eternal life.

(4) Good Deeds without Merit

On the other hand, good deeds performed by one in the state of mortal sin are supernaturally dead from the beginning. Such works never were quickened by the life of divine love, they never were meritorious. Once a deed is done, that same deed cannot be repeated. No amount of penance can infuse life into deeds which never had it. "And if I distribute all my goods to feed the poor, and if I deliver my body to be burned, yet do not have charity, it profits me nothing" (I Cor. 13:3).

Each man is allotted a certain time to work out his salvation, to merit an eternal reward by good deeds. Each moment of that time spent in mortal sin is wasted for all eternity. Every such moment is so completely beyond recall that not even a miracle of mercy could restore it, for this would involve the contradiction of having something both dead and alive at the same time under the same circumstances. It is for this reason that a sinner can place himself outside the pale of divine mercy by obstinately rejecting grace and clinging to his sins. The tragedy is magnified when we consider the wonderful power of grace, through penance, to wipe life's slate clean, and the measureless mercy of God that impels him to offer that grace to every one who needs it.

5. The Parts of the Sacrament of Penance

We have seen that the acts of the penitent are the *proximate* matter of the sacrament of penance, as anointing with chrism is in confirmation and washing with water in baptism. The **form** is the sacramental absolution of the priest. Penance seeks to re-establish the balance of justice and to reconcile the sinner to God. Sins are not atoned simply by fulfilling the sentence of a judge; the discretion of the sinner and the will of an offended God must be considered in penance. In view of this, three acts are required of the penitent:

1. He must have the will to atone for his sins, and this is done by **contrition.**

2. He must submit to the judgment of the priest who stands in God's place, and this is done by **confession.**

3. He must make amends according to the decision of God's minister, and this is done by **satisfaction.**

These are the parts of the sacrament, and each will be studied separately.

A. Contrition

Contrition is *deliberate sorrow for sins which includes the purpose of confessing and of making satisfaction for them.* The Council of Trent declares: "Contrition . . . is a profound sorrow and detestation for sin committed, with a resolution of sinning no more."[7]

Contrition is an act of the virtue of penance whereby the hardness of man's attachment to sin is crushed or broken. It is so called from the Latin *contritum* or *contritio,* which signify a crushing, breaking or undoing of something.

(1) Kinds of Sorrow for Sin

One can be sorry for sin on several grounds, very unequal in value. These give rise to this division:

[7]Council of Trent, Sess. XIV, Chap. 4, 1551; Denz. 897.

Sorrow for Sin
{
  Supernatural—based on some motive of faith.
  {
    Perfect contrition—a sorrow based on the love of God.

    Attrition—a sorrow based on some lesser supernatural motive, e.g., fear of hell.
  }

  Natural—natural remorse based on some worldly motive, e.g., the disgrace or natural evil effects due to sin.
}

Natural sorrow or remorse is not sufficient for the sacrament of penance, which pertains to the supernatural order.

Attrition, however, combined with the reception of penance is sufficient for the forgiveness of sin.[8] Such sorrow is a morally good act, even when based upon fear of hell. While this is the least noble of supernatural motives, it is undeniably supernatural, because the existence of hell is accepted on divine faith. Further, attrition includes a detestation of sin, which is a means of avoiding hell; finally, it directs this detestation of sin toward the avoidance of hell. This sorrow for sin is similar to the fear of a slave; contrition is like the reverent fear of a devoted child.

Perfect *contrition* suffices to remit all sins, even when confession is impossible, provided that the desire for the sacrament is included in the contrition. For contrition breaks the attachment of the will to sin. Consequently, the proper object of contrition is man's actual sins, each of which is an act of his will, and it affects only sins actually committed. But it does not extend to original sin (this is not an act of the individual's will), nor to future sins which may or may not be committed, nor to the sins of others. Contrition can and should extend to each personal actual sin. No sin can be forgiven without it—in sacramental penance attrition becomes contrition through the power of the sacrament—for this would mean that the will would both cling to and detest the same sin at the same time. This is clearly impossible.

[8]*Ibid.,* Chap. 5; Denz. 898.

(2) The Qualities of Contrition

It is generally taught by theologians that the contrition or attrition required for penance must have four qualities:

1) It must be **true and formal** sorrow, not something external and pretended, imagined or implicit.

2) It must be **supernatural.** This means that it must originate with the inspiration of grace and not through natural effort, and it must be motivated by some consideration known by the light of faith, and not by some natural realization of guilt.

3) It must be **supreme**—in the sense that the penitent must regard sin as the greatest evil, and must be prepared to endure any evil rather than lapse into it again. This does not require an intense *feeling* of sorrow, but rather a *conviction* of the evil of sin.

4) It must be **universal,** extending to all mortal sins without exception which the penitent has committed. It is fruitless to confess venial sins without contrition.

(3) Purpose of Amendment

Implied in all true contrition is the **purpose of amendment,** which is *the resolve not to sin again.* On the one hand, the purpose of amendment is not merely a wish to avoid sin; on the other, it is not a promise or vow never to sin again. Sometimes a penitent proposes amendment by a distinct act of the will; more often, his purpose of amendment is contained in his act of sincere contrition. True contrition and the purpose of amendment are like the two sides of the same coin and are just as inseparable.

Without a purpose of amendment, there can be no true contrition. Without true contrition or attrition, there can be no forgiveness of sin. While an implicit purpose of amendment is sufficient, it is better for the penitent to make an explicit intention to amend, one which is centered on some special sin. Any intention is more efficacious in proportion to its particular determination.

Theologians generally list three qualities of the purpose of amendment:

1) It must be **firm** regarding the present determination of the will, although it may be weak regarding the future. It is not the same as a constant or persevering determination, nor is it a guarantee against sin. Many who measure the future in terms of their own strength betray a serious lack of trust in God's providence.

2) It must be **efficacious,** that is, it must include the sincere will to employ the ordinary safeguards against sin, e.g., prayer and caution. Further, it must include the will to avoid the free, proximate occasions of sin. Finally, it must include the will to repair the damage done by sin, as far as this is possible.

3) It must be **universal,** i.e., including a resolve to avoid all mortal sins.

In cases where a penitent confesses only venial sins, or even mortal sins which have been absolved previously, the purpose of amendment is as essential for the validity of the sacrament as is true sorrow. In these cases, the purpose of amendment must embrace at least one of these possible resolutions:

1) To avoid all venial sin.

2) To avoid one specific venial sin.

3) To correct one kind of sin, e.g., lying.

4) To avoid all deliberate venial sin.

5) To diminish the number of venial sins.

Perhaps the most common cause of failure to overcome habits of venial sin is lack of due attention to the purpose of amendment.

B. Confession

The second act of the penitent is the telling of his sins, or confession. Confession is *the telling of the personal sins one has committed after baptism to an authorized priest for the purpose of obtaining absolution.* When Christ instituted the sacrament of penance, he gave his priests power to forgive and to retain sins. This means that he instituted the sacrament in the form of a judgment, and a judgment requires the hearing and weighing of evidence. Thus, the act of confessing is an integral part of the sacrament. This is evident in the Scriptures (cf. Jas. 5:16; I Jn. 1:9; Lk. 17:14), and it has been declared a matter of divine law by the Council of Trent.[9]

(1) Obligation of Confessing

Confession, then, is necessary for salvation for any who after baptism have the misfortune to fall into mortal sin. This general obligation which arises from divine law is made more specific by the law of the Church: "Every one of the faithful of either sex, upon reaching the age of discretion, i.e., the use of reason, is bound to confess sincerely all sins at least once a year" (Can. 906). This law refers specifically to mortal sins. This is quite distinct from the obligation to receive Holy Communion during Eastertide (Can. 859), but, in practice, the two are generally fulfilled at the same time. A sacrilegious or invalid confession does not fulfill the obligation (Can. 907).

While it is clear that the ecclesiastical law of confession binds only once each year (most practically computed from one Easter until the next), we may well inquire if the divine precept to confess binds at other times.

It is commonly taught that the divine precept of confession would oblige anyone who is in actual or probable danger of death. The precept would also become binding in the face of special circumstances such as the following:

1) Whenever someone in mortal sin wishes to receive Communion.

2) Whenever a mortal sinner is required to be in the state of grace, and he cannot be morally certain of evoking perfect contrition; for instance, before marriage or confirmation.

3) When it becomes morally impossible to overcome a grave temptation without the special grace of penance; for instance, in the face of temptation to a seriously evil habit.

While the time for fulfilling the ecclesiastical law of confession is fixed within the limits of one year, there is no set time fixed for the fulfillment of the divine precept in itself. As already explained, this divine obligation may begin to bind by reason of some special neces-

[9]Sess. XIV, Chap. 5; Denz. 899.

sity for being in the state of grace at a particular time. In general, however, it seems best to say that none are bound to confess as soon as they fall into serious sin, although delay in these matters is very dangerous.

(2) The Qualities of Confession

St. Thomas selects from the writings of saints and theologians sixteen qualities which should characterize a perfect confession, and explains the meaning of each. Confession should be:

1: *discreet*—prudent discretion gives greater weight to graver sins.

2: *free*—confession must always be a voluntary act.

3: *sincere*—it should proceed from a right intention.

4: *courageous*—truth must not be forsaken through shame.

5: *marked by shame*—it must not be a boastful account of sin.

6: *sorrowful*—it must spring from interior penance.

7: *humble*—it must be an acknowledgment of misery and weakness.

8: *truthful*—it must be free from all lies and deception.

9: *open*—it must be free of ambiguity and vagueness, yet free of coarse or offensive language.

10: *simple*—it must be free of superfluous words and comments, especially about others.

11: *entire*—nothing pertinent should be omitted.

12: *accusatory* of the penitent—it should not be an excuse for sinning.

13: *manifestive* of a readiness to obey—the confessor's advice should be followed.

14: *secret*—confession in the present discipline of the Church is not public, and no one is obliged to use an interpreter in confessing (Can. 903).

15: *frequent*—confession should be used to *preserve* the life of grace in the soul, and not only to recover it.

16: *prompt*—no one should remain freely in the state of sin. St. Gregory remarks that he who promised forgiveness to penitents did not promise tomorrow to sinners.

(3) Integrity of Confession

Integrity means completeness or wholeness. With reference to confession, integrity means the telling of all mortal sins. There are two kinds:

Confession is

Formally integral—when it includes all the mortal sins which the penitent can and should confess here and now, when all circumstances are taken into consideration.

Materially integral—when it includes each and every mortal sin committed after baptism and not yet directly forgiven.

1. Formal integrity. Formal integrity is absolutely essential for the validity and lawfulness of confession. This is clear from the teaching of the Council of Trent that "penitents must disclose in confession all the mortal sins of which they are conscious after a diligent examination of conscience, even if these sins be most hidden and committed against the last two commandments only. Moreover, even those circumstances which change the species of the sin must be mentioned in confession."[10]

The following must be confessed in order to have formal integrity:

a) The *specific kind of mortal sin committed.* This is called technically the ultimate moral species. E.g., fornication, not "impurity"; blasphemy, not "vulgar language"; detraction, not "unkind speech"; etc.

b) The *number* of mortal sins, as far as is morally possible. E.g., if the exact number is forgotten, a close approximation will do ("about 7" would indicate something between 5 and 9), or the duration of a habit with the number of falls per day or per week.

c) The *circumstances which change the kind* of sin. E.g., that one stole from the *poor,* sinned with another who was *married,* etc.

---

[10]Council of Trent, *loc. cit.*

d) The *external act of sinning*. E.g., it does not suffice for a thief to confess "I intended to steal," or for a fornicator to say "I entertained impure desires."

e) Any *external evil effect which was foreseen or intended* as the result of the sin. E.g., "I lied about someone and seriously damaged his reputation," "I read an obscene book and committed a sin of unchastity by myself."

2. Material integrity. For legitimate reasons, material integrity may sometimes be lacking. The reason is that material integrity is sometimes impossible, and Christ does not bind anyone to what is impossible. The reasons excusing from material integrity are physical or moral impossibility.

1) *Physical impossibility* is considered to exist in these and similar cases:
   a) extreme sickness;
   b) lack of speech, e.g., in mutes or in those whose language the confessor cannot understand;
   c) lack of time for confession, e.g., during wartime;
   d) invincible ignorance or forgetfulness.

2) *Moral impossibility* exists when a complete recital of mortal sins would result in some grave moral inconvenience. This inconvenience must be **extrinsic** to confession, and only **accidentally** associated with the confession that must be made here and now. Difficulties intrinsic to confession, like shame, or the loss of the confessor's esteem, do not excuse from material integrity. Moral impossibility is considered to exist in these and similar cases:
   a) danger of violating the seal of confession; e.g., in a crowded hospital ward, others could easily overhear the penitent;
   b) grave danger to life resulting accidentally from this confession; e.g., in time of an epidemic the life of the penitent, the confessor or of some third party may be jeopardized by the contact needed for confession.

If formal integrity was lacking, it must be repeated in its entirety, because sins are not forgiven by invalid confession. If material integrity was lacking, the sin or sins inculpably omitted must be mentioned in the next confession.

C. Satisfaction

Satisfaction is the final part of penance. To make satisfaction is itself an act of virtue that pertains to justice, for it implies a voluntary compensation for an injury inflicted. In making satisfaction for sin, the compensation is not quantitatively, but only proportionately equal. Yet when man makes whatever satisfaction he can, God accepts this as sufficient to regain the divine friendship.

Mortal sins partake of infinity because they are offences against an infinite God. Man's satisfaction also shares in infinity, because it is dependent upon the infinite mercy of God and because it is inspired by the infinite power of divine grace. Grace gives infinite value to human satisfaction. Clearly, then, no one remaining in the state of mortal sin can make any satisfaction for his past sins.

The Council of Trent teaches that "it befits divine mercy that sins not be forgiven us without any satisfaction, lest having thus found an occasion for thinking sins to be light, we fall into graver sins (such as insulting and contemning the Holy Spirit), storing up wrath for ourselves on the day of wrath."[11] That this is the plan of divine justice is clearly indicated in many passages of the Scriptures. (Cf. Gen. 3:16 ff.; Num. 12:14 f., 20:11 f.; II Kings 12:13 f.)

For any human activity to be satisfactory for sin, two things are required:

1) it must be *good,* i.e., capable of procuring God's honor;
2) it must be *penal,* i.e., involving some loss to the sinner.

Satisfaction may be made in God's sight through the grace of Christ in several ways:

1) By freely undertaking penance for sin.
2) By patiently bearing the temporal punishment sent by God.
3) By doing the penance assigned by the priest in confession.

The three principal acts of penance are almsgiving, fasting and prayer. Each of these produces a distinctive result, and each is aimed at uprooting one of the principal causes of sin. This is made clear in the following graph:

[11]Sess. XIV, Chap. 8; Denz. 904.

Principal Penances	Results	Uproots (I Jn. 2:16)
Almsgiving	surrenders possessions	concupiscence of the eyes
Fasting	surrenders pleasures	concupiscence of the flesh
Prayer	surrenders mind and heart to God	pride of life

(1) The Sacramental Penance

The sacramental penance imposed by the confessor is a means whereby the penitent satisfies for the temporal punishment due to his sins by freely performing good acts that are penal. *It is to be noted that the eternal punishment due to mortal sin is forgiven by the sacrament itself; the penance is designed to remit temporal punishment.*

The penance assigned in confession produces four good results according to the teaching of the Council of Trent:

1) It reminds the penitent that sin is a serious evil deserving heavy penalties.
2) It puts the sinner on his guard against falling into the same sins again.
3) It serves as a remedy to heal the weakness resulting from past sins and helps to break down evil habits.
4) It associates the penitent in the satisfaction that Christ made for all, and gives renewed assurance that if we suffer with Christ we shall also be glorified with him.[12]

Under ordinary circumstances, confessors are bound to exercise their power and to assign a penance to all who confess. The penance imposed should be proportionate to the kind of sins confessed and to the ability of the penitent.

[12]Council of Trent, *loc. cit.*

There are cases in which no penance is assigned because none could be fulfilled, e.g., when the penitent is in danger of death. There are also certain cases in which the penance is considerably lightened, e.g., when the penitent is infirm, or when the confessor willingly undertakes to perform part of the penance himself.

(2) *Acceptance and Fulfillment of the Penance*

Just as the confessor is obliged to assign a penance, so the penitent is obliged to accept and to fulfill any reasonable penance that may be imposed. Satisfaction is an integral part of the sacrament, and whoever wishes to receive it must fulfill its essential requirements.

Should a penitent forget what penance was assigned, it becomes impossible to fulfill, unless he can conveniently return to the same confessor. If the confessor imposes a time limit for the penance, it must be observed. If no limit is set, the penance should be said as soon as conveniently possible. While there is no special obligation to fulfill the penance before receiving Holy Communion, this is certainly the best course to follow in practice.

It is most unwise to treat sacramental penances lightly or to run the risk of forgetting them. No amount of privately undertaken penance has the same efficacy in satisfying for the temporal punishment due to sin as the sacramental penance has. The sacramental penance enjoys a unique power in this regard. Other voluntary penances will contribute to satisfaction, but they do not substitute for the penance assigned by the confessor.

6. The Recipients of Forgiveness

To answer the question as to who are capable of receiving the forgiveness of sins, the virtue of penance must be distinguished from the sacrament.

The sacrament of penance may be received by any baptized Christian who has committed some personal sin, either mortal or venial, after his baptism, and who is capable of performing the three essential acts of contrition, confession and satisfaction.

The virtue of penance extends beyond those who have committed actual sins. Like other virtues, penance is infused into the soul at baptism along with sanctifying grace. Even those among the baptized who have not committed personal sins (infants, for example) have both the power and the habit of penance.[13] They cannot actually exercise penance, however, because sin, which is the material upon which penance works, is lacking. It must not be thought that the habit of penance in the innocent is useless, because it endows them with a special perfection and makes them radically capable of sorrow and satisfaction should the need ever arise through the commission of actual sin.

Penance is present among the blessed in heaven, but it operates differently than in this life. Among the blessed the act of penance consists in gratitude for the mercy God shows in forgiving sin.

Strictly speaking, there can be no penance among the angels. Good angels are innocent of sin and their wills are fixed in goodness. Fallen angels cannot be forgiven because their wills are fixed in evil. The virtue of penance can exist only where there is the possibility of forgiveable sin; it can be exercised only where there is sin to be forgiven.

7. The Minister of the Sacrament of Penance

Under this heading, we will examine three important considerations: the power of the keys, excommunication and indulgences.

A. The Power of the Keys

The gates of heaven were closed to mankind by the sin of our first parents. There are three keys to these gates. The first is the key of authority possessed by the Blessed Trinity; the second is the key of excellence possessed by Jesus Christ; the third is the key of ministry, possessed by the ministers of Christ's Church who are the dispensers of his sacraments. (Cf. Matt. 18:17 f.; Jn. 20:23).

---

[13]It should be recalled that Christ, being absolutely impeccable, did not possess this virtue, nor would it be found, according to many theologians, in Our Lady.

In order to administer the sacrament of penance validly and lawfully, two things are required in the minister: holy orders and jurisdiction.

(1) Holy Orders

The minister of penance must be ordained to the priesthood. This is required by divine law and is contained in the official teaching of the Council of Trent.[14] Thus no deacon, subdeacon, cleric in minor orders, nor any layman has the power to absolve from sin validly.

In absolving from sin, the priest acts as a minister of Christ who judges and pronounces sentence. The absolution he grants is not his own, but Christ's. Therefore, the personal worthiness of the priest does not affect the validity of his absolution. That power is conferred by the Holy Spirit at ordination, and it operates independently of the personal sanctity, or lack thereof, of the priest.

(2) Jurisdiction

The sacrament of penance was instituted in the form of a judgment. Now every valid judgment requires that the judge have jurisdiction over his subjects. Ecclesiastical jurisdiction is the power of ruling, judging and coercing baptized persons in matters pertaining to their spiritual welfare and supernatural happiness. Jurisdiction allows the priest to exercise validly the power to forgive sin which he received at ordination. Without jurisdiction, then, the absolution of a priest is of no avail.[15]

There are two kinds of jurisdiction regarding the sacrament of penance, ordinary and delegated.

1) **Ordinary jurisdiction** is annexed to some duly obtained ecclesiastical office, e.g., the episcopacy. The Holy Father and the Cardinals have ordinary jurisdiction over all the faithful. The Holy Father may limit the jurisdiction of everyone else. Local Ordinaries, such as bishops, have ordinary jurisdiction in their territories and dioceses, and over their own subjects even out-

---

[14]Sess. XXIII, Chap. 1; Denz. 957.
[15]See the Church's doctrine on jurisdiction as enunciated by the Council of Trent, Sess. XIV, Chap. 7; Denz. 903.

side their territories. Parish priests and those who serve in their place have ordinary jurisdiction over their parishioners, both within and outside their parishes.

2) **Delegated jurisdiction** is granted either by law or by an authorized individual, without being annexed to any ecclesiastical office. Cardinals and parish priests may not delegate their jurisdiction to others. The law delegates jurisdiction to any priest to absolve validly and lawfully any penitent who is in danger of death. Military personnel mobilized for war are considered to be in danger of death, and they may be absolved by any priest anywhere. The Local Ordinary may delegate jurisdiction to priests who are not his own diocesans and to religious, provided they are known to be competent in theology. Delegated jurisdiction may cease in various ways, e.g., it may be revoked, or it may expire when it is limited to certain times.

It is thus easy to understand that priests when traveling will often not have jurisdiction in the dioceses through which they are passing. Should a layman request such a traveler to hear his confession, the priest would have to refuse, not because of any impairment of his priestly powers, but simply because he had not sought faculties to hear confessions from the Ordinary of that place.

Jurisdiction may be limited in various ways. Faculties to hear confessions may exclude certain penitents from the confessor's jurisdiction; e.g., special jurisdiction is required to hear the confessions of nuns. Jurisdiction may be limited to a certain place; thus a retreat-master may be limited to hearing confessions in the college where he conducts the retreat. Jurisdiction may be limited to a certain time, as when faculties are granted for six months. Jurisdiction may also be limited with regard to certain sins.

This last type of restriction requires a brief explanation.

(3) Reservation

Reservation is the limitation of a case to some special tribunal so that absolution from such cases may be granted only by the authority who made the reservation, or by his successor, superior or delegate (cf. Can. 893). The purpose of reservation is to preserve discipline in the Church and to create a greater barrier against certain sins. There is a parallel in civil law where certain crimes are tried only before special tribunals. All reservation of cases involving the laity comes either from the Holy Father or from the Local Ordinary. A bishop, for example, could reserve to himself absolution from the sin of attending some specific anti-Catholic motion picture, or of sending children to some school where anti-Catholic doctrines were taught. Reserved cases are quite rare, and confessors are made aware of them so they know exactly how to guide the penitent who may have been involved in these difficulties. When anyone is in danger of death, all reservation ceases, and any confessor may absolve him.

B. Ecclesiastical Penalties

An ecclesiastical penalty is a punishment inflicted by the Church for some offense. These penalties are attached to external and sinful violations of certain laws, and not to internal acts. They are inflicted both for the reparation of harm done to the social order and for the correction of those who break the law.

The entire matter of ecclesiastical penalties is a complex problem in moral theology and canon law. Here we present only a summary of basic considerations with particular reference to penalties which may be incurred by laymen.

The more common type of ecclesiastical penalties are known as **censures**. These are medicinal penalties by which, because of obstinate violation of some law of the Church, a baptized person is deprived of certain benefits which are either spiritual or connected therewith, until he repents and obtains absolution (cf. Can. 2241). It is a teaching of faith that the Church has the power to inflict censures.[16]

(1) Excommunication

Excommunication is a censure by which a person is deprived of communion with the faithful of the Church (cf. Can. 2257). An excommunicated layman may not lawfully receive the sacraments; he

---

[16]The Council of Constance condemned the errors of John Wyclif, the English heretic, which denied this power to the Church. See Sess. VIII (1415), nn. 11 ff.; Denz. 591 ff.

is excluded from sharing in the prayers offered by the Church for all the faithful, and from indulgences; he may not act as sponsor at baptism or confirmation; if under a condemnatory or declaratory sentence by Church authority, the excommunicate is also deprived of ecclesiastical burial.

Absolution from most kinds of excommunication is reserved to different courts, from the Local Ordinary to the Holy See itself. Confessors are aware of these technical matters and are able to offer competent advice to any who may be excommunicated.

Excommunication of varying degrees of gravity is attached to these crimes: profanation of the Blessed Sacrament; embracing of heresy, schism, or apostasy, which includes the profession of Communism; joining the Freemasons and other similar societies; marrying before a non-Catholic minister; marrying after obtaining a civil divorce; entering marriage with an agreement to rear children in a non-Catholic religion; deliberately having children baptized by a non-Catholic minister, or educated in a non-Catholic sect; effectively procuring an abortion.

(2) Interdict

Interdict is a censure by which the faithful, while remaining in communion with the Church, are forbidden the use of certain sacraments and other sacred things (cf. Can. 2268, § 1). The effects and extent of interdicts are usually fixed in each case by the superior who inflicts them, but the following rules apply generally.

(1) **Local interdict** forbids the celebration of divine offices and the administration of sacred rites in the place under interdict. Certain great feasts are usually excepted. All solemnity and special functions are forbidden. However, the sacraments are available privately, Mass is offered once each day, and the Blessed Sacrament is reserved. It is the *solemn celebration* of these things which is forbidden.

(2) **Personal interdict** is similar in effects to excommunication.

(3) Conditions of Censures

In order to incur a censure, the sin to which they are attached must be mortal both objectively and subjectively, i.e., it must be grave and the sinner must know and intend it as such. It must be certain and not doubtful; it must be an external sin, because censures are not attached to internal sins, as, e.g., the desire to embrace heresy. Also, the sinner must be aware that a special penalty is attached to his crime. In general, whatever would excuse from grave fault will also excuse from censure.

C. Indulgences

An indulgence is a remission in the sight of God of the temporal punishment due for sins whose guilt has already been forgiven. It is granted by ecclesiastical authority from the spiritual treasury of the Church outside the sacrament of penance. To the living, it is granted in the form of absolution from temporal punishment; to the faithful departed, it is granted in the form of suffrage (cf. Can. 911).

Indulgences do not remit either mortal or venial sin. They affect only sins whose guilt has already been forgiven, either in the sacrament of penance or in other ways. Indulgences remit *temporal* punishment in the sight of God, so that it need not be endured again either in this life or in purgatory.

In a previous section we saw that temporal punishment may be remitted in various ways. Indulgences are among these. Their efficacy is derived from the satisfactory merits of Christ and the saints, which are stored in the spiritual treasury of the Church. The existence of this spiritual treasury, and the possibility of vicarious satisfaction (by which one member of the Church may pay part of another's debt through the union of charity), are the two doctrinal foundations of the teaching on indulgences.

The Church enjoys direct jurisdiction over her living members. Just as she absolves them from eternal guilt in the sacrament of penance, so does she absolve them from temporal punishment by indulgences. Lacking jurisdiction over the faithful departed, she offers indulgences for them by way of suffrages applied to their needs.

In terms of their effects there are two kinds of indulgences:

1) **Plenary indulgences** remit all of the temporal punishment due to sin when received by one having the necessary dispositions.

2) **Partial indulgences** remit some portion of the temporal punishment due to sin. It is commonly taught that a partial indulgence of seven years remits the temporal punishment that would be satisfied for by a canonical penance of that duration in the practice of the early Church.

The following are the conditions necessary for gaining indulgences:

1) An *intention* of gaining the indulgence. A habitual intention suffices to gain indulgences personally; at least a virtual and explicit intention is required to apply them to the souls of others.

2) The *state of grace* and perfect union with the Church. The unbaptized, the excommunicated and mortal sinners cannot gain indulgences.

3) The *prescribed work*, e.g., visiting a particular church or altar; saying certain prayers; etc. These must be performed exactly, personally, and not when it comes under some other obligation. Thus a visit to some church is not fulfilled by attending Mass there on Sunday; another visit would be required.

4) When confession is prescribed, it must be made even by those guilty only of venial sin. It may be made within eight days before or after the day on which the indulgence is granted. One confession suffices for all indulgences to be gained in that period.

5) The same rules as in the preceding paragraph apply to the required reception of Holy Communion.

6) When, to the prayers or good works prescribed for gaining an indulgence, there is added the condition "of praying according to the intention of the Supreme Pontiff," it suffices to recite the Our Father, Hail Mary and Glory once for the intention of the Holy Father. When all these conditions are not required, those that are required are stated.

7) All prayers prescribed for gaining indulgences must be said orally (i.e., with at least a movement of the lips forming the words, though not necessarily audibly), except in the case of mutes who may offer them mentally, and of ejaculatory prayers.

8. Penitential Discipline in the Church

A. Introduction

Before concluding our study, something should be said concerning the history of the sacrament of penance. It may seem strange, both that the history of this sacrament should be treated only after the theological study has been completed, and that this sacrament should receive a special historical treatment at all. To explain adequately the reasons for taking up its history after having expounded its theological aspects would require a discussion of the role of the history of dogmas; this is manifestly impossible here. However, the direction of the answer can and should be pointed out.

Penance, like the other sacraments, is an object of faith. Belief in this sacrament has always existed in the Church. Aside from all historical questions concerning it, we believe that Christ established the sacrament of penance to forgive sin. Theology studies what the Church has proposed as revealed with regard to this sacrament. The historian may then search for evidence of this belief in the early Church, for indications of a developing understanding, and for information concerning the practice of the Church in various places and at different times. In this way the historian can help us to understand our faith and our theology better.

Penance requires a special historical treatment because there is great historical difficulty with regard to it. Those who do not accept this sacrament on faith attempt to justify their rejection of it by arguing that the priestly power to absolve was unknown in the primitive Christian communities and is not mentioned in any early patristic text. They say that the reconciliation of penitents was concerned only with the external forum and had nothing to do with a purification of conscience, and that priestly intervention in the forgiveness of sin was in the form of prayer or intercession, not in the form of a declaration of forgiveness.

These assertions in no way distress the historian of dogmas. He knows that the sacrament of penance has been part of Christian teaching since the beginning, whether historical evidence can be discovered to prove it, or not. He knows that no historical evidence has been nor ever can be produced to prove the contrary. Yet because of his desire to know and manifest the truth, even the particular truths of history, he sets out to see what history does have to say about the theory and practice of this sacrament. As a good historian he is well aware of the fact that historical events cannot be isolated. Because a historical event is no longer historical if taken out of context, he realizes that the sacrament of penance cannot be studied apart from the totality of Christian life.

Today the confessional is an integral part of every church. It was not so in the beginning. The fact that the sacrament of penance was not administered then as it is now, that it did not play the same role in the life of the Christian, was due to the fact that circumstances were different then from what they are today. The sacrament of penance is essentially a juridical tribunal. Judges reasonably judge more harshly or more easily depending upon the conditions of society. In the early Church most Christians were adult converts of mature stability of disposition, and were filled with the enthusiasm of recent conversion. Anyone who acted on his convictions and professed Christianity in those days of cruel persecution knew that his goods and even his life were in peril. Men and women of such supernatural outlook did not look upon sin lightly. By baptism they were cleansed of all the sins of their youth. But what did the Church do about them, if they did sin seriously after their baptism?

B. Penance in the New Testament

There are clear and unmistakable instances in the New Testament of Christ's forgiving sins. It is also clear that Christ gave this power to the apostles, the power to bind and to loose being plainly conferred in the eighteenth chapter of St. Matthew's gospel. To argue that this refers only to ecclesiastical faults is refuted by St. John's gospel (20:21-23), where Christ clearly confers upon the apostles the power to forgive or to retain sin. First, Christ makes evident that the power being conferred is the power he himself has exercised: "As the Father has sent me so I send you." Then he grants this power by conferring his Spirit. It is not a case of granting mere administrative authority. He is giving a real supernatural power. "When he had said this, he breathed upon them, and said to them, 'Receive the Holy Spirit; whose sins you shall forgive, they are forgiven them; and whose sins you shall retain, they are retained.'" Therefore, he adds to the commission to *preach* penance, long since clearly given, the special mission for the *forgiveness* of sins. The apostles are made capable of doing for sinners what they had seen their Master do. What he did by his proper power, they would do as delegated ministers. But although he could see into souls and discern their dispositions, his ministers would have to learn the dispositions of penitents from their sincere manifestation of conscience.

The reality of the pardon granted by the apostles and their successors (the objective element) always remains related to the dispositions of the penitent (subjective element). But the pardon granted to those rightly disposed is the true cause of divine forgiveness. What is done on earth is accepted in heaven. If the pardon granted by the ministers of Christ was merely an ecclesiastical reconciliation which would give no assurance of internal reconciliation, and would have nothing directly to do toward effecting an internal reconciliation, then there could be no significance attached to the acceptance of the reconciliation in heaven.

Here, too, is made plain the necessity of submitting serious sins to the power of the keys, the necessity, that is, of confession. This power is not to be used arbitrarily. A judgment is to be made, and judgment requires knowledge. The judge must know the faults which are either to be forgiven or not forgiven, and the disposition of the culprit. It is certainly unfitting to forgive someone who retains an affection for his evil ways. In this act of judgment which is essential to the sacrament we find the radical difference between penance and the first sacrament of Christian initiation, baptism.

The Scriptures give no instance where the apostles exercised their power to forgive sins. This is not to be wondered at, because the Acts of the Apostles are not greatly concerned with the daily life of the Christian communities but rather with the expansion of Christianity. Furthermore, the epistles are devoted to specific points of doctrine and to certain local incidents. Despite the great role penance was to play later, it was given but a small part in the life of the early Church.

C. Penance in the Infant Church

However, the historian, even abstracting from his faith, can safely presume the presence of the sacrament of penance in the earliest life of the Church, although in a less developed form than our present sacramental rite. We do not expect that the Church came forth from the Cenacle as fully developed as Minerva issuing from the brain of Jupiter; but the sudden emergence from its infant side of a completely new limb would have certainly shocked the faithful. Before the year 180, there is practically no textual evidence of the existence of a real penitential discipline.[17] There are, however, texts which date from the end of the second century until the middle of the third century which clearly manifest a penitential discipline functioning in regular fashion.[18] In these written documents, there is neither discussion of its beginning, nor is there any complaint against it as an innovation.

That an ecclesiastical function of this kind was the result of some kind of spontaneous generation about the year 180 seems improbable to the historian and impossible to the theologian. On the other hand, there is no reason to conclude that a well-developed discipline existed earlier despite the lack of textual evidence for it. It *is* reasonable, however, to conclude that some embryonic form of penitential discipline did exist and that it developed as circumstances demanded. The important point is that the exercise of the power to absolve (as it begins to appear in documents) never gives the impression of being a novelty.

[17]There may possibly be reference to sacramental penance in the *Didache*, "Doctrine of the Apostles" (c. 70-90, 120-150?), Chap. 4, n. 14, Chap. 14, n. 1, and in St. Clement's *Epistle to the Corinthians* (c. 96-98), Chap. 51-53; but these allusions are so vague and incomplete that little can be deduced from them.

[18]*The Shepherd of Hermas* (c. 150) contains a whole series of instructions on the necessity and efficacy of penance, although it is a difficult work to interpret; his doctrine is echoed by Clement of Alexandria (+ c. 216). Origen's (+ c. 255) teaching on penance is especially valuable for information concerning the Church's early discipline.

D. Penitential Discipline in the Third Century

Early in the third century we find clear reference to penitential discipline in the writings of Tertullian (+ c. 240/250)[19] and Hippolytus (+ 235)[20] and in the famous (lost) edict of Pope Callistus discussed by both writers. The edict seems to have stated that, after penance had been performed, the sin of adultery was to be forgiven. Actually to grant forgiveness for this sin (always recognized in theory as pardonable) seems to have been an innovation. Moreover, it is made clear that this forgiveness is to be granted but once. This second point is not, however, anything new; even at the time of St. Augustine (+430) the sacrament of penance was ordinarily received but once in a lifetime.[21]

The reasoning behind such rigor can be understood only if we remember the points mentioned above concerning the life of the early Christians. They felt that no human being could prudently judge that a Christian who had seriously sinned, done penance and been pardoned, and then fell again into the same sin, possessed the necessary dispositions for again receiving pardon. This fact clarifies a very important point concerning the sacrament of penance. Even today no priest may absolve a penitent unless he is morally certain that the one confessing is truly sorry for his sin and has a true purpose of amendment. Circumstances of time have resulted in authoritative ecclesiastical decisions to the effect that it is possible to be morally sure of such contrition even in one who has sinned repeatedly. This was not considered possible by the early Church.

The earliest documents concerning penitential discipline clearly state that sacramental absolution cannot be granted to those guilty

[19]Converted to Catholicism about 195, this brilliant Roman advocate placed his considerable talents at the service of Catholic truth. But his mystical bent attracted him to Montanism, a heretical sect extremely rigorist in its moral teaching, which held that sins committed after baptism were not to be forgiven. His *On Penance* exposes the Catholic practices, but a work of his Montanist period, *On Chastity*, is a violent attack on Catholic penitential doctrine in general and Pope Callistus in particular.

[20]Hippolytus also attacked St. Callistus on the grounds of "leniency" in penitential discipline (*Philosophumena*, "The Refutation of All Heresies," Bk. IX, Chap. 12). But he was a bitter personal enemy of the pope, and a puritan to boot; his reproaches are certainly exaggerated and lack little historical authority.

[21]Cf. the letter of Pope St. Siricius (+ 399) to Himerius of Tarragona, 6.

of certain sins, such as murder, apostasy and adultery. Those guilty of these sins were required to live out their days as penitents, and were left to the mercy of God. No one can say whether this discipline was universal or whether it was primitive, but it held sway for many years and in many places. Indeed, no one denied that the Church could forgive these sins in principle, and, *a fortiori*, it was never held that these sins were irremissible in themselves.

The question has been raised whether there existed in the early Church some form of private penitential discipline for secret sins. No evidence for the existence of such a discipline has been found. It is possible, of course, that bishops remitted public penances in some cases and absolved without public ritual, but there is no evidence of any recognized provision for private penance before the fifth century.

From early writings, especially St. Hippolytus, St. Cyprian and Origen, it is possible to reconstruct the penitential discipline of the third century clearly. The subject was a Christian guilty of a grave sin, either public or secret. If secret, the existence of the sin was publicly known by the absence of the guilty one from Communion; in those days all Christians except those excluded by sin ("excommunicated") partook of the sacred banquet. A voluntary confession was made to the bishop. It seems that in the case of a secret sin, the confession of the kind of sin was not made public, but the fact of the confession was made public. Since the fact that the Christian had sinned was already known, this public announcement of his reconciliation with God and the Church did him no spiritual damage.

There is evidence that the sinner often secretly consulted the bishop or a priest concerning the best manner of making his confession. After his confession, the sinner was separated from the Christian community and subjected to public humiliation, fasts, etc. A protracted satisfaction seems always to have preceded reconciliation. Reconciliation was publicly effected by the imposition of hands.

Tertullian, Hippolytus, St. Cyprian and Origen do not exhaust the third century literature on penance, but they do give its tenor, which was one of extreme severity. The fact that for nearly four centuries the Church refused to grant sacramental absolution more than once in a lifetime conveys forcefully the idea of how far the penitential discipline of the Church has progressed today.

E. The Origin of Private Penance

It was never the practice of the Church to remit sin without confession. Normally when a secret sin was confessed privately, the confession was also kept secret. When we speak here of private penance, we refer to private confession, private satisfaction, and private absolution.

As early as St. Augustine a distinction was made between sins of malice and sins of ignorance or weakness. When such distinctions became clearer, priests commonly began to judge that certain sins did not warrant public satisfaction and absolution, but that satisfaction and absolution could be taken care of privately. The practice of repeated reception of the sacrament of penance developed from this, since only public penance was unrepeatable. The practice of private penance developed first in the British Isles and was first brought to the continent by St. Columbanus and other Irish monks. From the fact that St. Augustine of Canterbury (+ c. 604) had no dispute with the British on this question (end of sixth century), it is evident that the practice was early known on the continent.

During the Carolingian period, the following principle was evolved: for occult sins, private penance; for public sins, public penance. Private penance came to be accepted as useful to the spiritual life. Alcuin recommends the practice to young people as a means of overcoming sin. By the ninth century the practice of annual confession had become quite common. All the books on penance of the Carolingian reform make it clear that public and private penance are but different modes of the same sacrament, and that both have the same purpose—the remission of sin.

The revival of learning and especially of theology in the eleventh century helped the speculative theology of penance catch up with its practice. The law of secrecy of the confessional came into being, and the Fourth Council of the Lateran (1215) legislated annual confession for all the faithful. The role that the Celtic and Anglo-Saxon monks played in spreading the custom of private penance was revived by the Friars Minor and the Friars Preachers, who diffused the custom of frequent confession and confessions of devotion.

F. Conclusion

This brief survey of the history of the development of the doctrine of the sacrament of penance should produce an awareness of two things:

1) Catholic scholars are well acquainted with the difficulties raised by opponents of the Church and can easily show that none of these difficulties are in any sense conclusive.

2) The confession of one's sins to a priest for the purpose of obtaining absolution is a very serious matter. Absolution is not some kind of miracle spot-remover to be used in cleaning up for Sunday. It is sacramental forgivness to be asked for only by a penitent who is truly sorry for his sins and willing to take every reasonable measure to avoid sinning again; it is to be granted only by a priest who is morally certain that the penitent is well disposed to receive the sacrament.

9. Summary and Conclusion

Penance offers the security of divine forgiveness of sins committed after baptism. The sacrament demands the exercise of the virtue of penance, but goes beyond it in its effects. The universality of the efficacy of this sacrament is symbolic of the infinite mercy of the Sacred Heart, for any sin whatsoever can be blotted out in penance if only the sinner will be truly sorry. This necessary sorrow must be expressed ordinarily by confession and satisfaction.

The true nature of the security of forgiveness is emphasized in the care with which the Church must administer the power of the keys which she received from Christ. Her laws, seen through the eyes of faith, are intended to guarantee the security of forgiveness to all, and not to withhold it from any who are worthy through sincere sorrow.

Extending the saving hand of Christ, the Church brings forth from her treasury an abundance of spiritual merits in the form of indulgences which complete the healing of the wounds of sin. So great is her mercy that she penalizes certain delinquents through excommunication and interdict in order to safeguard the sincere faithful from spiritual contagion and to recall to their spiritual senses her errant children.

The sacrament of penance is beautifully symbolized by the figure of Christ who stands at the gate of the sinner's heart and knocks, asking only for the sins which no man should desire to retain, wishing not to punish, but to forgive them.

A number of practical conclusions derive from the Church's teaching on penance, but all of them cannot be treated here. However, the following is a sampling.

1. When John the Baptist passed through the Jordan valley to prepare for the coming of Christ, the Jews to whom he preached were scandalized at his approach. For, although they were steeped in wickedness, they covered themselves with justice. Because of their blindness they considered sin to be linked with the performance of external works alone; for them, it was only a question of ritual and legal impurity rather than of moral impurity. In later years St. Paul tried to shake them from this artificial self-righteousness. He remarks: "For they, not knowing the justice of God and seeking to establish their own, have not submitted themselves to the justice of God" (Rom. 10:3).

John the Baptist came to reprove and replace this ignorance; his manner of dress and his manner of preaching were both designed to give mankind an example of repentance and confession. And because the Jews, for the most part, would not turn from their sins, they turned their backs on Christ. If they had pondered over their sins, Christianity would have had an easier beginning, for in seeking forgiveness of sin, they would have sought out the Redeemer from sin.

2. "The omnipotent God sometimes permits his elect to fall into offences, that he may give hope of pardon to others who lie down despairing in their guilt, if they will but turn to him with their whole

hearts; to such as these he opens the way of justice, because of their tears of repentance.

"Let us then be earnest in our repentance. Let us wash away with tears, and with fruits worthy of repentance, the evil we have committed. Let not that time be lost that is in mercy given to us, for we who see so many healed from their sins, what have we here but a pledge of heavenly mercy, in Jesus Christ our Lord who with the Father and the Holy Spirit, liveth and reigneth world without end. Amen."[22]

3. There is a vast difference between the moral and physical evils suffered by man. A broken arm does not affect every bone in the body: it is not a broken leg or back or neck, nor does it set off a chain reaction of similar injuries. Sin, on the other hand, since it is an offence against God, has infinite repercussions in the spiritual order. Despair arising from one sin can be the fuse which will ignite hundreds of other sins. The challenge offered by Christ to human nature does not consist in *restraining* from sin, but in totally *refraining* from sin.

4. Never underestimate the power of the priesthood in the confessional. A priest's ministerial work behind the confessional screen brings him in closer contact with souls than any other duty he may have. His intimate association with the Holy Spirit is never more apparent than when he says, "I absolve you. . . ."

5. In the ages before Christ, the history of sin as recorded in the Old Testament was the history of man's degeneration. Man was created to the image and likeness of God, but time and self-will marred this likness. When Christ united human flesh to himself, he reminded man of his original dignity and at the same time restored man's right to the title, "heir of heaven."

6. Each sacrament is a special remedy for sin. A sincere examination of conscience before confessing will tell us our predominant faults, and if we confess them aright, with true contrition and a firm purpose of amendment, we will receive through the sacrament the special graces that will enable us to eradicate this barrier between ourselves

[22]St. Gregory, Homily, *Vigil of the Fourth Sunday of Advent.*

and God. That is why the frequent reception of the sacrament comes so highly recommended to us by the Church and by her saints.

BIBLIOGRAPHICAL NOTE

St. Thomas' tract on Penance can be discovered in the *Summa,* Part III, Questions LXXX-XC inclusive, and in the "Supplement" to the *Summa.* As a complement to these studies the student should also read "Penance," by Augustine Klass, S.J., in Volume III of the English translation. A more popular approach to the sacrament of penance is the book *Penance, the Most Human of the Sacraments* (Ottawa: University of Ottawa Press, 1954), by Louis N. Boutin. Another work called *Sin and Penance* (St. Louis: Sands, 1932), by Rev. V. Galtier, is a semi-technical account of the sacrament and well worth reading. *Pardon and Peace,* by Alfred Wilson, C.P., (New York: Sheed & Ward, 1947) is a work the student will find of great practical value.

A multiple essay in the periodical *Altar and Home,* XXIV (1957), 3-30, contains several excellent articles on penance. They are entitled, "Sacrament of Peace"; "Hand of God"; "Beauty of Confession"; "Intimate Sacrament"; "Sin and Song"; "Shame of Christ"; and "Our Brother Has Come Back."

Two chapters in Volume II of *The Teaching of the Catholic Church* should be a great aid to the student. They are "Sin and Repentance," by E. J. Mahoney, and "The Sacrament of Penance," by H. Harrington.

CHAPTER FOURTEEN

Extreme Unction and Holy Orders

1. Introduction

The fifth and sixth sacraments of the Church listed by the Council of Trent are extreme unction and holy orders. Only for the sake of pedagogical convenience are these two sacraments treated in the same chapter, for there is no extrinsic ordination of one to the other, nor any reason even of fittingness why they should be considered together. Extreme unction is, in a sense, the perfecting of penance, since it brings to ultimate perfection at the hour of death the freedom from sin and the effects of sin which is inaugurated by baptism and intensified in the sacrament of divine pardon. Holy orders, on the other hand, may be compared with matrimony, in the sense that both are primarily social sacraments, the first providing for the perpetuation of members of the Mystical Body of Christ, the second establishing the apostolic continuity of the hierarchy who govern and teach those members and re-enact Christ's mediatorship.

Two quite different sacraments, then, will be studied in this chapter according to the order and the principles already theologically determined for the sacraments in general.

479

THE LAST ANOINTING

Death is the most important time in life. The instant of death witnesses the eternal fixing of the will upon good or evil. The time immediately preceding death, then, is of inestimable importance.

The Church exercises maternal solicitude over the growth and preservation of the life of grace in the souls of her children throughout their earthly journey. And in keeping with the importance of the occasion, she exercises more special care over those whom illness brings to the threshold of death. This special solicitude is manifested in the administration of the sacrament of extreme unction, which is a part of Christ's guarantee that he would not leave us orphans, especially in our hours of greatest need.

Extreme unction complements the work of penance in the remission of sin. In the early years of the Church's existence, there were not many heretical attacks against this sacrament. But during the Middle Ages and the period of the Reformation, the true doctrine was impugned, and the Church found it necessary to promulgate dogmatic decrees about the existence and nature of this sacrament.

Following St. Thomas, our investigation of extreme unction will be undertaken under the following headings:

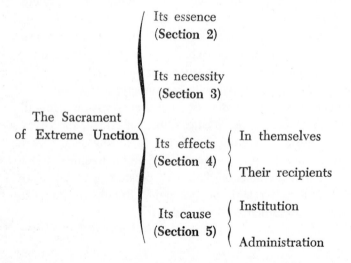

The Sacrament of Extreme Unction
- Its essence (Section 2)
- Its necessity (Section 3)
- Its effects (Section 4)
  - In themselves
  - Their recipients
- Its cause (Section 5)
  - Institution
  - Administration

2. The Essence of Extreme Unction

Extreme unction is *a sacrament of the New Law through which, by means of anointing with blessed oil and the prayer of the priest, health is conferred on the soul and sometimes on the body of one of the faithful who is both seriously ill and capable of grave sin.*

Every sacrament of Christ is an outward sign causing an inward grace, and is composed of two elements, **matter** and **form.** In extreme unction, the *remote* **matter** is olive oil specially blessed either by a bishop, or by a priest having special faculties from the Holy See. This oil is required for valid administration of the sacrament. The *proximate* **matter** consists in the use or application of the remote matter. In this sacrament the proximate matter is the anointing of the sick with blessed oil on the various senses and parts of the body. **The form is the** words used while anointing: "By this sacred anointing and his most tender mercy, may the Lord forgive you whatever sins you have committed by sight (hearing, smell, taste, speech, touch, walking). Amen."

A. The Matter

St. Thomas finds special suitability in oil as the matter of this sacrament. The spiritual healing which comes at the end of life should be complete, because no other follows it, and it should be gentle, to nourish the hope of which the dying stand in so much need. Olive oil, penetrating with its emollient effect to the interior of a thing and spreading over it, symbolizes both the completeness and the gentleness required.

Ordinarily, the anointings are to be made on the eyes, lips, ears, nostrils, hands and feet. Priests are anointed on the backs rather than the palms of the hands because of the previous anointing at **ordination. In case of necessity, a single anointing on the forehead or one of the senses suffices.**

B. The Form

The form of many sacraments is expressed as a declaration: "I baptize you"; "I absolve you." But the form of extreme unction is a petition: ". . . may the Lord forgive you. . . ." There are two reasons for this difference. The recipient of this sacrament is deprived of his strength, and he needs the help of prayers. The dying are about to rest in the hands of God alone, and it is fitting that we commit them to his care by our prayers.

3. The Necessity of Extreme Unction

A. The Purpose of the Sacrament

An important conclusion follows from the theology of this sacrament: **Extreme unction should not be delayed until there is extreme danger of death. It should be administered** *as soon as possible* **in a dangerous illness and while the recipient is in possession of his senses.** It is no charity to defer extreme unction until the subject can no longer consciously appreciate the comfort of the sacrament, thereby depriving him of the opportunity to receive its full spiritual efficacy. Unfortunately these considerations are only too often forgotten by the family of the sick Christian, whose anxiety for the natural health of the one they love may temporarily obscure spiritual and supernatural considerations.

Since it is not certain when the soul departs from the body, extreme unction may be administered conditionally for at least one-half hour after apparent death, and longer in some cases.

B. Repetition of the Sacrament

This sacrament cannot be repeated during the same illness, unless the sick person has recovered after he was anointed, and again fallen into danger of death. If a patient survives for a month, it is generally held that this period represents the cessation of the previous danger, and the sacrament may be repeated.

4. The Effects of Extreme Unction

A. The Effects Themselves

Each sacrament is instituted to attain one principal effect, although it may produce other effects consequently. All sacraments cause what they signify and signify what they cause. Hence the principal effect of extreme unction must be learned from its signification.

(1) Its Principal Effect

Just as baptism is a kind of washing, extreme unction is a kind of medication, and the purpose of medicine is to cure sickness. The chief effect of this sacrament is to cure the sickness of sin. As baptism is a spiritual regeneration and penance a spiritual resurrection, so extreme unction is a spiritual healing or cure.

Now every cure presupposes life in the one who is cured. Hence extreme unction is not a sacrament of the dead designed as a remedy against original or mortal sins which deprive the soul of spiritual life; rather it is a sacrament of the living, presupposing the state of grace in the recipient. It is designed to cause an increase of sanctifying grace, and thus to cure the soul of the weakness that is the result of original or actual sins which have *already* been forgiven. Hence extreme unction should always be preceded by confession (or, if this is impossible, by an act of perfect contrition), if the recipient is in the state of mortal sin; the practice of confessing before receiving this sacrament, even if one is not conscious of serious sins, is highly to be recommended.

Every sacrament imparts a special grace designed to assist the recipient in acquiring the distinctive benefits of the particular sacrament. Extreme unction provides a special grace which strengthens the soul against all evils, past, present and future, and which remits venial sins and destroys the remnants of past sin.

(2) Its Secondary Effects

There are two secondary effects of this sacrament. The first is the restoration of bodily health in those cases where such recovery is expedient for the good of the soul. The second is **the remission of mortal sin** for which the invalid has at least habitual attrition when, without fault, he has omitted confession and perfect contrition.

It is to be noted that the sacrament of penance requires at least an act of attrition exteriorly manifested for the forgiveness of mortal sin. Extreme unction, however, requires only habitual attrition to produce this effect secondarily. Hence, it is more important to anoint a dying person who is unconscious than to grant him conditional absolution, and every care must be exercised to see that such people receive extreme unction.

The effects of extreme unction may be seen clearly in this outline:

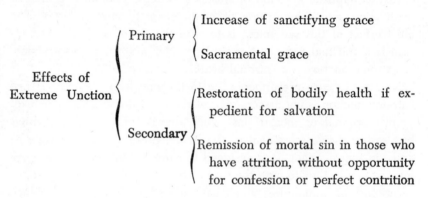

Effects of Extreme Unction

Primary
- Increase of sanctifying grace
- Sacramental grace

Secondary
- Restoration of bodily health if expedient for salvation
- Remission of mortal sin in those who have attrition, without opportunity for confession or perfect contrition

B. The Recipients of Extreme Unction

Any one of the faithful who is in danger of death from sickness or old age after attaining the use of reason can receive this sacrament. When there is doubt whether the sick person has reached the use of reason, whether he is truly in danger of death, or whether he is already dead, the sacrament is to be conferred conditionally. This condition is expressed by the priest, who precedes the form of the sacrament with the words, "If you are alive," or, "If you are capable."

In view of this doctrine, extreme unction is not administered to:

1) The unbaptized.

2) Infants and those who never reached the use of reason.

3) Those in danger of death from some cause other than sickness (e.g., soldiers before battle, criminals before execution, passengers in danger of shipwreck).

4) Those who remain willfully impenient in mortal sin. (But if there is any doubt of this, the sacrament is to be administered conditionally.)

5. The Cause of This Sacrament

A. Its Institution

The principal scriptural reference to the sacrament of extreme unction is found in the Epistle of St. James (5:14 ff.): "Is any one among you sick? Let him bring in the presbyters of the Church, and let them pray over him, anointing him with oil in the name of the Lord. And the prayer of faith will save the sick man, and the Lord will raise him up, and if he be in sins, they shall be forgiven him."

A possible allusion to this sacrament is made by St. Mark, who says of the mission of the apostles: "And going forth, they preached that men should repent, and they cast out many devils, and anointed with oil many sick people, and healed them" (6:12-13).

The effect intended in the administration of all the sacraments is the healing of the disease of sin. As is evident from the text of St. James, just such an effect is obtained by the use of this sacred rite. Thus, it is truly a sacrament.

The first mention among the documents of the Church of extreme unction as a sacrament is found in a letter written by Pope St. Innocent I to the Bishop of Gubbio in 416.[1] In its instruction on the sacraments, the Council of Florence, 1438-45, enumerated extreme unction among them, and gave specific information about its matter, form and administration.[2] At the Council of Trent an authoritative dogmatic declaration was issued.[3] The following are the principal points contained in the chapters and canons which this great Council of the Church devoted to extreme unction:

[1] Denz. 99.
[2] Denz. 700.
[3] Denz. 907-910; 926-929.

1) Extreme unction is Christ's special provision for his children at the crucial hour of death when Satan strives most vehemently to destroy them.

2) The Apostolic Tradition transmitted to the Church teaches that this is a true and proper sacrament of the New Testament instituted by Christ.

3) In the words of Sts. Mark and James (cf. *supra*), Christ teaches the matter, the form, the proper minister and the effects of this sacrament.

B. Its Administration

The minister for the *valid* administration of extreme unction is any priest, and no one who is not a priest. This is clear from the words of St. James, "let him bring in the presbyters of the Church." The Council of Trent has defined that this term "presbyters" refers exclusively to priests and bishops.[4]

In addition, the Code of Canon Law limits those who can *lawfully* administer extreme unction. The principal directive states that the pastor of the place where the sick person is staying, or another priest who has his express or reasonably presumed permission, is the lawful minister of the sacrament.[5]

THE SACRED SEALING

Holy orders is absolutely and necessarily divine in its origins. It impresses an indelible character upon the soul of its recipients, and thus sets the ministers of the Church apart from the laity. Historically, various errors have impugned this concept. In the Middle Ages, certain heretics taught that the powers of the priesthood originated with the faithful rather than with God. Some of these ideas were developed during the period of the Reformation. More recently, however, the Church has witnessed a different trend among those who have extended the notion of the priesthood of the laity beyond

---

[4]Sess. XIV, Chap. 3 and Can. 4, "Extreme Unction"; Denz. 910, 929.
[5]Can. 938. Other provisions are made by Can. 514 and 1368.

legitimate bounds, with a consequent diminution of the significance of, and respect for holy orders.

In order to safeguard the sacredness of the ministry, the Church has promulgated a great number of laws pertaining to holy orders. Much of this legislation deals with the selection and training of candidates and other highly technical matters. These considerations are extraneous to the purpose of the present study, and will be omitted. Following the general lines of St. Thomas' treatment, our consideration of holy orders will be presented according to this division:

Holy Orders
- Its essence (**Section 6**)
- Its necessity (**Section 7**)
- Its effects (**Section 8**)
  - In themselves
  - Their recipients
- Its cause (**Section 9**)
  - Institution
  - Administration

6. The Essence of Holy Orders

A. Its Definition

Holy orders is *a sacrament of the New Law whereby certain spiritual powers are conferred together with the grace to perform ecclesiastical duties worthily.*

St. Thomas, following Peter Lombard, employs the ancient definition that holy orders "is a seal of the Church whereby spiritual power is granted to the one ordained."[6] In the active sense, ordination is the action which confers a spiritual power and institutes a hierarchy of diverse grades in the Church. Thus it is an outward sign, a "conferring of a seal," of an inward grace and of spiritual

[6] Cf. *Supplement,* q. 34, a. 2.

power. As a sign instituted by Christ to give grace, holy orders is a sacrament.

B. The Parts of the Sacrament

Holy orders comprises seven parts. There are the major orders of priesthood, diaconate and subdiaconate, and the minor orders of acolyte, exorcist, lector and porter. The older theologians and some moderns hold that subdiaconate and the minor orders are truly sacraments, whereas certain more recent theologians deny this. Similarly, the older theologians regarded the episcopacy as the fulfillment of the priesthood, whereas recent theologians see it as a distinct order. Neither opinion is certain, although the Council of Trent in defining that holy orders is truly a sacrament makes no distinction among the various orders.[7]

Clerical tonsure, which is a ceremonial clipping of part of the hair of the head, is not a part of holy orders. By tonsure, aspirants are inducted into the clerical state and affiliated to a particular diocese if they are not religious; they are made subject to the laws for clerics, sharers in clerical privileges, and fitted for the reception of holy orders.

The practice of the Church in conferring orders led to various theological opinions about the matter and form of the different orders. In 1947 the Holy Father Pius XII issued an apostolic constitution on the subject which determined the imposition of hands as the matter for the episcopacy, priesthood and diaconate, and certain designated words from the Prefaces of the different ceremonies as the form. The matter, form and powers of the seven orders are represented in the graph on the opposite page.

7. The Necessity of Sacred Orders

Jesus Christ is pre-eminently a priest. By the very fact of his Incarnation, he became the perfect mediator between God and men who would offer the perfect sacrifice for the redemption of mankind.

---

[7]Council of Trent, Sess. XXIII, "On Holy Orders" (Denz. 959); cf. Denz. 963.
[8]Cf. Denz. 2301.

Order	Matter	Form	Power
Priesthood	Imposition of hands.	"We beseech thee, almighty Father, grant the dignity of the priesthood to this thy servant; renew in his heart the spirit of holiness, that he may hold the office, the second in importance, which he has received from thee, O God, and by the example of his life point out a norm of living."	Consecrate the Eucharist; forgive sins; administer sacraments not reserved to bishops; nourish the faithful by teaching and example.
Diaconate	Imposition of hands.	"Send forth upon him, we beseech thee, O Lord, thy Holy Spirit, by whom he may be strengthened in faithfully discharging the works of thy ministry through the gift of thy sevenfold grace."	Assist the priest immediately at solemn Mass; sing the Gospel; preach with permission of Ordinary; baptize solemnly and distribute Communion with special permission.
Subdiaconate	Handling of empty chalice & paten; handling of book of Epistles.	"Behold whose ministry is entrusted to you. Therefore, I exhort you so to conduct yourselves that you may be able to please God." "Receive the book of Epistles, and have the power of reading them in the holy Church of God, both for the living and for the dead, in the name of the Father and of the Son, etc."	Prepare matter for consecration in sacred vessels; serve as minister in solemn Mass; sing the Epistle; wash used corporals and purificators.
Acolyte	Handling of unlighted candle in candlestick and of empty cruets.	"Receive the candle and candlestick, and know that you are appointed to light the lights of the church in the name of the Lord." "Receive the cruet to minister wine and water for the sacrifice of the blood of Christ, in the name of the Lord."	Assist the subdeacon at solemn Mass; carry cruets at altar; light candles.
Exorcist	Handling of book of exorcisms.	"Take and commit to memory, and have the power to lay your hands upon the possessed, whether they are baptized or catechumens."	Expel demons. (Public exorcism requires permission of Ordinary.)
Lector	Handling of book of Lessons.	"Receive, and be readers of the word of God. If you fulfill your office faithfully and profitably, yours will be the reward of those who have duly administered the word of God from the beginning."	Read psalms and lessons in church; catechize; bless bread and first fruits.
Porter	Handling the keys.	"So act as if about to give an account to God of the things which are kept under these keys."	Guard the doors to admit the worthy and exclude the unworthy.

The perfect sacrifice of the perfect priest was confined in time and place to the first Good Friday on the hill of Calvary. But this sacrifice had to be extended to many if the divine plan of salvation was to become a reality. To extend the effects of that sacrifice and to apply its fruits down the ages and across the world, Christ instituted holy orders as a means for the continuation of his priestly work among men.

The divine architect leaves his impress upon his works so that they might mirror his likeness and perfection. Thus do the works of God proclaim his reality and his perfections to his creatures. The hallmark of divinity is order, and all creation is so ordered that the higher provides for the lower. This unity in diversity is the foundation of the beauty in the universe, and it is a reflection of the beauty of God. In order that this beauty should not be lacking in the Church, Christ established holy orders, so that some in the Mystical Body should deliver the sacraments to others. Thus they are made like to God in a most special way by co-operating with him, even as in a physical body some members act upon others.

According to the economy of salvation designed by divine wisdom and divine love, therefore, holy orders is necessary, not (except in very special circumstances) for the individual Christian, but for the Church of Christ. "In regard to the whole community," St. Thomas points out, "man is perfected . . . by receiving power to rule the community and to exercise public acts. Corresponding to this in the life of the spirit is the sacrament of order, according to the remark of Heb. 7:27, that priests offer sacrifices not for themselves only, but also for the people."[9]

8. The Effects of the Sacrament

A. The Effects Themselves

Like all sacraments of the living, holy orders causes an increase of sanctifying grace in the soul of the recipient. In addition, it confers a special sacramental grace which enables the recipient to discharge

[9]*Summa*, III, q. 65, a. 1.

his special spiritual duties. Holy orders also confers an indelible character upon the soul, which is a ministerial power whereby those ordained are deputed to their sacred functions. It is certain that a sacramental character is conferred in the priesthood and diaconate. It is the opinion of St. Thomas and of many reliable theologians (but by no means of all), that a character is impressed with the subdiaconate and the minor orders as well.

The different powers conferred by holy orders are included in the graph representing the various elements and parts of the sacrament. It should be noted that all of these powers and functions are related to the Eucharist. Now the Eucharist is the sacrament of unity in the Church, and this indicates that holy orders is a social sacrament, given as a remedy to the whole Church, and not as a personal favor to an individual.

B. The Recipients

The candidate for holy orders must fulfill certain conditions. Some of these are required for *valid* reception of the sacrament, while others are required for *lawful* reception.

(1) Conditions for Valid Reception

To receive holy orders validly, the one to be ordained must be a baptized male person with at least the habitual intention of receiving the sacrament.

The condition requiring an intention at least habitual is common to the reception of all the sacraments, for without this intention the reception would not be a human act.

The condition of being of the male sex may require some explanation. This is founded upon the teaching of St. Paul: "Let women keep silence in the churches, for it is not permitted them to speak, but let them be submissive, as the Law also says" (I Cor. 14:34). "For I do not allow a woman to teach, or to exercise authority over men; but she is to keep quiet" (I Tim. 2:12-13). The entire Christian tradition bears this out, for Eve did not discharge any sacerdotal function, nor is even the Blessed Virgin honored with any priestly title.

St. Thomas observes that it is as necessary that the recipient of orders be a male as that the recipient of extreme unction be sick. For just as extreme unction signifies essentially a kind of healing that would be meaningless for those in good health, so holy orders signifies an eminence of degree that cannot be signified by the female. Nor is this a misogynous attitude. It is simply a recognition of the divinely instituted and profound difference between the sexes, each of which is enabled to make a distinctive contribution to the building up of Christ's Mystical Body. It is no more an affront to womanhood to declare that women are incapable of the priesthood than it is an affront to declare that men are incapable of being the mothers of families. It may be remarked that while the unique glory of women is motherhood, there is a special distinction for those mothers whose sons are raised to holy orders.

Likewise, unbaptized males are incapable of receiving holy orders. Baptism imprints a character upon the soul which gives the subject the power to receive the other sacraments. Without this basic character, no other sacrament can be received validly.

(2) Conditions for Lawful Reception

Over and above the conditions required to receive holy orders validly, certain others must be fulfilled to receive the sacrament lawfully. If any of these are lacking, the sacrament is truly received, but such reception is contrary to the law, and hence, sinful.

Some of these conditions are established by divine law; others by the law of the Church. Each group will be examined briefly.

1. **Divine legislation.** For lawful reception of holy orders, divine law requires four things: the state of grace; the right intention; probity of life; and divine vocation.

    1) *The state of grace.* As a sacrament of the living, holy orders requires that recipients be in the state of grace. For anyone knowingly to receive orders in the state of sin would be a sacrilege, but the orders would still be received validly.

    2) *The right intention.* This is not the same as the intention (at least habitual) to receive orders which is required for validity. Rather this is a matter of the *purpose* one has in receiving

orders. The laws of the Church warn superiors not to ordain those who give evidence that they desire the priesthood for some motive other than the purpose of promoting God's glory and of saving souls through the exercise of the sacred ministry. Especially to be deterred are those suspected of desiring personal gain in the priesthood. The Church has established an elaborate inquiry to assure that candidates for the priesthood are properly motivated.

But even if a candidate were motivated by the worst possible intentions in receiving orders, he would still receive them validly, and could exercise them validly, if all conditions for validity were present. The priesthood is for the people, and no amount of personal unworthiness on the part of the priest can deprive those who need his ministrations. A priest forbidden the exercise of his office in punishment of crimes is still able to grant valid absolution, and he may do so lawfully if a dying Catholic asks him.

3) *Probity of life.* Everyone called to the priesthood is called to be a worthy priest. This means that he must give positive signs of virtue. Those who lead others in divine things should be examples of their own teaching. Purity, obedience, charity toward others are indispensable for the worthy exercise of the priesthood. These and other qualities are diligently investigated by authorities before promoting a candidate to orders.

4) *Divine vocation.* A priest is a mediator between God and men, and the dispenser of divine mysteries. But no one may lawfully undertake to dispense the goods of another without his authorization. Hence a divine vocation is required for holy orders. This is emphasized by St. Paul: "And no man takes the honor to himself; he takes it who is called by God, as Aaron was" (Heb. 5:4).

Among the more prominent signs of a divine vocation are these:

a) A good intention to honor God and promote the salvation of oneself and one's neighbor.

b) The ability to discharge ecclesiastical tasks. This includes requisite health and the ability to complete successfully the studies required of students for the priesthood.

c) A life of virtue and perseverance in grace. The best guarantee of a virtuous future is a virtuous past. Candidates for the priesthood must give positive signs that they are both willing and able to live a life of grace and virtue constantly. From the outset, candidates for the priesthood are given special direction calculated to lead them to the degree of spiritual perfection and stability requisite for the worthy fulfillment of their ministry.

d) An official call or summons by the legitimate ecclesiastical superior. In every ceremony of ordination there is the official call or "vocation" by the ordaining prelate. Those are said to be called by God who are called by the legitimate rulers of his Church.

2. **Ecclesiastical legislation.** In addition to the qualities required by divine law for the worthy reception of holy orders, the Church makes further stipulations. These are very frequently complex, and designed to protect the sacredness of the ministry. There are eight requirements:

1) *Testimonial letters* from designated authorities who testify to the candidate's qualifications must be presented to the ordaining prelate.

2) *Canonical age* must be attained. For subdiaconate, twenty-one years; for diaconate, twenty-two; for priesthood, twenty-four years completed.

3) *Required knowledge* is demanded in different degrees for the different orders. Reception of tonsure and minor orders requires the completion of the course in philosophy and the beginning of the study of theology. Subdiaconate is not ordinarily conferred until near the end of the third year of theology. The diaconate is not conferred until the fourth year of theology has begun, and the priesthood only after the first half of the fourth year of theology. All the above studies must be completed successfully in seminaries approved by the Holy See.

4) *Examinations* dealing with the orders about to be received (and also on certain theological tracts in the case of major orders) must be passed successfully.

5) *Reception* of minor orders must be preceded by a *retreat* of three days. A six day retreat is required for major orders.

6) *Intervals* determined by law must be observed between the reception of the various orders so that the candidate is led gradually to the priesthood.

7) A *title to sufficient and suitable support* that will guarantee that the cleric will be able to devote himself entirely to the work of Christ's Church is required for ordination. Some of the common titles are: service to the diocese for which one is ordained; poverty or solemn profession for religious clerics. These titles guarantee that a diocesan cleric will be able to find decent support in exchange for his labors in his diocese, and that a religious will be provided for by the institute to which he belongs.

8) *Freedom from irregularities and impediments to orders.* This is a highly technical subject of interest only to clerics and their superiors, and no treatment of it is necessary here.

9. The Cause of Holy Orders

A. Its Institution

That holy orders is truly a sacrament is clearly taught in the Scriptures. "Do not neglect the grace that is in thee, granted to thee by reason of prophecy with the laying on of hands of the presbyterate" (I Tim. 4:14). "For this reason I admonish thee to stir up the grace of God which is in thee by the laying on of my hands. For God has not given us the spirit of fear, but of power and of love and of prudence" (II Tim. 1:6-7). Here we have described a sense-perceptible sacred action (the laying on of hands), the *proximate* matter of the sacrament, and the pronouncing of an accompanying prayer (cf. Acts 6:6), the words or form, by a duly constituted minister (the presbyterate; St. Paul himself). This whole ceremony is significative of the passing on of the priestly power of Christ, and confers grace for this sacred office on its recipient. As the Council of Trent declares: "Since it is very clear from the testimony of Scripture, from the Apostolic Tradition, and from the unanimous consent of the Fathers, that grace is conferred by sacred ordination, which is effected by words and external signs, no one should doubt that order is truly and properly one of the seven sacraments of holy Church. . . ."[10]

As a true sacrament, holy orders must have been instituted immediately by Christ himself, although it would seem that he left the specific determination of its matter and form to his Church, so that proper adjustments could be made in accordance with changing circumstances. Neither Sacred Scriptures nor the Church informs us for certain of the exact moment of its institution. But it seems likely that Christ instituted this sacrament at the Last Supper when he said to the apostles, "Do this in remembrance of me" (Lk. 22:19; cf. I Cor. 11:25).[11]

B. The Minister of the Sacrament

The ordinary minister of holy orders is a consecrated bishop, and no other. The episcopacy is the perfection of priestly power by which a bishop is enabled to dispense the priesthood to others. Simple priests do not have this power.

In certain cases determined by law, an extraordinary minister who is not a bishop may confer tonsure and the minor orders.

Generally speaking, the ordaining bishop is the Ordinary of the place where the candidate was born, or where the candidate has his residence. Exceptions to this general rule are provided in the law.

10. Summary and Conclusion

In the sacrament of extreme unction we glimpse the Divine Healer; in holy orders we see the Eternal Priest. Both are indications of the unfailing care with which God surrounds his children.

[10]Sess. XXIII, Chap. 3, "On Holy Orders" (Denz. 959); cf. Denz. 963.
[11]Cf. the Council of Trent, Sess. XXII, Can. 2; Denz. 949.

The hour of death brings fear and uncertainty into every heart. Death may sometimes be the lesser of evils, but it is always an evil. Faced with death, men realize the inadequacy of all human succor. Only God, the master of life and the conqueror of death, can fortify and console the soul in the face of death.

This strength and consolation is abundantly provided in **extreme** unction. It lends divine strength for the final struggle; it brings divine consolation with the knowledge that the remnants of sin are destroyed as a preparation for eternal life. So important is this sacrament that every Christian should pray daily that he may **receive it** in the hour of his death, and each should do everything possible to procure it in time for the faithful who are dying. Extreme unction is the final sign of Christ's care in this life, the last application of his saving grace to the soul.

The saving work of Christ is continued through his priesthood, inseparably united to Christ himself in the Eucharist. The priest is a mediator between God and man, a dispenser of divine gifts. Nowhere is his mediation seen more clearly than in his eucharistic ministry, wherein he offers mankind through and with Christ to God, and where he brings God to men in return. It is true that the priest is for the people; it is also true that the priest is for God. No one is ever a priest solely for himself.

Humanly speaking, then, the priest sets out on a lonely journey. He must remain in the world, else his priesthood does not avail those for whom he is ordained. He must not become of the world, worldly, else his life beclouds the brightness of the divine image he is called to reflect, not only by what he does, but also by what he is. His ordination makes him a servant of the eucharistic Christ, and his heart must accept this destiny, for no other fulfillment shall ever be given him.

The Church must be solicitous for good priests, and she must train them well. She prays that they may increase both in number and in quality. But if, unhappily, a choice must be made, the quality is always to be preferred. It is unthinkable that Christ would not give the grace of divine vocation sufficiently to insure an adequate priesthood. Yet there are many places where the number of priests is far short of the needs. Perhaps the defect is to be found in the home and in the hearts of young men. Grace is a gift, not a compulsion, and some there are who reject it. Then there are homes in which the seed of the divine vocation is smothered by the weeds of worldly cares, weeds cultivated perhaps by the very parents who should be solicitous for the true happiness of those whom they thwart.

The priesthood is a great sign of contradiction, for it is a living declaration of the dependence of man upon Christ, and especially of the priest himself upon Christ. To acknowledge this dependence is to go against the grain of nature with its heritage of pride from the primal sin. To do this occasionally is not much; to do it as a way of life is quite another thing, and few are chosen. Yet only thus can mankind return to God through Christ whose kingdom is for the childlike in soul. Christ the Priest has provided the means through holy orders by which the fruits of his redemption are applied that bring the elect to life everlasting.

Two practical points are offered in particular for the thoughtful consideration of the student.

1. "My eyes have seen vanities, but now let them be shut to the world, and open to thee alone, my Jesus; and pardon me all the sins I have committed by my seeing.

"My ears have been open to detraction, profaneness and unprofitable discourses: let me now give ear to thy word, to thy commands, and to thy call; and pardon me, O Jesus, all the sins I have committed by my hearing.

"I have taken delight in the perfumes of this world, which are nothing but corruptions: now let my heart and prayers ascend like incense in thy sight, and pardon me, O Lord, all the sins I have committed by my sense of smell.

"My tongue has many ways offended, both in speaking and tasting; now let its whole business be to cry for mercy: pardon me, dear Jesus, all the sins I have committed by words, or by any excess in eating and drinking.

"My hands have offended in contributing to many follies injurious to myself and to my neighbor: now let them be lifted up to heaven in testimony of a penitent heart; and pardon me, O Lord, all the sins I have committed by the ill use of my hands.

"My feet have gone astray in the paths of vanity and sin: now let me walk in the way of thy commandments; and forgive me, O Lord, all the sins I have committed by my disordered steps."[12]

2. "For the social needs of the Church Christ has provided in a particular way two sacraments which he instituted. Through matrimony . . . provision is made for the external and properly regulated increase of Christian society . . . through holy orders men are set aside and consecrated to God, to offer in sacrifice the eucharistic Victim, to feed the flock of the faithful with the bread of angels and the food of doctrine, to guide them in the way of God's commandments and counsels, and to strengthen them with all the other supernatural helps."[13]

BIBLIOGRAPHICAL NOTE

A consideration of the sacrament of extreme unction is taken up in the "Supplement" to the *Summa*, Questions XXIX-XXXIII. For a more popular review of the doctrine, the book *Extreme Unction* (New York: The Macmillan Co., 1931), by John P. Ardendzen, is well worth reading. *Extreme Unction* (St. Louis: B. Herder Book Co., 1927), by Adrian J. Kilker, is a canonical treatise on the subject, although it also contains a consideration of the dogmatic, historical and liturgical aspects. A brief article in the *Theology Digest*, IV (1956), 185-188, called the "Meaning of Extreme Unction," by P. De Letter, would also be a helpful source for a deeper insight into this sacrament.

The tract on holy orders is treated in the "Supplement," Questions XXXIV-XL. For an easier approach to this teaching, the book *The Christian Priesthood: or the Sacrament of Order* (New York: The Macmillan Co., 1931), by Charles Cronin, gives an excellent digest

[12]Rite used in the anointing of the sick as found in the *Roman Ritual*.
[13]Pope Pius XII, *Mystici Corporis* (Paulist Press trans.), 7.

and explanation of the important doctrinal points concerned with the priesthood. Another book which is highly recommended is *Holy Orders and Ordination* (St. Louis: B. Herder Book Co., 1928), by J. Tixeront.

A short but solid study of orders is the essay, "The Seven Orders of Christ," by J. Crehan in *Theological Studies,* XIX (1958), 81-93. Consult also *The Teaching of the Catholic Church,* Volume II, Chapter XXIV, "The Sacrament of Order," by Very Rev. Canon C. Cronin.

CHAPTER FIFTEEN

Marriage in Christ

1. Introduction

The importance of matrimony in the Christian life is self-evident. To dwell on its importance would seem to stress the obvious. Yet it may legitimately be asked if many of those who will agree to its importance have a grasp of the profound truths that make it so. Beyond the economic, sociological and legal aspects of marriage there lie the truly radical reasons for its importance. These reasons are spiritual; they are based upon the revelation made by Jesus Christ; they are properly the province of theology.

While it is true that marriage is a many-faceted reality and that many diverse areas of knowledge make vital contributions to our understanding of it, the most fundamental realities concerned are spiritual and theological. Divorced from the theological doctrine on marriage, even a study of the canon law which regulates marriage so minutely will fail to unfold the fulness of its meaning. As St. Thomas points out, law is an extrinsic principle of human action: it is a guide for acting, not a principle of being. Christian marriage is a sacrament, a channel of grace, and grace is an intrinsic principle of divine life in man. From the Church's law we receive divine guidance; from grace we receive divine assistance, which works interiorly to conform men to the image of God, not only in what they do, but also in what they are.

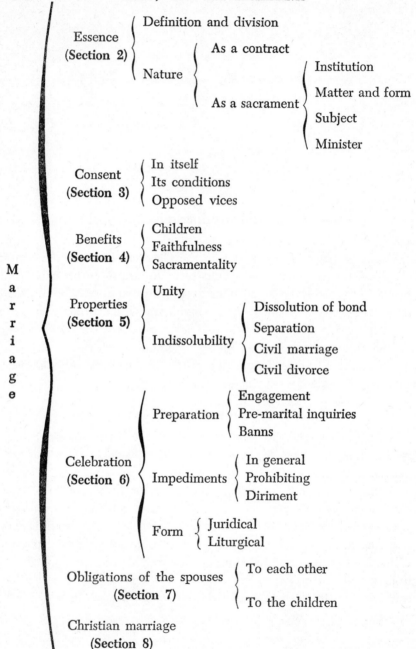

Marriage

- Essence (Section 2)
  - Definition and division
  - Nature
    - As a contract
    - As a sacrament
      - Institution
      - Matter and form
      - Subject
      - Minister
- Consent (Section 3)
  - In itself
  - Its conditions
  - Opposed vices
- Benefits (Section 4)
  - Children
  - Faithfulness
  - Sacramentality
- Properties (Section 5)
  - Unity
  - Indissolubility
    - Dissolution of bond
    - Separation
    - Civil marriage
    - Civil divorce
- Celebration (Section 6)
  - Preparation
    - Engagement
    - Pre-marital inquiries
    - Banns
  - Impediments
    - In general
    - Prohibiting
    - Diriment
  - Form
    - Juridical
    - Liturgical
- Obligations of the spouses (Section 7)
  - To each other
  - To the children
- Christian marriage (Section 8)

An understanding of Christian marriage requires a synthesis of theological and canonical knowledge as a basis. Such a synthesis is herein offered within the framework of the teaching of St. Thomas. Since the time he wrote his profound treatise there has been a certain amount of theological development and a great deal of canonical change. However, the basic principles remain unchanged, and the framework within which he developed his doctrine is grounded upon principles so universal that it remains today an ideal reference for the necessary synthesis.

Most professional treatises on marriage are designed for the use of the clergy whose duty it is to safeguard the sanctity of this sacrament. Much of the technical data of these treatises is of little value to the generality of the laity under ordinary circumstances. The matter here presented will emphasize rather the role of the laity in marriage. For this reason, certain canonical technicalities will be omitted, while others will be abbreviated. On the other hand, the theological consideration of the nature and function of the sacramental grace of marriage will be developed in some detail.

2. The Essence of Matrimony

A. Its Definition and Division

(1) Nominal Definition

Several different words are used to describe the fundamental idea of marriage; they express different aspects of the reality:

1) Referring to its essence, it is called **conjugal union,** because marriage is essentially a conjunction of two.

2) Referring to its cause, it is called **nuptial union,** because marriage is caused by the ceremony in which the bride is "veiled off" from potential union with other men ("nuptial" comes from *nubere,* which means "to veil").

3) Referring to its *effect,* it is called **matrimony,** from *matris munus,* which means "the duty of motherhood."

(2) *The Real Definition*

Two distinguishable realities are expressed by the term "marriage," since in the natural order it is a contract and in the supernatural order it is a sacrament of divine institution.

The classical definition of the **natural contract of marriage** is: *the marital union of a legally competent man and woman involving the undivided sharing of a common life.* The elements of this definition are the following:

1) Its essence is found in the *union of one man with one woman.*

2) It is a *marital* union, not simply a contract of friendship, or business, or concubinage; the very term (from *maritus*, which means "husband") signifies a noble union for the raising of a family.

3) That the man and woman must be *legally competent* implies that not every man and woman can enter into such a contract with one another.

4) It involves the *undivided sharing of a common life,* which indicates the exchange of the mutual obligations and rights which refer to the raising of a family. Therefore, a common "bed, board, and dwelling" pertain to this natural conjunction of man and woman, as well as a loving union of souls and sharing of goods.

The natural contract of marriage is part of the natural law in this sense: the inclination to form such a contract is provided by nature itself, even though its fulfillment is under the dominion not of nature but of man's free will. Moreover, nature provides not only for the existence of offspring but for their necessary care until they are capable of providing for themselves. Thus nature teaches human beings the natural truth: a lifetime together is necessary for parents to provide for their children. Mother and father each have their separate and important parts to play in accomplishing this work.

Since marriage is necessary to society it is not, of course, an obligation which falls directly upon each individual. But each individual must take some part, indirect though it may be, in fulfilling an obligation which rests upon the community, unless the fulfillment of some higher purpose provides an exemption.

(3) The Real Definition of the Sacrament

By faith we know that marriage is a true **sacrament** instituted by Jesus Christ.[1] It may be defined as: *a sacrament of the New Law in which, through the lawfully exchanged consent of the contracting parties, grace is given to them for the proper and Christian fulfillment of the duties of matrimony.* The following points are included in the definition:

1) One of the seven sacraments *of the New Law.*

2) *The lawfully exchanged consent of the contracting parties* expresses the matter and form of the sacrament; this mutual consent, as we shall see, is essential to the marriage contract. This phrase also indicates that the ministers are the contracting parties themselves.

3) *In which grace is given,* etc., indicates the special bond established between the partners and the special sacramental graces bestowed to enable them to fulfill in a Christian manner the duties arising from the married state.

Thus it is easy to see that the essence of the sacrament of matrimony is found in the matrimonial contract itself, which is made by the blessing of Christ a special channel of divine grace (Can. 1012).

(4) The Kinds of Marriage

To discuss this great sacrament intelligently, we must make certain distinctions and clarify certain terms. Thus we must distinguish between the act of contracting matrimony, and the state of matrimony which is the result of the contract. These divisions are also of great importance:

1. **As to** *dignity* **marriage is called:**

1) *Legitimate,* when unbaptized persons are validly married (Can. 1015, § 3).

2) *Ratified,* when baptized persons are validly married, but since the contract was made have not been joined in physical union (Can. 1015, § 1).

3) *Ratified and consummated,* when the partners of a ratified marriage have been joined in the flesh (*ibid.*).

---

[1] Cf. the Council of Trent, Sess. XXIV, Can. 1 on matrimony; Denz. 971.

2. As to *celebration* marriage is called:
    1) *Public,* when it is celebrated openly in the form prescribed by the Church.
    2) *Secret,* when it is celebrated in the form prescribed by the Church, but in secret without banns being published or registration in the parish records.
    3) *Clandestine,* when not celebrated in the form prescribed by the Church.
3. As to *validity* marriage is called:
    1) *Valid,* when all the conditions for a true marital contract are present.
    2) *Invalid,* when one or more of the necessary conditions are lacking.
    3) *Putative,* when the marriage is actually invalid, but one or both of the partners are in good faith. It is putative until both partners are aware of the nullity (Can. 1015 § 4).

These terms and divisions should be kept in mind, since they will be used in explaining the various theological and legal aspects of marriage which will be discussed.

B. The Nature of the Contract of Matrimony

We have seen that since marriage is necessary for the continuation of society it is provided for by the law of nature. On the other hand, the obligation of matrimony does not fall upon every individual. In what, then, does this natural institution consist? This we must know so that we may determine where true marriage exists. To do this we must recall the distinction between the *act* of contracting marriage and the matrimonial *state.*

The essence of the **act of contracting marriage** consists in *the mutual consent, exteriorly manifested, whereby a man and a woman give and accept mutually the exclusive and perpetual right over each other in regard to acts which are of themselves suitable for the generation of children.*

The *mutual consent* is the adequate efficient cause of the marriage. This man does not have to marry this woman; but if they do marry, it is their mutual consent to *this kind of a union* which effects the marriage (Can. 1081, § 1). If the right to the procreation of children is withheld by either party, there is no marriage.

The essence of the **state of matrimony** consists in *the perpetual obligation of the spouses to perform mutually those duties which follow from the legitimate matrimonial contract.* The obligation to provide the circumstances in which children can be properly brought into the world and properly reared (such as the sharing of "bed, board, and dwelling") cannot be evaded without the consent of the public authority, granted for a just cause. The obligation, however, to perform the acts ordained to the procreation of children arises when the other spouse desires to exercise the right of these acts.

The question of whether the actual exercise of the acts pertains to the essence of marriage presents itself at this point. The answer is that, like a common dwelling, the *exercise* of these acts pertains to the perfection of marriage, not to its essence. The answer becomes clear when we advert to the fact that these things are licit only after marriage itself is essentially present. Therefore, they do not themselves belong to the essence of marriage. Adam and Eve were truly married in Paradise; Mary and Joseph were truly married.

C. The Sacrament of Matrimony

Since this is an involved question, a proper understanding of the answer requires the separate consideration of several factors. We will consider first its institution, then its matter and form, its subject, and finally the minister of this sacrament.

(1) The Institution of Matrimony

Marriage is an institution of the natural law. The specific good which this natural institution seeks to accomplish is the continuation of the human race by the procreation and rearing of children. What constitutes a satisfactory education of children varies according to conditions. Therefore, more or less is required of matrimony as more or less is required for the education of children. Since in the New Law children are to be reared in the grace and divine love which is brought into the world by Christ, and this is a supernatural work, supernatural help is especially necessary to fulfill the tasks imposed by matrimony. For this reason the natural institution of marriage was raised by Christ to a supernatural level; Christ made it a sacrament.

Three things are necessary for a sacrament of the New Law, and all of them are found in Christian marriage:

1) *An external sign.* In matrimony this is the expression of mutual consent. This sign signifies something sacred, namely, the union of man and wife, itself significative of the union of Christ and his Church (cf. Eph. 5:23).

2) *A sign which causes grace.* St. Paul says of marriage that it "is a great mystery—I mean in reference to Christ and to the Church" (Eph. 5:32). Christian marriage is mysterious precisely because it signifies the union of Christ with the Church. Christ is united to the Church by supernatural grace, which he, as Head of the Church, causes and infuses in his members. Thus, too, Christian marriage is instituted to cause supernatural grace in the partners.

3) *A sign divinely instituted.* This is implicit in the Pauline text, since only God can make purely natural things the causes of supernatural grace.

When did Christ institute this sacrament? Christ spoke of marriage at different times, and theologians maintain that he instituted the sacrament gradually.

1) He sanctified and consecrated matrimony by his presence at the wedding in Cana (Jn. 2:1-11).

2) He sanctioned the essential properties of marriage, unity and indissolubility, and restored it to its original perfection (Matt. 19:3-9).

3) After the resurrection Christ definitively instituted marriage as a sacrament together with the other sacraments (cf. Matt. 28:20; Mk. 16:15 f.).

It is defined by the Church that marriage is a true sacrament and that it confers grace.[2]

[2]Cf. the Council of Trent, Sess. VII, Can. 1; Denz. 844.

(2) The Matter and Form of Matrimony

We have seen that each of the sacraments is composed of two elements, the matter and the form. Certain teachings of the Church must be noted in order to understand how these elements are found in matrimony.

It is the teaching of the Church that the mutual consent of the contracting parties, expressed by words of the present tense, is the efficient cause of matrimony.[3] It also teaches that for the faithful the contract and the sacrament are one and the same thing; they cannot be separated.[4] Moreover, every marriage between Christians is a sacrament.[5] From this it follows that whatever is the matter and form of the contract will be the matter and form of the sacrament as well.

In contracts the externally expressed willingness to exchange something is the material element. The externally expressed acceptance of this offer is the formal element. With it the contract is made. In matrimony the groom offers to the bride dominion over himself in those things which pertain to the generation and rearing of offspring. This offering is the *matter* of the contract. Its acceptance by the bride is the *form*. Since by its very nature the contract is mutual, the bride also makes the offer and the groom accepts. With this the contract and the sacrament are complete. From this doctrine several practical conclusions follow:

1) Whenever two baptized persons (including heretics) validly marry, they receive the sacrament of matrimony no matter what their wish may be, since for Christians the contract and the sacrament are inseparable.

2) Since matrimony is essentially a contract, what pertains to contracts pertains to matrimony. Thus, for example, it is possible to contract marriage by proxy (Can. 1088).

3) Since for Christians the contract is the sacrament, the Church alone can legislate concerning its essence. The power of the state is limited to the civil effects (Can. 1016).

[3]Council of Florence, *Decree for the Armenians;* Denz. 702.
[4]Cf. the allocution of Pope Pius IX, *Acerbissimum Vobiscum*, Sept. 27, 1852; Denz. 1640.
[5]Cf. the encyclical of Leo XIII, *Arcanum divinae sapientiae*, Feb. 10, 1880; Denz. 1854.

4) The marriage of infidels becomes a sacrament immediately on the baptism of *both* parties, but since it is a mutual contract it cannot be more strict or more sacred on the part of one than it is on the part of the other party. Therefore, it is never a sacrament for one and not for the other. Marital consent does not have to be renewed when the second partner is baptized, but it is advisable that the nuptial blessing be sought.

(3) The Subjects or Recipients of the Sacrament of Matrimony

Those who are to be married must fulfill certain conditions in order that the marriage be **valid**. These conditions being fulfilled, further conditions must be present in order that the marriage be not only valid but also **lawful** and its reception **fruitful**.

1. **For valid reception the subject must:**
   1) be *baptized,* and this must be true of both partners (see above).
   2) have the *intention,* at least implicitly, of receiving and administering the sacrament. Baptized persons could not have the intention of making a marriage contract without implicitly intending the sacrament, even though they may deny that they intend the sacrament.
   3) be free from all *diriment* (i.e., invalidating) impediments. These impediments may arise from the natural, the divine, or the ecclesiastical law.
   4) be *present,* personally or by proxy (Can. 1088, § 1).
   5) if either party is a Catholic the marriage must take place according to the *juridical form* prescribed by the Church.

2. **For lawful and fruitful reception the subject who fulfills the above requirements must also:**
   1) be free from *prohibiting* impediments, since they gravely oblige Christians in conscience.
   2) be *confirmed,* unless they are unable to receive this sacrament without grave inconvenience (Can. 1021, § 2).
   3) be in the *state of grace,* since matrimony is a sacrament of the living. It is not obligatory but it is strongly advised that

those about to be married receive the sacrament of penance
and the Holy Eucharist (Can. 1033). It is fitting that they
should receive at the marriage ceremony itself. While it has
long been customary for members of the wedding party to
receive Communion, the laudable custom is being established
in many places of encouraging the guests as well to communicate together with the bridal couple.

4) observe *the rites and ceremonies of the Church* (Can. 733, § 1).

5) listen reverently to the *counsel of their parents,* especially if
they are minors. In the choice of a state of life or of a marriage partner obedience to parents is not required. Yet it is
the better part of prudence to seek and consider well the advice of parents regarding such matters. Pastors are required
to attempt to deter minors from marrying without the consent of their parents and may not assist at such marriages
without consulting the Ordinary (Can. 1034).[6]

(4) The Minister of Sacramental Matrimony

Since for the baptized the contract of marriage is the sacrament,
those who make the contract are the ministers of the sacrament. This
must be the case since the Church recognizes marriages performed,
under certain conditions, without a priest (Can. 1098). The priest
who officiates does so as the Church's principal *witness.*

Because matrimony is a sacrament of the living, those who receive
it while in the state of serious sin commit a sacrilege. Yet even though
they are ministers of the sacrament they do not commit an additional
sacrilege, since they are not ministers officially consecrated for divine worship.

3. Matrimonial Consent

The essence of the act of marriage is matrimonial consent. It requires
special attention since the quality of consent is the first thing to
be judged in assessing the validity of a marriage. The points of inquiry
are outlined thus:

[6]The Ordinary, in most cases, is the bishop of the diocese or his vicar-general.

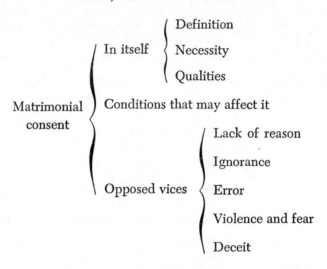

Matrimonial consent
- In itself
  - Definition
  - Necessity
  - Qualities
- Conditions that may affect it
- Opposed vices
  - Lack of reason
  - Ignorance
  - Error
  - Violence and fear
  - Deceit

A. Matrimonial Consent Considered in Itself

(1) The Definition of Consent

The Code of Canon Law states: "**Matrimonial consent** is *an act of the will whereby each party gives and accepts an exclusive and perpetual right over the body for acts which are of themselves suitable for the generation of children*" (Can. 1981, § 2).

1) *An act of the will*—indicates that consent must be **free.**
2) *Each party*—indicates that it is a **bilateral** contract.
3) *Gives and accepts a . . . right over the body*—indicates the **essential object** of the contract, which is the mutual exchange of marital rights.
4) *For acts which are of themselves suitable for the generation of children*—indicates that the contract is **limited** and does not grant absolute and unqualified rights over each other.
5) *An exclusive and perpetual right*—indicates the essential properties of matrimony: **unity** and **indissolubility.**

(2) Its Necessity

The Code of Canon Law states: "The consent of the parties, lawfully expressed between persons who are capable according to law, makes the marriage; and no human power can supply this consent" (Can. 1981, § 1). Since the consent makes the marriage, and since consent is a free rational act or it is nothing, it is obvious that a free rational act of consent must be expressed by both parties or there is no marriage. The parties must, of course, be free to consent to such a contract. A marriage without such consent is as impossible as a square circle.

(3) Its Qualities

Valid matrimonial consent must be:

1) **True and internal,** i.e., both parties must sincerely intend to accept the matrimonial obligations.
2) **Free,** i.e., consent must be given with sufficient knowledge and deliberation, and without error, violence or grave fear.
3) **Mutual and simultaneous,** i. e., it must be the consent of *both* parties expressed *at the same time.*
4) **Present.** Consent regarding the future causes engagement, not marriage.
5) **Externally manifested.** A bilateral contract cannot be purely internal. If possible the consent should be expressed in words since this is the normal manner of manifesting one's mind.

B. Conditions Which Affect Consent

A **condition to a contract** is *a circumstance upon which one or both of the contracting parties desired the validity of his consent to depend.* Since matrimony is both a sacrament and a contract no condition can be placed which is not in accord with its nature as either sacrament or contract. A condition contrary to its essence clearly invalidates matrimony. Matrimony may never be celebrated lawfully under a condition unless (1) there is a serious reason for doing so, and (2) the Ordinary has granted his permission. If any condition is contemplated in marriage, it is imperative that the matter be discussed well in advance with the priest who is to officiate at the wedding.

It is well to remember that a condition may express the will *not to accept* an obligation; in this case, if the obligation is essential to matrimony, the sacrament is invalidated. On the other hand, a condition may express the will *not to make use of* the marital right; since this would place no obligation on the other party, the contract would not be invalid. Of course, it is never permitted to keep a condition secret from the other party, since marriage is strictly bilateral. Nor, since it is a legal contract, can a condition be placed which cannot be proven in a court of law.

C. Vices Opposed to Consent

There are six factors which can destroy matrimonial consent. These, called **the vices opposed to consent,** are: lack of reason, ignorance, error, violence, fear and deceit. Many of the suits brought in the matrimonial courts to have marriages declared null are based upon one or more of these vices. They often present intricate canonical problems and can be treated here only in brief summary.

(1) Lack of Reasoning Power

Since consent is a human act, and since the making of a human act requires reasoning power, those who are actually deprived of the use of reason for any cause are unable to contract marriage. This includes those who are completely intoxicated, drugged, hypnotized, or insane. Those who have temporary fits of insanity or who are mentally defective only in some respects may be able to consent to marriage, but in practice it is considered that there is room for doubt in such cases as to the validity of such consent.

(2) Ignorance

Since ignorance is a lack of required knowledge, ignorance invalidates marriage only when it concerns what is essential to the marriage contract. The minimum knowledge required is that marriage is a permanent union for the procreation of children (Can. 1082 § 1), and that children are begotten by physical co-operation between the spouses. This minimum knowledge is presumed in those who have reached the age of puberty, but like other legal presumptions it gives way before proof to the contrary.

(3) Error

Error is a false judgment which affects matrimonial consent. In this matter the most useful division of error distinguishes:

Error of fact—a false judgment about a fact relevant to the marriage.

Error of law—a false judgment about the nature, properties, or essential goods of marriage itself.

1. Error of fact. If this false judgment is about the identity of the person, it renders the marriage invalid by natural law (Can. 1083, § 1). However, when the error is about some personal quality which does not affect the substance of the contract (e.g., age, nationality, race, etc.) it does not invalidate consent (Can. 1083, § 2). On the other hand, there are personal qualities which can affect the substance of the contract, and error of this kind would be invalidating. Such a situation is, however, exceptional.

2. Error of law. When this error concerns the essence of matrimony, it is the same as ignorance. When it is about the properties of marriage—such as unity, indissolubility, the sacramental character of marriage—it does not invalidate the marriage unless one of these goods is positively excluded (Can. 1084).

(4) Violence

Violence is an external force repugnant to the recipient. By natural law marriage which results from physical violence is invalid. It excludes the freedom necessary for consent.

(5) Fear

Fear is mental anxiety caused by an imminent or future danger. Contracts are not usually invalid as a result of fear, but in the case of marriage the public authority which is the Church has legislated that a marriage entered as a result of grave fear unjustly caused by an intelligent agent is invalid (Can. 1087, § 1). Note that the fear must be *grave*, at least as far as the one who suffers it is concerned; it must be *unjust*, i.e., caused by one who has no right to do so or by means he has no right to use; it must be caused by *an intelligent agent* and not by a natural force such as a bolt of lightning; and there must be *no alternative except marriage*. Lesser fear would not invalidate marriage, even if it should be the cause of the contract (Can. 1087, § 2).

(6) Deceit

Deceit is a simulation of true and internal consent to marriage and can occur in three ways:

1) By expressing consent which is *not really intended;* this excludes true consent and so invalidates the contract (Can. 1086, § 2).

2) By intending *not to assume* the essential obligations of matrimony; this invalidates the contract, which cannot be separated from its essential obligations (*ibid.*).

3) By intending *not to fulfill* the obligations; while this is a grave sin and an unjust deception of the other party, it does not invalidate the contract.

4. The Goods and Goals of Matrimony

The **goods of matrimony** are the benefits to the partners which result from lawful marriage. Principally they are children, fidelity and the sacrament. Other secondary goods, such as the preservation of the family name, economic advantages, peace and friendship among families, etc., may also result from marriage.

The same goods, viewed as advantages leading the unmarried to embrace the married state, are called the **goals of marriage**.

A. The Goals or Ends of Matrimony

The goals of matrimony may be outlined thus (Can. 1013, § 1):

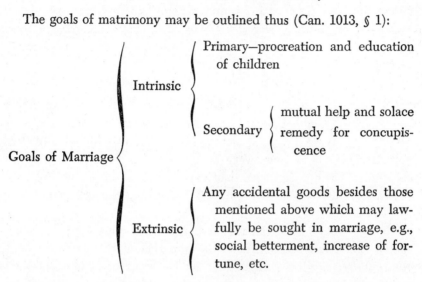

Goals of Marriage

Intrinsic

Primary—procreation and education of children

Secondary

mutual help and solace
remedy for concupiscence

Extrinsic

Any accidental goods besides those mentioned above which may lawfully be sought in marriage, e.g., social betterment, increase of fortune, etc.

The *intrinsic goals* of marriage are those which in the redeemed state of mankind belong to marriage of its very nature. They are not subject to any human control, including that of the parties themselves.

The Church has recently condemned the errors of those who teach that anything other than the procreation and education of children is the primary end of matrimony, since this is established by Almighty God himself.[7] The Book of Genesis makes clear that, subordinated to the primary end, mutual help and solace for the partners is also intended in matrimony (2:18). Nature and God intend man and wife to assist one another by mutual love, by help in household affairs, and by the co-operative division of labor in providing for the needs of the family and the training of children.

Since marriage was instituted before the fall, before concupiscence had come into the world, it is clear that the relief of concupiscence is not the primary end of matrimony. Yet St. Paul tells us that in the present state of mankind this important subordinate effect is one of the goals of matrimony (I Cor. 7:2,9). Concupiscence is relieved

[7]Cf. Gen. 1:28; the encyclical of Pope Pius XI, *Casti Connubii*, Dec. 31, 1930; Can. 1013, § 1; *Acta Apostolicae Sedis*, XXXVI (1944), p. 103.

both by the grace of matrimony and by the ennobling of carnal desire which takes place as a result of this holy union.

It is not wrong to desire other goals as a result of matrimony, but they must never be opposed to the intrinsic goals which are essential to this state.

B. The Goods or Benefits of Matrimony

The *Instruction before Marriage* in the Roman Ritual tells those about to be married that "if true love and the unselfish spirit of perfect sacrifice guide your every action, you can expect the greatest measure of earthly happiness that may be allotted to man in this vale of tears." This wonderful promise is fulfilled in the goods or benefits of matrimony.

Marriage requires the same regulation as every other virtuous undertaking. The first requirement is the intention of the right end, and thus *children* are listed as the first good of marriage. The second requirement is the right use of the means to the end, and so *fidelity*, by which the spouses are true to one another, is the second good of marriage. Finally, since marriage is a spiritual reality by which the spouses work out their salvation in union with one another, it has been made a "sacrament," a source of grace, which is the third good of matrimony. Each of these goods deserves individual attention.

(1) Children

In the fulfillment of this primary essential end of marriage—the procreation and education of children—marriage is brought to its perfection. To compensate for the great sacrifices involved in raising a family, Almighty God has granted the unique joys of parenthood, which none but parents can experience. Sharing in this way in the divine work of creation and providence brings a satisfaction, a wholeness and completeness, to a mother and father that the unmarried and childless can never know. Our Lord himself remarks that the pains of childbirth are swallowed up and forgotten in the joy that fills a mother's heart as a result of the knowledge that she has brought a child into the world.[8]

[8]Cf. Jn. 16:22.

(2) Fidelity

Fidelity means *the faithful keeping of the marriage promises*. It is the root of marital security and trust. As a contract marriage involves the virtue of justice, by which rights and duties are properly ordered. Fidelity is the keeping of the contract by which exclusive right over the body's powers of generation is granted by each spouse to the other. This contract is kept by making use of these powers only in union with one's partner, and by granting to one's partner the use of these powers whenever it is reasonably requested by word or sign. The deep personal union of marriage is symbolized and expressed by the exclusive co-operation of the partners in marriage in performing the acts which of their nature are ordained to the generation of children. An ancient ritual of marriage indicates this, calling forth these words from the bride and groom: ". . . with my body I thee worship." Worship implies complete subjection, reverence and tribute. In this sense the body is offered in worship not to another body, in the manner of an animal, but to a person. The holy beauty of sexual union in marriage is found in the deep spiritual union between two persons symbolized and expressed by the physical union of bodies.

(3) The "Sacrament"

The justice expressed by fidelity is the foundation of Christian marriage, but the union is perfected by charity. **The profound spiritual reality signified by fidelity is the "mystery" or the "sacramentality" of marriage. The** term "sacrament" in this sense—of one of the goods of matrimony—is used in quotation marks to indicate that it does not refer to the fact that matrimony is one of the seven sacraments. Rather is it a more primitive meaning of the term, signifying mystery, as in the text of St. Paul.[9] St. Augustine sees the absolute indissolubility of Christian marriage as an immediate consequence of its mysterious sacredness. Quoting St. Paul's assertion that Christian marriage is a symbol of the unbreakable union betwen Christ and the Church, he says: "Without doubt the effect of this symbolism is

[9] Cf. Eph. 5:32; St. Paul also seems to insinuate here the elevation of marriage to the rank of a sacrament of Christ.

that man and wife, when united in marriage, preserve an inseparable union."[10]

Just as fidelity refers to the unity of marriage, so the "sacrament" has reference to its indivisibility and to whatever results from marriage's signifying the union of Christ with his Church. Sacramentality is the most excellent good of marriage because it is the direct effect of divine institution, and because it pertains to the order of grace.

5. The Properties of Matrimony

Now we must consider unity and indissolubility from another aspect, namely, as properties of marriage (cf. Can. 1013, § 2).

A. The Unity of Marriage

Unity signifies that *one man is united to one woman*. Polygamy is completely excluded from Christian marriage since it is destructive of family peace, destroys the equality of partnership in conjugal relations, and destroys the image of the union of Christ and his Church. Polygamy is of two types:[11]

Polyandry—the union of one wife with many husbands—is absolutely contrary to the natural law. For one man can provide a woman with as many children as she can bear; furthermore, paternity would be uncertain in such marriages.

Polygyny—the union of one man with several wives—is, on the other hand, contrary not to a primary but to a secondary precept of the natural law. It admits of dispensation by God, a dispensation granted to the Jews by the Mosaic Law before Christ restored marriage to its original unity and purity. Polygyny is not contrary to the primary end of marriage (namely the procreation and rearing of children), but it is contrary to the secondary ends mentioned above under the generic term, polygamy.

---

[10]*On the Nuptial Union and Concupiscence,* Bk. I, Chap. 10.
[11]The terms are given here according to modern usage, as found in the dictionary.

B. The Indissolubility of Marriage

Indissolubility consists in this, that *the marriage bond is not broken until the death of one of the partners.* Since it pertains to the natural law, it is a property of all marriages, Christian and natural. By a dispensation of God, the Mosaic Law tolerated divorce and remarriage, but this was revoked by Christ (cf. Matt. 19:5 f.). No more than a bare outline of the teaching of the Church on this important matter can be attempted here.[12]

(1) The Dissolution of Marriage

The Church is given the power by God to dissolve certain marriages in some cases. But an important distinction must here be recalled: **to dissolve a marriage** is something quite different from a **declaration of nullity.** In the latter case the Church declares that, because of some impediment or defect in the original contract, *no marriage ever took place.* Sin may have been committed, scandal may have been given, but these things have nothing to do with whether valid marriage was contracted or not, and it is the determination of this last point which is the concern of the marriage court. Catholics are sometimes heard to complain when they hear of some prominent person, who has been "married," perhaps several times, being married in the Church. But one should realize that their sins do not disqualify them from marrying validly. If they have never been validly married, they cannot be refused valid marriage no matter what their past life has been.

Here our concern is not with invalid marriage but with the dissolving of a valid marriage. Three points must be made:

1) *Valid marriage which is* **ratified** and **consummated** (refer to the definitions given in Section 2, A above) can be dissolved by no human power and by no other cause than death (Can. 1118). Contrary to the misunderstanding of the words of Christ by certain Protestant churches and by the Orthodox church, the

[12]It must be remembered that the application of this teaching is a complicated procedure of which only experts are capable. Applying marriage legislation is no do-it-yourself project.

Church by its infallible authority teaches that not even adultery renders possible the dissolving of such a marriage. "What God has joined together, let no man put asunder" (Matt. 19:6).

2) *Marriage between two baptized persons or between one baptized and one unbaptized person,* **provided it has not been consummated,** *is dissolved by solemn religious profession or by a dispensation from the Holy See* (cf. Can. 1119). This implies legally acceptable proof that the marriage was never consummated and a grave reason for the dissolution. Since a married person cannot be accepted by a religious order without a dispensation, in either of these cases the Holy See must act.

3) *Legitimate marriage between unbaptized persons, even if consummated, can be dissolved* in favor of the faith *by virtue of the Pauline privilege* (cf. Can. 1120; I Cor. 7:12-15). The application of this privilege is highly technical and can only be made by qualified experts.

(2) *The Extent of Indissolubility*

The living of a common life together by the married couple is a serious and essential obligation of their marriage. Only a just cause can possibly excuse the married partners from the fulfillment of this obligation. The degree of their separation from one another—total and perpetual, total but temporary, partial separation—will require proportionately more serious justifying reasons in the eyes of God and the Church as their living apart is more complete.

Unless it is clear to all concerned that separation is the lesser of two evils, no effort should be spared to reunite the disaffected couple. Since the supervision of marriage has been placed by Christ in the hands of his Church (for marriage is a sacrament and a sacred thing), the Ordinary (usually the local bishop or his representative) must always be consulted and his approval obtained. In certain extraordinary cases, this may be anticipated. This is a delicate and complicated matter, and common sense dictates that those who are considering separation consult their pastor, his assistant or another priest before taking up the matter (as they must) with the competent ecclesiastical authority.

(3) Civil Marriage

Although in modern times the state often exceeds its authority in making legislation concerning marriage, the Catholic should be well aware of the fact that only the Church has authority over what is essential in marriage. The powers of the state are limited to civil effects. Catholics are permitted to do what the state requires for achieving the civil effects of marriage (in some European countries this requires going through a civil ceremony before a civil official), but they must be aware that for Catholics true marriage is not effected by the civil authority. Since such a requirement has never been made in the United States the problem does not arise here; the officiating priest acts also as the civil official and signs the civil documents, which are returned to the civil authorities to be kept on record.

But it should be clearly noted—Catholics are sometimes found to be under a false impression in this regard—**non-Catholics, who are free from invalidating impediments and have the intention of contracting true marriage, do contract valid marriage before a civil official.** In this country non-Catholic ministers act in this capacity just as Catholic priests do. Non-Catholic marriages are presumed to be valid unless proven otherwise.

(4) Civil Divorce

Civil divorce is certainly not what it pretends to be, namely, the dissolution of a marriage so that a new marriage may be contracted by the parties involved. But the immediate object of such a legal action is to dissolve the **civil effects** of marriage, and in certain circumstances this may be desirable. Hence a judge, a lawyer and even spouses may legitimately involve themselves in such a process. The obligations of each may be briefly noted.

1. The judge. The Catholic judge may pronounce a civil divorce in cases where the marriage is certainly invalid. But ordinarily, if he can do so without grave inconvenience, a Catholic judge should seek to be relieved of trying divorce cases. If this cannot be done, he should make it as clear as possible that his judgment is limited to civil effects when, according to law, he must pronounce a divorce in regard to a valid marriage. His co-operation is then remote and material, and when necessary such co-operation can be given, lest Catholics be excluded from an office in which much can be contributed to the common welfare. Since the divorce laws in this country are generally not enacted out of hatred for the Church, the judge's remote and material co-operation should not usually give rise to scandal. In all cases, however, the local directives of the Ordinary must be observed.

2. The petitioners for divorce. The Catholic who petitions for a civil divorce must always have the consent of the Ordinary. This consent may be given when a marriage has been declared null in the ecclesiastical courts or dissolved by the authority of the Church. Sometimes it is also given when separation has been approved by the Ordinary. This is done for the sake of the legal effects and the custody of the children. To seek a divorce for any reason without the consent of the Ordinary is gravely sinful.

3. The lawyer. As a general rule, a lawyer acts legitimately when his clients are acting legitimately. A lawyer may never take a case to court for Catholics who do not have the permission of the Ordinary to file a petition for divorce.

Since a lawyer enjoys greater freedom than a judge in refusing a case, he may take a case for non-Catholics only in the following instances:

1) If the client's marriage is manifestly invalid.
2) If there are real reasons for *separation,* and the only practical method of securing it is through civil divorce.
3) If the client wishes merely to file a cross-petition to prevent the divorce or to protect his rights.

6. The Celebration of Marriage

A. Marriage Preparations

Numerous books have been prepared on this subject, one whose importance is, fortunately, becoming more and more to be recognized.

We are concerned with the subject here, however, only from the point of view of what is strictly necessary according to the teachings of theology and canon law. From this restricted aspect, the preparations for marriage are three: betrothal, pre-nuptial investigation, and the publication of the banns.

(1) Betrothal

We are not concerned with the simple engagement which usually precedes marriage, but with solemn engagement according to the form prescribed by law. This practice is becoming more common; it has the approval of the Church; in many cases it is to be recommended. However, those who enter such an agreement should be clear as to what they are undertaking.

Betrothal is *a mutual promise, legitimately given, of future marriage, exchanged between persons who are legally capable.* It must be made in writing, dated and duly signed by both parties and by the pastor or Ordinary, or, in their absence, by two witnesses. It creates a grave obligation in justice to live up to its terms and makes marriage with another party *unlawful.* It makes betrothal with another party *invalid.*

The parties may freely agree to end the agreement, or it may be dissolved as a result of some important circumstance coming into existence or becoming known which would have prevented the original making of the contract. If one party seriously offends against chastity with another or unduly defers marriage, the other party is free of the contract. The Holy See may dispense at the request of one party, or one party may dissolve the contract by choosing a more perfect way of life, even if that should be simply a private vow of chastity.

(2) Pre-nuptial Investigations

These investigations, concerning the freedom of the parties to marry, must be conducted by the pastor who has jurisdiction in regard to the marriage. In order to allow sufficient time for these investigations he should be approached *at least* **one month** in advance of the desired time for the wedding.

(3) Publication of the Banns

Unless dispensed by the Ordinary, public announcement of the proposed marriage must be made in the parishes of the parties who intend to marry on three successive Sundays or holydays of obligation. The banns are not published for a mixed marriage. What is important to note here is the **grave obligation** on the part of anyone who knows a reason why the marriage should not take place to make the reason known to the parish priest or the Ordinary. This obligation holds unless it is known that the pastor is already aware of the matter, or unless it would result in grave harm to the person making the revelation or other innocent parties, or it is known only through a sacramental or professional secret. Even if a promise confirmed by oath has been made to keep the matter secret it must be revealed.

B. The Impediments to Marriage

A **matrimonial impediment** is *any external circumstance affecting the persons of the spouses which, by a disposition of law, hinders them from validly or licitly contracting marriage.* If an impediment arises only from ecclesiastical law it does not bind the unbaptized. Impediments are either *invalidating* or *prohibiting.* The former render marriage impossible, the latter make it illegal though valid. The impediments need not be discussed at length here, though they will be mentioned to the extent necessary to warn against company-keeping with one with whom marriage would be illegal or invalid.

(1) Invalidating Impediments

According to the present legislation of the Church, there are thirteen **invalidating impediments.** Some of them flow from the natural law or from divine positive law and, therefore, can never be dispensed from. Others are ecclesiastical, and dispensations from them are given under certain conditions.

From the natural law itself it follows that impotency (lack of ability to perform the marital act), blood relationship in the direct line or in the first degree of the collateral line, and the bonds of an already valid marriage eliminate the possibility of contracting valid marriage. They cannot be dispensed from.[13]

By ecclesiastical law the impediment of blood relationship is extended to the third degree of the collateral line. Other relationships from which marriage is excluded: blood relatives in the direct line and to the second degree of the collateral line of a deceased wife or husband; blood relatives in the first and second degree of the direct line of a partner in an invalid marriage or notorious concubinage; spiritual relationship established by baptizing or acting as sponsor for baptism; legal relatives as a result of adoption where this is a civil impediment.

Furthermore, by ecclesiastical law a baptized Catholic cannot contract marriage with an unbaptized person. Nor can a subdeacon or a religious in solemn vows contract valid marriage. If a woman has been abducted for the purpose of marriage, marriage cannot take place. People who have committed adultery together with a promise of marriage (even civil), or who have co-operated in the murder of the valid marriage partner of one of them, are impeded from contracting valid marriage. Girls under fourteen and boys under sixteen are not able to enter valid marriage.

All of these ecclesiastical impediments are sometimes dispensed, though some of them only very rarely. Good reasons must always be present for such a dispensation.

(2) Prohibiting Impediments

Prohibiting impediments make marriage illegal though valid. The only ones we need consider are mixed religion and simple vows. Any simple vow—whether a private vow or taken in a religious community—which is contrary to entering the married state makes marriage a grave sin and illegal. The existence of such a vow must be made known during the pre-nuptial investigation.

1. Mixed marriages. We have seen that a baptized Catholic cannot contract marriage with an unbaptized person. A baptized Catholic can contract marriage with a *baptized* non-Catholic, but such a contract is illegal and a grave sin.

---

[13]See the exceptions for valid but not consummated marriage in Section 5.

The Church detests mixed marriages.[14] They imply (when both are baptized) a communication in the administration of a sacrament with a non-Catholic. They are always a grave danger to faith—a successful and harmonious mixed marriage is, in the long run, often a worse danger to the faith than an unsuccessful one. The faith of the children is bound to be weaker than it would be if both parents were Catholic; it may well die out in the second or third generation. To be sure, examples of cases in which this did not happen can be easily given. But so can those of people who have taken arsenic and lived; yet no one would propose these exceptions as an argument for deliberately eating arsenic.

Because the Church grants a dispensation for marriage with a non-Catholic for a just and grave cause, a Catholic can be excused for keeping company with a non-Catholic, but only if there be a just and grave reason for doing so. Many young Catholics seem to think that there is no objection to keeping company with a non-Catholic. This does not make sense. Company keeping is always at least remotely ordained to marriage, and they are forbidden by the Church to marry a non-Catholic.

When a dispensation is granted for a mixed marriage, the non-Catholic must provide promises in writing, both not to interfere deliberately with the faith of the Catholic party and to rear the children in the Catholic faith. There must be moral certainty that these promises will be kept or the dispensation will not be granted.

Catholics who enter a mixed marriage are excommunicated:

1) if they participate in a religious marriage ceremony before a non-Catholic minister either before or after their marriage in the presence of a priest;

2) if they agree, even implicitly, that some of the children will be educated outside the faith;

3) if they knowingly have their children baptized by a non-Catholic minister or educated or enrolled in a non-Catholic religion.

---

[14]The remarks which follow apply both to the marriage of a Catholic and an unbaptized person and to the marriage of a Catholic and a baptized non-Catholic; the first is *invalidated* by law, the second *prohibited* by law.

2. Other prohibiting impediments. Catholics are also forbidden to marry Communists, notorious apostates, or members of secret societies. Priests are forbidden without grave reason to officate at the marriage of a public sinner who refuses to confess before the marriage.

3. Practical procedure. If there is any suspicion that one of the impediments might be present, a priest should be consulted. It would save much grief if such a consultation were made by one of the parties well before the question of marriage comes up. These impediments are established by God and the Church to guard the happiness and well-being of the faithful. Happiness could not conceivably be found in a union impeded by divine or natural law. Where an impediment arising from ecclesiastical law is found, the wisdom of the Church attests that public and private welfare is not served by such a union, and that it would normally lead to unhappiness. When a dispensation is granted it is because evidence is present that it is the lesser of two evils to do so.

C. The "Form" of Marriage

By natural law it is sufficient for the marital contract that the parties manifest mutual consent. However, since marriage is a matter of great concern to the common welfare, those who have the care of the common welfare have the right and duty (in accord with the kind of care that belongs to them to exercise) to legislate concerning marriage in such a way as to protect the rights of the community.

For her own children the Church has prescribed a particular way in which the marriage must be performed. This **juridical form** must be observed by them in order that they may enter into a valid marriage. It requires the presence of official witnesses to the contract—the pastor or Ordinary (or a priest delegated by one of these), and at least two witnesses possessing the use of reason (cf. Can. 1094). It is unlawful (unless for a grave cause the Ordinary judges otherwise) for non-Catholics, the excommunicated, persons declared infamous by law, adolescents, and militant Communists to act as witnesses. This form binds all who have ever been baptized Catholics or received into the Catholic Church, even though they have since left the Church. It binds them even should they contract marriage (with or without a dispensation from the impediments of mixed religion or disparity of cult) with a non-Catholic.

Non-Catholics, when they contract marriage among themselves, are not, of course, bound to this form. As far as the form is concerned, marriage of non-Catholics, whether civil or religious, is recognized by the Church as valid. On the other hand, those bound to the form cannot contract valid marriage in a civil court or before a non-Catholic minister. If they attempt to do so they are living in concubinage, their children are illegitimate, and they are reputed as public sinners. If the attempt at marriage is made before a non-Catholic minister acting in a religious capacity, they are excommunicated.

Except in cases of necessity, Catholics are also bound to the liturgical rites, for marriage is a sacrament, a sacred ceremony. These ceremonies are usually completely excluded for mixed marriages. The nuptial blessing is ordinarily excluded during Lent and Advent.

7. The Obligations of Man and Wife

We shall first consider the obligations of married people to one another, then their obligations toward their children.

A. The Duties of the Spouses to Each Other

(1) The Conjugal Debt

The principal duty of spouse to spouse is to render the conjugal debt when it is reasonably asked. There is a matter of strict commutative justice involved here. To refuse the request on rare occasions would not seem to be a serious injustice (unless there is danger of incontinence), but to render the debt habitually in a grudging or unpleasant manner is equivalent to denial. If husband and wife freely and mutually agree for the sake of some real bodily or spiritual advantage to abstain from this relationship for a time, there is no sin involved; such abstention may well be virtuous. If the request is unreasonable, it may, of course, be refused. If there is doubt in the matter the advice of the confessor should be sought.

Conjugal intercourse is a holy and meritorious act as long as the following conditions are fulfilled: (a) There is true penetration and deposit and retention of the seed; (b) the primary purpose, namely, conception, is not efficaciously excluded (though, if there be a good reason, it does not have to be desired); and (c) it be under circumstances which will not be an occasion of scandal to children or others. Minor acts, such as looks, touches, kisses, etc., are legitimate to the spouses as long as they are ultimately ordained, not simply to venereal pleasure, but to the marriage act and the expression of mutual love and affection. Ordinarily they are venially sinful if ordained only to venereal pleasure. To seek complete satisfaction outside the normal marriage act is gravely sinful.

(2) Marital Chastity

Sins of incontinence with a third party or with oneself are sins against justice as well as against chastity. Sins of birth prevention (often incorrectly called *birth control*) with one's partner are gravely sinful, whether artificial means are used or not. By such sins God is excluded from the family and matrimonial grace is cut off. Society, family life, the children and the spouses themselves are gravely harmed. What was intended by God as the supreme expression of mutual love, of mutual self-giving, becomes an act selfishly ordained to personal pleasure. What was intended as a tender tribute to the spouse ("With my body I thee worship") becomes a sordid *use* of the one for venereal pleasure who should be dear above all others.

A false and unwarranted notion exists that "rhythm" or "periodic continence" is the "birth control method of the Church." Nothing could be further from the truth. The Church neither recommends nor approves the practice, indeed she counsels against it. Under certain conditions it seems not to militate essentially against marital chastity and is, therefore, permissible.

A pre-marital agreement to limit the conjugal right to periods during which the wife is naturally sterile would invalidate the marriage, though an agreement to so limit the use of the right would not. The limitation of the use of the right to the sterile period is, at least, not seriously sinful (and may be without sin at all) if the following conditions are present:

1) There is a serious reason for avoiding the fecundity of the union while at the same time continuing to engage in the union.
2) There is complete mutual agreement to this practice.
3) It is in no serious way an occasion of sin for either party.
4) The danger of frustrating the secondary ends of marriage, such as mutual aid and love, is not significant and proximate.

Rhythm is only a last resort alternative to keep married people from serious sin. When the conception of children is inadvisable the Church counsels abstinence, not without realizing that it can easily demand true heroism. The Church knows that, to the extent that they depend upon God, her children are capable of great heroism.

(3) Other Duties of the Spouses to One Another

The spouses are to live together and share one another's life. Where the husband fixes his home, there the wife's home ought to be. The husband must rule his family without bossiness, but with good example, friendly persuasion and counsel. Only rarely should it be necessary for him to use full authority toward his wife, but when authority is necessary he neglects his duty if he does not use it. His duty, also, is to provide to the extent of his ability for the necessities of life according to the social status of the family.

The wife must remember that next to God she must love her husband above all others, and that she must be loyal to him in every way. The care of the household and the training of the children in virtue is in a special way her province. To desert these duties for work outside the home which is not absolutely necessary (however gainful it might be), or for social activities, manifests a childishly selfish failure to measure up to the nobility, dignity and responsibility that is hers as a Christian wife and mother.

B. The Duties of Parents to Their Children

This book is not a manual of handy methods for the rearing of children; obviously only the most general principles can be set down here.

The parents who brought children into the world must provide for those children physically and spiritually until they have reached the degree of maturity necessary to provide for themselves. It is not simply a waiting period. They must be trained by the parents to assume the responsibilities of maturity. The physical needs of children are obvious, but they are less important than their spiritual needs. Parents must remember that their work is never done until their children are in the kingdom of heaven. When their children are mature they can do little more than pray for them. During their childhood they must provide a truly Christian atmosphere in the home so that children can grow with a habitual love and reverence for what is holy and good. They must provide for their children a Catholic schooling to the fullest extent possible. This includes the college and university. Parents must, however, realize that they have no right to dictate to their children in the matter of the choice of a state of life or of a marriage partner.

In the rearing of their children excessive indulgence must be avoided as well as excessive harshness. Nor should parents be unduly ambitious for their children, for this too often results in leaving them rich in this world's goods but spiritually impoverished.

8. Christian Marriage

Having studied the moral and canonical aspects of marriage, we must now state precisely the manner in which Christian marriage differs from marriage among the unbaptized. What does it mean to the Christian man and wife, *as man and wife,* that their marriage is a sacrament and not merely a natural contract?

A. The Sacrament of Matrimony

The very purpose of the sacraments is to give grace, to unite man to God. Since this union must be effected in various ways depending on the various states or conditions normal in human life, the special sacramental grace of each sacrament unites man to Christ in a special way and for a special purpose. The sacrament of matrimony unites a man to Christ through the very union established with his wife in marriage, and the wife through the union with her husband. Their very union becomes symbolic of Christ's union with the Church. Together man and wife must live their life (in a very real sense there is but one life between them), and the purpose of life on this earth is to work out salvation. Therefore, together man and wife work out their salvation. Since the purpose of their union is so sacred, it is fitting that Christ should have raised it to the supernatural order so that it might itself be a principal means of attaining salvation.

The vast difference between natural and supernatural marriage is apparent, even when expressed in these general terms, but if we recall a distinction made in Chapter Nine concerning the sacraments in general, we will be able to make more specific our study of the effects of the sacramentalizing of matrimony in the lives of the spouses. Any sacrament, we have seen, can be considered in three ways:

Sacramentum tantum—the sacrament only, the external signifying rite.

Res et sacramentum—reality and sacrament, the reality immediately caused by the sacrament which itself signifies the ultimate reality.

Res tantum—the reality only, the ultimate effect signified and produced by the *sacramentum tantum* together with the *res et sacramentum*.

We shall consider the sacrament of matrimony under each of these aspects.

(1) The "Sacramentum Tantum" of Matrimony

When a man and woman marry, they do so by expressing mutual consent to exchange the rights to one another's body in regard to the acts of generation. The unique natural union thus created has been raised by God to the dignity of a sacrament. That means it has been given supernatural powers of signification and it has been enabled to achieve supernatural effects. By the institution of Christ this natural union symbolizes the mystical union between Christ and his Church, the redemptive Incarnation. The human love which effects this union becomes a wonderful symbol of divine love. The baptized man and woman, in effect, celebrate the nuptials of God and man, express in their mutual acts of love the immortal love of Christ toward his Bride.

The very ceremony by which this is achieved becomes a religious sign, a liturgical action. In their expression of consent true and supernatural worship is offered to God by the spouses and by the Church. The sublimity and dignity of this Christian action as compared with a pagan exchange of consent is recognized immediately by all who look with the eyes of faith. But this figure, sublimely significative of the union between God and man, is not only itself holy, it is *effective* of holiness. For the sacraments are God's instruments as well as God's signs, and through them he showers upon man the copious blessings of the life and death and resurrection of the God-man.

(1) The "Res et Sacramentum" of Matrimony

The natural bond created by a natural exchange of consent is the inseparable union of souls in which the essence of matrimony is to be found. This union, primarily for the benefit of offspring, is also ordained to the perfection of the spouses themselves. Thus matrimony is primarily a social or common good, rather than a matter of private advantage.

Since God does not provide less for the order of grace than he does for the order of nature, and since a more noble cause will achieve a more noble effect, sound theology leads to the conclusion that the first effect of sacramental union is a **sacramental bond,** intrinsically superior to the natural bond, because it is supernatural. This sacred union can provide for the birth and education of children in a holy and supernatural society, the Christian family.

This bond is both **res et sacramentum,** both *reality* achieved by that which is *sacramentum tantum* (the sacramentalized exchange of consent), and in turn itself the *symbol* of something more, a further reality, the *res tantum*. In this sacramental bond the union is immeasurably stronger, more holy, more noble than in the natural bond. It is a practical sign, and together with the *sacramentum tantum* it produces the sacramental grace by which marriage daily approximates, and in increasing perfection imitates, the union it symbolizes.

(3) The "Res Tantum" of Matrimony

The grace by which man can fittingly accomplish all the works that a marriage "contracted in the faith of Christ" requires, is the final effect produced by this sacrament. By divine institution man and wife receive power over one another to secure the ends of matrimony; consequently they receive the graces without which the fitting execution of marital functions would be impossible.

B. The Effects of Matrimonial Grace

Each sacrament rightly received either begins the life of grace in us or intensifies it. Not essentially differing from sanctifying grace, the sacramental graces realize in a special way, determined by the end of the particular sacrament, the common end of man's sanctification and his imitation of Christ.

What, then, is matrimonial grace? We may answer this question by asking: what is the sacred symbolism of matrimony? It is a visible manifestation of the union of Christ and his Church. The special modification in sanctifying grace wrought by the sacrament, therefore, is a **grace of conjugal union,** a grace that will enable the spouses to live a life together which will make visible the sacramental bond symbolic of Christ's bond with his Bride. Beyond the union of each spouse to God (a common effect of all sanctifying grace), the sacramental grace of matrimony effects the union of the spouses to one another and of the man and woman so united to God. As St. Thomas states: "Grace is conferred by this sacrament by which they belong to the union of God and the Church; this is most necessary for them, for they must so deal with carnal and worldly matters as not to destroy their union with Christ and his Church."[15]

Matrimonial grace, then, supernaturalizes the love of the spouses for each other; in addition, it supernaturally orders them to the prac-

[15]*Summa contra Gentiles*, Bk. IV, Chap. 78.

tice of those particular virtues which will perfect their union, which make of their married life a living image of Christ and his Church. This will mean, on the one hand, the overcoming by grace of the disorders inherent in man since the fall which are obstacles to so perfect a union. On the positive side, this grace will bring a special increase of infused virtues and gifts and a right to the actual graces which divinely inspire and direct the virtuous action demanded of the sacramental union.

We will discuss each of these aspects of matrimonial grace in detail.

(1) The Healing of the Wounds of Sin

The sacraments are special remedies for the defects left by past sins, original and actual, defects which are obstacles to the promptings of grace and to virtuous action. Christ's power works in the sacraments to heal and expiate, to subdue the rebellion of the lower powers against reason and restore proper order among them. By this sacramental healing the soul of the Christian becomes apt for further increase of grace and sensitive to the impulses of the Holy Spirit.

The special obstacle to grace which Christian marriage must face and overcome is that of sexual concupiscence. Even natural marriage, by providing the opportunity for the legitimate use of sexual pleasure, provides some remedy for the disorder so frequently found in this great human drive. But it merely touches the surface of the radical disorder consequent upon sin. It cures the acts of concupiscence but leaves concupiscence itself untouched. Sacramental marriage penetrates to the very root of this disorder. While it does not completely repress the rebellion of the lower powers, it appreciably reduces it. Thus the married Christian is more capable of resisting temptation, of acting virtuously; he is freer of the impediments to actual grace and to the workings of the virtues and the gifts.

This is a fact of tremendous importance in the daily lives of the married faithful, and a most potent and practical motive for their preserving themselves in the state of grace—or recovering that state, if they should unhappily fall, as quickly as possible. Let us repeat: only matrimonial grace produces this radical suppression of concupiscence. And it should be recalled that that grace will be restored to the truly penitent and contrite sinner through the sacrament of penance (Denz. 2193).

(2) The Special Increase of Graces

Christian marriage must be worked out in a set of concrete circumstances bewildering in variety and varying in difficulty. Through the sacrament, habitual grace is specially adapted to achieve Christian virtue in the circumstances of married life.

1. The virtues of Christian marriage.

1) Primary among all virtues is *charity* toward God and neighbor. The natural love of spouses is perfected in conjugal charity whereby their mutual love will be best expressed in their concern to be of help one to another in the practice of virtue.

2) The virtue of *hope* by which they count on God not only for "eternal life" but for "the means to attain it" will be their safeguard in every crisis in the life of their family.

3) They will live by *faith,* an example to all of deep realization of the true goals of life.

4) Domestic *prudence,* differing in husband and wife according to their respective duties, will help them to make right decisions and rule their family for the best good of all.

5) The virtue of *justice* will be theirs, by which selfishness is suppressed, obligations cheerfully accepted and faithfully fulfilled.

6) The virtue of *religion* will create a Christian atmosphere in their home by common family prayers and devotions, by the reverent presence of religious images and customs in the home.

7) The *patience* needed to live a common life—to understand one another deeply, and their children, so that what could easily be causes of irritation become rather occasions of virtue—is a small but very important virtue for harmonious family living. Slow to anger, quick to forgive, disinclined to bickering and quarrels, harsh words and unnecessary criticism, the patient spouse indeed witnesses to the grace of matrimony.

8) Conjugal *chastity* will permit the spouses to give an example the world badly needs.

2. The gifts of the Holy Spirit. Over and above these special marital virtues, the special help of the gifts of the Holy Spirit will make the wedded life of the Christian spouses more truly divine. We have seen that these gifts are necessary for salvation, for they dispose the Christian to receive the inspirations of the Holy Spirit, and by means of these impulses divine action even in worldly matters becomes second nature, as it were, for the husband and wife. In God's design for married life the gifts will have a very special and essential part.

Wisdom will lead to an appreciation of the divine nature of their sacramental life together. *Understanding* gives them a deep penetration of the truths of faith, especially those which are most necessary to perfect their life together and the direction of their family. *Counsel* provides the assistance to handle with divine ease and assurance the innumerable domestic difficulties which are inevitable, especially in large families. *Piety* is of special importance because of the necessity (and difficulty) of exercising parental authority. *Fortitude* fills the spouses with confidence in divine wisdom and power, so that they are enabled to do God's will, knowing that he will provide where their resources fail. Through *fear of the Lord* the married couple will appreciate their **need** for full co-operation with God's grace, at the same time that they realize their right to his all-powerful assistance.

3. The actual graces of Christian marriage. Habitual grace and the infused virtues and gifts make us ready to act supernaturally. But actual grace, the grace of the moment, moves us from the capability of supernatural action into actual performance. Though they remain free to reject it, the spouses know that matrimonial grace insures that God's help will be forthcoming for any of the actions which their state of life requires. Knowing that God, their Father, is with them, they may say with St. Paul: "If God is for us, who is against us? Who shall separate us from the love of Christ?" (Rom. 8:31).

C. Conclusion

When the faithful give their sincere matrimonial consent, they open up for themselves a treasury of sacramental grace from which until death they may draw the supernatural strength to fulfill their duties and offices with fidelity, with holiness, with perseverance.

This sacrament not only increases the permanent principle of super-natural life, sanctifying grace, in those who place no obstacle, but it also gives them special additional gifts: good inspirations, seeds of grace, together with the augmenting and perfecting of natural faculties. Thus the spouses may appreciate interiorly (and not only know in an abstract manner) all that pertains to the state of matrimony, its goals and its duties; with firm conviction and efficacious will they may thus proceed to fulfill these goals and duties. Finally, this sacrament gives them the right to ask and receive the help of actual grace as often as the fulfillment of the duties of their state demands it.[16]

Thus will they find the blessings of marriage to be daily increased by an abundance of divine grace; and living in the pursuit of piety, they will not only spend this life in peace and tranquillity, but will also rest in the true and strong hope of reaching and possessing, through the goodness of God, that life which is eternal.[17]

'For this cause a man shall leave his father and mother, and cleave to his wife; and the two shall be one flesh.' This is a great mystery— I mean in reference to Christ and to the Church.

—Eph. 5:31-32

9. Summary and Conclusion

"Christ the Lord, the 'Institutor and Perfecter' of the sacraments, by raising the matrimony of his faithful to the dignity of a true sac-rament of the New Law, made it a sign and source of that peculiar internal grace by which it perfects natural love, it confirms an indis-soluble union, and sanctifies both man and wife.

"And since the valid matrimonial consent among the faithful was instituted by Christ as a sign of grace, the sacramental nature is so intimately bound up with Christian wedlock that there can be no true marriage between baptized persons without it being by that very fact a sacrament.

"Nevertheless, since it is a law of divine providence in the super-natural order that men do not reap the full fruit of the sacraments which they receive after acquiring the use of reason unless they co-operate with grace, the grace of matrimony will remain for the most part an unused talent hidden in the field unless the parties

---

[16]Encylical of Pope Pius XI, *Casti Conubii*, Dec. 31, 1930; Denz. 2237.
[17]*Catechism of the Council of Trent*, Bk. II, Chap. 8.

exercise these supernatural powers and cultivate and develop the seeds of grace they have received. If, however, doing all that lies within their power, they are docile to grace, they will be able to bear the burdens of their state and to fulfill their duties. By such a sacrament they will be strengthened, sanctified and in a manner consecrated. For, as St. Augustine teaches, just as by baptism and holy orders a man is set aside and assisted, either for the duties of Christian life or for the priestly office and is never deprived of their sacramental aid, almost in the same way (although not by a sacramental character), the faithful once joined by marriage ties can never be deprived of the help and the binding force of the sacrament. Indeed, as the holy Doctor adds, even those who commit adultery carry with them that sacred yoke, although in this case not as a title to the glory of grace, but for the ignominy of their guilty action, as the soul by apostasy, withdrawing as it were from marriage with Christ, even though it may have lost its faith, does not lose the sacrament of faith which it received at the laver of regeneration.

"These parties, let it be noted, not fettered but adorned by the golden bond of the sacrament, not hampered but assisted, should strive with all their might to the end that their wedlock, not only through the power and symbolism of the sacrament, but also through their spirit and manner of life, may be and remain always the living image of that most fruitful union of Christ with the Church, which is to be venerated as the sacred token of most perfect love.

"All these things, venerable brethren, if considered attentively and with a lively faith, if the extraordinary benefits of matrimony—offspring, conjugal faith and the sacrament—are viewed in their true light, no one can fail to admire the divine wisdom, holiness and goodness which, while respecting the dignity and happiness of husband and wife, has provided so bountifully for the conservation and propagation of the human race by a single, chaste and sacred fellowship of nuptial union."[18]

A few conclusions can be added to this summary of the doctrine on Christian marriage.

---

[18]Encyclical of Pope Pius XI, *Casti Connubii*, Dec. 31. 1930; Denz. 2237.

1. Many of America's divorce problems can be traced back to a false notion of obedience. The subjection that a wife owes to her husband does not consist in a kind of marital slavery. She does not lose her liberty as a human person: rather, she finds a new liberty, a consummate dignity, founded upon her role as wife, mother and companion to her husband. However, the so-called social equality of the modern man and woman has had tragic repercussions in family life. Woman, in an attempt to free herself from the duties of marriage, has enslaved herself by the chains of immodesty, negligence and personal sorrow. If woman would recognize the importance of true obedience, obedience to the will of the divine plan, she would find peace of conscience in a confused world.

2. "The Lord cast a deep sleep upon Adam: and when he was fast asleep, he took one of his ribs and filled up flesh for it. And the Lord God built the rib which he took from Adam into a woman: and brought her to Adam. And Adam said: 'This now is bone of my bones and flesh of my flesh; she shall be called woman because she was taken out of man.' Wherefore a man shall leave father and mother and shall cleave to his wife: and they shall be two in one flesh."[19]

3. The exemplar for every Christian marriage is the marriage of Mary, the Mother of God, and Joseph the carpenter. Their marriage, truly made in heaven, was characterized by the virtues of charity, humility and patience. What more is necessary for perfect companionship?

BIBLIOGRAPHICAL NOTE

A thorough treatment of this subject can be found in Volume III of the English *Summa*, Questions XLI-LXVIII. A technical summary of this doctrine has been written by J. E. Marr, O.P., in his essay "Christian Marriage," which has been appended to Volume III of the *Summa*. Several books can be suggested for their more popular view of the Church's teaching and for the practical conclusions at which they arrive. They are: *A Guide to Catholic Marriage* (Milwaukee:

---

[19]Gen. 2:21-24.

The Bruce Publishing Co., 1955), by Clement S. Mihanovich, *et al.;* *Christian Marriage* (New York: Sheed and Ward, 1933), by George H. Joyce; *The Meaning of Life and Marriage* (Westminster, Md.: The Newman Press, 1954), by Friedrick E. von Gagern; and *Marriage* (New York: Longmans, Green and Co., 1942), by Dietrich von Hildebrand.

But no doubt of primary interest to users and readers of this text will be a companion volume on marriage written for the college student as part of the series. *Toward Marriage in Christ*, by T. C. Donlan, O. P., F. L. B. Cunningham, O.P., and Augustine Rock, O.P., (Dubuque: The Priory Press, 1957) is a short but thorough study constructed on the same principles as the present volume.

An excellent piece entitled, "Marriage and Spirituality," by M. R. Newland, can be found in the periodical *Integrity*, VI (1950), 24-33. Another essay on this sacrament, "Christian Marriage," by E. J. Mahoney, is in Volume II of *The Teaching of the Catholic Church*.

CHAPTER SIXTEEN

The Mystical Body of Christ

1. Introduction

The subject of the Church is of primary importance today on two levels: (1) the strictly theological, and (2) the level of lay instruction. It is important on the theological level because many of the great problems facing contemporary theologians depend for their solution upon principles of **ecclesiology** (from *ecclesia,* church; therefore, the study of the Church). And it is important on the level of lay instruction because the modern layman is called upon to take a more active role than formerly in the work of the Church's apostolate.

The purpose of this chapter is to present in orderly fashion the teaching of the Church about herself. The doctrine here explained is firmly rooted in the ecclesiological teaching of St. Thomas[1] and has been developed in line with the pronouncements of the Church and the teachings of modern theologians. Special reference will be made to the profound doctrinal encyclical of Pope Pius XII, *Mystici Corporis Christi*.[2] The reliance of Pope Pius XII on the Angelic Doctor's theology concerning the Church, the Mystical Body of Christ, is sufficient assurance that St. Thomas' method of presenting the basic principles concerning this subject, so widely discussed and so profoundly studied in our time, can be followed with confidence.[3]

In this chapter, our concern with the Church is essentially a dogmatic one. Since the Reformation, much of the writing concerning the Church has been apologetic rather than dogmatic. Heretical attacks on the visible Church by those who rejected it, the "reformers," necessitated such a defense. But this preoccupation with the visible Church directed attention away from her inner reality and, indeed, led (at least in practice) to the distorted view that the invisible Church and the visible Church are not entirely coterminous. The impression was created in many minds that a person could somehow be a member of the invisible Church (the "soul" of the Church) without being at the same time a member of the visible Church

---

[1] As Père Congar, perhaps the leading ecclesiologist of our day has pointed out, "In reality everything in the thought of St. Thomas has an ecclesiological phase, and the author of an essay on his theology of the Mystical Body has gone so far as to say that this doctrine is the heart of his theology. The reason is that the Church is not a separate reality, something outside the Christian-Trinitarian mystery, outside the anthropologic, christologic, sacramental thing which is the subject of theology. So much is this true, that I am forced to ask myself if it be not a deliberate act on St. Thomas' part that he has refused to write a *separate* treatise *De Ecclesia*, seeing that the Church pervaded his theology in all its parts. I am indeed inclined, personally, to think so." Cf. "The Idea of the Church in St. Thomas Aquinas," *The Thomist*, I (1939), 358.

[2] The references to this encyclical are to the English translation published by The Paulist Press. The same translation has been published by the National Catholic Welfare Conference, but with different paragraph numbering. The NCWC has also published another translation with still a third paragraph numbering and with no indication (e.g., date, edition, number, etc.) by which one NCWC translation can be distinguished from the other. There is, therefore, no way of clearly indicating to the student where these quotations can be found in the NCWC editions.

[3] One third of the references of *Mystici Corporis* (other than those to Sacred Scripture and papal documents) are to St. Thomas. Indeed, with the exception of the Fathers of the Church and one reference to St. Robert Bellarmine (who, more than any other doctor, wrote *ex professo* on ecclesiology), St. Thomas is the only theologian quoted, his teaching being directly referred to by the Holy Father fifteen times.

(the "body" of the Church). It seemed almost as if there were two Churches, one visible and the other invisible.

Such a doctrine, of course, was never taught by Catholic apologetes. But the relegation of the study of the Church almost entirely to the realm of apologetics did tend to satisfy many with a somewhat superficial and extrinsic concentration upon the visible and organizational elements in the Church. For a long time a profound dogmatic study of the Church precisely as a mystery of faith was neglected.

Keeping in mind the dependence of our doctrine concerning the mystery of the Church on the encyclical *Mystici Corporis,* and on the teachings of St. Thomas Aquinas and the best modern theologians, we shall follow this order:

The Mystical Body of Christ

- The problem of the Church **(Section 2)**

- The Church in itself **(Section 3)**
  - Definition
  - Division (no real division)
  - Foundation
  - Membership in the Church

- The Church as mystery **(Section 4)**
  - Necessity of the Church
  - Christ, its Head
  - The Whole Christ
  - The soul of the Church

- The Church as visible institution **(Section 5)**
  - Its form
  - Its infallibility
  - Its properties
  - Its head

- The Church and other societies **(Section 6)**

2. The Problem of the Church

A. Introduction

Every heresy is fundamentally a rejection of the Church. Since Christ commissioned the Church to teach the truth at all times and in all places, anyone who rejects the truth, rejects the Church. Furthermore, the Church is such a prominent reality in the Scriptures that all who call themselves Christians are forced to offer some explanation of it. Their problem is to explain the Church in such a way that their own special doctrines can be brought to light. The defense of the Church as the infallible teaching authority, as the divinely appointed mediator between God and man and the administrator of the sacraments and offerer of sacrifice, and as ruler and disciplinarian of the faithful on their pilgrimage to eternity—all this is the work of apologetics. Yet in the last analysis there would be nothing to defend unless there were first something to believe. For, above all, the Church is a mystery of the faith: "I believe in one, holy, Catholic and apostolic Church"; "I believe . . . in the holy Catholic Church."

The apologetic of the Church does not demand a theological exposition of the mystery of the Church, but it does demand an acceptance of this mystery. Here, however, we are concerned with a theological explanation of the mystery of the Church, not with apologetic arguments which offer a rational defense of the Church's visible hierarchical organization. The purpose of this study is to know more fully the Mother of our supernatural life and growth. For she is the one who feeds us and nurses us back to health. It is she who shows us the way to our goal and disciplines us when we stray from the path. She presents, in the best possible light, what good there is in us to our eternal Father.

The first result of this study should be the stimulation of an intense love for the Church. It should also lead us to a deeper understanding of those who reject the Church and to a greater tolerance for them, even during their most vicious attacks. The more intimately we understand the mystery of the Church, the better we can appreciate the ignorance of those from whom this mystery is hidden.

Those who do not have the faith see the Church as a vast, powerful and demanding human organization, and judge it from that point of view. At this level it is not surprising that many unkind things have been said to discredit the Church.

B. Non-Catholic Idea of the Church

Let us consider, for a moment, the basic concept of the Church entertained by non-Catholic Christians. By doing so, the importance of striving to understand its *inner* reality will be readily evident. Only this inner reality, a mystery known by faith alone, can give meaning to the external manifestation of the Church. The external manifestation of the Church can be called "the Church as institution," for the Church as institution is the visible sign of an inner reality, a divine mystery. To judge it, then, from a purely natural point of view is to miss its true significance. The Church known through faith is an entirely different reality from the Church known through reason alone. For the Church known through faith is an objective reality, while the Church imagined by those not blessed with the gift of faith is fictional in character.

Catholics often entertain the superficial notion that the absurdity of the essential Protestant position, first formulated by Martin Luther, can be easily manifested by one simple question: "Where was the Church of Christ from the apostolic ages until the time of Martin Luther?" This shallow idea misses Luther's point entirely. Basically, his position on the Church, and that of Protestants since his time, is this: "Christ neither intended to establish nor did he establish a tightly knit visible organization under the authority of pope and bishops. The humanly organized hierarchy set itself up as a middle-man between the faithful and God. It claimed to be the exclusive dispenser of all favors granted by God to men and the exclusive channel through which men could offer sacrifices to God. But since, by and large, the hierarchy had long been composed of good, sincere and self-sacrificing men, its role as sole mediator had not been seriously challenged."

By Luther's time, however, the functions of the hierarchy had become so intimately connected with material administration that many self-seeking men, with little or no concern for spiritual values, seized the centers of power in order to gain material advantages. Because this undesirable element was present in the hierarchy, Luther concluded that the hierarchy in itself was essentially evil. Then he followed up his hastily drawn conclusion by leading a widespread popular movement "to liberate the Christian from an intolerable bondage and to restore him to direct communication with God and his Christ." Although Luther's position can be shown to be untenable, even without appealing to the proofs of faith, it is by no means absurd nor can its error be exposed by a clever turn of phrase.

A detailed discussion of the numerous and often nebulous notions espoused by various non-Catholic religious leaders concerning the Church would take us too far afield. Yet the presentation of their basic position which we have endeavored to formulate makes clear the importance of our having a profound appreciation for the Church. This appreciation will support her position not only in the marketplace but also in our own faith-transformed souls.

C. The Meaning of the Church in Our Lives

As the basic confusion of Protestant teaching on the Church should suggest, it is ever of the deepest importance that we realize fully the meaning of the Church in our own lives. Our salvation depends upon the Church, for through the Church Christ continues to live in our midst and to share his divine life with us. This he does by making us his members. Our divine Savior chose the Church as *the* means of extending his redemption in time and space.

If Jesus Christ had intended his short life on earth merely as a means of providing mankind with an inspiring story and a collection of salutary maxims, he would not have had to found a church. Men would undoubtedly have established a society for the preservation of these values on their own initiative. Even the devotees of Sherlock Holmes have done that for their hero. Such a society, however, would be a human organization, one which could be revised, suppressed, reformed or reorganized at will. Its influence on the lives of its members would, necessarily, be confined within limits. It could hardly be a necessary means of achieving union with God. Indeed, a society of this kind could not directly achieve union with God at all. Union with God comes only through a personal religious experience. Members of a church founded by man could merely exchange ideas on the ways of effecting this experience. A church of this kind could group men together to engage in individual worship, but it could not reasonably require its members to attend common worship, since in such a church there would be no truly *common* worship. This society could even understand the existence of rival societies, societies which would approach the Christian message from another point of view, even though it might deplore this plurality as falling short of the ideal of fraternal unity as proclaimed by Christ.

But if, on the other hand, Christ intended to accomplish something truly supernatural in the redemption of man, that work would either have to be confined within the narrow limits of the time and space circumscribed by his earthly existence, or would have to find extension in a true extension of himself. His story and his maxims were not a sufficient legacy for men. His message and his maxims are not of themselves salvific. He himself had to come to us. Therefore, his saving work can transform us today only if he is with us personally. He promised to remain always in the world. Such a promise would have been empty had he intended to fulfill it merely by remaining, as Dr. Johnson did, the subject of a book. He promised to remain, and remain he did.

Christ living in the world and our living in Christ, in the Mystical Body of Christ—this is what the Church means, and this is the subject of our study.

3. The Nature of the Church

A. Its Definition

The Church, we have seen, is the divinely appointed means by which men are associated with the redemptive work of Christ. Therefore, its purpose is to lead men to salvation. But this does not sufficiently tell us what the Church is. Pope Pius XII states that the

Church is "a society whose Head and ruler is Christ," and is the Mystical Body of Christ.[4]

Although narrower definitions of the Church are in vogue today, since St. Augustine the universal Latin tradition holds that the Church is substantially one and unbroken from Abel to the end of the world, and is "the congregation of the faithful."[5] Thus St. Thomas says:

> As in a man there is one soul and one body, yet a diversity of members, so the Catholic Church is one body and has different members. The soul which enlivens this body is the Holy Spirit, which is why, after faith in the Holy Spirit, we must have faith in the Catholic Church, as is made plain in the Creed. When we speak of *Church* we signify *congregation;* when we speak of *Holy Church* we signify *congregation of the faithful;* when we speak of a *Christian* we signify a *member of that Church*.[6]

The important point for the student to note is that the word "Church" probably conveys to him the notion of "Church of Rome," the visible Church and especially its visible aspects. Such a signification is, of course, quite apt as far as it goes. However, the traditional concept of "Church," a concept which more fully responds to reality, places greater emphasis on the mystery of the Church and includes all the stages of the Church's development.

From a somewhat different point of view it seems practical to mention Journet's three meanings of the word "Church."[7]

1) In the **restricted** sense it refers to the faithful, the believing and receiving Church, those to whom the teaching Church is ordered. It should be remembered that the pope and bishops, since they too must be saved, are members of the faithful.

2) In the **intermediate** sense, the word "Church" refers to the entire Church, which is made up of hierarchy (precisely as hierarchy) and faithful, and which is subject to Christ as its Head.

---

[4]*Mystici Corporis,* 64.

[5]St. Augustine, *Commentary on Psalm 36, Sermon 3,* 4: "From the beginning of time all the just who have ever existed have had Christ as their Head, since he whom we believe to have already come they believed would come, and as we are saved by our faith in him, they were saved by theirs."

[6]*Expos. in Symbolum,* Art. 9.

[7]Charles Journet, *The Church of the Word Incarnate,* Vol. I, *The Apostolic Hierarchy* (New York: Sheed and Ward, 1955), 45 ff.

3) In the **broad** sense, the word "Church" refers to the **total** Mystical Body which includes both head and members. The context will indicate the sense in which the word is being used.

B. Division of the Church

There is no division in the Church; the Church is one. However, a *quasi-division* can be made according to the various ways in which the Church can be considered. The more important elements of this division are:

1) The distinction between the Church as **visible** and the Church as **invisible.** It is not possible, for example, to belong to the visible Church and not belong to the invisible, or *vice versa,* because they are one and the same thing. Yet one can visibly belong (or seem to belong), while invisibly one is not truly a member. Or one can invisibly belong while not seeming to belong.

2) By reason of time we can distinguish the **Church of the Law of Nature** from the **Church of the Old Law,** and we can distinguish both of these from the **Church of the New Law.**

3) A distinction between the **Church Teaching** and the **Church Taught** can also be made.

4) Since all who are joined to God through Christ are members of the Church, this term must include those in heaven, the **Church Triumphant;** those in purgatory, the **Church Suffering;** and those who are still engaged in the struggle on this earth, the **Church Militant.**

We are concerned here with the Church Militant. Other divisions could be suggested, but what the student must remember is that the Church is one. None of these divisions divides the Church into several churches or even into truly separable parts. The divisions are made solely for convenience in study.

C. The Foundation of the Church

The Church which was foreshadowed in the Old Law was brought to full reality by Christ. The manner in which he is the founder of the Church is made clear in *Mystici Corporis,* in which Pope Leo

XIII is quoted as noting three stages in the foundation of the Church: "The Church which, already conceived, came forth from the side of the second Adam in his sleep on the cross, first showed herself before the eyes of men on the great day of Pentecost."[8] The Church was prepared by Christ during his public life by his teaching, his selection of the apostles, his appointment of a Vicar on earth, his establishment of baptism and the Eucharist, as well as by his other works. It was born from his side. Commenting on this, St. Ambrose says: "And it is now that it is built, it is now that it is formed, it is now that it is created. . . . Now it is that arises a spiritual house for a holy priesthood."[9] And finally, on the day of Pentecost the Spirit whom he had promised to send was poured out upon the apostles to strengthen the Church and to make its supernatural office and mission evident.

D. Membership in the Church

Since Christ is the only way to the Father, and since the Church is the Mystical Body of Christ, the question of membership in the Church and of the necessity of this membership for salvation is of primary importance. Many knotty problems are connected with this question, but we will discuss only the basic principles involved, together with their applications to the more common situations.

Pope Pius XII has stated categorically: "Only those are really to be included as members of the Church who have been baptized and profess the true faith and who have not unhappily withdrawn from body-unity or for grave faults been excluded by legitimate authority."[10] The meaning is clear. *To possess* **actual** *membership in the Church, in the Mystical Body of Christ, one must profess the one true faith, be baptized, and not have left the Church or been excommunicated.* Yet it is certain that actual membership in the Church is not necessary for salvation. The traditional adage, "Outside the Church there is no salvation," is to be interpreted as Van Noort interprets it,

[8]Nn. 27.
[9]St. Ambrose, *Commentary on the Gospel of St. Luke*, II, 87.
[10]*Mystici Corporis*, 23.

when he says, "Anyone who *by his own fault* lives and dies outside the Church will definitely be damned."[11]

Such an interpretation is demanded when one considers this important statement of Pope Pius IX:

> It is known to us and to you that those who are invincibly ignorant with regard to our holy religion, if they dutifully fulfill the natural law and its precepts which are inscribed by God in the hearts of all men and are prepared to be obedient to God, and if they live an honest and upright life—that such men can, by the operating power of divine light and grace, attain eternal life. For God, who fully understands the minds, souls, thoughts and habits of all men, will not by reason of his supreme goodness and clemency permit anyone who is not voluntarily guilty of sin to suffer eternal damnation.[12]

Thus it is possible for men to have some kind of salvific union with the Church without being actual members. This possibility is considered in *Mystici Corporis* where Pope Pius XII answers the objection that, if it is possible for those invincibly ignorant of the Church to be saved, missionaries should not be sent to them, because through the preaching of missionaries their invincible ignorance might be rendered culpable. He says: "For even though unsuspectingly they are related to the Mystical Body of the Redeemer in desire and resolution, they still remain deprived of many precious gifts and helps from heaven, which one can only enjoy in the Catholic Church."[13]

E. The Necessity of the Church

It is clear from what has been said about the nature of the Church that the necessity of seeking salvation through the Church is not only a necessity arising from a precept, i.e., a direct command from Christ. As far as the necessity is one of precept, it is fulfilled by those who belong to the Church merely by implicit desire.[14] But

---

[11]*Dogmatic Theology,* Vol. II, *The Church,* translated and revised by John J. Castelot, S.S., and William R. Murphy, S.S. (Westminster, Md.: The Newman Press, 1957), 265.

[12]Encyclical *Quanto conficiamur moerore,* August 10, 1863; Denz. 1677.

[13]*Mystici Corporis,* 117.

[14]Letter of the Holy Office to Archbishop Cushing, 1949; cf. *The Church Teaches* (St. Louis: Herder, 1955), 279.

the necessity of belonging to the Church is also a **necessity of means.**
The means are not absolutely necessary, as Pope Pius IX notes in
the passage just cited, but they are so important that without them
there remains slight chance of attaining the end.

4. The Church as Mystery

We have already seen that the Church is a mystery of faith, an
object of our belief. This arises from the fact that the Church is something essentially supernatural, a projection of the Incarnate God himself in time and space. The Church is identified with the Mystical
Body of Christ. However, confusion sometimes arises when an author
uses "Church" in a restricted sense and "Mystical Body" in a wide
sense in the same passage, or vice versa. Such phraseology is in-
accurate and should be avoided.

But in themselves the two terms remain interchangeable, describing
one and the same supernatural reality. *Mystici Corporis* clearly
teaches this. But because some tried to avoid accepting this teaching, Pope Pius XII says in *Humani Generis:* "That the Mystical Body
of Christ and the Catholic Church in communion with Rome are
one and the same thing is a doctrine based on revealed truth, and
as such was set forth by us in an encyclical a few years back."[15]

We shall consider the mystery in three sections:

1) Christ its Head, in which we shall study the relevance of Christ
   to the Church;
2) The Whole Christ, in which we shall study how the Church
   is Christ's body and, indeed, his Mystical Body;
3) The Soul of the Church.

A. Christ, the Head of the Church

(1) Christ, the Way to God

We studied the capital grace of Christ in an earlier chapter. However, let us consider this mystery again, precisely as it results in his
being the Head of the Mystical Body. Christ is our way to God.

[15]Denz. 2319.

The moral part of the *Summa* is concerned with the motion of rational creatures, precisely as they are images of God, toward God. This motion is realized only by participation in the capital grace of Christ. Thus in Question 93, Article 4 of the First Part of the *Summa*, St. Thomas speaks of the degrees of realization of the image of God in man. After treating of the development of this image— that is to say, the return of the rational creature to God (Second Part of the *Summa*)—St. Thomas returns to the same degrees in Part Three of the *Summa*, this time in the context of participation in Christ (Question VIII, Article 3).

Father Congar makes this admirable statement of the case:

> In the world of grace, a kind of Platonism is valid, for Christ contains in himself the fulness of the species grace, in a way similar to that in which the archtype of man, in Plato, contains the fulness of human species. So that, if other individuals are to receive grace too, they may only do so in dependence on Christ and, if these be men, whose unique Savior is the God-given Christ, they may only receive it from Christ and in virtue of sharing, and participating in his own grace.[16]

Christ is the "new Adam," the new head of the human race. Just as the brilliant colors of the spectrum are contained in the white light which the spectrum analyzes, so also every effect of grace which appears in the Church, now and forever, is contained first in him. Indeed, the Head recapitulates the members so perfectly that St. Thomas tells us that Christ plus the Church adds up to Christ alone, just as God plus the world adds up to God alone.[17]

(2) Work of Christ as Head of the Church

Christ's role as Head of the Church is considered at length in *Mystici Corporis* (nn. 35 ff). Christ is Head because he holds the highest place, and he rules and governs the Church. He instructs by precept, counsel and warning. Not only did he confer upon his apostles and their successors a threefold power which enables them to teach, to govern and to lead men to holiness, he himself guides and governs his people directly and personally. He watches over in-

---

[16]*Art. cit.*, 341-342.
[17]*In IV Sent.*, d. 49, q. 4, a. 3, ad 3.

dividuals and exercises his providence over the universal Church; he provides special helps and special vocations for the preservation of his work. As we shall see later, he rules visibly through his Vicar on earth. Through his human nature Christ humanizes the divine life communicated to man. Therefore, he is truly able to be the Head because in his humanity he is of like nature with the body. He enlightens his Church and communicates power to it. All holiness comes from him.

B. The Whole Christ

How foolish to love; or how wise. For when we love we subject ourselves to the object of our love. We need what we love. Because he chose to love us, Christ needs his members. Christ joined with his members, the Mystical Body of Christ, has been called "the Whole Christ." Pius XII says:

> Dying on the Cross he left to his Church the immense treasury of the Redemption; towards this she contributed nothing. But when those graces come to be distributed, not only does he share this task of sanctification with his Church, but he wants it in a way to be due to her action. This is a deep mystery, subject of inexhaustible meditation; that the salvation of many depends on the prayers and voluntary penances which the members of the Mystical Body of Jesus Christ offer for this intention and on the assistance of pastors of souls and of the faithful, especially of fathers and mothers of families, which they must offer to our divine Savior as though they were his associates.[18]

Only the life of Christ in us as members of his Mystical Body enables us to make real progress toward God. Therefore, the Church is the whole economy of the return of man to the God from whom he came. There is no other happiness for man, no other goal. Union with God is the sole worthy objective of man's pilgrimage, an objective which cannot be obtained by his natural powers. Man can reach this objective only by participation in the grace of Christ. He must live the life of Christ, belonging in some way to the Mystical Body of Christ. The whole moral teaching of St. Thomas is, in this sense, ecclesiological. The prologue to the second question of the *Summa* reads:

[18]*Mystici Corporis*, 46.

Because the chief aim of Sacred Doctrine is to teach the knowledge of God, not only as he is in himself, but also as he is the beginning of things and their last end, and especially of rational creatures, as is clear from what has been already said, therefore, in our endeavor to expound this science, we shall treat: (1) of God; (2) of the rational creature's advance towards God; (3) *of Christ, who as man is our way to God.*

The concept of the "Whole Christ" is based upon the unity between Head and members which results from the participation of the members in the life of the Head. This share in the divine life makes a true movement toward God possible to the members and makes the members acceptable to God. Thus St. Thomas considers the whole of Christian morality to be Christocentric, because as man Christ is our way. The unity of head and members produces a **mystical body**. It is not a natural (or physical) body because each member retains individual subsistence and maintains intact his own personality.[19] On the other hand, it is not just a moral body, since its unity does not depend merely on having a common end and a common co-operation for the attainment of that end. Rather:

This collaboration is supplemented by a distinct internal principle, which exists effectively in the whole and in each of its parts, and whose excellence is such, that of itself it is vastly superior to whatever bonds of union may be found in a physical or moral body. This is something not of the natural but of the supernatural order. Essentially, it is something infinite, uncreated: the Spirit of God, who, as the Angelic Doctor says, "numerically one and the same, fills and unifies the whole Church."[20]

This leads us to the consideration of the "soul of the Church."

C. The Soul of the Church

As in a man there is one soul and one body, yet a diversity of members, so the Catholic Church is one body and has different members. The soul which quickens this body is the Holy Spirit; and that is why, after faith in the Holy Spirit, we are required to have faith in the Catholic Church, as the Creed itself makes clear.[21]

[19]Cf. *Mystici Corporis,* 65.
[20]*Ibid.,* 66.
[21]St. Thomas, *Expos. in Symbolum,* Art. 9.

This teaching, namely, that the Holy Spirit is the soul of the Church, is found in the writings of the Fathers of the Church[22] and is clearly expressed by Pope Leo XIII in his encyclical *Divinum Illud*. The idea is developed at some length in *Mystici Corporis*. Yet the Holy Spirit must not be considered as having the same relationship to the Mystical Body as the soul has to a material body. Theologians, following the example of St. Thomas, speak of the Holy Spirit as the "quasi-soul" of the Church. It is more accurate to say that the Holy Spirit *inhabits* the body which is the Church than to say that the Holy Spirit *informs* it.

The Church's life is drawn from the Holy Spirit. Actually its life, however, is a created (homogeneous) reality, supernatural charity. Faith, the indispensable foundation of charity, unites us imperfectly to God by knowledge. Charity unites us perfectly to God by love. And it is God's knowledge and God's love which is the life of the Trinity. To participate in this divine knowledge and love is to share in the life of the Trinity. Therefore, as Congar points out, the Church is, in a sense, an extension or manifestation of the Blessed Trinity; it is the mystery of God in man: God, coming from God and returning to God, taking up humanity into himself.[23]

The union of humanity to divinity in Christ is a personal union, one which precludes a human personality. Human nature was assumed by the divine Person in such a manner that one being resulted. The union of human beings to the Blessed Trinity in the Mystical Body is of such a nature that all share the same divine life but each remains an individual person. This union is modelled on that of the Blessed Trinity itself. For in the Blessed Trinity a community of persons fully and perfectly share a common life. That is why Christ's prayer, "that they may be one *even as we are* . . . that they also may be one in us" (Jn. 17:11 and 21), is in the fullest sense of his meaning applicable to creatures. Thus the Church is one with the very oneness of God. He has formed, together with himself, a divine family of mankind. This great truth is the source of three truths which are already known:

[22]Cf. S. Tromp, S.J., *De Spiritu Sancto anima Corporis Mystici. I. Testim. ex Patribus graecis. II. Testim. ex Patribus latinis.* (Rome: Gregorianum, 1932).
[23]M. J. Congar, O.P., *Divided Christendom* (London: Geoffrey Bles, 1939), 56.

1. **The Church is not only one but** *unique.* There can be no other Church since her oneness is the unique oneness of the unique God.

2. **The unity of the Church comes, not from the members, but from God.** Therefore, no matter how many members separate themselves from the Church, her unity is not destroyed nor even diminished by their departure.

3. **Since the Church is the sharing of Christ's divine life there can be no salvation except in her and through her.**

5. The Church as Visible Institution

> It is clear how grievously they err who arbitrarily picture the Church as something hidden and invisible, as do they also who look upon it as a mere human institution with a certain disciplinary code and external ritual, but lacking power to communicate supernatural life. No; the Mystical Body of Christ is like Christ, the Head and exemplar of the Church, "who is not complete, if only his visible human nature is considered, or if only his divine, invisible nature . . . , but he is one through the union of both and one in both. . . ." Thus the Word of God took unto himself a human nature liable to sufferings, so that he might consecrate in his blood the visible society founded by him and "lead man back to things invisible under a visible rule."[24]

The phrase of Jesus to the Samaritan woman at the well, "But the hour is coming, and is now here, when the true worshippers will worship the Father in spirit and in truth" (Jn. 4:23), has been seized upon and interpreted out of context by some who call themselves Christians but who do not acknowledge the visible headship and authority of a visible Church. The basic position of all non-Catholic Christians rejects either completely or partially the idea of a divinely instituted hierarchy, which is the principle of authority, the teacher of truth, and the source of sacramental grace in the Mystical Body of Christ.

A. The Hierarchy—the Form of the Church

(1) The Mystery of Belief

The hierarchy is the form of the Church. Since Christ wished to retain direct contact with the faithful, he determined that some men

---

[24]*Mystici Corporis,* 69.

be associated with himself as mediators between God and man. He wished some men to govern others in the supernatural order just as some men govern others in the natural order. Using the Scriptures and Church history, apologetics develops arguments which show that the claims for a purely human origin of the hierarchy are specious and that strong evidence points to divine origin. Perhaps stronger evidence can be found in the fact that, in a world of changing institutions, the hierarchy has always been impervious to the attacks of its enemies. "For if this plan or work is of men, it will be overthrown; but if it is of God, you will not be able to overthrow it" (Acts 5:38-9).

But we are not directly concerned with apologetic arguments here. Rather we are concerned with the hierarchy as a deep mystery of belief. It is the divinely chosen instrument of the divine power working among men. Like sacramental signs, it is visible, but only with regard to its existence and a small part of its reality. It is the *form* of the Church.

(2) Visible Organization

The Church is a visible organization. Its enemies, along with the indifferent and the faithful, know that the pope and bishops rule a vast organization which, no matter what is thought of it, does exist and function in the midst of men. To its enemies, the Church may appear as a blight on the world; to the indifferent, as a rather silly and quite senseless means of satisfying the emotional needs of men. But to the faithful it is the external sign of a profound and sacred reality, God working in the lives of men. Its form, therefore, the hierarchy, is likewise visible, and has a much deeper reality than can be appreciated by the senses. The jurisdictional and sacramental power exercised by God through the instrumentality of the hierarchy keeps God in contact with his people.

Those who become popes and bishops remain men, and because they remain men, they need the ministration of the Church in order to attain their own salvation. Not even a pope can absolve himself from his sins. The hierarchy, therefore, belongs to the company of the faithful, and it is the faithful who are the **material cause** of the Church.

The hierarchy is the form divinely impressed upon the Church, precisely because it is the minister of salvation, possessing and exercising the priestly and kingly and prophetic offices of Christ for the salvation of men.

In a human being the form is the soul. Why is this not true of the Mystical Body? First of all, we must remember that the term "body" is used analogically. While the unity of the Mystical Body is more than a mere moral union, it is not a physical union. Perhaps it would avoid confusion if, in reference to the Church, the terms *quasi*-form and *quasi*-soul were used.

(3) *Perpetuity of the Form*

Christ, the Head and source of all life in the Church, on Pentecost fulfilled (cf. Acts 2:1-4) his promise (cf. Jn. 15:15,26; 15:26; 16:7-16) to send his Spirit to vitalize the Church. His Spirit is, therefore, the **uncreated soul** of the Church, because in the Holy Spirit, the Spirit of Christ, is found the font from which the Church draws her life. The Spirit was granted in a special way to the apostles (Jn. 20:23; also note that the texts indicated above—Jn. 14 through 16—are spoken at the Last Supper to the apostles alone). The mission given to Christ by his eternal Father is extended and continued in and through the apostles. "As the Father has sent me, I also send you" (Jn. 20:21).

The apostles recognized fully their power to designate successors and their authority to pass on to them the Holy Spirit, with the power to celebrate the Eucharist, to forgive sins and to rule the Church. (Cf. II Tim. 1:6; Titus 1:5 ff.). Moreover, it is obvious from the final words of St. Matthew's gospel, "I am with you all days, even unto the consummation of the world," that the commission of Christ would not die out with the apostles. Therefore, the apostles and their successors (the hierarchy) are the divinely appointed channels through which the Holy Spirit infuses into the souls of the faithful a created share in the divine life, which is grace and charity. Thus, *grace* and *charity*, precisely as they pass through the hierarchy with its sacramental and jurisdictional power (Journet calls it "jurisdictionally orientated sacramental grace"[25]) constitutes the **created soul** of the Church.

[25]*Op. cit.*, 512-3, 515.

(4) Order and Jurisdiction

Sometimes the distinction is made between the "hierarchy of orders" and the "hierarchy of jurisdiction." But this is a distinction not between two hierarchies but between two offices of the one hierarchy. Divine life is both begun and substantially increased in the souls of men through the ministerial power of sacred orders. Yet the existence of ministerial power is not alone sufficient for maintaining divine life. The power of orders must also function through the jurisdictional power. Faith is not enough. One must know what to believe. One must know what to love, what to do. Thus, the same hierarchy through which divine life comes must direct its development. This it does by the power of jurisdiction. Taken in its wide traditional sense, jurisdiction includes the power to speak with divine authority in both speculative and practical matters; to be teacher and law-giver. This power of jurisdiction, in turn, rests upon the power of orders. The Church does not grant the exercise of jurisdiction except to one who has the requisite power of orders.[26]

> Bishops, then, must be considered as the nobler members of the universal Church, for they are linked in an altogether special way to the divine head of the whole body and so are rightly called "principal parts of the members of the Lord"; what is more, as far as each one's own diocese is concerned, they each and all as true Shepherds feed the flocks entrusted to them and rule them in the name of Christ. Yet in exercising this office they are not altogether independent, but are duly subordinate to the authority of the Roman Pontiff; and although their jurisdiction is inherent in their office, yet they receive it directly from the same Supreme Pontiff. Hence, they should be revered by the faithful as divinely appointed successors of the apostles.[27]

B. The Infallibility of the Church

(1) Meaning of Infallibility

Through her active principle, the hierarchy, the Church teaches men what they must believe and instructs them in what they must do. Moreover, Christ has promised to remain always with the Church

---

[26]Cf. Augustine Rock, O.P., *Unless They Be Sent* (Dubuque: Wm. C. Brown Co., 1953, and London: Blackfriars, 1955), 123 and 140 ff.
[27]*Mystici Corporis*, 44.

(cf. Matt. 28:20). Therefore the Church cannot possibly teach an error in matters concerned with revelation. Nor can the Church universally misguide the faithful, causing them to turn away from their salvation. To agree that the Church is incapable of erring when it hands down decisions on matters of faith and morals is to concede that the Church is infallible. These infallible decisions require the full and absolute assent of everyone.

(2) Objects of Infallibility

All the religious truths contained in the sources of revelation are the primary object of revelation. Furthermore, the Church is infallible with regard to any other truth which is so intimately connected with the truths of revelation that to make an error about it would seriously endanger revealed truth. Therefore, it is theologically certain that the Church is infallible about:

1) theological conclusions (drawn from one revealed principle and one principle known by natural knowledge);

2) dogmatic facts (although not themselves revealed, they must be admitted lest something which is revealed be either contradicted, or made incapable of being proposed); e.g., that Trent was a true general council; that a certain proposition is contained in a certain book, etc.;

3) general Church discipline; i.e., the Church cannot make laws contrary to faith or morals, nor can it make laws which would, of their nature, lead souls away from their eternal destiny;

4) the approval of religious orders (taken in the strict sense of the term), since such approval states that the way of life of the order is suited to acquiring perfection;

5) the canonization of saints, since the formula of canonization plainly asserts, in terms which *commit* the authority of the Church, that the person involved is indeed in heaven and should be venerated by all.

Infallibility is not a positive influence impelling the Church to teach a truth. It is merely a negative assistance of the Holy Spirit, which, by any suitable means, prevents the official teachers of the Church from teaching error in matters of faith or morals. It implies, however, much more than the inerrancy of the Church's teaching. It implies that the Church *cannot* err in its teaching.

(3) The Magisterium of the Church

The *magisterium* or teaching authority of the Church is either solemn or ordinary. The solemn magisterium, which through the centuries has defined very few truths, is a solemn statement made by the pope or by a general council in conjunction with the pope, that binds the faithful to hold and believe a certain truth (e.g., the definition of papal infallibility by the Vatican Council with the approval of Pope Pius IX; the definition of the Assumption of Mary by Pope Pius XII). Those truths which are commonly taught by the **Church teaching** and commonly received by the **Church taught** are proposed by the ordinary magisterium. Truths so taught are to be believed by all. Pius XII says in *Humani Generis*: ". . . these matters are taught with the ordinary teaching authority, of which it is true to say: 'He who hears you hears me'."[28]

C. The Properties of the Church

The Church is one, holy, Catholic and apostolic. These four terms are familiar to all Catholics. They are found in the Nicene Creed among the objects of our faith. Yet most Catholics are more familiar with their visible manifestation, and with the apologetic argument based on them: "The Church of Christ should be one, holy, Catholic and apostolic. But the Roman Catholic Church is all of these. Therefore, the Roman Catholic Church is the Church of Christ."

We are not concerned here, however, with the apologetic value of these qualities. We are concerned with these qualities as they are **properties** of the Church, rather than **marks** or **notes** (properties externally manifested).

(1) The Church Is One

We have already seen that the Church of Christ must be uniquely one because the Mystical Body is a communication of the divine life,

[28]N. 29.

which is one and unique; "one Lord, one faith, one baptism" (Eph. 4:5). Therefore, this unity is *social*, for there is one jurisdiction, one government and one obedience. Moreover, this unity is *symbolic* (in the sense that symbol means creed), since there is but one faith and one teaching to which all must assent. Finally, this unity is *liturgical*, for the essential form of worship and the means of salvation are common to all.

Thus, the **unity** of the Church can be defined in this way: *A property of the Church by which the Church is undivided in itself and divided from everything else in the profession of supernatural faith, in hierarchical rule and in divine worship.*

(2) The Church Is Holy

Great mischief has been worked in the Church by those who have misunderstood the property of holiness which belongs to the Church, a property which must belong to the Church since she is the Mystical Body of Christ. The history of the Church is witness to the development of various heresies based on the erroneous notion that personal virtue rather than sacramental ordination and apostolic commission give title to power and authority in the Church. Aside from being contrary to the plan of Christ, systems based on this notion have been completely unworkable and have invariably created such confusion among their adherents that the sects disintegrated within a comparatively short time. Personal virtue cannot be assessed by natural means. An attempt at assessing virtue by natural means turns the curious into detectives and the self-righteous into hypocrites.

The property of holiness does not mean that every member of the Church, or even every official, will be outstanding in personal virtue. Cockle will grow up with the wheat and bad fish will swim with the good (cf. Matt. 13). **Holiness** is *that property which perfectly directs the Church's doctrine, sacraments and members to the divine good.* Her doctrine and her sacraments are holy and productive of holiness. There has always been a deep holiness in her members. The task of the apologist is to furnish evidence for these statements and to answer objections against them, but our concern is with the meaning of holiness as a property of the Church.

(3) *The Church Is Catholic*

Because of the property of **Catholicity**, the Church is found essentially the same everywhere and in all ages. One day it will be completely diffused through all nations. For the present it is sufficient that it be conspicuously present everywhere. St. Thomas notes that the notion of Catholicity extends to other than geographical factors. It includes men of all kinds and all conditions; no one is left outside. Furthermore, the Church is universal in time, enduring from Abel to the end of the world, after which she shall continue to endure in heaven.[29]

(4) *The Church Is Apostolic*

When we speak of **apostolicity** we speak of the unbroken continuation of doctrine, worship and government, from the time of the apostles in whom the Church was constituted, to our own era. As Msgr. Journet points out, apostolicity is the power that gives birth to the Church. It signifies a mediation or a chain of dependence which begins with the power of the Trinity, passes first into the humanity of Christ, then into the sacramental and jurisdictional power of the apostolic body (which is uninterruptedly continued in the hierarchy), and finally into the Christian people. In this sense of the word apostolicity would be the supernatural power (*formal aspect*) which comes down from God (*first efficient cause*), then from Christ (*instrumental cause conjoined to the divinity*), then from an apostolic body preserved by an uninterrupted succession (*instrumental cause separate from the divinity*), in order to form the Church (*final cause*) among men (*material cause*).[30]

Considered, however, strictly as a property of the Church, **apostolicity** may be defined as *that property of the Church by which she continues through a legitimate, public and unbroken succession of pastors from the apostles, in a oneness of doctrine, sacraments and government.* History can attest to this mark of the Church. Yet in a deeper sense, what is passed down is a mystery of faith pertaining

[29]Cf. *Expos. in Symbolum*, Art. 9; see also St. Cyril of Jerusalem, *Eighteenth Catechesis*, 23.
[30]Cf. Charles Journet, *op. cit.*, 527.

to the created soul of the Church. The sacramental powers, jurisdictional power, sacramental grace, as well as the divine truth entrusted to the apostles, remain in the Church. Although committed to the apostles, this divine endowment belongs to us by reason of our firm belief in the apostolicity of the Church: *credo in . . . apostolicam Ecclesiam.*

D. The Visible Headship: The Pope and the Bishops

(1) Primacy of the Pope

> Now since the social body of Christ has been designed by its founder to be visible, . . . everyone must be able to see the Supreme Head, who gives effective direction to what all are doing in a mutually helpful way towards attaining the desired end, that is, the Vicar on earth of Jesus Christ. As the divine Redeemer sent a Paraclete, the Spirit of Truth, who in his name should govern the Church in an invisible way; similarly he commissioned Peter and his successors, to be his personal representatives on earth and to assume the visible government of the Christian community.[31]

Apologetics proves that Peter was given a true primacy over the other apostles and over the whole Church. Since this primacy is passed down to the successors of St. Peter, the Supreme Pontiff over the whole Church, the Bishop of Rome, possesses a true and absolute primacy.[32]

This primacy grants true jurisdiction, not mere directive power. It is universal both with regard to matters of faith and morals and with regard to discipline and government. The power of the pope is direct and episcopal. That is, the pope is the proper bishop of every bishop and of every one of the faithful. His power is not merely used to make sure a command is carried out. He directly commands without the mediation of the Local Ordinary. A council of bishops which does not include the pope is neither superior to, nor equal to the pope. Nor can a council of bishops limit the power of the pope. Indeed, even a council of bishops which includes the pope can never wield more power than the pope alone.

[31]*Mystici Corporis,* 76.
[32]Cf. Vatican Council, Sess. IV, *Dogmatic Constitution on the Church of Christ,* Chap. 3; Denz. 1831.

The pope is, of course, bound by divine law to use his power with wisdom and prudence. Still, no power on earth has the authority to judge him.

(2) Infallibility of the Pope

Since the Supreme Pontiff possesses fulness of power over the whole Church, and since the Church is infallible, it follows that the pope is infallible. This was defined by the Vatican Council.[33] The infallibility of the pope is directly concerned with the *teaching office* and refers only indirectly to any other activity. The pope is infallible when he speaks *ex cathedra* (from the throne). The throne of a bishop is primarily the chair of a teacher. Therefore, to speak infallibly, the pope must speak precisely as pope, using the fulness of his authority. His message must include the element of universality, for when he speaks precisely as pope, using the fulness of his authority, he speaks to the whole world. Nevertheless, the pope can speak to the whole world, as pope, without intending to make the fullest use of his authority. This is often the case in the papal encyclicals. The faithful are bound to respond to an infallible pronouncement with a true and unconditional internal act of faith.

Note that even with regard to papal statements which do not use the fulness of pontifical authority, the consent of the faithful is demanded. Pius XII says:

> Nor must it be thought that what is expounded in encyclical letters does not of itself demand consent, since in writing such letters the popes do not exercise the supreme power of their teaching authority. For these matters are taught with the ordinary teaching authority, of which it is true to say: "He who heareth you, heareth me" (Lk. 10:16); and generally what is expounded and inculcated in encyclical letters already for other reasons appertains to Catholic doctrine. But if the Supreme Pontiffs in their official documents purposely pass judgment on a matter up to that time under dispute, it is obvious that the matter, according to the mind and will of the same Pontiffs, cannot be any longer considered a question open to discussion among theologians.[34]

(3) Power of Individual Bishops

By divine ordination, subordinate pastors are associated with the Supreme Pontiff in ruling the Church. These pastors are called

---

[33]Cf. *ibid.;* Denz. 1839.
[34]*Humani Generis* (Paulist Press), n. 29; Denz. 2313.

bishops. At the time of their episcopal consecration they receive the fulness of the priesthood and become ordinary ministers of the sacraments of holy orders and confirmation. When appointed to a diocese, a bishop, by divine right, possesses ordinary jurisdiction over the territory of that diocese. The pope cannot suppress the office of bishop, nor interfere with the normal jurisdiction of a bishop over his see. Each bishop possesses the power to teach and to rule his own see.

Nevertheless, this power is subordinate to that of the pope. This is obvious from what has been said of the pope's supreme universal jurisdiction. Since the pope is the supreme head of the hierarchy it would be manifestly absurd for a bishop to possess true jurisdiction in the Church without the consent of the pope. Indeed, since the promulgation of *Mystici Corporis* it has been certain that "although their [the bishops'] jurisdiction is inherent in their office, yet *they receive it directly* from the same Supreme Pontiff."[35]

The teaching authority of the bishop in his own diocese is not protected by infallibility. And yet his teaching authority is not to be ranked simply according to the value of his arguments or his erudition. Unless weighty reasons prove the contrary, the authority of the bishop in doctrinal matters must be accepted by his subjects.

(4) Power of the Bishops Collectively

The college of bishops in union with the Bishop of Rome is infallible. In other words, the college of bishops shares the same infallibility of the Church with the pope. This does not mean, however, that the pope depends on the bishops for his infallibility. This collective teaching of the bishops does not have to be produced in a general council. In *Munificentissimus Deus* (the Apostolic Constitution of Pius XII defining the Assumption) the pope says:

> And, since we were dealing with a matter of such great moment and of such importance, We considered it opportune to ask all Our Venerable Brethren in the episcopate directly and authoritatively that each of them should tell us what he thought in his own words. Hence, on May 1, 1946, We gave them our letter *Deiparae Virginis Mariae,* a letter in which these words were contained: "Do you, Vener-

[35]N. 44; italics added.

able Brethren, in your understanding, wisdom and prudence, judge that the bodily Assumption of the Blessed Virgin can be defined and proposed as a dogma of faith? Do you, with your clergy and people, desire that it should be?"

But those whom "the Holy Spirit has placed as bishops to rule the Church of God" (Acts 20:28) gave an almost unanimous affirmative response to both these questions. This "outstanding agreement of the Catholic prelates and the faithful" (*Ineffabilis Deus, Acta Pii IX,* Pars I, Vol. 1, 615) affirming that the bodily Assumption of God's Mother into heaven can be defined as a dogma of faith, since it shows us the concordant teaching of the Church's ordinary doctrinal authority and the concordant faith of the Christian people which the same doctrinal authority sustains and directs, thus *by itself and in a way altogether certain and free of all errors, manifested this privilege as a truth revealed by God* and contained in that divine deposit which Christ has delivered to his Spouse to be guarded faithfully and to be taught infallibly. Certainly this teaching authority of the Church, not by any merely human effort but under the protection of the Spirit of Truth, has carried out the commission entrusted to it, and that in such a way that it presents them undefiled, adding nothing to them and taking nothing away from them. For, as the Vatican Council teaches, "the Holy Spirit was not promised to the successors of Peter in such a way that, by his revelation, they might manifest new doctrine, but so that, by his assistance, they might guard as sacred and might faithfully propose the revelation delivered through the apostles, or the deposit of faith" (Constitution *De Ecclesia Christi,* Chap. 4; Denz. 1836). Thus, from the universal agreement of the Church's ordinary teaching authority we have a certain and firm proof, demonstrating that the Blessed Virgin Mary's bodily Assumption into heaven . . . is a truth that has been revealed by God and consequently something that must be faithfully and firmly believed by all the children of the Church. For, as the Vatican Council asserts, "All those things are to be believed by divine and Catholic faith which are contained in the written word of God or in tradition, and which are proposed by the Church, either in solemn judgment or in its ordinary and universal teaching office, as divinely revealed truths which must be believed" (*ibid.,* Chap. 3; Denz. 1792).[36]

6. The Church and Other Societies

A. The Claims of the Church

The Church is a visible organization existing in the workaday world. Faith is not required to recognize it as an organization. But

---

[36]The entire text is from the translation of *Munificentissimus Deus* by Msgr. Joseph C. Fenton, S.T.D., as published in *The Thomist,* XIV (1951), 6-7.

faith is required to understand the relationship of the Church to other societies. The claims of the Church, claims her very nature requires her to make, often seem to be sheer arrogance to the man without faith. The Church's claims have been the cause of diverse attitudes among non-Catholics, attitudes ranging from suspicion to the passing of death sentence. The Church claims to teach with divine authority, to be superior to the state in spiritual matters and independent of the state's authority, and to have the right and duty to legislate for her children.

Misunderstanding can arise on each and on all of these points, and it easily results in hatred. A basic misunderstanding of the Church is unavoidable in non-Catholics. Every effort should be made, of course, to present the Church in a favorable light and to try to live at peace with all men. However, the unwillingness of all men to accept us peacefully should occasion no surprise. "And you will be hated by all for my name's sake" (Matt. 10:22).

B. Harmony of Church and State

The Church, like the state, is a perfect society. That is to say, it contains within itself the necessary means for achieving its purpose, a purpose of ultimate consequence. However, Church and state must meet in the man who belongs to both. Therefore Church and state are destined by the divine plan to work in harmony to aid man in the attainment of his goal. This does not mean that Church and state must be united in the European manner. We are not concerned here with practical problems connected with the Church-state relationship. But we can note that some kind of positive harmony between them is necessary for true peace in society.

7. Summary and Conclusion

The Church can be considered either as a visible organization or as a mystery of faith. It cannot truly be understood as a visible organization without recognizing it as a mystery of faith; nor can there be fruitful investigation of the mystery unless its visible manifestation be taken into consideration. Yet it is the one same Church founded by Christ to lead men to salvation. It is the Mystical Body of Christ in which the salvific work of Christ is given extension in time and place. It is not a physical body whose members have no individuality, nor is it a moral body in which each member lives a separate life. It is a *mystical* body in which each member retains his personality, yet shares one common life, the life of the Head, who is Christ. The uncreated soul of the Church is the Holy Spirit, the divine life by which the members live. The created participation of divine life in the members, the created soul of the Church, is divine grace, whose principal fruit is charity.

It is manifest that the form of the Church is hierarchical, and that its infallible magisterium is exercised through the hierarchy. Because of the hierarchy it maintains its unity, its holiness, its catholicity and its apostolicity. Moreover, through the hierarchy the life of the Church is communicated from Head to members. Finally, the Church is a perfect society which as mystery and as visible organization exists among the other societies of men. To those who believe in her nothing is more beautiful, nothing more lovable. To those who believe in her she is the Mystical Body of Christ, the dwelling place of the faithful, the New Jerusalem, the hope of salvation.

> *If I forget you, Jerusalem,*
> *may my right hand be forgotten!*
> *May my tongue cleave to my palate*
> *if I remember you not,*
> *If I place not Jersusalem*
> *ahead of my joy.*[37]

The doctrine of the Mystical Body of Christ gives rise to many practical conclusions. Here are a few of them.

1. Christ died for us. He is a King who gave up his earthly life in order to establish an eternal kingdom. At the last judgment, we, the members of the Mystical Body, shall be grouped around our King and he will say to us, "Come, ye blessed of my Father, possess you the Kingdom prepared for you from the foundation of the world"

[37]Ps. 136:5-6.

(Matt. 25:34). Notice the words, "possess you the Kingdom," for they have a profound significance. Subjects live in a kingdom; they occupy it but can never possess it. Only kings can possess kingdoms. Therefore, it shall be as kings with Christ the King that we will one day sit with him on an eternal throne, there to enjoy a reign without end.

2. From the beginning of her existence, the Church has manifested tremendous vitality. Throughout the centuries she has been persecuted and cruelly tormented. She has been deprived of her goods and she has been denied her rights. Her pastors have been expelled from godless nations. They have been tortured and murdered for her sake. And yet the consummate skill of earthly power, a power which has left the ruins of whole nations in its wake, has not been able to destroy or crush the life of the Mystical Body. For the Mystical Body has Christ as its Head and no man can lay waste the work of God.

3. Because the Church is a perfect society, she has the inalienable right to govern herself, to throw up bulwarks of defense when she is attacked, and to insure her perpetuity through the members of the Mystical Body. The Church's rights derive from her right to exist. Even her power to govern herself came from God, for St. Paul said to the elders of Ephesus: "Take heed to yourselves and to the whole flock, wherein the Holy Ghost hath set you as guardians, to rule the Church of God, which he hath purchased with his own blood" (Acts 20:28).

4. The liturgy gives expression to the most divine function of the Mystical Body, the sacrifice of the Mass. The Mass is offered by the Church and in her offering all her members participate. Therefore, all who co-operate in any way with the Church—priests and faithful alike—share in the fruits of the eucharistic sacrifice.

5. "'Authoritarianism' excludes the citizens from all effective participation in, or influence upon the formation of the will of society. Consequently it splits the nation into two categories, the rulers and the ruled, and the relations between the two are either purely mechanical as the result of force or have no more than a biological basis. . . . The nature of ecclesiastical authority has nothing in com-

mon with this authoritarianism; the latter can claim no point of resemblance to the hierarchical constitution of the Church."[38]

6. As love of Mary is a criterion of the Christian's love of her Son, so also is love of the Church. The marks of true love of the Church will be faithfulness to her directives, respect and reverence for her pastors, generosity toward her needs, self-sacrifice in her service, awareness of her interests and a willingness to defend them.

7. It is as members of one Body that we reach the kingdom of heaven; the life of the Christian is not individual and self-centered but social, corporate and centrifugal. For most, this will be lived as members of a parish, and the measure of their co-operation in the life of the parish—its liturgical and spiritual life, of course, but its social and charitable life as well—is a practical index of their living the life of Christ.

BIBLIOGRAPHICAL NOTE

Books and articles without number have appeared in recent years on the Mystical Body and on the Church. For the most part books on the Church are written from an apologetical point of view and are concerned principally with the Church as institution, while books on the Mystical Body are more concerned with less visible aspects of the Church. Books written before *Mystici Corporis*, even by the most reliable authors, must be read in the light of the teachings enunciated in that important encyclical, which is itself the most important bibliographical item for this chapter.

The Pauline teaching is explained in F. Prat, S.J., *The Theology of Saint Paul* (Westminster, Md.: Newman, n.d.), Vol. I, 300-309; Vol. II, 275-308. The essentials of Thomistic ecclesiology are briefly stated in the valuable and penetrating article of M. J. Congar, O.P., "The Idea of the Church in St. Thomas Aquinas," in *The Thomist*, I (1939), 331-359. A wealth of valuable material on the Mystical Body is to be found in the works of Emile Mersch, S.J., *The Whole Christ* (Milwaukee: Bruce, 1938) and *The Theology of the Mystical*

[38]Address of Pope Pius XII to officials of the Sacred Roman Rota, October 2, 1945.

Body (St. Louis: Herder, 1951), but they must be read carefully in the light of the encyclical and keeping in mind the general principles of theology as learned thus far. The many articles on the Church by Msgr. J. C. Fenton which have been appearing since 1944 in the *American Ecclesiastical Review* are theologically solid and clearly expressed. The two volumes of Msgr. Charles Journet's *The Church of the Word Incarnate* (New York: Sheed & Ward, 1955) contains much material of great value.

Among many other books and articles which could well be mentioned just a few are listed here: De Lubac, *Catholicism* (New York: Longmans, 1950); de Montcheuil, *Aspects of the Church* (Chicago: Fides, 1955); K. Adam, *The Spirit of Catholicism* (revised ed.; New York: Macmillan, 1954); Clérissac, *The Mystery of the Church* (New York: Sheed & Ward, 1940); Hasseveldt, *The Church: A Divine Mystery* (Chicago: Fides, 1954); Van Noort, *Dogmatic Theology*, Vol. II: *Christ's Church* (trans. and revised by J. J. Castelot and W. R. Murphy; Westminster, Md.: Newman, 1957); Suhard, *Growth or Decline? The Church Today* (South Bend: Fides, 1949); and in G. D. Smith (ed.), *The Teaching of the Catholic Church* (London: Burns Oates & Washbourne, 1947), the two articles: "The Mystical Body of Christ" by E. Myers, in Vol. II, 659-690; and "The Church on Earth" by A. Graham, in Vol. II, 691-732.

Also the articles: "Identity of the Mystical Body and the Catholic Church," by J. Beumer, *Theology Digest*, IV (1955), 53-58; "Sacramental Incorporation into the Mystical Body," by J. T. Dittoe, *The Thomist*, IX (1946), 469-514; "Mystery of Christ's Incarnation and His Mystical Body," by K. B. Adam, *Orate Fratres*, XIII (1949), 337-344, 392-399, 433-440; and "*Mystici Corporis* and the Soul of the Church," by J. I. McGuiness, *The Thomist*, XI (1948), 18-27.

CHAPTER SEVENTEEN

The Consummation of the Work
of the Incarnate Word:
The Glorification of the Just
and
The Punishment of the Damned

1. Introduction

Few subjects evoke as much interest and arouse as much curiosity as the topic of life after death. Even those who strive to settle the matter by the expedient of denying its reality find themselves reluctantly interested when it is discussed. Among people who profess any religion, the subject of immortality and the many questions it raises have always commanded attention. Practically every religious creed contains some teaching about life after death, and some appear to be almost exclusively concerned with the matter.

When the imagination is allowed to serve as a guide to knowledge about immortality and its problems, disaster, in the form of misconception, superstition and ignorance, is sure to result. The strange beliefs heralded over the centuries bear eloquent and sad testimony to this truth. For here is an area of knowledge set beyond the limits of human investigation and experience. Death remains the land "from whose bourne no traveler returns" to unveil its mysteries. Certain knowledge of these things must be accepted from the only teacher who is competent to make disclosures. That teacher is God himself, and his lessons must be accepted through divine faith. That faith, proposed by the authority of Christ's Church, is the only reliable source of knowledge about life after death.

We propose here to present a summary of the salient points of the teaching of faith on what are called the "last things"—death, judgment, heaven and hell. The teaching will be based upon the Scriptures, the official declarations of the Church, and the common teachings of her theologians under the guidance of St. Thomas Aquinas.

The theological treatment of the last things is technically called "eschatology," from the Greek *eschatos* meaning ultimate or last events. For St. Thomas, eschatology is considered precisely from the aspect of its relation to Christ who "has shown to us in himself the way of truth by which, arising from the dead, we are able to arrive at the happiness of immortal life" (*Summa*, III, Prologue). Immortal life, then, is the goal which men attain through Christ who is both God and man. The joyous participation in eternal happiness is a benefit won for the just by the suffering, death and resurrection of our Savior.

Our supreme guide is found in an injunction of the Council of Trent which exhorts bishops to proclaim the true doctrine on purgatory, and counsels that "they should not permit anything uncertain or having the appearance of falsity to be preached or written. And they should prohibit as scandalous and harmful to the faithful whatever pertains to a kind of curiosity or superstition. . . ."[1]

---

[1]Sess. XXV, *Decree on Purgatory;* Denz. 983.

The material of this chapter will be treated in this order:

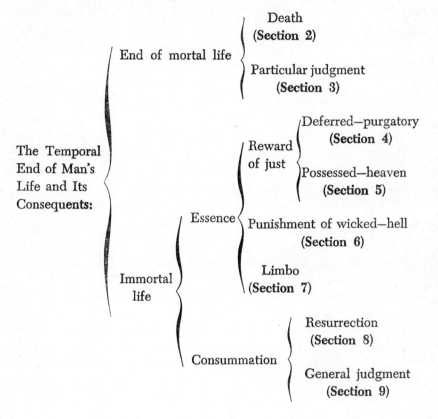

The Temporal End of Man's Life and Its Consequents:

- End of mortal life
  - Death (Section 2)
  - Particular judgment (Section 3)
- Immortal life
  - Essence
    - Reward of just
      - Deferred—purgatory (Section 4)
      - Possessed—heaven (Section 5)
    - Punishment of wicked—hell (Section 6)
    - Limbo (Section 7)
  - Consummation
    - Resurrection (Section 8)
    - General judgment (Section 9)

2. The Significance of Death

Any question raised about a future event must necessarily receive the answer, "Maybe." The future is always uncertain. There is one exception to this rule, and that is the question, "Shall I die?" To this question the answer is an unequivocal, "Yes." Death is the only real inevitability in life.

A. The Teaching of Revelation

In the Christian tradition, life is regarded as a time of trial and preparation for death, and the future state of unending happiness or damnation depends upon the result of the earthly pilgrimage. This truth has always been taught by the Church. While it is nowhere solemnly defined as an article of faith, the contrary view that the future life may admit of further trial, of amendment and penance, has been condemned as heretical. This false teaching was part of a heresy known as Origenism which was condemned by the Second Council of Constantinople, A.D. 553.[2]

The final decisiveness of death in determining man's state for all eternity is clear from many passages in the Scriptures. This is conveyed by Christ's description of the last judgment (Matt. 25:31-46); it is clear in the parable of the rich man and Lazarus (Lk. 16:19-31). Many texts from St. Paul confirm the teaching that men will be judged by what they have done in this life, and that death ends the time for probation (cf. II Cor. 5:10, 6:2; Gal. 6:10; Heb. 3:13).

B. The Teaching of Theology

This life is the time of probation, the time of choice between good and evil. At the instant of death, the soul is rendered immobile, incapable of altering its final choice. This is in accord with the changeless choice of man's free will, determining his state for all eternity.

But in view of the fact that all human choices are changeable during this life, we may well ask why the final choice should be unchangeable. Why is it impossible to change from good to evil or from evil to good after death?

(1) The Choice of End

It has been shown in the second volume of this series, Chapter One, that the choice of a supreme goal, of a final end, governs all other choices. The final goal is regarded as supremely desirable, and it is loved with the strongest love, in the sense that a man will forsake anything else in order to have what he loves most. The choice of a final end is always permanent *of itself*, because only something

---

[2]See also the condemnations of Origen's teaching which were approved by Pope Vigilius (540-555); Denz. 203-211.

more desirable could supplant it; but this involves a contradiction, since by definition the final goal is desirable above all others, and no one can seek two ultimate ends at one time.

While life lasts, however, man is extremely changeable. The final end, unchangeable *of itself,* may be changed *on the part of him who desires it.* This he does by exaggerating the desirability of false goals while minimizing the goodness of the true goal. Man is free to refuse to consider the defects of the former or the perfections of the latter. It is thus that man can turn from the love of God to the love of some evil, which is radically a kind of self-love. Throughout this life, man is under a natural necessity to seek whatever he desires under the aspect of happiness. It is unnatural to desire evil or sorrow for its own sake. But man remains free to choose whatever he thinks will make him happy, even if it cannot really do so, and he is free to make this choice the supreme goal of his life.

(2) The Choice in This Life

During this life all knowledge begins in the senses. From the data supplied by the senses, the intellect abstracts its ideas. The will can desire only what is presented to it by the intellect. Thus it is that man arrives at his idea of happiness. Now happiness is objectively identical with the possession of God, but subjectively men may seek happiness in anything they choose. The senses are subject to changing impulses and to changing dispositions. Thus there is a constant flux in the primary source of man's knowledge. This changeableness, which is a part of the instability of corporeal existence, is at the root of man's ability to change his ultimate goal as long as the soul remains united to, and dependent upon the body.

(3) The Eternal Choice

At the instant of death, all this changes. The body is separated from the soul, which becomes subject to the laws of spiritual beings. No longer is it dependent upon the senses; no longer does it strive for happiness under the aspect of an abstract notion of happiness. The separated soul, like an angel, by one single act of intelligence and will which exhausts its capacity for the final goal, clings to a concrete object which it conceives as its ultimate happiness, and it does this without any possibility of change. In the instant of death, the soul becomes fixed upon the object of its final desire during the last instant of life.

If man at the instant of death preferred God to all else, his will is fixed upon God for all eternity. But what of the sinner? Upon what can his will be fixed? Surely the money, the pleasures, the power, that entice the sinner's love throughout life will not continue to exist beyond the grave. But the sinner does not love these things *in themselves,* but rather *for himself.* All sin is a way of loving oneself not wisely but too well, and the unrepentant sinner's eternity will be spent with himself, with his own ego, whom he served throughout life in preference to God. The sinner strives throughout life to promote what he considers his self-interest, and in eternity he receives the full measure of the choice he has made.

St. Augustine provides a profound summary of these truths: "Two loves have built two cities, the love of self even to the contempt of God, and the love of God even to the contempt of self. The former has built the city of evil, of disorder, of confusion, the infernal Babylon; the latter the city of order and of peace, the eternal Jerusalem."[3]

Cardinal Billot, S.J., points up this difference:

> These are the two supreme loves; they are opposed to one another as contraries, and all other loves are subordinate to them. These also are the two final ends between which we must make our choice while this life lasts. On the one side is God, holding in our hearts a higher place than our very selves, and therefore loved above all things, virtue's last end; on the other hand is self, raised even over God's head, the idol of our adoration, obedience and service, the final end of vice and sin. To whichever of these two ends the soul is actually bound at the moment of death, to that must it remain bound—by its own nature and of necessity—for all eternity. And since our last end governs all our actions, since all that is good or evil in the will depends upon it, the necessary result is, for some, an unchangeable fixation in evil and moral disorder, and for others an equally unchangeable stability in good and the beauty of order, with happiness arising from the impossibility of ever failing.[4]

[3]*The City of God,* Bk. XIV, Chap. 28.
[4]"La Providence de Dieu," *Etudes,* 1923, 397.

3. The Judgment of Each Individual

The Church's belief in the particular judgment was already explicit by the time of St. Augustine: "Souls are judged as soon as they leave their bodies, even before they appear before that other tribunal where they will have again to be judged together with their reassumed bodies, and whence they will pass to torments or to glory in the same flesh as they had lived on earth."[5]

A. The Fact

While the fact of a particular judgment of each soul immediately after death is not solemnly defined, it is clearly taught by the ordinary *magisterium* of the Church, and this suffices to make it an article of faith.[6]

References to judgment in the Scriptures refer explicitly to the general judgment, but they implicitly refer to a particular judgment at the moment of death. Thus they contain the notions that each man will be judged according to his works and that his eternal destiny will have been settled before the last day. In the parable of the rich man and Lazarus (Lk. 16:19 ff.), it is clear that the condition of each is fixed forever, and it is also clear that the incident occurs before the general judgment.

It is not conceivable that souls would be left in a state of uncertainty about their eternal fate. Pope Benedict XII has defined that the souls of the just enter at once into heaven if they are completely purified at the time of death, and that the souls of sinners go immediately into hell.[7] This teaching clearly supposes that they are judged individually.

B. Its Meaning

It is widely held among theologians that a special grace of conversion is offered to sinners at the hour of their death. Under no cir-

---

[5]*The Soul and Its Origins*, Chap. 4, n. 8.
[6]*Humani Generis;* Denz. 2313.
[7]*Benedictus Deus;* Denz. 530 f.

cumstances may this be construed to mean that the separated soul is offered some final trial wherein it may choose God or self *after* death. Nothing can be done once the soul is separated from the body. But the exact moment at which that occurs is often impossible to determine, and the last rites are administered after the onset of apparent death because life may very well linger.

(1) *The Nature of the Particular Judgment*

The exact manner of the particular judgment is not known with certitude, but something of its nature can be deduced from the way in which separated souls can acquire knowledge. The only source of new knowledge for a separated soul is divine illumination. Thus at the moment when body and soul are separated, God illumines the mind so that it has a clear, objective and unbiased look at itself—it knows itself for what it is in the sight of God. This "judgment" of God is impressed in somewhat the same way that the natural sense of right and wrong is impressed upon each awakening conscience. The soul does not confront its Judge face to face; rather, there is a ray of divine light that enlightens the mind to see itself clearly, without evasion or sham.

The particular judgment, then, is simply *a certification or registration of the unchangeable state of decision in which death finds the soul.* Immediately, the separated soul goes to its proper place: if it is perfectly purified, to heaven; if further purification is required, to purgatory; if it is turned from God, then to hell.

(2) *The Place of the Separated Soul*

To explain how the separated soul is located anywhere is very difficult. An angel is wherever he operates, but the separated soul most probably can act upon external things only when reunited to the body. It seems the better opinion to say that God's justice assigns the soul to its proper dwelling-place by a kind of local restriction in the intellectual order. Thus the knowledge of individual things by the soul would be restricted to the objects contained in the place to which it is assigned, and to the events that take place here.

4. Purgatory—Deferred Reward

The Catholic doctrine on purgatory was consistently taught by the ordinary *magisterium* of the Church until the thirteenth century. Up to that time, there had been no need for any solemn declaration on the subject; like many other doctrines contained in the Sacred Tradition handed down from apostolic times, it was included among the articles of faith accepted by all members of the Church.

A. Teaching of the Church

At the time of the Second Council of Lyons (1274), which was the fourteenth ecumenical council of the Church, Pope Gregory X was concerned with the reunion of the Eastern Church which had been in schism since the ninth century. To prepare the way for this event a profession of faith was drawn up to clarify certain doctrinal matters, among them the doctrine on purgatory.[8] In 1438 the Council of Florence reissued this profession of faith as a dogmatic and infallible definition of the Church's teaching:

> If those who are truly penitent depart from this life in the charity of God before they have made satisfaction by worthy fruits of penance for their sins of commission and omission, their souls are cleansed by purgatorial sufferings after death. And the suffrages of the living—namely, the sacrifice of the Mass, prayers, alms-deeds and other works of piety which the faithful have been accustomed to offer for each other according to the established usages of the Church—are profitable to those departed souls for the relief of their sufferings.[9]

Still later the doctrine on purgatory was impugned in a manner almost ferocious by the Protestants. In reply, the Council of Trent reaffirmed the existence of purgatory and the efficacy of suffrages for those detained there.[10] Earlier, the same Council had decreed: "If anyone shall say that, after receiving the grace of justification, every repentant sinner's sin is so wholly forgiven and the debt of eternal punishment so completely remitted that there remains no

[8]Cf. Denz. 464.
[9]Denz. 693.
[10]Sess. XXV, *Decree on Purgatory;* Denz. 983.

debt of temporal punishment still to be paid either in this world or in the next in purgatory, before the gates of heaven are open to him, *let him be anathema*."[11]

Thus two things are defined: first, the existence of a state of purification for souls after this life; secondly, the efficacy of our prayers and good works in hastening the process of purification.

B. Testimony of Scripture

Several passages are cited from the Scriptures to prove, **at least** indirectly, the existence of purgatory (cf. I Kings 31:13; II Kings 1:12; Tob. 4:17; I Cor. 15:29). There are two passages, however, which are more explicit than any of these.

(1) Evidence from the Old Testament

In the Second Book of Machabees (12:32 ff.) the victory of Judas Machabeus over Gorgias is related. After the victory, Judas found concealed in the garments of some of his fallen soldiers idolatrous objects which they had stolen from the temple of Jamnia. Such thievery was a grave offense against the Law. The survivors, "betaking themselves to prayers, they besought him [God] that the sin which had been committed might be forgotten. But the most valiant Judas . . . making a gathering, he sent twelve thousand drachmas of silver to Jerusalem for sacrifice to be offered for the sins of the dead, thinking well and religiously concerning the resurrection. For if he had not hoped that they that were slain should rise again, it would have seemed superfluous and vain to pray for the dead. And because he considered that they who had fallen asleep with godliness, had great grace laid up for them. It is therefore a holy and wholesome thought to pray for the dead, that they may be loosed from sins."

This clearly shows that there is a middle state between heaven and hell in which souls not perfectly purified are detained and that we can aid in their purification by placating God's justice through our good works and prayers.

---

[11]Sess. VI, *Canon 30 on Justification;* Denz. 840.

(2) *The Testimony of Christ*

In the gospel according to St. Matthew, Christ declares that "whoever speaks against the Holy Spirit, it will not be forgiven him, either in this world or in the world to come" (12:32). This implies that some sins can be expiated in the next world, and that there is a penalty to be paid for some sins in the next life. This is the sum and substance of the doctrine on purgatory.

C. Interpretations of Theologians

At the beginning of this chapter, the decree of the Council of Trent was cited in which idle curiosity and superstitious speculation about the after life were forbidden. In keeping with that decree, we will present only a few matters on which there is more common agreement and which are completely free of the matters forbidden by the Church.

(1) *The Pains of Purgatory*

Many theologians indicate that there is a twofold pain in purgatory: the pain of being deprived of the vision of God, and some kind of penal suffering.

1. **The deprivation of the sight of God.** Of the two sufferings of this state, this is surely the worse. But in view of the fact that all in purgatory are absolutely certain of one day seeing God, how can this be a great suffering? It may be faintly likened to the disappointment one experiences when a dear friend is greatly delayed from an important meeting, or to the growing gnawings of hunger when a meal is long deferred. This deprivation is accentuated in purgatory for two reasons: first, the souls there are separated from the body and have no physical surroundings to distract them from their loss; secondly, they have a burning realization that the time has already passed for their joyous union with God—the remains of their own sins render them temporarily unfit to see him.

2. **The penal suffering of purgatory.** Nothing has ever been defined about a suffering in purgatory that may be compared to the

fires of hell. There is some certainty that such punishment exists, but it is equally certain that we know nothing of its nature.

3. The meaning of purgatorial suffering. Whatever sufferings exist in purgatory are designed for the salvation of the repentant sinner. They will exercise him in humility and charity so that he may grow progressively more worthy of his eternal reward. These sufferings are completely different from the despairing and fruitless sufferings of hell which are entirely penal. The pains of purgatory are uplifting and sanctifying.

4. The severity of purgatorial suffering. It is the opinion of St. Thomas that the least suffering of purgatory is greater than the greatest pain of this life. The reason, he says, is that desire is more ardent in purgatory, and hence its frustration more painful, and also because the souls there suffer directly without the cushion, so to speak, of bodily protection.[12] This is an echo of the teaching of St. Augustine in his commentary on Psalm 37. St. Bonaventure teaches that, even though the least pain of purgatory is not necessarily more intense than the greatest earthly pain, still for one and the same sin the sufferings of purgatory are more severe than their punishment in this life would have been.[13]

And what reason underlies this thinking? Simply that the pains of purgatory, although endured willingly in charity and hope, are less meritorious than penances on earth. This life is the time of mercy and forgiveness; the next world is the place of judgment and retribution. This should lead all the faithful, first to do penance for their sins during this life; secondly, to practice devotion to the holy souls who can only suffer and who are incapable of aiding themselves.

(2) The Duration of Purgatory

As to the duration of purgatory, we are sure only that it will end with the general judgment when all will enter their final reward. How long must souls remain in purgatory? There is no way to know, for purgatory lies in eternity, beyond the borders of time, and here clocks and calendars are of no avail. The Church allows Masses to

[12]*Appendix to Supplement,* q. 2, a. 1.
[13]*Liber IV Sententiarum,* d. 21, q. 4.

be offered for all the departed who are not canonized saints. We know that souls are hastened from purgatory by our good works and prayers. We are certain that penance done in this life will shorten the sufferings of purgatory. Beyond those things, we know nothing for sure. But these facts are a sufficient guide for the devout Christian.

(3) The Joy of Purgatory

It must never be forgotten that purgatory is a place of great spiritual joy. All souls there are absolutely certain of salvation, they are the recognized friends of God. There is no doubt, no uncertainty in purgatory. Further, there is no possibility of sin among the souls in purgatory, for God is the only object of their increasing desires and their burning charity. They are free from venial sins, cleansed of them the moment they enter this state.[14] According to St. Catherine of Genoa, only the joys of heaven surpass those known in purgatory, but they coexist with expiatory and sanctifying sufferings in such a way that one does not diminish the other.

5. Heaven—Eternal Happiness

Purgatory is a state in which beatitude is temporarily deferred; it is a place of preparation and expectation. Heaven is a state in which beatitude is possessed; it is a place of achievement and fulfillment.

A complete and perfect knowledge of heaven is not possible in this life. "Eye has not seen nor ear heard, nor has it entered into the heart of man, what things God has prepared for those who love him" (I Cor. 2:9). Yet the certainty of eternal happiness is provided by the Scriptures and guaranteed by the authoritative teaching of the Church. Moreover, reason enlightened by faith is able to perceive some faint idea of a twofold glory in heaven: an essential and unchanging glory, and an accidental and secondary glory which can increase until the time of its consummation.

---

[14]Such is the teaching of St. Thomas. Cf. *Appendix to Supplement*, q. 2, a. 4.

A. Teaching of Sacred Scripture

The Scriptures frequently speak of eternal life as the reward and the happiness for which we must strive. This happiness is God's own infinite and beatifying glory. It is manifested in the elect who are raised up to see and to partake of the glory given by the Father to the Son.[15]

St. Paul teaches that the charity whereby we love God, ourself and neighbor in this life endures even into the next, where God is the essence of heavenly happiness. Faith, however, will cease at our entrance into heaven, and will give way to a direct vision of God in which we will know him as we ourselves are known.[16]

St. John's teaching centers around the idea of the divine sonship which we share through adoption. By this we become co-heirs with Christ. On earth, this process is begun by grace, and it will be consummated in the next life by glory. We will become like to Christ because we will see him as he really is. Thus there will be fulfilled the words of Christ which tell us that eternal life is to know the true God and Jesus Christ whom he has sent. The faith of this life will give way to vision, and a knowledge of the divine Son will cause us to resemble him.[17]

B. Teaching of the Church

In his constitution *Benedictus Deus,* Pope Benedict XII summarizes the teaching of Scripture and tradition by declaring that the blessed in heaven "see God's essence directly, and face to face, and thus the souls of the departed enjoy the divine nature, and are thereby rendered truly happy in the possession of eternal life and peace."[18] A more precise meaning is given to this teaching by the words of the Council of Florence. ". . . the elect will see God himself clearly, as he is in his unity and trinity."[19]

---

[15]Cf. Jn. 17:22-24; I Pet. 4:4; Rom. 5:2, 2:18; II Cor. 4:17; Col. 3:4.
[16]Cf. I Cor. 13:8-12; II Cor. 5:6-8.
[17]Cf. I Jn. 3:1-2; Jn. 14:6-9,21, 17:3.
[18]Denz. 530.
[19]*Decree for the Greeks,* 1439; Denz. 693.

C. Theological Explanation

(1) The Essential Joy of Heaven

How can the immediate vision of God make a human soul supremely happy? To see God is beyond any human power. But by a special gift known as the "light of glory" the soul is raised to heights impossible to unaided nature. This gift raises and strengthens the soul so that it may enter into an intuitive union with the Uncreated Light which is God. This results in the closest possible union in the order of knowledge. Now God's distinctive and intimate life consists in knowing, loving and delighting in himself. The soul does not lose its individuality; it is not absorbed into God. Yet it partakes of God's own life, knowing and loving him in a way comparable to that in which he knows and loves himself. This is to be caught up into the inexpressible joy of the Blessed Trinity; it is to take hold of God, to possess him in himself. Between God and the blessed there is a union as intimate as that between the mind and the idea it conceives. The entire soul is penetrated by God, filled with perfection, held by divine love and filled with divine joy. Just as iron plunged into fire absorbs the very nature of the flames, so does the soul become like unto God. *Heaven is to know, to see, to live in an ecstasy of the divine illumination and love.*

This is the essential joy of heaven. But how can a finite and limited being enjoy such union with the infinite God? The theologians tell us that the blessed see God *entire* but not *entirely.* That is to say, God is seen in such a way that the blessed see the infinite being of God, but they see it according to the limits of their own being which cannot encompass divinity. The act of seeing God and its mode are limited by the nature of a creature, but the object seen is truly the infinite being of God.

(2) The Accidental Joys of Heaven

In their vision of the Godhead, the blessed will also see whatever concerns them and whatever they may rightfully wish to know. All reality is mirrored in divinity, and this is open to the gaze of those in heaven. They will penetrate the meaning of the mysteries of faith which they believed during life. They will see the nature of the Mystical Body of which they are triumphant members, the nature of the sacraments by which they were directed to salvation. They will also have a clear knowledge of the wonders of creation to a degree that will satisfy every natural desire of the soul. They will know whatever concerns themselves, their loved ones, or their labors. They know of the prayers offered in their honor, and the progress of works in which they were interested on earth.

(3) Degrees of Glory

We know that there are degrees of glory in heaven, for the Father's house has many mansions, and star differs from star in glory.[20] This different participation in glory is rooted in the different degrees in which the "light of glory" is given to each. The measure, however, is not some earthly endowment, but divine charity, "for the greater the charity the more ardent is the desire, and it is from the ardor of the desire that arises the capacity of receiving what is desired."[21] There are also differences among the things seen by the blessed in the divine essence, because all do not share the same desires. Such diversity is not necessarily a form of inequality. The basic principle governing all these things is this, that in God the saints will each find the full satisfaction of all desires.

(4) Further Joys

Two further points are worthy of mention. One of the great sources of accidental joy among the blessed is the companionship they share with one another. In heaven the Communion of Saints becomes a communication among saints.

After the general resurrection, the bodies of the just will be reunited with their souls. More will be said of this later, but for the present, let it suffice to mention that some spiritualization will have to take place in the senses of taste, olfaction and touch. But the more lofty senses of sight and hearing will operate by listening to the heavenly chorus and by seeing the glorious bodies of Christ and all his saints.

[20]Cf. Jn. 14:2; I Cor. 15:41.
[21]St. Thomas, *Summa*, I, q. 12, a. 1.

6. Hell and Hell-fire

Our knowledge of hell is derived from three sources: first, from divine revelation and Catholic faith; secondly, from theologically certain truths; thirdly, from commonly accepted truths proposed by theologians. We will investigate each of these sources briefly.

A. The Teaching of Faith

Explicit divine revelation and the authoritative teaching of the Church contain three points regarding hell: first, the existence of hell and its eternity; second, the damnation of sinners who die without repentance; third, their condemnation to a double punishment, consisting in the loss of the vision of God and in a positive penal torment.

(1) The Existence of Hell

Christ himself taught the reality of hell as a place of eternal torment. "Depart from me, accursed ones, into the everlasting fire which was prepared for the devil and his angels . . . and these will go into everlasting punishment. . ." (Matt. 25:41, 46). "It is better for thee to enter into life maimed, than, having two hands, to go into hell, into the unquenchable fire, 'Where their worm dies not, and the fire is not quenched'" (Mk. 9:42 f.). In his epistle, St. Jude speaks of "everlasting chains under darkness . . . the punishment of eternal fire . . . the storm of darkness has been reserved forever" (vv. 6, 7, 13). St. Paul frequently mentions the eternal exclusion of the damned, for example: "Now the works of the flesh are manifest, which are immorality, uncleanness, licentiousness, idolatry, witchcrafts, enmities, contentions, jealousies, anger, quarrels, factions, parties, envies, murders, drunkenness, carousings and suchlike. And concerning these I warn you as I have warned you, that they who do such things will not attain the kingdom of God" (Gal. 5:19-22). Finally, in the Apocalypse, St. John frequently refers to the eternal fires and torments of hell. The unending duration of these punishments is explicitly stated: "And the smoke of their torments goes up forever and ever;

and they rest neither day or night. . . ." (14:11). "And the devil who deceived them was cast into the pool of fire and brimstone . . . and they will be tormented day and night forever and ever" (20:9 f.).

(2) Damnation of Sinners

These dread torments are reserved for sinners who die without repentance. This life is the time of mercy and forgiveness, but only for those who seek it. "Unless you repent, you will all perish in the same manner" (Lk. 13:5). Whenever the Scriptures speak of works of kindness and charity, and of the forgiveness of injuries as meriting pardon of our sins from God, it must be understood that sincere repentance is presupposed as a necessary condition.[22] Consequently, no matter what good works a man may have done, if he dies refusing to repent and clinging to mortal sin, he will go to hell.

(3) The Pains of Hell

The essential pain of hell is the eternal deprivation of the vision of God, which exiles the wicked far from the home to which they once were called. This is the "exterior darkness" into which are cast those who had been called to be the "children of light." This is what theologians call *the pain of loss*.

In addition, there is a positive torment called *the pain of sense*. This is alluded to as an unquenchable fire, a bottomless pit of smoke, fire and brimstone, a gnawing worm. Both the fallen angels and the separated souls of the damned even before the resurrection suffer from this pain of sense. Yet they are without bodily senses, so it is certainly not a pain such as we would experience during this life. It is some fearsome positive punishment which the Scriptures call "fire," the precise nature and action of which we will discuss in a later section. Faith teaches that, in addition to the pain of loss, there is this other distinct positive torment in hell.

B. The Teaching of the Church

The truths contained explicitly in the Scriptures are confirmed by the authoritative declarations of the Church. One of the earliest pro-

[22]Cf. Tob. 4:11; Dan. 4:24; I Pet. 4:8; Jas. 5:20; Matt. 6:12-15; Lk. 9:4.

nouncements comes from a provincial council held at Constantinople in 543, the canons of which appear to have been approved by Pope Vigilius. "If anyone shall say or hold that the punishment of devils and wicked men is temporary and that it will cease at some future time, or that the devils and the wicked will be restored and re-established in their former state, *let him be anathema.*"[23]

The universal **condemnation** of all unrepentant sinners is explicitly taught in several declarations. "We further define," Pope Benedict XII stated in the constitution *Benedictus Deus* (1336), "that according to the usual ordination of God the souls of those who die in a state of mortal sin go down immediately after death into hell, there to suffer eternal torments."[24]

The First Council of Lyons in 1245 clearly taught that there is a **positive torment** in hell besides the loss of the vision of God. "If anyone dies without repentance in the state of mortal sin, he will without doubt be tormented perpetually in the flames of an everlasting hell."[25]

Thus the Church authoritatively teaches: *1) there is a hell of eternal punishment, 2) into which all unrepentant sinners are sent, 3) to undergo a twofold pain of the loss of the vision of God and of a positive torment as well.*

C. Theologically Certain Teachings

Truths are said to be theologically certain when they are deduced from a doctrine of faith by a process of reasoning. The certitude of these truths is not as great as the certitude of faith, although they depend upon its certitude. To deny the truths of faith is a sin of heresy; to deny theologically certain truths is a grave sin of error.

1) Basing their reasoning upon passages in the Scriptures and upon certain declarations of the Church, theologians deduce that **the punishment of the wicked will be proportioned to the gravity of their sins.** The Church teaches that the rewards of

---

[23]*Canon 9 against Origen;* Denz. 211.
[24]Denz. 531.
[25]From the letter of Pope Innocent IV (1243-54) to the Bishop of Tusculum, apostolic delegate in Greece; Denz. 457.

the just will be proportioned to their merits, and this is a teaching of faith.[26] Nothing is officially declared, but it is deduced that the same rule applies to the wicked; so the worse and more numerous the sins, the graver and more severe the punishments in hell.

2) From the fact that the pains of hell are eternal, theologians deduce the conclusion that they are constant. There is no progressive and indefinite mitigation of the sufferings of the damned. St. Thomas offers an enlightening insight into this matter by observing that there is evidence of mercy in hell, not by a total relaxation, but by a partial alleviation, in the sense that the pains are not as severe as deserved. Further, St. Thomas opines that this mitigation is accorded especially to those who during this life showed mercy to others.[27]

D. The Reality of Hell-fire

It is very commonly taught that hell's fire is real. This is not explicitly revealed, nor is it deduced directly from some revealed truth. Yet it is a teaching held by the greatest theologians, and it would be rash indeed to deny it.

(1) The Reality of the Fire of Hell

To say that hell's fire is real is not to make a declaration explaining its true nature. It is not to say that it is a physical or material fire such as we know on earth. Rather, we say that hell's fire is analogous to earthly fire—that there is a comparison between the two, that they both resemble and differ from each other.

The language of Scripture clearly suggests this, for it speaks with great realism of the pain of sense in hell. To claim that this is merely the remorse of conscience does violence to the words of Scripture when they are considered in their totality. To interpret this as some kind of "spiritual fire" is to speak an absurdity, for a "spiritual fire" is inconceivable.

[26]Cf. the Council of Florence, *Decree for the Greeks* (Denz. 693); cf. also Matt. 10:15, 11:21-24; Lk. 10:12-15, 13:47-48; Apoc. 18:6-7.
[27]*Summa*, I, q. 21, a. 4, ad 1; *Supplement*, q. 99, a. 5, ad 1.

The fire of hell is neither metaphorical nor spiritual; it is real. The word "fire" or "flame" is used to describe the pain of sense of hell no fewer than eight times in the gospels and thirty times throughout the New Testament. This indicates that the pains of hell are most closely allied to the torment of burning flames, which are the most terrible we know.

(2) Earthly Fire and Hell-fire

Yet certain differences must be kept in mind. Earthly fire is the result of chemical combustion; hell's fire is kindled by the wrath of God. Earthly fire afflicts the soul only through the body; hell's fire attacks the soul directly. Earthly fire may be quenched or it may die out; hell's fire endures forever. Earthly fire gives light; hell's fire produces gloom and darkness. Earthly fire consumes; hell's fire burns, but does not destroy its victims.

E. Some Theological Speculations

Beyond what has been already explained, the Church has no official teaching on hell, nor are further theological conclusions drawn from revelation with certitude. While theologians are practically unanimous in teaching over the centuries the reality of hell's fire, there are many different explanations given of its nature and operation, and also of the pain of loss. Here we will present a brief summary of what seems to be the best opinion on these matters.

(1) The Fire of Hell

St. Thomas maintained that the fire of hell is of the same nature as the fire we know on earth, and that it is a physical fire, but not precisely the same kind of fire we know, for it needs no kindling nor is it kept alive by fuel.[28]

This fire serves as the instrument of divine justice, and by the power of God it can act directly upon spirits in a way similar to that by which the material signs of the sacraments produce their effects upon the soul. Besides its natural power, the fire of hell is endowed

[28]*Supplement*, q. 97, a. 6.

with a special efficacy by God, whereby it is able to grip and restrain spiritual beings, depriving them of their freedom and prevent-
ing them from acting where and as they desire.[29] It is not only a
prison, however, but it penetrates the fallen and lost souls to paralyze
them at the very core of their being. Hence the damned are subjected to torment by a being inferior to themselves, and this gives
rise to great frustration and hatred.

How this fire will afflict the resurrected bodies of the damned is
a very mysterious matter. By being used as an instrument of divine
justice, it is raised up, so to speak, to fit this lofty purpose. The fire
of hell is able to torment the bodies of the damned without consum-
ing or destroying them. It produces upon these bodies, not the scars
and blisters of earthly flame, but rather an extremely severe emotional disturbance that is acutely felt throughout the entire body, and
which results in a constant violent movement. Thus will they suffer
a sensation similar to burning, but they will not be consumed.

But although the fires of hell are the most dreadful of physical
torments, they hold second place among the pains of the damned.
The worse affliction is the pain of loss.

(2) The Pain of Loss

To understand something of the magnitude of this pain, we must
recall what was said at the beginning of the chapter about the importance of the desire for the final goal. This desire causes and regulates all others. Now once men die, as a result of the particular judgment they see clearly what their true end should be. Freed of bodily
distractions, the separated soul comes to a painfully acute realization
of the role of God as the first and necessary principle of all love and
desire in the world, and especially of eternity. To those free of all
taint of sin, this realization becomes a means whereby the joy of
seeing God is increased beyond any earthly attainment. To those who
must still expiate sins in purgatory, it becomes a source of pain that
accentuates their separation from God, and this is the root of their
satisfactory sufferings.

[29]*Supplement*, q. 70, a. 3.

To those who choose to serve self at the expense of serving God—to the damned—the realization of God's place in the order of love is the source of the greatest internal torment; by this insight their spirit is rent internally in an eternal frustration. The damned are impelled to reach out for God, but they are imprisoned by their own selfishness. They are at war with themselves in the very act that should bring happiness. Compared to this, the actual tearing of the body limb from limb is but a feeble image of suffering.

A cold, speculative and unsaving faith enlightens the minds of the damned without warming or comforting their hearts. By this faith they are able more fully to appreciate the lofty supernatural joys of which they have deprived themselves forever. Thus even knowledge, man's great treasure on earth, becomes an instrument of torture in hell. The final curtain of death prevents any repentance or any turning back. St. Thomas compares the damned to a man seething with rage and bent upon murder. Of a sudden, he is forcibly overcome; his passion mounts as his frustration increases, he is denied the evil deed he desires most. Yet he continues to cling to his desire for murder, and his only sorrow is that he cannot accomplish it. So, too, the damned are locked forever in their evil desires, and their fatal sorrow is that these failed to bring them the happiness they hoped for. Theirs is a despairing and fruitless punishment, bringing terrible remorse but not repentance.

Just as the pain of sense varies according to the degree that men turned sinfully to the love of creatures during this life, so there is a difference in the pain of loss proportioned to the degree to which they turned away from God. Yet how can there be degrees in a suffering that consists in a lack of the vision of God? Do not all in hell lack God utterly? A comparison may help a bit. All exiles are deprived of home and country, but more distant exile is worse than that which is closer to one's native land. Destitution deprives men totally of material resources, but some who are destitute are not only bereft of possessions, but are also loaded with debts which add a special note of hopelessness to their misery. In somewhat the same way, a greater deprivation is inflicted upon those who sinned more often and more deliberately.

F. St. Thomas' Conclusion about Hell

It is commonly agreed among Catholic theologians that the obduracy of the damned is rooted in the fact that all actual and habitual grace is withheld from them. But St. Thomas goes a step further. He maintains that the damned are refused grace because of the obduracy of the state of evil in which they have rooted themselves. *God does not give them grace because they have deliberately chosen to make themselves incapable of receiving it.* The withholding of grace, then, is attributed more to God's wisdom than to his justice. Just as it is more accurate to say that a squared circle cannot be made than to say that God cannot make a squared circle, so it is more accurate to say that grace cannot be accepted by the damned than to say that God will not give them grace. The offer of grace to a will immovably fixed in evil would be a foolish gesture, contrary to God's wisdom.

It is a sobering thought to reflect that heaven would be more painful than hell itself to a soul fixed deliberately in evil. The ultimate reason for hell is to be sought in the sinner, not in God. On God's part, hell is less severe than the malice of the damned warrants. While it is indeed a fearful thing to fall into the hands of the living God, it is still more fearsome to plunge oneself into the sins that earn the divine wrath.

Hell is a monument to creatures' declaration of independence from their Creator. The presence of each sinner therein is a work he can claim wholly for himself. And what has he prepared by his malice? A place haunted by the shadows of eternal death, wherefrom is excluded the orderliness for which nature itself cries out, wherein is found unending horror.

7. Between Heaven and Hell: Limbo

Sacred Scripture is silent about any middle state between heaven and purgatory on the one hand, and hell on the other. But the Scriptures speak only of the eternal destiny of those who are capable of moral actions and who are able to choose between good and evil. They make no mention of unbaptized children who are incapable of actual sin, nor of those adults who must be classed as children.

A. The Existence of Limbo

Under the name of "Abraham's bosom" (Lk. 16:24), mention is made of a dwelling-place of the just who died before the coming of Christ. But the only scriptural justification for a limbo of unbaptized infants and others must be sought in the general teaching on God's eternal justice. On the other hand, the tradition of the Church, expressed in the writings of the Fathers, pontiffs and great theologians, asserts that there is a place in the next world for the unbaptized wherein they neither see God nor suffer any pain.

While there has never been an authoritative declaration positively teaching the existence of limbo, the denial of its existence has been censured, and its existence is held as theologically certain.[30]

St. Thomas teaches that the souls in limbo do not undergo any "pain of sense," but that they can attain the degrees of perfection which are consequent upon human nature by reason of its own native principles. Because they never had the light of faith, they cannot suffer from a "pain of loss" of which they are not aware. They are in a state of a kind of painless possession of their natural perfections. The penalty for original sin, then, is to be deprived, albeit unknowingly, of the supernatural joy made possible by the free gift of God through Jesus Christ. This is so great a loss that we cannot say that those in limbo are in a state of beatitude. But as there was no personal guilt in them, so neither is there any personal realization of what they miss.

B. The Inhabitants of Limbo

Who are in limbo? Theoretically, we can answer: all those who die with original sin only. Practically, it is not easy to determine just who these are.

Certainly the unbaptized who die before attaining the use of reason, and those unbaptized adults who never reach the use of reason, are in limbo.

---

[30]Cf. the Letter of Innocent III to the Archbishop of Arles, 1201 (Denz. 410); the constitution *Auctorem Fidei* of Pius VI, condemning the false teaching of the Jansenists that limbo was a "Pelagian fable," 1794 (Denz. 1526); *Appendix I to Supplement*, qq. 1, 2.

Some have held that good pagans who are invincibly ignorant of the faith and who, nonetheless, lead good lives will go to limbo. But we know that no one can observe all precepts of the natural law without the help of grace, nor can anyone repent of his sins without the aid of grace. How, then, could such a "good pagan" exist in fact? This theory must be rejected.

Again, it has been claimed that there are many in the world who, through no fault of their own, remain spiritual dwarfs after reaching adulthood. Such people are able to carry on all kinds of worldly affairs, to marry and raise families, to engage successfully in business. Yet, according to the theory, they remain stunted spiritually because of unreligious education, bad example, and other forces over which they have no control. They are the modern secularists, the activists who have no time for thinking, especially about God and his judgment. Yet could we not apply to these men the condemning words of Christ? "In them is being fulfilled the prophecy of Isaias, who says, 'Hearing you will hear, but not understand; and seeing you will see, but not perceive. For the heart of this people has been hardened, and with their ears they have been hard of hearing, and their eyes they have closed; lest at any time they see with their eyes; and hear with their ears, and understand with their mind, and be converted, and I heal them'" (Matt. 13:14-15).

Practically speaking, it is most difficult to speculate about the possible inhabitants of limbo. Perhaps it is wiser to leave this matter to God, whose ways are not our ways. The sentiment of St. Robert Bellarmine contains practical advice for all in this matter: "Our pity regarding their eternal state does nothing for them; but on the other hand, the strength of our determination to convert and baptize them profits them immeasurably. Moreover, we ourselves lose much if, because of a fruitless sentimentality towards either adults or children, we defend obstinately anything contrary to the Scriptures or the Church. In this matter [of limbo and its inhabitants] we should not be carried away by any human consideration, by which so many are wont to be swayed; rather should we consult the teaching of the Church Councils, the Scriptures and the Fathers, and then follow it."[31]

[31]*The Sinful State*, Chap. 2.

8. The Resurrection of the Dead

The belief of the Church in the resurrection of the dead is expressed in several professions of faith, among which the best known is the Apostles' Creed. It is mentioned many times over in the New Testament in unmistakable terms.[32] One of the many authoritative pronouncements of the Church on the general resurrection is found in the dogmatic declaration of the Fourth Council of the Lateran, 1215: "He [Christ] will come at the end of the world to judge the living and the dead, and to render to all according to their works, whether to the reprobate or to the elect; who all will arise with their own bodies that they have in this life, to be rewarded according to their works, whether good or evil, the wicked to go into eternal punishment with the devil, the good to receive everlasting glory with Christ."[33]

In other words, all men will arise on the last day, and they will have the same bodies they had during this life. This is eminently reasonable, because the same body which shared in the deeds of life should share in their reward or punishment.

A. The Theology of the Resurrection

Working on the data contained in revelation, theologians offer some conclusions about the resurrection.

1. This resurrection is miraculous. No natural power can bring it about. Nature causes a body by generation, never by restoring it. Hence, while it is true that the separated soul naturally tends to be united to a body, nature itself cannot bring about this reunion. Divine power is required.

2. Man will arise with the same body he had in this life. When it is said that "the dead will arise again with the same bodies they had had in this life," it means that they will be the same bodies *numerical-*

---

[32]Cf. Jn. 5:23, 6:39-44; Mk. 12:26; Rom. 5:6; II Cor. 5; Phil. 3:11; I Thess. 4:15; I Tim. 2:16; Heb. 11:35.

[33]This is an explicit denouncement of the Albigensian heresy which, based on the doctrine that matter was intrinsically evil, taught false notions about the resurrection of the body and life after death. Cf. Denz. 429.

ly. In view of the fact that the resurrection is miraculous there should be no difficulty in seeing that the same divine power that formed the body originally will reform it in the resurrection.

This truth is clearly expressed by the Roman Catechism:

> It is of vital importance to be fully convinced that the identical body which belongs to each one during life, though corrupt and dissolved into its original dust, will be raised up again to life. It is a truth conveyed by the Apostle when he says: "This corruptible body must put on incorruption" (I Cor. 15:53), evidently designating by the word *this,* his own body. It is also clearly expressed in the prophecy of Job: "In my flesh I shall see my God, whom I myself shall see, and mine eyes behold, and not another" (19:26).
>
> Further, this same truth is inferred from the very definition of resurrection; for resurrection, as Damascene defines it, "is a return to the state from which one has fallen" (*On the Orthodox Faith,* Bk. IV, Chap. 27).
>
> We have said that the body is to rise again, that "each one may receive what he has won through the body, according to his works, whether good or evil" (II Cor. 5:10). Therefore, man is to rise again in the same body with which he served God, or was a slave to the devil; that in the same body he may experience rewards and a crown of victory, or endure the severest punishments and torments.[34]

3. Immortality. We learn from the gospels that the elect will arise immortal, that is, that their bodies will be endowed with an interior principle of incorruptibility which makes them unable to die. This is expressly stated by Christ (Lk. 20:34-36).

B. The Qualities of Risen Bodies

Theologians conclude that all risen bodies, whether of the elect, the damned, or those in limbo, will be incorruptible. Yet the damned will derive no joy from this prerogative, for it is ordained to the ceaseless enduring of torment.

In risen bodies all nutritive and generative functions will cease, simply because the state in which they live has no need for them. The organs remain intact, because the bodies arise whole and entire, but they will not function. In the after life, the soul will rule the body; it will no longer serve it.

[34]*On the XI Article of the Creed,* nn. 7, 8.

Finally, the bodies of the blessed in heaven will be endowed with certain qualities which the damned will lack. These are four in number:

Qualities of Glorified Bodies

Impassibility—security from all injury and corruption (cf. I Cor. 15:42).

Subtlety—complete domination of the body by the soul making it independent of all things material (*ibid.*, 5:44).

Agility—unresisting obedience to the soul's commands, with a speed of movement comparable to thought (*loc. cit.*).

Clarity—translucency in the body originating in the soul, similar to that of Christ on the Mount of Transfiguration (*loc. cit.*).

C. Christ, the Cause of Our Resurrection

Christ is the mediator betwen God and men, and it is through Christ's sacred humanity that divine gifts are bestowed upon men. Men cannot be delivered from spiritual death except by the gift of grace bestowed by Christ. Similarily, they cannot be delivered from bodily death except through the resurrection wrought through Christ. At baptism our conformity to Christ is begun. This conformity increases with the growth of charity; it extends to our conformity to his death. Its consummation is reached when we are conformed to his glory through the resurrection, when he works in us in the same way that he healed the leper by the touch of his hand (Matt. 8:3).

9. The Second Coming of Christ

The Scriptures frequently comment on the general judgment, which will take place on the last day when the Son of God will bring to consummation the work for which he became man. At that time, Jesus

Christ himself will act as judge, passing sentence upon all.[35] The entire scene is described in detail by St. Matthew (25:31-46). The epistles of St. Paul are filled with references to the judgment, and the Apocalypse offers a prophetic description (20:7-15; 21:5).

The faith teaches two things: the certain fact of a general judgment, and the person of the judge. This is summed up in the Nicene Creed, which declares that "Jesus Christ will come again in glory to judge both the living and dead."

Theologians study all the aspects of this doctrine to distinguish the certain from the probable so that the truth may be more clearly seen. These are some of their conclusions.

1. The fittingness of the general judgment. St. Thomas explains that, while death puts an end to man's earthly existence, that existence does continue to be dependent upon the future in many ways.[36] For instance, a man's reputation seldom corresponds to his actual worth; families often fall away from the high standard set by the father; men's deeds live after them, so that we continue to benefit from the faith of the apostles and to suffer from the heresy of Arius; even the body will sometimes receive an undeserved honorable burial and sometimes suffer a shameful neglect. All such things are the objects of human activity. Some pass quickly; others endure. But before God they form a perpetual reality, awaiting the final verdict of God, who will set all things in order according to justice. This judgment will glorify God, Christ and the saints.

2. The day of judgment. The circumstances of the judgment and the signs preceding it are very uncertain, and St. Thomas interprets the scriptural references to these things very broadly.[37] To follow his example will save men much futile speculation about the hidden affairs of God.

3. The nature of the general judgment. There will be two aspects to the general judgment: the discussion of the merits and demerits of each, and the passing of sentence.

[35]Cf. Matt. 7:22-23, 13:37-42, 16:27, 24:30; Mk. 13:34-37; Lk. 12:36-48, 21:34-36.
[36]Cf. *Supplement*, qq. 87, 89.
[37]*Supplement*, q. 88.

1) *The discussion of the merits of the blessed* will not raise any doubts as to their state. That matter is determined for all in the particular judgment at the moment of death. But this discussion will show how good triumphs over evil in the lives of the elect, and will thus manifest God's justice.

The discussion of the damned will manifest whatever good they may have accomplished, and it will also manifest divine justice by showing how they are justly excluded from the city of the saints.

The judgment of inquiry will be made of all whose lives contained an admixture of good and evil. This includes practically all men. Infants who die before attaining the use of reason are excluded, as are any who may have passed their lives without offence.

2) *But all will submit to the judgment of reward or punishment.* Those who enter heaven will receive the judgment of reward. All who are excluded from heaven will receive the judgment of punishment.

Thus will Christ finish the work he came to do, by bringing the elect to the reward he purchased for them, and by sentencing to punishment those who rejected his saving grace.

10. Summary and Conclusion

"I am the Alpha and the Omega, the beginning and the end" (Apoc. 1:8). Something of the fulness of the meaning of this may be glimpsed at the end of a course in theology, which culminates with a consideration of the last things. For the immediate urgency of divine reality in daily life becomes clear through the contemplation of divine truth. Christ came to save mankind from sin, and this he did by showing us in his own person the way of truth, by which we may attain to the happiness of eternal life by rising again.

Death is the portal through which all must pass. But life is not taken away, it is only changed by the passage. That change is certified in the particular judgment. For those who freely chose to follow the way marked out by Christ, the reward of his eternal companionship is at hand. To those who are perfectly prepared it is given at once in heaven; for those who must still prepare themselves by expiation, the reward is deferred through purgatory. To such as reject the way of Christ by preferring themselves to him, there is prepared a place where they can be left to themselves, bereft of God, forever in torment. For those who were unable to follow Christ's way only because of original sin, a place of separation from him is prepared which is free of the pain that comes from malice alone. All are called to appear at his judgment, and for this they are clothed once again in the flesh which is their natural abode.

For all, Christ is the Alpha, the beginning; for every creature must somehow be a reflection of his creator according to the pattern who is Christ. For all, Christ is the Omega, the end. For those who reject his mercy, he is the end, for, even unwillingly, they stand as a manifestation of his divine justice. For those who follow his mercy, he is also the end, but the end of salvation, in which they taste forever the fulness of the benefits which he came to bestow on the human race.

This doctrine suggests these conclusions.

1. The whole sacramental system of the Church is a reality which embraces all of time; in the present the Mass and sacraments recall the past in order to engender the future. Thus the true Christian (and many today have lost this essential viewpoint of the faith) is one whose deep roots in the Savior's past are productive of present blossom which is a pledge of, and a straining forward to the fruits of the future. In brief, the fundamental Christian attitude is an eschatological one. "I await the resurrection of the dead," he says in his *Credo,* "and the life of the world to come. Amen."

The Church's liturgy emphasizes this point. The great liturgical cycle of feasts which memorialize the events of Christ's presence among us is not a closed circle; it is not an empty repetition year after year of memorial services for past events, not only the reiteration of those mysteries so that we may relive them and share in them in the present. Above all it is a mounting spiral of sacramental participation, by which each feast as compared to the corresponding feast of the preceding year brings us ever closer to the coming of Christ, both in terms of time and of preparation. Advent prepares our souls, not only to celebrate Christ's past coming among us, but more especially his second coming; in Lent we again await this coming, of which his resurrection was the first fruit and always remains the pledge.

By truly living the mysteries of Christ, then, by sharing more deeply in them from one Mass to the next, we, with the Church, can draw ever nearer to "the day of the Lord."[38]

2. For your deeper reflection on the great mysteries of the times to come, consider these thoughts of the Fathers:[39]

EUSEBIUS, from *Catena of Greek Fathers*:

"For now is the end of all perishable life, and, according to the Apostle, the outward appearances of this world will pass away and a new world will follow, in which, in place of the visible luminaries, Christ himself will shine as the Sun and King of a new creation; and so great will be the power and splendor of this new Sun, that the sun which now shines and the moon and the other stars will grow dim before the face of this greater Light."

HOMILY OF ST. EPHRAEM, CONFESSOR AND DOCTOR,
On Patience, the Second Coming, and the Last Judgment:

"But what shall we do, I ask you, when God will come down in anger and dread wrath, and sit on the throne of his glory, and summon to him all the earth, 'from the rising of the sun to the going down thereof,' and all the ends of the earth, so that he may judge his people, and render to each according to his works? Oh, woe! woe! What kind of people shall we be then? In what state of mind shall we be, when naked and fearful we shall appear there, delivered to that dread tribunal? Woe! Woe! Woe is me! Where now is the pride of the flesh? Where now is vain and useless beauty? Where, all human delight? Where then, shameless and impudent boldness? Where the

---

[38]For a fuller development of these points, cf. A.-M. Roguet, O.P., *Holy Mass: Approaches to the Mystery* (Collegeville, Minn.: The Liturgical Press, 1953), Chapter XIII, "Memorial of Times to Come," and Chapter XIV, "Masses in Succession."

[39]These excerpts are taken from *The Sunday Sermons of the Great Fathers*, translated and edited by M. F. Toal, D.D., I, 5, 15-16, 21-23, with the permission of the publishers, Henry Regnery Company, Chicago, Illinois, 1958.

delight of sin, sordid and unclean? What then of those who wallow in the wickedness of lust, 'of that which is filthy'? Where then will they be who worship with drum and wine and dance, but the works of the Lord they have not considered? What then of those who have passed their lives in sloth and disorder? Where then will be the enticements of pleasure? All these things shall have passed away, and like a little cloud shall have been dissolved.

"Where then shall avarice be, the desire of earthly possessions, from which rises up hardness of heart? Where the monstrous pride that despises all things, and thinks to itself that it alone exists? Where now the vain and fleeting success and glory of men? Where then human might? Where now is the tyrant? Where the king? Where the prince? Where the leader? Where the magistrate? Where are they who revelled in luxury, who gloried in the multitude of their riches, and despised God? In that moment, look up; they shall be struck dumb, they shall be utterly confused and shaken. 'Fear will seize them; their pains as of a woman in labour. With a vehement wind thou shalt break them in pieces.'

"Where then will be the wisdom of the wise? Where all their vain cleverness? Woe! Woe! They are terrified; 'and they were troubled and reeled like a drunken man; and all their wisdom was swallowed up.' Where now the learned? Where the scribe? Where the recruiting officer of this foolish world? My brother, what shall we be then, and in what state of soul, as we render an account of all things, big and little, that we have done, even to the least—for even for an idle word we shall render account to the just Judge? What must we do, that in that hour we may find mercy before him?

"And with what joy shall we be filled, if we are directed to the right hand of the King? What must we be like when the just embrace us there? When, I repeat, they shall embrace thee there, Abraham, Isaac, Jacob, Moses, Noah, Job, Daniel, the holy prophets, the apostles, the martyrs, who all were pleasing to God in the days of the flesh? And whomsoever you have heard of, and whose life you have admired, and whom you now wish to look upon, they will come to thee, and embrace thee, rejoicing in thy salvation. What manner of men must we then be? Of what kind shall be that unspeakable delight which we are to receive, when the king shall with joyfulness say to those who will be on his right hand: 'Come ye blessed of my father, possess the kingdom prepared for you from the foundation of the world.'

"Then, my brother, then will you receive the kingdom of beauty, the crown of all your desires, from the hand of the Lord, and reign with Christ for ever. Then you will receive for your inheritance the gifts, 'which God has promised to those who love and serve him.' From thenceforward you will be secure, no longer filled with anxiety. Be mindful, my brother, of what kind of a person it must be, to whom it will be given to reign with Christ in heaven. Reflect upon what it means to dwell forever in the light of his countenance, to possess the source of all light. 'For then you shall no more have the sun for thy light by day, neither shall the brightness of the moon enlighten thee,' but Christ will be thy unfailing light, and God thy glory. Behold, my brother, what glory he has laid up for those who fear him, observing his commandments."

HOMILY I OF ST. GREGORY, POPE AND DOCTOR,
Given to the People in the Basilica of the Holy Apostle Peter:

"But let this be far from the faithful, far from the hearts of those who believe through their faith that there is another life, and who love it in very deed. Let them grieve over the ruin of the world who have planted the roots of their hearts deep in the love of it, who neither look for the life to come, nor are even aware that it is. But we who have learned of the joys of our heavenly home must hasten to it as speedily as we may. We should desire to go there with all haste, and to arrive by the shortest way. And with what miseries does not the world urge us forward? What sorrow, what misfortune is there, that does not press upon us? What is this mortal life but a way? And what folly would it be, let you carefully consider, to be weary with the fatigue of the way, and yet not eager to finish the journey!

"We must carefully keep in mind that in the doing of these things it is the invisible Judge that moves the breath of the faintest breeze, that awakens the storm from even one small cloud, or razes the foundations of so many buildings. But what shall happen when the Judge shall visibly appear, and when his anger burns against the wicked, if we cannot now endure his wrath when he inflicts upon us the least tempest? Before the face of his wrath what flesh shall stand, if he it is that moves the wind, and shakes the earth, incites the storms, and lays low so many buildings? Paul, reflecting on this severity of the Judge to come, says to us: 'It is a fearful thing to fall into the hands of the living God.' The psalmist gives voice to the same reflection: 'God shall come openly, our God, he shall not be silent, and round about shall be a mighty tempest.' Tempest and fire shall accompany the severity of this justice, because the tempest shall search out those whom the fire will burn.

"Beloved brethren, keep that day before your eyes, and then whatsoever may seem burthensome will become light in comparison. Of that day is it said by the mouth of the prophet: 'The great day of the Lord is near, it is near and exceeding swift; the voice of the day of the Lord is bitter, the mighty man shall there meet with tribulation. That day is a day of wrath, a day of tribulation and distress, a day of calamity and misery, a day of darkness and obscurity, a day of clouds and whirlwinds, a day of trumpet and alarm.' Of this day the Lord has spoken by the mouth of the prophet Aggeus: 'Once again and I shall move not alone earth, but heaven.'

"Behold, as we have said, he moves the tempest, and the earth cannot endure it. What will it do when he moves the heavens? What can we say of the terrors we now see, except that they are but heralds of the wrath to come? And let us keep in mind that these present afflictions are as far below the last tribulations, as is the person of the herald below the majesty of the judge he precedes. Reflect with all your mind upon this day, my dearest brethren. Remedy what is now defective in your present life. Amend your ways. Conquer evil temptations by standing firm against them. Repent with tears of the sins you have committed. For the more you make ready against the severity of his justice by serving him in fear, the more serenely shall you behold the Coming of that Eternal Judge, who with the Father, and the Holy Spirit, liveth and reigneth, world without end. Amen."

BIBLIOGRAPHICAL NOTES

St. Thomas' treatment of what are known as The Last Things, viz., Death, Judgment, Heaven and Hell, comprises thirty questions in the "Supplement" to the *Summa* plus three questions contained in two appendices. All of this material was originally written in his commentary on the *Sentences* of Peter Lombard, and was culled by editors to complete the *Summa*. An excellent commentary on this material which incorporates much in the way of doctrinal development is available in *Life Everlasting*, by Reginald Garrigou-Lagrange, O.P. (St. Louis: Herder, 1952). In addition, there are several other books dealing generally with the same themes: Martin Jugie, A. A., *Purgatory* (Westminster: Newman, 1950); A Father of the Society of Jesus, *The Happiness of Heaven* (Westminster: Newman, 1950); Martin D'Arcy, S.J., *Death and Life* (New York: Longmans, 1942); J. P. Arendzen, *What Becomes of the Dead?* (New York: Sheed & Ward, 1951); Robert Gleason, S.J., *The World to Come* (New York: Sheed & Ward, 1958); R. Guardini, *The Last Things* (New York: Pantheon, 1954).

There are several pertinent articles to be found in *Theology Digest*: William A. Van Roo, S.J., "Infants Dying Without Baptism," III (1955), 3-9 (including a bibliography); P. M. Soullard, O.P., "Can Infidels Be Saved?," *ibid.*, 134-138; Y.-B. Trémel, O.P., "Man Between Death and Resurrection," V (1957), 151-156; Ch.-V. Héris, O.P., "A Theology of Suffrages for the Dead," *ibid.*, 172-175. "Limbo—A Theological Evaluation," by G. J. Dyer, appears in *Theological Studies*, XIX (1958), 32-49. Finally, a penetrating and lucid discussion of many aspects of the problems of eschatology was presented serially in *The Sign* magazine during 1949 by Aloysius McDonough, C.P.

APPENDIX

A Scriptural Harmony
of the Life of Christ

A Scriptural Harmony
of the Life of Christ

	Matthew	Mark	Luke	John	Others
I. Birth of Christ			2:1-7		
A. Manifestations of His Birth					
1. To the shepherds			2:8-20		
2. To Simeon and Anna			2:22-38		
3. To the Magi	2:1-12				
B. Legalities Attendant upon His Birth					
1. His circumcision	1:25		2:21		
2. His presentation			2:22-38		
C. Baptism of Christ by John	3:13-17	1:9-11	3:21-22		
II. Christ's Life					
A. Christ's Manner of Life					
1. He lived among men					
a) in Judea at Jerusalem	21:1-11	11:15-17	19:29-44	2:13-15	
b) in Judea outside Jerusalem			18:35-44	4:4-42	
c) in Galilee	4:13-16	1:40-45	6:6-11	4:43-45	
d) in Phoenicia and Decapolis	15:21-39	7:24 8:10			
e) in Perea	9:1-2			10:40-42	
2. He lived a life of prayer	14:23	1:35 6:46	6:12 9:18 11:1		
3. He lived a life of poverty	8:20				II Cor. 8:9
4. He conformed to common social customs	11:19		14:1	2:1-11 9:16	
5. He conformed to the law	15:17-18 21:47				Gal. 4:4-5
B. Christ's Temptations	4:1-11	1:12-13	4:1-13		
C. Christ's Teachings					
1. Source of his teachings					
2. He teaches with authority and power	7:28-29	1:22	4:32	7:14-24	

3. Sermon on the Mount	5:1 7:27		6:20-49	
4. Parables				
a) on the Kingdom of God	9:14-17 20:1-16	4:30-32	13:20-21	
b) on membership in the Kingdom	25:1-30		7:36-50 10:25-37 13:22-30 14:15-24	
c) on the relation of King and subjects	17:23-36	15:1-32		10:1-18
5. Other teachings				
a) on humility		9:32-36		
b) on tolerance			9:49-50	
c) on avoiding scandal	18:6-7	9:42-49		
d) on avoiding occasions of sin				
e) on fraternal correction	18:15-18 18:21-22			
f) on the power of united prayer	18:19-20			
g) on the Eucharist				6:22-72
D. Christ's Miracles (based on the four-fold division of the subjects on which they were worked)				
1. On demons	8:28-34 9:32-34 17:14-30	1:23-28 1:34 3:11 5:1-20 9:13-18	4:33-37 4:41 8:26-39 9:37-44 11:14-23	
2. On heavenly bodies	27:45	15:33	23:44-45	
3. On men				
a) the blind	9:27-34 12:22 21:14	8:22-26	18:35-43	9:1-41
b) the centurion's servant			7:1-10	
c) the deaf and dumb	15:29-31	7:31-37		
e) dropsy			14:1-6	
f) the hemorrhage victim		5:25-34	8:43-48	
g) the infirm			13:10-17	5:1-15

	Matthew	Mark	Luke	John	Others
h) the lame	21:14				
i) lepers		1:40-45	5:12-16 17:12-19		
j) Malchus' ear	26:51-52				
k) paralytics		2:1-12	5:17-26	5:1-15	
l) Peter's mother-in-law	8:14-15	1:29-31	4:38-39		
m) the ruler's son				4:46-54	
n) the withered hand	12:9-13	3:1-5	6:6-10		
4. On irrational creatures					
a) curse of the fig tree	21:18-19	11:12-14			
b) draft of fishes			5:1-11	21:1-8	
c) multiplication of loaves	14:13-21 15:32-39	6:31-44 8:1-10	9:10-17	6:1-15	
d) calming of the storms	8:23-27	4:35-40	8:22-25		
e) changing water into wine				2:2-11	
E. Transfiguration	17:18	9:1-7	9:28-36		
III. The Passion and Death of Christ					
A. Palm Sunday: Entry into Jerusalem	21:1-11 21:14-16	11:1-11	19:29-44	12:12-19	
B. Monday in Passion Week	21:12-13 21:18-19	11:12-19	19:45-48		
C. Tuesday in Passion Week	21:19—25:46	11:20—13:37	20:1—21:38	12:37-50	
D. Wednesday in Passion Week: the Council and the Betrayal Plot	26:1-5 26:14-16	14:1-2 14:10-11	22:1-6		
E. Maundy Thursday					
1. Preparation for the Passover	26:17-19	14:12-16	22:7-13		
2. The Last Supper	26:20-35	14:17-25	22:14-38	13:1—17:26	I Cor. 11:25-25
F. Good Friday					
1. Gethsemani	26:36-56	14:26 14:32-52	22:39-53	18:1-12	
2. Jesus before Annas				18:13	
3. Jesus before Caiphas and the San-hedrin for the first time	26:57-66	14:53-64	22:54-55		

4. Peter's denials	26:69-75	14:66-72	22:56-62	18:14-27	
5. Jesus before the Sanhedrin for the second time	27:1	15:1a	22:66-71	18:28	
6. Jesus before Pilate for the first time	27:2	15:1b	23:1		
7. Jesus before Herod Antipas			23:6-12		
8. Jesus before Pilate for the second time and his sentence	27:15-30	15:6-19	23:13-25	18:39—19:15	
9. Way of the Cross and the Crucifixion	27:31-56	15:20-41	23:26-49	19:16-37	
10. The Burial	27:57-61	15:42-47	23:50-56a	19:38-42	
G. Saturday (Jewish Sabbath)	27:62-66		23:56b		
IV. Christ's Exaltation					
A. Resurrection of Christ					
1. The empty tomb					
a) the women go to the grave	28:1-7	16:1-8	24:1-8	20:1	
b) Mary Magdalen informs Peter and John of the empty tomb				20:2	
c) the other women inform the apostles	28:8		24:9-11		
d) Peter and John go to the tomb			24:12	20:3-10	
2. The appearance of Jesus					
a) to Mary Magdalen and the other women	28:9-10	16:9-11		20:11-18	
b) to Peter			24:34		
c) to the disciples at Emmaus		16:12	24:13-32		
d) to the apostles in the absence of Thomas			24:36-43	20:19-23	
e) to the apostles in the presence of Thomas		16:14		20:24-29	
f) to many of the brethren		16:15-18			I Cor. 15:4-8
g) to the apostles in Galilee	28:16-20			21:1-23	
B. Ascension of our Lord		16:19-20	24:50-53		Acts 1:9-12

INDEX

Accidents, 377, 380 f., **384 f.**,

Action in Christ,
  kinds of, 180
  merit of, 180 f.
  unity of, 179-181

Adoption,
  divine, 190 f.
  nature of, 190 f.

Adoptionism, 43 f., **46 f.**
  anathematized, **51**

Adoration, civil, **193**
  kinds of, 193
  of Christ, 193-**196**
  religious, 193

Advent, 288

Agility, 241

Albigensianism, **603**

Amendment, purpose of, **452 f.**

Annunciation, 288

Apollinarianism, 55 f., 132

Apologetics, 10
  early Christian, 39

Apostolate,
  meaning of, 354 f.
  preparation for, 354-**359**
  works of, 358 f.

Arianism, 50 f., 59, 132

Ascension, effects of, **245 f.**

"Assuming,"
  by a person, 121
  by divine Persons, 121-**124**
  notion of, 120-122
  possibility of, 123 f.

Assumption, 278-280
  definition of, 279
  Immaculate Conception **and,**
    279
  order of, 132-134

Attribution, 451

Authority,
  absolute, 16
  moral authority of Christ, **16**

Banns of marriage, 526

Baptism, 326, 328, 331-346
  administration of, 343-**346**
  bibliography on, 364 f.
  ceremonies of, 337 f.
  character of, 342
  conclusion of, 362 f.
  definition of, 334
  effects of, 340-342
  form of, 336 f.
  institution of, 343 f.
  kinds of, 346
  matter of,
    proximate, 335 f.
    remote, 334 f.
  minister of, 343-344
  necessity of, 338-340
  of Christ, 207 f.
  physical nature of, 334-337
  sponsors for, 345 f.
  summary of, 361

Betrothal, 525

Birth of Christ, 204-206
  and his mother, 204 f.
  and the Law, 207
  circumstances of, 205
  manifestation of, 205 f.

Birth prevention, 531

Blessed Sacrament, *see* Eucharist

Body,
  of Christ, 129 f., 236
  qualities of risen, 604 f.

Bread for Eucharist, 372

620

Filiation, divine, 17

Forgiveness, 442 f.
  extra-sacramental, 445
  perfection of God's, 446
  recipients of, 460 f.

Gifts of Holy Ghost,
  in baptism, 341
  in Christ, 149 f.
  in Confirmation, 351
  in marriage, 539

Gnosticism, 39, 46
  refuted by St. Irenaeus, 40-42

God,
  freedom of, 78, 83
  goodness of, 78-81
  love of God for man, 80
  related to Incarnation, 78-82
  will of,
      antecedent, 89
      consequent, 89

Grace, 444 f., 447
  actual, 150 f., 539
  and the damned, 600
  capital, 151-155
  habitual, 134, 145-148, 161
  Mary and distribution of, 276-278
  Mary's fulness of, 259-271
  matrimonial, 505, 508, 536-540
  of Christ, 140, 145-148, 151, 260 f., 556, 586
  of conversion, 586
  of union, 118, 134 f., 143-146
      See also Hypostatic Union
  order of, 119
  sacramental, 309-312
  sanctifying, 310
  work of, 142 f.

Heaven, 233, 589-592
  degrees of glory in, 592
  existence of, 589 f.
  joys of, 591 f.
  Sacred Scripture on, 590
  teaching of Church on, 590

Hell, 237, 593-600
  Christ's descent into, 237 f.
  existence of, 593-595
  fire of, 596-598
  pains of, 594 f.
  separation from God in, 598 f.

Heresies, *see* Adoptionism, Albigensianism, Appollinarianism, Arianism, Docetism, Ebionites, Gnosticism, Manichaeism, Modalism, Monarchianism, Monophysitism, Nestorianism, Patripassianism, Sabellianism

Hierarchy of Church, 560-563

Holy orders, 327 f., 487-500
  bibliography on, 500
  character of, 491
  clerical tonsure and, 488
  conclusion about, 499
  definition of, 487
  effects of, 490-495
  essence of, 487 f.
  form of, 488 f., 495
  lawful reception of, 492-495
  matter of, 488 f., 495
  minister of, 496
  necessity of, 488-490
  parts of, 488
  penance and, 462
  recipients of, 491-495
  scriptural texts for, 495 f.
  signs of vocation to, 493 f.
  summary of, 497 f.
  valid reception of, 491 f.

Holy Spirit, 559

Homoöusios, 51 f.

Hope, 245
  in Christ, 148 f.

Human nature,
  alone can be assumed, 126 f.
  assumption by Christ of, 120-124